HENRY VIII

Henry VIII, school of Holbein, 1537

JASPER RIDLEY

HENRY VIII

CONSTABLE · LONDON

First Published in Great Britain 1984
by Constable and Company Ltd
10 Orange Street, London WC2H 7EG

Set in Monophoto Ehrhardt 11pt by
Servis Filmsetting Ltd, Manchester
Printed in Great Britain by
St Edmundsbury Press
Bury St Edmunds, Suffolk

British Library cataloguing in publication data

Ridley, Jasper
Henry VIII
1. Great Britain – Kings and rulers –
Biography
I. Title
942.05'2'0924 DA332

ISBN 0-09-465930-3

The illustration on the half-title page is:

The Royal Palace of Pleasance, or Placentia, at Greenwich, where Henry VIII was born: detail from a painting by an unknown artist

To my son Benjamin

By the same author

NICHOLAS RIDLEY
THOMAS CRANMER
JOHN KNOX
LORD PALMERSTON
GARIBALDI
THE ROUNDHEADS
NAPOLEON III AND EUGÉNIE
THE STATESMAN AND THE FANATIC

CONTENTS

ILLUSTRATIONS

ACKNOWLEDGEMENTS

I wish to thank Tony Mercer for driving me to Calais, Thérouanne, Eguinegatte, Bomy, Tournai, the Field of Cloth-of-gold, Gravelines, and Boulogne; Christopher Small, for taking me to Solway Moss and Liddisdale; Bill and Pamela Petrie, for allowing me to stay at their charming cottage at Cargill in Perthshire, where I wrote the first chapter of this book; Ann Hoffmann of Authors Research Services, for help with research; the librarian and staff of the London Library for their assistance at all times, and particularly during the siege of St James's Square; the staff of the British Library, the Public Record Office, and the Kent County Library at Tunbridge Wells; and my wife Vera and my son John for their help with the proof-reading.

JASPER RIDLEY
Tunbridge Wells
24 July 1984

SOURCES OF THE ILLUSTRATIONS

The illustrations facing pages 65, 96, 128, 129 and 289, and the double-page illustration between pages 400 and 401, are reproduced by Gracious Permission of Her Majesty The Queen. The illustration facing page 97 is reproduced by kind permission of the Marquess of Tavistock and the Trustees of the Bedford Estates. The illustration from the Pepys Library facing page 64 is reproduced by kind permission of the Master and Fellows of Magdalene College, Cambridge.

The detail from the Westminster Tournament Roll, facing page 33, is reproduced by courtesy of the College of Arms. The portraits facing pages 32, 193 and 288 are reproduced from the originals in the Kunsthistorisches Museum, Vienna. The detail on the half-title page is reproduced by courtesy of the National Maritime Museum, Greenwich. The miniature facing page 321 is reproduced by permission of the British Library, Department of Manuscripts. The portrait facing page 320 is Crown Copyright and is reproduced by permission of the National Gallery, London. The illustrations facing pages 160, 161, 192, 224, 225, 400 and 401 are reproduced by permission of the National Portrait Gallery, London. The frontispiece is reproduced by permission of the Walker Art Gallery, Liverpool.

The picture research was by John Hadfield.

Abate the edge of traitors, gracious Lord,
That would reduce these bloody days again,
And make poor England weep in streams of blood!
Let them not live to taste this land's increase,
That would with treason wound this fair land's peace!

Richmond, in Shakespeare's *Richard III*, Act v, scene iv

CHRONOLOGY

PRINCIPAL EVENTS IN HENRY VIII'S LIFE

1491	June 28	Birth of Henry.
1501	Nov.	Marriage of Arthur, Prince of Wales, and Catherine of Aragon.
1502	Apr.	Death of Arthur.
1503		Henry created Prince of Wales, engaged to Catherine of Aragon.
1509	Apr. 21	Death of Henry VII; accession of Henry VIII.
	June	Marriage and coronation of Henry and Catherine of Aragon.
1510	Aug.	Execution of Dudley and Empson.
1511	Jan. 1	Birth of a son to Henry and Catherine of Aragon (died on 22 Feb.)
	July–Sept.	Henry's visit to Nottingham.
	Aug.	Andrew Barton killed in sea-fight with English fleet.
	Nov.	Alliance of England, Spain and the Emperor Maximilian against France.
1512		Wolsey becomes Henry's chief minister.
	Apr.–Oct.	Disastrous English expedition to Fuentarrabia.
1513	July	Henry invades France.
	Aug.	Battle of Guinegatte; capture of Thérouanne.
	Sept.	Scots defeated at Flodden. Capture of Tournai.
	Oct.	Henry visits Margaret of Austria at Lille, and returns to England.
1514		Peace between England and France; Henry's sister Mary marries Louis XII.
	Dec.	Richard Hunne found hanged in Lollard's Tower.

1515	Jan. 1	Death of Louis XII; accession of François I as King of France.
	Feb.	Suffolk secretly marries Henry's sister Mary.
1515–16		Henry finances military operations of the Emperor Maximilian and the Swiss against France in Northern Italy.
1516	Feb.	Birth of Mary, daughter of Henry and Catherine of Aragon (later Queen Mary).
1517		'Evil May Day' riots in London.
1517–18		Henry leaves London because of the Sweating Sickness.
1518	Oct.	Treaty of London between England, France, Spain and the Empire.
1519		Death of Emperor Maximilian; Charles V elected Holy Roman Emperor, defeating François I and Henry. Birth of Henry Fitzroy, illegitimate son of Henry and Elizabeth Blount (created Duke of Richmond in 1525).
1520	May	Henry meets Charles V at Dover and Canterbury.
	June	Henry meets François I at Field of Cloth-of-gold.
	July	Henry meets Charles V at Gravelines.
1521	May	Execution of Buckingham.
	Aug.	Treaty of Bruges, secret alliance of Henry and Charles V against France.
	Oct.	Henry's book against Luther presented to the Pope, who grants Henry the title of 'Defender of the Faith'.
1522	June–July	Charles V's visit to England; England declares war on France.
1523		English invasion of northern France.
1524		Secret peace negotiations between England and France.
1525	Feb.	François I taken prisoner by Charles V's forces at Pavia.
	Aug.	Treaty of The Moor between England and France.
1526		Treaty of Madrid between Charles V and François I, who is released from captivity. Henry finances Holy League of the Pope and Italian states against Charles V. Angus and the pro-English party seize power in Scotland.
1527	May	Henry begins divorce proceedings against Catherine of Aragon.
1528	Jan.	England and France declare war on Charles V.
	Aug.	Angus banished from Scotland, where pro-English party loses power.
1529	June–July	Divorce proceedings at Blackfriars.
	Oct.	Wolsey's fall from power; Sir Thomas More appointed Lord Chancellor.

1530	Nov.	Arrest and death of Wolsey.
1531	Jan.	Convocation recognises Henry as Head of the Church of England 'as far as the law of God allows'.
	July	Henry separates from Catherine of Aragon, and cohabits openly with Anne Boleyn.
1532	May	'Submission of the Clergy'; More resigns as Lord Chancellor.
	Oct.–Nov.	Meeting of Henry and François I at Boulogne and Calais.
1533	Jan.	Henry secretly marries Anne Boleyn.
	May	Cranmer divorces Henry from Catherine of Aragon.
	June	Anne Boleyn crowned as Queen.
	Aug.–Dec.	Henry's negotiations with envoys of Lübeck.
	Sept.	Birth of daughter, Elizabeth, to Henry and Anne Boleyn (afterwards Elizabeth I).
	Nov.	Exposure of the 'Holy Maid of Kent' (executed in Apr. 1534).
1533–35		Resistance, and virtual imprisonment, of Catherine of Aragon and Mary.
1534	Apr.	Oath of Succession; arrest of More and Fisher.
	Nov.	Acts of Supremacy and Treasons.
1535	Jan.	Thomas Cromwell appointed the King's Vicegerent.
	May–July	Executions of the Carthusians, Fisher and More.
	Aug.–Dec.	Visitation of the monasteries.
1536	Jan.	Death of Catherine of Aragon.
	Feb.	Suppression of the smaller monasteries.
	May	Execution of Anne Boleyn; Henry marries Jane Seymour.
	June	Mary submits.
	Oct.	Outbreak of revolt in Lincolnshire and Yorkshire, the Pilgrimage of Grace.
1537	Jan.–July	Suppression of Pilgrimage of Grace and execution of rebels.
	Oct.	Birth of Prince Edward, death of Jane Seymour.
1537–9		Surrender and suppression of the larger monasteries.
1538		Negotiations for Henry's marriage to the Duchess of Milan or Mary of Guise.
		Campaign against relics; destruction of Becket's tomb at Canterbury.
	Nov.	Trial and burning of John Lambert.
	Dec.	Execution of Marquis of Exeter and others.
		Pope excommunicates Henry.
1539	Apr.	Henry's preparations against invasion threat.
	May–July	Act of the Six Articles passed in Parliament.
1540	Jan.	Henry marries Anne of Cleves.

	July	Execution of Cromwell and Barnes. Henry divorces Anne of Cleves and marries Katherine Howard.
1541	July–Oct.	Henry's visit to York.
	Nov.	Arrest and exposure of Katherine Howard (executed in February 1542).
1542	Nov.	English defeat Scots at Solway Moss.
1543	Feb.	Alliance of Henry and Charles V against France.
	July	Marriage treaty between England and Scotland.
		Henry marries Katherine Parr.
		Protestant heretics burned at Windsor.
	Sept.	Scots repudiate marriage treaty with England.
1543–45		War against Scotland; devastation of Scottish borders by English raids.
1544	May	English troops burn Edinburgh.
	July	Henry invades France.
	Sept.	Henry captures Boulogne. Charles V makes separate peace with France at Crépy.
1545	July	Threat of French invasion. Henry at Portsmouth. Sinking of the *Mary Rose*.
1546	June	Peace of Camp between England and France.
	July	Anne Askew and other Protestants burned.
	Dec.	Arrest of Duke of Norfolk and Earl of Surrey (Surrey executed in January 1547).
1547	Jan. 28	Death of Henry.

I

HENRY TUDOR AND HIS ENGLAND

IN the wet summer of 1491, on the eve of St Peter's Day, 28 June, Elizabeth of York, the daughter of Edward IV, the sister of the 'Princes in the Tower', the wife and Queen of Henry VII, gave birth to her third child, who became King Henry VIII. He was born in the royal palace of Greenwich, five miles south-east of London, in the county of Kent. He was therefore by birth a Kentishman, as he sometimes reminded his Kentish subjects in later years when they objected to paying their taxes.[1] When he was a few days old, he was baptised in the church of the Franciscan Observants at Greenwich, in the font which had been specially brought from Canterbury Cathedral, by Richard Foxe, Bishop of Exeter, who had been with his father in exile in France in the days of Richard III and was now Lord Privy Seal.

Henry VIII is perhaps the most formidable and famous King who has ever reigned in England. He was admired, feared and hated by Englishmen and foreigners in his lifetime, and for four hundred and fifty years after his death he has been remembered as a Gargantuan figure, as a handsome young King who was an accomplished musician, a patron of the arts, and a fine athlete, but who became a bloated old despot with a waist-measurement of 54 inches, a greedy tyrant who suppressed the monasteries and seized their wealth for himself, repudiated Papal supremacy and founded the Anglican religion and the Church of England, put to death the Carthusian monks and Sir Thomas More but also burned Protestant martyrs, who was one of the builders of the English navy and made England a great power, but above all as the husband of six wives, whose fate is remembered in the old child's jingle: 'Divorced, beheaded, died, divorced, beheaded, survived'.

Recently a new school of historians have presented a rather different picture of him, as a stupid, lazy blunderer, a 'bit of a baby', as Professor Elton has called him,[2] who was moved, first in this direction and then in that, by scheming courtiers and by his latest wife or mistress, and who would have failed in all his objectives if he had not been saved from disaster by able ministers like Wolsey and Thomas Cromwell, whom he sacrificed in due course to please some favourite who had made a fool of him. This is an interpretation which would have astounded his contemporaries, though it is perhaps only a disrespectful version of Pole's picture of a Catholic sovereign corrupted by Cromwell, and John Foxe's of a great and good King who was misled by the Papist Gardiner.

More than most men, Henry VIII was a product of his time. Only an early sixteenth-century King could have behaved in the way that he did. We can imagine Wolsey or Thomas Cromwell living as efficient administrators in other centuries, just as we can imagine Thomas More and Anne Askew being martyrs in other centuries, and Rich in another century changing sides with every change of régime; but it is impossible to imagine Henry VIII as anything except an absolute hereditary sixteenth-century monarch. His régime was in many ways remarkably similar to the totalitarian régimes of the twentieth century; but twentieth-century dictators have to attain their position either by making a successful revolution or *coup d'état*, or by climbing the political ladder within the system by currying favour with their superiors and choosing the right faction to support in the Politburo. It is difficult to imagine Henry VIII doing either of these things. It is equally difficult to imagine him as what he was born to be and might easily have become –Henry, Duke of York, the younger brother of King Arthur I. Would he have been a loyal subject, one of the chief props of his brother's throne? Or a successful usurper, wrongfully seizing it? Or an unsuccessful one, executed by King Arthur as a traitor? If he had done any of these things, he would not have been the same kind of man as the Henry VIII of history.

Elizabeth of York was beautiful, and according to the Spanish ambassador, 'a very noble woman', and much loved.[3] She was also the lawful heiress to the throne of England. But she was not the reigning Queen; she was the Queen Consort of Henry VII, whose right to the crown was very spurious. He could claim to be descended from Edward III, that lecherous King who had not only had many mistresses but had complicated English history by fathering twelve legitimate children by his lawful wife, Queen Philippa of Hainault. But several English noble families could claim descent from Edward III; the Plantagenets, the de la Poles, the Staffords and the Howards had a claim to the crown, as well as the Tudors.

The oldest inhabitants of England in 1491 could remember the days, more than seventy years ago, when the hero-king, Henry V, invaded France, won the glorious victory of Agincourt, and forced the King of France to give him his daughter, Princess Catherine, as a bride and to recognise him as his heir to the throne of France. But the invincible Henry V died of plague at the age of thirty-five. His son, Henry VI, after becoming King of England and France before he was a year old, grew up to be a saintly man who hated war and violence; while Catherine of France, the Queen Mother, left a widow at twenty, fell in love with a gentleman of her guard, the Welshman Owain ap Meredith ap Tewdwr, and married him. Like all Welshmen, Owain had a patronymic and no surname, but in England he took his grandfather's name, Tewdwr, as a surname, and was called Owen Tudor by the English. The son of Owen and Catherine, Edmund Tudor, married the eleven-year-old Lady Margaret Beaufort, the granddaughter of an illegitimate son of John of Gaunt and Katherine Swynford who had afterwards been legitimised by Act of Parliament. When she was fourteen, Margaret Beaufort had a son who by 1485 had become King Henry VII.

It was to him that England turned after thirty years of intermittent civil war. After the saintly pacifist Henry VI had lost France, the Yorkists won the Wars of the Roses; Edward IV became King, and murdered Henry VI. But when Edward died, and his brother Richard, Duke of Gloucester, began to exterminate the Yorkist nobility, the frightened Yorkists turned to the exiled Henry Tudor in Brittany, and offered to make him King on condition that he married the Yorkist heiress, Elizabeth of York. At Christmas 1483 Henry Tudor took an oath in Rennes Cathedral to marry Elizabeth, and in August 1485 he landed in Wales with an army composed chiefly of French, Breton and Scottish troops and commanded by a French general. Richard was defeated and killed at Bosworth; and Henry marched to London to be proclaimed king by Parliament.

But what claim did Henry VII have to the throne? It was so unsatisfactory that he and his supporters never clearly stated what it was. If he claimed by hereditary succession from Edward III through his mother, Margaret Beaufort, other claimants had a better hereditary title than he; the patent which legitimized the children of John of Gaunt and Katherine Swynford had stated that they were ineligible to succeed to the crown; and in any case, if Henry Tudor claimed to be king by hereditary succession, his mother, who was still living in 1485, should have become Queen before her son succeeded her as King. He made it clear that he did not claim the throne by the right of his wife, Elizabeth of York, by postponing his marriage to her until three months after he had been crowned King, and putting off her coronation as Queen for two years. He did not even claim to be King by right of conquest, having conquered the King of England with an invading army composed chiefly of the hated national enemy, the French. The Act of Parliament merely declared that he alone was the rightful King, while he himself announced that he was King by just hereditary title and by the Judgement of God revealed by his victory on the field of battle.

Four years after Henry VII died, the Florentine writer, Nicolo Machiavelli, wrote in his book *The Prince* that princes could be divided into those who inherited the throne in territories where their family had long been established, and those who obtained it by force of arms or by their own ability. He thought that it would be much easier for the first than for the second group to maintain themselves in power without being overthrown by their enemies.[4] Henry VII undoubtedly came into the second category.

In September 1486 Henry VII and Elizabeth of York had a son, Arthur, and in November 1489 a daughter, Margaret, before Prince Henry was born in June 1491. Princess Elizabeth, who was born a few years later, died at the age of three. Princess Mary was born in March 1496. Prince Edmund, born in February 1499, died at the age of sixteen months, and the last child, Princess Katherine, died within a few months of her birth in 1503. Meanwhile Henry VII was continually confronted with revolts in support of Yorkist pretenders. It was not until 1498 that his most formidable challenger, Perkin Warbeck, was finally defeated and captured. Three years earlier, Henry VII had executed Sir William Stanley, whose desertion of Richard III in 1485 had made Henry king, for Henry had found out that Stanley was a traitor conspiring with Warbeck. As the future Henry VIII grew up, the Tudor dynasty was still very insecure.

Henry VII thought that he would be safer the fewer powerful nobles there were to threaten his throne. He therefore decided to make the most of the depletion of the nobility in the civil wars. There had been sixty-four peers at the outbreak of the Wars of the Roses, but by 1485 there were only thirty-eight. This killing off of the nobility in war was not unprecedented, but Henry VII refused to remedy the situation by the usual practice of creating new peers. For the same reason, he did not appoint noblemen, in the usual way, to fill the great offices of state. Instead, he gave these offices to his infant children, leaving the duties of the offices to be carried out by deputies, whom it was unnecessary to enoble, but who could remain knights.

Having created his eldest son, Arthur, Prince of Wales when he was three, he appointed his second son, Henry, to be Constable of Dover Castle and Lord Warden of the Cinque Ports on 5 April 1493, when he was twenty-one months old. Soon afterwards the two-year-old boy was made Earl Marshal of England. In September 1494, when he was three, he was appointed Lord Lieutenant of Ireland; his Deputy was Sir Edward Poynings, the author of 'Poynings's Law' which brought Ireland under greater subjection to the English government. Seven weeks later, he went through the solemn proceedings of being created a Knight of the Bath. Next day, on 31 October, he was created Duke of York, which was the title adopted by the pretender Perkin Warbeck; and in December 1494 he was appointed Lord Warden of the Marches of Scotland, with the duty of organising the defence of the border against the Scots. In the following May, a month before his fourth birthday, he was made a Knight of the Garter.[5]

Henry, Duke of York, spent his childhood with his brothers and sisters in his mother's care at the royal houses near London, at Greenwich, Eltham, and the palace of Sheen, which was renamed Richmond after the title of Earl of Richmond which Henry VII had held before he won the crown. In June

1497, a few weeks before his sixth birthday, he was with the Queen at the house of his grandmother, Margaret Beaufort, in Coldharbour Lane in London, when news arrived that the Cornishmen, who had risen in revolt against the taxes imposed on them, were marching on London and had reached Farnham. Elizabeth of York hurriedly moved with her children to the safety of the Tower, and stayed there till the Cornishmen were defeated by the King's army at Blackheath.[6] Young Henry, Duke of York, learned at an early age about the danger of rebellion.

He was given an excellent education, having the famous poet John Skelton as his tutor, and learning at an early age to speak and write fluently in Latin and French, and adequately in Spanish and Italian. Skelton afterwards commemorated his achievement in a well-known verse:

> The honour of England I learned to spell . . .
> I gave him drink of the sugared well,
> Of Helicon's waters crystalline,
> Acquainting him with the Muses nine.[7]

Skelton taught him deportment, and how to behave on public occasions. In the late summer of 1499, when he was staying with his brothers and sisters at Eltham, he was visited by two young intellectuals, Lord Mountjoy and Thomas More. They brought with them Desiderius Erasmus, who was visiting England for the first time. In the absence of his elder brother Arthur, the eight-year-old Henry acted as the host, saying the appropriate words of praise and encouragement to the learned foreign scholar.[8]

Those who attach importance to hereditary factors in forming a man's character cannot find it easy to identify the ancestors whose genes make up the character of Henry VIII. Did he inherit anything from his shrewd, cautious father, with his quiet, painstaking methods and his low-key system of government? From his beautiful, docile mother, who was a faithful wife and a loving parent, and, according to the Spanish ambassador, allowed herself to be dominated by her mother-in-law?[9] From his grandfather Edward IV, rash, pleasure-loving and lascivious? From his other grandfather, the insignificant Edmund Tudor? From his very pious grandmother, Margaret Beaufort, who founded religious and educational establishments? From his maternal grandmother, the hard-boiled and ambitious Elizabeth Woodville, who induced Edward IV to risk his crown and renew the Wars of the Roses in order to marry her? From the Valois ancestors of Catherine of France, or the Welsh forbears of Owen Tudor?

Like Edward IV and Richard III, the Tudor monarchs ruled over a smaller territory than any of their predecessors and successors for four hundred years. For the first time since the eleventh century, the King of England's realm did not include even one French province, and he had not yet acquired Scotland and the British Empire or Commonwealth. He reigned over England, Wales and the Channel Islands. He bore the title of King of France, but when Henry VIII was born in 1491 the only part of France still held by the English was the Marches of Calais, a strip of territory around the town of Calais and the castle of Guisnes about eight miles in depth from the sea and stretching for about twenty miles along the coast. It was bounded on the south and west by the kingdom of France, and on the east by Flanders, a province of the duchy of Burgundy, which by 1491 had been acquired by the house of Habsburg and its head, the Holy Roman Emperor. But Edward IV and Henry VII, by short and successful campaigns in France, had induced the Kings of France to pay them a yearly pension on condition that they did not enforce their claim to the crown of France. The King of England had borne the title of 'Lord of Ireland' since the twelfth century, but effectually governed only an area which was roughly a semi-circle forty miles deep around Dublin.

Henry VII's three million subjects were vigorous, pugnacious, orthodox in religion, and pleasure-loving in their private lives. Many of them resembled, on a modest scale, the King's second son, Prince Henry. They were relatively prosperous in 1491. Nearly every summer they were hit by epidemics of plague or the Sweating Sickness which killed many of the population and improved the standard of living of the survivors, as the shortage of tenants and agricultural labourers kept rents low and wages high, despite all the attempts of Parliament and the Justices of the Peace to keep wages down by legislation. Foreign travellers visiting England were surprised to see how well the English labouring classes ate. The Englishman was famous throughout Europe for his hearty appetite. It was said that the English vice was overeating, as the German vice was drunkenness and the French vice lechery. 'Every country hath his peculiar inclination to naughtiness', wrote Stephen Gardiner, Bishop of Winchester, when arguing in favour of fasting in Lent, 'England and Germany to the belly, the one in liquor, the other in meat; France a little beneath the belly; Italy to vanity and pleasures devised; and let an English belly have a further advancement, and nothing can stay it.'[10]

The great majority of the population still worked on the land, but many people were dissatisfied to see the sheep encroaching on agricultural land, and enclosures reducing the number of common lands, in the interests of the wool trade of south-west England and East Anglia. But it made fortunes for many clothiers and brought prosperity to their workmen as the wool trade with Burgundy increased each year, becoming a more and more important factor in the economy and the foreign policy of England and Burgundy.

Fifty thousand people lived in the capital city, London, which stretched from Aldgate and the Tower in the east to Fleet Street and Temple Bar in the west, and was joined, by the houses along the strand of the River Thames, with Westminster at Charing Cross. On the north side, the built-up area reached as far as the village of Holborn, and to the south went across London Bridge – the only bridge over the Thames between Staines and the sea – to the town of Southwark on the south bank. If it could not compare with Paris and Naples, which had more than 200,000 inhabitants, it was one of the great cities of Europe. The second largest city in England, Norwich, had 13,000 inhabitants; but Bristol and Newcastle were the only other towns with more than 10,000. Ninety per cent of the population lived in villages and on the farms in the countryside.

The 50,000 inhabitants of London hated foreigners even more than other Englishmen did. The Londoners, unlike most of their compatriots, came into contact with foreigners, for many foreign merchants lived in London. As befitted foreigners resident abroad in that regimented society, they lived together in their national 'houses' under the watchful eye of their 'Governor', who saw to it that they did not break the laws or customs of their own country, and was responsible to the English government for their good behaviour in London. The merchants from the Hansa towns of north Germany and the Baltic lived together in the Steelyard. The French, Venetian, Spanish and Burgundian merchants had more freedom, but were likewise subjected to the control of their Governor. The hatred of the English, and especially the Londoners, for foreigners was well-known throughout Europe, and contrasted with the friendliness shown to them by the Scots. Foreigners who came to London expected to encounter open hostility from the people.

England was on the western edge of Christendom, and on the western edge of the known world, for only her island of Ireland, and the hostile kingdom of Scotland on her northern frontier, were between England and the world's end. If any Europeans had sailed to America more than five hundred years before, no one remembered it in 1491, when Columbus had not yet finished his preparations to sail from Spain on his first attempt to circumnavigate the world. After Columbus's voyage next year, Henry VII, who had refused to finance his expedition, sent John Cabot on a voyage which led to the discovery of Newfoundland; but though English fishermen went to Iceland and Newfoundland every year, and there was much interest in the tales that were told about America, the English did not think seriously of colonising it during Henry VIII's lifetime. They turned their backs on the Atlantic and confidently faced the other nations of Christendom to the south and east.

France had made a most unwelcome recovery during the lifetime of older Englishmen. Sixty years after Henry VI had been crowned King of France in Notre Dame in Paris, when three-quarters of France had been under English control, the French had not only thrown the English out of all France except the Marches of Calais, but had acquired Brittany by marriage and part of

Burgundy by conquest, and were preparing to send their armies deep into Italy to seize the duchy of Milan, dominate the Italian peninsula, and become the strongest military power in Europe. Maximilian of Habsburg had married the Duchess of Burgundy and acquired this great sovereign duchy which stretched from the Lake of Geneva to the Zuyder Zee and at the frontier town of Gravelines touched the English Marches of Calais. A Habsburg had for the third successive time been elected Holy Roman Emperor when Maximilian was chosen, and the Empire remained in their family for the next three hundred years. This gave them suzerainty over the Princes and free cities of Germany. The King of Denmark ruled over all Scandinavia, including his subject territories of Norway, Sweden and Finland. In Italy the Venetian republic and the Papal States were the strongest of the many independent sovereign states, while the kingdom of Naples was part of the territory of the King of Aragon. In the Iberian peninsula, the kingdoms of Aragon and Castile, united by the marriage of Ferdinand of Aragon and Isabella of Castile, co-existed with the two other Christian kingdoms of Portugal and Navarre and the Moorish Moslem kingdom of Granada.

The kingdom of Poland and the united kingdoms of Bohemia and Hungary guarded the eastern defences of Christendom. Beyond them was the vast grand-duchy of Muscovy, with its undeveloped Siberian hinterland, and the empire of the 'Great Turk', who had overrun the Eastern Roman Empire and threatened the Hungarian outpost of Belgrade. Beyond the Turk was the empire of the Shah of Persia, the 'Sophy', whose activities were watched with interest by the kings of Christendom because they always hoped that the Sophy would quarrel with the Turk and, by attacking him in his rear, prevent him from invading western Europe. Even further east were Cathay and the Moslem rulers of India, and in Africa, according to popular belief, there was the mythical Prester John, who was supposed to rule a large Christian empire, for the peoples of western Europe were dimly aware that there were Christian communities far beyond the confines of Christendom.

The Englishman had no doubt that, of all the countries of Christendom, his was the best; and he accepted its political and social system. A hundred years before, John Ball and his followers had asked the question: 'When Adam delved and Eve span, who was then a gentleman?' But at most times, most of the people accepted the inequality which was enforced by law and custom in every sphere, prescribing the costume and colours which the nobility, the gentry, the merchants, and the common people, and their wives, were allowed to wear, and the number of different dishes which each class was allowed to eat for dinner. Peers, unlike knights, gentlemen and everyone else, had the privilege of being exempted from torture during judicial investigation, and of being beheaded instead of hanged, drawn and quartered when convicted of high treason, though this did not help their wives, for peeresses, like all other women, could be burned alive if they committed high treason or murdered their husbands.

The people accepted regulations and government interference with their businesses and their social life. They needed licences from the authorities to export money, wool and other manufactures; they needed passports to go abroad, and licences to marry foreigners; they were compelled by law to go to church every Sunday and on the major holy days. They were forbidden to eat meat, butter or cheese on Fridays, Saturdays, in Lent, in Advent, on the Ember Days, and on the eve of the Holy days, unless they obtained a dispensation. All these licences and dispensations had to be paid for, not only with the prescribed fee to the King or bishop, but nearly always with additional sums as bribes to the priest or clerk who was in a position to grant or refuse the licence or dispensation.

The English, unlike their neighbours and enemies the Scots, had a strong respect for law. Although a substantial section of the population, consisting of criminals, vagrants, and noblemen's servants who had been discharged as redundant, did not wish to work, and preferred to defy the rules of their authoritarian society, the majority of the people expected the King to maintain order and punish malefactors with such severity that they would not dare to murder, rape or rob. This view may have been most strongly expressed by the gentry and the merchant class who had property to lose; but it was shared by many sections of the common people who did not want the little that they had to be taken by thieves.

To some extent, this respect for law and order went against the nature of the vigorous, hot-blooded, truculent English, who always loved a fight. When noblemen and gentlemen quarrelled, a few insults would lead them to draw their swords and start fighting; and the lower classes, who did not wear swords, set to, just as energetically, with cudgels and fists. But the chaos of the Wars of the Roses had caused a revulsion against civil war and anarchy. People believed in the necessity of strong government. Blood-feuds and open defiance of the law were largely confined to the lawless parts of the realm – Wales, the Border region of Northumberland, and Ireland.

The Church reinforced the Englishman's belief in inequality, restrictions on freedom, and respect for law. Its hierarchical structure emphasized the difference in rank between its legates, cardinals, metropolitans, bishops, deans and priests, and their order of precedence, powers and privileges. It meddled continually in the private lives of the people, inquiring about what they did, what they ate, and what they thought. It had a code of canon law which was legalistic, precise and complicated. The law of marriage was particularly complicated, and this made it possible for married couples to end their marriages and marry someone else, if they had the money to start expensive legal proceedings and the necessary influence with the ecclesiastical courts. The Church did not permit divorce, but marriages could be annulled as void because of the lack of free consent, the relationship of the parties, or a precontract entered into by one of them with someone else before the marriage. These bars to marriage could be got rid of by a dispensation; but it was still possible to annul the marriage later by proving that the dispensation itself was invalid because of some technical irregularity in the wording of the dispensation. In view of the complexities of the marriage laws, it was usually comparatively easy to find a reason for annulling a marriage, especially if the spouses and the ecclesiastical judge were eager to find one.

The attitude of the ordinary Englishman to his religion and his Church was contradictory. He fervently believed in Heaven, Purgatory and Hell, and interpreted the horrors of hell fire in the most literal sense. He believed that he could avoid hell fire, and eventually enter Paradise after a shorter or longer stay in Purgatory, by observing the sacraments of the Church and receiving absolution from a priest for his sins. He believed that the length of his stay in Purgatory would be reduced by the 'good works' that he performed during his lifetime. 'Good works' usually meant giving money to the Church and to monks, who, by praying for his soul, might shorten the period in which he suffered the tortures of Purgatory by ten thousand or a hundred thousand years.

Most Englishmen went to Mass every day, and had no doubt that, after the priest had spoken the words of consecration, the Body and Blood of Christ were really present, in substance, in the Host under the 'accidents' of bread and wine. They watched approvingly the religious processions which often went through the streets of their local town. They believed in 'creeping to the cross' on their knees on Good Friday, and in the ceremonies which were performed on other days in the Church calendar. They hoped and prayed that their patron saint, and other saints, would intercede for them with God if they showed reverence to the image of the saint in the churches and on the highway. They went from time to time to their nearest monastery to see and touch some relic, and sometimes went on a pilgrimage to the two most famous shrines in England, the shrine of Our Lady at Walsingham in Norfolk, and the tomb of Thomas Becket in Canterbury cathedral.

Becket was venerated throughout England and all Christendom as the most moving example of the triumph of the power of the Church over the secular royal power. Murdered in his cathedral by four knights, at the order of Henry II, on 29 December 1170, for upholding the privileges of the clergy against royal authority, he had triumphed in death when the public opinion of all Christendom had forced Henry II to do penance and submit to a flogging at his tomb on 7 July 1174. The anniversaries of the murder and of the King's repentance were holy days in England, and for three hundred years Kings, noblemen and great numbers of the common people came to Canterbury on horseback and on foot from all over England and Western

Europe – from London and the north across Blackheath and through Rochester, Sittingbourne and Faversham, from the west by Farnham along the Pilgrims' Way, from France, Flanders and Germany through the English territory at Calais to Dover and across Barham Down – to lay priceless jewels or humble pennies on St Thomas's tomb.

A small minority of Englishmen did not believe in pilgrimages, relics, praying to saints, confession of sins to a priest, or even in the Real Presence of the Body of Christ in the Host at Mass. They wished to read the Bible themselves, to interpret it on the basis of their own reason, to find their own way to God and not follow the path prescribed by the Church. These men and women were, in their different way and from nobler motives, like the vagrants and criminals: they were the non-conformist element in the totalitarian society which State and Church imposed on the people of England in 1491. They were prepared to defy State and Church, to outrage public opinion by mutilating the images and desecrating the consecrated Host which, in their opinion, it was idolatrous to worship, and to suffer imprisonment, penance, and an agonising death at the stake rather than revoke their beliefs. They placed the dictates of their own consciences above the laws of the King and the pronouncements of the ecclesiastical hierarchy.

They were the successors to the Lollards, the followers of Wycliffe, who had been condemned as heretics a hundred years before, and whose doctrines had been accepted by the Czech, Jan Hus, and had led to a violent revolutionary upheaval in Bohemia. A handful of them were to be found in England in 1491 among doctors of divinity and scholars in the universities, among artisans in London, Kent and East Anglia, more often in the towns than in the countryside, and hardly ever north of the Trent.

The secular and ecclesiastical authorities rightly regarded them as subversive and a threat to the established order, for their ideas eventually led – though not for another two hundred years – to the rejection of absolute monarchy and ecclesiastical hierarchy, and to new régimes based on the principles of personal freedom, religious toleration, and political democracy. Acts of Parliament of 1382, 1401 and 1414 laid down how they were to be dealt with: the King's officers were to arrest them and bring them before the court of their bishop, and if the bishop or his Ordinary condemned them as heretics, and they refused to make a public recantation and undergo penance, they were to be burned alive by the King's officers and the local JPs at the nearest market town. Ten of them were burned during the twenty-four years of Henry VII's reign, including one old woman of over eighty.

The ordinary Englishman had no patience with these martyrs, who threatened the established order and outraged his own religious beliefs. He thoroughly approved of persecuting them, and when they were burned in the market town, he took his small children to watch the burning.

Orthodox though he was, the Englishman was not very enthusiastic about the Pope. He accepted that the Pope was God's Vicar on earth, but he was also a foreigner, and so were all the officials in Rome who delayed for months or even years the appeals that went to Rome from the ecclesiastical courts in England, and who had to be bribed to obtain dispensations, divorces and appointments. The Pope was entitled to receive 'annates', or first fruits, the first year's income of any see after a new bishop was appointed, and his consent to the consecration of bishops had to be obtained. This led to conflicts between the Papacy and every Catholic King in Christendom. For two centuries the Holy Roman Emperors had engaged in a savage war against the Popes, and in the fourteenth century the King of France had imprisoned the Pope and deposed him. Compared to this, the Kings of England had only minor differences with the Popes, and had gone no further than to persuade their Parliaments, in the reigns of Edward III and Richard II, to pass Acts of Praemunire, making it a criminal offence, punishable with imprisonment for life, to assist the Pope or any foreign ruler to encroach on the rights of the King of England in his realm.

In practice, disputes between the King and the Pope, which were usually about the annates, were amicably settled, after some hard bargaining, by compromise. Both King and Pope had a healthy respect for each other. The King did not wish to be excommunicated, to have England placed under an interdict which forbade the clergy to hold any religious services, and for the Pope to call on foreign rulers to invade England and depose the King; but the Pope knew that the King could defy the excommunication, put to a painful death anyone who published the bull of excommunication in England, cajole or bully the English clergy into continuing to exercise their functions despite the interdict, and deter any foreign King from invading England, at the Pope's behests, by having a powerful navy and invincible English bowmen. Most Englishmen could be relied on to support their King against a foreign Pope.

Though the Englishman believed that priests had the power to absolve him from his sins, and to bring about the transubstantiation of bread and wine into the Body and Blood of Christ, he had a low opinion of the men who possessed this power. Perhaps it was because he believed that he needed the priest so much, and unconsciously resented this, that he was so ready to believe that priests were corrupt, lecherous and wicked. He had as low an opinion of the monks, in the 530 monasteries which were distributed in London, in Canterbury, in Oxford and Cambridge, in the county towns, and in remote parts of the countryside in every region of England and Wales. Although most of the monasteries contained fewer than a dozen monks, they provided employment for the people of the district and hospitality to the traveller; but the monks were hated as rapacious landlords, who enclosed commons and demanded high rents. Stories were always being told of the women smuggled into the monasteries for the pleasure of the abbots and the monks, of homosexuality between the brothers, and of abbesses and nuns in the nunneries who were regularly visited by their lovers.

In recent years, a school of historians have tried to show that the stories of the corruption of the Church at the outbreak of the Reformation have been greatly exaggerated, and that the English clergy in 1500 were less ignorant and less immoral than they had been in the fourteenth century. This comparison would not have impressed the people who lived in Henry VII's reign, any more than a Socialist today would be reassured if he were told that Margaret Thatcher is a less ferocious Tory than Castlereagh was in 1819, or than a Tory would be by the argument that he need not fear Tony Benn because he is less of a menace than Tom Paine was in 1792. The point was that the Englishman in 1491 had a vague but strongly-felt idea in his mind of what a priest ought to be, and he knew that in nearly every case the clergy did not remotely resemble this ideal.

Whether or not the clergy were immoral, they were certainly worldly. None of the bishops had ever performed the routine pastoral duties of a parish priest. They were nearly always canon lawyers, who had gone from their university to become the chaplain, secretary or legal official of a nobleman or bishop, and advanced from there to a post in the King's household and government. They very rarely celebrated Mass, and spent most of their time performing administrative and judicial duties if they were not at court, acting as members of the King's Council or serving him as an ambassador abroad. Lower positions in the diplomatic and civil service were filled by deans, canons and priests who had been granted a benefice with a dispensation for non-residence, so that they could live on the tithes and rents of the benefice while they performed their duties at court. The ordinary parish priest who did reside in his parish did not often set a good moral example to his parishioners. The law of the Church compelled priests to be celibate; but many priests in England in 1491 lived openly with their concubines and bastards in their vicarages, and the practice was usually winked at by the ecclesiastical authorities.

The Englishman made jokes about the vices of the clergy, but his jokes showed his disapproval. He accepted the fact that the King, the nobles and the clergy lived on the products of his labour, and that he was required to pay taxes, rents and tithes to maintain them; but he expected something from them in return. He expected nobles to be brave warriors and to protect him from enemies; and he expected the clergy to be virtuous – more virtuous than he himself would ever aspire to be.

He expected the King to provide firm government, to show himself to his people and impress them with his kingly presence and pomp; to hang robbers; to burn heretics who would bring down God's vengeance on a realm which allowed them to propagate their wicked doctrines; to keep his nobles in order and prevent them from starting another War of the Roses; to fight the national enemies, the French and the Scots; and to win wars, not lose them. The Englishman expected his King to do all these things without taxing him too much. He knew that it was his duty to obey his King, and he did so because of his respect for law and his religious beliefs, as well as from fear of the very painful consequences of resistance to royal authority.

His duty to the King meant more to him than his loyalty to his squire or nobleman. He respected the gentleman in his parish and the nobleman in his shire, as his social superiors, and thought it right that the King's orders should be transmitted, and the country governed, by the local noblemen, bishops and gentlemen, and not by upstart lawyers and officials. But only in exceptional circumstances would he support his local gentleman or nobleman against the King. Henry VIII could arrest and execute a Stafford, a Neville, a Dacre of the South, a Courtney, a Pole, and a Howard, without any of their tenants in Buckinghamshire, Sussex, Devon, Hampshire or Norfolk rising in their defence, as sixteenth-century Scots, and probably sixteenth-century Frenchmen, would have done if their local nobleman had been so treated.

But there was a strange ambiguity in the Englishman's idea of obedience to his King. If any nobleman with a plausible or semi-plausible claim to the crown – anyone descended from Edward III – could manage to make a revolution quickly, and to depose, imprison and assassinate the King, without involving the country in a long civil war, the Englishman was prepared to accept the situation and obey the usurper as his King. He seems to have regarded the usurper's victory as a proof that his claim to the throne was just and that God was on his side. It was the established practice in such cases to legalize the usurpation by an Act of Parliament which enacted that the usurper was the rightful King, though any lawyer should have questioned the validity of an Act of Parliament to which a usurper, not the King, had given the royal assent.

The Englishman was particularly ready to accept the usurper if the deposed King had been weak, effeminate, homosexual or a pacifist, especially if he had lost a war. These usurpations took place once in every lifespan, with curious regularity every seventy-two years. In 1327 the homosexual Edward II, having lost a war against the Scots, was deposed, imprisoned and assassinated. Seventy-two years later, in 1399, the effeminate Richard II, who had refused to continue the Hundred Years' War with France, was deposed, imprisoned and assassinated. Seventy-two years after this, in 1471, the saintly pacifist Henry VI, having lost all his territories in France, was finally deposed, imprisoned and assassinated. But seventy-two years after 1471, in 1543, Henry VIII was King. He was not weak, he was not homosexual or effeminate, he was not a pacifist, he had won his wars; and no one dared even to contemplate deposing, imprisoning and assassinating him.

2

THE PRINCE OF WALES

ALMOST from the beginning of his reign, Henry VII had planned a marriage alliance with Spain. The daughter of Ferdinand and Isabella, Princess Catherine of Aragon, was born in December 1485, and was nine months older than Henry's son Prince Arthur. In July 1488 a treaty was signed by which it was agreed that Arthur and Catherine should marry when they reached marriageable age. There were lengthy negotiations about the amount of Catherine's dowry; but the agreement for the marriage was confirmed by a new treaty in 1496. Catherine, who was growing up in Spain, was always referred to there as 'the Princess of Wales', and was preparing for the day when she would come to England. She was learning to drink wine, because the Spanish ambassador had warned Ferdinand and Isabella that the water in England was undrinkable.[1]

At last, in September 1501, Catherine sailed for England; she was never to return to her native country. On 2 October she landed at Plymouth, and set foot in the country where she was to undergo so much suffering. She moved by slow and dignified stages to London, and on 14 November she and Arthur were married in St Paul's cathedral. Henry, Duke of York, attended the ceremony, and walked up the aisle hand in hand with the bride.

Arthur was just fifteen, and Catherine nearly sixteen. During the next few years, and more dramatically twenty-eight years later, there were lengthy arguments as to whether their marriage had been consummated. There is some evidence that it was, but the verdict of history has been almost unanimous that it was not, partly because of the youth of the spouses, but chiefly because Catherine stated that she had never had intercourse with Arthur. Her reputation for virtue is so unassailable that her statement has been accepted without challenge. But the question is perhaps not so clear, because though Catherine would never have sinned by committing adultery or breaking the fasting laws, she was perfectly capable of lying and perjuring herself in the interests of her dynasty and of the Habsburg family to whom she transferred her allegiance after her nephew Charles V became King of Spain and Holy Roman Emperor.

Soon after their marriage, Arthur and Catherine went to Ludlow on the borders of Wales, where the Council of the Marches of Wales sat regularly, and tried to bring law and order to the unruly territory. In April 1502 Arthur died there, of an illness which his contemporaries called 'consumption', after less than five months of married life. His parents were broken-hearted, and Elizabeth of York fell ill at once. She was pregnant again, and gave birth to a daughter, Katherine, in January 1503; but a month later Elizabeth died, on her thirty-eighth birthday. There is no reason to doubt that Henry VII's grief was sincere, as there had never been any rumour of a quarrel between them. The new baby died a few months later.

Henry, Duke of York, had inherited the title of Duke of Cornwall when his brother died, and on 18 February 1503, a week after his mother's death, he was created Prince of Wales,[2] the title and revenues of the Duke of York reverting to the crown. Negotiations were already in progress for him to marry his widowed sister-in-law, Catherine; but for this, a dispensation would be required. If the marriage of Arthur and Catherine had been consummated, it raised the bar of 'affinity' to Catherine's marriage to Arthur's brother Henry; if it had not been consummated, it still raised the lesser impediment of 'public honesty'. But there was no reason to doubt that the Pope would grant the dispensation, and in September 1502 a draft treaty for a marriage between Henry and Catherine was drawn up.

The death of Elizabeth of York put Henry VII as well as his son Henry into the marriage market. He thereupon proposed that he himself should marry Catherine. He apparently fancied his young daughter-in-law, with her golden hair, her erect carriage, and her tiny hands and feet, and wanted her for himself; but her mother, Queen Isabella, was shocked. 'As this would be a very evil thing', she wrote to the Spanish ambassador in England, 'one never seen before, and the mere mention of which offends the ears, we would not for anything in the world that it should take place'.[3]

Henry VII was only forty-six in 1503, but even by sixteenth-century standards he was old for his age. He was often ill, and his eyesight sometimes troubled him. He had become very religious, and in Lent 1499 he attended a sermon every day and afterwards spent many hours in religious devotions.[4]

He was not a vindictive man, and his style of government was quiet and efficient, never using more cruelty or deceit than was necessary. When he captured Lambert Simnel, the young tradesman's son who led the first revolt against him and was crowned King of England in Dublin, he did not put him to death, but employed him as a servant in his household. When he defeated and captured a second and far more dangerous pretender, Perkin Warbeck, he spared his life, and it was only after Warbeck had twice tried to escape that he was executed. After defeating the dangerous revolt of the

Catherine of Aragon, by Miguel Sittow, c.1502

Henry returning from the joust, watched by Catherine of Aragon and her ladies.
Detail from the Westminster Tournament Roll at the College of Arms, c.1509

Cornishmen at Blackheath, Henry executed only three of the ringleaders, and pardoned all the other rebels. But at the same time that Warbeck suffered, Henry also executed Edward Plantagenet, Earl of Warwick, the son of Edward IV's brother, the Duke of Clarence, after he had kept Warwick a prisoner in the Tower for fourteen years, though Warwick's only crime was to be a descendant of Edward III and to have a better title to the crown than Henry VII.

He preferred, if possible, not to notice treasonable talk, rather than to ferret it out. Once, when he was ill, some of his highest officials at Calais discussed amongst themselves who would succeed him if he died. Some suggested the Duke of Buckingham, and some Edmund de la Pole, but no one mentioned Prince Henry. One of those present decided not to report the conversation to Henry VII, because he knew that the King did not like those who accused others of treasonable talk; for he usually assumed that the man reporting the treasonable words did so out of envy.[5]

Henry VII's greatest characteristic was his love of money; he amassed an enormous fortune and guarded it like a miser. Recently a school of modern historians has denied that he was very rich or avaricious; but none of his contemporaries had any doubt about it. The two Spanish ambassadors in London, Puebla and Ayala, who hated each other and disagreed about nearly everything else, both agreed on that point. In July 1498 Ayala thought that Henry, though very wealthy, was not as rich as he pretended to be; but eight months later he was writing to Ferdinand and Isabella that the King of England's revenues were increasing every day, and 'I think he has no equal in this respect.' Puebla stated that Henry had the reputation of possessing immense riches; and the Venetian ambassador wrote that though he was a King of 'vast ability', he was 'a very great miser'.[6]

This reputation is confirmed by the English chroniclers; and the Cornish rebels, and the MPs who, under Thomas More's leadership, resisted Henry's tax demands in 1504, all believed the same thing. 'He spends all the time when he is not in public, or in his Council', wrote Ayala, 'in writing the accounts of his expenses with his own hand'.[7] The picture of the King sitting in his counting house counting out his money, and making sure that every farthing was accounted for, impressed his English subjects and foreign rulers. He had only himself to blame if this was the image which he presented to the world.

He gave up the idea of marrying Catherine of Aragon himself, and concentrated on making as much money as possible out of the situation. On 23 June 1503 he signed a treaty with the Spanish ambassadors by which Henry, Prince of Wales, was to marry Catherine, and Ferdinand and Isabella were to pay an extra 100,000 scudos, in addition to the 100,000 scudos already paid, as a new dowry for the new marriage. The treaty stated that the Pope would be asked to grant a dispensation for the marriage, as Catherine's marriage to Arthur had been consummated. When Ferdinand heard about this, he was surprised, for he said it was well-known in England that the marriage had not been consummated and that Catherine was still a virgin. But he did not alter the wording of the marriage treaty, and ordered his ambassador in Rome to ask the Pope for a dispensation on the assumption that the marriage had been consummated.

Julius II, who had just been elected Pope, granted the dispensation on 26 December 1503, though he did not send the bull to England till October 1504. It dispensed with the bar of affinity created by the marriage of Arthur and Catherine, which had 'perhaps' been consummated.[8]

But there was a hitch in the negotiations for Henry's marriage to Catherine. In November 1504 Queen Isabella died. The throne of Castile passed to the daughter of Ferdinand and Isabella, Joanna, who was on the verge of becoming insane. Ferdinand continued to act as ruler of Castile as well as of Aragon as Regent for his mad daughter; but her husband, Duke Philip of Habsburg, who was the son of the Emperor Maximilian and his regent in the Netherlands, claimed the throne of Castile for him and her. The quarrel between Philip and Ferdinand made Henry VII reluctant to marry his son to Ferdinand's daughter; for he began to consider the possibility of making an alliance with Maximilian and the Habsburgs by marrying his daughter Mary to the infant son of Philip and Joanna, Prince Charles of Castile, who later became the Emperor Charles V. The trade between England and the Netherlands made any ruler of Burgundy a more desirable ally than the King of Aragon.

The result was that on 27 June 1505, the day before his fourteenth birthday, Henry, Prince of Wales, made a protestation in the eastern wing of the palace at Richmond before Foxe, the Bishop of Winchester and Lord Privy Seal, in the presence of several other members of the King's Council. He declared that the marriage contract between him and Catherine had been made when he was under age, and now that he was about to reach full age he refused to ratify it, and it was therefore null and void.[9] His protestation had certainly been drafted by the King and the counsellors. Ferdinand was indignant, but there was nothing that he could do.

In January 1506 Philip of Habsburg and his wife Joanna sailed from the Netherlands for Spain with a force of three thousand German mercenaries. On their way, their ships were driven ashore by storms at Melcombe in Dorset, and Philip was entertained by Henry VII at Windsor and Richmond. Henry and Philip made a treaty of alliance and a new commercial treaty between England and the Netherlands; and they agreed to extradite each other's rebels. As a token of goodwill, Philip offered to extradite Edmund de la Pole, the son of Edward IV's sister, who was a possible Yorkist claimant to the throne of England and had taken refuge in Philip's territories. Edmund had been condemned as a traitor in his absence by an Act of

Parliament; but Philip asked Henry VII not to put him to death. The King gave a written undertaking that he would not be executed, and he was handed over to the English officials at Calais and safely lodged in the Tower of London.

While Philip was in England, he made Henry, Prince of Wales, a knight of the Burgundian Order of the Golden Fleece.[10] In April, when the weather improved, he sailed to Spain, where he had some unfriendly meetings with Ferdinand. In September he died suddenly; some people suspected that Ferdinand had poisoned him.

As the various marriage negotiations dragged on, Henry VII vented his displeasure on Catherine of Aragon. He began to subject her to irritations and humiliations, and reduced her household allowance, so that she and her servants were in serious financial difficulties; then suddenly he switched, and showed his old affection for her, and increased her allowance. His attitude towards her changed according to whether his diplomatic relations with Ferdinand were improving or worsening.

Ferdinand decided to break off negotiations for Catherine's marriage to the Prince of Wales, and to ask Henry VII to send her back to Spain. Henry VII refused to let her go. It became clear to Ferdinand that she was being held in England as a hostage. He was afraid that Henry VII might poison her. By the summer of 1508 he had become so angry that he was threatening to declare war on Henry, 'to make a worse war on the King of England than on the Turks', even though this would mean that 'the world may perish'. But his ambassadors' reports had led him to believe that young Henry, Prince of Wales, was a very different kind of man from his father, and was in no way responsible for Catherine's ill-treatment. Ferdinand instructed his new ambassador in England, Fuensalida, to visit the Prince of Wales and assure him of Ferdinand's regard for him. Fuensalida found it impossible to gain access to the Prince. He reported that King Henry kept his son as closely guarded as if he were a girl, that he was locked in a building from which the only exit was through a door into a park where he was allowed to take exercise under the close supervision of his guard. Fuensalida also wrote that the Prince was so frightened of his father that he did not dare to speak in his presence, except to mumble a few words in reply when the King spoke to him.[11]

Henry VII was becoming increasingly unpopular. The Spanish envoy Londoño had written in 1498 that he kept his people in a greater subjection than they had suffered under any previous King, and the government grew even firmer in later years. The taxes were bitterly resented. Even more unpopular was the habit of Henry VII and his ministers of accusing his wealthier subjects of having committed some offence, and requiring them to pay a large sum of money as a recognisance, or bond, for their good behaviour. The King himself told Ayala that he imposed heavy taxes 'to keep his subjects low, because riches would only make them haughty'.[12]

He occasionally summoned some of his nobles and bishops to attend meetings of his Council; but he normally ruled his kingdom through a very small body of advisers, while the person who had the greatest influence over him was his mother, Margaret Beaufort. The chief instruments of his financial policy were Edmund Dudley and Sir Thomas Empson. Dudley was the son of a gentleman of Atherington near Climping in Sussex; Empson was of lower birth, for his father was a prosperous sieve-maker of Towcester in Northamptonshire. Both became barristers, MPs, and Speaker of the House of Commons, and entered Henry VII's service. Empson was knighted, and was appointed Chancellor of the Duchy of Lancaster, but neither he nor Dudley held any position which would account for their activities in extorting money from the King's subjects.

They seem to have been almost universally hated throughout England. They were accused of acting illegally when they extorted large sums of money from wealthy landowners under the recognisance system, and of not only obtaining this money for the King, but of enriching themselves in the process. According to the historian, William Camden, who wrote seventy-five years later, Empson once met a blind soothsayer, who could foretell the future. Empson asked him when the sun would change. 'When such a wicked lawyer as you goeth to Heaven', replied the soothsayer.[13]

In recent years, historians have discovered a little more about the activities of Dudley and Empson. Some of this new material seems to vindicate them to some extent, or at least to show that everything they did was justified by the law of England. Other documents confirm their high-handed methods. None of them explains why the people hated them so much more than Henry VII's other advisers. Perhaps Francis Bacon, relying no doubt on popular tradition, came nearest the truth when he stated that Empson had very rude manners. People often resent insult more than injury.[14]

The small group of Henry VII's confidential advisers did not include the Prince of Wales. He played no part at all in government. When Arthur was Prince of Wales, the King had sent him to preside over the Council of the Marches of Wales at Ludlow; but when Prince Henry was given his brother's title, he was not sent to Ludlow. Although he had been appointed Warden of the Cinque Ports, Lord Lieutenant of Ireland, and Warden of the Marches of Scotland at the age of three, now that he was old enough to perform, or at least to learn, the duties of these offices, they were taken away from him and given to various noblemen. He spent his time in the princely sports, riding, hunting, hawking, and jousting in tournaments. He greatly enjoyed wrestling, and became very proficient in the national sport of archery, which had made the English bowmen the most formidable military force in Europe. He could compete with the best archers of the King's guard.

Fuensalida's description of the Prince of Wales being held almost a prisoner by the King is probably an exaggeration; and it is even more difficult to believe the ambassador's story of how Henry VII once nearly killed his son Henry, and also attacked his daughter Mary, in a fit of rage because he was annoyed by a letter which he had received. But the story confirms other evidence that father and son did not get on well. According to Henry VIII's cousin, Lord Montagu, who knew him when he was Prince of Wales, his father the King did not like him. Montagu was unwise enough to say this, many years later, to his brother Sir Geoffrey Pole, in a private conversation, which was quoted against him when Henry VIII had Montagu executed as a traitor.[15] In view of the striking differences in the personalities of father and son, it is not surprising that their relations were strained.

The Prince of Wales, excluded from all share in government, could do nothing but wait for his father to die. He did not have to wait very long, though it was longer than many people expected. Henry VII's health was deteriorating rapidly. In the spring of 1507, when he was just fifty, he fell dangerously ill, and his courtiers were convinced that he would die. He recovered, but fell ill again in February 1508, and after recovering again, had another serious illness five months later in July. His physicians, in the usual language of the period, called his illness 'consumption'. On 24 March 1509 he collapsed, and the Venetian ambassador reported that he was 'utterly without hope of recovery'.[16]

The more ill he was, the more devout he became, and this final attack brought him to a state of great repentance. On 31 March he made his will, in which he expressed his penitence for his sins, and left money for ten thousand masses to be said for his soul. He stated that he wished reparation to be made to any subjects who had been unjustly expropriated, and appointed commissioners, including Dudley and Empson, to see that this was done. On 10 April he issued a proclamation cancelling all recognisances which had been entered into for less than £15 and granting a general amnesty to criminals.

On 20 April the Prince of Wales hurried to his father's bedside at Richmond. He afterwards stated that the dying King asked him to marry Catherine without any further delay; but we do not know what else they discussed. Henry VII lingered for another twenty-seven hours, but the end came at last; and on 21 April 1509, at the age of seventeen years and nine months, the Prince of Wales became King Henry VIII, King of England, King of France, and Lord of Ireland.[17]

3

THE YOUNG KING

HENRY VIII remained at Richmond for twenty-four hours, and on 23 April, St George's Day, travelled to London and took up his residence in the Tower. It had become an established custom for a new King to stay at the Tower during the few weeks which elapsed between his accession and his coronation, and never to live there again during the rest of his life. On the same day he was proclaimed King in the city by the heralds: and also on the same day, Dudley, Empson, and Lord Henry Stafford, the Duke of Buckingham's brother, were arrested and sent to the Tower, though not to that part of the building where the King was residing. A few days later, some of the most unpopular of Dudley's and Empson's friends and subordinate officials were also arrested, though the worst of them all, John Baptist Brimald, escaped and took sanctuary in Westminster Abbey.

On 23 April Henry granted a general pardon to all offenders, except seventy-seven people who were excepted by name in the proclamation. These included Dudley, Empson, Henry Stafford, and the subordinates of Dudley and Empson, and Edmund de la Pole, who had been in prison in the Tower since Philip of Habsburg handed him over to Henry VII. This was the second amnesty which had been granted within thirteen days, for Henry VII had granted a general pardon on 10 April. The ostensible reason for this second amnesty was that Henry VII's applied only to crimes committed before the day on which it was issued, and the new amnesty extended to crimes committed during the last eleven days of the late King's life. But the proclamation of 23 April did more than this: it superceded Henry VII's amnesty in the people's minds. They forgot that Henry VII had also granted a general pardon and remembered only that the good young King who had replaced the bad old King had pardoned the victims of his father's tyranny.

It was usual for Kings to begin their reign by granting an amnesty and releasing prisoners; but to arrest the most hated of the old King's ministers was an unexpected and striking sign of Henry VIII's desire to end the misgovernment of his father's reign. He also showed that he was determined to right the wrongs of the people by ordering that all cases of recognisances should be investigated, as Henry VII had directed in his will. Throughout the summer of 1509 and in the next few years, many sums of money unjustly forfeited under the recognisances were repaid.[1]

He was seen as a liberator of his people from oppression. Thomas More wrote a poem in which he just refrained from directly criticising Henry VII, but praised the new King for ending the 'tyranny' of the dead King's ministers. He acclaimed Henry VIII as 'the greatest, the best, and, to use a new and very honourable title for a King, the most loved'. More's friend, Lord Mountjoy, wrote even more enthusiastically to Erasmus about the virtues of 'our Prince, now *Henricus Octavus* [Henry VIII] whom we may well call our Octavius . . . Avarice is expelled from the country; liberality scatters wealth with a bounteous hand. Our King does not desire gold or gems or precious metals, but virtue, glory, immortality'.[2]

Henry's handsome physical appearance added to his popularity. He was very tall, about six foot three or six foot four, with broad shoulders. He had strong athletic limbs, and a very fair skin. He still wore his red-gold hair long, and was clean shaven, for shorter hair and beards had not yet come into fashion. Like another forceful statesman of later times, Bismarck, he combined an impressive presence with a thin, piping, high-pitched voice; and he must already have had those small, piggy eyes that Holbein painted, calculating and cruel.

However much the people disliked Henry VII, they expected their noble young King to show a proper respect for his father's memory, and Henry VIII took care to do so. He did not leave the Tower for eighteen days, until after Henry VII's funeral solemnities on 9 and 10 May. He himself did not attend the funeral, but this would have been unusual; funerals were a matter for priests and monks. Large numbers of them escorted the corpse in procession from Richmond to St Paul's, and next day to Westminster Abbey, where it was buried beside the body of Elizabeth of York.

The funeral sermon was preached by John Fisher, Bishop of Rochester, who had been for some years a member of Henry VII's Council, and was the closest confidant of Margaret Beaufort; he had persuaded her to endow several lectureships and colleges in his university of Cambridge. The sermon was a little defensive and apologetic in tone. Fisher praised Henry VII's piety and religious orthodoxy, and especially the sincerity with which he had repented of his sins, and the liberality of his religious and charitable gifts in his will. Margaret Beaufort was very pleased with the sermon, and asked Fisher to have it printed; but she did not live to see it published. She died seven weeks after the funeral. On her deathbed, she urged her grandson, the new King, to choose Fisher as his closest adviser, and always to follow his guidance.[3]

After the funeral, it was time for rejoicing. Henry VIII left the Tower, and engaged in festivities and amusements at Greenwich while preparations were made for his coronation. Meanwhile his Council and the ambassadors in London were wondering whether the new King would make any changes in England's foreign policy and alliances, and especially which foreign Princess he would marry. Would he, after all the long delays, marry Catherine, the Princess Dowager of Wales? Or would he choose one of the three alternative brides whom his father had thought might be suitable for him – Philip of Habsburg's daughter Eleanor, or the daughter of Albert, Duke of Bavaria, or Marguerite de Valois of Angoulême, the sister of François, Duke of Angoulême, who was the heir to the throne of France unless his cousin, the old King Louis XII, had a son? The Spanish ambassador, Fuensalida, was not optimistic about Catherine's chances; and some members of Henry's Council, especially the Archbishop of Canterbury, Warham, who was also Lord Chancellor, had doubts about the propriety of his marrying his brother's widow.

On 26 April the English ambassador in Spain, John Stile, wrote from Valladolid to Henry VII, for he had not yet heard that the King had died five days before. He warned him that King Ferdinand's anger at Catherine's treatment in England had reached a point where he was contemplating going to war. But soon after, reports reached Valladolid from France that Henry VII had died, and these were soon confirmed by Fuensalida's dispatches from London.

Ferdinand believed that the whole international situation had changed in his favour by the accession of the young King of England. He wrote to Fuensalida and Catherine, that he would no longer haggle about the dowry or other matters, and that in order to persuade Henry VIII to marry Catherine he would grant him all the concessions which he had refused to Henry VII, because he trusted the new King as he had not trusted his father. As for the doubts which existed in some quarters in England about the propriety of Henry marrying his brother's widow, Ferdinand pointed out that such a marriage was perfectly lawful because the Pope had granted a dispensation for it. He told Fuensalida to spare no money in bribing Henry's ministers if this would help matters, because the marriage of the Princess of Wales to the King of England was the most important business that ever was, or ever would be, entrusted to the ambassador.[4]

Ferdinand need not have worried; Henry VIII had decided to marry Catherine. He had always had good relations with her. The fact that she was six years older than he was not a serious drawback, and only Warham and a few others seemed to have any doubt as to the legality of the marriage. He wrote to Margaret of Austria that he had taken the decision because his father had told him, on his deathbed, to marry Catherine, and he would not disobey him, especially because it would help to bring about a grand alliance of

England, Spain, the Emperor and the House of Burgundy.[5] This was probably his real reason for marrying Catherine, for he was undoubtedly already thinking of forming an anti-French alliance, and of adding to his great popularity with his people by going to war with France.

He married Catherine on 11 June. In the sixteenth century, royal weddings were private affairs, and Henry's took place in the chapel royal at Greenwich. The ceremony was performed by the Archbishop of Canterbury, which Henry perhaps considered particularly advisable in view of the doubts which Warham had expressed about its legality. During the service, Warham put the formal question to him: 'Most illustrious Prince, is it your will to fulfil the treaty of marriage concluded by your father, the late King of England, and the parents of the Princess of Wales, the King and Queen of Spain; and as the Pope has dispensed for this marriage, to take the Princess, who is here present, for your lawful wife?' After Henry had answered 'I will', Warham addressed Catherine 'Most illustrious Princess', and put the same question to her, and she too replied 'I will'.[6]

On 21 June, Henry and Catherine came from Greenwich to the Tower of London, travelling not, in the usual way, by barge, but riding overland along the south bank for all to see them, into Southwark, and then across London Bridge and by Grace Church to the Tower. On Saturday 23 June they rode in a great procession through the streets of London, by Bread Street, past Grace Church, Cheapside and Cornhill, to Westminster, with the great officers of state, the King's household, and the Lord Mayor, the Aldermen, and the livery companies, along the streets decorated with cloth-of-gold, with virgins dressed in white, and priests waiting to cense the King and Queen as they passed. Henry, dressed in crimson velvet lined with ermine, and a coat of gold with diamonds, rubies and emeralds, rode on a richly accoutred horse, surrounded by his bodyguard; and Catherine followed a little way behind, in a litter with her ladies and train. The crowds cheered the King enthusiastically. 'The features of his body', wrote Edward Hall, who watched him ride by, 'his goodly personage, his amiable visage, princely countenance, with the noble qualities of his royal estate, to every man known, needeth no rehearsal, considering that for lack of cunning I cannot express the gifts of grace and of nature that God hath endowed him withal'.

Henry and Catherine spent the night at the Palace of Westminster, where there were jousts and a great banquet, and next day, Sunday, 24 June, the Feast of St John the Baptist and Midsummer Day, they proceeded in great state to Westminster Abbey, where they were crowned by Warham with all the traditional ceremonies. They returned to Westminster Hall for the coronation banquet. During the second course, Sir Robert Dimock, the King's Champion, rode into the hall, on horseback, and offered to fight to the death 'any person, of what estate or degree soever he be, that will say or prove that King Henry VIII is not the rightful inheritor and King of this realm'.[7]

Dimock had performed this ceremony in 1483 at the coronation of Richard III, and again two years later at the coronation of the man who had defeated and killed Richard and seized his throne. Having twice been King's Champion at the coronation of a usurper, he now issued his challenge for Henry VIII who, as the eldest surviving son of Elizabeth of York, was unquestionably the rightful King.

The highest of the secular officers of state at the coronation was the Duke of Buckingham, who the day before had been appointed Lord High Constable of England. Buckingham's brother, Lord Henry Stafford, was still a prisoner in the Tower on suspicion of treason, though no charge was brought against him. As a descendant of Edward III, Buckingham was a possible heir to the throne, and his name had sometimes been mentioned in political gossip as a possible King; but he was less likely to cause trouble if his brother was a hostage in prison. Soon after the coronation, Henry VIII released Henry Stafford, and said that he was sure that the rumours about him were unfounded;[8] and later in the year, Henry created him Earl of Wiltshire.

Empson was brought before the King's Council and charged with illegally extorting money from the people. In a long and reasoned speech, he argued that he had acted on Henry VII's orders, and that everything he had done was justified by ancient laws which were perfectly valid, even if some of them had been obsolete for many years. This was an awkward argument to deal with. But a new accusation was then made against him and Dudley: when they knew that Henry VII was dying, they had consulted their friends and asked them for support if their position was threatened. This could be construed as planning a rebellion, an act of high treason against the new King. In July, Dudley was indicted for high treason at the Guildhall in London; Empson was sent to his native county to be tried on the same charge at Northampton in October. Both were found guilty and sentenced to be hanged, drawn and quartered.

Henry did not order the sentences to be carried out for nearly a year. He may have thought it unsuitable to spoil the months of rejoicing and amnesty by having an important public execution, even of two notorious malefactors, in that happy summer of 1509. Dudley and Empson were held prisoners in the Tower of London; in January 1510, their conviction and sentence was confirmed by an Act of Parliament. Their subordinate officials who had been arrested at Henry VIII's accession were sentenced by the Council to be put in the pillory; but no attempt was made to force or trick Brimald to leave sanctuary, and he was allowed to go free.

Dudley wrote a book in the Tower, *The Tree of Commonwealth*, which he dedicated to Foxe and Sir Thomas Lovell, who was Chancellor of the Exchequer and Constable of the Tower. In it, he discussed the principles of good government which a ruler should pursue. He also wrote out a list of eighty-four cases in which he had oppressed Henry VII's subjects, and he asked Foxe and Lovell to make restitution to his victims. He described himself as 'the most wretched and sorrowful creature, being a dead man by the King's laws, and prisoner in the Tower of London, there abiding life or death at the high pleasure of my sovereign lord, to whom I never offended in treason or thing like to it to my knowledge, as my sinful soul be saved'.

Dudley tried to escape from the Tower. The plot was discovered, and this may have been a factor in Henry's decision to proceed to extremities. He commuted the sentence of hanging, drawing and quartering to the more merciful death by the headsman's axe. Dudley and Empson were beheaded on Tower Hill on 18 August 1510.[9]

None of the sixteenth-century chroniclers, nor any of the records unearthed by modern research, give any indication as to who was responsible for the decision to overthrow Dudley and Empson and put them to death. Wolsey, who would have been capable of it, was already in the royal service, but was not yet high enough to do it, or even to suggest it. It is difficult to believe that Foxe, Warham, Lovell or Ruthall, who were cautious and slow, and a few years later allowed Wolsey to downgrade them without a struggle, would have been capable of it. Fisher and Margaret Beaufort might have advised it; and it is even possible that Henry VII, wishing to prove to himself the sincerity of his repentance and thinking of the interests of his successor, advised his son on his deathbed, during their last talk, to sacrifice the most hated agents of his own policy to win the goodwill of the people.

But the responsibility and the final decision rested with Henry VIII, and perhaps there is no need to look farther than him. Young men of seventeen are capable of making up their own minds without asking anyone's advice, and of taking drastic and cruel action on their own initiative, even when they are not in the first flush of exultation at becoming an absolute monarch. The sudden overthrow and arrest of Dudley and Empson, the straining of the law to find them guilty of treason, and the decision not to show mercy but to put them to death, followed a pattern which was to be repeated on many occasions during Henry VIII's reign: it was unexpected, unjust and popular.

While Dudley and Empson waited in the Tower, not knowing whether they would live or die, Henry began the round of lavish entertainments and gorgeous displays which continued all his life and which so impressed his contemporaries. On every 'high holy day' a crowd of courtiers and petitioners assembled to see the King go to Mass. Henry was dressed in sumptuous clothes and wore expensive jewellery. On his way, he would pause to say a few words to ambassadors and noblemen to whom he wished to show a public sign of friendship, and graciously accepted petitions presented to him. Mass was followed by a great banquet, with the King sitting alone at his table and waited on by the high officers of state who were his carver and cupbearer; but sometimes important dignitaries and foreign visitors were invited to sit at his table as a mark of outstanding favour. The nobles and courtiers, and their ladies, sat at lower tables according to their rank. A large number of dishes were served, with extra courses and delicacies for the King and the nobility. There were enormous helpings of beef, venison, and chicken, and French wines from Bordeaux, not the ale which most Englishmen drank. The banquet ended with that expensive luxury, hypocras, a sweet liqueur imported from the Levant.

After the banquet, which usually began at 11 a.m. and lasted several hours, a great tournament was held, conducted according to the complicated rules of the game, with challengers and defenders, and shields and banners arranged in order of precedence, in the presence of the King and Queen and the lords and ladies of the court. As Prince of Wales, Henry had shown great skill in jousting; but at the jousts which were held during the coronation festivities, and later in the year, he sat with the Queen, watching with royal dignity from the seat of honour, as his father had done and other Kings did. There were risks involved in jousting, for though the participants were encased in heavy armour, and their faces covered with visors, and were separated from each other by a barrier on their left-hand side, accidents could occur with the lances, and the riders could fall from their horses. Would it be right for the King to take part in a tournament, or would it be incompatible with his royal dignity?

On the Twelfth Day of Christmas, 6 January 1510, Henry came in disguise to a tournament at Richmond and took part in it, showing great skill. All the spectators admired the unknown knight, and one of them recognised him and cried 'God save the King!'[10] As his participation had made him very popular, he regularly took part in tournaments from now on, and this played a part in creating the image of the gallant, athletic young King which made such a favourable impression, not only in England but throughout Christendom. But it was not a case of a headstrong young man, with no interest in politics or in his position as a King, rushing to take part in his favourite sport without thinking of the consequences. For all his bluff manner and his preference for vigorous measures Henry was cautious, and throughout his life reflected carefully, sometimes for years, on the results of an action before pursuing it. It took him longer to decide to take part in tournaments than to order the arrest of Dudley and Empson.

The tournaments, banquets and Masses were a feature of all the major holy days which recurred quite frequently throughout the year. As soon as Lent was over there was Easter, and in April St Mark's Day and the feast of St George, the patron saint of England. Eight days after St George's Day came May Day, when the people celebrated with Robin Hood games, which were apt to lead to disorder; but Henry and his court held the usual dignified banquet and tournament. Next came Ascension Day, Whitsun, and Corpus

Christi Day, and in June St Barnabas's Day, the Feast of St John the Baptist on Midsummer Day, and the Feast of St Peter on the 29th. The major feast of St Thomas of Canterbury was celebrated on 7 July, and St James's Day on the 25th. In August there was St Lawrence's Day and St Bartholemew's Day; in September the Nativity of the Virgin Mary, St Matthew's Day, and Michaelmas; in October St Luke's Day; in November All Saints, All Souls and Martinmas. In December the feasts of St Nicholas and the Conception of the Virgin, and St Thomas the Apostle's Day were followed by the Twelve Days of Christmas, with Christmas Day, St Stephen's Day, St John's Day, Childermas, the minor feast of St Thomas of Canterbury, New Year's Day, and Twelfth Day. The first of January was called 'New Year's Day', because three hundred years earlier the calendar year had begun on 1 January, though for several centuries 25 March had been reckoned as the first day of the year in England. New Year's Day was a particularly splendid occasion, when gifts were given; ambitious courtiers gave potential patrons the most expensive gifts they could afford, and observers carefully noted who had received gifts from the King and how expensive they were compared with those which he had given to other favourites. Later in January there was the Feast of St Paul, and in February Candlemas and St Mathias's Day; and on Shrove Sunday and Shrove Tuesday there were again festivities before the seven weeks' pause during Lent.

On the other days in the year, the King hunted. He usually rose late, not till 8 a.m., which was two or three hours after most of his subjects had risen. He was dressed by his servants and by the noblemen and gentlemen of his court whose duty and privilege it was to attend the dressing ceremony. As soon as he had been to Mass in his chapel, he was in the saddle leaving for the hunt; in winter, if the ground was too frozen or wet to make hunting possible, he went hawking. Only very heavy rain kept him indoors. It was usually late before he returned from hunting, only just in time for supper at 6 p.m.; for he never seemed to get tired, riding eight or ten horses in succession until they were exhausted, and sometimes following a stag or boar, or several stags or boars, for thirty miles.[11] At supper he replenished his energy by eating an enormous meal, and he also drank quite heavily from his stock of red wine from Gascony. Either before or after supper he spent an hour or so closeted with his secretary, who read the day's state papers and diplomatic reports to him, and received his instructions as to what to reply. Then the King settled down to his evening entertainments, sometimes attending masques, and dancing with the ladies, and sometimes playing cards – the game of cent, later called piquet – and gambling at dice with a small group of gentlemen of his household who were probably his closest friends. This gambling often went on until well after midnight, though most Englishmen were in bed soon after 9 p.m.

This daily routine did not leave him much time for governing his kingdom. Unlike his father, he did not attend the meetings of his Council or the smaller body of advisers which was sometimes called his 'secret council' or his 'privy council', though this term did not come into general use until twenty years later. It was not easy for his secretaries to persuade him to deal with his correspondence. He disliked writing letters, and he sometimes had to be urged several times before he agreed to copy out the letters which his secretary had drafted from him to foreign Kings, which international etiquette required should be written in the King's own hand. He disliked even reading letters, and wise people knew that if they wished to have a favourable reply from him, they must keep their letters short.

He would not deal with the day's correspondence, except in real emergencies, until he had gone out hunting; if he returned late from the hunt, as he often did, he refused to have the letters read to him until after supper. This could cause inconvenience, not only to the messenger who was kept waiting at court until the King had time to deal with the correspondence, but to the secretaries, ministers and foreign ambassadors whose routine or special arrangements were thrown into disarray as a result of the delay. But Henry had no cause to feel any compunction about this. The ministers and secretaries who wrote dispatches and handled state business while he hunted and enjoyed himself, were his servants, like the page who rose in the cold winter mornings to light the fire and warm the King's shirt in front of it.[12] He was their master, and it was their duty to serve him, not his duty to suit their convenience.

What duty did he owe to his servants, to his people? It is clear from everything that he wrote and said that he considered that his duty to them was to protect them against foreign enemies; to prevent the French and Scots from invading the realm and burning their homes, as his armies burned houses in France and Scotland; to ensure the safety and profits of his merchants at home and abroad; and to preserve law and order. More important than his duty to his subjects was the duty that he owed to his only superior, God; but this could be performed by observing the laws of the Church, by eating fish on the fast days and gorging himself on meat only on the other days, by going to Mass five times a day – or three times a day when he hunted[13] – by 'creeping to the cross' on Good Friday and performing the other ceremonies of the Church, and most important of all, by burning heretics who were guilty of pride, the sin of Lucifer, and who put their own opinions before the laws of the Church.

But the fact that Henry hunted all day and postponed dealing with his correspondence did not mean that he played no part in government. His closest advisers knew, though no one else did, that it was he who took the decisions. According to Gardiner, he sometimes took very important decisions rapidly while he was mounting or dismounting in the palace courtyard as he was leaving or returning from the hunt.[14] His business sessions with his secretaries may have taken only an hour of his day, but during this hour he decided what was to be done and told his secretary how to do it. He often corrected the wording in dispatches which had been drafted, and told his secretary to write to an ambassador ordering him to adopt a slightly different line. He involved himself in small details of government – at least in matters which interested him, like religious policy and foreign affairs – and if he had once been informed about a matter, he did not often forget it, and would ask what was happening about it, and made sure that his earlier directions had been carried out.

If he spent much more time in the saddle than in the council chamber, this was not only because he preferred pleasure to work, but also because it pleased his subjects. A King galloping through the countryside, covering thirty miles a day, was much more to their taste than a King sitting at the council board. It was also politically advantageous to dissociate himself from the government. If unpopular measures were introduced, if blunders were made, if the people were oppressed, this was not the King's fault, for the King had been out hunting in the fields. It was all the fault of hated, upstart ministers who had been running the country during the King's absence. When the King returned from hunting and realised what they had been up to, he would punish them and do justice to his subjects.

He was determined to shine as an intellectual as well as a sportsman, and to win the esteem of the partisans of the new culture as well as of those who loved the traditional martial and athletic pastimes of the age of chivalry. The ordinary English gentleman did not approve of books. 'By the body of God', said one of them to the humanist scholar, Richard Pace, in 1515, 'I would sooner see my son hanged than be a bookworm. It is a gentleman's calling to be able to blow the horn, to hunt and hawk. He should leave learning to clodchoppers'.[15] But the King liked books as well as the sound of the hunting horn.

The study of Greek, which had developed in Italy during the fifteenth century, had hardly begun in England when Henry VIII was born; but by the time he became King, a number of eminent intellectuals had appeared. Colet, Linacre, William Latimer, and Thomas More were flourishing under the protection of such powerful patrons of learning as Archbishop Warham and Bishop Fisher. These princes of the Church protected the scholars from the more conservative ecclesiastical officials in lower positions, who opposed the spread of humanist studies because it challenged traditional thinking and the authority of ignorant teachers.

Henry VIII was determined to be a greater patron of literature and the arts than Warham or Fisher or the Popes and Dukes in Italy. As well as encouraging the English humanists, he set out to draw the greatest foreign scholars to England. He persuaded Vives, the Spaniard, to come from Louvain, and Erasmus the Dutchman to come from Italy. Erasmus hated the sea-journey to England,[16] but he could not resist the invitation to visit the centre of culture which England was becoming under its brilliant young King, and he lived for five years in London and Cambridge. The German painter, Hans Holbein the younger, came to Henry's court. As for music, Henry was not only a patron but a composer. He wrote several musical compositions, including the songs 'Pastime with good company' and 'Helas Madam', the motet 'O Lord, the maker of all thing' and two five-part Masses; but there is no truth in the popular idea that he wrote the song 'Greensleeves'. He could play the lute, the organ and the virginals, and could sing well.

Henry's patronage of the arts, and his friendship with avant-garde intellectuals like Colet, Erasmus and More, is often seen as being inconsistent with his tyrannical behaviour in later years, and as a proof of the great change which occurred in him, and of the difference between the young and the old Henry VIII. But it is not surprising to find a dictator collaborating with intellectuals, and they with him. Intellectual and cultured statesmen can sometimes be ruthless men of action. They can admire the genius of intellectuals as well as making use of them as propagandists. In Tudor times, as in other centuries, intellectuals have had to rely on powerful individuals to protect them against the philistine masses; and eminent writers in modern times have admired savage autocrats, and have praised them in language almost as adulatory as the words in which Erasmus and More and other humanists wrote about Henry VIII.

There was an epidemic of plague in London during the late summer of 1509, and at the beginning of August Henry left the neighbourhood and went on a 'progress' to Hanworth, Sunninghill, Woking, Farnham, Esher, Enfield and Waltham before returning to Richmond towards the end of September.[17] He went on a similar progress in August and September nearly every year during the rest of his life, though sometimes he would go at other times, and stay away longer, to avoid the plague or the sweating sickness. He usually went by Oatlands near Weybridge, Woking, Guildford, Easthampstead and Abingdon to Woodstock, which was one of his favourite hunting lodges, and then east to Ampthill and north to Grafton in Northamptonshire, travelling back by Ampthill and Dunstable either to Windsor or to St Albans and his manors in Hertfordshire. But he changed his route if he heard that there had been an outbreak of plague or 'the sweat' near the places which he had planned to visit.

The fear, amounting almost to panic, which Henry showed about catching the diseases was partly due to the fact that until he produced a son and heir, his death would cause the gravest problems. The next in line to the throne was his sister Margaret, who had married James IV of Scotland; her accession would mean in practice that a Scottish King would be King of England, and this would certainly not be popular with the English. Next would come his other sister, Mary, still unmarried, but engaged to Prince Charles of Castile. This, too, would mean that England would be under a foreign ruler. But it was unlikely that either of Henry's sisters would be allowed to succeed to the crown without being challenged by the next in the line of succession, the Courtenays, the de la Poles, or, most probably, by Buckingham.

There was no doubt that the first duty of Henry and Catherine was to have a male child. Catherine was pregnant within a few weeks of their marriage, but in May 1510 she gave birth to a stillborn daughter. She was very distressed, and wrote to Ferdinand that it was regarded as a tragedy for the nation; but it was not her fault, it was God's will. She and Henry at once made another attempt, and on 1 January 1511 she gave birth to a boy, who was christened Henry. It was a splendid New Year's gift to the King and the realm, and the New Year's Day festivities were even more lavish than usual; but though Henry rode to the shrine of Our Lady of Walsingham to give thanks for the birth of a son, the baby died when he was seven weeks old.[18]

Not surprisingly, the vigorous, pleasure-loving young King was attracted by women. It was natural for him to have mistresses, as nearly all the other Kings did; but sex was the only sensuous pleasure in which Henry engaged discreetly and with at least some moderation. England in the early sixteenth century was not a country in which sexual promiscuity was regarded as lightly, by the aristocracy and other classes, as in the England of the Restoration, the Regency, and the twentieth century. Adultery and fornication might often be winked at among Kings, nobles and churchmen, but they were regularly punished in the ecclesiastical courts. Gluttony, not lechery, was the English vice; and Henry's subjects preferred not to know that their virtuous Christian King was committing adultery as well as hunting, jousting and banqueting. So, while he allowed his appetite for food to be well publicised, he kept quiet about his love affairs.

He probably went to bed with other women during the frequent periods when his Queen was in an advanced state of pregnancy; but if he did, he conducted the affairs with such discretion that only once was there any breath of scandal. In May 1510, in the closing stages of Catherine's first pregnancy, he was said to be pursuing the Duke of Buckingham's sister, Anne, who was the wife of Lord Hastings and one of Catherine's ladies-in-waiting. Anne's sister Elizabeth, Lady Fitzwalter, who was also one of Catherine's ladies, discovered that Anne was having secret assignations with Sir William Compton, Henry's Groom of the Bedchamber. Buckingham was sure that Compton was acting as the go-between in an affair between Anne and the King. He removed Anne from court, and sent her to a nunnery sixty miles away. According to the Spanish ambassador, Caroz, Henry was furious with Buckingham, and shouted angrily at him; he insisted that Catherine should dismiss Lady Fitzwalter, whom he accused of spying on him, and he also sent Lord Fitzwalter away from court.

Catherine did not accept the situation without a protest, and gave Henry a piece of her mind. She was a very strong-willed woman, and despite the reputation for meek submission which she afterwards acquired, she was capable, at least in her youth, of violent passions and strong resentments. But her quarrel with Henry soon subsided, and within a few days she was writing to Ferdinand that she thanked God and him for having given her such a husband as the King of England.[19]

Catherine's imperious temperament made her intolerant of the faults of her father's ambassadors. She had a flaming quarrel with Fuensalida, and with one of her Spanish ladies-in-waiting, during the difficult last months of Henry VII's reign, because they made adverse comments on her intimacy with her confessor, the friar Father Diego Fernandez. She wrote indignantly to Ferdinand, asking him to 'punish' Fuensalida. Ferdinand came down on his daughter's side. He wrote to Fuensalida and ordered him to prove his loyalty by adopting a submissive attitude towards Catherine, and by asking her pardon for having offended her, whether he was in the right or the wrong about the quarrel. When Caroz succeeded Fuensalida, he too became alarmed about the friar, and Catherine was soon asking Ferdinand to 'punish' Caroz.

Henry VIII adopted a tolerant attitude about Father Diego. Catherine was happier, now that she was Queen, than she had been as Princess Dowager of Wales, but she still sought spiritual solace from Diego. She was very close to him, and told him that she was pregnant before she told Henry. She spent a great deal of time alone with him, showed him many signs of affection in public, and enthusiastically praised him to others, particularly to his critics. Many people thought that her behaviour towards Diego was unwise, but Henry did not interfere. If he had believed that she was having a love affair with Diego, he would have reacted very strongly, for it was universally accepted that for a wife to commit adultery was a far more serious offence than when a husband did so; and adultery by a Queen, with the problems that it might raise for the succession, was everywhere considered to be a crime that should be punished by death. In England both the Queen and her lover would have been guilty of high treason. But Henry trusted Catherine. He did not become needlessly jealous, and he refused to draw the conclusions about her relations with her confessor that other people did.

For a long time, Ferdinand refused to allow Caroz to do anything against Father Diego. On the contrary, he ordered Caroz to make use of Diego's influence with Catherine to ensure that she continued to urge Henry to pursue a pro-Spanish foreign policy. But eventually Ferdinand received reports which convinced him that Diego was leading an immoral life, and in 1515 he accused Diego of fornication with harlots. The charge was investigated by Henry's confessor, Longland, the Bishop of Lincoln, and by the Earl of Surrey. They found Diego guilty. He was dismissed from his position as Catherine's confessor, and was sent back to Spain at Ferdinand's request. Diego wrote from Spain to Henry, denying the charge against him, stating that his life was in danger from Ferdinand, and offering to act as an English spy in Spain. His letter was apparently intercepted by Ferdinand's agents, and he was doubtless appropriately dealt with, for nothing further is known about him.[20]

4

GUINEGATTE AND FLODDEN

FROM the moment he became King, Henry VIII was thinking of going to war with France. His father's peaceful policy had kept England out of a major war for seventeen years; but war appealed to Henry VIII as peace had appealed to Henry VII, for he could distinguish himself and win glory in war. His nobles loved war for the same reason; and the common people had not forgotten the bygone days of Edward III and Henry V, of which their grandfathers had told them, when English armies won famous victories against the French, and it was said that every woman in England wore some jewel or trinket that her father, husband or lover had brought back as loot from France.

Henry gave a hint of what was coming at his first meeting with an envoy from 'the French King', as the English always called the King of France, because they thought that Henry VIII was the rightful King of France. Louis XII sent the fat and tactless Abbot of Fécamp to him in July 1509. The abbot began the conversation with Henry by saying that he had come because his King had received a letter from Henry asking him for peace and friendship. Henry flared up, thinking that this statement implied that he was afraid of the French King. He denied all knowledge of the letter, demanded to know which of his ministers had written it, and said that he would never ask for peace and friendship from the French King, who did not dare to look him in the face, still less to make war on him. He then walked out of the room, refusing to hear another word from the abbot. This account of the interview, by the Venetian ambassador, who was not present, is perhaps exaggerated, for Henry, however angry he might be, was never discourteous to foreign ambassadors.

The Venetian ambassador wrote that after the interview Henry went to watch riding at the ring, that sport in which riders, at full gallop, tried to put the point of their lance through a ring a few inches wide. The Abbot of Fécamp had been invited; but he found that no seat had been provided for him in the grandstand, and left. Henry then ordered a cushion to be brought for him, and the abbot returned and watched the entertainment.[1]

The incident between the King and the abbot became known, and was interpreted as a sign that Henry was preparing for war; but whatever Henry might say, he was always cautious before taking action. He took no further step towards war for the time being, and established friendly relations with the French; but his letter to Margaret of Austria of 23 June 1509, when he told her why he had married Catherine, shows that war against France was already in his mind.

Henry's Council was divided about peace or war. There were only two noblemen among his ministers, the Lord Steward of the Household, George Talbot, Earl of Shrewsbury, and the Lord Treasurer of England, Thomas Howard, who had been restored to the title of Earl of Surrey which he had forfeited for supporting Richard III but not to his dead father's title of Duke of Norfolk. Both Shrewsbury and Surrey were in favour of war, as were Surrey's sons, Lord Edward Howard, the Lord Admiral, and Lord Thomas Howard. Buckingham, who was not a member of the King's privy Council, was also strongly anti-French and in favour of war, and so was Queen Catherine. The churchmen on the Council – Warham, Foxe, Fisher and Ruthall, whom Henry VIII had appointed Bishop of Durham two days after he became King – were in favour of continuing the peaceful policy of Henry VII.

But the ground was dug from under the churchmen's feet by Pope Julius II, who was trying to build up an international coalition against France and was inciting his allies to war. France was the strongest military power in Europe, and other states were afraid of her. People everywhere laughed at the unheroic figure of the old invalid, Louis XII; but his armies, under valiant generals like Gaston de Foix and the gallant Bayard, '*le chevalier sans peur et sans reproche*', were dominating Italy and occupying Bologna in the Papal territories. King Ferdinand became alarmed at the French threat to Naples, and he made a league with the Pope and Venice against France.

Julius urged Henry to join the league. He put constant pressure on Cardinal Bainbridge, the Archbishop of York, who lived in Rome as Henry's representative at the Papal court. In April 1510 the Pope sent Henry a golden rose to show his regard for him and to encourage him to go to war.[2]

Ferdinand was delighted with Henry. He was getting old, his health was failing, he had developed a squint in his left eye, and the loss of a front tooth made him talk with a lisp. But he forgot his personal troubles in his satisfaction at the diplomatic success which he had achieved by Catherine's marriage to Henry. He thought that he had Henry in his pocket, that the young King would always follow his fatherly advice, and that England could be used to further the interests of Spain. His daughter encouraged his hopes; she wrote to him that he could be fully satisfied with the state of England and

Ireland, 'these kingdoms of Your Highness'.[3] It would be wrong to interpret Catherine's enthusiasm as evidence of a design on her part to make her husband a vassal of Spain; but neither she nor Ferdinand had any doubt that Henry would be completely under the influence of his father-in-law.

The chief impediment to Julius's plans was the hostility between the Emperor and his southern neighbours, the Venetians, with whom he had quarrelled bitterly about their rival claims to Verona and other frontier towns. Maximilian was hostile to France, but he made difficulties about joining a league with Venice. Instead, he and his daughter Margaret of Austria, who was his regent in the Netherlands, encouraged Henry to join the league against France which he refused to join himself. But Henry had no intention of becoming involved in a war with France until he could be sure of his allies. In January 1510 he wrote to Cardinal Bainbridge that he would not join the league unless both Ferdinand and Maximilian were in it.[4]

France's only ally was James IV of Scotland, whose kingdom on Henry's northern border was the most important factor in his foreign policy throughout his reign. Scotland suffered from two great disadvantages, the poverty of the country and its remoteness. The climate and the poor quality of the soil made the people far poorer than the English. There were only half a million inhabitants in Scotland – only one town had a population of over 5,000 – but the land could not provide a living for them all, and many of them emigrated. They were kept out of England by strict immigration laws; any Scot found in Berwick without a licence had his ears cut off and was branded in the face.[5] They were more welcome in other countries; many of them went to France, and some to Norway, East Prussia and Poland.

Like many poverty-stricken countries in modern times, Scotland had a small intellectual élite; it had three universities as compared to England's two, and eminent Scottish scholars taught in the universities of Europe. But Scotland remained for the people of other countries a barbaric and semi-mythical land, inhabited by 'wild Scots' in the north, and ending in a great field of stone and ice. Foreigners were fascinated by the stories they had heard of a strange kind of bird that was to be found in Scotland, which did not lay eggs but gave birth to its young by dropping them from the branches of the trees. The foreign writers never saw the bird; however far they travelled, they were always told that they would have to go even further north to find it.[6]

For more than three hundred years the Scots had been allies of the French against their common enemy, England; but geographical factors weakened the value of the alliance. It was not easy to travel between France and Scotland. Any Scot or Frenchman who entered England without a safe-conduct from the English government was promptly arrested and held indefinitely as a prisoner. Safe-conducts would be granted when relations with England were good, but refused if they were strained. If the safe-conduct was not granted, it was not only dangerous to travel overland through England, but it meant that the envoy or messenger who took ship from Leith or Dundee would be in serious difficulties if he encountered storms in the North Sea and could not put into port at Tynemouth, Hull or Yarmouth without being arrested. He faced the same difficulties if he sailed without a safe-conduct from Dumbarton down the west coast of England through the Irish Sea; while to sail far out into the Atlantic and pass to the west side of Ireland was much too risky to be even contemplated by any except the most daring seaman.

The international status of Scotland had risen sharply during the reign of James IV. He had set out to change the Scottish image and make Scotland one of the leading nations in Christendom. He built a navy; brought cannon from the Netherlands, including his great showpiece, 'Mons Meg'; opened gunpowder factories in Fife; and intervened in European politics. He had a splendid court, which included William Dunbar, David Lindsay, and other poets, and beautiful ladies, several of whom had love affairs with him. He was very religious, and, despite all the time that he spent in diplomacy, in inspecting his ships and his artillery, in hunting, and in pursuing women, he attended Mass several times every day.[7]

In 1503 he married Henry VII's daughter, Margaret; but the marriage did not lead to the good relations with England that many people had expected. He refused to repudiate the 'old alliance' with France, as Henry VII had hoped he would, and Anglo-Scottish relations became very bad during Henry VII's last years. They improved at first after the accession of Henry VIII; but it was obvious that they would come under strain if Henry went to war with France.

In the summer of 1511, Henry was informed about the activities of Andrew Barton, who was James IV's most able sea-captain. Like other Scottish sea-captains, Barton served in the King's navy on a part-time basis, combining it with trading as a merchant in his own ships. Barton's father had also been a shipowner, and thirty-five years before, one of his ships had been seized by a Portuguese fleet off the coast of Zeeland. James III protested to the King of Portugal, and demanded compensation for Barton; and as the Portuguese refused to pay, he granted letters of marque to the Bartons, which authorised them to seize any Portuguese ships until they had recovered the value of their captured ship. But he suspended the operation of the letters of marque in the hope that the Portuguese could be persuaded, by diplomatic pressure, to compensate the Bartons.

After James IV became King, he renewed the letters of marque on several occasions and then suspended them. In 1510 he again renewed the Bartons' letters of marque. Andrew Barton and his brother Robert seized and robbed Portuguese ships. Margaret of Austria arrested Robert Barton and threatened to hang him as a pirate, but James IV intervened and told her about the Bartons' letters of marque. Andrew Barton robbed a richly-laden Portuguese ship on her way to London. This alarmed the London merchants, who feared for the effect on London's trade if foreign shipowners were to think that they could not safely sail to London. Andrew Barton twice stopped an English ship and removed some of the goods on board on the grounds that they were the property of Portuguese subjects.

Henry sent orders to Lord Edward Howard to find and destroy Andrew Barton. Lord Edward and his brother Lord Thomas sailed at once in two ships to intercept Andrew Barton as he returned from the Netherlands to Scotland in his ship, *The Lion*. They came on him in the Downs on 2 August 1511. The two English ships were separated in the sea-mist, but Lord Thomas Howard chased *The Lion* and engaged her, while Lord Edward pursued and captured a smaller pinnace which was accompanying *The Lion*. A very fierce fight took place between Lord Thomas and Barton. After a brave resistance, Barton was shot by an arrow from an English archer, and the English then captured *The Lion* and its crew. Barton fell alive into his enemy's hands, but died almost immediately from his wound, which solved the problem as to whether the Howards and Henry were to hang him as a pirate or treat him as a prisoner of war. *The Lion*, with the prisoners, was brought into Blackwall.

Henry was on a progress through the Midlands, travelling through Northamptonshire and Leicestershire to Nottingham, where he stayed for three weeks before returning to the south by Coventry, Warwick, Woodstock and Windsor.* A messenger was sent northwards at once to tell the King about Barton's death and the capture of *The Lion*, while the prisoners were sent to York. There they were visited by Foxe, who had gone to Nottingham with the King. He told them that they were all pirates who should be hanged according to law, but that if they admitted their crime and begged for mercy, King Henry might grant them their lives. They all agreed to do so, and Foxe then informed them that Henry had pardoned them and would send them back to Scotland with a gift of money for each man, but that they would be hanged if they were ever caught committing piracy again.

It was a subtle question of law as to whether Andrew Barton was a pirate or a loyal Scottish sea-captain carrying out the orders of his King under lawful letters of marque. If in fact, as the English claimed, he had seized the goods of

*Hall states that it was at Leicester in June 1511 that Henry was informed about Andrew Barton's piracies and ordered the Howards to act against him; but this must be an error. Hall also states that the sea-fight with Barton took place on 2 August. Henry did not leave Windsor on his journey north till after 16 July. He was at Stony Stratford by 24 July, at Liddington in Rutland on 3 and 4 August, and in Nottingham by 9 August. There is no record of his having been to Leicester, but it is more than likely that he went there on his journey from Liddington to Nottingham. He might well have been at Leicester, between 4 and 9 August, when he heard about Barton's death and the capture of *The Lion*; and this might account for Hall's error.

English traders and of the subjects of other countries than Portugal, he was technically a pirate; but it was a little high-handed of Henry to order an attack on the King of Scots' great ship without first raising the matter with James by diplomatic means. Henry seems to have acted on the principle which has guided British admirals on many occasions in later times – that the chance to destroy a dangerous or potentially dangerous enemy warship must not be lost from an undue regard for the niceties of international law.

James sent a herald to Henry to protest at the death of Barton and to demand the return of *The Lion*. Henry replied that Barton was a pirate, that the death of a pirate should not lead to a quarrel between Princes, and that he was entitled to keep *The Lion* as lawful prize.[8]

James was indignant, but still hoped to avoid war with England. He did not wish to be drawn into the coming European conflict. He was particularly reluctant to take up arms against the Pope. Julius had summoned a General Council of the Church – the first to be held for seventy years – to meet at the Lateran Palace in Rome in May 1512. Louis XII refused to send representatives, and persuaded four cardinals to summon a rival General Council to meet at Bologna. Julius denounced Louis and his General Council at Bologna as schismatic. In July 1512 he issued a bull against Louis XII, which proclaimed that when Christ, after His incarnation and death on the cross, returned to Heaven, he left on earth a Vicar whose chief duty is to preserve the flock confided to him in the true religion and to expel those sheep which are infected and refuse to be cured. As the Devil, with his diabolical wiles, had ensnared Louis, King of France, and had instigated him to occupy Bologna and Ravenna and to call a schismatic General Council, the Pope had called on his beloved son Ferdinand, the King Catholic, and his beloved son Henry, King of England, to defend the Church, and had excommunicated all those who fought for the King of France.[9]

James IV refused to send delegates to the General Council at Bologna, and wrote to the Pope apologising for Louis' action and trying to excuse it. He wrote to the Papal court protesting that Henry, who called himself the Pope's soldier, was attacking and robbing his subjects. But the Pope issued a plenary indulgence granting pardon for all sins committed during the next six months to any soldier who fought for Henry or his other allies.[10]

For the first years after Henry's accession, Foxe and Ruthall were, or appeared to be, the most influential of Henry's ministers. Caroz wrote to Ferdinand in May 1510 that all government business was in the hands of the Bishops of Winchester and Durham: when he discussed the international situation with Henry, the King showed that he was Ferdinand's most obedient son; but he referred all details to Foxe and Ruthall, who were very slow in dealing with them. Caroz wrote that, in this respect, they were the exact opposite of the King, who was irritated by long, detailed discussion. But Caroz's letter makes it plain that neither Foxe nor Ruthall, nor Warham nor any of the other members of the Council, were in control of the government of England, and that they were merely executives who carried out Henry's decisions for as long as he trusted them to do so. In the summer of 1510, when Henry was moving cautiously towards joining the anti-French alliance, he told Caroz not to discuss relations with France with anyone except the Bishop of Winchester (Foxe). Caroz asked Henry if he confided in the Bishop of Winchester. 'Yes, at my risk', replied Henry. 'Here in England they think he is a fox, and this is his name'.[11]

Two new men were becoming influential at Henry's court. One of them was the Dean of Lincoln, Thomas Wolsey, and the other was a gentleman of Henry's bodyguard, Charles Brandon. Wolsey had entered Henry VII's service a few years before the old King's death, and had very ably carried out several diplomatic missions for him. Soon after his accession, Henry VIII appointed him to be his almoner, and in the autumn of 1511 he was made a member of the King's Council. He was far more energetic than the other counsellors, and in no time he was dominating the Council. In contrast to Foxe and Ruthall, Wolsey was a very fast worker; and he was always ready to take a short cut instead of proceeding through the proper channels if this would help expedite business, even if it meant breaking the regulations and treading on other ministers' corns. These qualities appealed to Henry.

According to George Cavendish, who a few years later became Wolsey's gentleman-usher, Wolsey gained the favour of Henry VIII because the other counsellors tried to persuade Henry to preside at Council meetings, as his father had done, and Wolsey encouraged him to go hunting and enjoy himself while Wolsey governed the country for him. Cavendish added that whereas the other ministers advised Henry to do what they thought he ought to do, Wolsey found out what Henry wanted to do, and then advised him to do it.[12] This was certainly an over-simplification; but Wolsey was just the minister that Henry required. He would carry out the duties of government very efficiently, and take the burden of state affairs off Henry's shoulders, while always informing Henry of what was happening and consulting with him, and always leaving the final decision to the King.

Charles Brandon was the son of William Brandon, who had been Henry VII's standard-bearer at the battle of Bosworth, and had been killed at Henry's side by Richard III himself. Charles was brought up at court, and was appointed to various positions in the King's household. Within a few months of Henry VIII's accession he had become a close friend of the King. He was Henry's companion at the hunt during the day and at the gaming tables at night. His bluff, jovial personality and unabashed manner pleased Henry, who created him Viscount Lisle.

In the discussions in the Council about peace or war, Wolsey, unlike the other churchmen, came down on the side of the nobles who wanted war. His influence, the wishes of the nobility, the pressure of the Pope and Ferdinand and Catherine, and last but not least Henry's personal preference and his sense of what would make him popular, crushed the opposition of the peace party in the Council. Henry decided to act without waiting for the Emperor. On 13 November 1511 he joined the coalition of the Pope, Ferdinand and Venice, and four days later he made a treaty with Spain by which he and Ferdinand agreed to go to war with France in defence of the Church and to compel the French King to surrender the Pope's town of Bologna. It was agreed that, as soon as convenient, Ferdinand would fight the French in Italy while Henry invaded France from the north; and in the meantime, a joint Anglo-Spanish force would attack Aquitaine, which by right belonged to Henry, before 30 April next. When Aquitaine was conquered, it would be annexed to Henry's realm.[13]

Maximilian was still dragging his feet, refusing to join a coalition with his Venetian enemies. Henry wrote to him urging him to play his part in the war against the worse than Turkish cruelty of Louis XII, who, though he dared to call himself 'the Most Christian King', had lacerated the seamless garment of our Lord Jesus Christ by invading the Papal states.[14]

In April 1512, Henry sent a force of 7,000 men to Spain, under the command of the Marquess of Dorset. The King went to Southampton to cheer them on their way. After going on board his ships, he wrote to Cardinal Bainbridge in Rome that there had never been a body of men more ready to die for the cause of the Church and the Holy Father, and that they regarded their French enemies as being Turks, heretics and infidels.[15] The soldiers landed at San Sebastian and joined 7,000 of Ferdinand's troops. There they discovered that Ferdinand's plan was not to invade Aquitaine and give it to Henry, but to seize the kingdom of Navarre for himself.

Henry had ordered Dorset to place himself under the command of the Spanish generals, and to obey Ferdinand as if he were his own King; but disputes broke out between Dorset and the Spanish commanders. Dorset agreed to participate in the invasion of Navarre, and the country was occupied without meeting much resistance. He then wished to invade Guienne, while Ferdinand chose to consolidate his position and complete the conquest of Navarre. Eventually Ferdinand proposed an invasion of France across the Pyrenees through Béarn from Pamplona; but Dorset advised an attack on Bayonne on the west coast.

The English soldiers, in their camp at Fuentarrabia, became more and more dissatisfied. They were not used to the hot climate, and were greatly put out by the fact that they could not get beer at Fuentarrabia. By the beginning of August they were on the point of mutiny; they refused to serve unless they were paid eightpence a day, and told their captains that they would only stay till Michaelmas. The English ambassador at Ferdinand's court, Stile, who had gone with the army to Fuentarrabia, wrote to Henry on 5 August and warned him about the situation: 'And it please your Grace, the greatest lack of victuals that we have is of beer, for your subjects had liefer for to drink beer than wine or cider, for the hot wines doth burn them, and the cider doth cast them in disease and sickness'.[16] Dorset decided that he had no choice but to march his mutinous troops back to San Sebastian and sail with them to England.

Henry was very angry when he heard of the events at Fuentarrabia, and ashamed when he received Ferdinand's reproachful letter. It was the second setback which he had suffered that summer. He had sent the Lord Admiral, Lord Edward Howard, to raid the coast of Brittany. Howard burned many Breton villages, but his fleet encountered the French navy off Brest, and in the action the largest of Henry's warships, *The Regent* of 1,000 tons, was burned with the loss of her captain, Sir Thomas Knyvett, and nearly all the crew.

Henry's first reaction to the news from Fuentarrabia was to order that all the mutineers should be hanged; but at the request of the Spanish ambassador he eventually decided to adopt a merciful attitude. The captains of Dorset's army were summoned to the King's palace at Westminster. Henry reprimanded them, and ordered them to ask forgiveness of the Spanish ambassador on their knees.[17]

The Fuentarrabia fiasco was to have serious long-term results. It made Ferdinand distrust the English, and began the process by which each of the allies in turn – first Ferdinand, then Henry, then Maximilian, and then Henry again – betrayed the others and conspired with France behind their backs. But neither the humiliation in Spain nor the defeat at Brest brought any discredit or unpopularity for Henry. The soldiers at Fuentarrabia had grumbled about Wolsey, holding him responsible for their hardships and the beer shortage; but they did not blame the King.

The defeats of 1512 would be forgotten if the King's great expedition against France was successful, and Henry made preparations to invade France in the summer of 1513. He made no attempt to conceal his plans, and to have the advantage of surprise, for this was to be first and foremost a propaganda expedition and a propaganda victory. In November 1512 he summoned a Parliament, which met in his palace at Westminster. He told the peers and commons that he himself in person, with an 'army royal', would invade his realm of France with fire and sword. By January the ambassadors in London were writing to their governments giving details of the naval preparations, and informing them that Henry would lead an army of 60,000 men to Calais by Easter. When Easter passed, and no invasion took place, the reports foretold that it would be in May, and later, that it would be in June.[18] Meanwhile Henry suffered another disaster in April, when Lord Edward Howard attacked the French fleet off Brest. The French were commanded by Admiral Prégent, whose name sufficiently resembled that of the mythical King of Ethiopia for the English to call him 'Prester John'. Howard himself led a boarding party which boarded Prégent's flagship, but the English were repulsed, and Howard was killed in the action.

Henry gave maximum publicity to the military preparations that were being made against the Scots. Like everyone of his subjects, he was confident that the English could always beat the French and the Scots at the same time; had not Edward III, a hundred and seventy years before, invaded France and won the glorious victory of Crécy, while an army, left behind in the North of England, had defeated and captured the King of Scots at Neville's Cross? But Henry made an attempt to preserve peace with James and to prevent an attack by the Scots in his rear. He told Nicholas West, his ambassador at Stirling, to assure James that he would be more willing to grant safe-conducts in future to Scottish merchants to travel through England, and to remind James that any ally of the French King would be excommunicated by the Pope. James said that if the Pope excommunicated him, he would appeal against the sentence. West asked him whom he could appeal to,for there was no appeal from the Pope's decision. James's sense of humour got the better of him; he laughed, and said that he would appeal to Prester John. West reported this to Henry, who wrote at once to the Pope to tell him of James's blasphemous threat to appeal from the Pope to Admiral Prégent's fleet.[19]

The final step in the creation of the alliance against France was taken on 5 April 1513, when the Emperor Maximilian at last agreed to join the league. But Ferdinand chose this very moment to betray his allies. Four days earlier, he had made a secret agreement with Louis XII for a truce, by which he agreed not to invade France during the next twelve months. Ferdinand assured Henry that he had not withdrawn from the alliance, but had only made a temporary truce with France; he said that he had done this because, being old and ill, he feared that he might die soon, and his confessor had told him that he should not allow his heir to succeed to the throne in the middle of a war. But he told his ministers that he had decided to withdraw from the war because he could not trust the English not to let him down, as they had done at Fuentarrabia.[20]

Ferdinand's action caused violent indignation in England, and there was an outbreak of hostility against Spanish residents in London; but the English were willing to fight the French without anyone's help, and the preparations for the invasion of France continued unchecked. The foreign merchants in England caught the enthusiasm of the native Englishmen. The Venetian merchant, Pasqualigo, wrote to his brother in Venice that there had not been a King more noble or more valiant than Henry for a thousand years.[21]

Only the intellectuals opposed the war fever. Their reason told them that it was wrong and absurd, and they had the imagination to realise what it would mean to the soldiers who were killed and maimed, to their widows, parents and families, and to the citizens and peasants whose towns and farms were burned and looted. Erasmus had had personal experience, in the

Netherlands, of the way in which mercenaries in the armies of Emperors and Kings behaved towards the civilian population; he believed that disputes between states should be settled peacefully by arbitration. He was particularly shocked that it was the Pope, the Vicar on earth of the Prince of Peace, who had deliberately instigated this major European war. But Erasmus kept quiet for the time being; he was always cautious not to offend the Kings who patronised him. Thomas More, who may already have been thinking of entering the King's service, showed his profoundly conservative instincts by going with the popular tide and writing a fiercely anti-French tract. Warham had made a speech in the House of Lords in favour of peace in February 1512, but since then had made no public comment.[22]

Only one of the intellectuals spoke out openly against the war. John Colet, the Dean of St Pauls, preached a number of sermons at Paul's Cross, the great open-air pulpit in the churchyard of St Paul's Cathedral, in which he denounced war in general terms as a sin. This was a risky course for Colet to pursue, because only a year before he had been denounced as a heretic by his enemy, Richard Fitzjames, the aged Bishop of London, though he had been completely exonerated after a hearing before Warham. Many people were angered at Colet's anti-war sermons.

On 25 March 1513 Colet preached the Good Friday sermon before the King at Greenwich. He condemned Princes who were eager to follow in the footsteps of Alexander the Great and Julius Caesar rather than in those of Jesus Christ, and he said that an unjust peace was better than a just war. Henry summoned Colet to come to his presence, but then, hearing that Colet was staying at the house of the Friars Observants at Greenwich, he walked over to the friary and talked to him in the garden about his sermon. He told Colet that he had not come to disturb him at his studies, but to relieve his own conscience, as he was perturbed by the fact that, when he was about to go to war, Colet should denounce war as an evil. Did not Colet recognise that there was such a thing as a just war? Colet agreed, but stressed the evils of war, and after he and Henry had had a long talk about the morality of war, Henry ordered wine to be brought, and told Colet that though he did not agree with all he said, he had the highest regard for him. According to Erasmus, who probably heard about the incident from Colet, Henry told his courtiers that every man had his favourite doctor, but that Colet was the doctor for him.[23]

It was an impressive picture – the handsome young King, who would soon be twenty-two, leading his people in a just war for the defence of the Church and the Holy Father, preparing to wage it in accordance with all the laws of chivalry, but strong enough and great enough to tolerate the expression of pacifist opinions and to respect the sincerity of his pacifist critics, knowing that they could not shake his subjects' loyalty and patriotism. Hardly anyone noticed that at this very time Henry quietly gave orders that his prisoner in the Tower, Edmund de la Pole, should be put to death in breach of the promise which his father had given to Philip of Habsburg that Edmund's life would be spared if he were extradited to England. Without any kind of legal proceedings, Edmund was taken out one day to the Tower green and beheaded, under the death sentence for high treason which had been passed by an Act of Parliament while he was a refugee abroad, eleven years before.

Perhaps Henry thought that his father's promise to spare Edmund's life did not bind his successor; according to Guillaume Du Bellay, who twenty years later was sent on a diplomatic mission to London but is not necessarily reliable on this point, Henry VII himself had said this to his son on his deathbed. Perhaps he argued that Pole had committed a new act of treason which absolved him from the promise. According to the Spanish scholar, Peter Martyr de Anglería, who was one of the few contemporaries to comment on the execution, Edmund wrote secretly to his brother Richard, who was fighting in the French King's army, urging him to invade England, and his letter was intercepted by Henry's officers.[24] Hardly anyone cared about Edmund de la Pole's fate, or even noticed what Henry had done, just as they did not notice the cruel piggy eyes of their tall, golden-haired hero.

At last the expedition was ready to sail, and on 15 June Henry left Greenwich with Catherine, and travelled by slow stages to Dover. He was taking Wolsey, Buckingham, Dorset, Essex and many of his nobles with him to France, as well as the officers of his household, including Charles Brandon, the new Viscount Lisle. Catherine would remain in England to govern his kingdom during his absence, with the help of a Council consisting of Warham, Foxe, Ruthall and some of the Judges. Surrey and his son Lord Thomas Howard were to command the army guarding the northern frontier from attack by the Scots.

Henry parted from Catherine at Dover, and embarked at 4 p.m. on 30 June.[25] It was a beautiful summer afternoon, and the sails of the three hundred ships of his navy seemed to fill the Channel; one of his officers wrote that it was a fleet such as Neptune never saw. The sea was calm, and he reached Calais at 7 p.m. He was welcomed with great pomp on his first visit to his town of Calais, and was escorted by the clergy through the decorated streets to the church of St Nicholas to give thanks for his safe arrival before proceeding to his lodgings.

It was just not too late in the year to launch the invasion, though at the most only four months of campaigning weather remained. In the sixteenth century, it was almost impossible to keep an army in the field after the end of October;* after this, the roads would be too wet and muddy for the soldiers to

*With reference to this, and to all other days of the year, it should be remembered that the Julian calendar, which was used all over Europe in Henry VIII's reign, was ten days behind our modern Gregorian calendar, and that when Henry and his contemporaries spoke of 31 October, they meant 10 November by our calendar.

march or for the carts carrying supplies to reach them; and there might be difficulties in finding shelter for the men during the colder weather. As it was much too expensive to pay the mercenaries while they remained inactive during the winter, the army had to be disbanded at the beginning of November, if not earlier; and if the war still continued, a new campaign had to be planned and a new army raised for the next summer.

Henry had therefore no time to lose before leading his men against the enemy. But his whole campaign in France was primarily a propaganda exercise, and he wasted three weeks of campaigning weather while he waited in Calais, going to Mass in St Mary's church in glittering processions, meeting foreign envoys, taking part in the usual tournaments and banquets, competing at archery with his guard in a garden and beating them all as he cleft the mark in the middle, knighting many of the gentlemen of his household, and pardoning petty criminals. It was not until 21 July that he marched out of Calais. On the same day the weather broke, and the fine weather gave way to a long period of rain and strong winds. The army camped the first night at Coulogne, in heavy rain and a gale. Henry stayed up till 3 a.m., walking around the camp and encouraging his men. 'Well, comrades', he said to them, 'now that we have suffered in the beginning, fortune promises us better things, God willing'.[26]

On the fifth day's march they entered French territory, and camped near Ardres. Some of Henry's German mercenaries set fire to some churches in Ardres, and the fire spread through the town. Henry had three of the Germans hanged. As the army advanced slowly towards Thérouanne, they met no open resistance, but the French were harrying their flank. On 27 July, when they were near Tournehem, they had their first and only hot day, which the soldiers remembered as 'dry Wednesday'; they encountered an enemy force, and fought for the first time in the great heat. They beat off the enemy, and continued their march. The rain returned, with thick fog on some mornings. They came to a stream which was so swollen with rain that the infantry hesitated to ford it, especially as the French were lurking near, ready to attack them while they were in the water. Henry dismounted, and waded into the river on foot, leading his horse by the bridle; and the men, encouraged by his bravery, followed him across.

It took them twelve days to march the twenty-five miles from Calais to within three miles of Thérouanne; but it then rained so hard for two days and nights that they could not move forward with the artillery, and it was not until 4 August that they were able to invest the town. Henry battered the walls with his twelve cannons, each of which was decorated with a picture of one of the apostles.

He prepared for a long siege. He had an impressive wooden pavilion built for himself before the walls; it was 125 foot long, with an iron chimney, and had at least six rooms. There were other wooden adjacent buildings for

The *Henry Grace-à-Dieu*, popularly known as the *Great Harry*. Watercolour drawing from the Anthony Roll, a series of drawings of some of Henry's fleet, including the *Mary Rose*, made by a nautical artist in 1546

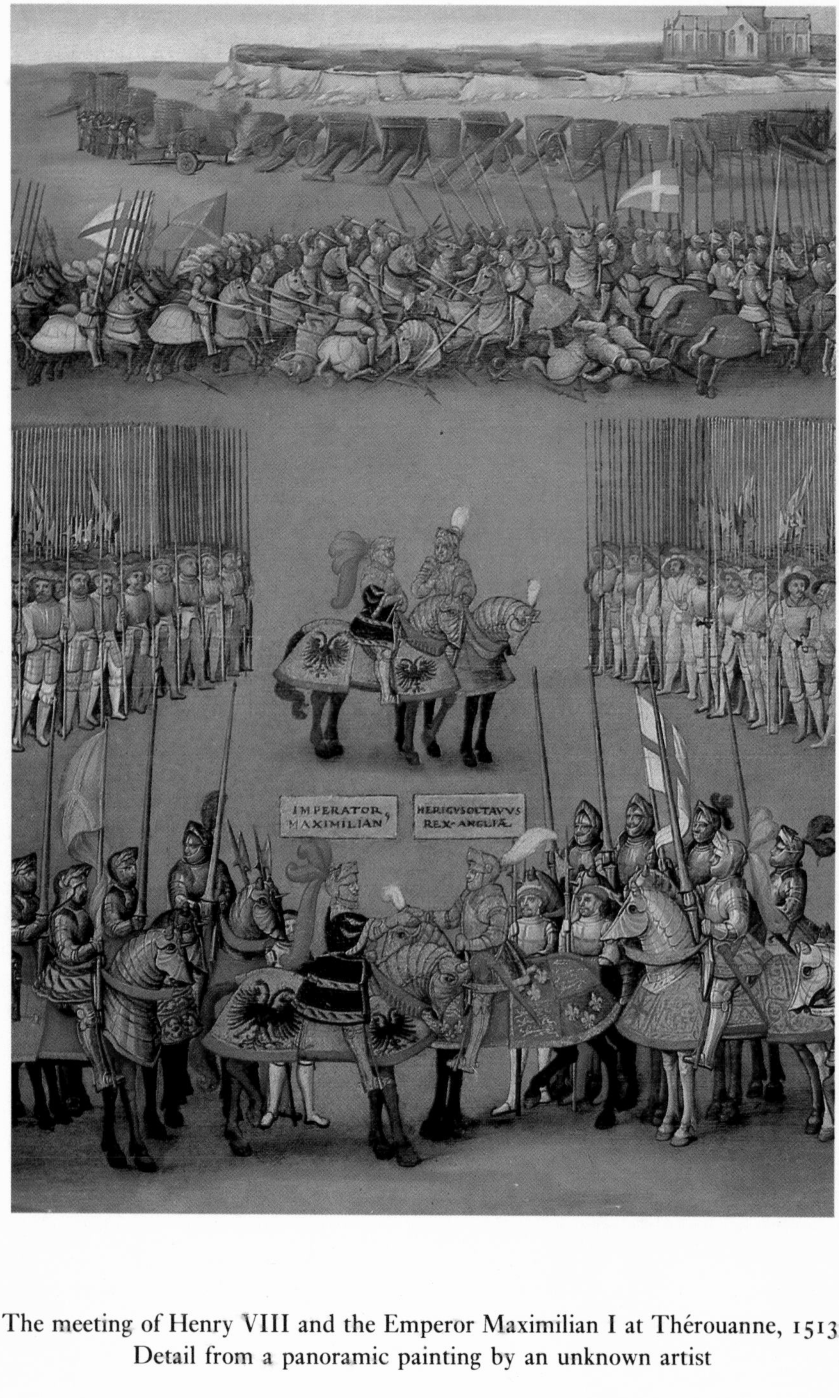

The meeting of Henry VIII and the Emperor Maximilian I at Thérouanne, 1513.
Detail from a panoramic painting by an unknown artist

Henry's counsellors and for visiting ambassadors. His officers were lodged in impressive and colourful tents. As usual, he was conscious of the propaganda effect, and wished the siege to be conducted as an impressive spectacle. The organisation of supplies, which was usually the weak point in sixteenth-century warfare, was managed very efficiently by Wolsey; according to one of Margaret of Austria's gentlemen who visited the camp, everything was in the hands of 'two obstinate men', Wolsey and Lord Lisle.[27]

The Emperor Maximilian, with a small Burgundian force, was at Aire, which was only six miles from Thérouanne but was across the frontier in Flanders. Henry went to Aire to meet him, and he and the Emperor greeted each other warmly. Maximilian came to Henry's camp at Thérouanne; he expressed his high regard for him, and offered to serve in Henry's army as a simple pikeman. This offer was not meant seriously, and was of course refused; but Maximilian, who was prepared to do anything to get money out of Henry, insisted in wearing the cross of St George, which was the uniform of Henry's men. He gave Henry the benefit of his advice about operations at Thérouanne, for he had much experience of siege warfare.

James IV had finally decided that he had no alternative but to enter the war on the side of his French ally. On 26 July he sent Lyon Herald to Henry with his declaration of war. The herald found Henry before Thérouanne on 12 August, and read out James's challenge. It gave, as the reason for declaring war, that Henry was invading the realm of James's ally, the King of France, and mentioned several other causes of complaint, including the killing of Andrew Barton. Henry, in his reply, accepted James's challenge, and criticised him for allying himself with a schismatic. Both James's declaration, and Henry's reply, were worded in the most courteous language.[28]

The French sent 8,000 men to force Henry to raise the siege of Thérouanne. The news that they were on their way reached Henry in his camp at Guinegatte (today Enguinegatte), on the high ground to the south of Thérouanne, on the morning of 16 August, and he and his army advanced to meet the French. The armies made contact near the village of Bomy. After the English artillery had thrown the advancing French into disorder, Henry sent his cavalry to charge the enemy. According to the chronicler Edward Hall, who wrote a detailed account of the campaign in France and must have received his information from soldiers in the English army, Henry wished to lead the cavalry charge in person, but was dissuaded from doing so by his nobles, and agreed to take up his position, at the Emperor's side, with the infantry in the rear. This was the story which reached England, and was what the people wanted to believe about their gallant King.

The infantry engaged in hand-to-hand fighting; but in a short time the French turned and fled, with their cavalry galloping away so fast that the French called the battle 'the Day of the Spurs'. Several French noblemen, including the Duke of Longueville, were taken prisoner, as was the great Bayard, while he was vainly trying to rally his men and prevent them from running away. Why the French, who had recently won convincing victories in Italy, should have put up such a pitiable exhibition at Bomy, is something of a mystery; but it was no surprise to the English, who had proved once again that they could always beat the French.

Henry treated the noblemen whom he had captured with great honour, and insisted that they should dine with him in his pavilion. He sent the Duke of Longueville and the other noble prisoners to England, where they were imprisoned in the Tower; but he released Bayard without a ransom as a mark of respect for Bayard's bravery, and merely required him to promise not to serve in the French army for six weeks. It was a great victory, and was rightly seen as such in England, though the people do not seem to have realised that the Burgundians played a part in it. Hall wrote that Maximilian and his men-at-arms served in Henry's army, wearing the red cross of St George; but he did not mention that 2,000 of Maximilian's soldiers fought in the battle.

Six days after the victory, the garrison of Thérouanne offered to surrender, and on 24 August Henry and Maximilian entered the town in triumph. They allowed the garrison to depart with their arms. The old Emperor gave pride of place to the young King in the streets and at the thanksgiving service in the cathedral. While Henry was in Thérouanne, four of his English soldiers went off to Aire, where they looted and fought with the local inhabitants. Henry ordered that two of them, who were brothers, should be hanged, but he allowed the other two, who were also brothers, to return to their units.

Henry offered to hand over Thérouanne to Maximilian; but as Maximilian was unable to garrison it, he burned it. The English writers placed the blame for this entirely on the Emperor, but Henry's soldiers helped the Burgundians to level the fortifications and the houses which could not be destroyed by fire.[29]

Henry and his army then entered the Emperor's territories, and advanced on Tournai, which the French had captured from Maximilian and held as an isolated outpost in Flanders. On his way, he went to Lille, where Margaret of Austria and Maximilian were staying with their court. Henry entered Lille in great state, wearing his crown, as if he were opening a Parliament at Westminster. He was loudly cheered by the people as he rode through the decorated streets.

He reached an agreement with Maximilian that if he succeeded in capturing Tournai, he could retain it for himself as part of his realm; and he agreed to advance another 200,000 crowns to Maximilian. After three days of festivities in Lille, he marched to Tournai, and arrived before the walls on 15 September.[30] Tournai was a large, prosperous and beautiful town on the River Scheldt, with several water-mills and bridges. Only half a dozen towns in England were as large as Tournai; the walk around the walls was a distance of three miles, and there were ninety-nine towers and steeples in the city, including all the fortresses and churches.[31] Henry invested Tournai, battered the walls with his artillery, and waited in his gold and purple pavilion till the garrison and citizens were starved into surrender.

James IV had crossed the Border near Coldstream with 20,000 men on 22 August. He had brought with him his magnificent Flemish cannons, which were dragged along the roads by 356 oxen and 150 soldiers. He gained an early success, quickly capturing Norham Castle, the most important of the English Border fortresses, which was supposed to be strong enough to withstand a long siege. He also took the smaller castles of Wark, Etal and Ford within a few days. He sent Sir William Heron, the owner of Ford Castle, as a prisoner to Scotland, and set up his headquarters at Ford, where he proceeded to make love to Lady Heron, while his illegitimate son, the twenty-two-year-old Archbishop of St Andrews, made love to Lady Heron's daughter. None of the contemporary chroniclers mention Lady Heron, but sixty years later the Protestant writers George Buchanan and Lindsay of Pitscottie told the well-known story of how Lady Heron patriotically became James's mistress in order to keep him inactive at Ford while the Earl of Surrey raised an army to march against him. They describe how Lady Heron and her daughter tricked James and his son into revealing his plan of campaign and into allowing Lady Heron to go to York, where she passed on the vital military information to Surrey.

It seems unlikely that Lady Heron had any influence on the campaign, for James probably never intended to penetrate very far into England, and hoped to fight and destroy Surrey's army somewhere in the neighbourhood of Ford. But the story of James, with his fatal weakness for women, being lured to his fate by the sexual wiles of an English Delilah, appealed to the Scottish Protestants of the 1570s. Pitscottie was prepared to give Lady Heron the credit of being motivated by the 'love she bore to her native country'; but she was nevertheless 'this wicked lady of Ford'. He attributed the Scottish defeat to the fact that 'the stinking adultery and fornication had a great part of their evil success'.[32]

Surrey, who had fought his first battle in the Wars of the Roses before James IV was born, was as vigorous as ever at the age of seventy. As he marched north, he took the great banner of St Cuthbert from Durham Cathedral, and had it carried at the head of his army, as it had been carried to victory against the Scottish invaders in 1138 and 1346. He sent a challenge to James to meet him in battle on Friday 9 September. Lord Thomas Howard added a challenge of his own, telling James that he had come to answer for the death of Andrew Barton, and that his men would give no quarter and would take no prisoners except James himself.

The battle that took place on 9 September was called by the Scots the battle of Flodden. The English, who knew the district better, correctly called it the battle of Branxton; but history has adopted the name that the losers gave it. If there had in fact been a battle fought at Flodden, the Scots might have fared better, for James and his army had established themselves in a good position at the top of Flodden Hill. But Surrey, leaving the Scottish army on his left flank, passed to their rear, and got between them and the Border; and James, thinking that the enemy was intending to invade Scotland, left Flodden Hill and marched his 20,000 men a few miles to the north-east to the village of Branxton, where he occupied the summit of Branxton Hill, which was lower than Flodden Hill. Surrey and his 13,000 soldiers were at the bottom of the hill.

James opened fire with his great cannons, but they were badly sighted, and shot harmlessly over the heads of the enemy. He then ordered his men to charge, and they took off their shoes and ran down the hill, led by the King himself. The smaller English cannons fired at the advancing Scots, but far more damage was done by the English archers, who for the last time in history played a decisive part in winning a battle. The Scots infantry carried long pikes, which might have given them an advantage over the English with their shorter bills; but the English cut through the wooden shafts of the pikes with their bills, and then killed the disarmed Scottish pikemen. The English, as they had promised, took no prisoners, and the Scottish losses were heavy. King James was killed in the fighting, and the dead included his son the Archbishop of St Andrews, another bishop, two abbots, twelve earls, fourteen lords – nearly all the Scottish nobility – as well as knights, gentlemen and the common soldiers. The English losses were not heavy. James's body was identified with difficulty, and was sent to London. It could not be buried anywhere, because James had been excommunicated.[33]

On 17 September a messenger, riding 'in post' with relays of horses, arrived in Henry's camp at Tournai with news of the victory over the Scots at Branxton. Henry immediately ordered a Mass of thanksgiving to be held in his pavilion.[34] Four days later, another messenger arrived from Catherine, and laid at Henry's feet a piece of cloth which had been cut from James IV's plaid. He also brought a letter from Catherine. 'I think your Grace shall see how I can keep my promise', she wrote, 'sending you for your banners a King's coat. I thought to send himself unto you, but our Englishmen's hearts would not suffer it. It should have been better for him to have been in peace than have this reward. All that God sendeth is for the best'.[35]

One success followed another. On the day that Catherine's messenger arrived with James's plaid, the garrison of Tournai surrendered, having heard that the French were unable to make any attempt to relieve them. The keys of the city were handed over next day, and on 24 September Henry rode in triumph into Tournai with great pageantry.[36]

Flodden was to have a decisive influence on events in Scotland and on the fortunes of Henry VIII for the next thirty-four years. In future centuries, Scots would speak with great pride of Flodden Field, and proudly boast – as so many of them could – of having an ancestor who was killed there. But in the short run it had a disastrous effect on Scottish morale. The achievements of James IV's reign, and the dream of Scotland taking her place as a great power in Christendom, were destroyed in those three hours of fighting on Branxton Hill. The mood of optimism was replaced by something like despair as lords and lairds thought of nothing but their own advantage and of surviving the chaos which, as always in Scottish history, accompanied the accession of an infant King.

In England, on the other hand, the double victories of Guinegatte and Branxton, and the capture of Tournai, established Henry's position for the rest of his reign. They made a great impression throughout Europe, and foreigners noted that Henry was not only the richest King in Christendom, but the one who had gained the greatest military glory. Once again, as in the time of Edward III, a King of England had successfully invaded France and at the same time a reserve army had beaten a superior force of Scots. For many years afterwards, Englishmen spoke proudly about the victory at Branxton, of 'the Scottish field' where the King of Scots was slain; and they gave the credit, not to Surrey, but to the King.

5

SUFFOLK AND MARY

HENRY remained for three weeks in Tournai, showing his benevolence to his new subjects, who were given forty days in which to take the oath of allegiance to him. On the first evening, Maximilian and Margaret of Austria arrived from Lille, and made a ceremonial entry into the city by torchlight. After a few days, Maximilian went on to Germany, leaving Margaret to be entertained at Tournai by Henry with the usual banquets and tournaments. Henry and Lord Lisle challenged all-comers in the tournaments, and distinguished themselves as defenders. One of Henry's gentlemen wrote that the King excelled over everyone, both in agility, in the breaking of spears, and in his nobleness of stature.[1]

Margaret of Austria was aged thirty-three. When she was seventeen she had married Catherine of Aragon's brother, Prince Juan, who had died a few months later. She then married the Duke of Savoy, who died within three years of the marriage, leaving Margaret a widow for the second time at the age of twenty-four, with no children of either marriage. During her stay in Tournai, Lord Lisle declared himself to be her devoted admirer, and she showed him many signs of her favour. Lisle's daughter by his marriage to his deceased wife was being educated at Margaret's court.

One day, Henry asked Margaret if she would be willing to marry Lisle. He told her that it was considered quite in order in England for a Princess to marry a subject; that she was not too old to remarry, as widows sometimes married when they were aged fifty or even sixty; and that Lisle, who was very much in love with her, possessed all the manly and Christian virtues. Margaret said that whatever the position might be in England, it was unheard of in the Netherlands for a Princess to marry a man who was not of royal blood, and if she were to do so, 'I should be dishonoured and holden for a fool, and light'. She added that she was fully aware of Lisle's great virtues, and if it were not for the fact that the marriage was impossible, she could think of no more worthy a husband than he.

One evening at Tournai, after a great banquet, Henry withdrew with Margaret to his chamber, and Lisle joined them. Lisle went on his knees to her, declared his love, and begged her to give him the ring that she wore. When she refused, he persisted, and gently took the ring from her finger, and refused to return it to her. She laughingly said that he was a thief, and asked Henry whether he had brought an army of thieves with him from England. Henry asked her to let Lisle keep the ring, and he would give her other rings to replace it. Next morning, when the stimulation of the wine at the banquet had passed off, Margaret became conscious of the scandal that might be caused if Lisle kept her ring; she asked Henry to order him to return it, and not to mention the incident. Lisle said that he would return the ring if she gave him a bracelet in exchange, and she agreed to do so.

Henry made another attempt, in Lisle's presence, to persuade Margaret to accept him as her husband. She said it was impossible, but that even if she could consider it, she would not accept Lisle's proposal without consulting her father the Emperor. Henry pressed her to accept Lisle at once. He said that he knew that Lisle would always be true to her, but ladies were fickle, and if he and Lisle returned to England without having obtained her promise, the Emperor would marry her to someone else during their absence. Eventually, Henry suggested that both she and Lisle should promise not to marry anyone else till they met again. Margaret said that she could safely do this, as she had no intention of remarrying.[2]

Henry was also visited at Tournai by Margaret's nephew, Prince Charles of Castile, who by the treaty of 1508 was to marry Henry's sister Mary when he reached the marriageable age of fourteen.[3] Charles's fourteenth birthday would be in the following February, and Henry wished the marriage between Charles and Mary to take place soon after this.

On 13 October, Henry left Tournai to return to England, and on his way to Calais he spent a few days at Margaret of Austria's court at Lille. He signed a new treaty of alliance with Margaret and the Spanish ambassador at Lille, by which Henry, Maximilian and Ferdinand agreed to launch a joint invasion of France before 1 June 1514. It was also agreed that Charles and Mary would be married in Calais before 15 May in the presence of Henry, Catherine of Aragon, Maximilian and Margaret of Austria. Henry promised Margaret that he would arrange for his Parliament to pass an Act vesting the succession to the crown of England in the children of the marriage of Mary and Charles of Castile, instead of in his elder sister Margaret, the Queen Dowager of Scots, and her son, James V of Scotland.[4]

On Henry's last day at Lille, there was a tournament, followed by a banquet in the evening. After the banquet, Henry and Lisle managed to trap Margaret behind a cupboard, where Lisle went on his knees to her and made another passionate declaration of love. Margaret's courtiers noticed what was happening behind the cupboard, and were outraged. Soon everyone was talking about the incident.[5]

It was just the kind of good, boisterous fun that appealed to Henry. And, after all, if it caused any scandal or political embarrassments, it would be Margaret, not he, who would suffer.

Henry sailed from Calais on 21 October, reached Dover the same day, and hurried 'in post' to Richmond, where he was reunited with Catherine. He spent Christmas at Windsor, with the usual festivities; in the tournaments, he and Lisle successfully defended against all challengers. Henry arranged for the body of James IV to be given honourable burial by the monks at Sheen, after he had persuaded the Pope to assume that James had given some sign of repentance as he lay dying on the battlefield, which enabled the Pope to release him from excommunication and to allow him to be buried in a church.[6] Henry had nothing now to fear from Scotland, where James V had succeeded to the throne at the age of seventeen months, and was in the custody of his mother and Regent, Henry's sister Margaret.

Henry celebrated Candlemas in 1514 by doing what his father had always refused to do, and creating a batch of new peers. Surrey was rewarded for his victory at Branxton by being granted his father's forfeited title of Duke of Norfolk. His son, Lord Thomas Howard, became Earl of Surrey. Brandon was created Duke of Suffolk, and his title of Viscount Lisle was given to Arthur Plantagenet, the illegitimate son of Edward IV. Arthur Plantagenet had married the widow of Edmund Dudley, and Henry now restored to the new Viscount and Viscountess Lisle the property which Dudley had forfeited to the King when he and Empson were executed. Henry also restored the lands of that other Yorkist pretender to the crown, the Earl of Warwick, Clarence's son, who had been executed with Perkin Warbeck by Henry VII in 1499. Henry gave them to Warwick's sister Margaret, the widow of Sir Geoffrey Pole, and created her Countess of Salisbury. Several knights and gentlemen of Henry's household were given peerages. Wolsey was appointed Bishop of Lincoln and Bishop of Tournai.

Henry fell ill during the winter, and his courtiers became alarmed, fearing that it would develop into smallpox; but he quickly threw it off, and rose from his sickbed 'as fierce as ever against France'.[7] The enthusiasm for the war was greater than ever. An official government spokesman in the House of Commons assured the MPs that in the coming campaign King Ferdinand would play his part and invade Guienne when Henry invaded Picardy, and that while the old decrepit French King was becoming increasingly infirm, Henry was like the rising sun and was growing stronger and brighter every day.[8]

But Maximilian and Ferdinand were much less enthusiastic for war, and the new Pope was in favour of peace. Julius II died in March 1513, and Giovanni dei Medici was chosen as Pope Leo X. Leo sent a ceremonial sword and a rose to Henry as a token of his appreciation of his services in the war in defence of the Church; but he also urged Henry to avoid vainglory and to work for peace and unity in Christendom in preparation for a crusade against the Turk. Henry assured Leo that he was not vainglorious, for he knew that God, who had given Saul the power to slay his thousands and David his tens of thousands, had alone made possible his victories over the French and the Scots; but he feared that a premature peace would endanger the true unity of Christendom, which must await the triumphant campaign against France which would take place in the summer of 1514.[9]

Henry had decided to send Suffolk to Margaret of Austria's court to make sure that she and Maximilian did not slacken in their resolve to invade France next summer. But an unfortunate difficulty had arisen. Rumours were circulating in England, the Netherlands, Germany and France that Suffolk was about to marry Margaret of Austria; and Margaret raised the matter with the English ambassador. She explained that she had shown great favour to Suffolk at Tournai and Lille because she knew how highly Henry regarded him, but that, despite the high opinion that she had of Suffolk's merits, she had always made it clear that she could not marry him. She asked Henry not to send Suffolk to her court, for the rumours would increase if she met him again. If he came, she would be forced to treat him with an aloofness which she would be most reluctant to have to show to him.

Henry wrote to Maximilian, expressing his regret that the rumour had arisen. He said he was sure that it had been spread by their enemies in order to cause a rift between them. It would be embarrassing to revoke Suffolk's appointment as ambassador to Margaret's court, as it had already been announced; but he agreed to do so, and to send Sir Richard Wingfield, the Deputy of Calais, instead. Suffolk assured Margaret's ambassador that it was not he who had started the rumour, and offered to remove his daughter from Margaret's court; but Margaret said that this would not be necessary.[10]

Margaret had learned the dangers of innocent flirtation. Some years later, when one of her gentlemen ventured to make advances to her, she ordered him to leave her court immediately.[11]

Suffolk had switched his matrimonial ambitions; and had another Princess in view. Henry's sister Mary, who was to marry the fourteen-year-old Prince Charles of Castile, was eighteen, and very beautiful. Gérard du Pleine, whom Margaret of Austria sent on a mission to Henry's court, may have been exaggerating when he wrote to Margaret that Prince Charles's bride, Princess Mary, was the most beautiful lady he had ever seen, that her conversation was delightful, that she was a graceful dancer, and very lively;[12] but many other men were impressed by her beauty. Henry realised that Mary was falling in love with Suffolk and he with her; but though he had told Margaret of Austria that it was possible in England for a Princess to marry a subject, he could not afford to forgo the use of Mary in a diplomatic marriage with Prince Charles of Castile which would cement the anti-French alliance.

Henry and Wolsey, who was now directing English foreign policy, were playing two cards at the same time. On the one hand they were urging Maximilian and Ferdinand to continue the war, to reject any peace overtures from Louis XII, and to ignore the Pope's appeal for peace; but they were also secretly considering the possibility of out-smarting their allies and making their own deal with France. From Louis XII's point of view, Henry was the greatest enemy and the real danger. While Ferdinand wanted only Navarre and Béarn, and Maximilian only frontier rectifications in the north-east, Henry claimed the throne of France and Louis' whole kingdom; and Henry, unlike Ferdinand and Maximilian, had defeated a French army. If Louis could make peace with Henry, he need not worry about Ferdinand or Maximilian, and he would therefore be willing to grant Henry very advantageous terms.

In February 1514 Ferdinand made another secret truce with Louis XII. Henry and Wolsey found out about it, and realising that Ferdinand would let them down again in the next campaign, entered into their own secret negotiations with the French. Maximilian, too, entered into negotiations with the French without informing Henry; and hoping to use the marriage of Charles and Mary as a lever to get more money out of Henry, he suggested that the date of their wedding should be postponed.

In May a report reached Maximilian and Margaret of Austria that Henry was negotiating with the French and was planning to break the engagement between Mary and Charles of Castile and marry Mary to Louis XII. When Margaret's ambassador raised this with Henry in May, Henry denied it, and urged that the marriage between Mary and Charles should be celebrated at once. But the Seigeneur de Bohier, the General of Normandy, was in London. He was supposed to be negotiating about the ransom to be paid for Henry's prisoner, the Duke of Longueville; but Maximilian's ambassador was not the only man who suspected that he was conducting secret peace negotiations with Wolsey.[13] Meanwhile the war went on. In February Admiral Prégent raided the Sussex coast; he landed in the flourishing fishing village of Brighthelmstone (Brighton), and burned it to the ground before the local levies could drive him off. In June the English retaliated by landing a force near Cherbourg and burning a few French villages.

Henry's shipbuilders had been building a new ship to replace *The Regent*. It was even larger than *The Regent*, half as large again, with 1,500 tons, four masts, with topgallant sails on three of them, eight decks one above the other, and 184 guns of various sizes. Henry invited all the ambassadors in London to come to Erith for the launching of the ship, with Queen Catherine, Princess Mary, the bishops and the nobles. When he and his party left, all the ship's guns fired a salvo in salute. The ship was named *The Henry Grace-à-Dieu*, which was the name originally given to *The Regent* when Henry VII built it in 1488. It became popularly known as *The Great Harry*.[14]

Henry had been in the best of spirits at the launching, and was particularly affable to Margaret of Austria's envoy, Gérard du Pleine; but when he granted du Pleine an audience at Eltham four days later, he spoke reproachfully about Maximilian's negotiations with the French and the delay in celebrating the marriage of Charles and Mary at Calais. Du Pleine politely said that Margaret would like to know what the General of Normandy was really doing in London.[15]

On 9 July Louis XII, at St Germain en Laye, agreed to the peace terms which had been negotiated by the General of Normandy. He agreed to pay a million gold crowns to Henry in addition to the 750,000 gold crowns already due under the treaties of 1475 and 1492; it would be payable by half-yearly instalments of 26,315 crowns to be paid at Calais on 1 November and 1 May each year till the whole sum was paid. Louis, whose wife, Anne of Brittany, had died in January, would marry Henry's sister Mary. He would pay 'pensions' to all the leading members of Henry's government as a token of appreciation for the part they had played in negotiating peace – 1,030 *écus d'or* per annum to the Duke of Norfolk, 1,000 *écus d'or* per annum to Suffolk and Wolsey, and lesser sums to Foxe, the Earl of Worcester, Compton, and other courtiers.[16]

This diplomatic volteface was negotiated as secretly, and announced to an astounded world with as little advance notice, as the German-Soviet Pact of 1939. On 29 July the General and the President of Normandy left St Germain en Laye on their journey to London. Next day Princess Mary, at Wanstead Manor, declared in the presence of Henry's counsellors that she repudiated her marriage contract with Prince Charles of Castile, and asked them to inform the King about her declaration. A few days later the French envoys arrived in London, and on 7 August they and the Duke of Longueville signed the peace treaty with Norfolk, Wolsey and Foxe. The peace was proclaimed throughout England on St Lawrence's Day and ratified by Henry on 20 August. The French envoys were of course entertained with the usual tournaments and banquets.[17]

Henry lost no time in having the marriage contract performed. The wedding took place at Greenwich on 13 August, with the Duke of Longueville acting as Louis XII's proxy. Immediately after the ceremony, the marriage was symbolically consummated. Mary went to her chamber, undressed in the presence of many lords and ladies of the court, and got into bed. The Duke of Longueville, who was in his doublet and a pair of red hose, removed one of his legs from his hose, got into bed with Mary, and in the presence of all the witnesses placed his naked leg over her body. The marriage was then declared to have been consummated.[18]

Maximilian and Ferdinand had the effrontery to complain that Henry had betrayed them by making a separate peace with France. Margaret of Austria told the English ambassador in Brussels, Sir Richard Wingfield, that she refused to believe that Henry had married Mary to Louis XII, and she sent an envoy to England to protest against it. It was obviously not what she would have expected from the gay young King who, less than a year before, had told her at Tournai and Lille that in England it would have been in order for a Princess to marry a handsome and gallant subject like Suffolk. Sir Edward Poynings, whom Henry had appointed Governor of Tournai, wrote to Henry that the marriage was so unpopular in Flanders that he feared that the people in the neighbouring districts would refuse to supply Tournai with provisions.[19]

The Flemish and Spanish critics of the peace naturally made fun of the fact that Mary was to marry the old and infirm Louis XII. His age and debility had been shamelessly used as a propaganda weapon against him by the English, Flemings and Spaniards during the war; and the idea that he should now appear in the role of bridegroom to the lovely eighteen-year-old English Princess caused great derision in Spain and the Netherlands. Peter Martyr de Anglería, at the court at Valladolid, wrote that everyone would be shocked that a beautiful girl of eighteen had been married to an old invalid suffering from leprosy; he imagined Louis XII 'licking his lips and gulping his spittle' in anticipation of his wedding night with her, but he thought that Louis would die from his exertions if he tried to consummate the marriage.[20]

Mary had at first refused point blank to marry Louis. She told Henry that she was in love with Suffolk and wished to marry him. Henry was torn between his great affection for his sister and for Suffolk, and what he considered to be his interests as a King and their duty as his subjects. As usual with Henry, cold political calculation won the day. He explained to Mary that the interests of his foreign policy and the peace of Christendom depended on her marrying Louis XII; but he pointed out that Louis was almost certain to die soon, and Mary would be left a young widow. He promised her that if she now agreed to marry Louis XII, he would allow her to marry the man of her choice after Louis' death.[21]

Mary was nevertheless in an unhappy mood when she left for France in September 1514. Henry travelled to Dover with her. On their journey they stayed at Canterbury, where Henry worshipped at the Rood of Grace at the Cross of St Augustine's, at St Augustine's shrine, at Our Lady Undercroft, at the high altar in the cathedral and at Becket's shrine there, giving at each of these sacred places an offering of one mark, or 13s. 4d., which was worth over £160 in terms of 1984 prices.[22] Mary embarked at Dover with her large retinue. Henry had sent Norfolk, Dorset, Surrey, Lord Herbert, Ruthall, and the Prior of St John of Jerusalem, Docwra, to escort her and to attend her wedding and coronation in France. The Earl of Worcester, West, and Sir Richard Wingfield were already in Paris, where Worcester had represented Mary at her wedding by proxy to King Louis. It was certainly no coincidence that Suffolk was not a member of the party.

Louis XII came to Abbeville to meet her, and according to the usual custom the proxy marriages were celebrated again by the spouses in person in Abbeville Cathedral on 9 October. They stayed for a fortnight in Abbeville before travelling by slow stages to Paris. Mary was now even more unhappy. She wrote to Wolsey complaining that her English servants had been taken away from her and replaced by French ones, and she reproached Norfolk for doing nothing to protect her from the ill treatment to which the French subjected her.

Henry's reaction was to send Suffolk to join his fellow-counsellors in France. There is little doubt that this was at Suffolk's suggestion. He was instructed to enter into important diplomatic negotiations with Louis XII; but the mission could have been confided to Norfolk, Ruthall or West, or even Surrey, who were already in France. Before Suffolk left, Henry spoke to him in his closet at Eltham; Wolsey was the only other person present. Henry asked Suffolk to promise that he would make no attempt to make love to Mary while he was in France, and Suffolk gave his word that he would not do so.[23]

Suffolk sailed from Dover on 20 October, three weeks behind Mary. Before embarking, he wrote to Wolsey that he hoped to be in Boulogne by noon and in Paris next day. It shows the optimism of his temperament that he could hope to travel the 140 miles from Boulogne to Paris in thirty-six hours, for forty miles was the most that a horseman would normally travel in a day on the rough roads, especially in the autumn mud, and even messengers riding in post could manage a hundred miles a day only with the greatest difficulty. But Suffolk caught up with Louis XII and Mary at Beauvais. At his first audience with the King, Louis was in bed and Mary was demurely sitting at the bedside.[24]

On Sunday 5 November Mary was crowned Queen of France in the abbey church at St Denis with great pomp. After the coronation the court went on to Paris. Mary was now a little happier, and Louis wrote on several occasions to Henry and Wolsey that he was very pleased with Suffolk.

Henry and Wolsey had instructed Suffolk to put a proposal to Louis in great secrecy. They suggested that England and France should go to war with Ferdinand and conquer Navarre and Castile. Navarre would be restored to France, and Henry would become King of Castile. Henry justified this by the argument that Ferdinand was only King of Aragon, and that at Queen Isabella's death the crown of Castile passed not to him as her husband but to her daughters Joanna and Catherine jointly, and that as Joanna was mad, Henry, as Catherine's husband, was entitled to seize Castile for Catherine. Henry would thus repay Ferdinand for his treachery, as well as acquiring a new kingdom and more military glory. Henry's biographer, Dr Scarisbrick, is probably right in thinking that this proposal was the first of many examples of how the desire for revenge played an important part in

Henry's policy.

It is quite possible that if Louis had accepted the proposal, Henry would have backed out at the last moment; but Louis had no intention of embarking on such a pointless enterprise. On 26 November he gave Suffolk his reply. If Henry really meant him to take the proposal seriously, he would consider it, but he thought that the cost of the expedition might well exceed the value of Navarre and Castile. Instead, he suggested that Henry, whose riches were so well-known, should help him to conquer Milan by lending him 200,000 crowns.[25]

Louis XII died on New Year's Day, leaving Mary a widow after eighty-three days of married life. The heir to the throne was Louis' cousin and son-in-law, François, Duke of Angoulême, unless Mary was carrying Louis' posthumous child and this child should turn out to be a boy. No one was surprised when Mary declared that she was not pregnant,[26] and the Duke of Angoulême was proclaimed as King François I. He was aged twenty, as athletic as Henry, and as fond of hunting and war. He also exceeded all his fellow-countrymen in his addiction to the French national vice. His court was considered to be the most immoral in Europe.

Mary observed the deep mourning which etiquette required of a widowed Queen. She sat beside Louis' corpse, and after the funeral sat in her chamber, dressed all in black except for a white nun's kerchief on her head. But a Venetian merchant in Paris, who saw her, wrote that even when she was in mourning she could never keep still, but moved her head constantly, and that she was the most attractive and beautiful woman he had ever seen.[27] The whiteness of her complexion particularly impressed the French, who called her '*la reine blanche*'.

Norfolk and the other English counsellors had returned to England after Mary's coronation, leaving Suffolk, West and Sir Richard Wingfield as ambassadors at the French court. They were discussing with François and his ministers the possibility of a summit meeting between Henry and François; and François' ministers raised the question of the return of Tournai to France and on what terms Henry would agree to this.[28] But while Suffolk, West and Wingfield wrote joint dispatches to Henry and Wolsey about these negotiations, Suffolk wrote private letters to Wolsey about Mary.

As soon as Wolsey heard, just after Christmas, that Louis XII's condition had worsened, he wrote to Mary that if he should die, she must take care not to commit herself in any way about a future marriage; she must wait until she heard from Henry and be guided by him in the matter. She assured Wolsey that she was no longer a child and would of course do what her brother required of her.[29]

Mary, Suffolk, the other English ambassadors, and the whole court went to Rheims for the coronation of François and Queen Claude on 25 January.

On the return journey to Paris, François asked Mary to go to bed with him; but she refused, and told him that she was in love with Suffolk and wished to marry him. François immediately accepted the situation, and said to Suffolk that he understood that he wished to marry Mary. Suffolk tried to deny that he would be so bold as to go into a foreign realm and try to marry its Queen without the consent of its King or of the King his master; but François said that Mary had revealed the secret, and promised that he would do what he could to help them to marry. It was in his interests to do so, because there was no available French Prince for Mary to marry, and if she married Suffolk, Henry would be unable to marry her to Charles of Castile or some other Habsburg or ally of Maximilian if he wished to make an anti-French alliance.

Suffolk wrote to Wolsey and asked him to persuade Henry to allow him to marry Mary. He stated that he knew that Wolsey was the only member of Henry's Council who would be willing to further the project; and he stressed the urgency of the matter, for if she did not marry him soon, François would renew his attempts to seduce her. Mary herself wrote the same thing to Henry; and she, Suffolk and François all wrote to Henry asking him to consent to the marriage.[30]

The first reaction from England was encouraging. Wolsey wrote to Suffolk stating that Henry was very sympathetic to the idea of him marrying Mary; but a few days later, Wolsey wrote again. He wrote that Henry was eager to persuade François to return Mary's dowry and her jewels, and he virtually said that if Suffolk could succeed in getting hold of the dowry and jewels, Henry would allow him to marry Mary, but that otherwise he would refuse his consent. Wolsey asked Suffolk 'substantially to handle that matter, and to stick thereunto; for I assure you the hope that the King hath to obtain the said plate and jewels is the thing that most stayeth His Grace constantly to assent that ye should marry his sister; the lack whereof, I fear me, might make him cold and remiss and cause some alteration, whereof all men here, except His Grace and myself, would be right glad'.[31]

It was obvious that Henry, despite his earlier promise to Mary that if she married Louis XII she could marry whom she wished next time, and despite his affection for her and for Suffolk, was determined to make as much money as possible from the situation. It was also clear that François I might make difficulties about returning the dowry and jewels. There were rumours circulating in Paris that there was a plan to marry Mary to the Duke of Savoy, or to send her to Flanders to marry someone else. Two friars came from England and visited Mary; they had been sent by those members of Henry's Council and by those English nobles who did not wish to see the upstart Suffolk obtain a royal bride. The friars advised Mary to abandon her plan to marry Suffolk, because Henry's Council would never consent to it.

The friars' message had exactly the opposite effect to what they intended. Suffolk and Mary decided to marry at once, and to confront Henry and

Wolsey with a *fait accompli*. It was a great risk to take; but they were probably right in thinking that it was their only chance of being able to marry. They were married secretly in the presence of only ten witnesses. Neither West nor Wingfield was informed, because Mary thought that the ambassadors would be embarrassed and might get into trouble with Henry if they knew anything about the marriage. By now, rumours that Suffolk was intending to marry Mary were circulating in the Netherlands. Sampson wrote to Wolsey from Ghent on 27 February that he supposed that the rumour was being spread for the dishonour of England; and Spinelly, another English envoy, wrote to Wolsey, also from Ghent and on the same day, stating that he was sure the story was a mischievous lie.[32]

On 5 March Suffolk wrote to Wolsey and told him what he and Mary had done. 'I am obliged to you next God and my master, and therefore I will hide none thing from you, trusting that you will help me now as you have done always. My Lord, so it is that when I came to Paris I heard many things which put me in great fear, and so did the Queen both; and the Queen would never let me be in rest till I had granted her to be married; and so to be plain with you, I have married her heartily, and have lain with her, insomuch as fear me that she be with child. My Lord, I am not in a little sorrow if the King should know it, and that His Grace should be displeased with me; for I assure you that I had rather 'a died that he should be miscontent'.[33]

Wolsey replied 'with sorrowful heart' that he had of course felt bound to tell the King, who was very angry with Suffolk; for Suffolk had dishonoured the King by marrying his sister and going to bed with her, and had broken the promise that he had given at Eltham to 'him which hath brought you up of low degree' to the rank of Duke. Wolsey wrote that he was very doubtful if Suffolk could do anything that would obtain him a pardon, but the only hope was for Suffolk and Mary, not only to write remorseful letters to Henry, but also to agree to pay Henry £4,000 a year out of Mary's dowry, which would allow them to retain the remaining £6,000 a year for themselves. Suffolk must also manage to persuade François to repay the 800,000 crowns of the dowry to Henry.[34]

Mary wrote to Henry and submitted the draft to Wolsey. She claimed that she alone was responsible for what had occurred, and stated that she had acted because the two friars had told her that Henry's Council would never allow her to marry Suffolk. 'Whereupon, Sir, I put my Lord of Suffolk in choice whether he would accomplish the marriage within four days or else that he should never have enjoyed me; whereby I know well that I constrained him to break such promises he made Your Grace, as well for fear of losing me as also that I ascertained him that by their consent I would never come into England. And now that Your Grace knoweth the both offences of the which I have been the only occasion, I most humbly and as your most sorrowful sister requiring you to have compassion upon us both and to pardon our offences'.[35]

Mary signed a document, 'freely' assigning to Henry all the plate and jewels which had been given her as her dowry when she married Louis XII. She persuaded François I to release some of them, including a great diamond with a pearl attached which was known as the 'Mirror of Naples'. On 16 April she and Suffolk left Paris and travelled towards Calais. From Montreuil, Suffolk wrote to Henry that he knew that Henry's Council wished to imprison him or even put him to death, but begging for mercy.[36]

When they reached Calais, they waited there while Wolsey and his secretary, Brian Tuke, drafted a suitable letter for Mary to write to the King. In it, she stated that 'I am now comen out of the realm of France and have put myself within your jurisdiction in this your town of Calais, where I intend to remain till such time as I shall have answer from you of your good and loving mind herein'. She again insisted that she, and not Suffolk, had been to blame.[37] This was necessary in order to counter the general impression that Suffolk, having risen in rank from a simple gentleman to a Duke, had insolently seduced a royal Princess for his further aggrandizement. His action was condemned by the people as well as by the nobility. He did not dare to leave the Deputy's house at Calais for fear of being lynched by the local inhabitants.[38] The story of the wicked ambassador who, on a mission abroad, basely betrayed his trust by eloping with the sister of the King his master, found its way into popular mythology, and in due course into children's fairy-tale books.

Henry forgave Suffolk and Mary. Having made his very satisfactory financial arrangement with them, he continued to show them every favour. As it transpired that Mary was not pregnant, as she and Suffolk had thought, Henry was able to safeguard his own reputation, and theirs, by suppressing all knowledge of their secret marriage in Paris and having another wedding at Greenwich, which he and Catherine attended. When Mary gave birth to a son at exactly the right time in March 1516, Henry and Wolsey were godfathers and Catherine was godmother.[39] Henry gave the child the name 'Henry', and when he was nine created him Earl of Lincoln. Suffolk and Mary afterwards had a daughter, Frances, who married the Marquess of Dorset and became the mother of Lady Jane Grey.

They fulfilled their promise to Henry, and duly paid him £1,000 every year till they had repaid £24,000 of Mary's dowry. They spent much of their time at their country house at Westhorpe in Suffolk, but were often at court. Mary, who was always referred to in England, for the rest of her life, as 'the French Queen', took a prominent part on state occasions, sometimes sitting at Henry's table with distinguished foreign guests. Suffolk continued to serve Henry as any other great nobleman did, attending at court and commanding armies in wartime against the French and the Scots. Mary died in 1533, when she was aged thirty-seven. Suffolk continued in Henry's favour as a courtier and general till he died, seventeen months before Henry, in 1545. After Mary's death he married Katherine Willoughby, who survived him and became a zealous Protestant, escaping from England illegally and at great risk to avoid being burned as a heretic in Queen Mary's reign.

So Suffolk succeeded in getting away with it, and did not forfeit his life or his freedom for marrying the King's sister without the King's consent. He was lucky in many respects. He was lucky to be one of the few people whom Henry regarded as a real personal friend. He was lucky in that although his conduct with Mary touched the King's honour, it did not arouse Henry's personal emotions and jealousies as it would have done if Suffolk had married a woman with whom Henry was in love. He was lucky in that he and Mary were abroad at the time, and that they could therefore find a priest who was prepared to marry them without Henry's consent, which surely no priest in England would have been prepared to do; and he was lucky in that, because of this, he had married Mary before he went to bed with her, and so could not be accused of having committed the sin and crime of fornication. He was lucky in that François I was sympathetic, and was prepared to return some of Mary's jewels. He was lucky in that, although a handful of noblemen resented him as an upstart, and public opinion condemned him, he was not bitterly hated by large sections of the people, as Wolsey and Cromwell were in later years. He was lucky in that none of the nobles who disliked him had any influence with Henry, and that the only man who did have influence, Wolsey, was tolerant of sexual peccadillos and not a fanatic for proprieties. He was lucky in that he was not descended from Edward III, so that no one could think that he had married Mary because he was secretly aspiring to gain the crown one day.

Above all, he was lucky in that he married Mary in 1515 and not in 1536 or 1541. Henry was basically the same Henry, as greedy and revengeful, at the age of twenty-four as he was at forty-five and fifty; but the political climate was very different in later years. If any courtier had secretly married the King's sister twenty years after Suffolk did, Henry and his ministers would have been much less inclined, and would have found it politically much more difficult, to overlook this affront to the King's authority.

6

WOLSEY

HENRY VIII was well represented at the Papal court in Rome. Cardinal Bainbridge, the Archbishop of York, had lived there as Henry's ambassador for five years, having of course received a dispensation for non-residence in his diocese of York. English interests were also represented in Rome by two Italian cardinals who had been given English bishoprics. Neither Cardinal Silvester di Gigli, the Bishop of Worcester, nor Cardinal Adriano di Castello, the Bishop of Bath and Wells, had ever visited their dioceses, but received the revenues of the sees as a reward for acting as Henry's agents in the Papal court. Adriano di Castello, whom the English called 'Cardinal Hadrian', was lucky to be alive, because he had been one of several men who had fallen violently ill at a party which he gave in his garden on the day in 1503 when Pope Alexander VI (Rodrigo Borgia) was taken ill. The Pope died a few days later, and it was widely believed, though almost certainly without justification, that the Pope had accidentally swallowed the poison which his son, Cesare Borgia, had intended should be drunk only by Hadrian.

One night in May 1514, when England and France were still at war, one of Bainbridge's agents saw Gigli's servant surreptitiously leaving, by the back lane, the house of the Bishop of Marseilles, the French ambassador in Rome. Bainbridge, who suspected that the Bishop of Worcester was betraying Henry and was in secret contact with the French, wrote and warned Henry. Six weeks later, Bainbridge died suddenly. His secretary, Richard Pace, suspected that he had been poisoned by his Italian chaplain, and he informed the authorities in Rome. The chaplain was examined under torture, and confessed that he had been paid by Gigli to poison Bainbridge. He then managed to get hold of a knife and committed suicide to prevent them from torturing him again. Gigli denied that he was involved, and said that the chaplain's confession was false, having been wrung from him by torture, and that in any case the chaplain was mad. The Pope decided that there was no evidence against Gigli, and exonerated him; and Henry concurred in the decision.[1]

Henry appointed Wolsey to succeed Bainbridge as Archbishop of York, and asked the Pope to consecrate him and also to make him a cardinal. As usual, Henry argued about the amount which should be paid to the Pope as annates when Wolsey was translated to York; and as usual, the annates question was settled by a compromise. Leo X made more difficulties about creating Wolsey a cardinal, for, unlike Julius II, he was anxious to conciliate France; but after holding out for over a year, he succumbed to the insistent demands of Henry and Wolsey, and sent the red hat to Wolsey. It was presented to him at a great ceremony in Westminster Abbey in November 1515.[2]

After Wolsey had completely dominated the government of England for two years, the position was regularised in December 1515 when he replaced Warham as Lord Chancellor. As Archbishop of Canterbury, Warham still had precedence in theory over Wolsey in the ecclesiastical hierarchy. Henry and Wolsey tried to remedy this by persuading the Pope to appoint Wolsey as his Legate *a latere*, which would give him power to override the authority of all the ecclesiastical authorities in England, including the Archbishop of Canterbury. This, too, the Pope was reluctant to grant to Wolsey, but he eventually did so in 1518.

Henry's courtiers, the English people, and the foreign ambassadors were all dazzled by Wolsey's wealth, splendour and power. In May 1515 Erasmus wrote that Wolsey was omnipotent with the King. In July, the Venetian ambassadors, Badoer and Giustiniani, wrote that he really seemed to rule all England. In January 1516, Giustiniani wrote that he was '*ipse rex*', the King himself, 'the King, author of everything'. In November, Giustiniani described him as being 'the beginning, the middle, and the end' of English foreign policy. In April 1517, the Papal Nuncio in London, Chieregato, wrote that the foreign ambassadors in London regarded Wolsey not as a cardinal but as another King. A fortnight later, Chieregato wrote again that Wolsey, because of his ability, ruled everything.[3]

The ambassadors were convinced that it was Wolsey who governed England while Henry hunted and enjoyed himself. Chieregato wrote that Henry devoted himself to amusements by day and night, and was interested in nothing except jousting and music, leaving all business to the Cardinal of York, for whom he had so much respect that he spoke only through the Cardinal's mouth. When the French delegation were in London in September 1518, Thomas More, who had just been appointed a member of the King's Council, told Giustiniani that Wolsey alone negotiated with the French envoys, and that when he had reached agreement with them, he called Henry's counsellors and told them what had been done, 'so that the King himself scarcely knows in what state matters are'.[4]

Henry was not the only King who went hunting and left an able churchman to conduct his foreign policy. François I, who spent even more time hunting than Henry, and even less time in dealing with state affairs, had an able Foreign Minister, Cardinal Du Prat; and Charles V, who also enjoyed hunting, but spent more time in the council chamber than either Henry or François, entrusted his diplomatic negotiations to his Piedmontese counsellor, Mercurino Gattinara. But no one spoke about Du Prat and Gattinara in the way that people spoke about Wolsey. They were regarded as able and influential ministers of their sovereigns, but not in any sense as their equals. The diplomats wrote about the policy and actions of the 'Most Christian King' of France and the 'King Catholic' of Spain; but they wrote about the policy and actions of 'the King and the Cardinal of England'.

Foreign Kings treated Wolsey almost as an equal. When they wrote personal letters to Henry, they wrote at the same time to Wolsey. In May 1519 Giustiniani stated that he had advised the Doge of Venice a hundred times that when he wished to write to Henry, he should write to Wolsey too; if the Doge was to write to only one of them, it would be better to write to Wolsey, lest Wolsey should resent the precedence conceded to Henry.[5]

But the foreign ambassadors did not, and could not, know the exact relationship between the Cardinal and the King. They formed their impression of Wolsey's omnipotence from what Wolsey himself told them and from his complete domination over all his colleagues in the government. Although Du Prat and Gattinara conducted the foreign policy of François and Charles, there were other important ministers at the French and Imperial courts who dealt with other aspects of policy. In England, Wolsey dealt with everything.

He did not, as is sometimes stated,[6] entirely dispense with the King's Council and with the privy Council which had governed the realm in the first four years of Henry's reign. He used the services of the other counsellors; on one occasion in 1518, Henry, who was away from London, offered to send some of his counsellors to him if he found it difficult to handle things without their assistance. He sometimes had Foxe, Ruthall and Warham with him when he spoke to foreign ambassadors; and meetings of the Council were still held from time to time. But Wolsey dealt with most affairs himself without bringing in his fellow-counsellors. Ruthall, who had been Foxe's colleague as chief minister before the advent of Wolsey, became in effect Wolsey's private secretary; as Cavendish wrote, Wolsey 'ruled all them that before had ruled him'. When meetings of the Council were held, as More told Giustiniani, Wolsey merely informed his colleagues what he had decided. After his fall, one of the accusations against him was that he hardly allowed the other counsellors to speak a word at the Council meetings.[7]

Wolsey did not adopt a modest pose, and make a pretence of being only a humble adviser to his King, as many powerful ministers have done. He did all he could to impress both his subordinate officials and the foreign ambassadors with his own power, with his wealth and ostentation, and the grandeur of his house at Hampton Court. He wrote to Gigli that neither Henry nor the English nobles would ever allow him to resign. When Giustiniani, in August 1516, asked to have an audience with Henry, who was away from London on a progress in Dorset, Wolsey told him that Henry did not wish to be troubled with foreign policy; and Giustiniani, fearing to offend Wolsey, agreed to transact the business with him and not with the King. When Giustiniani returned to Venice in October 1519, and reported to the Senate on his four years' mission to England, he said that when he first arrived in London in 1515, Wolsey would say: 'His Majesty will do so and so'. A few years later, he would say: 'We will do so and so'. By 1519 he was saying: 'I will do so and so'.[8]

As Wolsey spent most of his time at court, he could usually discuss matters with Henry without having to communicate with him in writing. But when Henry went on his progresses in August and September every year, Wolsey remained at his country houses at Hampton Court, or The Moor or Tyttenhanger in Hertfordshire; and on these occasions, and during the terrible epidemic of the sweating sickness in 1517 and 1518, when Henry stayed away from London for nearly a year, the King and the Cardinal wrote many letters to each other.

Some of these letters have survived, and reveal to us very clearly the relationship of Henry and Wolsey. It was a very different one from that which Giustiniani and Chieregato, or Cavendish, imagined. It was neither a case of a pleasure-loving King showing no interest in government and diplomacy, and automatically agreeing to everything that the all-powerful minister suggested, nor of a cowering, obsequious Wolsey being forced to resort to flattery and ruses to trick a stupid Henry into doing what Wolsey wanted. Their correspondence reveals a very successful collaboration between two intelligent men who had the same objectives and usually agreed about how to achieve them. It was a model relationship for any master and servant, or principal and agent. It worked exceedingly well for fifteen years. Between 1512 and 1527 they never had a quarrel.

Henry certainly did not take any interest in questions of administration or in Wolsey's judicial activities as Lord Chancellor; but in all major questions of policy, especially in foreign affairs, he was intimately involved. However much Henry preferred hunting, and however much Wolsey preferred it if he himself, and not Henry, handled foreign policy, international usage required Henry to grant personal audiences to foreign ambassadors; and Henry did not shirk this duty. Wolsey was not present at these interviews, and Henry, who had usually discussed with Wolsey beforehand what line to adopt, had to handle the interview himself. He did this very effectively in his own special way, with courtesy, with bluff bonhommie, with an occasional display of ill-temper, perhaps genuine or perhaps contrived, and with a mixture of disarming frankness and deliberate lying. His tactics were impressive; in March 1517 Giustiniani wrote to the Doge: 'I consider that His Majesty is much more free and sincere in judging what is right than the Cardinal'.[9]

We know from Henry's and Wolsey's letters that when any important policy decision had to be taken, Wolsey would advise Henry what ought to be done. In nine cases out of ten, Henry agreed; but occasionally he did not, and gave Wolsey his reasons for pursuing a different course. Wolsey hardly ever accepted this without coming back with new arguments to reinforce his original proposal and to persuade Henry to change his mind. Henry then sometimes gave way and did as Wolsey wished, and sometimes insisted on adhering to his former opinion. The final decision always rested with Henry, and Wolsey never expected anything else; but Wolsey was always prepared to argue against Henry's point of view, and did not merely advise Henry to pursue the course which he wished to pursue, as Cavendish wrote. His letters to Henry were of course written in respectful language, but there was nothing obsequious about them. They confirm the statements from such varied sources as Erasmus, More, and Cranmer, that Henry did not want flattery or submissiveness in private, but expected his intimate advisers to speak their minds freely and to tender their honest advice.

The King and the Cardinal were completely united in their objective – to increase Henry's power at home and abroad, by maintaining law and order and the absolute royal authority in the kingdom, and by raising the prestige and influence of Henry and of England in international affairs. It is strange that Pollard and other eminent modern historians should have thought that Wolsey's aim was to further the interests of the Papacy. Wolsey never cared a whit for the interests of the Papacy. He wanted very much to be elected Pope, but only so that he could use his position as Pope in Henry's interests; and Henry was just as keen as Wolsey that Wolsey should be chosen. Wolsey regarded the Pope as he regarded every other foreign ruler, as a potentate to be helped, opposed, manipulated, deceived and betrayed according to which course would benefit the interests of Henry and of England. He was usually in conflict with the Papacy, and was hated by all the Popes with whom he had to deal and by most of the College of Cardinals and officials of the Papal court. This was why he could not obtain more than a few votes in the two elections in which he was a candidate for the Papacy.

Henry and Wolsey were also in general agreement about the means to be used to achieve their aim. They were in favour of war against the national enemy, France, as long as it was a short and successful war; but they did not wish to get involved in a long war, least of all in a war without allies. When they went to war, they hoped to win propaganda victories, but to leave the worst of the fighting to their allies; and they were always on the look-out for an opportunity to betray their allies by making an advantageous separate peace with the enemy before their allies could betray them in the same way. After Henry had gained the glory of his victories over the French and Scots in 1513, he and Wolsey did not wish to push their luck too far, and were happy to avoid war if they could gain their objectives by peaceful means.

They tried their best to set foreign rulers at each other's throats, and to draw the greatest advantage from the wars of other nations. They were not in the least interested in liberating Eastern Europe from the Turk. They wished to gain the crown of France for Henry if they could obtain it without a prolonged war; but if this could not be done, they were prepared to accept money to waive Henry's claim to it. They wished to draw Scotland out of the French and into the English orbit, and hoped to achieve this without war by patient diplomacy, by subverting Scottish traitors, by a mixture of blandishments and threats, and by an occasional raid across the Border.

They both liked pomp and display, and understood the propaganda value of what would today be called 'prestige projects'. Henry was perhaps more conscious than Wolsey of the need to gain popular support. Henry was never afraid to take unpopular measures when he thought that these were necessary or advantageous, but he was more eager than Wolsey to satisfy the feelings of his people as regards war with France, the attitude towards the clergy, and other matters, although he was prepared to stamp mercilessly on unpopular minorities.

Henry and Wolsey were completely at one in dealing with the new international situation that arose in the spring of 1515 after the accession of François I. Instead of the old decrepit Louis XII, there was a French King who was even younger than Henry, as athletic, as fond of hunting, and as eager to win glory in war. Before Louis died, negotiations had begun for a summit meeting between him and Henry, and after the accession of François I both Henry and François became eager to meet. They developed a great interest in each other and a desire for friendly personal competition. The first result was a change in men's fashions, and the reintroduction of the beard into Western Europe after an absence of just over a hundred years. When Henry heard that François had grown a beard, he decided to imitate him, and soon had a fine, golden beard to match his red-blonde hair.[10]

The season got underway with the usual festivities on the high holy days. On St George's Day, Henry attended a chapter of the Knights of the Garter at Richmond. He was always fascinated by the ritual of the Order of the Garter, of which he had been made a member when he was four years old; it appealed to that side of his character which loved the old romantic ideals of chivalry. He nearly always attended in person every year at the meeting of the chapter on St George's Day.

The Doge and Senate of Venice had sent two new ambassadors, Giustiniani and Pasqualigo, to France and England. They arrived in London in time to be presented to Henry at Richmond on St George's Day. They found Henry dressed in the robes of a Knight of the Garter, standing beside a gilt chair, and surrounded by eight lords. Pasqualigo thought that he was the most handsome Prince in the world, with his auburn hair and a skin and complexion as soft as a beautiful woman's. He wore a cap of crimson velvet, a doublet striped in white and crimson, in the Swiss fashion, scarlet hose, a gold collar with a very large diamond, and a mantle of purple velvet with a train that stretched for more than four Venetian yards. Pasqualigo and Giustiniani were pleased to find that Henry could speak reasonably good Italian as well as perfect Latin.[11]

A week later, the Venetian ambassadors, with their diplomatic colleagues and all the court, were in Greenwich for the May Day festivities. They went from the palace to a wood near Shooter's Hill, being watched by an enormous crowd of onlookers. Henry and his guard were dressed in green livery and carried longbows in their hands as if they were Robin Hood and his merry men. The Queen and her ladies were there, and bowers with singing-birds had been placed in the wood.

Henry came into the bower where Pasqualigo was sitting, and began talking to him in French. He was most interested to know that Pasqualigo had been at the French court, and he asked him about François I. Henry spoke in very typical vein. He asked Pasqualigo: 'The King of France, is he as tall as I am?' Pasqualigo said there was only a little difference. 'Is he as stout?' asked Henry. Pasqualigo said no. Then Henry asked: 'What sort of legs has he?' Pasqualigo said they were thin. At this, Henry 'opened the front of his doublet, and placing his hand on his thigh, said; "Look here; and I have also a good calf to my leg"'. He told Pasqualigo that he was very fond of François, and that during the war he was three times very close to him, but that François 'would never allow himself to be seen and always retreated'. Having thus made an implied slur on François' courage, he added that he was sure that François had done this only out of obedience to King Louis, who did not wish a battle to be fought.

They left the wood, and returned to the palace for a sumptuous banquet, eating off gold plates of enormous value. After dinner, they listened to music before attending a tournament in which Henry jousted with great energy. Giustiniani's secretary, Sagudino, thought that he looked like St George on horseback, but that Queen Catherine was ugly rather than otherwise, though her ladies-in-waiting were very handsome.[12]

Henry's badinage with Pasqualigo about François I did not mean that he had any real hostility towards François, or wished to put an end to the friendly relations with France which had so recently been established. Nor was he unduly alarmed at the preparations which François was making to renew the war in Italy for the recovery of Milan. Louis XII had told Suffolk in November 1514 that he was planning an expedition into Italy in the spring, and Henry had not reacted. But there was one area in which English and French interests were in serious conflict, as François had realised immediately on coming to the throne. In March 1515, when he spoke to Giustiniani in Paris, he said that he was friendly to Henry, but that he foresaw difficulties with him about Scotland; for Henry expected him to withdraw French protection and friendship from Scotland, which he would never agree to do.[13]

While Henry was chaffing Pasqualigo in the wood near Greenwich about François' legs, John Stewart, Duke of Albany, was on the point of sailing from France to Scotland. Albany was James IV's cousin; his father was a younger son of James II of Scotland, his mother was a French Countess, and through his wife, who was also a French Countess, he was related by marriage to Pope Leo X. He had been sent from Scotland to France at the age of three, and lived there for the next thirty years till François I decided to send him back to his native country. His first language was French, and he could speak only a little Scots or English; but as a loyal servant of the King of France, he reluctantly undertook the duty of challenging the position of Henry's sister Margaret as regent for the three-year-old James V.

Margaret Tudor, the Queen Mother, was aged twenty-four when she was left a widow after Flodden, with the infant James V, and James IV's posthumous son in her womb. Henry was thinking of marrying her to the Emperor Maximilian; but she fell in love with Archibald Douglas, Earl of Angus, who was a young man of her own age, and married him in August 1514, less than a year after the death of James IV. Henry did not oppose the marriage; it gave her the support of the powerful Douglas family, and Angus and his brother Sir George Douglas became the mainstay of the pro-English party in Scotland. Angus was supported by Lord Home, whose lands in Berwickshire were too near the Border for him to wish to oppose the English, and by the Earl of Arran and the Hamiltons; but Margaret's marriage to Angus aroused the fear and envy of the other Scottish lords. The Scottish Parliament decided that by marrying Angus she had forfeited her right to be 'Governor' (regent) for her son, and that Albany, as the King's nearest adult relative, should be Governor.

François I agreed to send the reluctant Albany to Scotland, and Albany landed at Dumbarton on 18 May 1515. With the support of all the Scottish lords except the Douglases, the Homes and the Hamiltons, he besieged Margaret and James V in Stirling Castle. Margaret was forced to surrender to Albany, who took her and the King to Edinburgh.

Henry and Wolsey were in a difficulty. They knew that if they went to war, they could again defeat the Scots in a battle; but they did not wish to incur the trouble and expense of trying to conquer and occupy Scotland south of the Tay. Their first reaction to Albany's seizure of power was to plot with Margaret for her to escape with James V and bring him to England; but the Warden of the Marches of Scotland, Lord Dacre of the North, reported that this would be impossible. Margaret, who was pregnant with Angus's child, pretended to reach an agreement with Albany, but sent secret messages to Henry, begging him to arrange for her own escape into England, even if she could not bring the King with her. Henry felt unable to refuse her request, and with Dacre's help she crossed the Border in September and arrived at Harbottle Castle near Otterburn in Northumberland.[14]

Margaret was one of three Queens in Henry's family who were pregnant in the autumn of 1515. Mary the French Queen was expecting Suffolk's child, and, most important of all, Queen Catherine was pregnant for the fifth time. Margaret's baby came first. Her daughter was born at Harbottle Castle on 8 October; she wrote and informed Albany that she had given birth to 'a Christian soul being a young lady'.[15] When the young lady grew up, she married the Earl of Lennox and became the mother of Lord Darnley, the husband of Mary, Queen of Scots.

Four months later, Catherine gave birth to a daughter at Greenwich at 4 a.m. on Monday 18 February 1516. She was the only one of Catherine's six children to live for more than a few weeks, and became Queen of England and the notorious 'Bloody Mary'. Catherine's failure to produce a son was a great disappointment to her and to Henry; but Henry, who became very fond of his daughter, was pleased that at least one of his children was strong enough to survive; and he was, as always, optimistic. When Giustiniani congratulated him and Catherine, Henry said: 'We are both young; if it was a daughter this time, by the grace of God the sons will follow'.[16]

The baby of Mary and Suffolk was the last to come. Their son was born on 11 March.[17]

Margaret fell dangerously ill at Harbottle. When she recovered from the effect of a difficult childbirth, she fell ill with sciatica. She heard at Harbottle that her younger son by James IV had died in Edinburgh at the age of twenty months. Henry allowed the rumour to spread that Albany had murdered him, and that Albany was also planning to murder James V and seize the throne of Scotland. Albany, on his side, warned the Scottish lords that Henry was plotting to kidnap James V and take him to England.

In the spring of 1516, when Margaret was well enough to travel, Henry invited her to come to London. He went to Tottenham to meet her, and she stayed at his court for nearly a year. Suffolk and Mary were also often at court, and the Queen of Scots and the French Queen played a prominent part in the festivities and banquets at court, with Henry dancing with both his sisters in the masques which took place in the evenings.

Henry and Wolsey had clearly lost this round in Scotland. They contented themselves for the moment with sending a personal letter of protest from Henry to François. They also decided to keep Albany on tenterhooks about the measures which they would take against him. Albany, who was certainly anxious to avoid war with England, offered to renew the truce on the

Borders. Henry and Wolsey told Lord Dacre to refuse the offer, and to tell Albany that Henry did not recognise him as being Governor of Scotland. When Albany stressed his desire for friendship with England and his readiness to negotiate on any outstanding differences between the two realms, Dacre contemptuously replied that if Henry wished to negotiate about Scotland, he would negotiate with Albany's master, the French King, and that the only way in which Albany and the Scots could placate Henry was by repudiating their alliance with France. In March 1516 Giustiniani reported to the Doge that an English invasion of Scotland was imminent. Perhaps Henry and Wolsey had deliberately given him this impression; but they had no intention, at this stage, of resorting to force.[18]

They decided to hit at François by instigating and financing the Emperor and the Swiss to fight against him in Italy. Their most useful ally was Matthias Schinner, the Cardinal of Sion. This energetic and wily old churchman was the son of a Swiss peasant; he had risen to become Bishop of Sion, a see which carried with it the temporal government of the canton of Grisons and the rank of a Prince of the Holy Roman Empire. Schinner had been chiefly responsible for inducing a majority of the Swiss cantons to fight against Louis XII in the last Italian war. The tough Swiss mountaineers were famous throughout Europe as valiant and ferocious soldiers who were respected and feared, both when they fought for their own cantons and as mercenaries in the armies of other rulers. They would do the fighting if Henry provided the money for their wages.

Henry was universally considered to be by far the richest King in Europe. The fact that he had executed Dudley and Empson and cancelled some of the recognisances which they had extorted, did not prevent him from benefitting from the money which they had amassed for Henry VII. This was popularly believed to amount to the enormous sum of £4,000,000; and though the ambassadors at his court thought that it was probably an exaggeration to say that he was as rich as all the other Kings of Europe put together, they had no doubt that he was much richer than anyone of them.[19] The view of Henry's contemporaries about his great wealth has been questioned by modern historians who have been trained to think of wealth in terms of national output and economic growth; but to the man of the sixteenth century, a rich King was a King who had gold in his coffers. Henry VIII had much more gold available than Maximilian and Charles of Castile, not only because of the hoard which he had inherited from Henry VII – much of which had been spent on his ostentatious displays, and even more on the war of 1512-13 – but also because the English, though they sometimes grumbled about taxes, were much more ready to pay them than the virtually independent German states or the unruly provincial authorities in Spain.

Maximilian was heavily in debt, and did not find it easy to persuade the Fuggers of Augsburg or the bankers of Antwerp to lend him money; but

Henry and Wolsey were prepared to do so if he would fight against the French in Italy. Henry's ambassador at Maximilian's court was a veteran diplomat of the old school, Sir Robert Wingfield, a gallant soldier who appealed to Maximilian much more than any bishop would have done. Wingfield became a close friend of the Emperor as he accompanied him on his travels for a period of seven years. They hunted the wild swine in Alsace together, and Wingfield rode beside Maximilian when they went to Mass in the church at Hagenau. Wingfield, like most other English gentlemen, believed that the French were always the enemy; he did not like the peace with France that Wolsey, the churchman, had negotiated. He thought that the French had always betrayed England, ever since Philip Augustus had plotted against Richard Coeur de Lion and King John, and that there could be no peace in Christendom until Henry VIII reigned as King of France.[20]

Henry and Wolsey decided to supplement Sir Robert Wingfield's straightforward diplomatic activities by sending Richard Pace to arrange for the transfer of money to Maximilian on condition that he fought the French in Italy. Pace was a very clever young churchman, a learned humanist scholar, a friend of Erasmus and More, who as Bainbridge's secretary in Rome had acquired a knowledge of subtle and devious diplomacy which Wingfield could never learn. Henry and Wolsey knew that Maximilian, for all his love of hunting and of romantic mediaeval chivalry, was reputed to be 'the wisest Prince this day living',[21] and they remembered how once before he had negotiated with the French behind their backs. They did not trust him, and they did not trust the honest Sir Robert Wingfield not to be fooled by his imperial hunting companion.

While Wingfield, Pace and Cardinal Schinner were travelling through Bavaria and Switzerland, egging on Maximilian and the Swiss against France, Henry and Wolsey in London were applying the pressure to Giustiniani. The Venetians were relying on François' help to force Maximilian to surrender Verona to them, and were intending to pursue a policy of friendly neutrality towards France in the Italian war, even if they did not join in on the French side. But Henry and Wolsey had a lever to use against the Venetians, who particularly valued their trade with England. They had been granted the privilege, which was denied to other foreign traders, of shipping goods from England in their own vessels, despite the law which provided that all exports from England must be carried in English ships. The Venetian galleys sailed from Venice, with the wares they had brought from Smyrna, through the Straits of Gibraltar to the Portuguese and Spanish ports, and on to Southampton and London.

Henry and Wolsey, in frequent talks with Giustiniani, tried to convince him that it would be in the interests of Venice to forgo her claim to Verona, to become reconciled with the Emperor, to prefer the friendship of England to that of France, and to join Maximilian and the Swiss in an anti-French alliance. Most of the discussions with Giustiniani were carried on by Wolsey, but Henry himself often granted the ambassador an audience, at which he reinforced Wolsey's arguments. Both the King and the Cardinal sometimes lost their temper. According to Giustiniani, Wolsey once laid hands on the Papal Nuncio, and almost resorted to physical violence.[22] Henry never went as far as this, and on the whole was a little more courteous and restrained than Wolsey.

As early as March 1515, Henry had warned Giustiniani's predecessor, Badoer, against François. 'This King of France is indeed a worthy and honest sovereign, but he is nevertheless a Frenchman and not to be trusted'. When Giustiniani arrived in London to replace Badoer, Henry repeated the warnings to him. 'I am aware that King Louis, although my brother-in-law, was a bad man. I know not what this youth may be; he is, however, a Frenchman, nor can I say how far you should trust him'.

At the end of June 1515, Giustiniani told Henry that François was at Lyons and on the point of invading Italy. Henry brushed the idea aside. 'The King will not go into Italy this year, though he circulates reports to this effect', said Henry, who added that François would not dare to cross the Alps because he was afraid of Henry. 'My belief is, if I choose he will not cross the Alps, and if I choose he will cross'.[23]

François crossed the Alps six weeks later, and entered Milan; but to the south of the city he encountered a strong Swiss army which the Cardinal of Sion had sent against him. A fierce battle took place at Marignano on 13 September, which the Swiss nearly won, but ultimately lost. When Giustiniani gave the news to Henry and Wolsey, they were sceptical, and said that they had received reports that the Swiss had defeated the French in Italy, and that François had been killed. When the news of Marignano was confirmed, Henry and Wolsey did not hide their annoyance.[24]

They did not invite the French ambassador to the official launching of another new warship at Woolwich on 25 October, though Giustiniani was invited to attend and took part in the great banquet which was held on board the galley. She had 120 oars, 207 guns, and could hold nearly a thousand soldiers. Giustiniani wrote that she was three times the size of the largest Venetian galley, and that the firepower of her guns was so strong that he thought that no town on earth could resist a bombardment by them. Henry was dressed in a vest of gold brocade, breeches of cloth-of-gold, and scarlet hose, and he wore round his neck a gold chain more than four fingers in width carrying a gold sea-captain's whistle a yard long, which he blew with great gusto. Queen Catherine was present, with Henry's sister the French Queen; who named the ship *The Virgin Mary*; but she became generally known as *The Mary Rose*.[25]

After the defeat at Marignano, the Swiss cantons made peace with François; but Henry and Wolsey authorised the Cardinal of Sion to promise the Swiss 120,000 crowns of Henry's money if they repudiated the treaty and raised a new army to fight against the French under the Emperor's command. The news reached Schinner in Constance just in time to prevent ten cantons from joining the French side, and it enabled Schinner to persuade six cantons to raise troops to fight for Maximilian. Henry and Wolsey sent another £20,000 to Maximilian, but ordered Pace not to let Maximilian have it until he left for Italy with his army.

In February 1516, Maximilian marched from Augsburg to Trent, and invaded the duchy of Milan. Schinner, Pace and Wingfield accompanied him. The French retreated towards the city of Milan. Schinner wrote the good news to Wolsey, but he was worried that Henry's money had not arrived to pay the Swiss soldiers. He urged Wolsey, if there was any hitch in the arrangements for the bankers to transfer the money to Trent, to take the risk of sending horsemen to carry it from Antwerp to Trent in gold bullion sewn into the lining of their doublets, because there would be serious trouble with the soldiers if the money did not arrive soon.

On 23 March, the Emperor reached the River Adda. The French general, the Duke of Bourbon, had not enough men to contest the passage of the river, and withdrew his army into the suburbs of Milan and prepared to defend the city. But Henry's money still had not come, though Pace assured Maximilian that it would arrive at any hour. On 25 March, Maximilian summoned Pace and Wingfield to his tent, and told them that he had heard from his spies in France that François had offered to abandon the Scots and allow Henry to control Scotland, if Henry would withdraw from the anti-French alliance. Maximilian accepted Pace's assurance that there was no truth in the story; but that night, he sent again for Pace and Wingfield, and told them that, as Henry's money had not arrived, he had decided to retreat from Italy and dissolve his army. Pace persuaded him to wait a little longer for the money, for he was sure that if Maximilian retreated, he and all Christendom would be lost.

In the middle of this conversation, a messenger arrived from the Duke of Bourbon inviting the Emperor to come to Milan to have a drink with him. Maximilian refused the invitation, and sent the Margrave of Brandenburg to Bourbon to challenge him to meet him in battle next day, but as Bourbon would not stir from his defensive positions, Maximilian felt obliged to retreat.[26] He recrossed the Adda and continued to retreat till he reached Trent, while Bourbon's army, pursuing him, defeated the Swiss at Lodi. The Swiss, furious that they had not been paid their wages, seized Pace as a hostage, telling him that they would hang him if Henry's money did not come. The money arrived at Trent at the beginning of May – six weeks too late.[27]

François told his ambassador in London to inform Henry of his victory, and to say that he was sure that Henry, his good brother, would be delighted to hear of his success.[28]

The news of Maximilian's retreat reached London on 17 April. Henry and Wolsey, who as late as 20 April were bluffing it out and boasting to Giustiniani of the Emperor's advance on Milan, were forced to admit that they had suffered a reverse in Italy. They changed their line of argument to Giustiniani, warning him that François was planning to double-cross Venice about Verona and to make a deal with Maximilian at her expense.[29]

Pace thought that Maximilian's retreat from Milan was as great an act of treason against the Princes of Christendom as was Judas's treason against Christ; and Wolsey agreed that it was an event 'redounding much to the Emperor's dishonour'. But in the new situation, Henry and Wolsey agreed for the first time to negotiate with Albany, on condition that this did not involve recognising him as Governor of Scotland.[30]

Maximilian chose this moment to ask Wingfield and Pace for another 60,000 florins. In order to encourage them to pay it, he offered to cede the duchy of Milan to Henry when he had conquered it from the French; and he also promised to abdicate as Holy Roman Emperor and to use his influence with the Electors of the Empire to elect Henry as Emperor in his place. Henry was not impressed. There was no prospect of Maximilian even attempting to recover Milan from the French; and as for the offer of the Holy Roman Empire, Henry's advisers pointed out that, apart from the fact that it would involve Henry and England in heavy liabilities, it was doubtful whether Henry was eligible to be Emperor, for his realm had never been part of the Empire.[31]

Henry and Wolsey transmitted to Wingfield and Pace, through the Fugger bank at Augsburg, the money for which Maximilian had asked; but they told Pace not to pay it over to Maximilian, nor even to tell him that it had arrived, until there were signs that another Swiss force was being raised to fight the French. Pace therefore refused Maximilian's request for the money. Wingfield, without consulting Henry or Wolsey, promised his friend the Emperor that it would be paid. The Cardinal of Sion had meanwhile told Maximilian that he had discovered from agents in England that Pace's reports were turning Henry and Wolsey against Maximilian. The Emperor thereupon ordered Pace to leave his court, and Wingfield wrote to Henry that he thought Maximilian's conduct was justified.

Henry was very angry. He sent a severe reprimand to Wingfield; but he still hoped that Maximilian would fight against the French, and there was no one else who was prepared to do so. He reluctantly agreed to honour the promise that Wingfield had made on his behalf, and authorised him to pay over the money to Maximilian; and he retained Wingfield as ambassador at Maximilian's court, although Wingfield offered to resign. But he sent another churchman, his chaplain Dr Knight, to replace Pace as a watchdog over Wingfield at the Emperor's court.[32]

King Ferdinand died on 23 January 1516. When Henry heard the news in

François I, by Joos van Cleve, c.1530

Mary Tudor, with her second husband, Charles Brandon, Duke of Suffolk

the middle of February, Catherine was on the point of giving birth to her baby, and Henry suppressed the news for a few days in case her safe delivery might be imperilled if she heard about her father's death.[33] Ferdinand was succeeded as King of Aragon by his grandson, Prince Charles of Castile, and Charles took over Ferdinand's position as Regent of Castile for his mad mother Joanna, who lived on for nearly as long as Charles himself. He was one month short of his sixteenth birthday. He remained in the Netherlands, where he had lived all his life, and went hunting while his kingdoms were governed for him by his Council in Brussels.

The members of his Council pursued a pro-French neutrality, and made things as difficult as possible for the English garrison at Tournai. Henry and Wolsey warned Maximilian that the counsellors were French agents in François' pay, and urged Maximilian to dismiss them from office;[34] but Maximilian found excuses for not doing so. In reality, they were only carrying out Maximilian's policy, for Maximilian did not wish to have a war on his hands in Flanders and Italy simultaneously, and hoped that the pro-French policy of Charles's Council would prevent the French from invading the Netherlands while he was fighting them in Lombardy.

To encourage Maximilian and the Swiss to renew the war against François, Henry and Wolsey assured them that Henry would participate in a joint invasion of France: he himself would lead an army royal to invade northern France from Calais while the Swiss attacked in the south-east. At the beginning of May 1516, Margaret of Austria's ambassador was informing her that Henry was very eager to invade France; but three weeks later, Wolsey wrote to Gigli that, though Henry himself wished to invade, his Council thought that the invasion should be postponed until the Swiss were ready to launch an attack from Italy. About the same time, Wolsey wrote to Pace at Trent, urging him to try, 'by good policy and wise drifts', to induce the Swiss to ask Henry to excuse them from invading France, as they did not wish to advance beyond Milan.

Dr Scarisbrick, in his biography of Henry, suggests that there was a serious disagreement between Henry and Wolsey on this point. He believes that, while Henry ardently wished to invade France, Wolsey opposed this, and schemed with Pace to use the Swiss reluctance to invade France from Italy in order to deter Henry from invading from Calais.[35] It is quite possible that Henry was more eager than Wolsey to invade France, because he was usually more receptive than Wolsey to the feelings of the people; he knew that if the people had to pay taxes to finance a war against France, they expected to see their gallant King play a personal part in it. But there is no evidence at all of any disagreement between Henry and Wolsey about the invasion, or that Wolsey's letter to Pace was written without Henry's knowledge. It is much more likely that both Henry and Wolsey hoped to lure the Swiss into expressing a reluctance to invade France in order to give

Henry an excuse for backing out of his promises to Maximilian, than that Wolsey would commit to paper a plan by which he and Pace would plot with the Swiss to deceive Henry.

In August, Charles of Castile's Council in the Netherlands signed a treaty of friendship with François I at Noyon. Henry and Wolsey again urged Maximilian to dismiss Charles's counsellors, and on 29 October 1516 made a new military alliance with Maximilian and Charles, which was concluded with the Cardinal of Sion in London. Henry offered to meet Maximilian at Calais and help him expel the pro-French members of Charles's Council; but Maximilian, after temporizing for several months, himself adhered to the Treaty of Noyon and made peace with France in February 1517. At the same time, he sold Verona to the Venetians.[36]

Giustiniani went to Greenwich to tell the news to Henry. He could not come from London by barge, as the river was blocked by ice, and he had to ride overland, along the frozen, dangerous roads. When Henry heard what Maximilian had done, he put on a cheerful face. 'How can this be?', he said to Giustiniani, and after repeating this several times, he said: 'Verily, the Emperor has been deceived by the King of France'. Then, smiling broadly, he added: 'Whoever has been deceived, it is not your Signory,* who has obtained Verona'.[37]

Henry was persuaded by Cuthbert Tunstal, a very able churchman whom he had sent to the court of Margaret of Austria, to conceal his anger and remain ostensibly on friendly terms with Maximilian; but Knight reported from Maximilian's court in February 1517 that Maximilian had urged Charles of Castile that they should together double-cross both the French and the English, and had said to Charles: '*Mon fils, vous allez tromper les Français, et moi je vais tromper les Anglais*'.[38] This famous remark, which is sometimes quoted as a proof that Maximilian had made fools of Henry and Wolsey, seems rather to show the efficiency of the English spies.

François retaliated for Henry's hostile acts by refusing to perform his promise to return the dowry which Princess Mary had brought when she married Louis XII, giving as his excuse for breaking his word that Mary and Suffolk had tricked some French officials into letting them have the diamond, the Mirror of Naples, without François' authority.[39] François also encouraged and gave financial help to Richard de la Pole, the son of Edward IV's sister, who, since the execution of his brother Edmund by Henry, was the Yorkist pretender to the throne of England. Richard styled himself Duke of Suffolk; but Henry and his agents called him 'White Rose'. He had served in the French army in the war of 1513; but after Louis XII made peace with Henry, White Rose left for Metz in the Emperor's territories. The French now renewed their contacts with him.

Henry, like all dictators, had an extraordinary fear of even the smallest and weakest group of refugees who were working against his régime from the

*The 'Signory' was the name given by the English to the government of Venice.

safety of foreign countries. He tried to persuade foreign governments to extradite them to England, or at least to refuse to grant them asylum; and he spent a surprising amount of money in hiring agents to spy on them, to infiltrate themselves into their houses, and to attempt to kidnap or assassinate them. After relations between Henry and François deteriorated in 1515, Henry's agents reported that François was planning for White Rose to invade England with 15,000 French soldiers. They also feared that François would send him with an army to Scotland.[40]

Henry's desire to destroy Richard de la Pole was even stronger than his love of music. He was always eager to persuade eminent musicians to come to his court. He was very pleased when Dionisius Memo, the organist of St Mark's Cathedral in Venice, agreed to come in September 1516. He also invited the Flemish lute-player, Hans Nagel, in February 1516. Nagel had formerly been friendly with Richard de la Pole, and thought it advisable to disclose the fact to Henry, and to ask for a pardon for having associated with the traitor, before setting foot in England.

When Henry heard this, he thought that Nagel could be more usefully employed in spying on White Rose than in playing the lute at Greenwich. As there would, in any case, be no musical evenings during Lent, Henry's agents in Brussels told Nagel to postpone his departure for England until after Easter, and in the meantime to go to Richard de la Pole at Metz, renew his friendship with him, and send reports to the English embassy about Richard's negotiations with the French King and his contacts in England. When Nagel had sent his reports, he would be granted his pardon and could come to England.[41] It is not clear why a distinguished musician was prepared to take a few weeks off from his work to engage in espionage activities. Perhaps he feared to offend the powerful King of England by refusing, even from the safety of the Emperor's territories; or perhaps Henry had some hold over him, for some of Nagel's Flemish musician friends were already in England.

Henry and Wolsey had had the worst of their contest with François. The idea of financing Maximilian and the Swiss to fight against the French had not been a good investment; but it is an exaggeration to write off the whole of Henry and Wolsey's foreign policy in 1515 and 1516 as a complete failure. The presence of Maximilian and his army in northern Italy, and the threat that Maximilian would raise another army and continue the war, had probably deterred François from advancing further into Italy and occupying Naples; and in 1517 Henry was able to reach a satisfactory compromise over Scotland. Though François did not agree to withdraw Albany from Scotland, he recalled him to France on indefinite leave, though he retained the position of Governor of Scotland. At about the same time, Margaret the Queen Mother returned to Scotland. A regency Council of Scottish lords governed the kingdom. François had in fact retreated without loss of face. In the area that really mattered, Henry had held his ground.

7

EVIL MAY DAY

HENRY'S relationship with the Papacy had deteriorated since the war for the defence of the Church against the schismatic Louis XII, and the day in May 1514 when thousands of Londoners had seen Henry, dressed in a gown of purple satin and a doublet of gold brocade, go in state to St Paul's to receive the sword and cap which the Pope had sent him as a tribute to his valour in the war.[1] Pope Leo X wished to unite the Kings of Christendom in a crusade against the Turks; and he did not wish to offend the King of France, whose armies could dominate Italy. He eventually agreed, after a long delay, to make Wolsey a Cardinal; but he refused to grant Henry the title of 'Defender of the Faith' for Henry to parade against the King of France's title of 'the Most Christian King' and the King of Spain's of 'the King Catholic'. He refused Henry's request, after Flodden, to downgrade the status of the Archbishop of St Andrews as a metropolitan and place his see within the province of the Archbishop of York. When François I invaded Italy, Leo had a meeting with him at Bologna after François' victory at Marignano; he would not allow François to kiss his foot, and offered him his cheek instead.[2]

The call for peace in Christendom and a crusade against the infidel was much talked of in Western Europe in 1516. Sultan Selim of Turkey was engaged in a war with the Circassian rulers of Syria and Egypt; and this was thought to be a good opportunity for the Christian powers to attack the Turk. The more imaginative armchair strategists drew up plans for a campaign led by all the twenty Princes of Christendom, with Henry, François and Maximilian leading their armies through the Balkans, while the King of Poland attacked the Turks across their Russian frontier, and the King of Portugal marched right across North Africa to help the Sultan of Egypt, who would be his ally against Selim. Both the Sophy of Persia and Prester John of Ethiopia would join the alliance. Jerusalem would be liberated, and, after victory, Anatolia would be partitioned between Maximilian and the Sophy, who, it was hoped, might perhaps become a Christian.[3]

Henry and Wolsey paid lip-service to the idea mean it seriously. Giustiniani tried from time to crusading enthusiasm; for although the Venetians ca trade with the Turks, had a colony of Venetian mercha were the only Christian state to have a diplomatic Constantinople, they regarded the Turks as powerful neighbours, and thought that the Venetians' position would be if the other Christian states adopted a resolute anti-Turkish pos Venice traded profitably with the Turks. Henry sometimes told the etian ambassadors that he was eager to go on a crusade; on one occasion, he said that he intended to lead his army in person into Jerusalem.[4] But he always hastened to add that this would have to wait until peace had been secured in Christendom, which could only be achieved by overthrowing the power of France.

Giustiniani several times reported that Henry and Wolsey did not seem interested when he talked about the Turkish menace. Henry cheerfully dismissed it by saying that the Turk would never dare to attack in the west because he was afraid of the Sophy. When Giustiniani told him, in 1516 and 1517, of the Turkish advance into Syria and Egypt and their capture of Cairo, Henry did not seem interested. Once he laughingly said that the Venetians need not worry about the Turks, as they had done very well for themselves by their friendship with the Turks. He told Giustiniani that there was little to be feared from the Turks, and more from bad Christians. 'Write to your Signory', said Henry, 'to be more apprehensive of a certain other person than of the Great Turk', and he thereupon confided in Giustiniani that his spies had discovered that François was planning to attack Venice. Wolsey told Giustiniani that Venice was in greater danger from the Christian Turk than from the true Turk.[5]

Another scandal in Rome brought Henry and Wolsey into a new conflict with the Pope. In May 1517 Leo X arrested two cardinals whom he accused of trying to poison him. A few days later, he accused Cardinal Hadrian and another cardinal of being involved in the plot. Hadrian's first reaction, on being accused of the crime, was to burst out laughing. He then denied the accusation, but afterwards admitted that he had heard about the plot but did not take it seriously. The Pope offered to exonerate him if he paid him 25,000 ducats. Hadrian thereupon fled to Venice, from where he protested his innocence, while Leo kept his offer open.

When Henry and Wolsey heard about the incident, they demanded that Hadrian should be deprived of all his offices, including his bishopric of Bath and Wells. Henry protested that it was an affront to his honour that his representative in the College of Cardinals should be accused of attempting to murder the Pope; but an additional motive for his attitude was that Wolsey wished to be made Bishop of Bath and Wells in Hadrian's place, so that he [illegible] enjoy the revenues of the see in addition to his income as Archbishop of York and Bishop of Tournai. Leo did not wish to punish Hadrian or deprive him of his see as long as there was any chance that Hadrian would pay him the 25,000 ducats. Henry and Wolsey continued to demand that Hadrian be deprived, and they protested to Giustiniani because the Venetian government had granted Hadrian asylum in Venice and had intervened in his favour with the Pope.[6]

The latent hostility of Englishmen to the foreign Pope and the corrupt clergy was never far below the surface. From time to time, Wolsey reminded the Papal court that Henry was a more devoted son of the Church than any other Prince, none of whom had rendered better service to the Church in the last war; and proceedings were regularly taken against heretics. Fitzjames, the Bishop of London, was a particularly active persecutor. Two heretics were burned in London in 1511 for denying the Real Presence in the Eucharist; but most of Fitzjames's victims recanted. If a heretic recanted, it was the invariable practice to spare his life; he was ordered to 'carry his faggot', that is to say, to make a public recantation of his opinions at Paul's Cross or some other specified place, and to undergo some penance, usually a short term of imprisonment. It was only if the heretic refused to recant that he was excommunicated as a heretic by the bishop's court, and handed over to the temporal authorities for burning. But if a heretic, after recanting and carrying his faggot, was guilty of heresy a second time, he was sentenced, as a relapsed heretic, and this time he was burned whether he recanted or not.

Fitzjames thought out an additional penance for a heretic who recanted and carried his faggot. He was ordered to wear at all times, for the rest of his life, a picture of a faggot sewn on his outer garment as a distinguishing badge of infamy.[7] This was in imitation of the yellow badge which every Jew who had not converted to Christianity was obliged to wear throughout Christendom. It did not apply in England, for the Jews had been expelled from England more than two hundred years earlier; but in Venice, where hatred of Jews was particularly strong, they were required to wear the more distinctive yellow hat. No Jew with his yellow hat could venture out in Venice without being subjected to insult. Henry used the services of several Jews, both as theologians and as intelligence agents; and in 1529 his ambassador in Venice asked the Doge and Senate to exempt an eminent Jewish physician from the obligation to wear the yellow hat. The French ambassador and the Papal Nuncio made the same request, and the Doge and Senate agreed as a gesture of goodwill to the foreign sovereigns.[8]

The ordinary Londoner thought it right that sacramentaries should be burned if they denied the Real Presence; but they were irritated by the excessive zeal with which Fitzjames and his officials denounced as a heretic anyone who made the least criticism of orthodox doctrine. The people had every sympathy with Richard Hunne, a merchant living in Whitechapel just outside the city walls, when he refused to allow a greedy priest to cheat him; and if Hunne had once been accused of reading heretical books, including an old Lollard Bible in English, they did not hold this very strongly against him. Hunne's infant baby died when it was a few weeks old. The parish priest refused to bury the baby until Hunne gave him the winding-sheet in which the baby's corpse had been wrapped; for a priest who performed the funeral service was entitled to the winding-sheet as his fee. Hunne disliked priests and knew some law. A priest was entitled to claim, as his fee, the deceased's winding-sheet; but in this case the winding-sheet did not belong to the dead baby, but to Hunne.

The priest eventually buried the baby's corpse, but he prosecuted Hunne in the ecclesiastical courts for refusing to give him the winding-sheet. Hunne complained to the King's Council, alleging that by bringing the proceedings the priest had exercised a power which was derived from a foreign sovereign, that is to say the Pope, and was therefore guilty of the criminal offence of a *praemunire* by encroaching on the King's authority in his realm, and liable to imprisonment for life. This was a ridiculous suggestion, for the clergy's power to bring proceedings in the ecclesiastical courts had never been questioned under the Statutes of Praemunire. The Bishop of London's Chancellor, Dr Horsey, then accused Hunne of heresy. Hunne was arrested and imprisoned in the tower in St Paul's Cathedral where heretics were usually imprisoned when awaiting trial, and which was known as the Lollards' Tower. Two days later, on 4 December 1514, Hunne was found hanged in his cell. The jailers said that he had committed suicide.

The London coroner ordered an inquest to be held. The evidence showed that Hunne had bled as he died; but no drop of blood was found on the clothes which he was wearing. The noose around his neck was made of silk, but his neck had been broken. His hands were not tied when his body was found, but there were marks on his wrists which suggested that they had been tied shortly before. On this and other evidence, the coroner's jury returned a verdict that Hunne had been murdered by his jailers, on the orders of the Bishop's Chancellor.

Dr Horsey and the jailers were indicted for murder in the Court of King's Bench. Meanwhile Horsey and Fitzjames continued the heresy proceedings against the dead Hunne. He was posthumously found guilty of heresy, and excommunicated, and his corpse was publicly burned as a heretic at Smithfield. This was the accepted procedure when a heretic was convicted after his death; but Hunne's friends claimed that Fitzjames and Horsey were guilty of a *praemunire* in burning Hunne's corpse.

In the spring, the question was raised in the Convocation of Canterbury by the Abbot of Winchcombe. He claimed that the privileges of the clergy had been infringed by the prosecution of Horsey for murder in the Court of King's Bench. The Abbot was opposed by Dr Standish, a learned friar who was one of Henry's chaplains. It was surprising to find Standish appearing as a champion for the anti-clerical cause, for he was not only strictly orthodox and especially rigid in his doctrinal views, but was very conservative on all religious issues and a staunch opponent of Erasmus, More, and all the humanists who supported the new culture. But as a royal chaplain he doubtless knew the King's attitude towards those who challenged the jurisdiction of his courts to try all his subjects, and he was duly rewarded for his opposition to the Abbot of Winchcombe when he was appointed Bishop of St Asaph three years later. Standish was denounced in Convocation for infringing the privileges of the clergy.

Eventually, in the autumn of 1515, the case was argued at Blackfriars before Henry, Wolsey and the judges. Warham suggested that the dispute might be referred to the Papal court in Rome; but Henry intervened. 'We are, by the sufferance of God, King of England, and Kings of England in times past never had any superior but God; know therefore that we will maintain the rights of the crown in this matter like our progenitors'. At the conclusion of the arguments, Henry ordered Wolsey to investigate and decide the dispute. This had the double advantage of enhancing Wolsey's prestige and of passing the responsibility from the King to the Cardinal; but there can be no doubt that Wolsey consulted Henry as to what his decision should be. A compromise solution was found which would avoid, as far as possible, antagonising either the ecclesiastical hierarchy or public opinion in London. The coroner's verdict, the posthumous proceedings for heresy against Hunne, and the indictment for murder against Horsey and the jailers, were all upheld; but the plea of Not Guilty by Horsey and the jailers was accepted by the prosecution, and they were sent away from London and given other employment in the West Country.[9]

The Londoners' hatred of foreigners took a more ugly form in the riots of 'Evil May Day' in 1517. Resentment had been building up against the 'strangers' who were there in such large numbers, not only in the city but all around – in Southwark, Westminster, Temple Bar, Holborn, St Martin's, St John Street, Aldgate, Tower Hill and St Katherine's – where they bought up all the food in the markets so that Englishmen had to go hungry. The Londoners hated not only the arrogant Frenchmen, who insulted the English – one of them bullied a shopkeeper into selling to him two pigeons which had already been sold to an English carpenter – but also German merchants who imported leather goods, baskets, chairs and tables and sold them in England, ruining the businesses of English leatherers and carpenters, and making their artisans unemployed. There were the Venetians, who shipped goods from London in their own galleys, which injured English shipowners; and there was the Lombard who had persuaded an Englishman's wife to leave her husband and live with him. This Lombard had friends at the King's court, where he had been heard joking with Sir

Thomas Palmer about his success in seducing the woman.

A second-hand dealer named John Lincoln decided to set matters right. He urged Dr Standish to denounce the foreigners in his Easter sermons; but Standish said that he would do no such thing, as it would be meddling in politics. But Lincoln persuaded the vicar of St Mary's in Spitalfields, Dr Beal, to preach against the foreigners in his sermon in Easter week to a great congregation in the fields outside the city. Beal denounced the aliens who stole Englishmen's livelihoods and seduced their wives and daughters; he said that even birds expelled interlopers from their nests, and that men were entitled to fight for their country against foreigners.

By the end of April, London was full of rumours that the people would rise and kill the foreigners on May Day. Giustiniani went to Wolsey, who promised to take precautions to prevent trouble; but as Giustiniani was still dissatisfied, he went to Richmond on 29 April to tell Henry about his anxieties. Henry promised that all foreigners would be protected. In view of the likelihood of disorders, Wolsey ordered the Lord Mayor and the city officers to enforce a curfew on the eve of May Day, when large crowds always assembled and trouble sometimes occurred. Some young apprentices broke the curfew. When the watch tried to arrest one of them, a riot broke out, and soon thousands of young people were attacking foreigners and burning their houses. Thomas More, who was Under-Sheriff of London, tried to persuade some curfew-breakers in another part of the city to disperse peaceably. He seemed to be on the point of succeeding when one of the apprentices threw a stone at him, and here, too, rioting developed.

News about the rioting was sent at once to Henry at Richmond. He rose at midnight, and assembled the soldiers of his guard. He sent a messenger to London with the news that he was coming in person at the head of an army to restore order; but in fact he did not leave Richmond. He had no intention of becoming embroiled in a riot, and as usual he arranged for subordinates to do the unpopular things. He ordered the Duke of Norfolk to gather an army and enter London as soon as possible.

The rioting continued all night and on the morning and afternoon of May Day. The hated Frenchmen were the chief target of the rioters. Several were assaulted in the street. The French ambassador escaped, when his house was attacked, by hiding in a church steeple. Giustiniani's house was unharmed. The London watch was quite incapable of dealing with the rioters. The Constable of the Tower opened fire on them with his cannon, but only shot a few rounds and did no damage to the city. In the afternoon, the Duke of Norfolk arrived with two thousand soldiers, and suppressed the disorders. Several hundred people were arrested. Nearly all of them were young apprentices; according to Edward Hall, who sympathised with them, the priests, the serving men and the watermen fled when the soldiers came, leaving the apprentices to become the scapegoats. John Lincoln was arrested, but Dr Beal escaped.

Henry and Wolsey took a very serious view of the May Day riots. The prisoners were summarily tried at the Guildhall four days after the riot, not by the usual London judges, but by a special tribunal appointed by the King and consisting of the Duke of Norfolk, his son the Earl of Surrey, the Earl of Shrewsbury, and the Lord Mayor. It had been expected that they would be tried for riot; but the charge was high treason under an Act of Henry V's reign, which made it treason to stir up hostility against subjects of a state with which the King was at peace. The 279 defendants were all tried on the same day. They included priests and husbandmen as well as apprentices; some of them were only thirteen years old. There was great sympathy for the young apprentices among the people of London; but Norfolk had brought 1,300 soldiers to keep order on the day of the trial.

All the defendants were found guilty. Some of them were sentenced to be hanged, drawn and quartered, but sentence on the majority was deferred. Those condemned to die were executed next day and their corpses left hanging on the gibbets at Aldgate, Whitechapel, Gracechurch Street, Leadenhall, Newgate, Aldersgate, Bishopsgate and elsewhere. According to Chieregato, more than sixty were executed; but Hall, whose strong sympathies for the rioters would not lead him to minimize the number of victims, is probably right when he states that thirteen were executed on 5 May.

John Lincoln and three others were tried separately on 6 May and sentenced to be hanged, drawn and quartered next day. After Lincoln had been executed, it was announced that the King had commuted the death sentences on the other three; and the people cried: 'God save the King!'

Some days later, an impressive ceremony was staged at Westminster Hall. Henry arrived from Greenwich, with Wolsey and Queen Catherine and his counsellors and nobles. All the convicted rioters were brought before him with halters around their necks. Wolsey asked him to pardon them, but Henry refused. As the prisoners wept and begged for mercy, Wolsey again begged Henry, on his knees, to pardon them, and Queen Catherine added her prayers to Wolsey's. At last Henry agreed to grant them their lives and freedom, and they were set free after they and all the nobles and people present had thanked the King for his great mercy.[10]

For the first time since he became King, Henry risked his popularity with the people by his severe repression of the anti-foreign rioters of Evil May Day. The resentment felt against the foreigners; the sympathy for the young apprentices; the grief of the parents when their boys of thirteen were executed; the feeling that in many cases the more innocent had been punished while the more guilty escaped; and the tales, which Hall reported, of the brutality of Surrey's soldiers who suppressed the disorders, all aroused great sympathy for the rioters. Even Giustiniani's secretary, Sagudino, though himself a target, as a foreigner, for the rioters' hatred, was shocked that so many young boys should be executed when no one had been killed by the rioters. But Henry wished to show the foreign merchants that they could safely come to London and carry on their business there; and, even more important, he would not tolerate anarchy in his realm, or any defiance of his royal authority and laws. He was justified in treating the riot as an act of high treason, not only in strict law under the Act of 1414, but because the preacher and the other agitators who had incited the rioters had clearly urged them to take the law into their own hands. Beal had called on them to defend their nests against interloping birds and to fight, as true Englishmen, for their country. Henry had to show them that Englishmen were only entitled to fight for their country when their King ordered them to do so.

His display of authority did him no harm. The people were shocked and saddened, but they did not blame Henry. Hall wrote about the brutality of Surrey's soldiers towards the Londoners, and the bias shown by Norfolk at the trials; but nowhere does he criticise Henry. He mentions only that when it was announced that the death sentences were commuted, the people cried: 'God save the King!'

A few days after Evil May Day in London, a riot broke out in Southampton. Foxe, who had retired to his diocese of Winchester, wrote to Wolsey that it was a very small affair, because the severe punishment meted out to the London rioters had deterred many evil-minded people in Southampton from joining in the disorders. In view of this, Foxe thought that the Southampton trouble-makers could be dealt with leniently, and that it would be sufficient to imprison the ringleaders before releasing them on recognisances. There were also riots in various places in Hampshire, Berkshire, Wiltshire and Somerset, where the weavers were angry that they were being paid their wages in goods and not in money. The serious drought added to the discontent.[11]

But the people's troubles did not prevent Henry and Wolsey from giving a particularly lavish reception to the ambassadors of Charles of Castile who came to London to sign a treaty of friendship with Henry in July 1517. If Henry and Wolsey were angry with Maximilian and Charles for having made peace with François, and if there were rumours circulating abroad about riots and risings in England, this made it all the more necessary to dispel all doubts and dissatisfaction by sumptuous tournaments and banquets. In the jousts on St Thomas of Canterbury's Day, Henry rode eight courses against the Duke of Suffolk; they fought with such vigour that Giustiniani compared it to the battle between Hector and Achilles. Both Henry and Suffolk broke their lances against the other's armour in every one of their eight encounters. Between the courses, Henry rode over to a window from which Queen Catherine, Mary the French Queen, and all the most beautiful ladies of the court were watching him, and made his horse rear and curvet as he performed feats of horsemanship before the eyes of the admiring ladies. At the banquet, Henry did not sit alone at his table, as he usually did, but honoured four other diners by inviting them to sit with him. Queen Catherine sat on his right, and his sister the French Queen on his left. Wolsey sat on Catherine's right, and Charles's ambassador, the strikingly handsome young Duke of Luxemburg, sat on Mary's left. The other ambassadors sat with Henry's nobles at lower tables. They sat at table for seven hours and ate more than twenty courses.[12]

Within a month, the social life of the court was disrupted by a serious outbreak of the sweating sickness. The disease attacked people suddenly as they sat in their houses, lay in bed, or walked in the street. They sweated profusely, and died, some after about four hours and some after ten or twelve hours; 'some merry at dinner and dead at supper', wrote Hall. If they survived for twenty-four hours, they were saved, and recovered quickly. Their best chance of survival was to lie down on their backs, well wrapped in warm blankets, in a moderately heated room which was neither too hot nor too cold, with their arms crossed on their chests to prevent air reaching their armpits. Those who took a cold drink to appease the fever invariably died.[13]

By the end of July 1517 the sweating sickness was claiming many victims. Four hundred died in Oxford in a week. According to Hall, in some towns half the people died, in others one-third.

Henry would in any case have left London on a progress in August and September, but because of 'the sweat' he remained at Windsor throughout the autumn. The Michaelmas law term in London was cancelled, and public functions and festivities at court were abandoned; but Henry rejected the suggestion that all fairs should be banned, lest the people resented being deprived of one of their few consolations in this sad time. Henry himself took all precautions to avoid the disease, particularly after some members of his household caught it. His Latin secretary, the Italian Ammonio, died of the sweat in the middle of August.

The very cold winter did not stop the spread of the disease. In November, several of Henry's servants died of it. The Christmas festivities were cancelled. Henry refused to receive ambassadors, and isolated himself from everyone, being attended by only three or four servants. Apart from a few brief visits to Esher and Newhall in Essex, he remained at Windsor throughout the winter. The sweating sickness continued in the spring. In March there was a case of the sweat near Windsor, so Henry moved to Abingdon, and then to Woodstock. He did not return to Greenwich until the beginning of August 1518. Where the sweating sickness was concerned, the tall blonde hero-King, the champion of the jousting lists, was far from heroic, and was determined to avoid all possible risks.[14]

The riots and the drought of the summer of 1517, the bitter winter which followed, and the terrible toll of the sweating sickness, caused more misery and discontent among the people than at any time since Henry's accession to the throne. Many people blamed Wolsey, whose pomp and arrogance had made him even more unpopular with the courtiers and nobility than he was with the common people. But Henry would hear no criticism of him. When Sir Robert Sheffield, the Speaker of the House of Commons, came to Henry and complained that Wolsey was persecuting him, he was sent to the Tower on a charge of insulting a member of the King's Council. In February 1518 he was brought before the Council; and though the charge of insulting Wolsey was not proceeded with, he was sent back to the Tower for having accepted money from men accused of murder. He was eventually pardoned by Henry after he had admitted his offence and had begged for mercy.[15]

During the period of exactly a year that Henry was in the country avoiding the sweat, he hardly ever saw Wolsey; but his respect and affection for him was as high as ever. In April 1518 he warmly praised Wolsey to the courtiers at Woodstock; and throughout the year of the sweating sickness, he showed the greatest concern for Wolsey's health and safety.[16]

By the summer of 1518, it seemed that the Pope's ideal of a universal peace in Christendom was about to be realised. As Charles of Castile and Maximilian had made peace with François, there was nothing left for Henry and Wolsey but to do the same. The problem of Scotland had been settled quite satisfactorily for Henry, and he was also able to solve the question of Tournai. In the five years in which Tournai had been part of his realm, it had caused him a great deal of trouble. The citizens revolted against the taxes which he imposed, and Welsh units in the garrison had mutinied because of dissatisfaction with their pay. He dealt with both the revolt and the mutiny in his usual way: after hanging a few of the ringleaders, he pardoned the other rebels and mutineers with the maximum of publicity.[17]

François was eager to buy back Tournai from Henry, and offered to do this as soon as he became King. The negotiations lapsed after the rift between François and Henry in the summer of 1515, but they were resumed three years later. Charles of Castile and his Council in the Netherlands were not pleased at the prospect of having the French again in Tournai; they protested to Henry against the negotiations, and thought that if Henry wished to sell Tournai, he should sell it to them. But Henry had no reason to feel any obligation to Charles and his family, and he sold Tournai to France in the summer of 1518. The purchase price of 600,000 *écus d'or* was added to the pensions due from France to Henry under the treaties of 1492 and 1514. At the same time, Wolsey divested himself of the bishopric of Tournai, which had involved him in difficulties with a French nominee who claimed to be the lawful bishop and had succeeded in preventing Wolsey from obtaining a large part of the revenues of the see. Wolsey resigned the see to the French bishop in return for an additional pension from François.[18]

The approach of peace in Christendom encouraged the Pope to renew his attempts to organise a crusade against the Turk. He sent Cardinal Campeggio, the Bishop of Salisbury, as his Legate to visit the courts of Maximilian, François and Henry to urge them to commit themselves to the crusade, or at least to induce their clergy to vote money for it. But Henry and Wolsey, while professing their devotion to the Pope and their enthusiasm for the crusade, pointed out that under the Statutes of Praemunire it would be illegal for a Papal Legate to enter the realm without the King's consent; and they made it clear that Henry would only give his consent on two conditions. He and Wolsey had been trying for some years to persuade the Pope to grant Wolsey legatine powers which would make him the supreme ecclesiastical authority in England, overruling the authority of Archbishop Warham and all bishops and abbots in the kingdom. They insisted that Wolsey should be appointed co-legate along with Campeggio. The Pope agreed to this, though he insisted that Wolsey's legacy, as was the usual custom, should last only for a limited time and should expire, as Campeggio's legacy would, at the end of Campeggio's visit to England. The Pope agreed that Wolsey should be the senior Legate. He would be named before Campeggio in all official documents; he would be in the place of honour on the right, and Campeggio on the left, when they walked side by side; and on state occasions he would sit in a larger chair than Campeggio.

The second condition on which Henry and Wolsey insisted was that the Pope should deprive Cardinal Hadrian of the bishopric of Bath and Wells and grant it to Wolsey, with the usual dispensation for non-residence and pluralities, thus allowing Wolsey to hold it together with the archbishopric of York. The Pope reluctantly agreed to this; but when Campeggio arrived in great state at Calais, Hadrian had still not been deprived. Henry therefore ordered that Campeggio should be detained at Calais and not permitted to cross the Channel until Hadrian had been deprived. Campeggio waited for a month at Calais, and it was not until 23 July that he was allowed to sail and land at Deal, after Hadrian had at last been deprived of his bishopric and his cardinal's hat and degraded from the priesthood.[19]

Hadrian was so frightened that he would be murdered by Henry's agents that he went into hiding and was never heard of again. There were rumours that he had taken refuge with the Turk in Constantinople; but he probably remained in Venice or in some village in the Venetian republic until he died a few years later.

Campeggio proceeded in state, by slow stages, from Deal to London. Henry received the two Legates, Wolsey and Campeggio, at a great ceremony at Greenwich, doffing his hat to them and making a welcoming speech in Latin. There were the usual ostentatious receptions and banquets; but they were surpassed by those held when Bonnivet, the Admiral of France, and his fellow-delegates arrived in London on 24 September. The treaty with France was signed on 2 October. Henry's daughter Mary, who was aged two years and eight months, was to marry François' five-month-old son, the Dauphin, when they had both reached the age of fourteen. Tournai was sold to France; and though there was no provision about Scotland in the treaty, Bonnivet reluctantly promised Henry and Wolsey that Albany would not be allowed to return there.[20]

On the same day, another treaty was signed in London between the representatives of Henry, François, Maximilian, Charles of Castile and the Pope. It provided that the four temporal sovereigns, at the request of the Pope, had agreed to form a Holy League to resist Turkish aggression against Christendom, and to make peace with each other. If any of the four powers committed aggression against one of the others, all the other powers would declare war on the aggressor. Any other Christian state was free to join the treaty and the guarantee against aggression during the next eight months. There was a special provision in the treaty by which Henry and François agreed that if either of them were attacked by a third power, the other King would lead an army in person to help repel the aggression.[21]

After the treaties were signed, Bonnivet and the French representatives remained in London for another week of festivities. Bonnivet was an admiral who spent more time at court than at sea. He was a great friend of François and emulated his amorous exploits, though he had failed in his attempt to seduce François' sister, Margaret, Duchess of Alençon; when he crept into her bedroom one night, he retired defeated, with his face badly scratched – an exploit which she recorded some years later, when she was Queen of Navarre, in her book *The Heptameron*.[22]

He was in his element in the festivities in London and Greenwich. On Sunday 3 October, the day after the two treaties were signed, Henry went in great pomp to St Paul's, and after Wolsey had celebrated Mass – a thing which he very rarely did – Henry and the ambassadors took the oath at the high altar to observe the terms of the treaties. The Bishop of London then entertained the King and the ambassadors to dinner. In the evening, Wolsey gave a supper party at his house at York Place in Westminster. In the middle of the party, twelve men and twelve women arrived, dressed as mummers in gorgeous costumes and wearing masks. After dancing together, they unmasked, and revealed that Henry and his sister Mary were the leaders of the mummers and the others were all lords and ladies of the court.

On the Tuesday, Bonnivet represented the Dauphin at the ceremony at which he was engaged by a precontract to Princess Mary. The two-year-old Princess was brought into the Queen's Great Chamber at Greenwich, and Bonnivet, on behalf of the five-month-old Dauphin, slipped a gold ring, with Wolsey's help, over Mary's finger.

The festivities culminated in a great tournament on the Thursday; Henry broke eight lances in the jousts. That evening there was a supper at which Henry sat at table with a number of guests. After the Dukes of Buckingham, Norfolk and Suffolk and the Marquess of Dorset had held the bowl of water while he washed his hands, he took his seat in the centre of the table, with Queen Catherine, Wolsey and Campeggio on his right, and his sister Mary, Bonnivet and the Bishop of Paris on his left, with the three Dukes facing them, and a lady sitting next to every lord. There were 82 gold vases and 52 silver drinking cups on the table. During supper a pageant was performed by actors, showing the defeat of the Turks by the Christians. After the pageant, servants entered with a shaker six feet long, in pure silver, which threw out confectionery for the guests to catch and eat. The party went on till 2 a.m. The cost of entertaining the French envoys came to over £5,000 – about £1,500,000 in terms of 1984 prices – which included £1,000 spent by Henry in gambling with his guests at dice and cards.[23]

Henry and his people were awaiting an even greater event than the peace treaty. Catherine was pregnant for the sixth time. Henry was first told at the beginning of July, when he and Catherine were living at Woodstock to avoid the danger of the sweating sickness. Henry had travelled to Greenwich with a very small escort to meet Wolsey to discuss state affairs with him; and Pace, who was acting as his private secretary, wrote to Wolsey a few days later that when Henry returned from Greenwich to Woodstock, the Queen 'welcomed him with a big belly'. Henry ordered that a *Te Deum* should be held at St Paul's in London to give thanks, and took every precaution for Catherine's safety. He insisted that she should travel as little as possible, and should only do so when this was necessary to avoid the risk of the sweat. The Pope was informed, and prayed that Catherine should have a son. Giustiniani thought that if she gave birth to a male heir, Henry would feel freer to go in person on military expeditions, including the crusade.

Catherine was delivered on the night of 10 November 1518. It was a still-born girl.[24]

8

THE DESTRUCTION OF BUCKINGHAM

DURING Catherine's pregnancy, Henry had been having an affair with one of her ladies-in-waiting, Elizabeth Blount, the daughter of Sir John Blount of Shropshire, and a relative of Lord Mountjoy. According to Hall, Henry fell 'in the chains of love' with her because she excelled all others 'in singing, dancing, and in all goodly pastimes'.[1] Henry conducted his love affairs with such discretion that we do not know when she first became his mistress; but in the summer of 1519 she gave birth to his son. The child was given the name of Lord Henry Fitzroy, and grew up to be a healthy lad. The position was frustrating for the King: despite all his efforts to father a male heir, the only one of his children who had been a boy and had survived was illegitimate.

Henry was very fond of Elizabeth Blount. When she married Gilbert Talboys, the son of Sir John Talboys, he gave her many gifts of land and money.

The Emperor Maximilian died in January 1519. The election of his successor as Holy Roman Emperor rested with the seven Electors of the Empire, who, when Maximilian died, would meet at Frankfort-on-Main to elect the new Emperor, though the successful candidate would be known officially as the King of the Romans until his coronation as Emperor by the Pope. On two occasions when Maximilian was trying to borrow money from Henry, he had offered to abdicate as Emperor and to arrange for Henry to succeed him;[2] but in fact he had been promising large bribes to the Electors to ensure that his grandson, Charles of Castile, was elected as his successor.

When Maximilian died, Charles was a strong favourite. Of the seven Electors, the twelve-year-old King Ladislaus of Bohemia and Hungary was engaged to marry Charles's sister Mary, and could be relied upon to support Charles. Maximilian had bought the votes of the Margrave of Brandenburg, of the Margrave's brother the Archbishop of Mainz, and of the Archbishop of Cologne, by offering the Margrave a royal Habsburg Princess as a bride, and enormous sums of money to the two Archbishops. But the other three Electors – the Duke of Saxony, the Count Palatine of the Rhine, and the Archbishop of Trier – were uncommitted; and François I decided to try to bribe them to choose him instead of Charles. One factor in François' favour was the attitude of the Pope, who did not wish Charles to become Emperor. Charles, as King of Aragon, ruled the kingdom of Naples, and the Pope did not wish to see Naples to the south of him and the Empire to the north of him in the hands of the same ruler.

Henry and his advisers thought that even if they could induce the Electors to choose Henry as Emperor, which was very unlikely, this would not be to his advantage, for it would involve him in responsibilities and difficulties in Germany without bringing any tangible benefit to him or to England. He therefore decided not to compete with Charles and François. But as the date for the election at the end of June drew nearer, the competitive sportsman and the gambler in Henry could not bear to be left out of the contest, and he decided to see if he could beat both Charles and François by a last-minute intervention. On 17 May, Pace hurriedly left London for Frankfort. His instructions from Henry and Wolsey were to discover whether there would be any support for Henry's candidature, and if so, to make arrangements with the German bankers to have the money available to buy the votes of the Electors. Pace was not to do anything to help either Charles or François win the election, but was to mislead Charles's supporters into thinking that Henry was helping Charles, and François' into believing that Henry was using his influence on François' side.

At Frankfort, Pace spoke to the Archbishop of Trier, who encouraged him to hope that he might vote for Henry in the Conclave of Electors; but Pace became increasingly aware of the difficulties which Henry faced. When he asked the banker, Hermann Rinck, to make the arrangements for bribing the Electors, Rinck discovered that the Electors would insist on being paid in cash, and would not rely on Rinck's bond unless he produced his authority from Henry issued under the Great Seal of England. Pace also realised the enormous sums that would be required to get Henry elected, for François had spent 200,000 crowns in bribes, and Charles had spent 1,500,000 gold florins (£266,666). There was also a very strong feeling in Germany that they should not have a Frenchman as Emperor, and bands of armed men were assembling, determined to prevent any candidate except Charles from being chosen. Pace thought that the Germans would be equally angry if Henry were elected, and that he himself might be killed.[3]

When Wolsey received Pace's reports, he became convinced that Henry should not put himself forward as a candidate, and he sent his chaplain, John Clerk, to Windsor, where Henry was staying, to persuade the King to agree. Clerk had a long talk with Henry on the evening of 12 June, but found it hard to persuade him not to stand. At last Henry said that he would not decide that night, but would sleep and dream on it and tell Clerk his decision in the morning; and at 1 a.m. Clerk wrote to Wolsey: 'As touching his enterprise of the Empire, I have reasoned as deeply as my poor wit would serve me, not varying from your instructions; but His Grace, as methinketh, considereth no jeopardies'.[4]

But by the morning Henry had realised that he had in any case left it too late. The Electors were on the point of going into the conclave at Frankfort, and Pace and all foreign ambassadors were ordered to leave the city and withdraw to Mainz until after the election. Henry and Wolsey sent orders to Pace not to spend money on Henry's candidature, but to pay small bribes to the Electors on condition that they told Charles that it was because of Henry's efforts on his behalf that they had decided to vote for him, and to suppress the fact that Pace had suggested to them that they might vote for Henry.

At the last moment, news reached Frankfort that the Pope had withdrawn his opposition to Charles's candidature; and there was also an outbreak of plague in Frankfort which made the Electors eager to leave the city as soon as possible. So on the second day of the conclave, on 28 June, they decided at 7 a.m. to elect Charles of Castile as King of the Romans. When the news reached England, Henry congratulated Charles and conveyed his condolences to François, without telling either of them that he himself had hoped to be a candidate.[5]

One aspect of the situation worried the wiser statesmen. Ten years before, Western Europe had been ruled by four elderly and cautious sovereigns; now Maximilian, Ferdinand, Louis XII and Henry VII had been replaced by three young men, all thirsting for military glory. Henry VIII, at twenty-eight, was the oldest of the three; François I was twenty-five, and Charles V nineteen.

But Henry was no longer seeking military glory. His immediate objective, and Wolsey's, was to remain neutral between François and Charles and to draw the greatest possible advantage from the conflict between them. It was generally realised that the contest in the election at Frankfort was only the beginning of a long rivalry between Charles and François, for their interests conflicted in at least three areas – in Lombardy, Burgundy and Navarre. Henry and Wolsey would wait for international developments, and in the meantime enjoy being wooed by both sides, though tradition, the anti-French feeling in England, and the wool trade with the Netherlands, all made Charles, not François, Henry's natural ally.

After Bonnivet's visit to London in October 1518, François suggested that he and Henry should have a personal meeting. But Henry and Wolsey wished to make him wait for this privilege, and to flirt with Charles at the same time. François proposed that he and Henry should meet in the summer of 1519; but Henry and Wolsey said that it would be impossible to arrange the meeting before 1520. By the autumn of 1519, the French and English representatives were engaged in lengthy discussions about the arrangements for the meeting, their chief anxiety being to ensure that their King was not put at a disadvantage and did not lose prestige as compared with the other King. Such questions as to whether the meeting should be held on English or French soil, and consequently which King would do the other the honour of visiting him; whose shield should hang higher at the tournaments which would be held; the number of lords and gentlemen who would accompany Henry and François; and which of them would take the place of honour on the right when they walked together, were endlessly discussed. Eventually Henry suggested to François that they should leave it to Wolsey to make the arrangements, not in his capacity as Henry's Lord Chancellor but in his neutral position as Papal Legate. François was so eager to steal a march on Charles by meeting Henry, that he agreed to appoint Wolsey as his proxy to make the arrangements for the meeting.

Wolsey decided that it should take place on the frontier between France and the Marches of Calais, between Guisnes and Ardres; that both Kings should be accompanied by an equal number of attendants; that after they had met on the frontier, Henry should visit François' wife, Queen Claude, at Ardres at the same time as François visited Catherine of Aragon at Guisnes; that after these first meetings, Henry and François would freely visit each other at Ardres and Guisnes; that when they were on English soil, Henry would grant François the place of honour on the right, and François would repay the compliment by placing Henry on the right when they were in France; and that Henry would be in Calais, ready for the meeting, no later than 31 May 1520. Extensive preparations were made in England for the meeting. The lords and gentlemen who were to accompany Henry were told how many mounted and unmounted attendants they should bring with them, according to their rank; and many workmen were employed building the pavilions on the frontier where the meeting was to be held.[6]

Henry and François also made their own informal agreement. They were eager to see each other's beards, and agreed not to shave off their beards until after the meeting. But Queen Catherine did not like Henry's beard, and he shaved it off to please her. François was disappointed when his ambassador reported that Henry had broken the bargain, but accepted Henry's explanation of why he had done so; and François assured him that their friendship rested in their hearts, not in their beards.[7]

When Charles heard that the meeting was to take place, he did not object, but was eager that he himself should also meet Henry, preferably before Henry met François. This gave Henry and Wolsey another opportunity to boost Henry's prestige. Charles, who had gone to Spain after he became King of Aragon and Castile, was planning to return by sea from Spain to the Netherlands in the spring of 1520. Henry invited him to visit England on the way. This meant that at their first meeting he would have the honour of being the host, while the Emperor would be the visitor. Charles agreed to this rather than miss the chance of meeting Henry. It was agreed that before Henry sailed to Calais at the end of May, he and Charles should meet at Canterbury, and that they should meet again after Henry's meeting with François. Charles invited Henry to visit him at Bruges. Henry said that this would not be possible, but that in July, after his meeting with François, he would meet Charles for the second time on the frontier of the Netherlands and the Marches of Calais between Calais and Gravelines, and would spend some days with the Emperor at Gravelines in Charles's territories and at Calais.

These plans were nearly wrecked by the contrary winds which kept Charles's fleet at Corunna throughout April and the first half of May, for Henry could not break his word to François to be in Calais by 31 May.[8] But the wind changed just in time. On 21 May, Henry and Catherine and their escort left Greenwich and arrived in Canterbury on the 25th. Next day Charles landed at Dover. Wolsey and other counsellors were rowed out to meet his ship and to escort him to the castle; and later in the day Henry, with a small escort, rode from Canterbury to Dover. Charles had already retired to bed, but hearing that Henry had arrived at the castle, he rose and came out of his chamber to meet Henry on the stairs as Henry walked up to his room. After they had warmly embraced, Henry went to the priory in the town, where he stayed the night, leaving the Emperor and his attendants in sole possession of the castle. From Henry's point of view, Charles's arrival could not have been better managed. Not only did the Emperor do him the honour of visiting him on his home ground, but it was Wolsey, not Henry himself, who welcomed Charles to English soil, while Henry's first meeting with Charles was – or appeared to be – a warm, spontaneous greeting on the castle stairs.

Next day, Whit Sunday, 27 May, Henry and Charles rode together from Dover to Canterbury, where Charles met his aunt Catherine for the first time in his life. She went with him and Henry in state to Mass in the cathedral. They entered the cathedral by walking over a carpet of purple velvet, and prayed at Becket's tomb. After two more days of banquets and Spanish dances, Charles left Canterbury and sailed from Sandwich to Flushing.[9] Henry and Catherine went to Dover, and on 31 May – the last day if Henry was to perform his promise to François – they sailed with a fleet of twenty-seven ships to Calais.

They were accompanied by Wolsey, Buckingham, Suffolk, Foxe, Fisher, and all the lords of England, only Norfolk remaining in London to take charge of affairs at home. Henry's escort amounted in all to 3,997 persons and 2,087 horses, Catherine having an additional escort of 1,175 persons and 778 horses. On 5 June they rode to Guisnes, and two days later, on Corpus

Christi Day, Henry and François met on the frontier in the Val Dorée between Guisnes and Ardres. The first enthusiastic meeting of the two Kings was far from spontaneous; every detail had been planned and agreed between Wolsey and François' ministers. Henry approached from Guisnes and François from Ardres, and both Kings stopped when they were in sight of each other. Then, leaving their escorts, they both galloped forward, and met exactly on the frontier, where they embraced two or three times on horseback, then dismounted, and embraced again.

Henry's masons and carpenters had built a temporary palace in the fields between Guisnes and Ardres. The base was of stone, the walls of brick up to a height of twelve feet from the ground, and the rest of wood. The building had four sides around a central courtyard, one side for Henry, one for Catherine, one for Wolsey, and one for Mary and Suffolk. Three of the rooms were larger than any room in Henry's palaces in England. The great chamber was 124 feet long, 42 feet wide, and 30 feet high. The dining room was 80 feet long, 34 feet wide, and 27 feet high, and the drawing room 60 feet long, 34 feet wide, and 27 feet high. The rooms were hung with cloth-of-gold, which was everywhere in evidence, and caused the meeting-place to be called, almost from the first day, the Field of Cloth-of-gold. There was also a chapel, filled with priceless gold and jewelled statues and crucifixes, and a cellar with three thousand butts of the most expensive wines. The building was surrounded by 2,800 tents for the members of Henry's and François' party; but François himself lodged at Ardres.

The meeting lasted for seventeen days. On most days the weather was hot and sunny, but twice the jousts had to be postponed because a very strong wind blew dust in the riders' eyes. Apart from the events in the buildings at the meeting-place, François on several occasions visited Henry and Catherine at Guisnes, while Henry visited Queen Claude and Margaret, Duchess of Alençon, at Ardres. The French and English gentlemen present made a display of Anglo-French friendship. Once a somewhat heated dispute broke out between Henry's and François' officers as to which King's shield should hang in the place of honour on the right above the lists where a tournament was taking place. When Henry heard about this, he ordered that his shield should be placed on the left, and François' in the place of honour. Henry with three English knights, and François with three French knights, met all challengers at the tournaments. François was slightly grazed on his cheek, but Henry was luckier; he was unhurt when a lance was splintered against his hand.

According to the Sieur de Fleuranges, who was one of the three French knights who jousted with François and Henry, on one occasion during the meeting when Henry visited François in his pavilion, he challenged François to a wrestling match. François, who was as skilled a wrestler as Henry, accepted the challenge; and though Henry scored a few points, François eventually threw him to the ground. Henry immediately challenged François to a second round; but there was no time for this, as supper was on the point of being served. Not surprisingly, no English writer referred to his King's defeat in the wrestling match; but there is nothing improbable in Fleuranges' story.

The meeting ended on Midsummer's Eve, 23 June, with a Mass which Wolsey celebrated in great state in the chapel built on the Field of Cloth-of-gold. Next day, Henry and François said goodbye, and Henry returned to Calais. It was decided to build a permanent chapel on the site of the meeting, to be called 'The Chapel of our Lady of Peace'.[10]

A fortnight later, Henry met Charles V on 10 July on the frontier between Calais and Gravelines, and was his guest at Gravelines before entertaining Charles at Calais. It was a modest affair compared with the meeting with François; the meetings in Gravelines and Calais lasted only four days, and Henry and Charles were each accompanied by only two hundred persons, less than one-twentieth of the numbers in attendance at the Field of Cloth-of-gold. But for Charles it at least cancelled out the diplomatic success which François had scored by his meeting with Henry; and for Henry, it left him with his options still open. He and François signed a new treaty on the Field of Cloth-of-gold, renewing the contract for the marriage between Henry's daughter Mary and the Dauphin; and Wolsey firmly scotched the suggestion by François that Albany should be allowed to return to Scotland. At Gravelines and Calais, Henry signed a new treaty with Charles, by which he agreed not to make any new treaty with François or any other power without Charles's consent; and Charles likewise agreed not to make any such treaty without Henry's consent.[11]

Henry and Wolsey were well aware that the universal peace was precarious, and that war between Charles and François would probably break out in the summer of 1521. Under the treaty of 1518 they would then be bound to help the victim of aggression, and they did not know who this would be. Meanwhile they were careful not to allow François to gain any advantage at England's expense. When Henry returned from his meetings with François and Charles, he went hunting in Berkshire, staying at Windsor Castle and as a guest of the abbot at Reading Abbey. Pace told Wolsey that on every day except holy days Henry rose at four or five o'clock in the morning and hunted till nine or ten at night; but this was perhaps an exaggeration on Pace's part, for the sun set soon after 7 p.m. Pace, who worked much harder than Henry but had less physical energy, thought that Henry was converting the sport of hunting into a martyrdom. But when Henry returned from hunting, he inquired eagerly about the report that the French were fortifying Ardres, which François had promised him, at the Field of Cloth-of-gold, that they would not do. Wolsey energetically raised it with the French, and François, who was determined to keep on good terms with Henry, promised that the work should be stopped.[12]

Henry's popularity at home and his prestige abroad were as high as ever. No one praised him more lavishly than the intellectuals, who exceeded any courtier in sycophancy. Thomas More, who had entered into a contest in chauvinism with the French author Germain de Brie, wrote in a pamphlet against de Brie that Henry had purified his realm from avarice, rapine and falsehoods. Erasmus, who had not the excuse, like More, of being one of Henry's subjects and ministers, eulogised Henry in nearly every letter that he wrote to an Englishman. Writing to Henry himself, he praised him for being the author of the universal peace, for repressing robbers, for advancing learning among his clergy, and – a month before the birth of his bastard son – for his fidelity to his marriage vows.[13]

In England, very occasionally a note of criticism was now heard. A man at Shaftesbury was denounced by his neighbours for saying, at Candlemas 1521, to a soldier discharged from Henry's army: 'Ah, Sir, have ye been with Mr Harry King? A noble act ye did there. Ye spent away my moneys, like a set of vagabonds and knaves'. Three months later, the parson of Rampsham in Dorset was accused of saying that Henry was no more worthy to be King than his father was, because Henry VII was 'a horsegroom and a keeper of horses'.[14]

The uncertainty about peace or war in Europe affected Henry and Wolsey's policy in Ireland and Scotland. Both Ireland and the Border with Scotland were areas where, unlike in the other parts of his realm, Henry was unable to enforce law and order. The Irish chiefs acknowledged Henry as Lord of Ireland, but in practice defied the authority of the King's Deputy in Dublin, and often carried on private wars against other chiefs, against the English settlers in the Pale, and sometimes against the King's government.

In 1520 Henry appointed the Earl of Surrey as Deputy of Ireland; but Surrey found that he could not adopt against the Irish chiefs the firm and brutal methods that he had used against the London apprentices after Evil May Day. He was confronted with a rebellion by O'Neill, the most powerful chief in Ulster, and informed Henry that troops would have to be sent from England if the revolt was to be suppressed.[15]

There was always trouble on the Scottish Border. Good order was maintained in the county palatine of Durham, which was under the government of the Bishop of Durham; in the flourishing port of Newcastle; and in the district near the coast, along the road from Newcastle to the garrison town of Berwick. But further west, in Tynedale and Redesdale, robberies, and killings in blood-feuds between rival families, were daily occurrences. The ordinary legal process of justices of the peace and assizes did not apply there; but from time to time the Lord Warden of the Marches would send a raiding party into Tynedale or Redesdale in the hope of seizing some notorious criminal and bringing him to Newcastle to be tried at the assizes and executed there; but the offender usually succeeded in escaping into Scotland.

The Marches were divided into the Eastern, Middle and Western Marches. The Eastern Marches, with their headquarters at Berwick, faced the Scots of the Merse, Jedburgh and Kelso. The Middle Marches, at Carlisle, faced the Scots of Liddisdale, which was always the most turbulent of the Border regions; and the Western Marches, also centred at Carlisle, faced the Scots across the Solway in Dumfriesshire and Annandale. The English Borderers not only robbed and killed each other, but often crossed the Border and raided Scotland; and the Scottish Borderers raided England as well as carrying on their feuds with their fellow-Scots. In peace time, the Wardens of the Marches tried half-heartedly to stop these border violations, and three or four times a year met their Scottish counterparts on a 'truce day', which was held alternately on the English and Scottish side of the Border. At these meetings, the English Warden complained to the Scottish Warden of the incursions by the Scots, and promised to try to prevent the raids into Scotland by the English Border robbers; and the Scottish Warden made reciprocal complaints and promises.

The disordered state of Scotland during the minority of James V had repercussions in Redesdale and Tynedale, which in the 1520s were more lawless than they had been for many centuries. Here, as in Ireland, Henry and Wolsey reluctantly accepted the situation. They had the consolation of knowing that in wartime the outlaws of Tynedale and Redesdale would do good service in the army against the Scots.

Apart from the constant troubles on the Borders, Henry received repeated complaints from his sister Margaret that since her return to Scotland she was being kept short of money by the Scottish lords, who were withholding her dowry from her. She asked Henry to intervene with the Scots on her behalf, and to send her money, for otherwise she might have to seek help from his enemies. She had taken a violent dislike to her husband, the Earl of Angus. This was annoying for Henry, because Angus and the Douglases were his most important supporters in Scotland.

In view of the possibility that war might break out in Europe and that England might become involved, Henry and Wolsey did not wish to send troops to deal with the trouble in Ireland and on the borders of Scotland. Henry explained to Surrey that he could not afford the cost of putting three armies in the field at the same time, and that Surrey would therefore have to deal with O'Neill and the Irish by policy and not by force. Though he did not send an army to Ireland at this time, he ordered the gentlemen of Cheshire, Lancashire and Wales to muster their tenants for a campaign in Ireland, so as to make O'Neill and the Irish believe that he was about to send an army against them; but he explained to Surrey that this would in fact be bluff, and that Surrey would have to play for time and be conciliatory towards O'Neill.

Henry conferred a knighthood on O'Neill, and sent him a gold collar as a gift.[16] No statesman has been more aware than Henry VIII that politics is the art of the possible.

As Henry and Wolsey were just as reluctant to use force in Scotland, they made use of François, knowing that François wished to keep on good terms with Henry so that Henry would not ally himself with Charles. In January 1521, François informed the Scottish lords that Wolsey had made it plain that he would never allow Albany to return to Scotland, and François urged the Scots to reconcile themselves to this fact. In April, Henry and Wolsey decided that it would be to their advantage to extend the truce with Scotland; but they thought that it would be bad for Henry's prestige if the initiative came from them. They therefore instructed Sir William Fitzwilliam, Henry's ambassador in France, to try to arrange that the request to extend the truce should come from the Scots; Henry would then agree to it in order to please François. They told Fitzwilliam that he was not to seem too eager for peace with Scotland; on the contrary, the more they seemed to be bent on war, the more François would urge the Scots to ask for a truce, as he would be anxious to avoid being drawn into a conflict with Henry. The plan worked just as Henry and Wolsey had hoped. The Scots asked Lord Dacre, the Warden of the Marches, for an extension of the truce, and Henry agreed.[17]

Neither the nobles nor the people of England were happy about the policy of friendship with France, which they attributed to Wolsey. No one was more strongly opposed to it than the High Constable of England, the Duke of Buckingham. He had never been one of Henry's closest friends, but he was often at court, where he had lost money to the Duke of Suffolk in archery competitions and at dice, and had once lost £14 to Henry at a game of tennis. He hated Wolsey as an upstart butcher's son, as well as disapproving of his pro-French policy. Polydore Vergil, who hated Wolsey, wrote that on one occasion, when Wolsey had dared to wash his hands in the same bowl of water in which Henry had just washed his, Buckingham was so angry that he poured the bowl of water over Wolsey's shoes. But this is not very likely, for Buckingham's letters to Wolsey were written in most respectful language.[18]

Buckingham had quarrelled with his surveyor, Knivet. According to Polydore Vergil, this was because Knivet had oppressed Buckingham's tenants, and Buckingham had dismissed him from his post at the tenants' request. Others said that Knivet was angry because Buckingham had cheated him out of his inheritance. Someone else hated Buckingham even more than Knivet did; for this person – it was probably Buckingham's chaplain, but may have been his confessor – wrote an anonymous letter to Wolsey accusing Buckingham of high treason.

The surveyor, the chaplain and the confessor were interrogated. They said that Buckingham had objected to going to the Field of Cloth-of-gold and having to pretend that he liked the French whom he met there; that he had often railed against Wolsey; that he had said that he was sorry that he missed the opportunity some years ago, when Henry VII was ill, of chopping off the heads of Wolsey and Sir Thomas Lovell; that he had listened to astrologers who had foretold that he would one day be King; that he believed that if Henry died, Parliament would offer him the crown; that he had said that if he were ever sent to the Tower, his friends would raise ten thousand men within a few days to set him free; and that he had thrown out hints that he might do to Henry VIII what his father had tried to do to Richard III.

Were these allegations true? They might be; and it was wiser to take no chances where so powerful a nobleman, and a descendant of Edward III, was concerned. Henry and Wolsey were always prepared to believe the worst, and had taken the precaution of keeping not only Henry's tennis opponent Buckingham, but his boon companion and brother-in-law Suffolk, under close observation, and laying traps for them. A year or so earlier, Henry had written about it to 'mine own good Cardinal' in his own hand. He explained that as he found it tedious and painful to write letters, he was sending a messenger to tell Wolsey verbally about certain business. 'Nevertheless to this that followeth I thought not best to make him privy, nor none other but you and I, which is that I would you should make good watch on the Duke of Suffolk, on the Duke of Buckingham, on my lord of Northumberland, on my lord of Derby, on my lord of Wiltshire, and on others which you think suspect, to see what they do with these news. No more to you at this time, but *sapienti pauca*. Written with the hand of your loving master, Henry R.'[19]

It was some years since a great nobleman had been put to death, and the execution of the first Duke in England could have as wholesome an effect on the aristocracy as the execution of the London apprentices had had on the rioters in Southampton. Buckingham owned very large estates. He had the manor of Thornbury in Gloucestershire, which was his principal residence when he was not at court; his impressive house at Penshurst in Kent, where he had recently entertained the King; his town houses in London and Calais; and manors and lands in twenty-four counties valued at £6,000. All this would be forfeited to Henry if Buckingham were convicted of high treason, and would be available not only to fill Henry's coffers but to reward all the courtiers and officials who served the King without wages in the hopes of receiving one day some of the forfeited lands of a traitor in addition to the more regular income that they obtained from taking bribes. And did Henry still bear a personal grudge against Buckingham because, ten years before, the Duke had sent his sister to a nunnery to prevent Henry from seducing her?

In April 1521 Buckingham, who was at Thornbury, received an invitation to come to court. He set out with his attendants, visiting the shrine of Our Lady of Eyton near Reading on the way. As he rode on towards London, he noticed that some soldiers were following him at a discreet distance; but he was not seriously worried about this. He spent the night at an inn at Windsor; and next morning, as he sat down to breakfast, he saw an officer standing outside the door of the room. He asked the officer why he was standing there, and the officer said he was carrying out the King's orders. At this, Buckingham turned very pale.

He had recovered his spirits by the time he reached Westminster, though he now expected the worst. At Tothill steps he took a barge to go to Greenwich, but stopped at York Place and asked to speak to Wolsey. When he was told that Wolsey was unwell and could not see him, he asked for wine, saying that he would have one more cup of wine at the Cardinal's expense. After drinking the wine, he re-entered his barge and went down-river. As he passed London Bridge, his barge was stopped and boarded by the captain of the King's guard and some soldiers, who were waiting for him there. The captain arrested him on a charge of high treason and took him to the Tower.

His son-in-law, Lord Abergavenny, and Henry Pole, Lord Montagu, whose sister had married Buckingham's son, were also arrested and charged with being accessory to his treason. Montagu was Abergavenny's son-in-law. His mother, Margaret Pole, Countess of Salisbury, was the cousin of Henry VIII's mother, Elizabeth of York, and sister of the Earl of Warwick whom Henry VII had executed in 1499.

Buckingham and his supporters, and nearly all the people, were convinced that it was Wolsey who had been responsible for his arrest: the butcher's son had laid low the greatest nobleman in the realm. But the examination of Buckingham was conducted by Henry himself. Wolsey was not present when Buckingham was brought before the King and confronted with his chaplain, his confessor and his surveyor and the other witnesses who testified to the rash words that he had uttered in a number of private conversations over the years, and which could be interpreted as proof that he was planning to usurp the throne from Henry's young daughter if Henry died, and that he was therefore guilty of high treason.

He could only be convicted of high treason after a trial before his peers in the House of Lords. He was related to many of them. Apart from his connections with Abergavenny and the Poles, one of his daughters had married the Earl of Surrey and another the Earl of Westmorland. He was not tried by the full House of Lords, but by the Court of the Lord High Steward. This was an established practice by which the King selected only a number of the peers to sit as judges at the trial; it was not until after the revolution of 1688 that treason trials before the Court of the Lord High Steward were prohibited. Norfolk presided, sitting with Suffolk, Dorset, Shrewsbury, and twelve other peers, and Docwra, the Prior of St John of Jerusalem. Surrey and Westmorland did not sit on the court.

None of the nobles on the court wished to be thought of as a sympathiser of a man who was charged with high treason. Moral pressure, obedience to the King, and personal admiration for Henry played a bigger part than fear. Henry had no doubt of the result of the trial. His secretary, Pace, made a note on the back of a letter: 'The King is convinced that Buckingham will be found guilty and condemned by the lords'.[20]

Buckingham pleaded not guilty, but the court unanimously found him guilty. The sentence of hanging, drawing and quartering was commuted to beheading by Henry. Five hundred soldiers surrounded the scaffold when Buckingham died with great bravery on Tower Hill on 17 May. Three strokes of the axe were needed to cut off his head.[21]

In France and the Netherlands, rumours were circulating that a revolution had broken out in England; but Henry's ambassadors assured François and Charles that there was no truth in these stories, that Buckingham was the only nobleman who had been disloyal, that Lord Abergavenny and Lord Montagu had been foolish rather than wicked, and that the nobility and people of England were all loyal to Henry. Abergavenny and Montagu were pardoned, after they had granted some of their lands to Henry and to Wolsey.[22]

In the same week in which Buckingham was executed, England officially took note of the new phenomenon which was changing the face of Christendom. Martin Luther first challenged the authority of the Pope by exposing one of the worst scandals in which the Papacy and the Church had ever been involved. Albert of Brandenburg, the twenty-five-year old Archbishop of Magdeburg and Bishop of Halberstadt, wished to become Archbishop of Mainz, one of the Electors of the Holy Roman Empire, so that he could obtain enormous bribes from Maximilian to vote for Charles of Castile. He required a dispensation to hold the see of Mainz as well as his other two bishoprics, and another dispensation to be for the third time a bishop under the canonical age of thirty. The Pope made him pay 10,000 ducats for a dispensation which would enable him to make such great profits. To help him raise the money to pay for the dispensation, the Pope announced that a pardon for past and future sins would be granted to anyone in Germany who contributed money to the repair of St Peter's cathedral in Rome; but in fact the money was to be used, not to repair St Peter's, but to enable Albert to pay for his dispensations, after part of the proceeds had been paid to the banking firm of the Fuggers for their help in providing facilities for transmitting the money to Rome.

On 31 October 1517 Luther nailed his Ninety-five Theses to the church door at Wittenberg, and put forward the proposition that Papal indulgences could only remit the need for penance and not the guilt of the sin itself, which only God could pardon. Neither the force of Luther's arguments nor the scandalous circumstances which had given rise to them were relevant in the minds of the Pope and the Church hierarchy; for Luther had questioned the authority of the Pope, and that was sufficient to damn him. During the next three years, Luther was driven by the denunciations of the authorities to adopt a more extreme position, and directly to attack the power of the Pope. His three great tracts, *The Freedom of a Christian Man*, the *Appeal to the Nobility of the German Nation*, and *The Babylonian Captivity of the Church of God*, which were published in the summer of 1520, aroused great enthusiasm in Germany, where a popular mass movement broke out against the Pope and the exploitation of Germany by Rome, which had the support of several German Princes.

All the sovereigns of Europe supported the Pope against Luther. The Kings had often quarrelled with the Popes about money and foreign policy; but a popular movement which attacked Papal authority was a seditious threat to the social order of Christendom which could soon lead to revolutionary attacks on the authority of Kings and on the privileges and property of the nobility and the wealthy classes. This aspect of Lutheranism, on which Thomas More and other Catholic propagandists were to place so much emphasis, especially after the outbreak of the Peasant War in Germany in 1525, caused fear from the beginning in the ecclesiastical and secular Establishment, and made Henry VIII, like his brother Kings, a determined enemy of Lutheranism.

Erasmus, who sympathised with Luther's criticism of the Church, but feared revolutionary violence and the anti-intellectual instincts of the masses who followed Luther, tried to preserve a neutral position. He feared that the Church, by persecuting Luther, would drive him to further extremism; he wished to prevent the Pope from sending Luther to Hell and taking half Germany with him. In July 1520 Erasmus went to Gravelines with Charles V for Charles's meeting with Henry, and travelled with the Emperor and King to Calais when the meeting continued there. He spoke to Henry in Calais, and urged him to restrain the anti-Lutheran indignation of the Pope and the authorities; but he had no success. He found Henry as friendly and charming as usual, but determined to act against Luther. According to Luther's supporter, Myconius, whose information may be unreliable, Henry slapped Erasmus on the back and asked him why he did not publicly defend Luther; and when Erasmus said that he felt unable to venture into theological disputation on the matter, Henry said: 'You are a good fellow, Erasmus', and sent him away with a gift of forty ducats.[23]

A fortnight before Erasmus's talk with Henry at Calais, the Pope had issued a bull excommunicating Luther; and in the autumn he sent his Nuncio to promulgate the bull in Germany and the Netherlands. In December, Luther publicly burned the bull at Wittenberg before a cheering crowd. The Pope appealed to all the Kings of Christendom to make a public declaration against Luther by burning his books, prohibiting everyone from reading them, and persecuting Lutherans as heretics. Henry and Wolsey were not prepared to do so until they had obtained what they wanted from the Pope – the renewal of Wolsey's appointment as Papal Legate in England on a permanent basis. When the Pope reproached them for lack of zeal against Lutheranism, Wolsey replied with the ridiculous argument that he had no legal power to act against Luther until he was appointed Legate.[24]

After some months of bickering, the Pope renewed Wolsey's legatine powers for another two years; and on 12 May 1521 the anti-Lutheran demonstration that the Pope desired was staged at Paul's Cross in the presence of Wolsey and a crowd which the Venetian ambassador's secretary estimated at thirty thousand. Fisher preached for two hours on the wickedness of Luther and his heresies; during his sermon, Luther's books were thrown into a fire. It was then proclaimed that anyone who read them would be guilty of heresy.[25]

Henry had decided that he himself would write a book against Luther, and by May 1521 he had nearly finished it. His *Assertion of the Seven Sacraments* was a short book of some thirty thousand words, written in Latin. It was published in London in July. Very few of Henry's contemporaries believed that he had really written the book himself. Some thought that Wolsey had written it; others believed that More or Fisher was the author. Luther was convinced that Edward Lee had written it. But according to More, though he and other theologians helped Henry with the research and contributed suggestions, Henry wrote the book himself.

Many modern scholars, like Henry's contemporaries, have refused to believe this; but though Henry was bored by state papers and disliked writing, and even reading, letters, he was fascinated by theological controversy. No one who reads his drafts and corrections of the articles of religion and doctrinal treatises which were issued in the last years of his reign should be surprised that he was already capable, fifteen years earlier, of writing *The Assertion of the Seven Sacraments*. When Pace arrived at Greenwich in April 1521, he found him avidly reading a copy of Luther's latest book which Wolsey had sent him. He took many hours off from hunting to sit in his closet studying the authorities which More, Fisher and Lee had assembled for him, and writing his book.[26]

The style of the book also suggests that Henry was the author. It reads like the work, not of a professional theologian, but of an intelligent amateur. The quotations from Scripture and the patristic texts are kept to a minimum, and the arguments are put briefly, clearly, logically and forcibly. Although Henry denounces Luther with some vigour as 'this impious fellow', 'this new doctor', 'this little saint', 'the little monk', his language falls far short of the polemical insults which mark most of the anti-Lutheran tracts of the period.

After defending the practice of granting indulgences – it was wrong of Luther 'to excite men to confide in the riches of their own penitence and despise the treasures of Holy Church and the bounty of God' – Henry turned to the question of Papal supremacy. He treated it as being self-evidently true. 'I will not wrong the Bishop of Rome so much as troublesomely or carefully to dispute his right, as if it were a matter doubtful', for Luther 'cannot deny but that all the faithful honour and acknowledge the sacred Roman See for their mother, and supreme'. As regards the sacrament of the altar, Henry rejected Luther's insistence that the wine as well as the bread should be given to the congregation. He had no objection to the administration of the sacrament in both kinds, but put forward the orthodox view that, as this was an inessential matter, the present system of giving only the bread to the laity should continue, and no one should denounce it until the Church ordered otherwise. If Luther attached so much importance to carrying out the words of Scripture, why did he not insist that the Eucharist should only be administered at supper time?

How could Luther deny that marriage was a sacrament, merely because it was not stated to be so in the Bible? 'You admit no sacrament unless you read its institution in a book!' Marriage, wrote Henry, was the first of all sacraments to be instituted, because the first man, Adam, was married; and it was at a wedding that Christ performed his first miracle. 'If all generation out of wedlock is damnable, the grace of marriage must needs be great, by which that act (which of its own nature defiles to punishment) is not only purged, to take away the blemish; but is so much sanctified that, as the Apostle testifies, it becomes meritorious'. But why, asked Henry, 'search we so many proofs in so clear a thing? especially when that only text is sufficient for all, where Christ says "Whom God has joined together, let no man put asunder". O the admirable word! which none could have spoken, but the Word that was made flesh!'

Above all, Henry denounced Luther for encouraging sedition. He quoted with approval the passage from St Augustine: 'The power of the King, the right of the owner, the instruments of the executioner, the arms of the soldier, the discipline of the governor, and the severity of the good father were not instituted in vain', and added: 'But I forbear to speak of Kings, lest I should seem to plead my own cause'. He went out of his way, in two places in his book, to refer to the superiority of men over women, which was so clearly laid down by Christian doctrine that even when a Christian woman had married an infidel husband, she was commanded by the Church to obey him.[27]

In October, a beautifully bound copy of the book was presented to the Pope in Consistory by John Clerk, Henry's ambassador in Rome. The grateful Pope thanked Henry, his 'most dear son in Christ', who had formerly defended the Church with his sword and was now defending her with his pen; and in order to confirm Henry in his most holy purposes and to augment his devotion, he granted to him and his successors the title of

'The Field of Cloth-of-gold'. Detail from a painting by an unknown artist, c.1520

Charles V, by an unknown artist, c.1527

'Defender of the Faith'. He assured Henry that if anyone should ever try to deprive him of this new title, such a person would incur the indignation of Almighty God and of the holy Apostles, Peter and Paul.[28]

9

THE GREAT ENTERPRISE

NEITHER the internal threat from Lutheranism, nor the external threat from the Turk, could cause the Princes of Christendom to remain at peace for long. As Henry and Wolsey, and many other observers, had feared, hostilities broke out between Charles V and François I in the spring of 1521. Robert de La Marck, the ruler of the territory of Bouillon and Sedan on the southern borders of the Netherlands, made a raid across the frontier and attacked Charles's territories. Charles sent his general, the Count of Nassau, to drive him out, and Nassau invaded La Marck's territories. François then intervened in support of La Marck.

Charles alleged that François had committed aggression against him, and asked Henry to come to his aid under the terms of the Treaty of London of 1518. Henry offered to mediate between Charles and François. At this juncture, François, in retaliation for Nassau's invasion of Sedan, invaded Charles's kingdom of Navarre, which Ferdinand of Aragon had captured from France in 1512. The French quickly overran Navarre until they reached Pamplona, which held out for Charles in a long siege.

There could be no doubt that François was the aggressor, for even if La Marck's initial inroad into the Netherlands and the subsequent escalation in Sedan could be considered as a comparatively minor incident, the French invasion of Navarre was a deliberate act of war against Charles. The first reaction of Henry and Wolsey was to do all in their power to preserve peace, for they had no wish to be drawn into war on either side, and feared that a situation was developing in which they would be forced to go to Charles's aid under the Treaty of London. They repeatedly urged François to suspend his military operations in Navarre, and to submit his dispute to their mediation.

But Henry and Wolsey soon had another idea. It arose from the fact that it was now clear that Catherine of Aragon was very unlikely to have another child, and that Henry would therefore never have a legitimate male heir. If his one surviving legitimate child, Princess Mary, became Queen after his death, the only way to prevent revolution and civil war among her nobility would be for her to marry a foreign Prince. She was engaged to marry the Dauphin, but a French King would be very unpopular with the English people; so Henry and Wolsey considered the alternative of marrying Mary to Charles V, who was only sixteen years older than she, and would still be young enough to father her children when she reached marriageable age.

This proposal involved a fundamental change in English foreign policy, the abandonment of neutrality and manoeuvre between Charles and François, and a permanent alliance with the traditional trading partner, Burgundy. Henry would repudiate Mary's marriage contract with the Dauphin, after obtaining the necessary dispensation from the Pope; would agree to marry her to Charles when she reached the age of fourteen; and would declare war on François. Henry and Charles would launch a simultaneous invasion of France from Calais, the Netherlands, Italy and Spain, which François would be unable to resist. When the French had been defeated, Charles would annex the provinces of Burgundy which France had seized in 1482, some border regions along the eastern frontier, and Guienne on the Spanish border; and Henry would become King of the rest of France in François' place. Once again, as in the days of Henry VI, the King of England would reign in his realm of France. After Henry's death, Charles and Mary would reign together as King and Queen of England, France, Spain and the Empire, which in due course would pass to their heirs after them. It was indeed a 'Great Enterprise', which was the code name by which the project was called.

Charles was not enthusiastic about the proposal. He felt that as François had committed aggression, Henry was automatically bound, under the Treaty of London, to come to his help without asking him to agree to any new treaty. He therefore proposed that he and Henry should first make a military alliance against François, and then proceed in due course to negotiate a closer unity. But Wolsey made it plain that it was to be all or nothing: unless Charles agreed to the marriage with Mary and the complete destruction of France as an independent kingdom, Henry would pursue a policy of neutrality and would act as an impartial mediator.[1]

Henry and Wolsey now resorted to one of the most calculated acts of deception in English diplomatic history. They proposed that Charles and François should send representatives to attend a conference at Calais, at which Wolsey would preside, in an endeavour to find a peaceful solution to the conflict between Charles and François; but while Wolsey would be ostensibly acting as the impartial mediator at Calais, he would also be engaging in secret negotiations with Charles to form a military alliance for the utter destruction of France. As the alliance with Charles could not be negotiated only through ambassadors, it was agreed that Wolsey should meet Charles at Bruges; but French suspicions might be aroused if Wolsey left the conference at Calais to visit Charles. An elaborate plot was therefore concocted, with Henry's express approval, between Wolsey and Charles's Chancellor, Gattinara, who was attending the Calais conference, with the object of pulling the wool over the eyes of François' Chancellor, Cardinal Du Prat, the leader of the French delegation at Calais. Gattinara would announce, at the conference, that Charles had ordered him to break off the negotiations and walk out of the conference. Wolsey would urge him, in the interests of peace, to continue the negotiations; but Gattinara would say that he had no authority to do so. Wolsey would then propose that he should go to Bruges with Gattinara in order to try to persuade Charles to allow Gattinara to return to the conference table.

The conference opened at Calais at the beginning of August 1521, while fighting was going on around Calais on the frontier between France and the Netherlands a few miles from the town. Everything went according to Wolsey's plan. After Gattinara had threatened to walk out of the conference, he and Wolsey left for Bruges, while Du Prat and the French delegates remained at Calais.[2] On 25 August, Wolsey and Charles made the secret treaty for the military alliance against France, by which it was agreed that Henry and Charles would invade France with 40,000 men each, Henry from Calais and Charles from the south, no later than 15 May 1523.

Meanwhile, as the invasion could not be mounted for twenty-one months, the treaty would be kept strictly secret while Wolsey continued to work for a truce at Calais on terms which would be acceptable to Charles. This would not only lull French suspicions while Henry and Charles secretly made their military preparations, but would mean that François would continue to pay the instalments of Henry's pensions which were due from France under the treaties of 1492, 1514 and 1518, and which were payable on 1 May and 1 November in each year. But if no truce was agreed at Calais before the beginning of November 1521, Henry would then declare war on François.[3]

Wolsey wrote nearly every day from Calais and Bruges to Henry, who was on his usual August progress. He kept Henry informed of every trick by which he deceived Du Prat and the French representatives. Pace, who was with Henry and acting as his secretary, wrote to Wolsey that Henry was delighted with Wolsey's 'singular diligence and high wisdom', and thought that if he himself had been at Bruges, he could not have managed things more to his liking. At the end of August, contrary winds prevented ships from crossing the Channel to England, and Henry at Guildford heard nothing from Wolsey for four or five days. He was worried, for he was impatiently waiting for news of the progress of the negotiations in Bruges; but he ordered Pace to tell Wolsey that he did not blame him for his failure to write, as he knew that it was solely due to the wind, and not to Wolsey's negligence.[4]

When Henry heard that the secret treaty with Charles had been signed, he was very pleased. On 4 September Pace wrote to Wolsey: 'I assure Your Grace of one thing, that the King's contentation with all your acts cannot be so well painted with a pen as it is imprinted in his heart'.[5]

On his return to Calais, Wolsey resumed his attempts to deceive Du Prat and the French. For three months, the conference continued in session, with Wolsey acting the part of the impartial mediator who was trying to persuade both the French and the Emperor's delegates to make concessions, while at the same time he passed on to Gattinara useful items of military intelligence which he had discovered about the French defences in the neighbourhood of Calais, and about favourable opportunities for a surprise attack on the French garrison town of Ardres. He was, however, sincere in his attempts to persuade both sides to agree to a truce, for he and Henry did not wish to go to war with France until the spring of 1523. Charles was not eager for a truce, for his armies captured Bouillon, Peronne and Tournai, and he was winning the war in Flanders. François was ready to make a truce, but only on the basis of the *status quo*, with each side retaining what they held. Charles would not agree unless the French evacuated the territory which they had conquered in Navarre, or at least the town of Fuentarrabia; and under the terms of the Treaty of Bruges, Henry would have to declare war on France if a truce was not made by November.[6]

Wolsey, who had been working under heavy strain for many months, fell ill during the Calais conference. Henry showed the greatest solicitude for his health, getting Pace to write regularly for news of Wolsey's illness and recovery.[7]

Wolsey had been surprisingly successful in fooling the French about the reasons for his mission to Bruges; but the extreme secrecy with which the negotiations there had been conducted aroused suspicions, and rumours of war between France and England began to circulate. Many of the English scholars at Paris University decided to return to England;[8] and the English merchants asked Henry whether it would be safe for them to sail to Bordeaux to buy the wines of Gascony, as they usually did twice a year, in the autumn and at Candlemas.

This led to a disagreement between Henry and Wolsey. On 1 September, Pace wrote to Wolsey that Henry was anxious about the risk to the merchants' ships if they sailed to Bordeaux, for the rumours of war might lead François to seize or detain them; on the other hand, if the ships did not make their usual autumn journey to Bordeaux, would not François deduce that war with England was inevitable, and act accordingly? Wolsey replied from Calais on 4 September. He advised Henry to allow the ships to sail to Bordeaux. He did not think that François would seize the ships, because he would not wish to quarrel with Henry while he was engaged in war with Charles; and as Du Prat had told Wolsey at Calais that François trusted Henry before all other Princes, Wolsey was sure that the French had no suspicions about the secret treaty between Henry and Charles. Wolsey suggested that, for once, Henry should allow the French merchants, this year, to export goods from England in French ships. This would draw many French ships to English ports, and Henry could then seize them as a reprisal if the English ships were seized at Bordeaux.

Henry was not convinced by Wolsey's arguments. Pace wrote from Woking on 9 September that Henry was very doubtful as to whether the English ships should go to Bordeaux. Wolsey persisted; he wrote on 15 September, urging Henry to allow the ships to go, for otherwise François would realise that Henry was about to declare war on him, would stop the pensions due to Henry, and would prepare for military operations. Henry then reluctantly accepted Wolsey's advice. The matter was finally closed when Pace wrote on 4 October: 'It was lately the King's pleasure to dispute with Your Grace, and now it is his pleasure to hold his peace'.[9]

It was Wolsey, with his usual optimism and daring , who was in favour of taking the risky course in order to gain the military advantage of surprise. It was Henry, a great gambler at the dicing table but always cautious in politics, who was unwilling to risk losing the ships; and it was Henry who was more reluctant to risk offending his merchants by wrongly advising them to pursue a course which could cause their financial ruin.

Henry and Wolsey also disagreed in their assessment of the military situation in Flanders and of the diplomatic negotiations at Calais. Again it was Wolsey who was optimistic and favoured a daring policy, and Henry who was more pessimistic and cautious. In October, Charles sent part of his army that was invading north-east France to besiege the French garrison at Tournai. Wolsey congratulated Charles on his decision; Henry thought that Charles had been very rash to divide his army.[10] When Tournai fell in November, both Henry and Wolsey were delighted, though François refused to pay Henry that part of his pension which was due for the sale of Tournai; he said that he would not continue paying Henry for Tournai now that he no longer had it.

Wolsey was quite confident that he could persuade both François and Charles to agree to a truce. He thought that he would be able to persuade Charles by showing him that it would be to his and Henry's advantage to postpone hostilities till the spring of 1523, when they would be able to attack France together; and he thought that he could persuade François by telling him that unless he agreed to a truce, the other members of Henry's Council would insist that England joined in the war on Charles's side under the provisions of the Treaty of London. Henry did not believe that Wolsey would be able to arrange a truce, for he thought that Charles and François were too far apart to reach any agreement. He was also worried about his own position if, as Wolsey was proposing, he should be appointed as the conservator of the truce. Would this not mean, he asked Wolsey, that he would have to take an oath to do all in his power to preserve the truce? And would he not violate this oath when he declared war on François, or alternatively, if he failed to declare war, would he not violate the oath which he had sworn to observe the Treaty of Bruges with Charles? Wolsey assured Henry that he had considered this point, and that Henry need not worry: it was only the parties to a truce, not the conservator of it, who had to take an oath to preserve it.[11]

As it turned out, this time it was Henry who was right. As Charles refused to agree to a truce unless François evacuated Fuenterrabia, and as François refused to do this, Charles ordered Gattinara to walk out of the Calais conference, which ended without a truce having been agreed. Before Wolsey returned to England on 28 November, he signed a new secret treaty with Gattinara at Calais. It was agreed that when Charles sailed from the Netherlands to Spain in the spring of 1522, he would visit Henry on the way, and that during his stay in England Henry would declare war on France. One clause in the treaty provided that Henry and Charles would punish all enemies of the Church and the Catholic faith in the territories which they won from France.[12]

Henry was very grateful to Wolsey for his efforts at Calais and Bruges. He told Pace that he thought that Wolsey must have spent £10,000 of his own money during the negotiations. He wrote Wolsey a letter of thanks in his own hand. Shortly before Wolsey returned to England, the Abbot of St Albans died. Without even consulting Wolsey, Henry sent a letter to the Pope asking him to appoint Wolsey as the new Abbot, with the necessary dispensations to hold the abbey along with his archbishopric of York and his bishopric of Bath and Wells.[13]

But Leo X died before he received Henry's request. Henry and Wolsey used all their influence to secure the election of Wolsey as Pope; but the result of the election depended chiefly on Charles V. Charles had promised Wolsey at Bruges in August that he would urge the 'imperial cardinals', as his supporters in the conclave were known, to vote for Wolsey instead of for Cardinal dei Medici, whom he had previously decided to support. When his ambassador in London visited Henry and Wolsey at Richmond on 16 December, the ambassador found Henry 'anxious beyond what I can express' that Charles should use his influence to get Wolsey elected. But very few of Charles's cardinals voted for Wolsey; and after Medici and other cardinals had repeatedly failed to secure the necessary majority, the Flemish Cardinal Adrian, who was Bishop of the Spanish see of Tortosa and had been Charles's tutor, was elected, to everybody's surprise, on the fourteenth ballot. He became Adrian VI – the last non-Italian to be chosen Pope for 456 years.[14]

Did Charles double-cross Wolsey and give secret orders to his ambassador in Rome not to canvass on his behalf? It was not easy to know what Charles was doing or planning; for this young Emperor, not yet twenty-two years of age, with his protruding jaw, his dowdy clothes, his slight stammer, his silent and reserved manner, with an appetite for food which was nearly as large as Henry's, and a lust for women which was nearly as strong as François', was as wily a political manipulator as any of his fellow-sovereigns. He had two objectives: the aggrandisement of his house of Habsburg, and the economic prosperity of the merchants in his territories. His devotion to the Church, his loyalty to the Pope, his hatred of heresy, his sympathy for the Catholic martyrs persecuted by Turks and heretics, and all feelings of personal gratitude, loyalty and revenge, had to give way to what he believed were the interests of his house and his duties to his subjects.

While Henry and Wolsey were preparing to betray François, Charles was already considering the possibility of betraying Henry. The whole policy of Henry and Wolsey depended on the future marriage of Charles and Mary; but in January 1522 Charles instructed his ambassador in Portugal to urge the King of Portugal to keep at least one of his daughters unmarried, so that Charles might marry her, as he would prefer to marry a member of his own family. He ordered his ambassador to keep this very secret, as it was important that Henry and Wolsey should not hear of it.[15]

But the preparations for joint military action against France continued, and during the winter of 1521–2 Charles's ambassadors in London were discussing strategical plans with Wolsey. Henry was cautious. In July 1521, when the idea of an alliance with the Emperor was being formulated, Henry had asked Wolsey's advice on a plan which, he said, was his own idea; would it be feasible for his navy and Charles's, at a suitable moment, to launch a sudden attack on the French fleet which would completely destroy it? Wolsey replied that he thought it an excellent idea, but that it should be deferred till the allies were ready to begin the war.[16]

But as Henry reflected on the plan which he had suggested, he became conscious of the difficulties. On 31 January 1522, Wolsey strongly urged Charles's ambassadors in London to carry out the attack; if the French fleet were destroyed, the war would be won, as France's trade would be ruined, and it would take six or seven years for the French to build another fleet. When the ambassadors went to Greenwich three days later, and discussed the proposal with Henry, Wolsey, and three of Henry's counsellors, Henry pointed out all the difficulties, and seemed to be much less enthusiastic about the plan than Wolsey. Henry said that the success of the operation would depend on a favourable wind; and that it would be impossible to destroy the French navy at one blow; for the ships were dispersed in several ports – Brest, Honfleur, Dieppe and Havre – and some of these ports were so strongly defended that they could only be captured by a larger army than it would be practicable to embark on the English and imperial ships. The plan was abandoned.[17]

On 23 May 1522, Charles left Brussels on his journey to Spain, and four days later sailed from Calais to Dover, being escorted across the Channel by an English fleet manned by ten thousand soldiers. Wolsey went out in his barge to meet Charles in Dover harbour, and brought him to Henry in the castle. Charles was accompanied by a train of 2,044 nobles, gentlemen and servants, who complained of the very unsatisfactory accomodation in Dover and of the dreadful weather; and nearly all Henry's nobles and courtiers, with their servants, had come to Dover. Henry rode with Charles by Canterbury, Sittingbourne and Rochester to Greenwich, where Queen Catherine awaited them. A few days before Charles arrived in England, Henry had sent a herald to declare war on France.[18]

There were the usual tournaments, banquets and masques at Greenwich; and there was great enthusiasm when the herald arrived on 5 June to report that he had given François the 'defiance' – the declaration of war – at Lyons a week before. On 6 June, Charles and Henry rode together through London, being welcomed by the Lord Mayor and all the city dignitaries one mile outside the city walls at St George's Bar, and riding in great state through Southwark and the richly decorated streets of London to St Paul's, where they attended Mass before going to their lodgings in Henry's palace at Bridewell. Next day they played tennis at Baynard's Castle, another of Henry's houses in the city. They partnered each other in a doubles match against two of Charles's most high-ranking courtiers, the Prince of Orange and the Margrave of Brandenburg, with the Earl of Devonshire and Lord Edmund Howard acting as ball-boys. The match was abandoned as a draw after they had played eleven games.

The King and the Emperor were entertained at a banquet by Wolsey at York Place, which was afterwards called Whitehall, and attended Mass in Westminster Abbey. They were also entertained by the Duke of Suffolk and Mary the French Queen at their town house in Southwark. They then went by Richmond and Hampton Court to Windsor, where Charles hunted, and was installed as a Knight of the Garter. After spending a few days at Windsor, Henry escorted Charles to Southampton.[19] At Windsor and at Bishop's Waltham he signed three new treaties with Charles by which they agreed to invade France, not to make a separate peace with François, and that Charles would marry Mary when she reached the age of twelve in six years' time.[20] On 6 July, Charles sailed from Southampton for Corunna.

Henry and Wolsey wasted no time in starting military operations against the French. Though the main invasion was planned for next summer, Henry sent the Earl of Surrey to Calais with an army to link up with the Emperor's army and do the greatest possible damage to the enemy in the few weeks remaining for campaigning. Surrey's troops crossed the French frontier near Ardres on 4 September. It was a very different operation from the last occasion on which Henry invaded France. In 1513, he had led, in person, an army which observed all the rules of chivalrous war, and any soldiers who set fire to houses were hanged. Now, while Henry himself went hawking in Essex and Hertfordshire, he sent Surrey to wage what the French general, the Duke of Vendôme, called 'very foul war', burning castles, towns, villages, farms, and even a church which looked 'more like a house of war than the house of God'.

Surrey advanced fifty miles into France, going as far as Doullens. At Lottinghen, near Desvres, they burned everything in an area five miles long and eight miles wide. But they failed to take Hesdin, and after a month Charles's generals, who were more alarmed than Surrey at the prospect that the French might retaliate for the destruction by burning villages and farms in the Netherlands, decided to cease operations until next spring, and Surrey returned to Calais.

Despite Vendôme's indignation at Surrey's method of waging war, and the burning of his own castle, he agreed to Surrey's proposal for an exchange of prisoners. The English who returned from captivity at Montreuil reported that all the French there blamed Wolsey for the sufferings which had been inflicted on their countrymen.[21] Apparently no one in Montreuil thought that Henry was responsible. Both abroad and at home, it was always the Cardinal who was blamed, not the King.

Henry and Wolsey set out to win over, or knock out, François' two allies, Venice and Scotland. Wolsey put strong pressure on the Venetian ambassador, Suriano, to abandon France and join the anti-French alliance of Henry, Charles, the Pope, and the other Italian states; and Pace was sent to Venice to reinforce Wolsey's arguments there. Apart from their usual reluctance to endanger their trade with England, the Venetians were at a grave disadvantage, because Wolsey detained all their galleys in English ports on various pretexts, and made it plain that the ships would not be released until the Venetians joined the anti-French alliance. Henry left Wolsey to conduct this blackmailing operation; but on the few occasions when Suriano raised the matter with him, he fully supported Wolsey. After the ships had been detained for more than thirteen months, the Venetians gave in, and joined the alliance with Charles and Henry in July 1523.[22]

François sent Albany back to Scotland. In the autumn of 1522, Albany marched on Carlisle. Dacre was unprepared for an attack, and asked Albany for a truce. Albany could have taken Carlisle without difficulty; but the defeatism which had pervaded Scotland since Flodden, and their consciousness that François was in no position to help them, made them only too eager to seize any opportunity of appeasing Henry's anger and showing their desire for peaceful relations with England. Wolsey persuaded Henry to overcome his initial anger that Dacre had asked for a truce without his authority, and prepared for a campaign to devastate Scotland when the truce expired next year.[23]

The burning of the Boulonnais was only a preliminary for 1523, which was to be the year of the utter destruction of France. Matters certainly looked grim for François. He faced an alliance of England, the Empire, the Pope, the Italian states, and the Swiss, and a joint invasion of his kingdom from Calais, the Netherlands, Switzerland, Italy and Spain. But worse was to come. His leading general, the Duke of Bourbon, the Constable of France, entered into secret negotiations with Charles, offering to betray François by launching a revolt in his district of south-east France to coincide with the invasions, if Charles would give him his sister in marriage and a dowry of 100,000 crowns.

But Bourbon's defection, which should have been the knockout blow to François, did more than anything else to weaken his enemies. It caused mistrust between Charles and Henry. Charles did not tell Henry and Wolsey about Bourbon's offer; but Bourbon told them, and this immediately aroused their suspicions of Charles's intentions. Their fears increased when Henry's ambassador to Margaret of Austria, Dr Knight, reported that he had heard that Bourbon was planning to make himself King of France after François' defeat; for it had been agreed between Charles and Henry that, though Charles would annex some French territory in the east and south, Henry would become King of France.[24]

Henry and Wolsey sent Sir John Russell – a gentleman of Dorset who was making a successful career as a soldier, diplomat and courtier – to meet Bourbon secretly in France. Henry took a personal interest in the negotiations with Bourbon. He suggested that Bourbon should kidnap François when François went masked on some nocturnal excursion, or when he was out hunting, or on some other occasion when he was accompanied by only a few attendants.[25] Henry and Wolsey also insisted that Bourbon should recognise Henry as King of France. Bourbon agreed to do so; but Henry and Wolsey still feared that Charles and Bourbon were plotting together behind their backs.

Henry had again agreed to finance his allies in the war against France. The House of Commons, the Church, and the City of London were asked to grant money for the war; and although in every case there was some initial resistance to the large sums which were demanded, they all eventually responded with patriotic enthusiasm and agreed to contribute for a war against the French and Scots, and for sending abroad an 'army royal' led by the King himself. But in all the proclamations and dispatches which Wolsey wrote, it was always stated that the army royal would be led by the King 'or his Lieutenant'. Henry never really intended to go on the campaign, and sent Suffolk to command the army at Calais. Charles had promised that he would invade Guienne from Spain before the end of August 1523; but he did not do so.

Henry's strategical plan for the campaign was limited and practical: Suffolk, with the help of the navy, was to besiege and capture Boulogne. But

Bourbon and Charles proposed an alternative plan. Suffolk should link up with Margaret of Austria's army from the Netherlands and march straight for Paris, while Bourbon launched his revolt against François at the very moment when the allies crossed the French frontier. Bourbon also insisted that there should be none of the looting and burning of farms and villages which Surrey's army had carried out in the previous year, for this would alienate the sympathies of the French people who, he hoped, would join him in the revolt against François. Henry and Wolsey were very sceptical about this plan. They thought that it was a trick by Charles's commanders in the Netherlands to leave the English to do the fighting for them. But Count Buren, Charles's general, became increasingly aware of the difficulties of besieging Boulogne, and persuaded Wolsey to accept the more daring plan for the advance on Paris. Henry agreed, but continued to dislike the plan.[26]

The collection of the money for the war, the preparations for transporting the army to Calais, and the negotiations with Bourbon, all caused delay, and it was not until the beginning of September that everything was ready. Then, at the last moment, Bourbon's page betrayed him to François. Bourbon fled to Italy just in time to avoid being arrested by François as a traitor. Henry and Wolsey were now more suspicious than ever, for Charles appointed Bourbon commander-in-chief of his armies in northern Italy; and Bourbon refused the invitation of Henry and Wolsey that he should visit them in England with a view to his leading the invasion of France from Calais. It was obvious that Bourbon was entirely under Charles's control.

In August and September, Henry went on his usual progress, taking Sir Thomas More with him as his secretary, while Wolsey remained at Hampton Court and at his houses in Hertfordshire. More wrote repeatedly to Wolsey, telling him of Henry's opposition to the plan for the march on Paris. The King did not believe that it would be as easy as Buren supposed. He feared that the transport and victualling problems would present great difficulties; and he did not share Bourbon's confidence that the English and Burgundians would not encounter any French forces which would all be occupied in invading Italy. He believed that François would do what he himself would do if he were in such a predicament, and ensure for the defence of his own realm before invading other realms. As for Bourbon's insistence that there should be no looting or burning, Henry was doubtful if the English soldiers could be prevented from deserting if they had no prospect of loot. On 20 September, More wrote to Wolsey from Abingdon: 'The King's Highness thinketh that since his army shall march in hard weather, with many sore and grievous incommodities, if they should also forbear the profit of the spoil, the bare hope whereof, though they get little, was great encouraging to them, they shall have evil will to march far forward, and their captains shall have much ado to keep them from crying Home! Home!'[27]

At last, with only seven or eight weeks of campaigning weather left, Suffolk marched out of Calais on 19 September, and, linking up with Buren's army, headed for Paris. They advanced a hundred miles into French territory, crossed the Somme near Bouvain, and were within sixty miles of Paris. But by now it was the beginning of November; and, though Henry congratulated Wolsey on the success of the operation, his worst forebodings proved to be justified. François rushed troops to Paris, and the people prepared for a determined defence of the city. A sharp frost came early, and a hundred of Suffolk's soldiers died of cold and disease. This was followed by a thaw, and the Burgundian supply carts were bogged down in the mud. Margaret of Austria's ministers refused to risk sending money from Antwerp for the soldiers' pay so far into France along the unguarded roads. Suffolk and the Burgundian general decided to retreat, and Henry's army returned to Calais.[28]

While Suffolk was invading France, Surrey was raiding Scotland. Queen Margaret did her best to prevent the devastation; she wrote to Surrey that burning the Border districts would not persuade the Scottish lords to abandon Albany and the French alliance, because the lords laughed at the sufferings of the poor people. But Wolsey insisted that the raid should be carried out as planned. The decision was referred to Henry at Woodstock, and he ordered that the action should proceed; he thought that the Scots were playing for time, and criticised Surrey for having postponed the raid at Margaret's request. But he authorised Surrey to spare the lands of the Douglases and the Homes and other Scots who supported the English.

Surrey burned Haddington and Jedburgh, and the villages, farms and crops in the Merse and Teviotdale. Albany sent an army on a revenge raid into England; but though they attacked the English border fortress of Wark Castle, and penetrated into the inner court, they were driven out, and back across the Border. Englishmen could feel safe, for under the leadership of their great King they had sent an army deep 'into the bowels of France', and had inflicted great suffering on the Scots; while, according to Surrey, they had suffered less than ten shillings worth of damage in Albany's raid into Northumberland.[29]

Lutheranism was gaining ground in Germany. Charles persecuted Lutherans in Spain and the Netherlands, but the constitution of the Empire made it much more difficult for him to take similar action in Germany. The Duke of Saxony protected Luther in his duchy, where he was almost a sovereign Prince. From this refuge, Luther wrote a stinging reply to Henry's *Assertion of the Seven Sacraments*. His *Answer to King Henry of England* shocked most of his readers by the disrespectful language which he used about a King. He referred to him as 'Lord Henry, by God's ungrace King of England'; as 'dear Junker'; as 'King Harry'; and as 'Harry of England'.[30]

Henry thought that it would be beneath his dignity to reply to these attacks; but he encouraged his officials and supporters to counterattack on his behalf. The German Catholic theologians, Thomas Murner and Eck, and Bishop Fisher in England wrote learned books in defence of Henry against Luther. But something more was considered necessary – a vulgar and scurrilously abusive diatribe against Luther which would vilify and ridicule him in the eyes of the readers.

No King or Bishop could demean himself by writing such a work; but one man was willing, and indeed eager, to do so. He was not some obscure and low-grade guttersnipe tract-writer, but Henry's secretary, the eminent intellectual, Sir Thomas More, who hated Lutheranism and heresy with a fury which was all the greater because he himself, and his friend Erasmus, had formerly been critics of the corruption of the Church, and were regarded by many Catholics as having paved the way for Luther. More's *Answer to Luther*, which was published in Latin in London in December 1523, was a publication which for abuse and obscenity has no parallel even in the field of sixteenth-century theological controversy. It was published under the pseudonym of William Rosse. Great efforts were made to hide the fact that it was written by a member of Henry's Council, with More going to the length of forging a number of documents in order to prove the existence of the fictitious William Rosse.

Henry himself was therefore in no way connected with More's book. On the contrary, he wrote a most dignified letter to Duke Frederick of Saxony. He explained that he did not care in the least what Luther wrote about him; but he asked Duke Frederick to consider whether it was in his interests, and in those of his fellow-rulers, that he should give asylum in his territories to a man who wrote books attacking a King, and who stirred up sedition against ecclesiastical and secular authority. The Duke replied with a tactful and evasive letter in which he disclaimed liability for Luther's books and opinions.[31]

Thus Henry preserved his dignity and left the dirty work to More, just as he had stayed at Richmond throughout Evil May Day and left Norfolk and Surrey to suppress the London apprentices.

In September 1523, Pope Adrian died. Henry and Wolsey again urged Charles to use his influence to secure the election of Wolsey as Pope. Again Charles promised to do so, and again apparently did nothing to help Wolsey. His cardinals in the conclave voted for Cardinal Medici, who was elected, after forty-nine days, as Pope Clement VII. None of the cardinals were prepared even to nominate Wolsey in any of the ballots.[32]

The war against France was resumed in 1524. The year opened hopefully, for Charles's armies under Bourbon attacked the French forces in Lombardy, defeated them in a campaign in which the great Bayard was killed, and invaded Provence. Henry and Wolsey sent Pace and Russell with money for Bourbon; and as Pace accompanied Bourbon on his march westwards along the Mediterranean coast to Marseilles, he strongly urged Henry and Wolsey to invade northern France while François' armies were engaging Bourbon in the south, for Henry would never have a better opportunity to regain the crown of France.

But Henry and Wolsey did not move. They were as inactive during the campaign of 1524 as Charles had been during the invasion of 1523. On 17 July, Wolsey wrote to Pace. After stressing, at great length, the difficulties of launching an invasion in the north, Wolsey referred, in one sentence, to the real reason for Henry's inaction: the King doubted whether Bourbon's success would not bring more benefit to the Emperor, and to Bourbon himself, than to Henry.[33]

Wolsey was meanwhile conducting tentative peace negotiations in London with two emissaries from François' mother, Louise d'Angoulême. He told Charles that he was meeting the French representatives, and assured him that Henry would never make a separate peace with France without consulting him; but Charles was not happy about the presence of the French negotiators in London. Wolsey adopted a very tough attitude in the negotiations, saying that Henry would be satisfied with nothing less than the whole kingdom of France; and the French, on their side, though they offered large sums of money to Henry, stated that François would never agree to cede an inch of French territory. But they stayed in London for more than a year, living in the house of the brother of Wolsey's mistress. All the negotiations were carried on by Wolsey; but the French negotiators had discussions with Henry on at least one occasion at Wolsey's house at The Moor, and the King was fully informed about the talks.[34]

In Provence, the situation suddenly changed. Bourbon besieged Marseilles, but failed to take the city, and was driven back into Italy faster than he had come. François pursued him into Lombardy, captured Milan, and by November was besieging Pavia. It was perhaps because of Charles's set-back that Wolsey ventured to commit a very provocative act against him in February 1525. Charles's Flemish ambassador in London, Praet, sent a dispatch to Charles by his courier, who set out for Plymouth, intending to take ship for Spain. The courier was stopped late at night near Brentford by a party of constables under the command of Sir Thomas More, who detained the courier, opened his packet, and read the letter to Charles, despite the courier's protest against this violation of diplomatic immunity. More sent the letter to Wolsey. Praet had criticised Wolsey and his policy in the letter, and Wolsey summoned Praet before the King's Council, upbraided him for writing it, placed him under house arrest, and forbade him to write to the Emperor. Henry and Wolsey then complained to both Charles and Margaret of Austria that Praet had been sending lying reports which damaged Charles's relations with Henry. They asked Charles to recall Praet and replace him by another ambassador.

The diplomatic immunity of ambassadors was not so clearly established in 1525 as in later centuries; but both Praet and Charles regarded it as a breach of international usage, and a grave affront to the Emperor's honour. It was probably Wolsey, not Henry, who was responsible for the action against Praet. Never again, during the rest of his reign, did Henry ever intercept diplomatic correspondence and arrest a foreign ambassador, even when he was dealing with ambassadors and their sovereigns who were far more hostile to him than were Praet and Charles in 1525. But Wolsey would not have acted without Henry's knowledge and authority; and after Praet had been detained, Henry officially backed Wolsey's action. He spoke on the subject to the ambassadors of Margaret of Austria, and wrote in person to Charles to demand Praet's recall, taking the opportunity, in his letter, to emphasize his high regard for Wolsey.

Charles blamed Wolsey for the incident. He thought it wise to suppress his anger for the time being, and agreed to replace Praet; but he told Praet that he wished he were in a position to punish Wolsey.[35]

A fortnight after Praet's arrest, there was another dramatic change of fortune in the war. Bourbon defeated François at Pavia, and took him prisoner. Charles kept him in prison in Italy and Madrid for more than a year. Henry and Wolsey showed every sign of being very pleased when they heard the news of the victory at Pavia; and they had their own additional reason for satisfaction because Richard de la Pole, White Rose, was killed fighting for François in the battle. A *Te Deum* was held, with great pomp, in St Paul's, and Henry ordered that church bells should be rung and bonfires lit to celebrate the victory in every town in England;[36] but he and Wolsey knew that it made Charles complete master of the situation.

The decisive time had been reached in Henry's relations with Charles and François. Henry and Wolsey proposed to Charles that as François was a prisoner, this was the moment to invade France. If François were released and restored to his throne, he would seek revenge; so he and his successors should be deprived of it for ever, and Henry should be proclaimed King of France in their place. But Charles replied that he would not wage war against a prisoner. He had no intention of helping Henry to gain the throne of France, but meant to use his bargaining position as François' captor to his own advantage, without gaining any benefits for Henry.[37]

In the summer of 1525, Charles, who had not repaid the money which he had borrowed from Henry for the war, asked Henry to pay him immediately an instalment of 200,000 ducats of Mary's dowry, to advance the date of his marriage to Mary, and to send Mary immediately to his territories. As Henry and Wolsey refused to advance more money to their defaulting imperial debtor, the marriage contract between Charles and Mary was broken off, in effect by mutual consent, and Charles married the King of Portugal's sister.

In August, Wolsey at last reached agreement with the French representatives in London. Louise d'Angoulême, who was Regent of France during François' captivity, agreed to pay an enormous war indemnity, as well as all the arrears of pensions due to Henry under the treaties of 1492, 1514 and 1518, which had been suspended during the war, adding two million crowns to François' earlier debt to Henry. Louise thought that the terms were absolutely outrageous, but she had no alternative but to accept them.[38]

In January 1526, Charles made his own peace treaty with François in Madrid. François agreed to cede to Charles the provinces of Burgundy which France had annexed in 1482, as well as Tournai and other towns in Flanders, and to renounce his claim to the duchy of Milan in favour of Charles's supporters, the Sforza family. It was also agreed that François should marry Charles's sister. In March, François was released, and his two sons were surrendered to Charles as hostages for the observance of the treaty. Wolsey immediately set about doing all he could to instigate François to break it; and having previously financed the Emperor and his allies to fight against France, he now sent money to François' supporters in Italy to fight against Bourbon and Charles's other commanders.

All the diplomats and observers thought that Wolsey alone was responsible for this total reversal of English foreign policy, and modern historians have agreed with them; but though there is no record of what Henry thought about it, Wolsey certainly kept him fully informed, and Henry agreed with the new policy, though perhaps with some misgivings. In any case, in view of Charles's attitude, Henry had little choice except to make the best of the situation; and he knew that if things went wrong, Wolsey would get the blame.

10

THE HOLY LEAGUE

In the summer of 1525, Henry was aged thirty-four, and was beginning the seventeenth year of his reign. He had emerged triumphantly from his second war with France; for though he had not accomplished his lofty aim of winning the crown of France, he had imposed a very favourable peace on the French by which he obtained a great deal of money, in return for nothing except a promise on his part to try to persuade Charles V to release François I from captivity.

The Emperor Maximilian had not been the only European statesman who believed that Henry's chief interest in foreign affairs was Scotland;[1] and here things seemed to be going well for Henry in 1525. Henry's policy as regards to Scotland was simple and moderate: to break the 'old alliance' between France and Scotland, and to draw Scotland out of the French and into the English orbit of influence. He and Wolsey repeatedly made it clear to the Scots that they would never accept Albany as Governor of Scotland and would not tolerate his presence in the country; as long as Albany was in Scotland, the Scots would have no peace with England. But Henry would be prepared to live in peace with any Scottish government that sent Albany back to France and broke the French alliance.

To achieve this end, Henry and Wolsey adopted in turn a policy of threats, force and conciliation. Henry had insisted, despite his sister's plea, in ravaging the Merse and Teviotdale in the autumn of 1523; but almost at once he was offering the olive branch to the Scots. He informed them that although in past centuries the Kings of England had claimed to be overlords of Scotland, he would not revive this claim during the lifetime of his dear nephew, James V; he only wished to prevent Albany and the pro-French faction from assassinating his nephew or taking him as a prisoner to France.

Albany returned to France after his repulse at Wark Castle, and was given a command in François' army in Italy. Before he left Scotland, he arrested Angus and Sir George Douglas and sent them as prisoners to France; but in the summer of 1524 they escaped, and made their way to London. Angus had several discussions with Henry and Wolsey, at which it was agreed that he and his brother should return to Scotland and use their influence there to persuade the Scottish lords to break with France. Angus signed a treaty with Henry, and took an oath to serve Henry against everyone except his own King, James V, and to pursue pro-English policy.

Angus and George Douglas left London in October on their overland journey to Scotland; but before they reached the Border, Wolsey had heard from Queen Margaret. She was appalled at the prospect of her husband's return to Scotland, and wrote to Lord Dacre at Morpeth, appealing to him not to allow Angus to come. She said that she had persuaded most of the Scottish lords, including the Earl of Arran, to break with France and pursue a pro-English policy, but as all of them, especially Arran, hated Angus, they would revert to a pro-French line if Angus entered Scotland. To prove their goodwill, she and Arran arrested the Archbishop of St Andrews and the Bishop of Aberdeen, who were leading supporters of the pro-French party.

Dacre referred the matter to Wolsey at Hampton Court. Henry and Wolsey faced the problem which in every century confronts a great power in dealing with contending factions in its satellite states. Should they support Angus and the Douglases, who were completely under their influence but were regarded as traitors and English agents by the majority of Scots; or should they back a more moderate group who were eager to change sides and, for the moment at least, to pursue a pro-English policy? In view of the urgency of the matter, Wolsey acted without consulting Henry, who was at Ampthill. It was a difficult decision, but he ordered Dacre to detain Angus and Sir George Douglas in Northumberland and prevent them from entering Scotland, on some pretext or other, without letting them know that he was acting on Henry's orders. Angus and Sir George soon realised what had happened. They agreed to wait at Newcastle, but protested that if they were prevented from entering Scotland, this would discourage all Henry's friends there; and they won the sympathy of the English officials in Northumberland, including Surrey, who had recently inherited the title of Duke of Norfolk on his father's death.

Henry, who had now returned to Greenwich, decided that he could not sacrifice his staunch supporters in the hopes of pleasing his sister and vacillators in Scotland. He ordered that Angus and his brother should be allowed to return to Scotland, but urged Angus not to try to cohabit with Margaret. He was convinced that he had taken the right decision when he heard, a few days later, that Margaret and Arran had released the Archbishop of St Andrews and the Bishop of Aberdeen.

Things did not, of course, remain quiet in Scotland for long. In February 1525, Angus marched into Edinburgh with eight hundred armed men. Margaret and the young King retreated to the castle, from where she could bombard her husband's supporters with the castle cannon; but Angus and his men moved into the Canongate, where they were out of range. Henry's ambassador in Scotland, Magnus, arranged a truce, which lasted for more than a year, till Angus and the Douglases began fighting the Earl of Lennox and the Stewarts in the summer of 1526. A few weeks later, Angus succeeded in capturing James V, who was now aged fourteen, and became the real ruler of Scotland. Margaret said that he was holding the King as a prisoner. Henry and Wolsey were very pleased with the position. Henry congratulated Angus on his *coup d'état*, and promised him every assistance; but he could not prevent Margaret from starting divorce proceedings against Angus in the Papal court in Rome, and from becoming the mistress of Henry Stewart, a handsome young courtier.[2]

At home, Henry had several causes for anxiety. Lutheranism was not a serious threat, but the authorities were too alarmed by what had happened in Germany, where mob violence and image-breaking had led to a peasant revolt, to view with equanimity even the slightest signs of the seditious heresy taking root in England. The younger divinity scholars at Cambridge University were attracted by Lutheranism, or at least interested in it. Several of them met regularly at the White Horse Inn in Cambridge to discuss Luther's doctrines. The orthodox Catholics denounced these doctrines as 'the new learning', and called the White Horse Inn 'Germany'.[3] The authorities were also worried by the activities of German Lutherans among the Hansa merchants in the Steelyard in London, who smuggled Lutheran books into the kingdom.

Wolsey was not an ardent persecutor, and was considered by many of the bishops to be soft towards heretics; but under pressure from Warham, Fisher, Standish, and Henry's confessor Longland, the Bishop of Lincoln, he took spasmodic action against the Lutherans. He suggested to Henry that a new proclamation should be issued, ordering everyone who was in possession of Lutheran books to surrender them to the authorities by a certain day on pain of excommunication, and that an order might perhaps be made requiring all merchants and stationers to give recognisances not to import or stock such books. Henry agreed, and was particularly pleased with the suggestion about the recognisances, because he thought that many people would fear this threat more than excommunication.[4]

In 1525, a heretical book appeared which caused more panic among the authorities than any other manifestation of Lutheranism. It was William Tyndale's English translation of the New Testament. Tyndale, who was probably a gentleman from Gloucestershire, had studied divinity at Oxford and Cambridge, and had gone abroad to escape persecution as a Lutheran. His English New Testament contained some marginal notes in which he expressed his opinions about the errors of the Church. It was published illegally, in the face of great difficulties, in Cologne and Worms, and smuggled into England by the Hansa merchants and other travellers; the copies were often hidden in bales of cloth. Tyndale said that his object in translating the Bible into English was to make every ploughboy as knowledgeable in Scripture as the most learned clerk. This was precisely what most learned clerks did not wish to see.

The authorities in Church and State thought that the Bible in English was subversive. If, as the Church itself admitted, the Bible was the Word of God, it was a higher authority than the word of the Pope or the word of the King. If the common people could understand the Bible and read it for themselves, or have it read aloud to them by those of their friends who could read, they would interpret the Bible for themselves, and appeal to the Word of God, as they interpreted it, against the orders of the Pope and the King. The fears of the authorities were well justified, as the history of the next hundred and fifty years was to show; for nothing has done more than the publication of the English Bible to encourage freedom of thought and political democracy.

The Lutherans gained an important recruit when the Prior of the house of the Austin Friars of Barnwell in Cambridge, Robert Barnes, became a Lutheran. At Christmas 1525 he preached a sermon in Cambridge in which he criticised the practice of celebrating holy days, for which there was no authority in the Bible, and the pomp of bishops and cardinals, who should spend their money, not in ostentatious display, but in relieving the poor. In February 1526 Wolsey took action against Barnes and other heretics, who were forced to recant and carry their faggots at Paul's Cross. Another prominent Cambridge scholar who supported the new learning was Thomas Bilney, who travelled through the parishes of the diocese of Norwich, preaching against prayers to the saints.[5]

On 1 September 1525, Luther wrote to Henry, apologising for having written his book against him. He apparently wrote the letter on the advice of King Frederick I of Denmark, whose son was a Lutheran supporter; and in the summer of 1525, after the Peasant War in Germany, Luther was anxious to show that he did not wish to incite sedition against Princes. In his letter to Henry, he wrote that he had been led to believe that Henry's book had not been written by him, but by some crafty sophist who had made use of Henry's name, 'and especially that monstrous and notorious person, hated by God and man, the Cardinal of York, the plague of your realm'. Luther had heard that Henry was now beginning to favour the Gospel, and he offered to make a public recantation of his book if Henry would notify him in what form he wished the recantation to be made.[6]

As other people were later to learn, it never paid to appease Henry. Luther's letter gave him just what he wanted – the opportunity to appear as the stern judge, who, with the miscreant begging for mercy at his feet, felt unable to pardon his heinous crimes. He waited for nearly a year before replying to Luther. He then wrote him a long letter, which was intended to be read, not by Luther, but by the public who would read it when it was printed. Henry wrote that he would not have deigned to reply to Luther if Luther had not presumed to imply that he was becoming sympathetic to Luther's doctrines. He denounced Luther in the strongest terms, castigating his doctrine of justification by faith and not by good works, and particularly abusing Luther for his recent marriage to a former nun, in breach of the vows of celibacy which both he and she had taken. As for Luther's remarks about Wolsey, Henry wrote that it could only increase the high regard which he had for Wolsey to know that he was abused by a man like Luther. He repudiated Luther's offer to write an apology and a book praising him, for he did not care for Luther's praise, and would always defend the Pope and the Papacy against Luther's attacks. He ended by calling on Luther to end his unlawful association with the nun, and to retire to a monastery.[7]

Henry was faced with a more serious threat than the Lutherans. There was widespread dissatisfaction in England with the taxes which were imposed to pay for the war. Henry and Wolsey's policy of lending money – which was usually not repaid – to Emperors and other rulers to fight against the French, cost a great deal, and so to a lesser extent did the lavish entertaining at Henry's court, the expensive gifts to foreign ambassadors and Princes, and the diamonds, rubies and sapphires which Henry wore in the rings on his fingers and the chains around his neck. From Henry's point of view, this expenditure was not wasted, for his reputation for wealth was his greatest diplomatic asset; his agent in Brussels, Spinelly, reported to Wolsey that Henry's wealth was the chief reason for the respect with which he was regarded by foreign powers.[8] But his subjects had to pay for it; and though their willingness to pay was another factor which created respect for him abroad, that willingness had its limit.

In 1525, Henry and Wolsey decided to raise more money by appealing to the people to make a voluntary gift to Henry, in addition to the taxes that had been imposed on them by law. It was known as the 'Amicable Grant', and after Wolsey himself, and all the leading counsellors and courtiers had made their donations, great pressure was put on the people to pay. There was strong opposition in some districts in south-east England; at Tonbridge, Chelmsford, Stansted, Sudbury and Norwich, the inhabitants refused to pay. Around Otford, the people said that all the taxes had not gained one foot of territory in France; but at Canterbury they paid willingly.[9]

The most serious resistance was at Lavenham in Suffolk, where large crowds assembled and threatened the royal officials who had asked them to pay. Wolsey treated the matter as high treason, and ordered the Duke of Suffolk and the Duke of Norfolk to raise forces in the neighbouring counties to suppress the revolt. But the King's judges, who were often prepared to strain the law to please Henry, but were not prepared to disregard it entirely, advised Henry and Wolsey that the men of Lavenham had done nothing that amounted in law to high treason, and that they could only be proceeded against for riot. Norfolk arrested four of the ringleaders, and allowed the rest to go free, after they had knelt in their shirts and begged for mercy. He told them that they deserved severe punishment, but that Henry had chosen to be merciful; and the four ringleaders, too, were pardoned.[10]

There was also trouble because Wolsey, acting under his powers as Papal Legate and under the provisions of a Papal bull, suppressed twenty-two monasteries in order to use their assets to found a new college at his university of Oxford, which should become a famous seat of learning and ensure the immortality of his name. But, as Henry was to be reminded ten years later, when he suppressed monasteries on a much bigger scale, the suppression of religious houses was not the popular measure which might have been expected. Nearly all the vocal elements in the kingdom criticised the monasteries. The reforming zealots in the Church, the local gentry with their eyes on the possible spoils to be bought at cheap prices in forced sales, the witty humanist intellectuals, the ballad-singers and story-tellers, all denounced or mocked the monasteries, the lazy, lascivious or homosexual monks, and the nuns with their lovers and bastard children. But for the people, monasteries were something that they loved to hate. They complained of the monks as bad landlords, and spoke half-disapprovingly and half-jokingly about the immorality that went on in the religious houses; but when monasteries were suppressed, they resented a measure which caused local unemployment when the servants in the houses lost their jobs, which deprived the poor of alms, the travellers of hospitality, and the local inhabitants of what were, despite all the jokes and rumours, places of pilgrimage and worship. At Tonbridge, and at Bayham Abbey a few miles away, there were riots among the local inhabitants when the monasteries were suppressed; at Bayham, armed men assembled and put the monks back in the suppressed house, before the riot was put down.[11]

After using the assets of the suppressed monasteries to found his Cardinal's College at Oxford, Wolsey proceeded to found another Cardinal's College in his native town of Ipswich. Priests, choristers and scholars were installed to pray for the souls of Wolsey's father and mother and to educate poor boys of the district. Wolsey put great pressure, which sometimes amounted to threats, on abbots, nobles and wealthy merchants to induce them to pay money to provide for the expenses of the colleges. The Ipswich foundation aroused even more resentment than Cardinal's College at Oxford. To found a college at Oxford or Cambridge was a well-established practice; but the only reason to found a college at Ipswich was that Wolsey's father had been a butcher there.

The most serious problem for Henry was that he had no male heir. His anxiety about this seems strange to us today, who know the life-story of his second daughter, Elizabeth; but he did not have the advantage of historical hindsight in 1525, and could not foresee that it would be possible for a female sovereign to reign for forty-four years without marrying either a foreign Prince or an ambitious subject, and to succeed in averting civil war. Only once in the previous seven hundred years during which England had existed as a nation, had a Queen succeeded to the throne; and the experience of Matilda in the twelfth century had shown that a woman could not peacefully reign in England.

When Henry realised that Catherine of Aragon would not produce a son, he thought of ensuring the succession by marrying his daughter Mary to Charles V as part of the Great Enterprise; but when this project collapsed in the summer of 1525 and Charles repudiated the marriage contract, Henry had to find another solution. He considered the possibility of legitimising his illegitimate son, Henry Fitzroy. Having kept his affair with Elizabeth Blount very quiet, he suddenly publicised it, and made all his subjects aware of the existence of the child of their union.

On 16 June 1525, just at the time when the marriage contract between Charles and Mary was repudiated, Henry ennobled his son at a ceremony at Bridewell in London. The boy, who was just six, came into the room where Henry sat on a throne, surrounded by Wolsey, Warham, Norfolk, Suffolk and his other nobles. After Sir Thomas More had read out the patent, Henry created his son Earl of Nottingham. The boy then walked out of the room, and immediately came back and was created Duke of Richmond and Somerset.[12] Soon afterwards Henry appointed him to be Lord President of the Council of the North, which exercised the powers of the King's Council north of the Trent, and set him up with an impressive household at the castle of Sheriffhutton, some ten miles north-east of York, and in other houses in Yorkshire. Henry did not forget the new Duke's mother, and at about this time knighted her husband, Gilbert Talboys.

Henry had ended his affair with Lady Talboys some years before, and had taken a new mistress, Mary Boleyn. Here again there is no record of when the affair with Mary Boleyn began, for Henry carried it on so discreetly that only very few people knew about it. Mary's father, Thomas Boleyn, was the son of a knight of Norfolk, who had become a soldier, courtier and diplomat, jousting with Henry at the tournaments at court, serving in the army in wartime, and serving as ambassador to both François I and Charles V. He married Elizabeth Howard, the daughter of the victor of Flodden and the sister of the third Duke of Norfolk; but he does not seem to have been particularly close to his brother-in-law, or under his political influence. He lived at Hever in Kent, and was an influential figure in the neighbourhood. In 1525 Henry created him Viscount Rochford.

His two daughters, Mary and Anne, had both spent some years at the court of François I. François, who was a connoisseur in such matters, said on one occasion that Mary Boleyn was the most promiscuous lady at his court.[13]

She returned to England and became one of Queen Catherine's ladies-in-waiting. When she married Sir William Carey in 1520, Henry attended the wedding. She was probably Henry's mistress both before and after the marriage. After Henry married Anne Boleyn, there was a rumour that Lady Boleyn, the mother of Mary and Anne, had also been Henry's mistress at one time; but Henry denied this.[14]

It was in the same year, 1525, in which he created his bastard son Duke of Richmond, that Henry first seriously considered another way of producing a male heir – by divorcing Queen Catherine and marrying another wife. He afterwards stated that the idea that his marriage to Catherine was unlawful, because it was against God's law for a man to marry his brother's widow, was first suggested to him by his confessor, Longland; but Longland said that it was Henry, not he, who had first raised the matter.[15] Henry's story about Longland was an attempt to explain, not why he had doubts about the marriage, but why the doubts had not arisen long before. As early as 1502, Warham and other counsellors had been unhappy at the prospect of Henry marrying his dead brother's wife; but Henry had nevertheless married her, and since the marriage had never publicly voiced any doubts of its validity. He could not do so until he had ended his alliance with Catherine's nephew, Charles V.

Even then he raised the matter only in private with his confessor, for Henry and Wolsey were proceeding cautiously in their actions against Charles. They were encouraging François to break the terms of the treaty which he had been forced to sign as a prisoner in Madrid, sending lawyers to persuade him that no one is bound to observe a treaty imposed under duress; and Henry wrote to François, urging him to disregard the fate of his sons who were being held as hostages in Spain, and to do his duty as a King and defy Charles.[16]

Henry had never been alarmed at the warnings which he had so often received from the Pope about the threat to Christendom from the Great Turk. After Sultan Selim had defeated the Persians and conquered Egypt, his successor, Soleiman the Magnificent, made his preparations to attack the west. In 1522 he captured the Hungarian border town of Belgrade, and next year attacked the island of Rhodes, which was held as a Christian outpost in the east by the Order of the Knights of St John of Jerusalem. The fall of Rhodes shocked Europe. It touched Henry, because Docwra, the Prior of the Order of St John, was a prominent dignitary in England, where he sat in the House of Lords and served Henry as a counsellor and diplomat. But Henry could do nothing to help Rhodes, even if he had wished to do so.

In the spring of 1526, a vast Turkish army, which was estimated by the Christians at 300,000 men, invaded Hungary. The young King Ladislaus of Bohemia and Hungary could raise only 50,000 men to oppose the Turks, and he and the Pope appealed for help to all the other Kings of Christendom.

Henry was even less inclined than usual to do anything about the Turkish menace, because Ladislaus was Charles V's brother-in-law; and although Henry and Wolsey at first promised to send at least financial aid to Ladislaus, and received grateful letters of thanks from the Pope, Henry afterwards wrote to Clement VII that he regretted that he could do nothing to help Ladislaus, as Hungary was too far from England.[17]

On 29 August, the Turks annihilated Ladislaus's army at Mohacs. Ladislaus was drowned in the Danube while escaping from the battlefield. Eleven days later, the Turks entered the city of Buda, and massacred the population. When the news of Ladislaus's defeat and death reached London on 8 October, Wolsey sent the report to Henry at Ampthill. Dr Knight, who was acting as Henry's secretary, told Wolsey that Henry's eyes filled with tears as he heard of the disaster; but he consoled himself with Christ's words to Peter: '*Oravi, ne deficiat fides tua*'.* After returning to London, Henry wrote to the Pope on 23 October, telling him how he had wept when he heard the news of Mohacs, attributing the disaster to the disunited state of Christendom, and promising that when these divisions had been healed, and the Princes of Christendom launched the crusade against the Turk, he would be the first to march, in person, against the infidel.[18]

There is no reason to question the sincerity of Henry's sympathy for the young King Ladislaus; but he did not allow it to affect his anti-Habsburg foreign policy. Ladislaus's brother-in-law, Ferdinand of Austria, the brother of Charles V, succeeded to the throne of Bohemia and Hungary; but though he took possession of Bohemia, the Vojvoda of Transylvania, John Zapolya, made himself King of Hungary. Ferdinand and most of Christendom denounced Zapolya as a rebel and as a collaborator with the infidel.

But for Henry and Wolsey, it was enough that Zapolya was opposed to Charles's brother and might make trouble for the Emperor in the east. Henry sent Sir John Wallop to visit Zapolya, to encourage him to go to war with Ferdinand, and to offer him financial help. Ferdinand discovered about Wallop's mission; he stopped him at Wroclaw and sent him back to England. Henry and Wolsey succeeded in getting into contact with Zapolya through Italy, and Zapolya sent an envoy to London in the summer of 1527; but though Ferdinand continued to regard Zapolya as a rebel, peace was maintained between them.[19]

Henry and Wolsey were more successful in stirring up the Pope and the Italian Dukes to make war on Charles. The Pope became alarmed at Charles's complete domination of the whole Italian peninsula, and with encouragement and promises of financial support from Henry, he formed a Holy League to resist the Emperor. Four years before, Henry and Wolsey had blackmailed the Venetians into joining the Emperor in the anti-French alliance; now they

* 'I have prayed for thee, that thy faith fail not' (Luke xxii.32)

urged them to join an alliance with France against the Emperor.

Henry and Wolsey did not wish to be directly involved in war with Charles, and were eager to prevent the disruption of the very profitable trade between England and the Netherlands. In order to encourage the formation of the Holy League against Charles in Italy, they agreed that Henry should join the League and should be named the Protector of the League; but they insisted that Henry's adherence to the League should be kept secret for the time being, and should not be disclosed until Henry thought that the moment was opportune. Henry and Wolsey made every excuse to put off the date for announcing that Henry had joined the League. On 1 October, Knight, who was with Henry at Ampthill, wrote to Wolsey that Henry was glad to have received news from Italy 'whereby his entry into the League of Italy may be well, and with good colour, deferred without his dishonour, whereat His Highness is very glad'. Meanwhile Edward Lee, Henry's ambassador at Granada, assured Charles that Henry had not joined the League. Charles believed, or pretended to believe, it; he told Lee that he was sure that Henry would not join the League.[20]

Charles's forces defeated the armies of the League, and on 20 September entered Rome, and burned, looted and raped in the city. Next day, the Pope signed a truce with Charles's general. When the news reached England, Henry, who as usual was keeping in close touch with political events while he was on his autumn progress, returned from Dunstable with a small escort to discuss the situation with Wolsey. He advised Wolsey to brazen it out, to tell the Papal Nuncio and the French ambassador 'sharply' that the disaster had occurred because of the slackness of the Pope and of François in not acting more vigorously against Charles.[21]

While Henry wrote to Charles, urging him to make peace in order to prepare for a crusade of united Christendom against the Turk, he and Wolsey urged the Pope to break the truce, which he had made with Charles's general in Rome on the day after the looting of the city, on the grounds that he was not bound to observe a truce made under duress. They promised Clement that if he and his allies resumed the war, he would receive money from Henry to pay his mercenaries. Relying on this promise, the Pope and the League resisted the advance of Charles's armies, which were commanded by the Duke of Bourbon. Henry and Wolsey sent Russell, who two years before had carried money to Bourbon's army, to go again to Italy with money, but this time for the army that was fighting against Bourbon. There were the usual delays about the banking arrangements in Antwerp; and as Bourbon's army advanced, the Pope's ministers wrote desperately to Wolsey, telling him about the atrocities committed by Bourbon's mercenaries, who were desecrating the Host and perpetrating other outrages in the churches in the towns and villages through which they passed as they advanced on Rome.[22]

At the beginning of May 1527, Bourbon reached Rome and demanded free passage through the city. When the Pope refused, Bourbon ordered the assault on Rome. He was killed in the attack, but his men captured Rome, and killed, raped and looted for twelve days. Charles's Viceroy held the Pope in Rome as a virtual prisoner.

When the news of the sack of Rome reached England, Henry and Wolsey made the most of the atrocity for propaganda purposes against the Emperor. Henry wrote to the Pope expressing his horror at what had happened; and the English bishops wrote to the Spanish bishops, protesting against the actions of Charles's troops. Charles apologised to the Pope. Bourbon's army had consisted partly of Spanish troops, and partly of Italian and German mercenaries. In order to excuse the conduct of the soldiers of the Holy Roman Emperor, Charles's sympathisers spread the story that the Spaniards in his army had been secret Moslems who had retained their infidel beliefs after the Moorish kingdom of Granada was conquered by Ferdinand and Isabella thirty-five years before, and that the German mercenaries were Lutherans.[23] There does not seem to be any reliable evidence of this, but the story has persisted for more than four hundred and fifty years.

A week before the sack of Rome, Wolsey reached agreement with the French envoys in the negotiations which had been proceeding in London since the beginning of March. It was agreed that Henry's daughter Mary should marry either François I or his second son, the Duke of Orleans, and that Henry and François should unite to compel Charles to free François' sons and to repay the debt which he owed to Henry.[24] In these circumstances, in May 1527, Henry took what was to prove to be the most momentous decision in his life, and began divorce proceedings against Catherine of Aragon.

11

THE KING'S GREAT MATTER

No event in Henry's life has been studied so thoroughly as his divorce from Catherine of Aragon. Many of the documents had been published before the end of the seventeenth century, and in the next three hundred years the dispatches, letters, bulls, briefs and theological treatises which were written during the seven years that the divorce proceedings continued, have been analysed and debated by theologians, historians and biographers. But there is a great shortage of evidence to explain the reason for an event which occurred at the same time and was closely connected with the divorce – the fall of Wolsey.

Henry had fallen seriously in love with Viscount Rochford's younger daughter, Anne Boleyn, before the summer of 1527. Anne, like her sister Mary, had been brought up at the French court, but had returned to England just before the outbreak of war in 1522, when she was aged fifteen, and came to Henry's court. Soon afterwards Lord Percy, the Earl of Northumberland's son, who was living in Wolsey's household, fell in love with her, and she with him; but as Northumberland had arranged for Percy to marry the Earl of Shrewsbury's daughter, Mary Talbot, Wolsey ordered Percy to cease wooing Anne Boleyn, and arranged for Northumberland to take Percy back to Alnwick. According to Wolsey's gentleman-usher, George Cavendish, who was present when Wolsey scolded Percy for his infatuation with Anne, Wolsey acted on Henry's orders, because Henry was already in love with Anne, and wished to prevent her from marrying Percy so that he could have her for himself; but as Percy married Mary Talbot in 1524, the incident which Cavendish describes must have taken place before this, and it is unlikely that Henry was already thinking of marrying Anne at that time. According to Cavendish, Anne never forgave Wolsey for this, as Wolsey afterwards discovered to his cost.[1]

None of the people who knew Anne seem to have regarded her as being an outstanding beauty; but she was obviously very attractive to men, and if there is any truth in the story told by some of the contemporary Catholic writers, that she had six fingers on one hand,[2] this did not detract from her sexual charms. It was probably in about 1526, when she was nineteen, that Henry fell in love with her. Unlike her sister Mary, she refused to become Henry's mistress, and this increased his admiration for her.

When Anne was away from court, Henry wrote her love letters, usually in French.

'My mistress and friend, I and my heart put ourselves in your hands, begging you to recommend us to your favour, and not to let absence lessen your affection to us. For it were a great pity to increase our pain, which absence alone does sufficiently. . . . Seeing I cannot be present in person with you, I send you the nearest thing to that possible, that is, my picture set in bracelets . . . wishing myself in their place, when it shall please you. This from the hand of your loyal servant and friend, H. R.'.[3]

But Anne showed a reluctance to return to court, and Henry wrote again 'to my mistress'.

'Since my last parting with you, I have been told, that you have entirely changed the opinion in which I left you, and that you would neither come to court with my lady your mother, nor any other way; which report, if true, I cannot enough wonder at, being persuaded in my own mind, that I have never committed any offence against you; and it seems a very small return for the great love I bear you, to be kept at a distance from the person and presence of a woman in the world that I value the most; and, if you love me with as much affection as I hope you do, I am sure, the distance of our two persons would be a little uneasy to you. Though this does not belong so much to the mistress as the servant. Consider well, my mistress, how greatly your absence grieves me; I hope it is not your will that it should be so; but, if I heard for certain that you yourself desired it, I could do no other than complain of my ill fortune, and by degrees abate my great folly'.[4]

When she wrote him a discouraging letter, he was in great distress.

'By turning over in my thoughts the contents of your letters, I have put myself into a great agony, not knowing how to understand them. . . . I beseech you now, with the greatest earnestness, to let me know your whole intention, as to the love between us two. For I must of necessity obtain this answer of you, having been above a whole year struck with the dart of love, and not yet sure whether I shall fail, or find a place in your heart and affection. This uncertainty has hindered me of late from naming you my mistress, since you only love me with an ordinary affection; but if you please to do the duty of a true and loyal mistress, and to give up yourself, body and heart, to me, who will be, as I have been your most loyal servant (if your rigour does not forbid me) I promise you that not only the name shall be given you, but also that I will take you for my mistress, casting off all others that are in competition with you, out of my thoughts and affection, and serving you only. I beg you to give an entire answer to this my rude letter, that I may know on what and how far I may depend. But, if it does not please you to answer me in writing, let me know some place, where I may have it by word of mouth, and I will go thither with all my heart. No more for fear of tiring you. Written by the hand of him, who would willingly remain yours. H. R. immutable'.[5]

As she did not reply to his letters, he wrote again:

'Although, my mistress, you have not been pleased to remember the promise which you made me when I was last with you, which was, that I should hear news of you, and have an answer to my last letter; yet I think it belongs to a true servant (since otherwise he can know nothing) to send to inquire of his mistress's health; and, for to acquit myself of the office of a true servant, I send you this letter begging you to give me an account of the state you are in . . . and , that you may the oftener remember me, I send you by this bearer a buck killed late last night by my hand, hoping, when you eat of it, you will think on the hunter'.[6]

By the spring of 1527, Henry had decided to divorce Queen Catherine and marry Anne Boleyn, who as his wife and Queen would not only give him the satisfaction which she was now refusing him, but perhaps also a legitimate son and heir. It was almost certainly his own idea, which no one had suggested to him. The contemporary Catholic writers, and those of the next generation, believed that Wolsey was responsible for the decision to divorce Catherine, and for the Reformation which resulted from it, and that he did so in order to revenge himself on Charles V because Charles had not used his influence to make him Pope. But at the trial at Blackfriars, Henry stated that Wolsey, far from urging him to divorce the Queen, had tried to dissuade him from doing so. According to Cavendish, Wolsey went on his knees to Henry to beg him not to attempt to divorce Catherine.[7]

When the marriage of Henry and Catherine was first suggested twenty-five years before, after Arthur's death, there had been great doubt as to its validity, and it had been made possible only by the Papal dispensation granted by Julius II in 1503. If it could now be shown that this dispensation was invalid, because of some technical flaw, this would mean that Henry's marriage to Catherine had always been void, and that Henry, as a bachelor who had never married, was free to marry Anne Boleyn. But by 1527, if not earlier, Henry was conscious that another line of argument was open to him: even if there had been no irregularity in the dispensation of 1503, it would be invalid if Julius II had exceeded his Papal powers by granting it; and this would be the case if the marriage of a man to his brother's widow was prohibited by the law of God, and was not merely an impediment of the canon law which could be dispensed with by the Pope.

There was a clear and well-known indication that Henry's marriage to Catherine was against God's law in the biblical text from the Book of

Leviticus: 'If a man shall take his brother's wife, it is an impurity; he hath uncovered his brother's nakedness; they shall be childless'. True, there was a directly conflicting text in the Book of Deuteronomy: 'When brethren dwell together, and one of them dieth without children, the wife of the deceased shall not marry to another; but his brother shall take her, and raise up seed for his brother'.[8] Many of the early fathers of the Church had considered these texts, and, acting on the established principle that biblical texts must always be interpreted in a way that reconciles any conflict between them , the majority had interpreted the text from Leviticus as meaning that the bar on the marriage of a man with his brother's widow did not apply if his brother had died, leaving her childless. Only a minority of them had upheld the Leviticus ban in its full force, interpreting the Deuteronomy text as applying only to the Jews. But the plea that Henry's marriage to Catherine was against God's law because of the text from Leviticus, was certainly arguable, and was upheld by many theologians between 1527 and 1534. Dr Scarisbrick, who includes a learned analysis of the canon law of the divorce in his biography of Henry VIII, is surely not justified in saying that Henry, in putting forward the text from Leviticus, had not merely grasped the wrong end of the stick, but the wrong stick altogether.[9]

There was another point about the argument that the marriage of Henry and Catherine was against God's law. If Henry argued that the marriage was void because of some irregularity in the dispensation of 1503, this would have to be decided in the ecclesiastical courts, and ultimately, no doubt, in the supreme court of appeal, the Papal court in Rome. If he argued that the marriage was against God's law, this would apply whatever the Papal court in Rome might decide. Henry realised from the first that he had two ways of obtaining the annulment of his marriage – one way through the Pope, and one against the Pope; and this, as he also realised, meant either through Wolsey or against Wolsey. However loyal Wolsey might be to him, however much Wolsey had always subordinated the interests of the Papacy to Henry's interests, if Henry argued that no Pope had the power to permit his marriage to Catherine, he would be driven to rely on the anti-clerical forces which hated cardinals in general and Wolsey in particular. It might also mean flirting with Lutheranism, and encouraging those dangerous seditious elements who, by attacking the ecclesiastical Establishment, also endangered the secular Establishment, and, whatever they might claim now, could one day impugn the authority of Kings. It would mean leading his kingdom into schism, if not into heresy. Henry was reluctant to do this, but it was a course of action which could be adopted as a last resort.

Henry and Wolsey had been very close since 1512. We know from a hostile source, from More's son-in-law William Roper, that Henry was as intimate with Wolsey as he was with More himself.[10] But to a cold, callous, calculating political animal like Henry, there were advantages to be gained by sacrificing

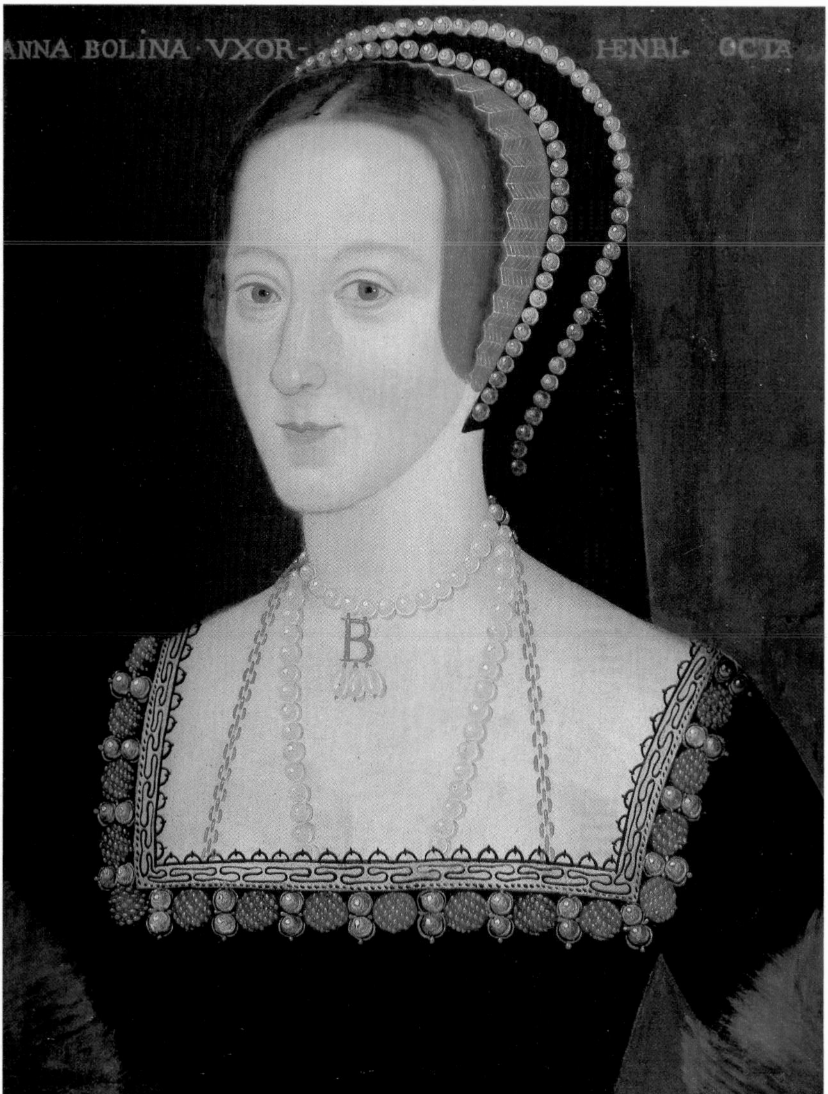

Anne Boleyn, by an unknown artist

Sir Thomas More, after Holbein, 1527

Wolsey. It would please the nobles who hated Wolsey as the upstart son of a butcher, and as the man whom they believed had been responsible for the execution of Buckingham and might any day strike again at another prominent nobleman. It would please the people who held Wolsey responsible for the high taxes that he had extorted from them on the pretext of paying for a patriotic war against the hated French, when really he was planning to ally England with the French, thereby endangering the wool trade with Burgundy. It would please those who did not like churchmen, who resented the pomp and pride of cardinals, and the power which Wolsey exercised as Papal Legate on behalf of the foreign Pope. It would even please Luther, whose offer of support Henry had so contemptuously rejected, but had not, perhaps, forgotten. Lutherans who thought that Wolsey was the plague of England, but who were ready to applaud Henry if he showed any signs of moving towards a Lutheran position, might, in the last resort – but only in the last resort – be useful allies for a King whose only principle was to advance his own interests.

Whatever Wolsey's first reactions may have been when Henry suggested divorcing Catherine, by April 1527 he was energetically looking for evidence which would help Henry's case. He sent officials to Winchester to question Bishop Foxe, who was nearly eighty, about the events which had taken place in 1501 and 1505, as to whether the marriage of Arthur and Catherine had been consummated, and whether it could be said that Henry had been forced by his father, against his will, to promise to marry Catherine.[11]

Henry and Wolsey worked out a plan by which Catherine could be divorced without being given any opportunity to contest the case, and without her or anyone else, except a handful of Henry's officials, knowing anything about it. Wolsey, acting under his powers as Papal Legate, would summon Henry to appear before a court composed of himself and Warham, on a charge of having unlawfully cohabited with his brother's widow when he was not lawfully married to her. Henry would plead guilty to the charge, and the court would then order him to separate from Catherine, and thus hold that his marriage to Catherine was invalid. Warham was probably invited to sit on the court with Wolsey because he had expressed doubts, twenty-five years before, about the validity of a marriage between Henry and Catherine.

When the court opened in Wolsey's house at York Place in Westminster on 17 May, only eight persons were present – Henry, Wolsey, Warham, and five lawyers, among them Wolsey's very able young secretary, Stephen Gardiner. The court sat again on 20, 27 and 31 May, but then adjourned and never met again. Apparently Henry or Wolsey realised that it was impossible to proceed by this secret method.[12] They decided to consult the bishops, and then in due course to apply to the Pope for the divorce. We do not know why they abandoned their original plan. Perhaps Warham refused to co-operate, for Henry afterwards stated that Warham was on Catherine's side in the divorce.

When the bishops were asked their opinion, most of them did what Henry and Wolsey expected of them, and said that the marriage of a man with his brother's widow was proved by the texts from Leviticus to be against God's law; but Fisher stated that the Papal dispensation of 1503 could not be void, because if there was a conflict between Leviticus and Deuteronomy, it was for the Pope to resolve it, as he had been given that power by Christ. By granting the dispensation, Julius II had impliedly ruled that the Deuteronomy text prevailed. The marriage between Henry and Catherine could therefore not be invalidated by any argument.[13]

Despite the efforts of Henry and Wolsey to keep it secret, Catherine had heard that Henry was taking steps to divorce her. She confronted Henry, and burst into tears; and when he told her that he had reluctantly reached the conclusion that their marriage was void and that they had been living in unlawful cohabitation for eighteen years, she made it clear that she would resist a divorce.[14] She also asserted, as she had always done, that her marriage with Arthur had not been consummated. Faced with these difficulties, Wolsey advised caution. He discussed the matter with Norfolk, Suffolk and Henry's chaplain, Richard Sampson, and suggested that no further steps should be taken till the Pope and François I had been consulted. Wolsey was about to set out in great state to visit François at Amiens to plan further action against Charles. He would be able to discuss 'the King's secret matter', as the divorce proceedings were called, with François at Amiens.

When Sampson told Henry about his conversation with Wolsey, Henry was not pleased with Wolsey's attitude. On 1 July, two days before Wolsey left London for Amiens, Henry sent Dr Wolman to York Place to tell Wolsey that he regretted that Wolsey was lukewarm about the divorce. Wolsey immediately wrote to Henry, assuring him, 'at the reverence of God, Sir, and most humbly prostrate at your feet', that no one was more eager for the divorce than he. He had merely pointed out to Sampson that if Catherine continued to deny that her marriage with Arthur had been consummated, this would not help her argument; because if her marriage to Arthur had not been consummated, this would raise the bar, not of 'affinity' but of 'public honesty', to prevent her subsequent marriage to Henry; and that as there had been no express reference to the bar of public honesty in the dispensation of 1503, it could be argued that the dispensation had not authorised Catherine's marriage to Henry.[15]

Although Henry fully appreciated the point, and used the argument on three occasions,[16] it was never emphasized in any of the many dispatches and books in which the case for the divorce was argued. No one attached any importance to it for four hundred and forty years, until Dr Scarisbrick, in his biography of Henry VIII in 1968, put it forward as the key argument which alone could, and probably would, have won the case for Henry. Dr Scarisbrick believes that it was not put forward because Henry, having thought out the argument based on Leviticus, was too stupid to realise that, although the Leviticus argument was unsound, this point which Wolsey had thought out could win his case; for whatever political influences might have been brought to bear on Clement, he would have been much more likely to hold for Henry if Henry had had a sound case in law. The opportunity was lost because Henry, with his 'pigheadedness', insisted on maintaining that Catherine's marriage to Arthur had been consummated, whereas he should, in his own interests, have accepted her assertion that it was not. Professor Elton has gone even further, stating that Henry 'failed to grasp the one suggestion of Wolsey's which could have assured immediate success'.[17]

This picture of Henry as the obstinate blunderer, who was too stupid to understand the point so brilliantly appreciated by the clever Cardinal, is quite untenable. It was Henry's shrewd political instinct and his common sense which made him base his case on Leviticus, and insist that the marriage of Arthur and Catherine had been consummated. The argument based on the omission of a reference to public honesty in the dispensation of 1503 was an extreme example of legal casuistry. Even if a dispensation from the greater impediment of affinity did not by implication extend to the lesser impediment of public honesty, the argument that a non-consummated marriage with Arthur was a bar to Catherine's marriage to Henry, whereas a consummated marriage was not, was a technical point so utterly devoid of merit that it could only have been accepted by a court that was determined to find some ground, however spurious, to hold for Henry. Even if the Leviticus argument was rejected by the majority of the early fathers of the Church, it was nevertheless very much stronger than this piece of sophistry which Wolsey put forward tentatively, but never seriously maintained.

As the text of Leviticus was always interpreted as applying only to a consummated marriage, Henry maintained that the marriage of Arthur and Catherine had been consummated, which Catherine always denied. Only two people knew the truth, for only two people knew whether Catherine had come to Henry's bed in 1509 as a virgin. These two people were Catherine and Henry. One of them was lying, and it was probably Henry. Once he had asserted that the marriage of Arthur and Catherine had been consummated, he could not accept her denial without admitting that he had lied.

There was an even more important reason why Henry could not adopt Wolsey's line of argument on the public honesty point. It would have meant staking everything on the hope of persuading the Pope to accept the argument, and throwing away the alternative possibility of invalidating the marriage to Catherine by appealing to God's law against the Pope. If, in the last resort, Henry led England into schism with the support of those who disliked the Pope, and appealed to the authority of the Bible against the authority of the Church, he could do so by putting the Word of God before a Papal bull; but he could not lead England into schism in order to maintain the principle that a dispensation from a greater impediment did not imply a dispensation from a lesser one.

Although we do not really know why Henry turned against Wolsey, all the contemporary writers agree that Anne Boleyn played the leading part in it; and there are many indications that Henry first began to lose confidence in Wolsey in the summer of 1527. On 18 May, Mendoza wrote to Charles V that Wolsey's position was in danger, that Norfolk and Tunstal, the Bishop of London, were the leaders of a group of Henry's counsellors who were working to overthrow him, and that Henry was thinking of appointing Tunstal Lord Chancellor in Wolsey's place.[18]

On 3 July, Wolsey left London for Amiens. On his way, he stayed at Rochester, where he tried to persuade Fisher to abandon his opposition to the divorce. He told Fisher that during the recent negotiations with the French envoys in London, the Bishop of Tarbes had raised some objection to Princess Mary's marriage to the Dauphin, on the grounds that Mary might be illegitimate if Henry's marriage to his brother's widow was against God's law. If the Bishop of Tarbes had in fact raised this issue, it is unlikely that he did so without some encouragement from Henry or Wolsey.[19]

When Wolsey reached Dover, he found that Henry had sent him a red deer to eat, which he himself had killed when hunting; and Henry's secretary, Dr Knight, wrote to him that Henry was very pleased with his efforts at Rochester to persuade Fisher to change his mind about the divorce. Wolsey stayed for eleven days in Calais, because of the wet and stormy weather in that very bad summer.[20] He received a letter in Calais from Knight, requiring his co-operation in a little plot which Henry had devised against Catherine. Henry was sure that Catherine would try to inform Charles that he had started divorce proceedings against her; and as he did not know that Mendoza knew and had already told Charles, he was determined to prevent Catherine from sending a messenger to Charles.

The King and Queen entered into a competition in deception. Catherine decided to send her Spanish physician, Francisco Felipez, to Spain with a letter to Charles. She told Henry that Felipez had asked for a passport to go to Spain to visit his mother, who was ill; but in order to lull Henry's suspicions, she pretended that she did not wish Felipez to go, and asked Henry to refuse him the passport. Henry saw through the trick, but pretended that he had been fooled, as he did not want Catherine to know that he wished to stop her communicating with Charles. He therefore granted Felipez the passport, but wrote to Wolsey in Calais, telling him to arrange with François to waylay Felipez as he passed through France, and to arrest him and confiscate any letter that he was carrying from Catherine to Charles. Wolsey wrote back that he could arrange for this to be done if Felipez travelled overland through France, but that he would be unable to stop him if he went from England to Spain by sea, and he urged Henry to prevent Felipez from travelling by sea. If Felipez went by sea, Henry's ambassador in Spain, Fitzwilliam, should be warned, so that he could stop and search Felipez between the Spanish port and Charles's court at Valladolid. But Felipez, having obtained the passport, travelled by sea and reached Valladolid safely in less than a fortnight. On 29 July, Charles wrote to Mendoza, informing him that Felipez had arrived with Catherine's letter, and how shocked he was to hear about the divorce proceedings. He added that he would do all he could to help the Queen his aunt.[21]

While Wolsey was in Calais, he received an unwelcome communication from the King. Henry had asked Wolsey to appoint a priest whom Henry favoured to a benefice in Calais which Wolsey claimed was in his gift as Lord Chancellor. Wolsey wrote to Henry that he had on three occasions presented one of Henry's nominees to a benefice in Calais, but that he wished to give this benefice to one of his own chaplains. Henry's chaplain, Wolman, replied on 26 July from Beaulieu in Hampshire, where Henry was staying. He wrote that Henry had been informed by two of his officials who had recently been in Calais that the right of presentation to benefices in Calais did not belong to the Lord Chancellor, but to the King, and that they had informed Wolsey of this, but that Wolsey had suppressed their report, and had not told Henry about it. Wolman wrote to Wolsey that the King 'is surprised that, without asking his pleasure, you should attempt to give away the said benefices, considering that you have formerly defended his title against all others; and his opinion of you is that you would rather yield part of what is due to your office than wittingly attempt anything against his prerogative which might be a precedent to your successors'. Wolman added that if in fact the right of presentation belonged to Wolsey, Henry thanked him for having presented his nominees; and that Henry, as the rightful patron, would always be willing to present Wolsey's chaplains if Wolsey asked him to do so.[22]

At Amiens, Wolsey was received with great honour by François, who treated him as an equal, not as the subject of a foreign King. He later went with François from Amiens to Compiègne for further talks and banquets. He agreed with François that Henry and François should instruct their ambassadors in Spain to demand from Charles that he should free François' sons, despite the fact that François had not performed the treaty and had announced that he did not intend to do so; and the French and English ambassadors were also to demand that Charles should repay the money which Henry had lent him to pay for the cost of the war. If Charles refused, the ambassadors were authorised, as a last resort, to declare war; but Henry and Wolsey hoped that this would not be necessary.[23]

Henry now took a step in his 'great matter' without consulting Wolsey. He sent his secretary, Dr Knight, to Rome to ask the Pope to grant him a conditional dispensation which would enable him, if his marriage to Queen Catherine should be declared a nullity, to marry the sister of a woman who had been his mistress; for, in the absence of a dispensation, Henry's adultery with Mary Carey would raise the bar of affinity to his marriage with her sister, Anne Boleyn. Knight wrote to Wolsey from Beaulieu that Henry was sending him to Rome, that he would be travelling through Compiègne, and that the King wanted Wolsey to arrange for him to have banking and other facilities on his journey. But Wolsey thought that it would be unwise for Knight to go to Rome, because Ghinucci and other officials at the Papal court were already handling Henry's case, and Knight's intervention could do more harm than good. Wolsey wrote and explained this to Henry, and added: 'If Your Grace will take a little patience . . . your intent shall honourably and lawfully take the desired effect'. He did not know the reason why Henry was sending Knight to Rome.[24]

When Knight reached Compiègne on 10 September, Wolsey took the responsibility of countermanding Henry's orders and ordered Knight to wait at Compiègne till Wolsey received Henry's reply to his letter. When Henry's reply came, it was not in the usual form of a letter from a secretary, but a personal letter from the King, written in the most friendly tone. Henry thanked Wolsey for his diligent service, 'which service cannot be by a kind master forgotten, of which fault I trust I shall never be accused, especially to yourward [towards you], which so laboriously do serve me'. But Henry added that after considering Wolsey's arguments, he had decided that Knight should go to Rome, because Henry had not sent an envoy to the Pope since his imprisonment by Charles's soldiers, and he thought it right that someone should go to express his sympathies for the Pope. Wolsey thereupon told Knight to go on to Italy, but to wait in Venice till the Pope's secretary, Cardinal Gambara, and Henry's Italian agent, Sir Gregory di Casale, told Knight that they had made the arrangements for Knight to gain access to the imprisoned Pope.[25]

It was the sort of disagreement about tactics which Henry and Wolsey had often had, and which had never in the past led to any ill-feeling between them. But Wolsey would have been worried if he had read the report of the incident which Knight wrote to Henry from Compiègne on 13 September, after the courier, Christopher Morres, had arrived there with Henry's letter to Wolsey; for Morres had also brought a letter from Henry to Knight. Knight wrote to Henry that he had read Henry's letter 'concerning your secret affair, which is to me only committed', and added:

'And where at my coming hither my Lord Legate [Wolsey] supposed to have so fully contented Your Highness, that by the coming of Christopher Morres I should have been by Your Grace countermanded, willing me therefore to abide and tarry for the said Christopher, I, for th'avoiding of suspicion, showed myself content so to do, being nevertheless determined to proceed in my journey, if the said Christopher had not come the next day; and now Your Grace's pleasure known, my Lord hath advised me to repair to Venice; which counsel cannot hinder Your Grace's purpose; for there being, if there be any possibility of access unto the Pope, I have commodity to pass by the sea, till within one hundred miles of Rome'.[26]

Henry was not only working with Knight behind Wolsey's back, but allowed Knight to write to him in the language of a fellow-conspirator against the Cardinal.

When Knight reached Rome, he found that Clement had escaped from the city, and had gone to Orvieto, where Knight had an interview with him on New Year's Day. Clement granted him the dispensation for Henry to marry the sister of his mistress if his marriage to Catherine was void, making it clear that this was without prejudice to the question of the validity of the marriage. Knight was the first of a stream of Henry's agents, both English and Italian, who pestered Clement throughout 1528; but neither he nor the others obtained anything except promises from the Pope. Wolsey, whatever he may originally have thought about the advisability of the divorce, was now exerting all his efforts to obtain it. He wrote again and again to Clement, stressing the purity of Henry's motives. It was quite wrong to suppose that the King was motivated by lust for a certain young gentlewoman; he was thinking only of his duty to provide his subjects with a male heir, in order to avoid civil war in England; and the young gentlewoman whom he intended to marry in order to produce the male heir was a model of virtue.

Almost from the beginning, Wolsey used the threat of schism in a barely concealed form. He reminded Clement that no King had been a more devoted son of the Church than Henry, the Defender of the Faith. If the Pope showed his gratitude by granting him the divorce, Henry would continue to render great services to the Church; but if the Pope was ungrateful and refused the divorce, thus imperilling the succession to the crown of England, Henry might be unable to prevent his indignant subjects from repudiating the Papal authority and setting up a schismatic Church.[27]

In February 1528, Wolsey sent Gardiner to Rome with another able young diplomat, Edward Fox. Travelling with the greatest possible speed through very difficult winter conditions, after being nearly shipwrecked during their thirty-hour crossing of the Channel, they covered the distance between Lyons and Orvieto in seventeen days, and reached Orvieto on 23 March.[28] They stayed there for three weeks, bullying the Pope and using increasingly threatening language. When Gardiner accused the Pope of ingratitude to Henry, Clement could only wipe away the tears from his eyes. Gardiner wrote to Wolsey:

'I said that I thought it God's will indeed, to the intent that, relation made by us of what condition men be here towards them who deserve everything, the favour of that Prince who now only favoureth them should be withdrawn and taken away, and that the Apostolic See should fall to pieces with the common consent and applause of everyone. At these words the Pope's Holiness, casting his arms abroad', agreed to Gardiner's demands, 'and therewith walked up and down the chamber, casting now and then his arms abroad, we standing in great silence'.*[29]

But the unfortunate Clement was under equally strong counter-pressure from Charles. If Henry could frighten the Pope with the threat of schism, Charles could frighten him with the prospect of another sack of Rome. The atrocity of May 1527 had been a political embarrassment to Charles, but also a useful reminder to the Pope and the cardinals of what could happen; if the Emperor were forced to order his troops into action against the Pope, then they might, to His Majesty's great regret, get out of hand, and loot, burn and rape in Rome for another twelve days.

Wolsey asked the Pope to grant him a decretal commission which would enable him, as Papal Legate, to try Henry's divorce case in England. Catherine found out his plan, and managed to communicate the information to Charles, whose ambassador protested to the Pope against allowing the case to be tried by so biassed a judge, and insisted that, as Catherine could not hope for justice in her husband's realm, the case should be tried in the Papal court in Rome. Clement's solution of his insoluble problem was to play for time by making contradictory promises to both sides; and he actually succeeded by these means in prevaricating for seven years. When Wolsey's agents asked him for the decretal commission, he delayed, adjourned the discussion, and eventually promised to grant it; when Charles's ambassador heard about this, and protested, the Pope promised that he would break his promise to the English representatives. The next time Clement promised to grant Wolsey the commission, Wolsey's agents insisted that he should promise not to break his promise. He promised this 'on the word of a Roman Pontiff',[30] and then promised Charles's ambassador that he would break this promise too.

At Palencia, the English and French ambassadors presented an ultimatum to Charles. He must release François from the terms of the Treaty of Madrid, under which François had agreed to cede the French provinces of Burgundy and to relinquish his claim to Milan; and as for the war indemnity of 2,000,000 crowns which François had agreed, in the treaty, to pay to Charles, François would pay only 1,200,000 crowns to Charles, and the balance of 800,000 crowns to Henry in satisfaction of Charles's debt to Henry. Charles must also release François' sons. Charles agreed, as his final offer, to waive his claim to the provinces of Burgundy, but insisted that François abandon his claim to Milan and pay him the whole of the 2,000,000 crowns; for though he admitted that he owed a debt to Henry, he disputed the amount, and said

*Some of the words in this passage in Gardiner's letter were written in Latin.

that Henry, by asking too much, had forfeited the whole sum under the usury laws. The French and English ambassadors then told their heralds to go to Charles and declare war, giving as the reason the fact that Charles had sacked Rome and was holding the Pope a prisoner. Charles, in his reply to the 'defiance', from Henry and François made an unprecedented attack on a subject of a foreign sovereign, saying that Wolsey was alone responsible for the declaration of war. He urged Margaret of Austria to arrange to smuggle leaflets into England, blaming Wolsey for the war.[31]

Henry and Wolsey were annoyed that war had broken out, and scolded Ghinucci and Lee, their ambassadors at Charles's court. They told them that though Henry had given them power to declare war, they had expected them to refer the matter back to him before doing so; and they accused them of having been stampeded into declaring war by their French colleague. They made an agreement with Margaret of Austria to allow trade to continue between England and the Netherlands, and took no military action whatever against Charles. The policy of Henry and Wolsey remained what it had been before the declaration of war: they would pay money to other states to fight against Charles in Italy without England being involved. They persuaded François and Charles to agree to a truce, which was signed at Hampton Court in June 1528, by which hostilities 'this side of the mountains' – that is to say, north of the Alps – were to cease for eight months, while the fighting continued in Italy.[32] There the French at first defeated the Imperial forces, and a French army, commanded by Albany, successfully invaded Charles's kingdom of Naples; but by the end of 1528, Charles's armies had gained the upper hand.

12

THE TRIAL AT BLACKFRIARS

HENRY's subjects had never been so angry with the government. The terrible summer of 1527 had badly hit the harvest, and there was a serious food shortage next winter. The farmers hoarded the little corn they had, and by June 1528 the price had risen from 1s.6d. to 2s.6d. a bushel. Commissioners were sent all over the country to inspect the farmers' stocks and force them to sell all the surplus corn that they did not need for themselves and their families. The outbreak of war with the Emperor aroused fears that an embargo would be imposed in the Netherlands banning the import of English wool, and the clothiers dismissed many of their workmen, thus causing unemployment in the districts which depended on the wool trade.

In the spring and early summer of 1528, there were riots among the unemployed workmen at Westbury, Taunton, Bridgwater, Colchester, and in Suffolk. But again, as in 1525, the Tonbridge district of Kent was one of the worst trouble-centres. The villagers of Tonbridge, Penshurst, Speldhurst, Bidborough and Sevenoaks marched together to Warham's palace at Knole, and presented him with a petition demanding that the King repay the money which the people had lent to him under the Amicable Grant three years before. Henry ordered Rochford and the gentlemen of Kent to find the man who had written the villagers' petition. There were rumours that the writer was Thomas Messer of Hawkhurst. He was arrested on a false charge of threatening the vicar of Hawkhurst in a quarrel, and then questioned about the petition; but nothing could be proved against him.[1]

A few weeks later, a more serious plot was discovered. Some working men at Goudhurst discussed a plan for seizing the local gentlemen at Bedgbury, Haddon and Scotney Castle, and holding them as hostages; then, having captured the armoury at Rye, they would march on London, join the discontented artisans there, and seize Wolsey. As it would be wrong to kill a cardinal, they would put him in a boat, pierce holes in the bottom, and send the boat out to sea with Wolsey in it. When they told a man of Cranbrook about their plan, he said that he knew fifty men of Cranbrook who would join them. But they had talked too much, and the ringleaders were captured and condemned to death for high treason at Rochester assizes.[2] Everywhere Wolsey was held responsible for all misfortunes – for the food shortage, the taxes, and the war with Burgundy.

To add to all the other troubles, there was a particularly virulent outbreak of the sweating sickness in June 1528. Henry, as usual, left London, and moved to Hertfordshire, first to Hunsdon and then to Wolsey's house at Tyttenhanger. Wolsey himself was at Hampton Court, where he caught the sweat, as did several ladies and gentlemen of the court – the Lady Marquess of Exeter, Sir Thomas Cheyney, Norris, Wallop, and others. One of Anne Boleyn's servants caught it, and Henry, to his great distress, felt obliged to send Anne away. She went to her father's house at Hever. Henry wrote to her about his anxiety, though he took comfort from the fact that women were much less likely to catch the sweat than men; but she and her brother George both caught it. Henry sent his physician, Dr Butts, to Hever to care for her. She and her brother survived, and, like all the other survivors of the sweat, recovered quickly; but her brother-in-law, Sir William Carey, died of it. Sir William Compton and other courtiers also died.

Henry had only a handful of attendants with him at Hunsdon. He withdrew to a tower, and stayed indoors, for it was thought that fresh air increased the risk of infection; and he attended Mass three times a day. One of the few people with him was his secretary, Brian Tuke, who had had the sweat, but had recovered. Tuke believed that fear was the chief cause of the sweat, for he noticed that Englishmen, who were so afraid of it, were the only people who caught it. In France and Flanders, it was called the King of England's sickness. When it raged at Calais, it never spread to Gravelines; and children never caught it, unless their parents talked to them about it. But when there was a rumour that a man had brought it from Sussex to London, a thousand people fell ill with it that night; and after it had reached London, whenever a healthy man came from London to a town and talked about the sweat, the same night all the town was full of it. The French ambassador, Jean Du Bellay, had also noticed that it was not as dangerous as it was supposed to be; for although 40,000 people had caught it in London, only 2,000 of them had died.

Henry was calmer than usual about the sweating sickness. As the danger increased, he became more philosophical and resigned to it, being perhaps encouraged by Tuke's attitude. Hennege, who was also at Hunsdon, wrote to Wolsey on 23 June that Henry was very merry. When he heard that there had been a case of the sweat in Wolsey's household at Hampton Court, he was most solicitous about Wolsey's well-being. He ordered Tuke to write a comforting letter to Wolsey, pointing out that there was little danger from the sweat if sensible precautions were taken, that few people had died of it, and that Anne Boleyn and her brother had recovered quickly when they had it. He advised Wolsey to move away from any district in which there was a case of the sweat, to have only a few people with him, 'to use small suppers and to drink little wine', and once a week to take the pills of Rosis. If Wolsey did catch the sickness, he should allow the sweat to escape and not keep it within his body, 'with more good wholesome counsel by His Highness in most tender and loving manner given to Your Grace'.[3]

Three weeks later, Wolsey received a very different kind of letter from Henry. The Abbess of Wilton had recently died, and the nuns of the convent had to elect her successor. Although these elections were supposed to be free, it was the usual practice for powerful patrons to indicate to the nuns the candidate whom they favoured, and Wolsey had for many years made a habit of doing this. He now sent his agent, Dr Bell, to Wilton to tell the nuns to elect their Prioress, Lady Isabel Jordan, as the new Abbess. But one of the nuns in the convent was Dame Eleanor Carey, the sister of Sir William Carey; and when Sir William was dying of the sweat, he made a last request to his sister-in-law, Anne Boleyn, to arrange for Eleanor to be elected Abbess of Wilton. Henry wrote to Wolsey and asked him to do this.

But Wolsey was not prepared to allow Anne's nominee to be promoted over the Prioress's head. He found out that many years before, Eleanor Carey had had two illegitimate children by a priest, and had more recently had a love affair with one of Lord Broke's servants. When Henry heard this, he wrote to Anne and stated that in view of Eleanor's past misconduct she would not be a suitable abbess; nor could he suggest to Wolsey that he appoint Sir William Carey's other sister, who had led an equally immoral life. But Henry had discovered that Isabel Jordan had also had lovers in the past; and he therefore ordered Wolsey to choose a fourth person as Abbess. Wolsey disregarded this instruction; and when Henry remonstrated, he expressed his regret, and wrote that he had not realised that Henry objected to the appointment of Isabel Jordan, though Henry had in fact made his attitude perfectly clear.[4]

Henry wrote a long personal letter to Wolsey from Ampthill on 14 July. He explained that 'the great affection and love' that he felt for Wolsey had led him to follow the doctrine of his master Christ, and say 'He whom I esteem, I castigate'.

'Wherefore whatsoever I do say, I pray think it spoken of no displeasure, but of him that would you as much good both of body and soul as you would yourself. Methink it is not the right train of a truly loving friend and servant, when the matter is put by the master's consent into his arbiter and judgment (specially in a matter wherein his master hath both royalty and interest) to elect and choose a person which was by him defended [forbidden]. And yet another thing which much displeaseth me more, that is, to cloak your offence made, by ignorance of my pleasure'.

He then proceeded to deal with another matter – the methods by which Wolsey was extorting money from the monasteries for his college at Ipswich.

'Since hitherto I have played both the part of a master and friend, methinketh, yet once more I must occupy the same, desiring you to take it in good part, for surely I do it upon no other ground, but for the wealth of your soul and mind; and because I dare be bolder with you than a great many that mumble it abroad'.

He wrote that it was being widely reported that Wolsey was extorting money from the religious houses unlawfully; and Henry had difficulty in believing that they had contributed to Wolsey's college at Ipswich from their own free will, in view of the reluctance which they had shown when they had been asked to make the Amicable Grant for the war against France. He ended the letter by assuring Wolsey that it was 'written with the hand of him that is and shall be your loving sovereign lord and friend, Henry R.'[5]

Hennege wrote to Wolsey on the same day, no doubt at Henry's orders, and told Wolsey that Henry had read his letter to him aloud to Russell and Hennege, and had then expressed the high regard which he had for Wolsey and the friendly spirit in which he had admonished him.[6] Wolsey replied with a submissive and repentant letter. Henry then wrote a friendly letter to Wolsey. He stated that the matter of the Abbess of Wilton was not very important.

'Wherefore, my Lord, seeing the humbleness of your submission, and though the case were much more heinous, I can be content for to remit it, being right glad that, according to mine intent, my monitions and warnings have been benignly and lovingly accepted on your behalf, promising you, that the very affection I bear you caused me thus to do. As touching the help of religious houses to the building of your college, I would it were more, so it be lawfully; for my intent is none but that it should appear to all the world, and the occasion of all their mumbling might be secluded and put away; for surely there is great murmuring of it throughout all the realm'.[7]

Wolsey expressed his gratitude to Henry, and stated that he would not accept any more gifts for his college from any monastery, however willingly it was offered; but he continued to disregard Henry's wishes about Wilton. He immediately sent Benet to Wilton to force the nuns, against their wishes, to elect Isabel Jordan as abbess. Benet imprisoned three or four of the nuns, and locked the doors of the nunnery to prevent anyone from entering or leaving till they had chosen Isabel Jordan.[8]

Wolsey was making no attempt to placate the nobility or the people; and he thought that he could keep Henry happy by writing humble letters of apology and by sending gifts to Anne Boleyn. Anne wrote him a delightful letter of thanks:

'My Lord, in my most humble wise that my poor heart can think, I do thank Your Grace for your kind letter, and for your rich and goodly present .... all the days of my life, I am most bound, of all creatures, next the King's Grace, to love and serve Your Grace'.[9]

Wolsey was convinced that he held a trump card in his hand: Henry's belief that Wolsey, and Wolsey alone, could persuade the Pope to grant him the divorce. Wolsey's agents in Italy at last succeeded, in July 1528, in badgering the Pope into granting a decretal commission to Wolsey to act as the judge in Henry's divorce case, despite the insistent demands of the Emperor's ambassador that the case should not be tried in England. But Wolsey realised that no one would believe that the court was impartial if he were the only judge in the case; so he asked the Pope to appoint Cardinal Campeggio, who was Bishop of Salisbury and had always been sympathetic to Henry's interests, to sit as Wolsey's fellow-judge.[10] This gave Clement an opportunity for further delays. Campeggio, who had the excuse that he was ill, travelled as slowly as possible from Rome to England.

Henry and Anne were impatiently awaiting his arrival. Anne wrote to Wolsey to ask when Campeggio would be arriving, and took the opportunity to inquire about his health. She wrote that she could never repay the great pains which he took for her, both day and night, 'but alonely in loving you, next unto the King's Grace, above all creatures living'. Henry added a passage in his own hand at the end of her letter:

'The writer of this letter would not cease till she had caused me likewise to set to my hand. . . . The not hearing of the Legate's arrival in France causeth us somewhat to muse; notwithstanding, we trust by your diligence and vigilancy (with the assistance of Almighty God) shortly to be eased out of that trouble. No more to you at this time; but that I pray God send you as good health, prosperity, as the writer would. By your loving sovereign and friend, Henry R.'

To which Anne added her signature: 'Your humble servant, Anne Boleyn'.[11]

While Henry waited for Campeggio, he received bad news from Scotland. James V escaped from the custody of Angus and Sir George Douglas at Falkland Palace, and joined Henry's old opponent, the Archbishop of St Andrews, at Stirling. They were supported by Queen Margaret, who had been granted a divorce from Angus by the Pope, and had married Henry Stewart. Angus and Sir George Douglas were tried, in their absence, by the Scottish Parliament on a charge of high treason for having plotted to deliver James V as a prisoner to Henry VIII. They were condemned to death, and their lands were forfeited to the King. James besieged Angus's castle of Tantallon on the sea near North Berwick; and though he failed to capture Tantallon, and the Douglases held out for some months in the Border regions, they were eventually forced to take refuge at Berwick.

Henry protested to James against the accusation that the Douglases had plotted to surrender James to him, and assured James that they were his loyal subjects. Dacre mustered men in Northumberland to be ready to intervene in Scotland, but Henry did not order them to cross the Border. After urging the Douglases to remain in Scotland and to fight against James's army, he granted them asylum in Northumberland when further resistance on their part was impossible. James protested to Henry that he was sheltering his traitors, but agreed to remit the death sentence imposed on them, though not their conviction for treason and the forfeiture of their property.[12]

It was a signal defeat for Henry. It showed clearly that now that James was aged sixteen, he would no longer be a pawn in the hands of Henry's agents.

Henry, on his progress at Easthampstead, sent Wolsey the only red deer that he had killed in ten hours' hunting in Windsor Great Park.[13] He was at Guildford when he heard that Campeggio had reached Paris, and on returning from hunting he wrote at 11 p.m. to Anne Boleyn:

'The Legate, which we most desire, arrived at Paris on Sunday or Monday last past; so that I trust, by the next Monday, to hear of his arrival at Calais; and then I trust, within a while after, to enjoy that which I have so long longed for, to God's pleasure, and our both comforts. No more to you, at this present, mine own darling, for lack of time; but that I would you were in mine arms, or I in yours; for I think it long since I kissed you. Written after the killing of an hart, at eleven of the clock; minding with God's grace tomorrow mightily timely to kill another, by the hand which I trust shortly shall be yours, Henry R.'[14]

It seems clear, from this letter, that Anne was still resisting him.

At last, on 29 September, Campeggio landed at Dover; but he had to travel in a litter because of his gout, and it took him another eight days to reach London. But Henry and Anne were disappointed in their hopes. Campeggio had received a letter in Paris from the Pope's secretary at Viterbo, telling him that in view of the Emperor's military successes in Italy, the Pope wished to do nothing which would give Charles an excuse to attack Rome. He was therefore ordering Campeggio to do all in his power to reconcile Henry and Catherine, and in any case not to give judgment in the divorce case without new and express instructions from Rome. When Campeggio informed his fellow-judge, Wolsey, about the Pope's order, Wolsey was shocked. He knew that this could have very serious consequences for himself.

Campeggio succeeded in spending nine months in London without starting the trial of the divorce. He was prepared to do anything except give judgement in the divorce case. He tried to persuade Catherine to enter a convent and submit to a divorce; when she refused, he tried to persuade Henry to abandon the divorce proceedings. He suggested that the Pope might grant a dispensation for Henry's daughter Mary to marry her illegitimate half-brother, the Duke of Richmond, who would be legitimised and would reign jointly with Mary as King and Queen after Henry's death. This offer satisfied nobody, and would probably have been retracted by the Pope if Henry had accepted it.[15]

As everyone in London seemed to know why Campeggio had come, Henry decided to inform his subjects officially about the divorce proceedings. He summoned the peers, the judges, the Lord Mayor and aldermen of London, and other dignitaries to his palace of Bridewell in London on 8 November, and made a long speech to them. He explained how necessary it was for the kingdom that he should have a male heir who would succeed him after his death, for otherwise there would be new wars like those between York and Lancaster which had formerly convulsed the realm. He said that he had been advised that he had been living in adultery with the Queen for twenty years, that she was not his wife, and that his dear daughter was a bastard. This had so disturbed his conscience that he had asked the greatest clerks in Christendom to advise him as to whether his marriage was lawful or not; this was the only reason why he had sent for Campeggio.

'And as touching the Queen, if it be adjudged by the law of God that she is my lawful wife, there was never thing more pleasant nor more acceptable to me in my life, both for the discharge and clearing of my conscience and also for the good qualities and conditions the which I know to be in her. For I assure you all, that beside her noble parentage of the which she is descended (as all you know), she is a woman of most gentleness, of most humility and buxomness, yea and of all good qualities appertaining to nobility, she is without comparison, as I this twenty years almost have had the true experiment, so that if I were to marry again, if the marriage might be good I would surely choose her above all other women. But if it be determined by judgment that our marriage was against God's law and clearly void, then I shall not only sorrow the departing from so good a lady and loving companion, but much more lament and bewail my infortunate chance that I have so long lived in adultery to God's great displeasure, and have no true heir of my body to inherit this realm'.[16]

All this, of course, was a lie; and most of Henry's subjects guessed it. There was strong sympathy for Catherine in London, especially among the women.[17]

In January 1529, the Pope fell seriously ill, and a report reached London that he had died. Henry and Wolsey put the strongest pressure on the cardinals to elect Wolsey as the new Pope. Henry's letter to Gardiner and his other agents in Rome went further than he had ever gone in impliedly threatening a schism. He stated that his divorce case could only be decided by the favour of the Head of the Church, for he was reluctant to have recourse to any special remedy, other than the authority of the See Apostolic, if he could find favour there according to his merits. He could only be sure of this if Wolsey were elected Pope, and no other Pope would be acceptable to him. Gardiner must offer any bribes which were necessary to secure Wolsey's election; if another candidate were chosen, Wolsey's supporters should withdraw from the conclave and elect Wolsey at a rival conclave in another town. Henry would be prepared to provide the money to pay three thousand soldiers to overawe the conclave and force them to vote for Wolsey; but he added that, in the last resort, he would be prepared to accept Campeggio as Pope.[18]

A few days later, it was known in London that the Pope had not died, and had recovered from his illness.

At last, on 31 May 1529 – more than two years after Henry had first begun the divorce proceedings – Wolsey and Campeggio opened their court at the Blackfriars church near Ludgate in London.[19] But Campeggio was determined to take advantage of every opportunity for delay which was provided by the notoriously slow procedure of the Roman courts; and after the first session, the court adjourned till 18 June. Henry and Catherine were both summoned to appear on that day. Henry came to the court, and through his proctor, Gardiner, submitted to the jurisdiction of the court; but Catherine, appearing in person and ignoring the proctors who had been appointed to represent her, knelt at Henry's feet and begged him to take pity on her, as she was a friendless foreigner in his realm. She said that she was his loving wife, and asked him to bear witness to the fact that she had come to his bed a virgin. She then turned to Wolsey and Campeggio, and informed them that she did not recognise the authority of the court, and appealed for the case to be heard by the court of the Pope in Rome. Her intervention caused a great sensation among the public, and aroused widespread sympathy for her.

It was very embarrassing for Henry, but he handled the situation as well as possible in the circumstances. He told the court, and the audience attending the trial, that he had always had the highest regard for Catherine, and that only the dictates of his conscience and his duty to observe God's law would have made him abandon so noble a woman. He did not answer her question as to whether she had come to his bed as a virgin.[20]

Wolsey and Campeggio rejected Catherine's appeal to 'advoke' the case to Rome, pronounced her contumacious for refusing to submit to their jurisdiction, and ruled that the trial should continue in her absence. They then sat for several weeks, hearing evidence as to whether Catherine's marriage to Arthur had been consummated twenty-eight years before. Aged lords, ladies, gentlemen and domestic servants told of what they had seen and heard on the wedding night in November 1501 – how the Prince of Wales had looked pale and seemed tired next morning, and that he had told the gentlemen of his bedchamber that he had been 'in the midst of Spain' during the night. But Henry's case received another set-back at the session on 28 June. Fisher, who was present, like the other bishops, as an observer at the trial, said that as the King had asked all the bishops, two years ago, to give their opinions about the divorce, he would now say that he believed that Henry's marriage to Catherine was valid. He thought that the Pope's dispensation of 1503 had removed all impediments to the marriage; and in any case a marriage should not be annulled, without overpowering reasons, after it had lasted for twenty years. Fisher's statement made a great impression on the public.[21]

Wolsey's great fear was that the Pope would comply with Catherine's request to advoke the case to Rome. This would be a disaster for which Henry would never forgive him. He wrote to Sir Gregory di Casale, one of his agents in Rome, that Casale must at all costs prevent the advocation of the case to Rome. 'For you may constantly affirm unto His Holiness that if he should at any Prince's suit grant the said advocation, he should not only thereby lose the King and devotion of this realm from him and the See Apostolic, but also utterly destroy me for ever'.[22]

But though Wolsey worked so desperately for the divorce, Henry suspected that he might be trying to prevent it. Two years before, Henry had suggested that Wolsey was not whole-heartedly in favour of the divorce;[23] and this suspicion increased as one snag after another arose to prevent him from obtaining the divorce and enjoying Anne as his wife.

Ever since January, François and Charles had been engaged in secret peace negotiations without informing Henry and Wolsey. In May they announced that Margaret of Austria would meet Louise d'Angoulême, who was the sister of Margaret's dead husband, the Duke of Savoy, in peace talks at Cambrai. Wolsey would have liked to go to Cambrai; but as he was detained in London by the divorce trial, Tunstal and More were sent instead.

Henry and Wolsey sent Suffolk to Paris to discuss the peace terms with François. But Henry had given Suffolk his own private instructions on another point. He told him to ask François whether Wolsey had said anything, when he was at Amiens and Compiègne, which indicated that he was opposed to Henry's divorce. François gave an ambiguous reply which was undoubtedly intended to sow suspicion of Wolsey in Henry's mind, and thus weaken the position of a minister who had done so much harm to France in the past: François said that when he had discussed Henry's divorce with Wolsey, the Cardinal had seemed to favour it, but that Henry should beware of trusting so powerful a minister. The French ambassador in London, Du Bellay, told Wolsey about François' conversation with Suffolk, and Wolsey protested to Henry in Suffolk's presence. Suffolk tried to excuse himself; but Wolsey's protest probably did him more harm than good in Henry's eyes, as it suggested that he was on very intimate terms with the French ambassador.[24]

As we read today the many letters which Wolsey wrote to the Pope and the Papal officials, and to Henry's agents in Italy, with his long, passionate, and sometimes desperate appeals to them to obtain the divorce which Henry desired, it seems extraordinarily unjust that Henry should have suspected that he was not working ardently for his cause. But though the letters that Wolsey wrote to Rome were strongly in favour of the divorce, how could Henry be sure that he was not also writing other letters, which he did not show to Henry, containing very different suggestions to the Pope? No one knew better than Henry what a consummate liar Wolsey was. He and Wolsey were in the position of two partners in fraud who could never be sure that the other was not double-crossing them. Henry knew how Wolsey had plotted with Charles to make war on France while he was making a show of friendship to Du Prat and the French delegates at Calais; how he had deceived Ferdinand of Aragon, Maximilian and Charles, and had twice made peace with the French while protesting that he would never do so; how only a few months before, he had arranged for Henry secretly to join the Holy League in Italy while he was assuring Charles that Henry would not join it. Was he now secretly telling the Pope to ignore the letters in which he pretended to be so eager for Henry's divorce? In fact Wolsey, however often he had double-crossed foreign sovereigns, had always been true to Henry. But could Henry be sure of this?

Events in Italy and Spain proved too strong for Wolsey. The Pope had finally decided to come down on Charles's side. On 29 June, his Nuncio in Barcelona signed a treaty of alliance with Charles, by which the Pope's nephew was to marry Charles's illegitimate daughter. The treaty was signed before news had arrived in Barcelona that Charles's army in Italy had defeated the French at Landriano. The Treaty of Barcelona and the victory of Landriano outweighed all the arguments of Wolsey's agents in Rome. On 6 July, the Pope informed Casale that he had decided to advoke Henry's divorce case to Rome; twelve months before, he had promised that he would never do so.[25]

The news of the Pope's decision reached Campeggio and Wolsey in London at eight o'clock in the evening on 22 July.[26] Next day, the court reassembled at Blackfriars. A rumour had circulated that the Legates would give judgement for Henry on that day; Henry himself was present, and the church was crowded with spectators. When the proceedings opened, Campeggio announced that in view of the number of documents which had to be examined, the court could not give judgement that day; and as it was impossible for the court to sit during the law vacations of the courts in Rome, the trial was adjourned until October. There was a shocked silence in the church, which was broken by Suffolk, who cried out angrily: 'It was never merry in England whilst we had cardinals among us'.

According to Cavendish, Suffolk's words were received in shocked silence by everyone in the hall. Then Suffolk repeated them in an even more violent tone. Wolsey replied that no man had less reason than Suffolk to complain of cardinals, for if there had not been one cardinal in England once, Suffolk would have lost his head – a reference to the fact that Wolsey's intervention had saved Suffolk when he married Mary the French Queen in 1515. Cavendish wrote that as soon as Suffolk began to speak these words for the first time, Henry walked out and went to his palace at Bridewell.[27]

Suffolk's outburst of anger was probably not spontaneous. He would hardly have ventured to say what he did about cardinals without consulting Henry, or at least saying enough to the King to receive a clear indication that such words would meet with Henry's approval. As Wolsey had received Casale's letter at 8 p.m. on the previous day, with the news that the Pope had decided to advoke the case to Rome, he must have known, or guessed, some twelve hours before, what Campeggio was going to do at the hearing on 23 July; and he would have told Henry, well in time for Henry to arrange for Suffolk's intervention, and to decide to walk out of the church at Blackfriars at the very moment when Suffolk began to speak.

Everyone knew what Suffolk's words meant, and the news spread at once through London, through England, and through Europe that Wolsey had fallen from power.[28]

13

THE DESTRUCTION OF WOLSEY

AFTER the sensational scene in the Blackfriars church on 23 July, Henry gave no indication that he was displeased with Wolsey. He remained for a week at Greenwich before starting out on a progress. Wolsey's secretary, Gardiner, had entered the King's service after distinguishing himself in his work for the divorce in Italy and as Henry's proctor at the trial at Blackfriars; and he wrote to Wolsey from Greenwich and from the houses where Henry stayed on his progress, assuring Wolsey that Henry was satisfied with the way in which he handled various matters of routine which arose during Henry's absence.[1]

On 2 August, Henry moved from Greenwich to Waltham, and Gardiner and his colleague Edward Fox stayed at the house of Master Cressy. A Cambridge doctor of divinity, Thomas Cranmer, was also staying in the house as tutor to Cressy's sons. At supper they discussed the King's divorce, and the deadlock that seemed to have been reached after the trial at Blackfriars. Cranmer suggested to Gardiner and Fox that the issue of the lawfulness of Henry's marriage should not be decided by the canon lawyers in the ecclesiastical courts, but by theologians in the universities.* Gardiner and Fox were sufficiently impressed by Cranmer's suggestion to mention the matter to Henry, and to arrange for Cranmer to meet the King at Greenwich some time later. According to John Foxe, Henry, after talking to Cranmer, said that Cranmer 'hath the sow by the right ear'.[2] Thus Gardiner was responsible for bringing into public life the hitherto unknown Cambridge scholar who was to become his bitter enemy for twenty years at the summit of power in Church and State.

As Henry proceeded on his progress, the official Papal decree arrived

*Ralph Morice, who some years later became Cranmer's secretary, wrote an account of this meeting for Archbishop Parker in about 1565. John Foxe slightly misunderstood what Morice had written. Foxe's well-known statement that Cranmer suggested an appeal to the universities is basically correct, but misses the point, which was the all-important one to Cranmer, that it was an issue for theologians, not canonists.

advoking the divorce case to the Papal court in Rome, thus prohibiting the court at Blackfriars from reopening in October.[3] News also arrived that a peace treaty had been agreed at Cambrai between Margaret of Austria for Charles and Louise d'Angoulême for François. Henry's representatives, Tunstal and More, were effectively shut out of the talks at Cambrai, and were not even able to obtain a copy of the treaty. It was a victory for Charles and a defeat for François and Henry. François agreed to abandon his claim to Milan and to cede Tournai and other towns in Flanders to Charles, though Charles agreed to allow François to retain the French provinces of Burgundy, while reserving his right to demand them at some time in the future. From Henry's point of view, the worst feature of the peace was that François agreed to pay to Charles the whole of the war indemnity of two million crowns due from him under the Treaty of Madrid without deducting the 800,000 crowns which Charles owed to Henry; and François agreed to accept liability for repaying Charles's debt to Henry.[4] This meant that Henry would get nothing from Charles. Henry adhered to the Treaty of Cambrai, as he had no alternative.

Henry had not shown any sign of annoyance with Wolsey; but Wolsey was worried at being out of touch with Henry at such a time. He wrote to Gardiner that he had matters which he wished to discuss with Henry, and suggested that he should visit him at Woodstock; but Gardiner replied that Henry was sure that Wolsey could just as well write to him about the matter.[5] Wolsey then found another excuse to visit Henry: Campeggio was on the point of returning to Rome and wished to take his leave of Henry and ask for his passport; and it was obviously fitting that Wolsey should accompany Campeggio to Grafton in Northamptonshire, where Henry was staying on his progress.

When Wolsey and Campeggio arrived at Grafton on 18 September, Campeggio was escorted to his rooms in the palace; but Wolsey was told that there was no room for him there, and that arrangements had been made for him to stay the night at the house of Master Empson – the son of the man whom Henry had executed nineteen years before – at Easton Neston, some three miles to the west of Grafton. This was a calculated affront to Wolsey. The courtiers were betting with each other as to whether Henry would agree to receive him. Most of them thought that the King would refuse to speak to him; but when Wolsey and Campeggio were presented, Henry greeted Wolsey with great warmth. He protested to Campeggio against the advocation of his divorce case to Rome, and then withdrew with Wolsey to a window – one of the alcoves off the long gallery where it was possible to sit apart. They talked together for a long time. Cavendish and the other people in the gallery, who could see Henry and Wolsey but could not hear what they said, saw Henry motion Wolsey to put his cap back on his head, which was a mark of special favour from the King. What thoughts were passing through

Henry's mind as he sat with Wolsey in the window? Was there a trace of the old affection, of sympathy, and of regret that these feelings must be subordinated to political self-interest and the art of kingcraft?

Wolsey stayed at the palace till nightfall, and then rode to Easton Neston, where he was visited by Gardiner, who had a long talk with him. Next morning, Wolsey went back to Grafton, and arrived just as Henry was mounting his horse in the palace courtyard as he prepared to ride to Hartwell to inspect a new park which was being made for him. Henry spoke to him in a most friendly way. He asked him to preside at a meeting of the Council in the palace, and afterwards to escort Campeggio on the first stage of his journey back to Rome. Then Henry said goodbye, and rode off to Hartwell Park. He never saw Wolsey again.[6]

Wolsey took Campeggio to his house at The Moor in Hertfordshire, and then returned to Hampton Court, while Campeggio remained for a few weeks at The Moor before returning to Rome. On 9 October, while Wolsey was sitting as Lord Chancellor in the Court of Chancery in Westminster Hall on the first day of the Michaelmas term, the Attorney-General appeared in the Court of King's Bench at Westminster, and charged Wolsey with having been guilty of a praemunire by exercising his powers as a Papal Legate in Henry's realm, thereby derogating from the King's royal authority.[7] The charge was brought under a statute of Edward III's reign, and the offence was punishable by imprisonment during the King's pleasure – which could mean for life – and forfeiture of goods. The statute had never been thought to apply in a case where a Papal Legate exercised his powers with the King's consent; but the anti-Papal feelings of the English common lawyers were now allowed full rein.

Henry, who was at Windsor, sent Norfolk and Suffolk to York Place to inform Wolsey that he was dismissed from his office as Lord Chancellor, and to require him to surrender the Great Seal of England. The rumour had spread in London that Wolsey had been arrested, and the river was full of boats with people who had come to see him taken to the Tower; but when he entered his barge, he went the other way, and was rowed up-stream to Putney, on his way to his palace at Esher. At Putney, he was overtaken by Sir Henry Norris, a gentleman of Henry's chamber, who brought him a ring from Henry.[8] This was not merely a token of Henry's regard; if a man received a ring from the King, it meant that he could not be arrested, except on the King's personal authority. If Wolsey were arrested by any officer, he need only show the officer the ring, and the case would be referred to Henry.

On the day that Wolsey was accused of the praemunire, Campeggio arrived at Dover on his way to Rome. The customs officials at Dover opened his baggage, and made an extensive search, despite his protests that this violated his diplomatic immunity as a Papal Legate. Campeggio believed that they had searched his baggage because they suspected that he was smuggling some of Wolsey's valuables out of the kingdom. He was so incensed that instead of embarking, he stayed at Dover and wrote a letter of protest to Henry.[9]

Henry sent a stinging reply to the protest. He wrote that Campeggio had no diplomatic immunity, because his status as a Papal Legate had ended when the Pope revoked the commission under which he had sat as a judge in the court at Blackfriars. Henry was surprised that Campeggio had dared to claim to be a Papal Legate when he had no authority to do so, for as Bishop of Salisbury he was subject to the laws of the realm. This was an implied threat to proceed against Campeggio under the Statutes of Praemunire. Henry then softened the effect of his remarks by regretting that Campeggio had suffered inconvenience from any excess of zeal by the officials at Dover, who were, however, acting within their powers; and he asked Campeggio to accept what had happened in a friendly spirit.[10]

Wolsey was tried for the praemunire in the Court of King's Bench. He pleaded guilty, and was sentenced to be imprisoned during the King's pleasure and to forfeit all his property to the King.[11] Henry did not enforce the sentence of imprisonment, and allowed him to remain at Esher.

Henry summoned a new Parliament, which met at Westminster on 3 November 1529. It was to sit for nearly seven years, and at Henry's instigation carried through a religious, political and social revolution. It was opened by the new Lord Chancellor, Sir Thomas More, with a violent denunciation of Wolsey as the 'great wether' among the sheep which the King, as a good shepherd, had driven out in order to save the flock. This metaphor, with its agricultural and Scriptural allusions, was well understood by the MPs; but it was necessary to explain why the good shepherd had allowed the wicked wether a free rein for seventeen years. More said that it was because Henry, until recently, had been too busy leading his victorious army in war to have time to find out what Wolsey had been doing. It was not a very convincing explanation, as Henry had last led his army in 1513. More and his colleagues in the House of Lords went a good deal further in inaccuracy a few weeks later, when they presented a petition to Henry, asking him to punish Wolsey for forty-four offences which included not only a long list of his political and personal misdemeanours, but also accused him of having deliberately breathed into Henry's face, when he knew that he had syphillis, in the hopes that he would infect the King.[12]

The Lord Chancellor and the peers would not have presented such a petition if Henry had not wished them to do so; but Henry, armed with the petition, was magnanimous to the fallen Cardinal, and was prepared to make a bargain with him. Wolsey voluntarily surrendered his houses at York Place, The Moor and Tyttenhanger to Henry, who allowed him to retain the house at Esher, which he held as Bishop of Winchester, and the property of the Archbishop of York in the north. He was then granted a pardon for his praemunire. He had already given his palace at Hampton Court to Henry a few years earlier, under a very satisfactory arrangement for Wolsey, by which he was granted a suite of rooms in the palace there and also at Richmond.

In December, Wolsey fell ill at Esher. Henry sent Dr Butts to care for him. He also sent him another ring as a gift, and Anne Boleyn sent him a jewel from her girdle as a token of her regard for him. When he recovered from his illness, he was allowed to move from Esher to Richmond. He began to hope that he might one day be restored to Henry's favour; but in March, Henry ordered him to go to his diocese of York, which he had never visited in the sixteen years that he had been Archbishop. He left Richmond, and travelled in state, at Henry's expense, to the Archbishop's palace at Southwell in Nottinghamshire, a few miles within the diocese of York.[13]

His greatest grief was the fate of his colleges at Oxford and Ipswich. The first of the many acts of praemunire to which he had pleaded guilty was his appointment of a vicar, under his powers as Papal Legate, on 2 December 1523; and all the property which he had held at any time since that date was caught by the forfeiture. The property which he had given to his colleges between 1526 and 1528 was therefore forfeited. After his lawyers had advised him that there was no way of getting round this legal ruling, he was reduced to writing appeals to Henry to allow the colleges to continue in existence, now that Henry owned their property. Henry's sympathy for Wolsey and his love of learning were in conflict with his greed for money and with the hopes of his courtiers that they could acquire the property of the colleges as gifts from the King or at low prices. He was also influenced by the widespread resentment of the methods which Wolsey had used to obtain the contributions to the colleges, and by the feeling that although there were established precedents for founding colleges at Oxford, the only reason for founding one at Ipswich was to glorify Wolsey.

Henry solved his dilemma in a way that brought the greatest benefits to himself, without any consideration for Wolsey or the inmates of the colleges. He decided that the Oxford college should continue, but that its name should be changed from 'Cardinal's College' to 'King Henry VIII's College', and that Wolsey's coat-of-arms should be removed from all the doorways and windows, and replaced by the royal arms. In 1546, Henry reorganised it, and its name was changed to 'Christ's Church'; it has continued to flourish for four hundred and fifty years.

But despite all the pleas which Henry received from many influential people, he insisted on suppressing the college at Ipswich, and sending away the teachers, scholars and servants to find, if they were lucky, employment and educational opportunities elsewhere. He sent agents to sell the assets and collect the rents due to the college from its tenants, and appropriated most of them for himself; but part of the property was sold at low prices to the courtiers and their friends. It was not to Henry's advantage to perpetuate the memory of Wolsey, a man whom he had destroyed and who was now being denounced in Parliament and throughout the country; and it would not be as easy at Ipswich as at Oxford to make the people forget that he had been the founder of the college. But by preserving King Henry VIII's College at Oxford and suppressing the Ipswich college, Henry could pose as a patron of learning, he could enrich himself, and he could win the goodwill of the courtiers and gentlemen whose support was more important to him than the gratitude of the teachers, choristers, gardeners and schoolboys of Ipswich.[14]

By overthrowing Wolsey, Henry was pandering to the anti-clerical movement which its opponents called 'Lutheranism'. The term 'Lutheran' was used in 1529 in three different senses. It was used in its accurate sense to mean those people who believed in Luther's theological doctrines – that man is saved by his faith, not by his good works; that there were three, not seven, sacraments; that at Mass the laity should be given the wine as well as the bread; that priests should be allowed to marry; and that although the body of Christ was 'really' present in the consecrated bread and wine, it was there, not by a transubstantiation of the bread, but along with the bread by consubstantiation. The term 'Lutheran' was also used in England to describe the followers of the Swiss reformer, Zwingli, who, unlike Luther, denied the Real Presence of Christ's body in the bread and wine, believing that it was only 'spiritually' or 'figuratively' present; although the Zwinglians, far from being Lutherans, were violently denounced by Luther for believing this heresy. After 1530, these more extreme reformers were usually referred to as 'sacramentaries' both by orthodox Catholics and by the Lutherans. The third use of the word 'Lutheran' was as a label attached to the far larger sections of the population who disliked the clergy and the foreign Pope, and who read, not Luther's theological theses, but the popular tracts which William Roy and Simon Fish were publishing in Germany and the Netherlands and were illegally smuggling into England. In these works, Roy and Fish mocked the priests who paid twenty pence a day to a whore who spent an hour in bed with them, and one shilling a day to pimps who provided them with the whores, whereas a man earned only fourpence, and a woman threepence, for a hard day's work in the fields.[15]

In this last sense, it was probably true to say, as the Pope's supporters did, that Anne Boleyn and her family were Lutherans. After Anne had become the immediate cause of Henry's repudiation of Papal supremacy, she was denounced, and acclaimed, as a Lutheran by both Catholics and reformers, who believed that she was the instrument of either Satan or of God in inducing Henry to break with Rome. There are at least some grounds for believing that Anne, with her father and brother, were anti-clericals at quite an early date. John Foxe wrote that Henry and Anne were reading and enjoying Fish's very successful *Supplication of the Beggars* (which urged that the clergy should spend their money in the relief of the poor and not amass it for monks to pray for souls) soon after it was published in 1528; and when Campeggio was at Henry's court at Easter 1529, he complained that heretical works were circulating openly among the courtiers.[16]

Suffolk was thought to be a 'Lutheran' sympathiser, but Norfolk always held orthodox religious opinions, and disapproved of what he called 'this new learning'.[17] He did not share the views of his niece, Anne Boleyn, and his brother-in-law, her father, whom Henry created Earl of Wiltshire in 1530.

Henry now embarked on a new policy which he pursued at many periods during the remaining years of his reign, of maintaining a balance of power in his government, and of counteracting a political move in one direction by a countermove in the opposite direction. At the time when he was encouraging the anti-clerical forces by overthrowing Wolsey, the last of the forty-four articles in the House of Lords' petition against Wolsey accused him of having prevented the bishops from persecuting heretics in the universities; and the bitterly anti-Lutheran Thomas More was appointed to replace him as Lord Chancellor. More's appointment contained another contradiction. It was the first time for seventy-five years that a layman had held the office of Lord Chancellor, which since 1454 had always been held by a churchman; and even the Lutherans, who knew what More would do to them, welcomed him as Lord Chancellor on the grounds that the appointment of a layman weakened the authority of the Church.

Henry was always skilful in his handling of men, but he surpassed himself in the ability with which he manipulated More; for More was intelligent enough to realise how he was being used. As a child, Henry had known More, and when he became King, and was acclaimed by the intellectuals as a great patron of learning and the arts, he decided to make use of the services of the brilliant English humanist. He appointed More to be a member of his Council, telling him that he hoped that More would be his loyal servant, but God's first.[18] This was certainly the way to get More on his side.

In 1523, when Henry and Wolsey wished to raise money for the war against France, More played his part, as Speaker of the House of Commons, in inducing the MPs to vote the money. More's son-in-law, Roper, tried afterwards to give the impression that More had been the MPs' spokesman in resisting Wolsey's demands; but it seems much more likely that More connived with Wolsey in tricking the MPs into doing what Wolsey wished, for at Wolsey's suggestion Henry rewarded More with a gift of £200 and by appointing him as his secretary.[19]

Henry saw a good deal of More after this, and became his close friend. As well as seeing More at court, he often visited More's house in the village of Chelsea. No two men could have been more different in character. More thought that it was barbaric to enjoy hunting animals; Henry spent the greater part of the day in hunting. More ate a little beef, eggs, milk, and vegetable foods; he usually drank water, to which he occasionally added a little weak beer. Henry ate enormous meals, with many draughts of Gascony wine. More wore a hair shirt, and whipped himself, and had a particular horror of sexual lust. Henry enjoyed all the sensual pleasures. More forbade cards and dice in his household, and thought tennis a waste of time; Henry played a vigorous game of tennis, and gambled half the night at cards and dice. They both liked books and theological controversy, and both, in their different ways, had a sense of humour.[20]

More realised the nature of Henry's friendship. On one occasion during the war with France of 1522–5, Henry visited More at Chelsea, and walked in the garden with his arm round More's neck. Roper was very pleased to see it, for he had never seen Henry show such intimacy to anyone except Wolsey. But More replied to Roper: 'I thank our Lord, son, I find His Grace my very good lord indeed, and I do believe he doth as singularly favour me as any subject in this realm. Howbeit, son Roper, I may tell thee I have no cause to be proud thereof, for if my head could win him a castle in France, it should not fail to go'.[21]

Henry first consulted More about his divorce in September 1527, a few weeks after he had taken the first steps in the case. He walked with More in the garden at Hampton Court, told him that he believed that his marriage to Catherine was against God's law, and asked him for his opinion on the point. More did not definitely commit himself, but expressed a provisional opinion that the marriage was valid; and though Henry arranged for More to discuss the question with various theologians who supported the divorce, More did not change his mind. Henry then told More that he would not employ him in connection with the divorce, but would use his services in other fields; and when he appointed More as Lord Chancellor two years later, it was on this understanding.[22]

As Lord Chancellor, More could render very useful services to Henry by counteracting the anti-clerical forces and showing to the Pope, the Emperor and the world that Henry could still be a zealous Defender of the Faith if the Pope did not provoke him too far by refusing him a divorce. As events slowly moved him in the direction of a breach with Rome, Henry was, as always, cautious. The King who had thought it safer in 1523 to besiege Boulogne than to march on Paris, and who pursued only limited objectives in Scotland, now threatened the Pope with schism, but hesitated to take the final step. For three years after the advocation of the divorce case to Rome, he sometimes bullied the Pope, and sometimes professed his devotion to him; he sometimes insulted the Papal Nuncio, and was sometimes particularly charming. He flirted with the Lutherans, and then stamped on them; he persecuted them at home, and encouraged them abroad. He offered the Pope the alternative of the stick and the carrot – the stick of English nationalism and anti-clericalism, and the carrot of More's persecution of Lutherans. If the Pope granted him a divorce, he would get the carrot; if he refused the divorce, he would get the stick.

After Parliament had duly passed an Act confirming the decision of the Court of King's Bench that Wolsey had been guilty of a praemunire – the practice of confirming a judicial decision by an Act of Parliament had become the established practice in proceedings against powerful dignitaries – the House of Commons sent a petition to Henry, complaining about the vices of the clergy, and asking Henry to reform them and bridle the power of the Church. The petition might be useful to Henry, but he did not grant it now. On the contrary, he thought it advisable to check the Lutherans who had been encouraged by the fall of Wolsey. They were going too far; in May 1530, the Bishop of Norwich, Nix, wrote to Warham that men who were arrested in his diocese for reading heretical books said that the King himself liked these books.[23]

On 24 May, Henry presided at a meeting on the east side of the Parliament chamber at Westminster, which was attended by Warham, More, Tunstal, Gardiner, Sampson, Wolman, Bell, Latimer, Dr Layton, and fifteen other divines and lawyers. It was decided to issue a proclamation against the writings and disciples of Luther. Every official, on taking office, was to swear an oath to exterminate heresy and to do all in his power to help the bishops to accomplish this task. The proclamation contained a list of books which were banned as heretical. Anyone who brought them into the country, or who failed to hand in to the authorities within twenty days any copy which came into his hands, was to be brought before the King's Council and punished. The books included Tyndale's New Testament, Fish's *Supplication of Beggars*, and all the books ridiculing the clergy which had been circulating in the country and at Henry's court.

The commissioners present at the meeting gave Henry their opinion about the desirability of translating the Bible into English. They stated that it was not necessary for salvation to read the Bible, because all men could be saved by the seven sacraments and by following the teaching, and obeying the laws, of the Church. It was therefore unnecessary to translate the Bible into English, and would indeed be undesirable to do so at the present time, when heresy was so prevalent; for if people read the Bible for themselves, they would discuss its meaning, which would encourage the growth of heretical doctrines. But whether or not to allow the Bible to be translated into English was entirely a matter for the King. Perhaps, at some time in the future, when heresy was not so prevalent, the King might order that the Bible should be translated into English, not by self-appointed heretics, but by learned bishops and divines chosen by the King. Until he decided to do this, it was an offence to read the Bible in the English translation of the Lutheran, Tyndale. Henry accepted the recommendations of the commissioners. In June, some of the banned Lutheran books, including Tyndale's

English New Testament, were publicly burned at Paul's Cross. The reformers were outraged at the burning of the Bible, which they denounced as blasphemy.[24]

After the divorce case was advoked to Rome, it proceeded more slowly than ever. Catherine now had the help of Charles's new ambassador in London, Eustace Chapuys, a young French-speaking priest from Savoy, who was one of Charles's most able diplomats. Through Chapuys and Charles, she urged the Pope to give judgement for her in his court in Rome as soon as possible. She also asked him to issue a bull prohibiting Henry and all his bishops from taking any step in the divorce proceedings in England, and ordering Henry to cease committing adultery with Anne Boleyn, pending the decision in the divorce case in Rome. It was now the turn of the impatient Henry to cause as many delays as possible in the divorce proceedings. Ghinucci, Sir Gregory and John di Casale, and a series of envoys whom Henry sent from England, urged the Pope not to issue any bull against Henry and not to proceed with the case in Rome. Henry argued that no King of England had ever been ordered to appear before a court outside his realm, and that his people would never accept such a thing; and if Catherine claimed that the case could not be fairly tried by any court in his realm, how could it be fairly tried in Rome, where the Emperor's influence was paramount? Henry therefore asked leave to send an 'excusator' to Rome to argue before the Papal court that the case should not be heard there. Long arguments then took place before the Papal court as to whether or not the excusator should be heard. It all took a very long time, with frequent adjournments, as the court could not sit during the long law vacations in Rome.

Clement continued to play his former game, using every excuse for delay, and promising everything to everybody. He promised Charles's ambassador that he would issue the bull ordering Henry to stop committing adultery with Anne, and that he would give judgement for Catherine. He then promised Henry's agents that he would not do this. Eventually he issued the bull against Henry, but refused to publish it. He suggested to Henry's agent, Carne, that he might grant Henry a dispensation to commit bigamy and marry Anne without divorcing Catherine; he said this would be less embarrassing than to give Henry the divorce.[25]

Henry had meanwhile acted on Cranmer's suggestion to consult the universities. He began at Cambridge, where Gardiner and Fox set to work in February 1530. They found that there was strong opposition in Cambridge to complying with Henry's wishes; but they eventually succeeded in obtaining the opinion that Henry required, after they had handpicked a number of university doctors, whom they knew supported Henry's case, to decide the question for the University. One of those selected was Hugh Latimer, who had attended discussions at the White Horse Inn, was a close friend of Bilney's, and was suspected of being a Lutheran. The University pronounced that a marriage of a man with his brother's widow was against the divine law, and that a Papal dispensation could not make it valid. In April, Longland, Fox and Bell encountered even stronger opposition at Oxford; but here, too, they succeeded in getting an opinion from the governing body of the University, by 27 votes against 22, that Henry's marriage was against God's law.[26]

Henry then approached the foreign universities. He won the support of François I by promising to support him against the Emperor; and François thought that it would be to his advantage to help Henry obtain a divorce from Catherine which would permanently damage Henry's relations with Charles. François not only helped Henry's case in Rome, where his ambassador reinforced Henry's argument that a King could not be required to appear before a court outside his realm; he also put strong pressure on the French universities to give their opinion that Henry's marriage was unlawful. In Paris, the theological faculty, the Sorbonne, was divided on the issue. The leading Catholic theologian there, Budé, supported Catherine's case; but after François had threatened to arrest Budé if he continued to support Catherine, the Sorbonne decided that Henry's marriage was against God's law. Charles's ambassador in Rome pointed out that the decision had not obtained the two-thirds majority of the doctors of the Sorbonne, which the University statutes required; but Henry and François ignored this requirement, and announced that the University of Paris had held for Henry. The Universities of Orleans, Angers, Bourges and Toulouse were easier to persuade, and all gave their opinion in Henry's favour.[27]

Charles arranged for the Universities of Alcalá and Salamanca to give their opinion that the marriage was valid; and his ambassador in Rome persuaded the Pope to issue a bull prohibiting any university from discussing the question while it was *sub judice* in his court in Rome. Henry sent Cranmer to join his other English and Italian agents in Rome, and they persuaded the Pope to suspend this prohibition and to allow the Italian universities to discuss the question. As the Italian universities were freer from political influence than the English, French or Spanish universities, there was scope for the giving and accepting of bribes; and Cranmer and his colleagues bribed the Universities of Padua, Ferrara, Pavia and Bologna to give judgement in Henry's favour.[28]

In July 1530, the House of Lords sent a petition to the Pope, asking him to grant Henry a divorce. It was signed by all the peers and bishops, including Wolsey as Archbishop of York; but the Lord Chancellor, More, did not sign. The petitioners warned the Pope that if he refused to grant Henry a divorce, great calamities might befall the realm, and they might be forced to take action on their own, independently of the Pope, to prevent this. Clement replied that he was shocked at this implied threat, and that he was sure that so pious a King as Henry had not sanctioned it.[29]

Henry himself blew hot and cold towards the Pope. When Charles went to Bologna in February 1530 to be crowned as Holy Roman Emperor by the Pope, Henry committed the great provocation of sending the Earl of Wiltshire, Anne Boleyn's father, to represent him at the ceremony, with instructions from Henry to tell Charles that Henry's marriage to Catherine was against divine law. According to the story that John Foxe wrote thirty years later, Wiltshire refused to kiss the Pope's foot, although this was a courtesy which even Kings and Emperors always rendered to the Holy Father. But in April, Henry wrote a very conciliatory letter to the Pope, in which he promised that, as the Pope had adjourned the divorce proceedings in the courts at Rome until September, he would take no step in England before September to further the divorce. When September had passed, Henry wrote a very bitter letter to the Pope, denouncing Clement for calling on him, a King, to appear before a foreign court outside his realm. [30]

There was still the problem of how to deal with Wolsey, who in September 1530 moved north from Southwell to his palace at Cawood, seven miles south of York. He waited there while preparations were made for his enthronement as Archbishop at a splendid ceremony in the Minster at York on 7 November. Henry felt a real pang of regret for Wolsey; but the courtiers who had overthrown him – Norfolk, Suffolk, Wiltshire and Anne Boleyn – knew that they could expect no mercy if he ever returned to power. He was said to be a reformed character, and to be devoting himself, for the first time in his life, to his pastoral duties in the villages of Nottinghamshire and south Yorkshire; but there were also reports that he was enlarging his palace at Southwell. Did not this prove that he was as ambitious as ever?[31]

Wolsey, as usual, was optimistic and ready to take risks. He sent his Italian physician, Dr Agostini, to make contact with the ambassadors of both Charles and François. He and Agostini employed three men to spy on Norfolk and to report to Wolsey what was happening at court. Unfortunately for Wolsey, the men were *agents provocateurs* in Norfolk's pay; and Agostini himself seems to have betrayed Wolsey to Norfolk. Henry was informed that Wolsey had been plotting against him with the French King and with the Pope, promising François to act in his interests if he returned to power, and urging Clement to give judgement for Catherine; for this would force Henry to get rid of Anne Boleyn and recall Wolsey, who alone would be able to patch up Henry's difficulties with the Pope.[32] These stories may have been lies instigated by Norfolk and the Boleyns; but Henry knew Wolsey well enough to realise that they might be true. In any case, it was always risky to leave an embittered man alive and free.

On 4 November, three days before Wolsey was due to be enthroned at York, the Earl of Northumberland arrived at Cawood and arrested him on a charge of high treason. Wolsey at first refused to acknowledge Northumberland's right to arrest him without express authority from the King; but

Thomas Wolsey, by an unknown artist

Pope Clement VII, painting from the studio of Sebastiano del Piombo, 1531/32

Master Walsh, a gentleman of Henry's privy chamber, had gone to Cawood with Northumberland. When Wolsey saw Walsh, he made no further resistance, for a gentleman of the King's Privy chamber had the right to arrest anyone without a warrant. Northumberland had been ordered by Henry to show every courtesy and consideration to Wolsey; he was to bring him to the Tower of London, but to allow him to travel as slowly as he liked, and to rest for as long as he wished at any place on the way. Wolsey was very ill, and took twenty-two days to travel from Cawood to Leicester. At Sheffield Park, Northumberland delivered him into the custody of Sir William Kingston, the Constable of the Tower, who treated him with as much consideration as Northumberland had done. Kingston told him that Henry still had a high regard for him, and had only ordered his arrest so that he could clear himself at his trial. 'Master Kingston', replied Wolsey, 'all these comfortable words which ye have spoken be but for a purpose to bring me in a fool's paradise. I know what is provided for me'.

Wolsey died at Leicester Abbey on 29 November. On the day before he died, he spoke to Kingston about Henry, in the presence of his usher, Cavendish, who twenty-seven years later recorded Wolsey's words in his biography of Wolsey. 'If I had served God as diligently as I have done the King', said Wolsey, 'He would not have given me over in my grey hairs'. He told Kingston that Henry was 'a Prince of a royal courage, and hath a princely heart. And rather than he will either miss or want any part of his will or appetite, he will put the loss of one half of his realm in danger. For I assure you, I have often knelt before him in his privy chamber on my knees the space of an hour or two to persuade him from his will and appetite, but I could never bring to pass to dissuade him therefrom'.

He said that if Kingston ever became a member of the Council, 'I warn you to be well advised and assured what matter ye put in his head, for ye shall never pull it out again'.

Kingston said to Wolsey that he had heard that he had some money hidden somewhere, and asked where it was. Wolsey said that the money did not belong to him, but to various other people, but that he would tell Kingston next day where it was. He died at 8 a.m. next day before he had told him.[33]

After attending Wolsey's funeral at Leicester, Kingston and Cavendish rode to Hampton Court, where Henry was in residence. They arrived there on 5 December. Kingston warned Cavendish that they were sure to be asked if Wolsey said anything before his death, and that it would be very dangerous for them both if they disclosed what he had said about Henry.

Next day, Cavendish was told that Henry wished to speak to him, and he went to the park, where Henry was shooting with bow and arrow at the butts. As Henry was occupied at his sport, Cavendish did not venture to approach him, but stood leaning against a tree, and waited. While he was standing there, lost in thought, Henry came up behind him and clapped his hand on Cavendish's shoulder. Cavendish knelt to him, and Henry, addressing Cavendish by his name, said 'I will make an end of my game and then I will talk with you'.

Henry finished shooting, handed his bow to the yeoman of his bows, and walked back to the palace without saying a word to Cavendish, who followed him at a discreet distance. Henry talked to Sir John Gage till he came to the garden postern gate; he then entered through the gate, which was closed behind him. So Cavendish walked away; but he had gone only a few steps when the postern gate reopened, and Sir Henry Norris came out, and called to Cavendish to come with him. They went in through the gate, and found Henry standing behind the door, dressed in a dressing gown of russet velvet furred with sables.

Cavendish knelt before Henry, and spoke to him for over an hour. Henry asked him if he knew anything about the £1,500 that Wolsey was supposed to have in his possession. Cavendish said that he thought he could tell Henry where it was. 'Yea can?', said Henry, 'Then I pray you tell me, and you shall do us much pleasure, nor it shall not be unrewarded'. Cavendish told Henry that Wolsey had given it to a priest, whom he named. 'Well then', said Henry, 'let me alone keep this gere [goings-on] secret between yourself and me. And let no man be privy thereof; for if I hear any more of it, then I know by whom it is come to knowledge. Three may keep counsel if two be away. And if I thought that my cap knew my counsel, I would cast it into the fire and burn it'.

Henry offered to employ Cavendish in his service in the same post of gentleman usher which he held in Wolsey's household, and said that Norfolk would pay Cavendish his whole year's salary in advance, 'which is £10, is it not so?' Cavendish said that it was, and that his wages were three-quarters of a year in arrears. 'That is true', said Henry, 'for so we be informed'. All this was typical Henry. He spent his time taking part in sports in the park; but he knew that Wolsey had £1,500 which was unaccounted for, and he knew what Cavendish's wages were and how far they were in arrears. He arranged to speak alone with Cavendish, and that only Norris should know that he had done so; and he had worked out an effective way of warning Cavendish to keep his mouth shut.

Cavendish was then called before the Council, who were meeting in the palace at Hampton Court, with Norfolk presiding. Norfolk asked Cavendish whether Wolsey had said anything before he died, because they had already questioned Kingston, who had told them that Wolsey had said nothing. Cavendish said that when Wolsey was dying, 'he spake many idle words', as men do when they are dying, but he could no longer remember them.[34]

Norfolk and the counsellors had discovered nothing from Cavendish in their interrogation in the Council chamber. Henry, when he had finished shooting at the butts, had found out what he wanted to know.

14

WHICH WAY?

FIFTEEN months had passed since the divorce case had been advoked to Rome, and no judgement had been given. Catherine was bitterly disappointed, and thought that the Pope had betrayed her. Chapuys urged Charles and the Nuncio in London to persuade the Pope to act; for he was sure that it was necessary to take a firm line with Henry. 'Gentleness makes these people harsh', he wrote to Charles on 4 December 1530, 'and harshness makes them gentle. For as long as the Pope acted graciously towards them, they threatened and defied him as outrageously as possible; but now that His Holiness has begun to tighten the reins, they have become as humble and mild as possible'.[1]

Henry was about to apply the stick again to the Pope, and to give the anti-clerical forces their head. In January 1531, his law officers announced that the whole clergy had been guilty of a praemunire by acquiescing in the exercise by Wolsey of his powers as Legate; for they had thereby been his accomplices in his usurpation of the King's power in his realm. Every bishop, dean and priest in England was therefore liable to be imprisoned for life and to have all his goods forfeited to the King. Henry stated that he would pardon them for their praemunire if the clergy in Convocation promised to vote him a large sum of money as a fine, and to recognise him as Supreme Head of the Church in his kingdom. The suggestion that the clergy had committed a crime against the King's laws, for which they must be punished by paying a fine to the King, because they had obeyed the all-powerful minister whom the King had appointed to rule over them, and whose authority he had enforced with his royal power, was so flagrantly unjust that Henry could never have put it forward had it not been for the fact that large sections of his nobles, gentlemen, merchants and the common people so hated the clergy that they were delighted to see them being the victims of a frame-up.

The Nuncio protested to Henry, and urged Convocation to refuse to pay; but on 24 January the Convocation of Canterbury agreed to pay Henry

£100,000 (£25,000,000 in terms of 1984 prices). They recognised him as Supreme Head of the Church of England, after adding the qualification 'as far as the law of God allows'.[2] Henry agreed to accept the additional words. This was good enough for a start.

Several churchmen protested to Henry against his assumption of the title of Supreme Head of the Church. They argued that no temporal Prince could be head of the Church. The most influential of the objectors was Tunstal, the Bishop of Durham. Henry wrote a friendly reply to Tunstal. He said that Tunstal had written in so humble a manner that he could not be offended with him; but he refuted Tunstal's arguments, and maintained that all Princes were the heads of the Church in their realms.[3]

The Pope, influenced perhaps by Chapuys's advice to the Nuncio, wrote to Henry on 5 January 1531 that, at Queen Catherine's request, he was herewith issuing an order to Henry which would be fixed to the gates of Bruges, Tournai and other towns in the Netherlands; this would be sufficient in law if Henry refused to accept the brief. He forbade Henry to marry any woman, and informed him that if he purported to do so, any children of this union would be bastards. He also forbade anyone to give judgement in the divorce case as long as the case was *sub judice* in his court in Rome.[4]

Henry had been warned in advance about the Pope's brief by his agents in Rome. When the Nuncio presented it to him on 6 February, he merely glanced at it, and said that it would be considered by his Council. He told the Nuncio that he knew that he had been urging his bishops to refuse to pay the fine for the praemunire or to recognise him as Supreme Head of the Church of England; but he had never been so charming to the Nuncio, or entertained him to so lavish a banquet.[5]

Henry had just acquired the services of another of those capable officials who had begun their career with Wolsey. Thomas Cromwell was a man of low social origin, the son of a shearman of Putney, and was aged about forty-five in 1530. Unlike the other able servants whom Henry had acquired from Wolsey, he was not a priest or a university doctor, and he had not been employed by Wolsey as a diplomat. He was a business man and a solicitor. He had spent some years in Italy in his youth, and had gained experience there and in the Netherlands of banking as well as law. He sat in the House of Commons as MP for Taunton, and had learned how to handle his fellow-members. Wolsey had employed him in connection with the dissolution of the twenty-two monasteries whose property had been acquired for the Cardinal's colleges in Oxford and Ipswich. When Wolsey fell from power, he employed Cromwell to make the best possible bargains for him with the King and with the courtiers. Henry formed a high opinion of Cromwell's abilities, and took him into his service; for though Henry had many able diplomats, he had no administrator and political manager of Cromwell's calibre. Here was another useful tool to be employed as an agent, and perhaps one day to be sacrificed as a scapegoat.

There are no reasons for believing that Cromwell had any great interest in the 'new learning' and in Lutheran doctrines in the days when he was serving the hated Cardinal. We know that as late as July 1529 he made a will in which he invoked the intercession with God of the Virgin Mary and all saints for his soul, and left money to be used in paying for prayers for his soul.[6] But he was probably always as anti-clerical as most Englishmen of his generation. After he had become Henry's chief minister, and played the leading part in the attack on the Church and on the Pope's supporters, the Catholics held him responsible for the anti-Papal policy. Cardinal Pole wrote in 1539 that after the fall of Wolsey, Henry was on the point of abandoning the divorce, and of submitting to the Pope's authority, when Cromwell appeared on the scene; he was an emissary of Satan who admired Machiavelli's book, *The Prince*. According to Pole, Cromwell suggested to Henry that he should proclaim himself Head of the Church of England, for then he could obtain a divorce from Catherine without bothering about the Pope.[7]

But there are several inaccuracies in Pole's story; and it is absurd to suggest that Henry put forward his claim to be Supreme Head of the Church of England at the suggestion of a man who had only entered his service, in a very subordinate position, a few months earlier.

At this time, when Henry was asserting his authority over the Church, the persecution of heretics had never been so severe. Warham and Fisher condemned Thomas Hitton for heresy; he had come to England from the Netherlands to arrange for Tyndale's New Testament to be secretly smuggled into the country. He was burned at Maidstone in February 1530 – the first heretic to be sent to the stake in England for nine years. In the spring of 1531, three more heretics were arrested and examined by More in his house in Chelsea; they accused More of flogging and torturing them.[8]

More was the driving force behind the persecution. The other persecutors – the bishops who sentenced the heretics, the sheriffs and justices of the peace who burned them, and the tradesmen who supplied the faggots for the fire – in most cases acted out of obedience, out of habit, out of a desire to show their efficiency and gain promotion, or simply because it was their job. But More was driven on by a passionate hatred of heretics, which was perhaps caused by a sense of guilt. Many people believed that he and his friend Erasmus were responsible for the present unrest because they had been the first to criticise the vices of the Church. Did More feel ashamed when he heard men say that Erasmus had laid the eggs which Luther hatched? Whatever the reason, More venomously attacked the Lutherans; he accused them of fornicating in churches, sneered at Hitton 'the Devil's stinking martyr', branded all Lutheran women as harlots, condemned the bishops for having been too lenient with heretics, and insisted that heretics must be put to a 'sore painful death' if they obeyed the dictates of their own consciences and not the commands of the Church.[9]

This suited Henry perfectly. More was getting rid of a few seditious heretics who were spreading subversion in Henry's realm; the burnings could be used to persuade the Pope that a King who was so zealous a Defender of the Faith deserved to be granted a divorce when he wanted one; and the persecutor who was arousing the hatred of the reformers was a man who opposed Henry's divorce.

At the same time as Henry was allowing More to burn heretics in England, he was in touch with the German Lutherans. Although he warned the Lutheran rulers to beware of radical religious trouble-makers – those reckless men who incited religious dissension and put themselves on a level with Princes – he encouraged them to make difficulties for the Emperor in Germany. In May 1530, Charles summoned a diet at Augsburg in the hopes of arranging an agreement between the German Catholics and Lutherans. Henry sent agents to offer money to the German Lutherans if they refused to compromise and resisted Charles; and he urged François to support them. He warned the German Lutherans that they would be utterly lost if they weakened in their opposition to Charles.[10]

He even got in touch with Tyndale, who in 1528 published at Marburg his book *The Obedience of a Christian Man*. Tyndale put forward in its extreme form the doctrine of obedience to 'the Prince' – that is to say, to the ruler of an independent sovereign state. God 'in all lands hath put Kings, governors and rulers in His own stead, to rule the world through them', wrote Tyndale. 'Whosoever therefore resisteth them, resisteth God, for they are in the room of God; and they that resist shall receive the damnation. . . . Neither may the inferior person avenge himself upon the superior, or violently resist him, for whatsoever wrong it be'. To resist a royal official was as wicked as resisting the King himself. Even if the King 'be the greatest tyrant in the world, yet is he unto thee a great benefit of God, and a thing wherefore thou oughtest to thank God highly'. The King 'may at his lust do right and wrong, and shall give account but to God only'.[11]

Two hundred years later, Strype wrote that when Henry read Tyndale's book, he commented: 'This book is for me and all Kings to read'. But More, in his very long books against Tyndale, argued that, though Tyndale pretended to uphold the royal authority, he was in fact seditious; for Tyndale stated that in one case only, it was necessary for a subject to disobey his Prince. If the King ordered his subject to contravene God's law, then the subject was entitled to disobey, though even then he must not actively resist the King, but must patiently submit to martyrdom. More argued that the suggestion that the individual should put the dictates of his own conscience before the King's commands was seditious. He fastened on the statement made by Barnes, who, after carrying his faggot and being released from prison, had gone to the Lutherans in Germany. Barnes had written that if a King ordered his subject to burn the Bible, the subject ought to disobey and face martyrdom. More pointed out that Henry had in fact ordered his subjects to burn Tyndale's English Bible; so the Lutherans were urging Henry's subjects to disobey him.[12]

Tyndale, like Luther and most of the other German Lutheran doctors, took a high-principled line about Henry's divorce. Disregarding their personal advantage and political expediency, they threw away the opportunity to be reconciled to Henry, and came out on Catherine's side.[13]

Henry appreciated the force of More's argument that to challenge the authority of the Church could lead to a challenge to the King's authority; but he ordered the English agent at Antwerp, Stephen Vaughan, to contact Tyndale and invite him to return to England and enter Henry's service. Vaughan wrote to Tyndale in Germany, and received a reply, which he sent to Henry, in which Tyndale expressed his devotion to the King, but wrote that he was afraid that if he returned to England he would be arrested, condemned as a heretic, and burned by More and the bishops. Vaughan wrote to Tyndale that Henry was prepared to give him a safe-conduct if he wished to return to England and serve the King.

In April 1531, Vaughan received a message from a friend that an unknown man wished to speak with him at a place in the fields outside Antwerp. When he went there, he met a man who identified himself as Tyndale. He told Vaughan that he regretted having offended Henry. He said that he had written his *Answer unto Sir Thomas More*, but promised not to publish it until Henry had read it. They talked until the light began to fade. Then Vaughan went back to Antwerp, and Tyndale walked off across the fields in the opposite direction. Vaughan thought that Tyndale would make a big detour and return to the town by another route, and that he had walked off in the opposite direction so that Vaughan should not realise that he was staying secretly in Antwerp.[14]

Tyndale sent Vaughan a copy of his book for Henry to read. Vaughan hesitated to send it to Henry, so he sent it to Cromwell, who gave it to the King. Henry read it, but decided that he could make no use of Tyndale. Cromwell wrote to Vaughan that Henry had praised him for his diligence in getting into contact with Tyndale and for sending the book, but that Henry 'nothing liked the said book, being filled with seditious slanderous lies and fantastical opinions'. Henry had formed the impression that Vaughan admired Tyndale; but Tyndale's book showed that he lacked 'grace, virtue, learning, discretion, and all other good qualities', and that his aim was 'only to seduce, deceive, and disquiet the people and commonwealth of this realm'.* Henry had therefore decided not to invite Tyndale to come to England, for if he came, he would try 'to infect and corrupt the whole realm

*These words were afterwards erased from the draft of Cromwell's letter.

to the great inquietation and hurt of the commonwealth of the same'.

Cromwell was obviously alarmed that not only Vaughan but he himself would be in trouble if Henry thought that Vaughan and Cromwell's friends were sympathetic to heretics. He urged Vaughan to take care, when he wrote to Henry, to 'show yourself his true, loving and obedient subject, bearing no manner favour, love or affection to the said Tyndale nor to his works in any manner of wise, but utterly to condemn and abhor the same'. If he did not, Vaughan would 'acquire the indignation of God and displeasure of your sovereign lord', and would cause his friends to regret that they had advanced him to Henry's favour.[15]

One of Tyndale's most devoted followers was a young man, John Frith, the son of an innkeeper of Sevenoaks who had become a bachelor of divinity at Cambridge, and had taken refuge in Germany from persecution in England. Everyone who met him admired his learning, the purity of his life, and his simple sincerity. Although Henry would have nothing to do with Tyndale, he ordered Vaughan to offer a pardon to Frith if he would renounce his heresies and return to England. Frith refused Henry's offer, and soon afterwards came illegally to England to arrange for the distribution of Tyndale's English New Testament. Sir Thomas More made every effort to catch him, and after Frith had evaded arrest for several months, he was seized at Milton Shore in Essex when he was on the point of embarking for the Netherlands, and imprisoned in the Tower.[16]

In July, Henry asked Charles to extradite Tyndale from the Netherlands, so that he could be tried in England for heresy and sedition. Charles replied that under the extradition treaty with England of 1506, heresy was not an extraditable offence; if Henry had evidence that Tyndale was a heretic, he should send it to the authorities in the Netherlands, who would then deal with Tyndale. But Charles wrote that he suspected that Henry's real motive in demanding the extradition of Tyndale was because Tyndale had written against his divorce, and for this reason he would refuse to extradite him.[17]

Henry had come down on More's side against Tyndale, but More had to pay the price. Henry had hitherto allowed him to keep silent about the divorce; but when Parliament was prorogued in March 1531, More, as Lord Chancellor, made a speech to both the House of Lords and the House of Commons. He said that although some people believed that Henry was seeking to divorce Catherine because he was in love with a certain lady, the only reason for his action was that he feared that his marriage to Catherine was against God's law – an opinion which had been upheld by eleven of the universities of Christendom. Chapuys realised that More had to make this speech if he was to remain in office and to continue to use his influence against the divorce and in Charles's interests. At Chapuys's suggestion, Charles wrote a letter to More, expressing his high opinion of him; but More asked Chapuys not to send him the Emperor's letter, for if he received it, he would have to show it to Henry, and it would then be impossible for him to continue serving Charles.[18]

Fisher was still writing book after book – he wrote seven in all – in support of Catherine's cause, despite all the pressures on him to desist. In February 1531, two members of his household and several beggars died after drinking broth which Fisher's cook had prepared but which Fisher himself did not drink. The cook was arrested, and accused of trying to murder Fisher by putting poison in the soup. He confessed that he had put some powder in the soup out of spite, hoping to cause a digestive upset to the members of the household; but he denied that he knew that the powder could cause death, or that he had any wish to hurt Fisher. The rumour spread around London that the Boleyns had paid the cook to poison Fisher, in order to prevent him from continuing to oppose the divorce; but, as usual, Henry himself was not blamed. Chapuys, who strongly suspected Anne and her father, was sure that Henry was too honourable to be a party to such an act.[19]

Henry was determined to show the world how deeply he deplored the crime. At his suggestion, Parliament passed an Act for the punishment of poisoners. It enacted that the Bishop of Rochester's cook was to be put to death by being immersed in boiling water till he died. The sentence was duly carried out.[20]

At Easter, Friar Peto, of the Franciscan Observants at Greenwich, preached before the King and the court. He said that Princes must beware of flatterers, who could lead them to follow the wrong path; and he mentioned how the Emperor Constantine, in the fourth century, had on one occasion refused to decide a dispute between two bishops because he believed that a temporal sovereign should never sit in judgement over churchmen. At this point, Henry interrupted Peto; he said that Peto was talking nonsense, and told him to continue with the main theme of his sermon. Henry afterwards spoke to Peto in a window. He tried to persuade him that he was wrong; but Peto would not change his opinion, and the conversation ended with Henry abruptly turning his back on Peto and walking away.[21]

Henry ordered that Peto should be confined under house arrest in the friary of the Franciscan Observants at Bedford; but soon afterwards, he granted Peto a passport to attend a meeting of Franciscans at Toulouse. Peto stayed abroad, writing books against Henry and supporting Papal supremacy. He did not return to England during Henry's lifetime.

During the summer of 1531, Henry varied between a tough and a soft attitude towards the Pope and the anti-clericals. On 23 April, he wrote a very strong letter to Benet, his agent in Rome: Benet was to tell the Pope that if he persisted in summoning Henry to appear before the court in Rome, this would lead to the destruction of Papal authority in England. Soon afterwards, the Pope wrote to Henry, appealing for aid against the Turks, and ordered the Nuncio in London to present the letter to Henry. The

Nuncio was almost afraid to go to court, for he knew how Henry was hardening against the Pope. Chapuys persuaded him to go, and Henry received him at Greenwich on 30 May. Henry was very courteous, but insisted on talking about the divorce, not the Turks. He said that the Pope was not a bad fellow, but he was a pawn in the Emperor's hands. If the Pope continued to insist that the divorce case be tried in Rome, he would defy the Pope, for the worst that the Pope could do would be to excommunicate him, and he did not care three straws for that. If the Pope injured him, he would avenge his wrongs by leading an army to Rome with the support of his ally, the French King. As for the Turks, Henry suggested that the Pope should ask his master the Emperor, not Henry, for help.[22]

Soleiman was preparing to invade Austria, with the help of his ally, the King of Hungary, John Zapolya. The Pope excommunicated Zapolya for supporting the infidel. Henry reacted vigorously in support of Zapolya. He sent a strong protest to the Pope, and stated that it was a very dangerous precedent to excommunicate a King. He wrote to the King of Poland, urging him to mediate in the dispute between Ferdinand of Bohemia and Zapolya, and told Chapuys that if the Turk invaded Austria and Germany, it would be Charles's fault for allowing his brother to quarrel with Zapolya.[23]

The persecution of heretics went on, with More more zealous than ever. He was helped by Stokesley, who had replaced Tunstal as Bishop of London when Tunstal was translated to Durham; for Stokesley was a great persecutor of heretics, though he was a loyal supporter of Henry's divorce. In August, Bilney was burned at Norwich. According to More, he recanted before he died, but this could not save him, for, having once before carried his faggot, he was a relapsed heretic. Bilney's supporters strongly denied that he had recanted. Two more of More's victims were burned in December. James Bainham, a barrister of the Middle Temple, who had been arrested and perhaps tortured at More's orders, was burned in April 1532. One of the charges against him was that he had said that St Thomas of Canterbury had been a traitor to his Prince. Bilney's friend, Hugh Latimer, who had rendered good service to Henry when Cambridge University gave their opinion about his divorce, was accused of heresy, but saved himself by a recantation. The Cambridge divine, Shaxton, was suspected of heresy by Nix, the Bishop of Norwich, because he questioned the existence of purgatory; but Henry ordered that Shaxton should be granted a licence to preach, as he had been examined and had shown that he was a good Catholic man.[24]

All over Europe, learned men were writing books about Henry's divorce. Cranmer, who had been appointed Anne Boleyn's chaplain, was one of several of Henry's English supporters who wrote a book to prove that the texts of Leviticus prevailed; and Henry asked German Lutherans, Swiss Zwinglians, and Jewish rabbis to write on the same theme. Erasmus, who as usual was determined not to fall foul of any powerful patron, refused to commit himself. Vives supported Catherine, and wrote to Henry that if he was anxious about not having a male heir, he should arrange for his daughter Mary to marry and for her son to succeed him.[25]

Henry himself wrote a book, *The Glass of the Truth*. Unlike his *Assertion of the Seven Sacraments* of 1521, it was published anonymously; but Henry let it be known that he was the author. Again, as with his earlier book, people refused to believe that he had written it himself; but he had in fact spent many hours working on it, as he wrote to Anne Boleyn: 'My book maketh substantially for my matter, in looking whereof I have spent above four hours this day, which caused me now to write the shorter letter to you at this time, because of some pain in my head, wishing myself (specially an evening) in my sweetheart's arms whose pretty ducks I trust shortly to kiss'.[26]

Catherine's position was becoming more difficult. She usually accompanied Henry when he moved from one house to another, but they lived in separate parts of the palace. She dined with him in public on holy days, but apart from this, he only visited her once every three days. He had changed his attitude to her, both in private and in public. At first he had adopted the attitude that she was a most noble lady whom he greatly loved and respected, but that unfortunately God's law forbade him to marry her. Now he treated her as a disobedient subject because she had appealed to the Pope to hear the divorce case in Rome, and to summon the King of England, who had no superior except God, to appear before a court outside his realm.

Henry was constantly in the company of Anne Boleyn. It was probably in the summer of 1531 that she at last consented to become his mistress. She began to behave in public as if she were his wife.

On 10 July Henry, who was at Windsor with Catherine, Anne and the court, wrote to Benet, ordering him to adopt a conciliatory attitude towards the Pope.[27] Early next morning, he left Windsor on a progress, with Anne and the court. He left a message for Catherine, telling her not to follow him. She wrote to him that she regretted that she had not known that he was leaving and had therefore not said goodbye to him, and assured him that she loved and respected him. He wrote in reply that she was unloving and disobedient, having appealed to the Pope to hear the case outside the realm, and having falsely pretended that her marriage to Arthur had not been consummated.

Henry and Catherine never met again. A fortnight later, he sent her a message that he was returning to Windsor, but that before he arrived she must leave the castle and go to the palace of The Moor. He reduced the number of her servants – an indignity which was always greatly resented by falling dignitaries. When Chapuys saw her a few months later, she had greatly aged in appearance, though she was only forty-six. On New Year's Day 1532 she sent Henry a gold cup as a New Year's gift. He refused to accept it, and returned it to her.[28]

The Nuncio and Chapuys urged Henry to treat Catherine more kindly, and not to force her to live apart from him. Henry replied that if, in fact, Catherine was his wife, as the Pope and the Emperor maintained, they should not meddle in disputes between husband and wife. When the Nuncio came to court on 26 January to deliver a brief from the Pope about the Turkish menace, Henry kept him waiting for three hours before receiving him. He accepted the brief, but did not look at it, and strongly criticised the Nuncio for having told the Pope that he was illtreating Catherine. He then went off to dinner without inviting the Nuncio to dine with him.[29]

On the day before this unfriendly interview, the Pope had written a letter to Henry which did not reach London until some weeks later. He wrote that he had been informed, though he could scarcely believe it, that Henry had sent his wife, Queen Catherine, away from court and was committing adultery with 'a certain Anna'. As Henry had hitherto been the Church's most zealous defender, he would remonstrate with him as a loving father before acting in the role of a judge. Did Henry not realise how the heretics would rejoice if Henry divorced a Queen who was the Emperor's aunt? This appeal had no effect on Henry, who simply ignored it.[30]

By the spring of 1532, Henry was taking two new drastic steps against the Pope. Parliament passed an Act abolishing the Pope's right to receive annates – the first year's income of every bishopric after a new bishop was appointed – and making it a praemunire for anyone to pay these annates to Rome; but a provision in the Act stated that the Act should not come into force for a year, and only then if the King so ordered. The House of Commons also drafted a petition against the clergy, as they had done in 1529; but this time the petition had the active support of Henry and his ministers. Cromwell helped to draft it, and used his experience as a political manager in the House of Commons to ensure that it was approved by the House. The petition demanded that the clergy should accept the fact that the King, the Supreme Head of the Church in England, had power to regulate all ecclesiastical proceedings. Convocation was not to discuss any subject without first obtaining the King's consent to do so; and the bishops' jurisdiction to try cases of heresy in their ecclesiastical courts was abolished. Henceforth, heretics were to be tried only by commissioners specially appointed by the King.[31]

When the bill to abolish the annates was introduced in Parliament, Henry told the Nuncio that he was not responsible for it, but that it showed how his people hated the Pope, and was the culmination of a resentment against annates which they had felt for a long time. The bill did not pass without opposition. Henry himself went three times to the House of Lords while it was being debated, in order to influence the peers and MPs to vote for it. When it became law, he wrote on 21 March to Ghinucci and his other agents in Rome. He told them that he could not prevent Parliament from discussing and passing the bill abolishing the annates, because the peers and MPs had freedom of speech and action with which he could not interfere; but the Act could not be brought into operation until he so ordered, and he had no intention of doing this unless the Pope's unreasonable behaviour left him with no alternative. He told Ghinucci to explain the position to the Pope and the cardinals in Rome, without allowing them either to hope too much or to despair too much about what he intended to do about the annates.[32]

There was considerable opposition to the MPs' petition against the clergy, not only from the churchmen themselves, but even from within Henry's Council. It was strongly opposed by More and Gardiner, whom Henry had appointed, with the Pope's consent, to be Bishop of Winchester in Wolsey's place. Henry showed his extreme displeasure with the attitude which More and Gardiner were adopting. Gardiner wrote a letter of apology, abandoned his opposition, and continued in Henry's service; More resigned as Lord Chancellor, ostensibly on grounds of ill health.[33]

On 15 May, Convocation accepted the MPs' petition; it became known as the 'Submission of the Clergy'. Next day, More placed the Great Seal of England in a white leather bag, and delivered it to Henry at 3 p.m. in the garden of York Place; and Henry appointed another layman and common lawyer, Sir Thomas Audley, to succeed More as Lord Chancellor.[34] Henry now spent much time at York Place, which soon afterwards became known as Whitehall. He enlarged Wolsey's palace, and engaged in the ostentatious building which he afterwards carried out at his other residences, at Newhall in Essex, at Woking, at Oatlands near Weybridge, and at Nonesuch near Ewell.[35]

Everything was ready for the break with Rome, the repudiation of Papal supremacy, and the proclamation of Henry as the only Head of the Church in his realm.

15

THE BREAK WITH ROME

HENRY had only to give the word, and the break with the Papacy would be complete; but he did nothing. He waited for another year to see what the Pope would do; and the Pope, too, did virtually nothing, despite all the pressure from Charles. It was five years since Henry had begun the divorce proceedings, and three years since the case was advoked to Rome; but Clement dallied and played for time till his annual excuse came round again – the long Roman law vacation which made it impossible to take any step in the divorce proceedings between the middle of July and the beginning of November.

It is impossible to know what the English people thought about Henry's divorce. There were no public opinion polls in the sixteenth century, and general elections were not fought between political parties on issues of policy. But Catherine and Chapuys believed that a majority of the people were against the divorce, and that if the Pope gave judgement for Catherine, the strength of public opinion in England would force Henry to comply with the judgement, to send Anne Boleyn away, and to resume his former relations with Catherine. As the long vacation approached again in 1532, Dr Ortiz, Charles's ambassador in Rome, urged the Pope to give judgement for Catherine at once, and to excommunicate Henry for committing adultery with Anne; but on 8 July, Clement in Consistory rejected this proposal and decided instead to inform Henry that his excusator's arguments had been rejected, and that he must appear by a proctor before the court in Rome on or before 1 November, or the court would proceed to try the divorce case in his absence.[1]

Ortiz was bitterly disappointed. He told the Pope that he would denounce him as a sinner on the Day of Judgement because he had refused to excommunicate Henry. But Henry was as dissatisfied with the Pope's decision as Ortiz, Charles and Catherine. The rejection of his excusator's plea angered him almost as much as if Clement had given judgement for

Catherine in the divorce case itself.[2] He was now living openly with Anne as husband and wife, and he spoke less and less about the divorce and more and more of the insolent usurpation of the Pope in summoning a King of England to appear before a court outside his realm.

Chapuys heard welcome reports of opposition to the divorce in England, of demonstrations against Anne Boleyn as she rode through the villages with Henry on his progress, of women who said that she was a harlot who should be burned. At Yarmouth in Norfolk some women took part in a riot which Henry assumed must have been instigated by their husbands. The Prior of the Crossed Friars of London said at dinner in the priory on St James's Eve that if, as people were saying, Henry was planning to dissolve many religious houses, he should be called, not Defender of the Faith, but Destructor of the Faith.[3]

The opposition hoped to stir up the strong superstitious feelings of the people by producing a holy woman to prophesy disasters unless the King changed course. She was Elizabeth Barton, the 'Holy Maid of Kent', who had first appeared in 1526 in the village of Courtopestreet near Aldington. She went into trances before the assembled villagers, writhing on the ground and groaning till a great voice was heard which seemed to be speaking from the pit of her stomach. She and all the onlookers were convinced that it was the voice of an angel sent by God. Her father confessor was Edward Bocking, a monk of Christchurch Priory in Canterbury, who persuaded her to enter the nunnery of St Sepulchre's in Canterbury.

Under Bocking's guidance, Elizabeth Barton heard the voice of the angel reveal to her that heretics should be suppressed and Tyndale's New Testament burned. Once, when two heretic monks were about to sail to the Netherlands to visit Tyndale, the angel bade her pray for a contrary wind, which blew with such force that their ship was unable to leave harbour. She made a favourable impression on Warham and Fisher. She went to see Wolsey, and warned him not to aspire to too great authority in Church and State.

It was probably in 1532 that she asked for an audience with the King. Henry was not easily impressed with holy men and holy women. Some years before, when he had met a famous Spanish holy man who was visiting England, he afterwards commented that the man seemed to be more a friar than a saint, with no learning but more than Spanish impudence.[4] But he agreed to see Elizabeth Barton. She told him that an angel sent from God had commanded her to come to him and warn him to amend his life, to take away none of the Pope's right, to destroy these new folks' opinions and the books of their new learning, and that if he married Anne Boleyn the vengeance of God would plague him. Henry listened patiently to all that she had to say, and seemed to be moved by her words; but after she had left, he gave orders that she was to be kept under observation.

Two months later, she came to Henry again, and told him that her angel had revealed to her that if Henry married Anne, he would die within a month, and that within six months the realm would be stricken by a great plague. Henry's officers continued to keep her under observation. She led them to Bocking and to several brothers of the Friars Observants of Greenwich and other houses who had preached in support of Catherine and against Henry's divorce.[5]

Soleiman was massing an enormous army of 250,000 men in Hungary, and was planning to invade Austria. When the Pope appealed to Henry for help against Soleiman, Henry said that the report of an imminent Turkish invasion was untrue; it had been circulated by Charles in order to make the Pope believe that he needed Charles's help to save Christendom from the Turk, and was therefore obliged to comply with Charles's wishes about Henry's divorce. But the Turks crossed the Austrian frontier in June 1532, and by the beginning of August Soleiman was besieging Graz. Charles, who was at Regensburg, prepared to march against the Turks, and appealed to all the other Kings of Europe for military, or at least financial, aid.

Henry appointed Cranmer as his ambassador to Charles, and ordered him to say that if English soldiers were sent to help Charles, they would not be in a fit condition to fight after so long a journey and in a climate so unlike their own; and history had shown that Englishmen fought much better against the infidel when they were commanded by their King in person. Henry was too busy at the moment to lead his men on a crusade, but he would do so at some time in the future; he regretted that he could do nothing at present. Charles told Cranmer that it was disgraceful that he and his brother Ferdinand were abandoned by all their brother-Kings in this hour of peril, but they would do their duty and save Christendom unaided.[6] Charles then marched at the head of his army against Soleiman, who raised the siege of Graz and retreated into Hungary after devastating the Austrian countryside.

From Henry's point of view, both Soleiman and the German Lutherans could perform a useful function by irritating Charles; but as he faced the prospect of the final break with Rome, he looked for a more effective ally, and turned to François I. Henry had thwarted François and financed his enemies in 1515, he had deceived him in 1521, ravaged his country in 1522, marched on his capital in 1523, fleeced him in the peace treaty of 1525, and left him in the lurch when he was his ally during the war of 1528. But he knew that François hated Charles more than he hated him, and he rightly believed that he could make use of François.

Henry hoped that François would not only be his ally against Charles, but would also help him keep the peace with Scotland, for he did not want a war with the Scots at such a time. During the summer of 1532, there were frequent border violations by the Scots. Henry ordered the Earl of Northumberland to put the gentlemen of the county and their tenants in a state of readiness, and decided to make use of the Douglases. Angus had been living in England for the last four years; he sometimes came to court, and on one occasion won £100 from Henry in a game of bowls at Abingdon. Until now, whenever Angus had promised to serve Henry, it had always been subject to the qualification that he would serve him against everyone except his own sovereign, James V; but this pretence was now abandoned. On 25 August 1532, Angus agreed, under oath, that as Henry was the supreme overlord of Scotland, he would serve him if Henry made war on Scotland; and Henry, in return, promised to pay Angus £1,000 a year until he was restored to his lands in Scotland.

Henry sent a herald to James V, assuring him of his wish to remain at peace; and James gave similar assurances to Henry. But spasmodic fighting continued on the Border throughout the autumn.[7]

In the summer of 1532, Henry paid great attention to the French ambassador, Jean Du Bellay, the Bishop of Bayonne, and arranged for him to see a great deal of Anne Boleyn. He invited Du Bellay to accompany him on his progress, and Henry, Anne and Du Bellay spent a whole day hunting together at Ampthill in July. Henry left Anne and Du Bellay in a place where they could shoot together with their crossbows at the deer as Henry and the huntsmen drove them past. Anne was particularly charming to Du Bellay, and presented him with a hunting costume and hat, a horn, and a greyhound, for greyhounds were the best hunting dogs. Du Bellay was sure that she would not have done this unless Henry had told her to do it, for 'what the said Lady does is always by order of my lord the said King'.[8]

Henry invited François to meet him, so that they could concert their plans against Charles. He suggested that the meeting should take place at Calais and Boulogne, and that though it would be on a less lavish scale than the meeting at the Field of Cloth-of-gold twelve years before, it should be a sufficiently impressive affair to capture the attention of the world. He and François decided to announce that the purpose of their meeting was to discuss measures for the defence of Christendom against the Turk; but they did not expect, or even wish , that anyone should believe this.

Du Bellay advised François that if he wished to win Henry's friendship, he should invite Anne to the meeting, as nothing would please Henry more. Anne was duly invited, and Henry asked Du Bellay to arrange for François' sister Margaret, the Queen of Navarre, to come as the chief lady on the French side. Du Bellay realised that Henry did not want François to bring his wife, Charles V's sister, to the meeting; for Du Bellay wrote that Henry hated the Spanish dress 'so much that he seems to see a devil in it'.[9] But Henry had better reasons than this for hoping that a lady who was Charles's sister and Catherine's niece would not be in Boulogne and Calais while he was talking to François there. François solved the problem by not bringing any ladies to the meeting.

In preparation for the meeting with François, Henry created Anne Marquess* of Pembroke at a ceremony at Windsor on 1 September. She came before Henry, who was attended by Suffolk, Norfolk and Du Bellay; she was 'in her hair' and dressed in a surcoat of crimson velvet furred with ermine, with strait sleeves; and Norfolk's daughter, Lady Mary Howard, bore her train. As she knelt before Henry, Gardiner read out her patent, and Henry invested her with her mantle and coronet. As well as the title, he granted her lands valued at £1,023.13s.2d[10].

Henry wished the meeting with François to take place as soon as possible. Sir Edward Guilford, the Lord Warden of the Cinque Ports, told Cromwell that it had always been the custom for the Five Ports to be given at least forty days' notice when the King was intending to cross the sea, and that it would take all this time to prepare the shipping for the party that Henry was taking with him to Calais, because the ships of the Cinque Ports were scattered in many places, some off Whitby, some in the Isle of Man, and some fishing off Iceland. But he summoned the Mayors of the Five Ports to his house at Halden, and arranged with them to expedite the arrangements as far as possible.[11]

Cromwell and Henry's ministers were meanwhile taking steps to ensure that the ladies and gentlemen who were to come to Calais would appear in suitable style. Henry was not taking Catherine to the meeting with François, but he ordered her to send her jewels for Anne to wear in Calais. This was not quite as outrageous an affront to Catherine as might appear. The jewellery of the Princesses of the royal family were considered to be at the King's disposal when he needed them to adorn the ladies whom he selected to take part in state occasions. He also called on his sister Mary the French Queen to send her jewels to Anne. But it is not surprising that Catherine resented it, and that Chapuys reported it to Charles in order to fuel the sense of outrage and indignation with Henry at the Emperor's court. Catherine sent the jewels, and let it be known that she had acted as an obedient wife.[12]

Henry now had a stroke of luck. On 24 August Warham died. His death had long been expected, but he had lived on till he was about eighty, and had been Archbishop of Canterbury for twenty-eight years. There was general surprise when Henry appointed Cranmer to succeed him. This quiet, scholarly, and rather timid man was so unambitious that he had not filled any of the university offices at Cambridge during his twenty-six-years' residence there, and had done nothing of note before he reached the age of forty; when he was on trial as a heretic twenty years later, he said 'that there was never man came more unwillingly to a bishopric than I did to that'. But he had made a favourable impression on Henry during the three years that he had

* Modern writers have commented on the fact that her title was 'Marquess', not 'Marchioness', of Pembroke; but Marquesses' wives, as well as Anne, were often referred to as 'the Lady Marquess', as well as 'the Marchioness'.

been in his service. He was also Anne's chaplain.

The supporters of Catherine and of the Pope believed at the time that Anne had been responsible for Cranmer's appointment as Archbishop of Canterbury, and that he was a Lutheran.[13] There is no doubt that he was already sympathetic to Lutheranism in 1532. During his residence in Germany as ambassador at Charles's court, he not only made contact with the Lutherans in Nuremberg, but actually married the niece of the wife of the eminent Lutheran theologian, Osiander, although the marriage of priests was illegal in England and to advocate it was regarded as a Lutheran heresy. Henry presumably did not know about Cranmer's marriage at this time, for he first raised the matter with Cranmer in 1543;[14] but whatever Henry may or may not have known about Cranmer, and however much Anne may have favoured him, the decision to appoint him as Archbishop of Canterbury, like all other major decisions of government policy, was Henry's. As he manoeuvred between the Pope and the heretics, as he defied the Pope and burned Lutherans, Henry, who in 1529 had decided that he wanted the anti-Lutheran More as his Lord Chancellor, decided in 1532 that he wanted the pro-Lutheran Cranmer as Archbishop of Canterbury. Cranmer throughout his life always professed the greatest devotion and indeed love for Henry; so it is clear that Henry knew just how to handle him, as he had known how to handle Wolsey and More and all his other ministers. For Henry, Cranmer was a loyal servant to be used and one day sacrificed, though Cranmer, unlike most of Henry's ministers, was not chosen as a sacrificial victim until after Henry's death.

Henry sent Hawkins to Regensburg to replace Cranmer as ambassador and to recall him to England, and then left for Calais with Anne, the thirteen-year-old Duke of Richmond, Suffolk, Norfolk, Cromwell, a number of peers and ladies, and some two thousand gentlemen and servants. As there was plague at Rochester, Henry went by water from Greenwich to Sir Thomas Cheyney's house at Shurland in the Isle of Sheppey, and then overland to Canterbury and Dover. At 5 p.m. on 11 October he embarked in *The Swallow*, and reached Calais five hours later. He stayed ten days at Calais, and on 21 October rode towards Boulogne for his meeting with François. Anne and the ladies stayed in Calais while six hundred lords, gentlemen and soldiers went with Henry to Boulogne.

Henry and François met on the frontier, two miles north of Marquise. They embraced five or six times without dismounting, and rode side by side and hand in hand for a mile, till they reached a fountain in a little copse, where they dismounted and drank some wine before continuing to Boulogne. As they entered the town they were greeted with the salute of a thousand guns which could be heard twenty miles away. Henry and François both stayed at the abbey. At dinner in the abbey, Henry's servants, as usual, knelt as they brought him the dishes, though François' servants, in the

French custom, stood to serve him. The meeting at Boulogne was meant to be an occasion for business rather than display; there were no tournaments or lavish banquets; but Henry played some tennis in Boulogne. Despite the modest scale of the entertainments, he displayed his wealth in his clothes. He wore a crimson satin doublet set with pearls which were said to be worth 100,000 crowns.

After spending three days in Boulogne, the Kings and their escorts rode to Calais on Friday 25 October. At Calais, Henry was able to outdo François by having everything bigger and better than at Boulogne. As they entered Calais, they were greeted by a salute from three thousand guns, though the guns were smaller than the thousand guns at Boulogne. François wore a doublet at Calais which was embroidered with diamonds worth more than 100,000 crowns, and the French lords and gentlemen were better dressed than the English; but Henry wore a robe of violet cloth-of-gold with a collar containing fourteen rubies, the smallest of which was as large as an egg, and fourteen diamonds which were smaller, with two rows of great pearls and a carbuncle as big as a goose's egg; the collar was worth more than 400,000 crowns. And, unlike at Boulogne, there were ladies at Calais – the English ladies who entertained and charmed François, the Dauphin, the King of Navarre, and all the lords and gentlemen in François' train.

François was lodged at Calais in the house of the merchants of the Staple, while Henry stayed with Anne in another house a little way away. François sent the Provost of Paris to the house with a gift for Anne, a diamond worth fifteen or sixteen thousand crowns. There were no tournaments, but bear-baiting and bull-baiting in the garden of François' lodgings. There was a wrestling match between the English and French gentlemen, which the English won.

On the Sunday evening, there was a ball. Seven masked ladies entered, and danced with François and his nobles. During the dance, Henry removed the ladies' masks, and revealed that they were Lady Mary Howard, Lady Derby, Lady Fitzwalter, Lady Rochford, Lady Lisle, Lady Wallop, and – first and foremost among them, eclipsing all the others with her beauty – the Lady Marquis of Pembroke herself. Anne danced with François for an hour.

François spent three days in Calais, and left on Tuesday 29 October for Paris. Henry escorted him as far as Marquise, where the Kings parted. The Duke of Richmond went to Paris with François to complete his education at the French court.[15]

As the official reason for the meeting was to discuss the defence of Christendom against the Turk, a treaty was duly signed at Calais on 28 October, by which Henry and François agreed that if the Turk attacked Europe again, they woud provide an army of 80,000 men, including 15,000 cavalry, to fight against him. Even in this somewhat hypothetical situation, Henry, as always, was to have the best of his bargain with François, for

François was to provide 53,000 of the 80,000 men, including 11,000 of the 15,000 horsemen. But far more important, from Henry's point of view, were the discussions about the divorce and Henry's relations with the Pope. Although François was so courteous to Anne at Calais, he suggested to Henry that it would be wiser not to defy the Pope by divorcing Catherine and marrying Anne; but Henry rejected this advice out of hand. He did, however, agree when François urged him not to bastardise his daughter Mary, and that if he insisted on going through with the divorce, Mary would be treated as legitimate. This would comply with the rule of the canon law that children of void marriages were legitimate if their parents were acting in good faith and believed that the marriage was valid. François promised to do all in his power to persuade the Pope to give judgement for Henry in the divorce case, and not to take any action against Henry; and Henry promised to come to François' help if he were attacked by Charles.[16]

The weather had been remarkably mild for the time of year in Boulogne and Calais; but after François had left, strong gales sprang up, which prevented Henry from crossing to Dover. When the gales stopped, fog came, and Henry could not sail from Calais till 12 November, when he embarked at midnight and reached Dover at 5 a.m. He spent some days inspecting the new fortifications at Dover, and reached Eltham on 24 November. Thanksgiving services for his safe return were held all over England.

Four days later, he gave audience to Chapuys. Both King and ambassador excelled each other in courtesy and duplicity. Henry assured Chapuys that nothing had been agreed at Boulogne and Calais which could harm the Emperor; and Chapuys assured Henry that the Emperor would be delighted to know that Henry and François were united in friendship and in their determination to resist the Turk. When Chapuys told Henry that Charles was going to meet the Pope at Bologna, Henry gave no sign of annoyance, and merely said that he hoped that the Pope's health would be good enough for him to meet the Emperor. But Chapuys was not really so happy, for the Lady Marquess of Exeter had sent him an unsigned letter informing him that Henry was planning to repudiate his allegiance to the Pope and to be divorced by his bishops in England.[17]

Charles had now arrived at Mantua on his way to Bologna, and Cranmer had accompanied him. Hawkins did not catch up with Cranmer till he reached Mantua on 16 November, when he told Cranmer that he had been appointed Archbishop of Canterbury. Cranmer left Mantua next day, but travelled very slowly. He told his judges at Oxford in 1555 that he took seven weeks over the journey home because he hoped that Henry would meanwhile forget about him and appoint someone else as Archbishop. But Henry sent Vaughan to escort Cranmer and hurry him up.

Cranmer had the excuse of the weather, for the roads of France were frozen. When Vaughan, after crossing from Dover, landed at Wissant, no one would hire out a horse to him, as the roads were too slippery, and he had to walk the twelve miles to Boulogne. There he managed to obtain a horse, but the horse slipped on the ice near Abbeville, and Vaughan hurt his leg, and had to wait at Amiens while he received medical treatment. He eventually met Cranmer at Lyons; but he could not persuade him to travel more than fifteen miles a day, and they did not reach London till about 10 January. According to the contemporary Catholic writers, Henry was at a bear-baiting when Cranmer arrived at Greenwich, and they professed to be very shocked that Henry had appointed Cranmer Archbishop of Canterbury at a bear-baiting.[18]

Nothing was happening about the divorce. As Henry did not send a proctor to the Papal court in Rome when it resumed the hearings after All Saints' Day, the Pope decreed that the case could continue in Henry's absence; but he refused the demands of Charles's agents that he give judgement for Catherine at once; nor would he excommunicate Henry, though Charles saw that he was informed of Henry's outrageous conduct in taking Anne to the meeting with François at Calais after Clement had ordered him to put her away. Catherine was in despair. She wrote to Charles: 'The thunders of the earth do not cast thunderbolts except to strike at me'.[19]

Then, at the end of January 1533, Anne realised that she was pregnant. If the baby was a boy, he could be the male heir that Henry so greatly needed. He must marry Anne before the baby was born so that it would be legitimate, and the sooner he married her, the better for the sake of propriety. He decided on his course of action. He would marry her at once, but keep the marriage secret; then an Act of Parliament would be passed, abolishing the right of appeal to the Papal court in Rome; then Cranmer, as Archbishop of Canterbury, would try the divorce case in England and give judgement that Henry's marriage to Catherine was, and had always been, void because it was prohibited by God's law, and the Papal dispensation of 1503 could not validate it. As Henry had never been married to Catherine, he was a bachelor in January 1533 and free to marry Anne. If anyone knew that Anne's sister, Lady Carey, had once been Henry's mistress, and ventured to suggest that this invalidated his marriage to Anne, the answer was that this impediment, being only an impediment of the canon law and not of God's law, had been overcome by the dispensation which the Pope had granted Henry in 1527 to marry the sister of a woman who had been his mistress if his marriage to Catherine should be held to have been void. As Anne's baby would be born less that nine months after the end of January, a rumour would be circulated, in due course, that Henry had married Anne on St Erkenwald's Day, 14 November 1532, though no one seems to have realised that this would mean that they had been married at Dover on the day after they returned from Calais.

But for the moment the marriage was to be kept very secret. Although Henry was about to repudiate Papal supremacy, and set up Cranmer as the first schismatic Archbishop of Canterbury, it was better to have everything in order, so that no legal objection could be raised against what he was about to do. He therefore wanted Cranmer to be the last English bishop to be consecrated under the authority of a Papal bull. He informed the Pope that he had appointed Cranmer as Archbishop of Canterbury, and asked Clement to authorise his consecration. He also asked him to expedite the issue of the bull, for usually many months elapsed between the appointment of a bishop by the King and the issue by the Pope of the bull for his consecration.

This raised the question of the annates payable for the see of Canterbury – the first year's income of the see, which amounted to £15,000. Henry thought that he might as well save this £15,000 if possible. As the Act of May 1532, which abolished the payment of annates to Rome, was not to come into force for a year, and then only if Henry so stipulated, the annates were still payable in Cranmer's case. Henry asked the Pope, as a favour, to waive the payment of the annates. There was nothing very unusual in such a request, for the amount to be paid as annates was always a matter for negotiation when a new bishop was consecrated; but Henry could not normally have expected Clement to agree, at a time when relations between them were so strained. On the other hand, Clement knew that if he refused to waive the annates, Henry might bring into operation the Act which abolished the payment of annates altogether.

Clement must know nothing about Henry's marriage to Anne until after he had granted the bull for Cranmer's consecration; and the secret was so well kept that we do not know today when the marriage took place. After it became known some months later, it was generally assumed that Cranmer had married them, though this was inconsistent with the general belief that they had been married on 14 November 1532. But Cranmer himself wrote to Hawkins that they were married about the time of the Feast of St Paul, 25 January 1533, that he had not married them, and that he did not know about the marriage until a fortnight afterwards.[20] So Henry and Anne did not tell even Cranmer, the Archbishop elect of Canterbury and Anne's chaplain, though he was at court at the time. We do not know who officiated at the marriage ceremony.

After six years of caution, Henry had at last decided to break with Rome, to take England into schism, and to take the first step on a path which led, probably inevitably, to England becoming a Protestant state with an official religion which was considered to be heretical by all the authorities, including Henry himself, in 1533. Anne's unborn baby was the decisive factor. The baby later became Queen Elizabeth I. She rendered the first of her many services to the Protestant cause when she was in her mother's womb.

While Henry waited for Clement to issue the bulls for Cranmer's consecration, he was very conciliatory to the Nuncio. When the Nuncio pressed him to send aid to save Christendom from the Turk, he said that he was a small Prince without power in a corner of the world by himself, but that he would do what he could. But there was always the implied threat of the stick as well as the carrot, of the Act against annates which he could bring into force. He ordered Benet in Rome to remind the Pope that he was the successor to St Peter, a fisherman, and that if a fisherman 'draweth his net too fast and too hard, then he breaketh it, and pulling it softly taketh fish good plenty'. The net had been pulled too tight in the case of the German Lutherans, 'Remember how the net broke in Pope Leo's days by the foolish handling of a Cardinal, who pulled and hauled and so rent the net that it is not yet made whole again, but rather rendeth more and more'. The Pope should remember that Princes are great fishes, and should be carefully handled; if the Pope refused to gratify Henry in so small a matter, no Prince in Christendom would tolerate the Pope's authority.[21]

Chapuys had no doubt that Henry had appointed Cranmer Archbishop of Canterbury in order that he should divorce him from Catherine and set up a schismatic Church. On 27 January, he wrote to Charles, who was with the Pope at Bologna, and told him this, and that Cranmer was said to be a Lutheran. The Nuncio in London also wrote and warned the Pope. On 9 February, Chapuys wrote again to Charles, and urged him to persuade the Pope to refuse to issue the bulls for Cranmer's consecration, to give judgement at once for Catherine in the divorce case, and to excommunicate Anne, which might be wiser than excommunicating the King himself. It would be a particularly good moment to act against Henry, while he was engaged in a war with Scotland. But if the Pope failed to act now, and allowed Cranmer to be consecrated, then Cranmer, Anne, and her father Wiltshire, who were all Lutherans, would persuade Henry to destroy the Church. It was now or never for the Pope.

Chapuys repeated his warning to Charles in two more letters, and informed him that he had heard that Cranmer had secretly married Henry to Anne. But on 21 February, the Pope, who was still with Charles in Bologna, issued the bulls for Cranmer's consecration, and agreed to waive his right to part of the annates. Chapuys wrote to Charles that all Catherine's supporters were disgusted that the Pope had issued Cranmer's bulls.[22]

Henry waited for only a few days after receiving the bulls before introducing a bill in Parliament abolishing the right of appeal to Rome in ecclesiastical cases. This would prevent Catherine from appealing against the judgement which Cranmer would shortly deliver. When Chapuys talked to Henry on 15 March as they walked for two hours in the garden at Greenwich, Henry spoke about the arrogance of the Pope in expecting even Kings to kiss his foot and claiming the right to depose them. He said that the Papal power was a threat to every Prince in Christendom.[23]

Sir George Throckmorton spoke in the House of Commons and expressed his doubts about the bill to abolish appeals to Rome; so Henry summoned him to court to discuss the matter with him and Cromwell. Throckmorton told Henry that it would be most inadvisable for him to marry Anne Boleyn, 'for it is thought ye have meddled both with the mother and the sister'. 'Never with the mother', said Henry. 'Nor never with the sister either', said Cromwell, 'and therefore put that out of your mind'. Henry said nothing; he left Cromwell to do the lying.[24]

Cranmer was consecrated Archbishop of Canterbury in St Stephens Church in Westminster on 30 March 1533. It was a necessary part of the consecration ceremony that the Archbishop should take an oath, swearing to be obedient to Pope Clement VII and his successors and to defend the Roman Papacy against all men. This raised a problem for Henry. He wanted Cranmer's consecration ceremony to be correct in every detail, so that no one could claim that he had not been properly consecrated; but as he knew that he would very shortly be asserting that the Pope had no authority in England, and that Cranmer would then do all that he could to overthrow the Roman Papacy, he did not wish his Archbishop to break his oath within a few months of taking office. As usual with Henry, he solved the problem by having it both ways; for it was certainly on Henry's instructions that Cranmer made his famous protestation, though the contemporary Catholic writers blamed Cranmer alone for it.

Before entering the church, Cranmer made the protestation in the chapter house at Westminster, in the presence of five lawyers. He declared that he did not intend to be bound by the oath of obedience to the Pope that he was about to take, if it was against the law of God or against our illustrious King of England, or the laws of his realm of England, and that he did not regard it as preventing him from taking any step which would increase the King's prerogative. He read the protestation aloud three times in the church, though most of the people in the audience there do not seem to have appreciated the significance of what he was saying. This is not surprising, and Henry and Cranmer may have relied on the fact that they would not notice.[25]

Two days after Cranmer's consecration, the bishops in the Convocation of Canterbury discussed the King's divorce, and decided that if the marriage between Arthur and Catherine had been consummated, then the marriage of Henry and Catherine was unlawful and void by God's law. Fisher was the only bishop to speak and vote against this resolution, which was also carried in the Lower House of Convocation by 14 votes against 7. On 3 April, a small group of canon lawyers reported to Convocation that they had carefully considered the evidence that had been given before Wolsey and Campeggio at the trial at Blackfriars in 1529, and that it proved beyond doubt that the marriage of Arthur and Catherine had been consummated.[26] Henry had decided that Cranmer could now give judgement for him without hearing any further evidence or argument, on the basis of the resolution of

Convocation and the decision of these canon lawyers.

On 11 April, Cranmer wrote to Henry, asking his permission to try his divorce case, as the rude and ignorant people were everywhere discussing it, and in view of its importance for the succession. Because 'it shall not become me, for as much as Your Grace is my Prince and sovereign, to enterprise any part of my office in the said weighty cause without Your Grace's favour obtained', he asked Henry, 'beseeching Your Highness most humbly upon my knees', to allow him to sit in judgement on the validity of his marriage to Catherine. Cranmer submitted the draft to Henry, who returned it with certain alterations which were designed to make Cranmer's language still more submissive and his request for permission to try the case more specific. In Henry's draft, Cranmer asked permission to try the case, not 'beseeching Your Highness most humbly upon my knees' but 'prostrate at the feet of Your Majesty'.[27] The phrase 'prostrate at the feet' was not an example of Henry's overweening vanity, but the accepted form in which a petitioner addressed the King, and by inserting it Henry was doing no more than to put Cranmer's draft into the proper language.

The change from 'Your Highness' to 'Your Majesty' was more significant. The accepted manner of addressing the King was 'Your Grace' or 'Your Highness', both of which were correct. The Emperor was always addressed as 'Your Majesty'. Henry was the first English King to make regular use of this title, which he adopted to show that he was Charles's equal, and emperor in his own realm, with no superior except God. He was perfectly content that the style 'His Grace' and 'His Highness' should continue to be used, but an occasional reference to 'His Majesty' was desirable; and nowhere was it more desirable than in this document at this time. With Henry about to repudiate the Pope's authority, when he was faced with the possibility of excommunication and perhaps rebellion, his royal authority must be emphasized to the uttermost; and as a litigant is normally regarded as being inferior to the judge, it was essential for Henry to show that, although he was appearing as a litigant before the Archbishop of Canterbury, he was nevertheless the Archbishop's superior.

Henry replied to Cranmer's letter next day. He wrote that 'ye, whom God and we have ordained Archbishop of Canterbury', had asked permission to try the divorce case, 'duly recognising that it becometh you not, being our subject, to enterprise any part of your said office in so weighty and great a cause, pertaining to us, being your Prince and sovereign, without our licence obtained so to do'. He had decided to grant Cranmer's humble petition. 'Albeit we, being your King and sovereign, do recognise no superior in earth, but only God, and not being subject to the laws of any other earthly creature', he would nevertheless allow Cranmer to try the case according to God's laws, 'to the which laws we, as a Christian King, have always heretofore, and shall ever, most obediently submit ourself . . . (our preeminent power and authority to us, and our successors, in this behalf nevertheless saved)'.[28]

Henry and his counsellors were very conscious of the opposition to the divorce in the country, and that the plan for Cranmer to try the case in defiance of the Pope's authority might arouse resentment in some quarters. They thought that it would be undesirable for the trial to be held in London, where there might be demonstrations by Catherine's supporters. Henry decided that Cranmer's court should sit at the priory at Dunstable, which was thirty-five miles from London, a day's ride. If anyone asked why the trial should be held there, it could be said to be convenient for Queen Catherine, who was living in Henry's manor at Ampthill. Cranmer summoned Henry and Catherine to appear before his court, in person or by proctor, on 10 May.[29]

Chapuys knew that the decisive moment had come. He had always believed that appeasement would encourage Henry, and that firmness would make him draw back; and as the Pope refused to do anything against Henry, and Charles was cautious, he resolved to act himself. It was a daring and risky policy, because it involved resorting very largely to bluff, making threats which he knew would not be implemented, and almost exceeding the authority which Charles had given him. It also entailed some personal risk to himself, for eight years before, when relations between Charles and Henry were much better than in 1533, Henry and Wolsey had violated the diplomatic immunity of Charles's ambassador, Praet, holding him under house arrest and threatening him with punishment. But apart from his sense of duty towards Charles and the Catholic religion, he had a strong personal sympathy and respect for Catherine and her daughter Mary, and wished to do what little he could to help them.

On 7 April, Chapuys went to court and asked for an audience with Henry. He met Norfolk and Wiltshire, who told him that Henry was too busy to see him; but after Chapuys had warned them that Charles would take a very serious view of a refusal by Henry to receive his ambassador, they arranged for him to have an audience with Henry two days later, on Maundy Thursday. Chapuys spoke very frankly and firmly to the King, who in reply used all the weapons in his armoury – theological argument, threats, and jocular good humour. Chapuys said that his duty to God and the Emperor required him to protest most strongly against the measures which were being taken in Parliament and in Convocation against Queen Catherine; and as Henry obviously had no regard for what men thought of him, as he despised them all, at least he should have regard to God. Henry assured Chapuys that he certainly had regard for God, which was why he was obeying God's law and refusing to cohabit with his brother's widow, and that he and his conscience were on excellent terms. Chapuys said that the world would think it very strange that Henry should put away his Queen after twenty-five years. Henry replied that twenty-five years was not such a long time, and that the world thought it even stranger that the Pope should grant a dispensation which he had no power to grant. When Henry said that he needed a son to ensure the succession, Chapuys pointed out that he could not be sure that he would have children by a second marriage. Henry protested at this, and asked three times if he was not like other men – '*s'il n'était point homme comme les autres*?' – and hinted that Anne was pregnant.

Henry asked Chapuys if he had been instructed by the Emperor to speak in this way, or if he spoke personally. This put Chapuys on the defensive; he said that Charles could not instruct him about events which had taken place only a week before, but that he was acting under the general power which the Emperor had given him to maintain friendship between him and Henry, and that nothing was more important for this friendship than the way in which Queen Catherine was treated. After a long discussion, Henry said that Charles had no business to interfere in English internal affairs, and that if the Emperor tried to use force against him, he would defeat him with the help of his allies. As for Catherine, he was no more her husband than Chapuys was.

At the end of their talk, Henry dismissed Chapuys most graciously, but continued to detain Chapuys's secretary, who had been present during their conversation, and spoke to him in private after Chapuys had left. He continued arguing his case with the secretary, and suggested to him that Chapuys's arguments had been fallacious; but the secretary said that he was not competent to discuss such matters. Norfolk and Wiltshire invited Chapuys and the secretary to dine with them, at court, but they refused.[30]

Next day, Chapuys wrote to Charles and advised him to send an army to invade England. He argued that the Pope would be fully justified in calling in the help of the secular arm against Henry and the English Lutherans, in order to end the scandal of the divorce and to prevent the kingdom from becoming Lutheran. The intervention would succeed, because it would be welcomed not only by the English people but by all the higher classes except the Duke of Norfolk and two or three others, so that Henry would have no leaders to command his army and no horsemen to serve in it. Charles need not fear François, who would certainly not go to war with him for Henry's sake. At the least, Charles should immediately break off diplomatic relations with Henry and expel the English ambassadors from Spain and the Netherlands.[31]

Catherine denied that Cranmer had any right to try her case, and consulted Chapuys as to what she should do. He advised her to refuse to attend the court, but not to challenge its jurisdiction, for this might make her liable to be prosecuted for a praemunire under the Act in Restraint of Appeals. On 6 May, four days before Cranmer's court was due to open at Dunstable, Chapuys made another daring intervention on Catherine's behalf. He wrote to Henry that as the Emperor had ordered him to act in Catherine's interests, he had constituted himself as her proctor, and in this capacity he challenged Cranmer's jurisdiction to try the divorce case. He was invited to appear before the King's Council next day, and argued with Wiltshire and the other counsellors, including Cromwell, who, Chapuys wrote, managed all the King's business. They told him that if any Englishman had written the letter which Chapuys had sent to the King, he would have been arrested and prosecuted under the Act in Restraint of Appeals, and that if Chapuys tried to act in a dual capacity as proctor for Catherine as well as ambassador, he might forfeit his diplomatic immunity; but they treated him with courtesy, speaking to him more in sorrow than in anger.[32]

Chapuys stayed away from court as far as possible, for he thought that Catherine's supporters would be discouraged if they thought that the Emperor's ambassador was on friendly terms with Henry. On two occasions, Henry invited him to hunt in his parks at any time he wished, but Chapuys refused the invitation.[33]

Cranmer did all he could to expedite the proceedings at Dunstable, for Henry wanted Anne to be crowned as his Queen on Whit Sunday, 1 June. But it was important that everything should be in order, and the court could not sit on the Rogation days or on Ascension Day. Henry and Cranmer made no pretence, between themselves, that Cranmer was acting as an impartial judge; he considered himself to be performing his duty to the King at Dunstable. He wrote regularly to Henry throughout the trial, assuring him that everything was proceeding according to plan, and that he would give judgement for him as soon as possible.[34]

On 23 May, Cranmer gave judgement that the marriage of Henry and Catherine was, and had always been, unlawful, that they must no longer cohabit as husband and wife, and that both of them were free to marry again. Five days later, at a very private hearing in his palace at Lambeth, he gave judgement that Henry had been lawfully married to Anne at the secret marriage ceremony four months earlier. On Whit Sunday, Anne was crowned in Westminster Abbey in a splendid ceremony, with a procession through the streets of London which was remembered by the citizens for many years. It was watched by thousands of interested, but silently hostile, spectators. Henry did not attend the coronation, for Kings were never present when their Queens Consorts were crowned separately; but he watched the procession from a hidden window where no one could see him.[35]

When the news of Cranmer's judgement reached Charles in Barcelona, he urged the Pope to give judgement for Catherine in the divorce case, to excommunicate Henry, and to issue a bull depriving him of his kingdom. Clement told Charles that he did not wish to do this unless he was sure that the bulls could be enforced; would Charles enforce them if he issued them? On 31 May, Charles's Council in Barcelona held a meeting to decide what action to take. They ruled out the use fo military force against Henry; the operation would be much too hazardous, and Henry would have the help of his various allies; war with England might endanger the Emperor's realms, particularly Germany, where the Lutheran Princes would enter the war on Henry's side. They also rejected the idea of a trade embargo against England, for this could easily lead to war, and would injure the interests of the Emperor's subjects in the Netherlands. The Pope must therefore be discouraged from imposing an interdict which would prohibit Christians from having any dealings with England, for this would mean a trade embargo.

Charles wrote to Chapuys, restraining his ardour and ordering him on no account to declare war on Henry. He also instructed Ortiz in Rome to press the Pope to excommunicate and deprive Henry, but not to proclaim the interdict against England.[36]

The modern Catholic writers, taking their cue from Catherine and Chapuys, have been very ready to blame the Pope for his weakness at every stage of the divorce case, and to hold him responsible, by his cowardice, for the fact that England became a Protestant state; but they have not pointed out that Charles V bears a heavier responsibility. Having made it impossible, at the beginning of the divorce case, for Clement to comply with Henry's wishes, and having egged him on against Henry at every turn, he refused, when it came to the crunch, to take any effective action, while continuing to urge the Pope to make himself a laughing stock by issuing unenforceable bulls.

16

THE PRINCESS DOWAGER

As soon as Cranmer had delivered his judgement, Henry ordered that Catherine should no longer have the title of Queen, but should be known as the Princess Dowager of Wales, to which she was entitled as the widow of Arthur, her only lawful husband. Her daughter Mary, who had been bastardised by the judgement, was no longer to be called 'Princess Mary', but 'the King's daughter, the Lady Mary'. When he sent Lord Mountjoy and other officials to Ampthill to inform Catherine of this on 4 July, she indignantly refused to accept the order. Seizing a pen, she struck out the words 'Princess Dowager' from the document which Mountjoy produced, and told him that Cranmer's judgement was illegal.[1] Her words would have been more than enough to ensure her arrest had they been spoken by any ordinary subject.

Mary, too, refused to recognise Cranmer's judgement, and insisted that she was Henry's legitimate daughter by a lawful marriage and was entitled to the rank of Princess. Henry had promised François at Calais that if he were divorced from Catherine, Mary would not be bastardised; but though he admitted to Chapuys that, under the canon law, she would be treated as legitimate because her parents had believed that they were lawfully married, he explained that this would cause difficulties about the succession to the crown, which was to be vested in Anne's children. He added that, in any case, Mary's disobedience justified him in disinheriting her, and he preferred the laws of his realm to the canon law.[2]

While Henry defied the Papal authority, he as usual counterbalanced it by action against heretics. That fine young man, John Frith, who charmed all who knew him, had been imprisoned in the Tower of London since Sir Thomas More's agents arrested him in the spring of 1532. The conditions of his imprisonment became less rigorous after More resigned office, but he was not released. After he had been a year in the Tower, he was denounced by a preacher at court, and Henry ordered that he should be tried for heresy.

Henry needed a Protestant extremist as a victim at this moment, to show foreign rulers and his orthodox Catholic subjects that though he might be a schismatic he was not a heretic. It would also serve as a warning to the heretics and Lutherans that they must not go too far. Frith denied the Real Presence in the Eucharist. This was the issue on which Luther had strongly denounced Zwingli; so Henry could rely on the support even of the Lutherans, those potential allies, in persecuting Frith.

In June 1533 Frith was examined by Cranmer and other commissioners. They found him guilty of heresy, excommunicated him, and delivered him to the secular arm for burning. On 17 June, Cranmer wrote to Hawkins that Frith 'looketh every day to go unto the fire'.

Tyndale wrote from the Netherlands to Frith in prison, telling him that his wife was prepared for him to suffer martyrdom. 'Sir, your wife is well content with the will of God, and would not for her sake have the glory of God hindered'. Frith was burned at Smithfield on 4 July. A London tailor, Andrew Huett, was burned with him. He was not as learned as Frith, but equally steadfast in denying the Real Presence. He had an easier death as they burned side by side, for the wind blew towards him and fanned the flames, which brought a quick death; but as it blew away from Frith, his fire burned slowly, and he suffered for a long time.[3]

Henry was in happy mood when he left on his annual progress. On 6 August, Sir John Russell wrote from Mr Weston's house at Sutton near Guildford that he had never seen Henry merrier than now.[4] From Sutton Henry went to Windsor, and on 17 August gave audience there to Chapuys and his colleague Sauch, who had come from the Netherlands. After Margaret of Austria's death in 1530, Charles appointed his sister Mary, the widow of King Ladislaus of Bohemia and Hungary, to succeed Margaret as Regent of the Netherlands; and Mary of Hungary now sent Sauch to England in haste. A dispute about taxation had arisen between Henry and the merchants of the Staple at Calais, and as a result Henry closed the Staple for a few months, and banned the export of wool from England to Calais. This meant that the wool could not reach the Netherlands.

Chapuys and Sauch complained to Henry that this was causing great hardship in the Netherlands, and asked him when the Staple would be reopened. Henry pretended to be surprised at the ambassadors' concern; surely the people of the Netherlands could obtain an alternative supply of wool from Spain, or make do with the fine cloths which they could import from France? When Chapuys and Sauch said that these supplies would not compensate the Netherlands for the loss of English wool, Henry said that if Charles and Mary of Hungary were so dependent on English wool, they must adopt a different tone towards him than they had done recently; he refused to give any indication of when he would reopen the Staple, as this was a matter between him and his subjects which did not concern Mary of

Thomas Cranmer, by Gerlach Flicke, 1545

Thomas Cromwell, Earl of Essex, after Holbein

Hungary.[5] The Staple was reopened soon afterwards; but Henry was encouraged by his talk with Chapuys and Sauch. If a few weeks' interruption in the flow of English wool to the Netherlands could so disturb Mary of Hungary, she and Charles would not enforce an interdict against England.

While relations between Charles and Henry were at their worst, seven warships of the Hansa town of Lübeck, under the command of Captain Marcus Meyer, were sailing across the North Sea towards London. Lübeck was one of the free cities of the Empire, but a few years before, a revolution had occurred there and had brought to power a radical government which was now under the leadership of Jürgen Wullenweber. The government of Lübeck adopted a very extreme position in religion, though their enemies were exaggerating when they denounced them as Anabaptists. Religious, political and commercial hostility had combined to bring about a state of undeclared war between the seamen of Lübeck and the merchants of Charles V's territories in the Netherlands.

Meyer sailed up the Thames and asked to be allowed to revictual and re-equip his ships. Henry allowed him to buy provisions in London, but not to remain there, because Lübeck was in effect waging war against the Emperor's subjects. Two small Spanish merchant ships were lying in the Thames. Meyer's men boarded them and robbed them, and sailed away with their loot.

Chapuys protested to Cromwell against this attack on the Emperor's subjects in English territorial waters, and demanded compensation for the Spanish merchants. Henry's first reaction was anger against the Lübeck captain who had affronted his honour by violating his neutrality and had embroiled him in yet another dispute with the Emperor at a time when he did not wish to provoke Charles. He told the Hansa merchants of the Steelyard in London that as Lübeck was a Hansa town he would hold them responsible for Captain Meyer's robbery, and that he would confiscate all their property in England, which was worth more than 5,000 ducats, unless they sent their ships after the Lübeck warships and brought the captain back to account for what he had done. The Hansa merchants' ships caught the Lübeck ships in the Downs; and though Meyer had 2,200 armed men with him, he agreed to return the loot and to come back to England, in order to prevent the reprisals which Henry was threatening to take against all the Hansa merchants. He was imprisoned in Dover Castle.

But Henry then had second thoughts. The Lübeckers were Charles's rebels and enemies, and if Henry could make use of them against Charles, he would be quite prepared to overlook their Anabaptist sympathies. He rejected Chapuys's demand for compensation; if the Spanish merchants whom Meyer had robbed were Charles's subjects, so were the Lübeckers. Why should Henry compensate Charles's subjects who had been robbed by other subjects of Charles? It was for Charles to compensate them, and to prevent his subjects from fighting each other. Chapuys tried to explain to Henry's counsellors the complicated legal structure of the Empire: the Emperor was protector of the Empire, including Lübeck, but the principalities and free cities of the Empire were independent states which might lawfully wage war against the Netherlands. He argued that Henry, as a neutral, was liable if his officers permitted a belligerent to attack his enemy in Henry's territory.[6]

In the autumn of 1533, Henry ordered that Meyer should be brought from Dover Castle to Westminster, and after Meyer had given his word of honour not to try to escape, he was allowed to stay at liberty at court. Henry granted Meyer an audience, and showed him great favour; he praised his valour as a sea-captain, and told his courtiers that he had a high opinion of him. After the government of Lübeck had apologised to Henry for Meyer's violation of English neutrality, Henry opened negotiations with Lübeck, through Meyer, about the possibility of forming an alliance against the Emperor. He made a public demonstration of his high regard for Meyer. On Sunday 7 December Meyer was standing among the courtiers and the public who as usual were waiting to see Henry pass on his way to Mass, and perhaps to speak to him. Seeing Meyer in the crowd, Henry called him over and immediatley knighted him. A few days later, he gave Sir Marcus Meyer a golden chain worth four or five hundred ducats.[7]

The Lübeckers put an interesting proposition to Henry. The kingdom of Denmark was on the verge of civil war. The Emperor's brother-in-law, King Christian II, having been thrown out of his Swedish provinces by the national revolution under Gustavus Vasa, lost Denmark too when he was overthrown by his uncle, Duke Frederick of Holstein, who made himself King of Denmark and imprisoned Christian in a fortress. In 1533 King Frederick died, and was succeeded by his son, Christian III, who continued to hold Christian II a prisoner. Christian III had made Denmark a Lutheran state; but this did not make him friendly to 'Anabaptist' Lübeck, or lessen the trade rivalries between the Danes and the Lübeckers. As Charles V was incensed at the deposition and imprisonment of his brother-in-law, Christian III was on the brink of war with both Lübeck and the Emperor. He was the ally of Gustavus Vasa, and preserved the traditional friendship between Denmark and Scotland, which did not please Henry.

Meyer and the government of Lübeck suggested to Henry that if he were to make an alliance with Lübeck, and if Christian III should be overthrown, a situation might develop in which Henry could intervene and make himself King of Denmark. This was still only a hypothetical situation; but Henry sent envoys to Lübeck to negotiate with Wullenweber.[8]

Anne's baby was born at Greenwich on 7 September 1533. To the joy of the supporters of the Pope and Catherine, it was a girl.[9] In view of all that Henry and his supporters had said about Catherine's failure to give birth to a surviving male heir, Anne's similar failure was a moral defeat for Henry, and was regarded by his enemies as God's judgement against him and Anne. But Henry was not the man to be disheartened by a set-back, or to show his disappointment to the world. He took even greater steps than he might otherwise have done to have his daughter, Elizabeth, proclaimed as the lawful heiress to the throne.

The birth of Elizabeth gave Henry an additional motive to attempt to force Catherine and Mary to submit. His treatment of them shocked Chapuys, Charles, and all the establishment of Papist Europe, and modern historians have been equally indignant. One could not expect a man like Henry to show any consideration for their feelings; but it would be wrong to suppose that he acted out of sadism or in order to please a spiteful Anne. As with most of Henry's actions, his object was political – to enforce absolute obedience to his royal authority. He offered to make a generous settlement of lands and money in Catherine's favour if she would accept the judgement of Cranmer's court and the title of Princess Dowager. If she had agreed to this, she would, after all, only have done what many other Queens had been obliged to do in similar circumstances, by submitting to a divorce when the King her husband considered this to be necessary for reasons of State. The refusal of Catherine and Mary to obey his orders and the laws of his realm was an act of disobedience, of rebellion, and in law a criminal offence which few sovereigns would have tolerated, though many Kings would not have forced the issue and closed all avenues of compromise, as Henry did.

In view of Catherine's defiant attitude, Henry ordered her to move from Ampthill to Buckden in Huntingdonshire. When Catherine asked that Mary should be allowed to live with her, Henry refused, on the grounds that they would encourage each other in their disobedience. He would not even allow Mary to visit her mother or to write to her, though Mary offered to submit her letters, unsealed, to Henry's officers to censor. Henry made it clear that Mary would be allowed to visit Catherine, and live with her, and would be granted many other favours, if they both submitted and accepted that Catherine's marriage to Henry was unlawful, that Mary was a bastard, and that Anne was Queen and Elizabeth heiress to the throne.[10]

Henry ordered Catherine to send him the christening robe which Mary had worn at her baptism seventeen years before, for Elizabeth to wear at her christening. This was a test of her obedience. Catherine did not send the robe.[11]

When Elizabeth was three months old, Henry ordered Mary to join the Princess's household as one of her ladies-in-waiting. Mary replied that she knew of no other Princess in England except herself, as Lady Pembroke's daughter had no such title. But she conceded that she could call the Lady Elizabeth 'sister', just as she called the Duke of Richmond 'brother'. After secretly consulting with Chapuys as to what she should do, she made a formal protest and then agreed to join Elizabeth's household. Chapuys told her to obey every order that she received from Henry, but to refuse to receive any letter in which she was not addressed as 'Princess'.[12]

In January 1534, Henry visited Hatfield, where the baby Princess and Mary were in residence. He showed his usual delight with the baby, but ordered that Mary should be confined to her room. She asked permission to speak to him, for she had always been fond of him, and he had formerly shown her much love; but he refused, because of her disobedience. When he left next morning, she went on to the roof of the house to look at him as he mounted his horse in the courtyard. He looked up, and she went on her knees and put her hands together as a salute to him. The gentlemen of his escort, who also saw her, pretended not to notice her; but Henry bowed to her, and raised his hand to his cap in salutation, whereupon all his gentlemen did so too. Henry then rode away.[13]

At Buckden, Catherine's chaplains, ladies and servants were loyal to her. They were ordered to take an oath that they would always address her as Princess Dowager, and not as Queen; but they refused, saying that they had sworn to serve her as Queen. In December 1533, Henry sent Suffolk and other officials to Buckden with orders to move Catherine to Fotheringhay. She refused to go, and locked herself in her room, and dared Suffolk to break down the door. Suffolk contented himself with arresting her chaplain, Abel, who was imprisoned in the Tower. Catherine's former chaplain, Friar Forest of the Friars Observants of Greenwich, had already been arrested. Catherine wrote to him that she would prefer to precede him than to follow him on the path to martyrdom for Jesus Christ.[14]

The Pope was still refusing to give judgement for her in the divorce case. This was partly due to François I, who was performing the promises that he had made to Henry at Boulogne and Calais. He urged the Pope not to give judgement for Catherine or excommunicate Henry, and said that he agreed with Henry that it was an affront to the honour of Kings that Henry's case should be tried at Rome. He had arranged to meet the Pope in the autumn of 1533 to negotiate a marriage alliance between his second son, Henry, Duke of Orleans, and the Pope's niece, Catherine de Medici; and he promised Henry that when he met the Pope he would use his influence with him on Henry's behalf. But this was not enough for Henry. He asked François to refuse to meet the Pope until the Pope abandoned his attitude of hostility towards Henry, and to refuse to marry his son to Catherine de Medici; but this was going too far. François refused to cancel the meeting or break off the marriage negotiations; but he continued to urge restraint on the Pope, although he assured him that he deplored Henry's defiance of the Papal authority and Cranmer's judgement at Dunstable.

François' efforts had their effect. As the long Roman law vacation approached again, for the sixth time since the beginning of the divorce proceedings, Clement again refused to give judgement and adjourned the divorce hearings until the beginning of November.[15]

François performed another service to Henry by exercising a restraining influence on James V, the only sovereign who was prepared to cause trouble for Henry in 1533. The raids across the Border had escalated into an undeclared war during the previous winter. In November 1532, 3,000 Scots invaded Northumberland and burned villages. The English retaliated on 12 December when Lord Dacre led an army of 2,000 local men into Scotland. They burned Douglas and twelve villages, and captured 2,000 cattle and a larger number of sheep. Sir Andrew Darcy wrote to Cromwell that the Douglases had planned the raid, which was the biggest that had been made in winter for two hundred years. James assembled a large force in order to hit back; but François strongly urged him not to attack England, and sent an envoy to Scotland in the hopes of mediating between Henry and James. François came very near to betraying his old Scottish ally in order to maintain his alliance with Henry. He informed Henry about James's preparations for war, and advised him to send a large army to the Border to deter the Scots from attacking, though he hoped that Henry would not order this army to begin hostilities against the Scots.

In earlier years, Henry had always refused to accept French mediation in settling his disputes with the Scots, and had claimed that his 'honour' required him to settle the issue by force of arms; but in his present difficulties he took a humbler tone. He sent commissioners to negotiate with the Scots and François' mediator at Newcastle. The Scots had occupied the fortified house of the Cawmills, or Eddrington, two miles north of Berwick, which the English had captured in the Border warfare some years before. They claimed that it was Scottish territory and should be ceded to James. As the English commissioners refused to agree, the peace talks broke down; but Henry and James agreed to a year's truce, leaving the Scots in possession of the Cawmills.[16]

The breach with Rome was complete. After Cranmer's judgement at Dunstable and Anne's coronation, there could be no going back. Henry no longer contemplated the possibility of a reconciliation with Rome, even if François and Clement himself still cherished the illusion that this might be possible. In May 1533 he brought into force the Act abolishing annates. A later Act of Parliament enacted that no foreigner could hold an English bishopric and deprived Campeggio and Ghinucci of their sees of Salisbury and Worcester. In June, Henry drafted an appeal to a General Council of the Church against any sentence of excommunication which the Pope might pass against him. This was an act of defiance, for the Popes had always maintained that it was heresy to claim that a General Council had power to hear appeals from the Pope. On 8 August, Clement threatened to issue a bull excommunicating and deposing Henry and to summon all the Princes of

Christendom to help enforce the bull. But he decided not to issue the bull until after he had met François, in the hopes that François would be able to arrange some compromise with Henry.[17]

François' interview with the Pope took place at Marseilles in November 1533. Henry sent Bonner to Marseilles to present to the Pope his appeal to the General Council. In view of the fact that the appeal was an act of defiance of the Pope, Bonner was a little afraid for his personal safety; but Henry ordered him not to mince his words when he spoke to the Pope, to do his duty to Henry and to rely on Henry's power to protect him. Bonner's interview with the Pope was stormy, but he came to no harm. François was incensed that Bonner had insulted the Pope when he was François' guest; he complained that he had been on the point of persuading the Pope to comply with Henry's wishes about the divorce when Bonner's rudeness wrecked everything. But François was probably deceived by Clement's usual false promises; and Henry no longer needed, or wanted, anything from the Pope. He ordered Wallop, his ambassador in France, to tell François that he and his nobles and subjects would 'give unto the Pope such a buffet as he had never had heretofore'.[18]

In his talks with the French ambassador in London, the Bailly of Troyes, Henry adopted a superbly confident and aggressive tone, to show that he was afraid of nobody, needed no foreign King's friendship, and was ready to defy the world. He told the Bailly that the Spaniards had been so buoyed up by their success in revictualling the garrison besieged by the Turks at Korun in Greece that they were now talking of invading England; if this was what they wanted, let them come, but many of them would not return. He criticised François for not breaking with the Pope, for not realising that Henry's friendship was worth more than the Pope's; though he did not blame François personally for this, but François' Council. François should not allow his Council to dominate him. Henry said that he himself was not governed by his Council, but governed them, for otherwise the Council would be King, and not he. He asked his counsellors for their opinions, but decided for himself, as every King ought to do.[19]

He suggested to the Bailly that if François was a loyal ally of Henry, as he claimed to be, he should seize the Pope in Marseilles and hold him as a prisoner in France until the Pope adopted a reasonable attitude towards Henry. The Bailly told him that François would never even contemplate such a thing.[20]

Cromwell, who had become Henry's chief secretary and had replaced Norfolk as the most important member of the Council, received regular reports from all over England of isolated opposition to Henry's policy, of support for Catherine, hatred of Anne, and shocked disapproval of the break with Rome and the slide into heresy. Reports came in of words spoken in monastery refrectories, in parish churchyards after Mass, but above all in inns. The reports were not sent by paid agents of a secret police, but by eavesdroppers who were either the King's loyal subjects, or zealous Protestants, or spiteful neighbours. Like most other forms of sixteenth-century government, the work of the secret police was carried out, not by paid professionals but by enthusiastic amateurs. Cromwell's information came almost entirely from voluntary informants who even in the twentieth century provide the main source of information about political dissidents to authoritarian governments.

The Holy Maid of Kent and Bocking and his associates were arrested one by one during the summer and autumn of 1533. They were examined by Cranmer and by Cromwell's officers, and revealed that the Holy Maid had been in touch with several prominent supporters of Catherine. It was impossible to prove that the Countess of Salisbury, who was Catherine's close friend, had ever met the Holy Maid; but Gertrude, Marchioness of Exeter – the clever daughter of Lord Mountjoy and the wife of Henry Courtenay, Marquess of Exeter, who was the grandson of Edward IV – was another of Catherine's friends, and sometimes provided Chapuys with useful information. She had met the Holy Maid, but only to discuss private family matters. Sir Thomas More had met the Holy Maid, but had been very cautious, and had advised her not to speak about any matter which concerned the King. Fisher had been less discreet, for he had talked to her about her angel's warning that Henry would die within a month if he married Anne.

In November 1533, Elizabeth Barton, Bocking, and four other priests and monks were charged with high treason for having said, and for inciting Elizabeth to say, that the King would die within a month if he married Anne. Legal difficulties arose at their trial, but they were sentenced to death by an Act of Attainder. They were paraded on a platform at Paul's Cross while the preacher denounced their wicked crimes; but Henry waited for five months before executing them. Henry pardoned the Marchioness of Exeter, who wrote to him that she had met that most unworthy, subtle and deceivable woman called the Holy Maid of Kent, but begged for mercy because she was a woman, and women's fragility and brittleness were easily seduced.

Fisher, More and Catherine's confessor, Abel, were charged with misprision of treason, of having failed to disclose the act of high treason which they knew that Elizabeth Barton had committed. Fisher argued that, as the Holy Maid had told him that she had spoken about the angel's warning to the King himself, he thought it was unnecessary for him to reveal this act of treason which was already known to the King; but his argument was not accepted, and he was convicted of misprision of treason, and sentenced to be imprisoned during the King's pleasure. He had, in fact, himself committed high treason; but the authorities did not know that he had urged Chapuys to persuade the Emperor to send an army to invade England and save the realm from heresy.[21]

The charge against More was dropped, after he had written to Henry assuring him that he had revealed all his contacts with 'the wicked woman of Canterbury'. In his letter, he expressed the hope that after death he would 'once meet with Your Grace again in Heaven, and there be merry with you'.[22] This reminder of the days when the two of them had joked together cannot have made any impression on Henry, for though he had allowed the charge of misprision of treason to be withdrawn, he was about to put More in a position from which there was no escape.

17

THE OATH

In December 1533 the Council issued an order declaring that the Pope had no more authority in England than any other foreign bishop and was in future to be referred to, not as 'the Pope', but as 'the Bishop of Rome'.[1] This was the repudiation of a fundamental principle which had been accepted in the English Church for nine hundred years; but the way had been so well prepared, and the breaking point approached so gradually since 1529, that there was hardly any open resistance. But Tunstal wrote to Henry, asking leave to express humbly his honest opinion in private. He wrote that he regretted a step which would separate England from the rest of Christendom, and reminded Henry that at the beginning of his reign he had played the leading part in a war in defence of the Pope and the Church against the schismatic French King, Louis XII.

Henry sent a superficially friendly reply. He wrote that he was always pleased to receive from Tunstal a frank expression of his honest opinion, because he knew that Tunstal was too conscious of the many benefits which he had received from Henry to wish to express opinions which were contrary to Henry's interests. He then entered at some length into the theological issues, arguing from old patristic texts that the Bishop of Rome had no authority over other bishops, and certainly not over Princes. He pointed out that by repudiating Papal supremacy, England would not be separated from the rest of Christendom, because large parts of Christendom had already broken with Rome; and he stated that he now realised that at the beginning of his reign he had, in his youth and inexperience, been tricked by the Bishop of Rome and his agents into making war against King Louis.[2]

Henry had no further trouble from Tunstal.

The decision that the Bishop of Rome had no authority in England was endorsed during the next few months by the Convocations of Canterbury and York and by the Universities of Oxford and Cambridge, and was enacted by Act of Parliament. The statute went further than the position adopted by

Convocation three years before, when it had been decided that the King was 'Protector and only Supreme Head of the English Church as far as the law of Christ allowed'. Henry was now declared to be, next under Christ, 'the only Supreme Head in earth of the Church of England'.[3]

The news from England at last convinced the Pope that he had nothing to gain by further delay. On 23 March 1534, nearly seven years after Henry had first started the divorce proceedings, Clement gave final judgement for Catherine in his court in Rome, ruling that her marriage to Henry was valid, and ordering Henry to resume cohabitation with her. Charles's supporters treated it as a great victory; they demonstrated in Rome that night, parading through the streets with shouts of 'Empire and Spain', letting off fireworks, and firing cannons. Ortiz wrote to Charles that this judgement for the Queen was the greatest of all his victories, for his victories in the field had been gained over men, but this was a victory over enemies let loose from Hell.[4] Henry, of course, ignored it, and it made no difference whatever to the course of events. For four hundred and fifty years, Catholic writers have argued that if the judgement had come a few years earlier, Henry would not have dared to defy it, and the cause of Catherine and Papal supremacy would have been saved; but it is rash to assume that Henry was bluffing at any time when he threatened, as he had first done in 1528, to take England into schism if the Pope refused him a divorce.

Henry decided that everyone of his subjects must be made aware that Papal supremacy had been replaced by royal supremacy. Every parish priest was required to erase the references to the Pope from the prayer books in his church, and if he forgot to do this, and a book was found in which the word 'Pope' had not been scratched out and made illegible, he was in trouble. The preachers were required to instil into their parishioners that the Bishop of Rome had no authority in England and that the King alone was head of the Church. The new doctrine was summed up in one sentence by the Dean of the Chapel Royal, Sampson: 'The Word of God is, to obey the King and not the Bishop of Rome'.[5]

In an age without television, radio and newspapers, but when everyone was required by law to attend Mass in his parish church every Sunday and holy day, the pulpit was the chief vehicle for political propaganda. It was a very effective one, especially as the preacher could bring the threat of hell-fire and eternal damnation as the ultimate deterrent, in addition to the fear of the stake, the rack, the gallows, the dungeons, the ear-croppings, the floggings and the stocks which an offender would suffer on earth. The government had always been aware of the power of the sermon and of the danger that a parish priest with unorthodox views could use his opportunities to spread sedition and heresy from the pulpit; and there was a danger, too, from anyone who tried to preach to the people in the churchyard as they left the church, or who erected a tub in his garden adjoining busy streets, or at fairs, and preached sedition or heresy there. It had therefore always been a criminal offence to preach without a licence from the bishop of the diocese, and the JPs had orders to arrest unlicensed preachers.

This system of control was not enough to deal with the new situation after the repudiation of Papal supremacy. Many of the clergy who had licences to preach were loyal to the Pope; and many priests with 'Lutheran' sympathies, who had hitherto not ventured to criticise established doctrines, now felt free to express their hatred of the Bishop of Rome. Some of the orthodox priests who in recent years had been the most ardent persecutors of heretics were known to be unhappy about the breach with Rome, and this gave their former victims and all the Lutheran sympathisers among the clergy the opportunity to denounce them as 'Papists'. But as Henry was as orthodox as ever on all points except the supremacy, these 'Papist' sympathisers could continue to denounce their opponents as Lutherans and heretics.

Henry could make use of these divisions between Papists and heretics, just as he could make use of the divisions between Charles V and François I. He could rely on the heretics to report to the authorities any case where a vicar said anything in a sermon which implied that he disapproved of the schism, who failed to scratch out the word 'Pope' in the prayer books in his church, or who, by design or from a slip of the tongue, spoke about 'the Pope' when he should have said 'the Bishop of Rome'. Henry could also rely on the Papist sympathisers to denounce any priest who criticised pilgrimages, prayers to the saints, or the doctrine of Purgatory, or who advocated any other heretical doctrine, especially if this man whom he was denouncing had recently denounced *him* as a Papist. Neither heretics nor Papists must be allowed to go either too far or not far enough; all must conform to the exact position which Henry had reached at the moment. It was also important to prevent the controversies between Papists and heretics from getting out of hand, and giving the impression to people at home and abroad that there were fundamental divisions, and a danger of religious civil war, in England.

At Easter 1534 Henry ordered Cranmer, Gardiner, Stokesley and Longland to cancel all preaching licences which they had issued in their dioceses of Canterbury, Winchester, London and Lincoln, and to forbid anyone to preach until he had been granted a new licence. In May, Henry issued an order in his own name extending this to every other diocese in the kingdom. The reason for the order was to ensure 'that our people may be fed with wholesome food, neither savouring the corruption of the Bishop of Rome nor led into doubt by novelties'.[6]

Before granting any priest a new preaching licence in his diocese of Canterbury, Cranmer inquired into the priest's reliability; and he entrusted the duty of examining applicants for preaching licences to Latimer, who only two years before had been denounced as a heretic by Hubbardine, an orthodox priest of Bristol. But since then, it had been reported that

Hubbardine had said that 'the Pope is King and Prince of all the world', and that if the King and the Mayor of Bristol walked down the street, the passers-by would say 'Knaves, knaves!' Cranmer appointed Latimer to preach at court in Lent 1534, despite the protests of Sampson, the Dean of the Chapel Royal, who thought that he was a heretic. Cranmer warned Latimer to be careful in what he said in his sermon, but not to waste any opportunity which the text of Scripture provided to condemn any ungodly practice. He also advised him not to preach for more than an hour or an hour and a half, in case the King and Queen became bored.[7]

In June 1534, Henry issued an order which forbade all preachers during the next twelve months from either criticising or defending the doctrines of Purgatory, the honouring of saints, going on pilgrimages, the working of miracles, justification by faith, and the marriage of priests.[8] The order helped the reformers more than their opponents. It had always been heresy to attack these established doctrines; but now, for the first time, the orthodox preachers were forbidden to defend them and to denounce those who criticised them as heretics. This would make it easier for Cranmer to introduce innovations in these matters at some future date, if he could persuade Henry to agree. From Henry's point of view, the less argument there was on controversial issues the better. Any religious revolution in England was to be a revolution from above, introduced when Henry wished and kept tightly under his control.

Henry and his counsellors found an even better way than the sermons of licensed preachers to ensure the obedience of his subjects. They were all to be personally committed to support the breach with Rome. In an age when it was almost universally believed that to violate an oath incurred eternal damnation, everyone in the kingdom was to be compelled to take an oath that they believed that Henry and Anne were lawfully married and that Princess Elizabeth and any other children that they might have were the rightful heirs to the throne. Anyone who refused to take the oath when invited to do so was to be guilty of a praemunire, and therefore liable to imprisonment during the King's pleasure. The King's counsellors, after taking the oath themselves, would administer it to their inferior officers. The sheriffs would administer it to the justices of the peace; the justices of the peace would administer it to the householders in their districts; the householders would administer it to their families and servants. Thus every man and woman in England over the age of fourteen would swear.

We do not know who first thought out this very effective method of compelling Henry's subjects to support him against the Pope – whether it was Henry himself, Cromwell, Cranmer, Edward Fox, or some underling who never received the credit for his idea either from his contemporaries or from future historians. But the decision to implement it was of course Henry's alone.

The measure was duly enacted by Parliament in March 1534, and the form of oath was drafted by Cranmer, Lord Chancellor Audley, Norfolk and Suffolk, who were appointed commissioners to enforce the Act. The oath stated that the swearer would bear allegiance to the King and to the issue of his marriage with Anne, 'and not to any other within this realm, nor foreign authority, Prince or potentate', and that he would obey and help to enforce this Act and all the other Acts passed by Parliament since 1529.[9]

The commissioners began at once with the London clergy, who on 13 April 1534 were summoned to Lambeth Palace and required to take the oath. Fisher and More were also summoned to attend that day. Fisher, More and Dr Wilson, the Archdeacon of Oxford and Master of Michaelhouse in Cambridge, refused to take the oath, and were sent to the Tower. All the other clergy agreed to take the oath, and Wilson, too, complied after a few months in prison. The oath was put to everyone in any position of authority, and to many other people all over the country. It seems unlikely that everyone over the age of fourteen was in fact required to swear; but we know that by July 1534, 7,342 persons had taken the oath, and this was certainly only a small proportion of the total number. Only a handful of persons refused to swear when the oath was put to them. Apart from Fisher and More, these included a number of Carthusian monks and Franciscan friars.[10]

Cranmer, who was a mild-mannered man, a compromiser by nature, and a perfect example of what would today be called a 'wet', thought of a compromise which he hoped would save More and Fisher. During the discussion at Lambeth, Fisher had said that he did not object to the operative part of the Act of the Succession, but only to the preamble, which repudiated Papal supremacy and stated that Henry's marriage to Catherine was unlawful. On 17 April, Cranmer wrote to Cromwell that as the Bishop of Rochester and Master More objected to the preamble of the Act of the Succession, could they not be required to swear only to the operative part of the Act without the preamble? He wrote that if Fisher and More took the oath, it would have a strong effect on Catherine and Mary and on others who objected to the oath, and would stop the mouths of the Emperor and other admirers of Fisher and More. The exact form of the oath which Fisher and More swore could be kept secret.[11]

Cranmer's suggestion was not only a well-meant attempt to save Fisher and More from perpetual imprisonment, but was also an ingenious scheme for enabling Henry to demoralise the Papist supporters by telling them that Fisher and More had capitulated. It would have entailed greater alterations in the wording of the oath than Cranmer suggested in his letter, and would have meant that Fisher and More would have sworn a completely different oath, swearing merely to uphold Princess Elizabeth and any other issue of Henry and Anne as the lawful heirs to the throne. More, unlike Fisher, had said nothing to suggest that it was the preamble to the Act of Succession to which he objected, and it is very unlikely that either Fisher or More would have accepted Cranmer's compromise proposal.

Still, the attempt to deceive the people into believing that Fisher and More had capitulated by allowing them to swear a secret oath which did not in fact involve their capitulation, was just the sort of manoeuvre which might have appealed to Henry as at least worth trying. In fact, he rejected it out of hand. Cromwell wrote to Cranmer that he had shown his letter to the King, who thought that if Fisher and More swore only to the succession and not to the preamble, this might be taken as a confirmation of the Bishop of Rome's authority and a reprobation of the King's marriage to Queen Anne. Cromwell informed Cranmer that the King had decided that Fisher and More should be required to swear the oath in its full form.[12] As usual, Henry's policy on this occasion was both simpler and more realistic than the course suggested to him by his advisers. If he had pretended that Fisher and More had submitted, he would have had to release them from prison; and if they had been free, Fisher at least would have made known the exact form of oath which he had sworn. If the secret about the form of their oath became known, it would be seen as a capitulation by Henry, not by Fisher and More.

Henry had probably another reason for his decision. The capitulation of Fisher and More might be less valuable than their imprisonment; for the knowledge that Henry was prepared to put such eminent men in the Tower could have a useful deterrent effect on the opposition.

Henry's next targets were Catherine and Mary. He had just received a request from Catherine to allow her confessor, her chaplain, her physician, and some of her ladies to join her at Buckden. He replied that he would send them to her if she submitted, relinquished the title of Queen, and swore the oath of the succession. If she did, both she and Mary would be well treated; if she refused, he might be driven to proceed against her under the laws of his realm, and Mary might be in danger. As Catherine was unmoved, he sent Edward Lee, the Archbishop of York, and Tunstal to her to emphasize the two alternatives which she faced. Tunstal was thus given the opportunity to prove that, despite the opinions which he had expressed in private to Henry five months before, he was nevertheless a loyal servant. Catherine indignantly rejected all proposals, interrupting Lee and Tunstal and insisting that she was Henry's lawful wife and Queen, as the Pope had given judgement in her favour. She reminded Tunstal that he had formerly supported her in the divorce case. He said that he had changed his mind, and advised her to do the same.[13]

Mary adopted an equally defiant attitude. She protested at being declared illegitimate and deprived of her title of Princess, and she refused to take the oath.[14]

Chapuys continued to do all he could for Catherine and Mary. In July

1534 he made a public gesture of support for Catherine which he hoped would cause the maximum embarrassment to Henry. He set off from London with a large escort to visit Catherine, who had been moved from Buckden to Kimbolton in Northamptonshire. He rode through London with his musicians playing, so as to attract as much attention as possible, and saw to it that everyone along his route should know that he was visiting Queen Catherine. When he was five miles from Kimbolton, he was met by a messenger from Catherine, who told him that she had been forbidden by Henry to receive him, and asking him to turn back. He complied with her wishes, having succeeded in his object of showing the people of England that the Emperor supported their rightful Queen. He returned to London by a different way, so that more people should know about his journey. But Chapuys knew that Charles would do nothing effective to help Catherine.[15]

The only foreign King who was showing any signs of readiness to act against Henry was his nephew James V, whose realm had been ravaged and dominated by Henry when James was a child. Now that James was twenty-two, he was pursuing a determined anti-English policy, alarming Henry by negotiating to marry a French Princess, assuring the Pope of his readiness to serve him against the schismatic King of England, and encouraging Chapuys and the opposition in England to hope that a Scottish invasion could trigger off an insurrection against Henry. As the one year truce which had been signed at Newcastle was about to expire, James sent envoys to London to negotiate a peace settlement. They took a firm line, and demanded that Henry should cede the Cawmills to Scotland.

In ordinary circumstances, Henry would have regarded such a suggestion as an affront to his 'honour'. But he did not want a war with Scotland in 1534. So he agreed to a peace treaty, which was signed in London in May, by which he ceded the Cawmills to James. The peace was to last for as long as both Henry and James were alive, and for a year after the death of the first of them, even if ecclesiastical censures were proclaimed against Henry or James.[16]

It was a good bargain for Henry, for he had surrendered one fortified house, which was already in Scottish hands, in return for a promise by James not to enforce any decree which the Pope might issue depriving Henry of his throne. But it was the first time since he became King that he had been compelled to cede territory to a foreign power, and the first time for many years that the Scots could claim to have won a war against England. Henry had to find a scapegoat for the setback. When the peace treaty with the Scots was signed in London, the Earl of Westmorland and the Earl of Cumberland were already on their way to arrest Lord Dacre, the Lord Warden of the Marches, on a charge of high treason for having secretly plotted with the Scots during the war and connived at their invasion of England. The two Earls knew that Dacre was very popular with his tenants and the local people in Cumberland, and they approached his house at Naworth with a smaller escort than they would normally have taken with them through that wild country, in order not to attract the attention of the local inhabitants; and for the same reason they separated, and approached Naworth by two different routes. But Lady Dacre, who was the daughter of Henry's powerful counsellor, the Earl of Shrewsbury, offered no resistance when Cumberland and Westmorland searched the house. She handed over all Dacre's papers, and sent petitions to Henry asking for mercy for her husband, until she and Shrewsbury received a warning from Cromwell not to attempt to interfere with the course of justice until Dacre had been tried according to law.[17]

Dacre was accused of having given military information to the Scots during the fighting in December 1532, and of having urged them to invade England in July 1533. During the English raids into Scotland, the lands of some of the Douglases had been ravaged by an unfortunate oversight of the local English commanders, and this was now said to have been done on purpose by Dacre because he knew that Angus was a loyal friend of King Henry. Henry's officials induced a grand jury at Carlisle to commit him for trial, and he was tried in the Court of the Lord High Steward by twenty of his fellow-peers in Westminster Hall on 9 July 1534. But the evidence against him was weak, and there was sympathy for him among the lords; and the peers unanimously found him Not Guilty.

It was the only occasion during Henry's reign on which a court acquitted a prominent political figure, who was put on trial by the government. It has often been cited, by authors who support Henry or Cromwell, to show that the state trials were not stage-managed, that judges and juries were not terrorised, and were prepared to acquit a defendant when they thought it right to do so. It undoubtedly shows that Henry could not always make powerful groups among his subjects do something that they did not wish to do, and that it was harder to persuade the nobility to agree to the execution of one of their number whom they believed to be innocent, than to persuade a London jury to convict priests and intellectuals whom they regarded as supporters of a foreign Pope against the King and laws of England. It also shows that, though Henry for once slipped up in Dacre's case, he knew when it was necessary to retreat. He ought not to have brought Dacre to trial; but realising the feeling for Dacre among the nobility, he did not try to bully them into convicting him, but allowed them to return a verdict of Not Guilty. It is clear that Henry agreed, however reluctantly, to accept the verdict, because the peers who unanimously acquitted Dacre included not only opponents of the government, like Exeter, Montagu and Darcy, but Henry's own counsellors, Norfolk, Worcester, and Queen Anne's father, Wiltshire, who would not have concurred in the verdict of Not Guilty without Henry's consent; and we know that the peers consulted Cromwell before delivering their verdict.[18]

But Dacre was not released from custody after his acquittal. A fortnight after the trial, he was brought before the King's Council and accused of having written some letters to the Scottish Warden of the Marches in 1532 and 1533 which he had not shown to the King or the Council at the time and which had not been disclosed at his recent trial. The letters contained perfectly legitimate comments on the truce negotiations, but could be held to have been, technically, unauthorised communication with the enemy. Dacre was warned that he might face a new prosecution for high treason on the basis of these separate treasonable acts with which he had not yet been charged, but that Henry would grant him a pardon for all acts of high treason which he might have committed in the past if he granted Henry lands to the value of £10,000. He accepted the offer.[19] Henry often made profitable bargains of this kind with men whom he was prepared to pardon, but he normally did so before they were brought to trial.

Henry had never had more than nominal control of Ireland outside the Pale, and had only been able to rule it through one or two powerful families. The greatest of these were the Fitzgeralds, whose head was the Earl of Kildare. Gerald Fitzgerald, Earl of Kildare, had on several occasions been arrested at Wolsey's orders and imprisoned in the Tower of London; but he was always restored to his post of the King's Deputy in Ireland, for no one else could effectively govern the country and prevent the native chiefs from rising in revolt. In the spring of 1534, Henry became alarmed that Papal agents would be sent to Ireland to incite insurrection, and he received reports which led him to believe that Kildare and his family would be the leaders of a revolt. He invited Kildare to court, but soon afterwards sent him to the Tower, where he died a few months later.

In June 1534 Kildare's son, Thomas, Lord Offaly, rose in rebellion. The government forces could not withstand him, and the Lord Deputy, Sir William Skeffington, and his counsellors, took refuge in Dublin Castle. John Allen, the Archbishop of Dublin, tried to escape to England, but his ship was driven back by the winds, and he hid in the village of Arlane on the north side of the Bay of Clontarf. Here he was found by Offaly and his men, and was murdered by the soldiers, who may or may not have been acting on Offaly's orders.

Offaly and his supporters got in touch with the Emperor. Conor O'Brien, Prince of Thomond, wrote to Charles, offering to raise 13,000 men to fight for him if he sent an army to Ireland. Charles hesitated to send an army, but sent his chaplain, who landed at Donegal in July 1534 and met the rebel chiefs. Offaly, who on his father's death in the Tower became Earl of Kildare, was in control of nearly the whole of Ireland, though the Mayor and citizens of Waterford held the town for Henry, and Skeffington repulsed Kildare's attack on Dublin. Chapuys reported that Henry was as much put out by the news from Ireland as he was delighted to hear that the Turkish fleet, under their admiral whom the Christians called Barbarossa, had captured Tunis.

Henry sent Lord Leonard Grey with an army to suppress the revolt, and the Irish rebels appealed to the Emperor for help. Charles's Council considered the matter as one of twenty-one items on the agenda at their meeting in Madrid on 31 October. They decided that there could be real advantages in sending a small force to aid the Irish; it would almost certainly prevent Henry from sending an army to help François if war should break out between France and the Empire. But obviously so important a decision would have to be referred to the Emperor when he had time to consider it; and in any case no help could be sent during the winter, and they would have to wait till the weather improved in the spring.

But by the spring the tide had turned in Ireland. In March the government forces captured Maynooth from Kildare, and put to death the rebel garrison who had defended it. By the summer of 1535, the revolt had been suppressed. Kildare surrendered, after Lord Leonard Grey, acting without authority from Henry, had given him his personal promise that his life would be spared.[20]

Terrifying events were occurring in Germany. In February 1534 a revolution broke out in Münster, and the local Protestant extremists, helped by an influx of recent immigrants from Holland, established an Anabaptist communist republic. The Anabaptists not only denied the Real Presence and the validity of infant baptism, and the manhood of Christ, whom they believed was God but not man; they also advocated the abolition of private property and the holding of all goods in common. The nobility and the gentry, and the wealthy merchants, were almost as alarmed by the developments in Lübeck as by those in Münster. Wullenweber's democratic republic of Lübeck was sending emissaries to stir up revolution in Denmark, winning over the artisans of Copenhagen and other towns, and inciting risings of the peasants in the countryside against the landowners. A military adventurer, Count John of Oldenburg, invaded Denmark with German soldiers, and with the encouragement and aid of Lübeck, to help the revolutionaries. He acted in the name of Charles's brother-in-law, the imprisoned former King, Christian II, the 'peasant King', as his supporters now called him; and a strange alliance was formed between Oldenburg, the Danish artisans and peasants, and 'Anabaptist' Lübeck, against the Lutheran King Christian III of Denmark, who was supported by the Lutheran Princes of Germany and by the Lutheran King Gustavus Vasa of Sweden, as well as by most of the Danish nobility and gentry.

Barnes, who had been condemned as a Lutheran heretic in London in 1526 and had only saved himself by a recantation, was now an influential preacher at Henry's court. He was cautiously putting forward Lutheran doctrines, telling his congregation that holy water blessed by a priest was no different from the water of the Thames. In the spring of 1534 he visited the Lutheran states of Germany, not, this time, as a refugee from persecution in

England, but as Henry's envoy, to offer Henry's friendship to the Lutherans, and to encourage them to make difficulties for the Emperor in Germany. Barnes was in Hamburg when the civil war in Denmark broke out in the summer of 1534. He wrote to Henry and Cromwell, urging them to make an alliance with Christian III and the Danish, German and Swedish Lutherans. He argued that if Henry and Christian III were united, England and a friendly Lutheran Denmark would be in control of both the western and the eastern halves of the North Sea.[21]

But there were advantages for Henry in allying himself with Lübeck rather than with Christian III. Christian, who had allies like Gustavus Vasa and the German Lutheran Princes, would never be wholly dependent on Henry; and the Lutherans had been troublesome about Henry's divorce, when nearly all of them had supported Catherine. The friendless revolutionaries of Lübeck would be less likely to oppose Henry if he were their only powerful supporter. So Barnes, who for the last few years had been soft-pedalling his religious opinions in the hope that he would be able to move Henry, very slowly, towards a Lutheran position, found that Henry had made an alliance with men who were so extreme that the Lutherans denounced them as Anabaptists.

On 2 August 1534, Henry's envoys signed a treaty with Lübeck. The Lübeckers agreed to support Henry against the Emperor, never to be reconciled with the Bishop of Rome, not to attend any General Council of the Church unless Henry agreed, to support the validity of Henry's marriage to Queen Anne, to maintain that the marriage of a man with his brother's widow was against God's law, and to use their influence to ensure that the throne of Denmark was disposed of in accordance with Henry's wishes. In return, Henry lent the Lübeckers 20,000 gulden. In November 1534, while the German and Danish Lutherans were saying that if the Anabaptists of Lübeck continued on their revolutionary path unchecked there would soon be no Prince or nobleman left in the world, Henry sent Christopher Morres, an expert gunner and military engineer, to Lübeck to give the Anabaptists the benefit of his technical advice. On one occasion, when Henry was exasperated with his lords at court, he told them that if they did not do what he wanted, he would abandon them and go and live in Lübeck.[22]

Captain Sir Marcus Meyer was commanding the Lübeck forces in Denmark and Scåne, the Danish territory across the Sound from Copenhagen, which is today the southern part of Sweden. During the winter of 1534-5, he had the worst of the fighting against the army which Gustavus Vasa had sent to help Christian III, and in January he was defeated and taken prisoner. He was imprisoned in the naval fortress of Varberg in Scåne; but by a daring plot, he succeeded in setting himself free, in killing the commander of the fortress, and in capturing it. He appealed to Henry for help, and offered to hold Varberg on his behalf. He also offered to hand over to Henry

Copenhagen and Elsinore, which were held by the Lübeckers and the Danish revolutionaries.

Henry did not intend to become too deeply involved in Denmark; but he thought it worth while to give Meyer a little help. He sent Bonner and Richard Cavendish to Varberg. Bonner, who had distinguished himself by braving Clement VII at Marseilles, was to become in Mary's reign the most hated of all the Papist persecutors of Protestants, the 'bloody Bonner' of Foxe's *Book of Martyrs*; but probably none of the martyrs whom he sentenced to be burned were as extreme as the heretics to whom be brought aid and comfort in Varberg in 1535. Bonner told Meyer that Henry was sending three ships to Varberg with ninety-two soldiers, ammunition for Meyer's cannon, and a splendid suit of armour which had been made for Henry himself, but which he was now sending as a gift to Meyer. Henry was also sending his coat-of-arms to be fixed over the gates of Varberg.

The ships never sailed. Before they were ready, news reached Henry of the defeat of the Lübeckers – that Christian III had besieged Copenhagen and Varberg and was on the point of capturing both places, and that a counter-revolution had broken out in Lübeck and had overthrown Wullenweber. Henry was happy to allow Bonner and Cavendish to accept a safe-conduct from Christian III to pass through his lines and leave Varberg, and to negotiate for the release by Christian of the English merchant ships which he had seized when it seemed as if Henry was about to send military aid to Meyer. By the autumn of 1535, both the Anabaptist régime in Münster and the democratic republic of Lübeck had fallen, though Meyer held out in the fortress at Varberg till the summer of 1536.[23]

In November 1534, Parliament passed an Act which declared that the King was Supreme Head of the Church of England. Another Act enacted that it was high treason to deny any of the King's titles, or to state, either in writing or by word of mouth, that the King was a heretic, a schismatic, a tyrant, or a usurper.[24] The effect of the two statutes was that anyone who denied that Henry was Supreme Head of the Church was guilty of high treason and could be put to death. It was now possible for Henry's officials to ask the opponents of the royal supremacy, who were already in prison for refusing to take the oath of the succession, whether they believed that the King was Supreme Head, and if they answered No, they could be executed.

On 29 April 1535, four Carthusian monks and two priests were tried for high treason in the Court of King's Bench in Westminster for having denied the King's title of Supreme Head of the Church of England. They were John Houghton, Robert Lawrence and Augustine Webster, the Priors of the Charterhouses of London, of Beaulieu in Nottinghamshire, and of the Isle of Axholme in Lincolnshire; Richard Reynolds, a monk of Sion, near Brentford in Middlesex, who was famous for his learning; and the two priests, John Haile and a very young man, John Ferne. When Reynolds was asked whether he believed that the King was the Supreme Head of the Church of England, he answered No, and said that he was supported by all the learned doctors for the past fifteen hundred years. 'I have all the rest of Christendom in my favour, I dare say even of all this kingdom, although the smaller part holds with you, for I am sure the larger part is at heart of our opinion, although outwardly, partly from fear and partly from hope, they profess to be of yours'. He was asked to say who his supporters were, and replied: 'All good men of the kingdom'. The other defendants all adopted the same attitude. The jury found them guilty, and they were condemned to be hanged, drawn and quartered.[25]

Even Reynolds, this stalwart Papal supporter, as he prepared to go to a terrible death at Henry's orders, did not blame Henry. He told his judges: 'I am sure that when the King knows the truth, he will be very pleased, or rather indignant against certain bishops who have given him such counsel'. He never knew that the most hated of all these bishops, Cranmer, wrote to Cromwell on the day after the trial and asked him to intercede with Henry for him and Webster. Cranmer thought that if Reynolds and Webster were sent to him, he might be able to convert them, and that their conversion would serve the King's interests better than their execution. But Henry rejected Cranmer's appeal. He wanted victims.[26]

The King pardoned Ferne on account of his youth, but the sentences on the other defendants were carried out on 4 May. For the first time in England, priests and monks were executed without being first degraded from their order. They were dressed in their monks' and priest's habits and dragged on hurdles from the Tower through the city of London, through Holborn, and out of the built-up area to Tyburn, which is today called Marble Arch. There the full sentence of the law was carried out. One by one, while their fellow-sufferers watched, they were hanged, cut down while still alive, and castrated; their bellies were cut open, and their bowels pulled out and burned before their eyes, while they were still living; and then they were beheaded.

The executions were as usual watched by a large crowd, which included some of Henry's leading courtiers. Henry's son, the Duke of Richmond, who was just sixteen, was there, with the Duke of Norfolk and the Queen's father and brother, the Earl of Wiltshire and Lord Rochford, and Sir Henry Norris and other gentlemen of the King's privy chamber. There were also five masked men, dressed in the costume of men from the Border districts, who were standing among the courtiers; and the rumour spread through the crowd that one of them was the King. But this was untrue.[27]

Papist Europe was deeply shocked at the execution of the Carthusians, and feared that worse was to come; for everyone expected that the Bishop of Rochester, nearly seventy years old and Queen Catherine's foremost champion, would be the next martyr. But first there were to be other executions. In 1533 Henry had burned the sacramentaries Frith and Huett just when he was completing the final break with Rome; now, as he was executing the leading supporters of the Papacy, he was also burning Anabaptists. Some Dutch Anabaptists had recently fled to England from the savage persecution in the Netherlands, and were making a few converts among their fellow-countrymen in London. It was just at the time when Henry was preparing to send ships to relieve Meyer at Varberg. But while Anabaptist warriors of Lübeck might perhaps be useful allies, the only useful function for Anabaptist refugees in England was to burn at the stake, in order to discourage Henry's subjects from thinking for themselves about religion, and to show the world that Henry was still a pious Catholic Prince, the Defender of the Faith who would not tolerate heretics in his realm.

In May 1535, twenty-three Dutch Anabaptists, three of whom were women, were tried for heresy at St Paul's. Some of them had recently come from the Netherlands, and others had been living in England for some time. Henry appointed two commissioners to act as their judges. One was Stokesley, the Bishop of London, who had always been an ardent persecutor of heretics; the other was Barnes, who had himself been condemned as a heretic in this same St Paul's nine years before. He hated Anabaptists as much as any Catholic did. If he could not persuade Henry to support the Lutherans against the Anabaptists in Denmark, he could help him to burn Anabaptists in England.

Stokesley and Barnes found all the defendants guilty of heresy. Nine of them recanted, and were deported to the Netherlands for Mary of Hungary to deal with. The other fourteen, who refused to recant, were sentenced to be burned. A man and a woman were burned at Smithfield on 4 June, and twelve were taken to various towns in England and burned there.[28]

The Catholics of Europe approved of burning Anabaptists, but were not impressed by what they considered was a hypocritical attempt by Henry to prove his orthodoxy. Their concern was for the Papists in England, above all for the Bishop of Rochester. They faced the perennial problem of a persecuted dissident's sympathisers abroad: would loud international protest make things better or worse for Fisher?

Pope Paul III, who had become Pope after Clement VII's death in September 1534, wished to do all he could to save him and to show the world that Fisher was supported by the full moral authority of the Apostolic See. On 20 May, the Pope in Consistory created seven new cardinals. Five of them were Italian officials at the Papal court, including Ghinucci. The sixth was Jean Du Bellay, who had been François' ambassador in England; and the seventh was Fisher.

Henry's agent in Italy, Sir Gregory di Casale, was horrified when he heard what the Pope had done. He was sure that it would enfuriate Henry against Fisher. Ortiz was pleased that Fisher had been given the red hat, as he thought it was a great gesture against Henry; but he wrote to the Empress that he feared that before Fisher heard about it, God would give him the true red hat, the crown of martyrdom.[29]

The Pope was shaken when Casale told him how deeply Henry would resent what he had done, and that his well-meant gesture had endangered Fisher's life. He asked François to use his influence with Henry in Fisher's favour. François said that he would do all he could to save Fisher, but was not optimistic. He told the Nuncio in France that Henry was a most difficult ally; he was sometimes so obstinate and arrogant that it was almost impossible to bear with him. 'Sometimes, indeed, he almost treats me as a subject', said François, 'he is the strangest man in the world, and I fear I can do no good with him; but I must put up with him, as this is no time to lose friends'.[30]

Casale's worst fears were realised. Henry was enraged when he heard that Fisher had been made a cardinal; he treated it as a challenge which he was bound to take up, and as an insult which he would avenge. He said that as Fisher had been given a cardinal's hat, he would cut off Fisher's head and send the head to Rome to have the hat put on it.[31]

Proceedings were brought against three more Carthusians of the Charterhouse of London, Humphrey Middlehurst, William Exmere, and Sebastian Newdigate. Strong pressure was put on them to accept Henry as Supreme Head. They were kept in their dungeon at Newgate fastened to posts in a standing position by chains around their necks, and half starved; but Margaret Clement, Thomas More's adopted daughter, and other devoted Catholic women somehow managed to enter the prison secretly and bring them food.[32]

Henry appointed seventeen commissioners to try the cases of Fisher and the three Carthusians. They included not only Audley, Suffolk, Wiltshire and Cromwell, but the Marquess of Exeter, whose wife, as Henry well knew, was so close to Catherine, Chapuys and Fisher. This was to be a test of Exeter's loyalty. The judges sat with a jury at Westminster Hall on 11 June to try Middlehurst, Exmere and Newdigate on a charge of high treason for having said that Henry was not Supreme Head of the Church of England. They were all found guilty, and sentenced to be hanged, drawn and quartered. Fisher was tried by the same court on the same charge on 17 June. He admitted that he had denied that Henry was Supreme Head of the Church of England, but argued that the statute made it high treason 'maliciously' to deny the King's titles, and he had not acted out of malice. This argument was rejected; he was found guilty, and condemned to be hanged, drawn and quartered. Henry commuted Fisher's sentence to beheading, but the Carthusians suffered the full penalty at Tyburn on 19 June. Fisher was beheaded on Tower Hill three days later.[33]

Henry was in excellent spirits. According to Chapuys, on the day after Fisher's execution, on Midsummer Eve, he rode thirty miles and then walked ten miles carrying a two-handed sword, with a group of friends, to some village in the country where he had heard that a pageant was to be performed showing good King Henry cutting off the heads of his disobedient clergy. He entered a house, from where he watched the show, and enjoyed it so much that he revealed himself to the spectators, and was loudly applauded. Chapuys's story is not confirmed from any other source.[34]

The last to suffer was Sir Thomas More. When he was asked whether he believed that the King was Supreme Head of the Church of England, he refused to answer, and argued that silence could not constitute high treason; but More had a conversation in his prison in the Tower with the Solicitor-General, Sir Richard Rich. According to Rich, More said, during their talk, that Parliament did not have the power to make the King head of the Church*. This could be interpreted as denying the King's title; and when More was brought to trial in Westminster Hall before commissioners who included Audley, Cromwell, Norfolk, and other members of the King's Council, he was found guilty of high treason by a London jury, though Rich's story was the only evidence against him. More said that Rich was lying. It is more likely that Rich committed perjury than that More for once slipped up and told Rich what he really believed; but the jurymen were not impressed by More's legal casuistry. As soon as they had given their verdict, More, in his final plea, admitted that he did not believe in the royal supremacy or in the validity of Henry's marriage to Anne, and said that all Christendom, except England, agreed with him.[35]

He was sentenced to be hanged, drawn and quartered, but Henry commuted the sentence to beheading. He was beheaded on Tower Hill on 6 July, the eve of the feast of St Thomas of Canterbury. As usual at executions, he was allowed to speak to the people before mounting the scaffold, but was told that the King wished him to be brief. He obeyed, and said only a few words, exhorting the people to pray for the King. He said that he had always tried to be the King's good servant, but God's first. Then the headsman did his work, and More's head replaced Fisher's on London Bridge.[36]

The executions in England shocked Christendom.[37] The rulers, churchmen and people of Catholic Europe were indignant at the execution of the Priors and monks and of Sir Thomas More, a former Lord Chancellor and a famous international scholar; but it was Henry's act in executing a cardinal, in deliberate defiance of the Pope, which stirred them most deeply. François informed the Nuncio and the other ambassadors at his court that he strongly condemned the action of his ally, the King of England. The Admiral of France, Brion, told the Nuncio that Henry's conduct towards Fisher 'was the most cowardly, infamous and grievous thing that had ever been done in

*The position is not seriously affected by a report from Rich to Cromwell, written on the day on which the conversation took place, which has been the subject of interesting analysis by Professor Elton.

the world'.[38] But the more the foreigners denounced Henry, the more he could rely on the support of his patriotic people. That typical Londoner, Edward Hall, was all on Henry's side against the cardinal who was so lamented by the Italian Pope, and wrote about Fisher's death with a joy that was barely concealed. 'It was said that the Pope, for that he held so manfully with him and stood so stiffly in his cause, did elect him a Cardinal, and sent the Cardinal's hat as far as Calais, but the head it should have stand on was as high as London Bridge or ever the hat could come to Bishop Fisher'.[39]

18

THE MONASTERIES

THE situation was looking dangerous for Henry in the autumn of 1535. The Pope informed the other Kings of Christendom that he intended to issue a bull depriving Henry of his throne for having put the Cardinal of Rochester to death, and he asked them to help enforce the sentence against Henry.[1] In England, a wet summer caused a bad harvest and a food shortage; Henry prohibited the export of grain to Calais, and imported it from the Netherlands. The Pope's supporters said that the weather was God's punishment on the realm for Henry's policy. An old husbandman, nearly eighty years old, trudging home through the rain from Worcester market on the Saturday before St Thomas of Canterbury's Day, said to a woman who was walking with him that there had been no good weather since 'the King began this business', and that there would be no better weather while he reigned; but when the local JP heard about the conversation, and questioned the old man, he could not explain what he meant by 'this business'. A neighbouring vicar in Worcestershire was more forthright; he said that the monks and others who were put to death in London were killed by men who were worse than Turks, Jews, heretics and Lollards.[2]

Many reports were sent to Cromwell of seditious utterances. A friar of Glastonbury said in a sermon in the abbey that all those who read 'the new books be lecherous and ready to devour men's wives and servants'. The curate of Harwich said that Henry was surrounded by 'knaves and churls' in his household, and that Dr Barnes was a 'false knave and heretic'. At Coventry, the copies of Acts of Parliament and royal proclamations, which had been publicly displayed, were torn down. The curate of Broughton in Oxfordshire said that the Pope was the sun, the King the moon, and the people the stars. A woman in Suffolk said that the Queen was a 'goggle-eyed whore'; and a man in Blisworth in Northamptonshire blurted out when he was drunk that he would like to see the King's head run along the ground like a football.[3]

But Henry was not dismayed. On the day before More was executed, he set out with Anne from Windsor on a progress which took him further west than he had ever travelled, to Tewkesbury, Gloucester and Bristol, and then through Wiltshire to Winchester, where he spent a month hunting and hawking in Hampshire. He sent his officers to Calais to strengthen the defences there; but Chapuys did not think that he was afraid of the Frenchmen, for he was spending more time dancing and talking to the ladies than ever before.[4] One lady in particular had attracted his attention. During his progress he stayed at the house of Sir John Seymour, Wolf Hall in Savernake Forest in Wiltshire, and met Seymour's daughter Jane. He already knew her, for she had been at court in attendance on both Catherine and Anne. According to Chapuys, she was of medium height, of no great beauty, and very pale, and she seems to have been very different in appearance and in character from Anne. By sixteenth-century standards, she was no longer young, being still unmarried at twenty-six. After Henry's visit to Wolf Hall, she returned to court with her brother Edward.

Anne had recently been behaving in an irresponsible way. She poked fun at the French ambassador, and laughed in his face. She insulted Norfolk in public. She was pregnant again, and Henry and his counsellors hoped for a son. She was in good spirits on the progress, and greatly enjoyed the weeks she spent hawking with Henry in Hampshire.[5]

Lord Leonard Grey came to Henry at Winchester, bringing with him the rebel Earl of Kildare. Henry was not pleased that Grey had promised Kildare that his life would be spared. He decided to act on the same principle which had guided him and his father Henry VII with regard to Edmund de la Pole: if he obtained custody of a prisoner by promising to spare his life, he would allow a decent interval to elapse before putting him to death. He gave audience to Kildare at Winchester, and allowed him to remain at liberty on condition that he stayed at court. Kildare did not trust Henry, and expected the worst; but Chapuys thought that as Henry had granted him audience and the freedom of the court, he would not afterwards put him to death. Henry waited until Lord Leonard Grey had returned to his post in Ireland, and then, only ten days after Kildare had arrived at Winchester, he sent him to the Tower. He waited for another sixteen months before giving the order for Kildare's execution.[6]

Henry took the attitude that his suppression of Kildare's revolt was a new conquest of Ireland, which gave him the right to override all laws and customs and rule arbitrarily as conqueror; but after consulting Cromwell, he decided to act through the Irish Parliament, which duly passed statutes granting him the lands of his defeated enemies, and extended to Ireland the Acts of the English Parliament concerning the succession and the royal supremacy. Statutes were also passed to destroy the Irish customs and to enforce the English way of life. The inhabitants were to speak English and teach the language to their children; they were to wear English clothes, and not the Irish mantle, in the street; they were to wear English caps; and they were to shave their upper lips and wear their hair long enough to cover their ears.[7]

Wullenweber was in Denmark when Charles V's agents carried out the counter-revolution in Lübeck. He travelled to Germany with 30,000 gulden in his purse, hoping to enlist mercenaries who would regain power for him in Lübeck. As he passed through the territories of the Archbishop of Bremen, he was arrested in an inn, identified, and imprisoned in chains in a dungeon at Rotenburg. He confessed, under torture, that he had received money from Henry, that he hoped to make Henry King of Denmark, and that he had ordered Meyer to erect Henry's arms over the gates of Varberg. He also confessed that he had been in touch with the 'King of Münster' – the Anabaptist leader, John of Leyden, who had governed Münster, but was now a prisoner in the hands of the victorious Catholics. The Catholic propagandists painted a lurid picture of a great international Anabaptist conspiracy of John of Leyden, Wullenweber and Henry. They said that it was the Anabaptists who had suggested to Henry that he should put Fisher to death.

Henry did his best for Wullenweber. He had no sympathy with Wullenweber's opinions, but he thought that it would be a blow to his prestige if he were unable to protect his allies. He protested to the Archbishop of Bremen on several occasions against Wullenweber's detention and treatment, and demanded that he be set free and allowed to go on his way with his 30,000 gulden; and he threatened to retaliate against the Bremen merchants in England. But the Archbishop would not be moved. He wrote to Henry that Wullenweber was a rebel against the Empire and an Anabaptist, and that if Henry took measures against the Bremen merchants in England, English subjects abroad might suffer. Wullenweber was beheaded in 1537 – a more merciful death than that accorded to most 'Anabaptist' revolutionaries in Germany.[8]

Henry and his counsellors thought that it would be advisable to counter the foreign propaganda campaign about the execution of Fisher and More. Cromwell wrote to Sir Gregory di Casale that Henry was not obliged to account to anyone except God for having put them to death; but he arranged for Gardiner, Morison and other writers to produce several books in Latin which justified their execution. Although the treason for which Fisher and More had been sentenced to death was only for denying that Henry was the Supreme Head of the Church of England, the propagandists now alleged that they had been plotting an insurrection against Henry.[9]

The Pope's denunciation of Henry was directed particularly at Henry's ally, François. Would François, who claimed to be a loyal son of the Church and to be shocked at Fisher's execution, help to carry out the Pope's sentence of deposition against Henry when it was published? François hinted that he might do so, but pointed out that Charles had taken no steps to stop trade between the Netherlands and England, and had recently allowed food to be sent to help Henry out of his economic difficulties. François said that if the Pope could persuade Charles to sign a treaty of friendship with him, and to join in measures against England, he would play his part, but that it would not be to the advantage of the Papacy and the Church if, by breaking his alliance with Henry, he allowed Charles to dominate Europe.[10]

Chapuys continued to urge Charles to act against Henry at once. But Henry ordered his officers to display notices in the royal forests, stating that those persons who had been granted permission to hunt in the forests could not do so until after the Emperor's ambassador had hunted there. Chapuys, who had repeatedly refused Cromwell's invitations to hunt in Henry's forests, thought that Henry had published the notices in order to make the people believe that he was on very friendly terms with the Emperor and his ambassador, and that the opposition could not expect to receive any help from Charles.[11]

Chapuys, like Catherine and Mary, believed that time was on Henry's side. They were worried that the propaganda campaign in England was having an effect. It was difficult to avoid hearing the anti-Papist sermons. The Carthusian monks were told, after the execution of their obstinate Priors and brethren, that Henry had graciously pardoned the survivors, on condition that all of them who were not sick listened three or four times a week to sermons preached by 'discreet and learned men' – that is to say, propagandists for Henry. People in London who were suspected of favouring the Pope were ordered to attend the sermons at Paul's Cross, where the preachers, week after week, denounced the wickedness and usurpations of the Bishops of Rome, and extolled the King, the Supreme Head, under Christ, of the Church of England.[12]

The repression was intensified. While Ortiz in Rome declared that Fisher's blood cried out to Heaven for vengeance, and asked the Pope to call for prayers for the saints who were fighting for the faith in England, Henry ordered that anyone who had a copy of Fisher's books must hand it in to the authorities within forty days.[13]

In January 1535, Henry had appointed Cromwell to be his Vicar-General and Vicegerent in ecclesiastical affairs. This gave him precedence over all the archbishops and bishops, and supreme powers over the Church. By creating such an office and giving it to a layman who was his chief secretary of state, Henry was making another gesture to emphasize the subordination of the Church to the King. It was also convenient that Cromwell, with his experience of business and the management of men, should be entrusted with the necessary powers to carry out the next step in the religious Reformation – the suppression of the monasteries. Cromwell had had experience of supressing monasteries in Wolsey's time, when he was in charge of the suppression of the twenty-two houses which Wolsey seized to finance his colleges at Oxford and Ipswich. It was widely believed at the time by the Catholics, and by the people as a whole, that it was Cromwell who suggested to Henry the idea of suppressing the monasteries. Pole went so far as to suggest that Cromwell persuaded Henry to repudiate the Papal supremacy by pointing out that if he did, he could then seize the wealth of the monasteries for himself.[14] This is most unlikely.

We do not know who first proposed the idea, but it was an obvious step to take, for it was in accordance with the religious principles of the Lutherans and appealed to the prejudices of the people and to Henry's greed. The monks spent most of their time praying for the souls of the dead in Purgatory, and the Lutherans did not believe in Purgatory or in the efficacy of prayers for souls; and the monks took vows of celibacy, which the Lutherans condemned. Many people believed that the monks were lazy shirkers who did not do an honest day's work, and hypocrites who lived immoral lives, and they were often considered to be bad landlords, though the suppression of the monasteries could cause local unemployment and resentment, as had been shown when Wolsey suppressed the monasteries in 1525. Henry was tempted by the idea of acquiring the monastic lands, for he would be able to give some of them as a gift, or for nominal sums, as rewards to leading courtiers, and to sell the bulk of them to the local gentry and to business speculators. He also hoped to acquire the valuable ornaments in the monastery chapels, the gold and silver plate and cups in their refrectories, and the valuable lead on the roofs of the houses.

The plan was for Cromwell, as the King's Vicegerent, to send visitors to inspect all the monasteries in England. It was confidently hoped that they would find many examples of immorality and mismanagement which would make it desirable to suppress the offending monasteries. Monks were to be permitted and encouraged to leave the monastery. Every monk under twenty-four years of age would be allowed to leave, on the grounds that he had taken his monastic vows when he was too young to appreciate their significance; and older monks would be granted licences to leave if they applied to the King's Vicegerent. The visitors, with the ostensible object of reforming the monasteries and suppressing vice there, would draft regulations for tightening the discipline of the houses in accordance with the old ideals of self-denial which had inspired the founders of the religious orders; and Cromwell and his agents hoped that this would make life in the monasteries so unpleasant that many monks would apply for licences to leave. Nunneries were to be visited in the same way, though there were far fewer nunneries than monasteries.

Cromwell chose as his visitors a number of lawyers, most of whom were in holy orders and had experience in the government service – Layton, Legh,

London, Tregonwell, and John ap Rice.* They began their visitation in August 1535, and did not have much difficulty in finding what they wanted. They had no success at Bradenstock in Wiltshire, where John ap Rice reported to Cromwell that after extensive inquiries they could find nothing discreditable against the Abbot; but at Farley, forty miles to the south, Layton found that the Prior had eight whores, and most of the monks also had whores, though a smaller number than the Prior. He also found cases of homosexuality between the brothers. Farley was a cell of the wealthy priory of Lewes, which had lands in fourteen counties; and the monks at Farley revealed to Layton that there was much vice at Lewes, with the Sub-Prior being particularly guilty. When Layton, moving east along the south coast, reached Lewes in October, he found not only homosexuality, but 'what is worse, treason'; for the Prior had made a sarcastic reference, in a sermon, to 'the authority of God the Father Almighty, the authority of the King, and the authority of Master Thomas Cromwell'.[15]

Layton was very lucky at Langdon Abbey at West Langdon near Dover, for when he arrived unannounced at the abbey, he found the Abbot in bed with a woman in the hut in the shrubbery. When Layton knocked at the door, the Abbot did not open it, but Layton broke it down with an axe, and found the Abbot's 'whore, alias his gentlewoman' hiding in a hole in the floor. He pulled her out, and sent her to Dover, with directions to the Mayor to imprison her in a cage or prison for eight days, and took the Abbot with him to Canterbury. He delivered him to the Prior of Christchurch, which with seventy monks was the largest monastery in England, and ordered the Prior to hold the Abbot there as a prisoner. The Prior and monks of Christchurch were eager to live down their connections with Bocking, and often sent gifts to Cromwell.[16]

Sometimes informers were prepared to volunteer information from anti-monastic zeal, or from spite. Six men found the Prior of the Crossed Friars in London in bed with a whore at eleven o'clock in the morning on a Friday in Lent. He paid them £30 to hush the matter up, but later tried to recover the money by alleging that they had libelled and blackmailed him; so one of the blackmailers denounced him to Cromwell.[17]

When the visitors could find nothing worse against the monks of a priory, they condemned them for the dirty condition of the monastery, as at Durford near Chichester, which Layton thought should be called 'Dirtford'. They denounced the Abbot of Shrewsbury for not repairing a leak in the roof of the chapel, and the Prior of St Swithuns in Winchester for the dilapidated state of the buildings.[18]

The visitors thought out ingenious ways of making life irksome for the monks. They forbade the Prior of Leeds in Kent to hunt. The Prior of Bath

*John ap Rhys, a Welshman, was usually called 'John Aprice' by his English contemporaries, and 'Sir John Price' by later historians.

was told that he must not speak to any woman, which made it impossible for him to question the woman plaintiff in a case in which he had been appointed to sit as a judge by the King. The monks of Cliffe and Osney were forbidden to leave the abbeys, which meant that they could not travel to collect their rents from their tenants or inspect their property. At Winchcombe, there were two gates to the abbey, the front gate leading into the town and the back gate into the fields. The visitors ordered that the back gate should be kept permanently locked, in order to prevent unauthorised entry into the abbey. The result was that when the monks collected the harvest in the fields behind the monastery, they had to bring it into the monastery by the front gate, after carrying it through the town, a detour of more than half a mile.[19]

When the monasteries in the North were visited, Layton found that they were even worse than those in the South, with more whores and more homosexuality. It was not the visitors, but a local JP, Sir Francis Bigod, who discovered the worst offence of the Abbot of Whitby. He was sending gifts to some priests and monks who were imprisoned in chains in York Castle for denying the royal supremacy. The Abbot's relief did not do much to alleviate their conditions, and after some months in prison one of the priests was persuaded to acknowledge that the King was Supreme Head, and to say that he had no more respect for the man in Rome – the Pope – than for any of the prisoners who were chained up with him in his prison.[20]

Very occasionally, the visitors not only admitted that they could find no fault with a monastery, but praised it. They reported that the nunnery of Catesby in Northamptonshire was very well-managed, and recommended that it should not be suppressed. When Henry heard about this, he was displeased, and suspected that the visitors had been bribed by the nuns to send this favourable report.[21] He was probably right.

After Cromwell had received the reports of the visitors on the state of the monasteries, a bill was introduced in Parliament to dissolve the smaller religious houses. Audley, the Lord Chancellor, and Rich, who was chosen as Speaker of the House of Commons, explained to the lords and MPs that the King wished to preserve all monasteries which lived up to the old, pure monastic ideal, but to suppress those in which vice flourished, as it would be better to entrust their assets to the King, so that he could use them for educational and charitable purposes. As it was clear that better discipline was maintained in the larger than in the smaller houses, all monasteries and nunneries which had an annual income of less than £200 should be suppressed, unless the King, in special cases, allowed some of these houses to continue. The MPs, moved to indignation by the visitors' reports of whoredom and sodomy, voted enthusiastically for the bill. Latimer, who was present, said in later years: 'When their enormities were first read in the Parliament House, they were so great and abominable that there was nothing but "Down with them!" '[22]

The intrigues and the wangling started immediately. The Priors of the houses which were liable to be suppressed contacted their influential friends, who offered gifts to Cromwell and other courtiers if the monastery was granted an exemption from suppression. On the other hand, local noblemen and gentlemen who claimed to have some connection with the monastery, either because they owned land in the neighbourhood or because their ancestors had founded it, asked to be allowed to buy it or lease it from the King at low prices. But so far there was not much profit to be gained from these transactions. Three-quarters of the monasteries and nunneries in England had an income of less than £200 a year, but these houses owned only a very small proportion of the monastic wealth of the kingdom.[23] It was the large, rich houses, not the smaller and poorer ones, that Henry wished to acquire; but he was approaching his objective indirectly, and was prepared to wait a few years for the wealth that he coveted.

Chapuys's repeated interventions on behalf of Catherine and Mary had at least prevented Henry from requiring them to take the oath under the Act of the Succession, or from proceeding against them for high treason if they denied that he was Supreme Head. But the strain was having its effect on the health of both mother and daughter. Henry had purged Catherine's household, and she was attended at Kimbolton by ladies, gentlemen and servants who had sworn an oath to address her as Princess Dowager; and as she refused to speak to anyone who did not treat her as a Queen, she withdrew to her room and had no dealings with anyone.[24]

The Marchioness of Exeter was still acting as Chapuys's spy at court. In November 1535 she told him that Henry was in a fierce mood, that he was planning to get rid of Catherine and Mary, and that he had threatened to make Mary an example of what would happen to people who disobeyed his laws. He had said that when he came to the throne there was a prophecy that at the beginning of his reign he would be as gentle as a lamb, and that at the end he would be worse than a lion, and he intended to see that this prophecy was fulfilled.[25]

Mary fell seriously ill under the tensions caused by her humiliating position as a lady-in-waiting to the infant Princess Elizabeth – 'the little bastard', as Chapuys and the Papal supporters called her – and by her distress at being separated from her mother and forbidden to write to her. She also feared that Anne's aunt, Lady Shelton, who was in charge of Elizabeth's household, would murder her at Anne's instigation. When Catherine heard about Mary's illness, she wrote to Chapuys and asked him to intercede with Henry to allow 'his daughter and mine' to come to her, so that she could nurse her with her own hands. Henry refused, and told Chapuys that he was sure that if Catherine and Mary came together, they would hatch some plot against him. He said that if Chapuys was worried about Mary's health, he could send his own physician to attend her. Chapuys refused this offer. He was a sincere friend to Catherine and Mary, but he was first and foremost the Emperor's ambassador, and knew that if Mary were to die, it would be much better for propaganda purposes if she were in the care of a physician chosen by Henry and not by him.[26]

Henry was justified in suspecting that Catherine and Mary were plotting with Charles. However understandable their attitude may have been, it came near to treason, at least in Mary's case. With all the passionate indignation of a high-spirited girl of nineteen, she repeatedly asked Chapuys to persuade Charles to intervene to save England from the heretics, which clearly implied armed intervention. Catherine expressed herself a little more cautiously, but despite all her protestations of devotion and obedience to her husband, she, too, wanted Charles to intervene. She certainly sometimes wrote to Chapuys saying that she would never resist Henry by force, and would never willingly be the cause of war; but were these letters, perhaps, meant to be intercepted and read by her jailers, and reported to Henry and Cromwell? We know that on at least one occasion, Chapuys smuggled to Mary the draft of a letter which he asked her to copy out and send to him, so that it could be read by the censors; and we know how cleverly Catherine had tried to outwit Henry over Felipez's journey to Spain in 1527.[27]

In the spring of 1535, Chapuys was eager to arrange for Mary to escape from England to the Netherlands. He discovered, through his contacts with her, that she was eager to go and was prepared to risk the attempt. He told Charles's minister, Granvelle, that the plan for her to escape 'is very hazardous, but would be a great triumph and very meritorious'. He thought that it should be possible, while she was staying in Princess Elizabeth's household at Eltham, to get her secretly out of the house at night, ride to the river, and take her by boat to a Spanish ship which would be waiting off the coast near Gravesend. But Charles was even more reluctant than usual to become involved in English affairs, for he was on the point of leading an expedition to North Africa to seize Tunis from the Turks. On 10 May 1535, he wrote to Chapuys that Mary's escape 'is a very difficult and hazardous matter, not to be attempted without good and sure means for its accomplishment; at all events, it would be inadvisable at this time'.[28]

The Emperor won a great victory at Tunis. Soleiman, who was engaged in a war in Persia with the Sophy, could not send reinforcements to Barbarossa; and in July 1535 Charles captured the port of La Goletta after fierce fighting, and a week later took the town of Tunis by storm. Barbarossa escaped with the greater part of his fleet and his treasure to his chief stronghold of Algiers; but Charles captured 82 of the Turkish ships and 20,000 prisoners, and was able to recoup some of the costs of his expedition by selling the prisoners as slaves. The news did not reach London till the beginning of September. Chapuys immediately sent a messenger to tell Henry, who was at the Seymours' house at Wolf Hall.

Henry showed every sign of being delighted. He gave Chapuys's messenger eight ducats as his reward for bringing the news, and Cromwell wrote on his behalf to Chapuys, warmly congratulating the Emperor; he said that Henry was as pleased as if the victory had been his own. Chapuys wondered how much larger a reward Henry would have given the messenger if he had brought news of Charles's defeat at Tunis, for he thought that, despite their pretence to the contrary, Henry and Cromwell had been as pleased as a dog who is thrown out of a window.[29]

Mary smuggled a letter to Chapuys, warning him that England would go to total ruin if the Emperor did not 'take brief order and apply a remedy'. He should act for the service of God, the peace of Christendom, the honour of her father, and compassion for poor afflicted souls, even though he was occupied with his 'not less triumphant than most necessary enterprise of Tunis'. By supporting the cause of her mother and herself, he would perform a service most agreeable to Almighty God and would acquire as much fame and glory for himself as by conquering Tunis or the whole of Africa.[30]

In September 1535, England was diplomatically isolated. There seemed to be a real danger of all Catholic Europe uniting against Henry, while the Lutheran Princes remained neutral. Henry was closely watching the international situation as he hunted in Wiltshire, and he reacted quickly to the danger. He appointed Gardiner to be resident ambassador in France, and ordered him to work for a closer alliance with François against Charles. If necessary, he was to offer François 200,000 crowns towards the cost of raising an army, though Gardiner was to do his best to get this sum reduced. If François invaded Italy, Henry would pay one-third of the cost of the war; if he invaded the Netherlands, Henry would pay 300,000 crowns within two years. But Henry did not propose to make any actual payments in cash. He merely offered to deduct these sums from the money which François owed him for his annual pensions under the earlier peace treaties.[31]

Henry also tried to repair his relations with the German Lutheran Princes, which had suffered as a result of his support for Lübeck. He hinted at the possibility of not only making a diplomatic alliance, but of reaching an understanding about religion, and raised their hopes that he might one day make England a Lutheran state. His old enemy Luther had been one of the few people abroad who had applauded the execution of Fisher; he wished that there were more Kings of England to kill cardinals.[32]

It was difficult for Henry to make a direct approach to Luther, but he sent a gift and a friendly letter to Luther's closest collaborator, Melanchthon, and proposed to the Duke of Saxony that Melanchthon should have discussions with some English theologians about their doctrinal differences. The Duke of Saxony agreed, and Henry sent Edward Fox and Nicholas Heath, who had been appointed Archdeacon of Stafford after having been the Boleyns' local vicar at Hever. Both Fox and Heath were sympathetic to Lutheranism. They held lengthy talks with Melanchthon at Wittenberg about private masses and the other points of difference between the Church of England and the Lutheran Confession of Augsburg.[33]

Once again, as in 1533, Henry could rely on the fact that Charles would take no effective action against him, and that François wished to have him as an ally. On 30 August, the Pope issued a bull excommunicating Henry and depriving him of his kingdom unless he repented and returned to his allegiance to the Apostolic See within two months; but he did not publish the bull, which was not to take effect for a year. Two months later, Francesco Sforza, Duke of Milan, died. This reopened the whole question of the future of the duchy which François had always coveted. Charles thereupon instructed Count Cifuentes, his ambassador in Rome, to urge the Pope not to publish the bull against Henry until he had discovered what François' attitude would be, and until Charles, who was on his way to Rome, had discussed the question with him. Charles was prepared to consider the possibility of allowing François' younger son, the Duke of Angoulême, to become Duke of Milan; but François also coveted the territory of his uncle, the Duke of Savoy, whose duchy included the port of Nice, and Piedmont; and the Duke of Savoy was Charles's ally.[34]

Sforza's death was good news for Henry, and he received more good news just before Christmas, when he heard from Kimbolton that Catherine was dying. He was sure that Catherine's death would remove the remote possibility that Charles would take action against him, and that Sforza's would soon lead to war between François and Charles. He would survive the danger of foreign intervention by bluff and bravado, and by skilfully sowing hostility between Charles and François without making any compromise, without wooing either of them for favours, but allowing them to quarrel among themselves and woo *him*, while he snapped his fingers at both of them.

Chapuys, who had also heard that Catherine was ill, asked permission to go to her. Henry agreed, but insisted that before Chapuys left for Kimbolton he must speak to him. On 27 December, Henry came from Eltham to Greenwich and met Chapuys in the lists, where a tournament was taking place. Henry greeted him warmly, put his arm around his neck, and took him to his chamber. He told Chapuys that after the Duke of Milan died, François had offered to invade Charles's territories if Henry paid the costs of the expedition, but that he had refused François' proposal, for he was an Englishman, not a Frenchman or a Spaniard to use such guile, and he would never incite one of his neighbours to attack another for his own advantage. This was in fact the reverse of the truth, because it was Henry who had suggested to François that he should finance him if he went to war with Charles.

Henry then told Chapuys that Catherine was dying, and said that after she was dead there would be no reason for hostility between him and Charles.

Chapuys merely replied that it would be a tragedy if Catherine died. He thanked Henry for allowing him to visit her, and asked if Mary would also visit her mother. Henry at first refused, but when Chapuys pressed him, he said that he would reconsider the matter. He knew that if he considered it for very long, it would be too late.[35]

Chapuys reached Kimbolton on 2 January, and spent four days with Catherine. He found her very distressed at the growth of heresy in England, and because several of her ladies had taken the oath to the succession; but Chapuys comforted her by reminding her that St Peter had renounced Christ and had later returned to the faith. When he left her on 6 January, she seemed to him to be recovering; but she died at 2 p.m. next day. Her Spanish physician believed that she had been poisoned, and that the poison had been contained in some Welsh beer that she had been given to drink. Chapuys either believed this, or pretended to believe it, and thanks to him the story was soon being told at the Spanish court and all over Europe. Catherine's English supporters believed, without the slightest reason, that the poison had been obtained and the murder planned by Henry's Italian agent, Sir Gregory di Casale.[36]

Henry ordered that she should be buried in Peterborough Abbey in suitable style. Elaborate preparations were made for the funeral of 'the right excellent and noble Princess, the Lady Catherine, daughter to the right noble and mighty Prince, Ferdinand, late King of Castile, and late wife to the noble and excellent Prince Arthur, brother to our sovereign lord King Henry VIII'. The corpse was carried in state to Peterborough, and, on the way, lay for two days at Sawtry Abbey, surrounded by 408 candles. Three bishops and six abbots received it at the church door at Peterborough. But Henry refused to agree to his Council's suggestion that there should be a hearse for Catherine in St Paul's in London; when they reminded him that his sister Mary the French Queen had had a hearse in St Paul's when she died in 1533, he replied that her case was different, because she had been a Queen. He sent mourning for the gentlemen of her household to wear at her funeral, but he himself wore yellow on the day of the funeral. He invited Chapuys to go to the funeral, but Chapuys refused, as she was not being buried as a Queen.[37]

Catherine's household was broken up at her death. Henry invited her Spanish physician to enter his service. The physician, who wished to return to Spain, was able to decline the offer by pointing out to Henry that if he entered Henry's service, it would encourage mischievous people to believe that he had poisoned Catherine at Henry's orders. Catherine's Spanish confessor, Athequa, who had been appointed Bishop of Llandaff, was not so fortunate. He tried to leave the country secretly, disguised as a sailor on a Flemish ship bound for Spain; but his servant, who was going with him, was overheard addressing him as 'My Lord', and he was stopped and identified. He was sent to the Tower, and was told that he would be tried for high treason for attempting to leave the realm without a passport; but as the lawyers advised that this did not constitute high treason, he was imprisoned in the Tower.[38]

Henry was now confident that he had nothing to fear from Charles. On the day after Catherine died, Cromwell wrote to Gardiner at Lyons that Henry wished him to adopt a tougher stand in his negotiations with François, because now that Catherine was dead, Charles had no further reason to quarrel with Henry. A dispute had arisen between England and France about the wine trade with Bordeaux. Henry was worried at the number of English ships which were lost on the voyage to Bordeaux in winter, and had prohibited the import of Gascony wines during the winter months. The French maintained that this was a breach of the commercial treaty, and in retaliation the authorities at Bordeaux detained the English ships which were in the harbour there. Henry offered to repeal the ban on the import of wines in the next session of Parliament, provided that the English ships were released first. The Admiral of France then said to Gardiner that it would be unwise of Henry to quarrel with François about so small a matter, when François had dissuaded the Pope from excommunicating and deposing him.

Henry reacted angrily to this, and adopted a high and confident attitude. He ordered Gardiner to tell the Admiral that he was a King of England who was more powerful than any of his progenitors, and had therefore no reason to fear an Admiral of France; nor did he need the help of any foreign ruler to protect him from the Pope or from anyone else. If the Pope issued a bull excommunicating and deposing him, it would be like the man who spat at his enemy when he was standing many yards away, and found that his spittle was blown back into his own face by the wind.[39]

Henry made no compromise with the German Lutherans. He refused to allow Fox and Heath to make any concessions about what the Lutherans called the 'three abuses' in the Church of England – private masses, at which the priest consecrated the bread and wine when no one else was present, and which, according to orthodox Catholic doctrine, benefitted the souls of all men, though none of them received communion; the administration of the bread alone, and not the wine, to the laity at Mass; and the prohibition of the marriage of priests. Melanchthon, on his side, refused to agree that the marriage of a man to his brother's widow was against God's law. After three months of argument, the talks ended without agreement, but in a friendly spirit, and it was decided that the discussions should be resumed in England at a later date.[40]

Henry tried to improve his relations with James V. He sent Lord William Howard to Scotland to invite James to meet him at York in the summer. As usual, Henry asked for a safe-conduct to be sent to his envoy; but James sent a safe-conduct which contained an unusual clause. It stated that the safe-conduct was granted on condition that Lord William Howard did nothing while he was in Scotland to encourage any 'strange opinions' about religion or to challenge the authority of 'the sacred Holy Church of Rome'. In a reply which was undoubtedly written after consulting Henry, Lord William stated that it was an affront to his King to include this condition in the safe-conduct, for no 'strange opinions' had been introduced into England, unless by 'strange opinions' was meant the correction of vice. He stated that although he had no instructions to make religious propaganda in Scotland, he would not refrain from speaking the truth if he were asked about religion. He refused to accept the safe-conduct, and was coming to Scotland without one, knowing that James would permit no one to harm the envoy of a King who was so loyal a friend and so formidable an enemy as Henry.

Howard reached Stirling safely in April 1536, and was well received by James; but though James at first seemed willing to meet Henry, the negotiations for the meeting broke down. James refused to go further south than Newcastle, and Henry would not go further north than York, because there would be no carriage, victuals or lodgings between York and Newcastle for the large escort which he would bring with him. He evidently expected James to travel through the same tract of country with a smaller escort.[41]

In February 1536, François suddenly invaded Savoy without warning. As soon as Charles heard the news, he realised that war with France was inevitable. On 29 February, he wrote to Chapuys from Naples that though he deplored the way in which Henry had treated Catherine and Mary, Chapuys must do everything possible to improve relations with him; and he urged the Pope not to publish the bull depriving Henry of his kingdom. The Pope reluctantly agreed, and Charles told Henry's ambassador, Pate, that it was only due to his efforts that the bull had not been published. Henry drew the conclusion that he had no need to placate the Emperor or anyone else. When François asked him to contribute to the cost of his campaign against Charles's ally, the Duke of Savoy, he refused to pay, and said that by his treaty with François he was only bound to help François if Charles invaded France.[42]

François had caught Charles off his guard. His armies advanced through the Duke of Savoy's territories, and by the middle of April had occupied the whole of Piedmont. By this time, Charles had arrived in Rome, and had discovered that François had made an alliance with the Turk against him. On 17 April, he made a speech to the Pope and the cardinals in the Consistory. He denounced François for making an alliance with the infidel, and offered to settle his dispute with François by single combat; the alternative would be a war to the death to save Christendom from the Turk and his ally.[43] As François did not accept the challenge, we do not know whether Charles meant it seriously, or whether he would have found some way of avoiding a duel with François. The alternative was merciless war. Henry was safe.

19

THE DESTRUCTION OF ANNE BOLEYN

On 24 January 1536, Henry took part in a tournament at Greenwich. During one of the jousts, he and his horse were thrown to the ground with such violence that the onlookers feared for his life. Chapuys thought that it was a miracle that he had not been killed, and believed that it showed that God was reserving him for a more dreadful punishment. François heard that Henry was unconscious for two hours after his fall; but Chapuys wrote that he was unhurt.[1] The theory which has been put forward by some modern writers, that the blow on the head which he suffered when he fell affected his mental health, and was responsible for his subsequent acts of tyranny, seems to be quite untenable.

Six days later, Anne had a miscarriage; her baby would have been a boy. Chapuys heard from Lady Exeter and his other informants at court that Anne told Henry that the miscarriage had been caused by the shock of hearing about his fall in the joust, and also because of her fear that she was losing his love, as he was paying constant attention to Jane Seymour. According to Chapuys, Henry was touched by her words, and left Greenwich, where he had been paying court to Jane Seymour, and came to York Place on St Matthias's Day to spend the holy day with Anne. Chapuys did not believe the story which the Marchioness of Exeter told him at third hand, that Henry had said that he believed that Anne had led him by witchcraft into marrying her, and that her failure to bear him a surviving son was proof that God condemned their marriage; but there is no doubt that by the end of January 1536, rumours were circulating at court that Henry would soon get rid of Anne and marry Jane Seymour.[2]

On 23 February, Chapuys had a secret meeting with Cromwell in a half-finished house which was being built for Cromwell in London. Cromwell told Chapuys that Henry wished to reestablish friendly relations with the Emperor, and they discussed how this could be achieved. Chapuys asked if Henry would be prepared to return to his obedience to the Pope, to legitimise

Mary and restore her to favour, and to make an alliance with Charles against the Turk and François. Cromwell said that Henry would certainly be prepared to make the alliance, and that he might well agree to the proposal about Mary, but that it would be difficult to persuade him to reestablish Papal supremacy. Chapuys and Cromwell had another meeting on 1 April. Cromwell said that Anne hated him and wished to have him beheaded, as she had hoped to have Wolsey beheaded. He said, with a grin, that though Henry was a very virtuous Prince, he was still interested in women, and asked Chapuys how he would react if Henry were to marry again. Chapuys replied that the world would never accept Anne as Henry's wife, but might perhaps be prepared to accept another lady as his wife.[3]

Jane, like Anne before her, was refusing to become Henry's mistress. At the end of March, Lady Exeter told Chapuys that Henry had sent a messenger from York Place to Jane at Greenwich with a letter and a gift of a purse full of golden sovereigns. Jane knelt as she took the letter, and kissed it, which was the correct way to receive a letter from the King; but she refused to accept the gift. She asked the messenger to return it to Henry, and to tell him that she was a gentlewoman of a respectable family, and that she would rather suffer a thousand deaths than lose her honour. She said that if Henry wished to give her money, he should wait until she was engaged to be married, and make a marriage settlement in her favour. When Henry heard what she had said, he fell more in love with her than ever. He praised her virtue, and said that he would prove the sincerity of his love for her by speaking to her only when some member of her family was present. Lady Exeter told Chapuys that Jane was being well trained by a group of courtiers who were very close to Henry and did not like Anne. They had warned Jane that she must not yield to Henry's desires unless he made her his Queen, and she quite agreed about this. This group of courtiers had also told her to let Henry know how greatly his subjects disliked his marriage to Anne.[4]

The cards were being stacked against Anne. She had again failed to produce a male heir, and again the Papists were celebrating her failure as a propaganda triumph. She was hated throughout the realm, and Henry could win the applause of the majority of his subjects if he got rid of her. She was a major obstacle in the way of an improvement in relations with the Emperor; Henry's most powerful minister, Cromwell, had turned against her; and Henry had fallen in love with another woman whom he wished to marry. If he married Jane, even the Papists would be forced to recognise this new marriage, for as Catherine was dead, it would be valid, whether the divorce from Catherine had been lawful or not; and if Jane bore Henry a son, or even a daughter, the child's legitimacy and right to succeed to the throne would be unchallengeable. The Lutherans would of course be distressed if Henry got rid of Anne, but this would not be the first time that he had annoyed the Lutherans.

On 3 March, Jane's brother Edward was appointed to be a gentleman of Henry's Privy Chamber. On the same day, Cromwell ordered his officials to compile a list of all the grants of land that Henry had made to Anne's father Wiltshire, and her brother Rochford, since 29 April 1522.[5] It would be useful for Cromwell to have this information readily available if they were convicted of high treason and their property was thereupon forfeited to the King. But, despite all the rumours, Lord Rochford had never played a more prominent part in the diplomatic and social activity at court. Both he and the Queen were still receiving requests and gifts from people who wanted their share of the monastic lands and other grants and perks.

Cromwell's negotiations with Chapuys had reached a stage at which it was appropriate to refer them to Henry, and on Easter Tuesday, 18 April, Chapuys went to Greenwich for an audience with the King. When he arrived, he was warmly greeted by all the lords of the Council, especially by Rochford; but he was annoyed that Rochford insisted on discussing what Chapuys called 'Lutheranism' with him. Chapuys refused to talk about the subject. During the last three years, Chapuys had carefully avoided meeting Anne, as his Emperor did not recognise her as Henry's Queen; but Cromwell now said to him that when they went to Mass with Henry in a few minutes' time, Henry would greatly appreciate it if Chapuys would kiss the Queen, which was a gesture of salutation among equals, though Henry would not insist on this if Chapuys objected. Chapuys said that he thought in the circumstances it would be better if he did not do it. When he met Anne as they entered the chapel, he bowed to her, and she acknowledged his bow with a curtsy. Henry had probably already decided to destroy Anne, but hoped to compel Charles's ambassador to acknowledge her as his Queen before he did so.

After Mass, Henry withdrew with Cromwell and Chapuys to a window, where they talked about the conditions which Chapuys had suggested to Cromwell would be acceptable to Charles as a basis for a new alliance. Henry adopted a very different attitude from Cromwell's. He said that it was no business of Charles whether or not he returned to his obedience to Rome, and that he had no intention of doing so; nor was Charles entitled to concern himself with Mary, for she was his daughter, and he could treat her as he liked. He would, in fact, treat her well, but he needed no advice about this from the Emperor; for 'God, of His abundant goodness, had not only made Us a King by inheritance, but also had therewithal given Us wisdom, policy and other graces in a most plentiful sort'. As for Charles's request for financial aid against the Turk, it was better to restore broken friendships before asking the former friend for money. Henry also rejected the proposal for an alliance with Charles against François. He said that François was entitled to Milan, and had more right on his side than Charles had in this war. If Charles wished to renew his alliance with Henry, he must first apologise for having tried to do him so much injury in recent years.

Cromwell was visibly put out by Henry's words, for Henry, at the last moment, had undone all the negotiations which Cromwell had been pursuing since Catherine's death.[6] Either Henry had changed his mind, or Cromwell had exceeded his authority in his preliminary talks with Chapuys, or – and this is the most likely explanation – Henry had allowed Cromwell to mislead Chapuys and to encourage false hopes, in order to humiliate the Emperor and make it clear that it was Charles who was wooing him. But Henry had judged the situation correctly. Charles would do him no harm, and would, on the contrary, offer more inducements to Henry the more Henry rebuffed him.

On 23 April, Henry attended the chapter of the Knights of the Garter on St George's Day, with Richmond, Norfolk, Wiltshire and Northumberland. There was a vacancy for a new knight to be elected. Rochford was one of the candidates, but Sir Nicholas Carey was chosen instead.[7] This was interpreted by some of the courtiers as a setback for Rochford, but it was not a very serious one.

Henry announced that he would go to Dover in the first week of May, to inspect the new fortifications which were being built there, and that the Queen would accompany him. They would leave Greenwich on the day after the tournament which was to be held there on May Day. After his recent fall from his horse, Henry did not take part in the tournament. Sir Henry Norris was the chief defender, and Rochford was the chief challenger.[8]

While the jousts were taking place, Henry's counsellors asked to speak with him urgently, and to everyone's surprise he left the tournament and went to Westminster. Here he was informed that the Council had discovered that the Queen had committed adultery with her lute-player, a youth named Mark Smeaton, with Norris, and with two other gentlemen of the Privy Chamber, Sir Francis Weston and William Brereton, and with her own brother, Lord Rochford. Smeaton was brought from Greenwich to the Tower that same evening, while the others were arrested and questioned at Greenwich by Norfolk and the other counsellors. Next day they were all sent to the Tower – first Norris, Weston and Brereton, then Rochford some hours later, and last of all Anne. Smeaton admitted his guilt, but all the others protested that they were innocent. Two other courtiers, Richard Page and Thomas Wyatt, the poet son of Sir Henry Wyatt of Allington in Kent, were also arrested; they had both been Anne's admirers in her youth.

It was late in the summer afternoon when Norfolk and other counsellors brought the Queen by barge from Greenwich. Her arrival was watched by crowds of gaping Londoners. All of them were surprised, and many of them rejoiced. As Anne entered the Tower by the watergate, she knelt and again declared that she was falsely accused.[9] She asked the Constable of the Tower, Sir William Kingston, if he was going to put her in a dungeon. He said that she would be placed in the room which she had occupied on the night before her coronation. Kingston wrote to Cromwell that she said to him: 'Master Kingston, shall I die without justice? and I said, the poorest subject the King hath, hath justice. And therewith she laughed'.[10]

It was said that the Countess of Worcester was the first person to warn the Council about what was happening. She reprimanded one of the ladies-in-waiting for her flirtatious conduct, and the lady replied that she behaved no worse than the Queen. Inquiries were made, and the counsellors learned that Smeaton had boasted of his success with the Queen and that her woman had stories to tell of conversations that they had overheard. They said that Anne had committed adultery promiscuously with Norris, Weston, Brereton and her brother; all of them apparently knew that they shared her favours with the others. They had laughed together about the King, for Anne had told them how unsatisfactory he was in bed, being almost impotent. They had plotted together to assassinate him, after which Anne would marry Norris and rule as Regent for her infant daughter Elizabeth. Their shameful and treasonable relationships had been going on for some time; according to one story which was widely believed, Norris was Princess Elizabeth's father.[11]

Anne said that Smeaton was lying, for he had only twice been in her chamber, once when she had ordered him to play for her at Winchester in October 1535, and the second time at Greenwich, two days before she was arrested. She found him standing in her presence chamber. She asked him why he was so sad, 'and he answered and said it was no matter'. She said: 'You may not look to have me speak to you as I should do to a nobleman, for you be an inferior person'. 'No, no, Madam', he replied, 'a look sufficed me, and thus fare you well'. Had she in fact been kinder to him than she made out? Or had he boasted of a triumph which he had not achieved, and sacrificed his life in order to destroy the haughty Queen who had scorned him, so that he and she and his more favoured rivals should all die together? Whatever his motives, he confessed in full, apparently without having been put to the torture.[12]

Smeaton, Norris, Brereton and Weston were tried on 12 May by commissioners who included Norfolk, Suffolk and other counsellors. Smeaton pleaded Guilty. The others pleaded Not Guilty, but were found guilty by the jury. They were all sentenced to be hanged, drawn and quartered. Anne and Rochford were tried three days later in the Tower before the Court of the Lord High Steward. Norfolk presided, and sat with twenty-six other peers, including Suffolk, Exeter, Dacre – who had himself stood trial before the same court two years earlier – and the Earl of Northumberland, who had been in love with Anne and had been loved by her before Henry had noticed her. But her father, Wiltshire, and Cromwell did not sit on the court.

The charge against her was that 'by sweet words, kisses, touches and otherwise' she provoked Norris to commit adultery with her, which he did at

Westminster on 12 October 1533 and at other times; that she committed adultery with Brereton at Hampton Court on 8 December 1533 and afterwards; with Weston on 20 May 1534, and with Smeaton at Westminster on 26 April 1535; that on 2 November 1535 and both before and after, she incited her brother, with his tongue in her mouth and hers in his, whereupon he, despising the counsels of God and all human laws, had the Queen at Westminster on 5 November 1535 and several times before and after; and that on 31 October 1535 she plotted with them to kill the King. She and Rochford pleaded Not Guilty. All the evidence was given in open court, but the allegation that she had said that Henry was impotent was written down on paper, and the judges ordered that it should not be read out. When the paper was handed to Rochford, he read it aloud, to the great displeasure of the judges.

Anne and Rochford were both found guilty. He was sentenced to be hanged, drawn and quartered, and she to be burned alive or beheaded, according to the King's pleasure. This was the accepted punishment for a woman convicted of high treason.[13]

She awaited her death in the Tower with composure. The letter which she is supposed to have written to Henry from the Tower is a forgery, written in the reign of her daughter Elizabeth.[14] She made no appeal at all to Henry; she knew him too well. She asked only to be shriven, and Cranmer was sent to hear her last confession of her sins.

Henry commuted the sentence of hanging, drawing and quartering in the case of all the convicted men, including the low-born Smeaton. They were all executed on Tower Hill on 17 May; Smeaton was hanged, and Norris, Brereton, Weston and Rochford were beheaded.[15] It would be interesting to know why Henry granted them the mercy of an almost painless death instead of forcing them to undergo the full atrocious sentence. It was probably because he knew them personally, for this seems usually to have been the criterion which determined whether or not a convicted traitor, who was not a nobleman, should be hanged, drawn and quartered.

Henry ordered that Anne should not be burned, but beheaded, and not on Tower Hill with the headsman's axe, but in the privacy of the green within the Tower, with a sword of the finest Flemish steel wielded by an executioner who was specially brought from St Omer. She obtained this much consideration from the husband who had once been so passionately in love with her.[16]

Her execution was postponed for forty-eight hours so that she could be divorced before she died. Henry wished his marriage to her to be declared a nullity so that their daughter Elizabeth would be a bastard. The marriage to Anne, which the whole population had been required to swear to uphold on pain of a praemunire, was now to be proclaimed void, and the child of the marriage, whom the people had sworn to accept as the lawful heiress to the crown, was to be pronounced illegitimate. This was to clear the way for the issue of Henry's forthcoming marriage to Jane Seymour, for otherwise, if Jane had a daughter and no son, Elizabeth would be the heiress in the eyes of those who supported Henry's divorce from Catherine, while Catherine's supporters would regard her as illegitimate. The bastardizing of Elizabeth had the drawback that until Henry and Jane had a child, the nearest heir to the throne would be James V; but this was to be surmounted by an Act of Parliament which empowered Henry to appoint anyone he wished to succeed him to the crown.

On 18 May, Cranmer sat as judge at Lambeth Palace to try Henry's petition for divorce against Anne. It was all done in proper form, and Anne was given notice in the Tower of the proceedings and was asked to appoint proctors to represent her at the hearing. It was not easy for Cranmer to find a reason for reversing his decision of three years earlier that Henry's marriage to Anne had been valid. There were two possible grounds for invalidating it: the existence of a precontract between Anne and the Earl of Northumberland more than ten years before, and the fact that Anne's sister Mary had been Henry's mistress. It would obviously be much more desirable if the precontract could be given as the reason, and Northumberland was asked whether he had been precontracted to Anne. Northumberland might have been tempted to give the reply which Henry wanted, had it not been for the fact that he had already sworn an oath in 1533 that there had been no precontract, and that if he now admitted it, he might be accused at some time in the future of having plotted with Anne to lure the King into an illegal marriage by suppressing the truth in 1533. On 13 May, Northumberland wrote to Cromwell denying that there had been a precontract.

Cranmer's solution was to try the case in private and to grant Henry a divorce without publicly announcing the reason for his decision. The secrecy strongly suggests that Henry's relationship with Anne's sister was the reason. Cranmer presumably found that the Bishop of Rome's dispensation of 1527, which allowed Henry to marry the sister of a woman who had been his mistress, was void, although Cranmer must have held in 1533 that it was valid.[17]

Anne was beheaded next day, after she had made a short speech on the scaffold. 'I pray God save the King, and send him long to reign over you, for a gentler nor a more merciful Prince was there never; and to me he was ever a good, a gentle, and sovereign Lord'. She neither admitted nor denied her guilt.[18]

It is impossible to know whether she was guilty. There was undoubtedly evidence against her and against the other defendants of improper behaviour, if not of adultery. But twenty-three years later, the Scottish Protestant, Aless, wrote to her daughter Elizabeth, a few months after she became Queen, that on the morning of Anne's execution he had walked at dawn with Cranmer in the Archbishop's garden at Lambeth, and that Cranmer had said that Anne was innocent.[19] If Aless's story is true, Cranmer's opinion is significant, as he had heard her last confession a few hours earlier.

Henry obviously believed that Anne was guilty. It was so greatly to his advantage that she should be guilty that he could not judge the case fairly; and this was one of the few occasions on which Cromwell, Lady Exeter, and Anne's other enemies may to some extent have forced his hand. As Cranmer wrote in his letter to Henry on the day that Anne was sent to the Tower, 'in the wrongful estimation of the world, Your Grace's honour of every part is so highly touched (whether the things that commonly be spoken of be true, or not)'.[20] After the rumours of Anne's infidelity had begun circulating at court, it was difficult for Henry to ignore them without compromising his own reputation; and it would have been foolish to ignore the reports of a plot by Anne, Norris and the others to assassinate him. These reports might be true, just as the accusations against Buckingham and Wolsey might have been true. It was always better to be safe than sorry; and Queens, like Dukes and Cardinals, could do no harm once their heads had been chopped off.

Once the decision had been taken to denounce Anne, it was essential to obtain a conviction; and as Henry waited confidently for news of Anne's trial, divorce and death, he acted as he often did at moments of tension: he went to parties at which there was wine, music and beautiful women. During the eighteen days which elapsed between Anne's arrest and her execution, he attended a party nearly every night, sometimes staying till after midnight, and returning to Whitehall by the river with his musicians playing on his barge. Jane Seymour went to many of these parties. According to Chapuys, he said that he believed that Anne had been had by more than a hundred men. 'You never saw Prince nor man', wrote Chapuys, 'who made greater show of his horns, or bore them more pleasantly'. His gaiety seemed to many people to be in bad taste. The Bishop of Carlisle admitted to Chapuys that he was shocked by Henry's behaviour at a party at the Bishop's house, at which Henry pulled out of his pocket some poems or a play whch he had written about Anne's crimes and punishment.[21]

On the day of Anne's execution, Cranmer granted him a dispensation to marry Jane, which was necessary because they were distant cousins, both of them being descended from Edward III. Henry stayed at Whitehall that day till a messenger brought him news that Anne had been beheaded, and then went at once to Jane, dressed in the brightest colours, and spent the evening celebrating with her. Next day Jane came secretly by barge to Whitehall, and she and Henry made a precontract of marriage; and ten days later, on 30 May, he married her privately. On the same day, he created her brother Edward Viscount Beauchamp.[22]

He first showed her off to the public as his Queen when they went together in state by barge from Greenwich to Whitehall on 7 June, and next day he took her with him to the state opening of Parliament. Audley, as Lord Chancellor, made a speech in Henry's praise; he was 'in wisdom and justice a Solomon; in body, vigour and strength a Samson; in appearance and beauty an Absalom'. In the House of Commons, Rich, the Speaker, compared him to the sun, whose rays have cleansed the filth and corruption wherever they shine.[23]

On the very day on which Henry was being so lavishly praised by Audley and Rich, he sent his niece to the Tower. At the beginning of June, he discovered that Norfolk's brother, Lord Thomas Howard, had made a precontract of marriage with Lady Margaret Douglas, the daughter of Henry's sister Margaret, the Queen of Scots, and Angus. Howard's conduct had been less heinous than Suffolk's when he secretly married Henry's sister Mary; but great changes had taken place in the kingdom and at Henry's court since 1515.

Howard and Margaret were arrested on 8 June and sent to the Tower. Margaret fell ill in the Tower, and was soon transferred to Sion Abbey, where she was held in confinement. In August, she wrote to Cromwell, assuring him that she was no longer in love with Howard; she asked him 'not to think that any fancy doth remain in me touching him'. She was released from the convent after sixteen months imprisonment in October 1537, two days before Lord Thomas Howard died in the Tower.[24]

The fall of Anne Boleyn had been welcomed with joy by the Papists. Chapuys was delighted to hear that the 'English Messalina' had blamed him for her downfall. The Emperor thought that it was clearly a revelation of the divine will. Granvelle wrote less piously to Chapuys that it was high quality music to his ears, and a worthy subject for laughter. Mary of Hungary wondered whether Anne was guilty, but thought that even if she were innocent, no injustice could be done to so evil a woman. Lord William Howard, in Edinburgh, was embarrassed to find that everyone at James's court, and particularly the Papist bishops, were jubilant at the news of Anne's arrest; he wrote to Cromwell, asking to be told 'the truth' – that is to say, what line he should adopt.[25]

The Papal Nuncio in Lyons thought that it was a great judgement of God; he heard that Cranmer and another heretic bishop, who had been protected by Anne, had fled abroad, and that Henry had abandoned his plans to dissolve the monasteries. In Rome, Ortiz exulted over Anne's fate; in Venice there were celebrations because God had shown Himself to be a rightful judge; and a servant of the Master of the Maison Dieu at Dover had heard that on the day before Anne was beheaded, the tapers which surrounded the sepulchre of Queen Catherine in Peterborough Abbey had miraculously lit themselves. But the Lutherans were anxious. Luther heard that Henry's new Queen was pro-Papist and that many changes for the worse were about to take place in England. Melanchthon considered that Anne's fall was a great tragedy, though this did not prevent those champions of English Lutheranism, Barnes and Shaxton, from applying in good time for their share of the forfeited lands of Anne and Norris.[26]

Five days after Anne's execution, Cromwell had an interview with Chapuys, and told him that if Mary could be persuaded to submit and recognise Henry as Supreme Head of the Church, she would be received at court, and an Act of Parliament would be passed declaring her heiress presumptive to the throne if Henry had no children by his marriage to Jane Seymour. Chapuys urged Cromwell to find a way in which Mary could submit without offending her conscience. On 26 May, Mary who was at Hunsdon in Hertfordshire, wrote to Cromwell that though she had 'perceived that nobody durst speak to me as long as that woman lived, which is now gone', she hoped that it would now be possible for her to be restored to her father's favour. She wrote again to Cromwell on 30 May, thanking him for all he was doing for her, and asking to be allowed to visit Henry; and on 1 June she wrote to Henry himself, begging him 'as humbly as child can' for his blessing and acknowledging all her faults, 'humbly beseeching Your Grace to consider that I am but a woman and your child, who hath committed her soul to God and her body to be ordered in this world as it shall stand with your pleasure'. But she received no reply.

She wrote again to Cromwell on 7 June, asking him whether Henry 'of his princely goodness and fatherly pity' had accepted her letter and had withdrawn his displeasure from her. This time she received a reply from Cromwell: the King her father had forgiven her offences. Henry's counsellors thought that the matter was settled. Sir John Russell told Sir Anthony Browne, Henry's Master of the Horse, and Sir Francis Bryan that an Act would be passed legitimising her and declaring that she would be next in line of succession to the crown after any sons or daughters who might be born to Henry and Jane. Lady Hussey, the wife of Lord Hussey, the Chamberlain of Mary's household, spread the good news, and soon it was the talk of the court. But Henry's only action was to send the Duke of Norfolk, the Earl of Sussex, and Sampson, who had been appointed Bishop of Chichester, to inform Mary that he required her to take the oath of supremacy recognising him as Supreme Head of the Church of England.

Mary had been in poor health for some time, and in addition to her other troubles was suffering from toothache and a bad cold in her head. But she refused to take the oath, though the lords threatened her, saying that if they had such a disobedient daughter they would knock her head against the wall until it was as soft as baked apples. She wrote to Cromwell that she would follow his advice 'in all things concerning my duty to the King, God and my conscience not offended . . . but if I be put to any more (I am plain with you as with my great friend) my said conscience will in no ways suffer me to consent thereunto'. On the same day she wrote to Henry 'in as humble and lowly manner as is possible for me', asking for his pardon, 'humbly prostrate before your most noble feet'. Cromwell wrote back at once and told her that her submission was inadequate and unacceptable, as she had shown her 'contempt of God, your natural father, and his laws'.[27]

Henry had reacted strongly when Norfolk and his colleagues informed him of Mary's refusal to take the oath. He told his counsellors that he had decided to send her to the Tower, and that if she refused to take the oath, she would be prosecuted for high treason and executed. The counsellors were shocked, and begged Henry, on their knees, not to take this action against her. According to a letter which was written by some Protestant refugees abroad to Mary in 1556, just before she gave the order that Cranmer should be burned for heresy, it was Cranmer who finally persuaded Henry not to put her to death. The story is confirmed by Cranmer's secretary, Ralph Morice, who told it to John Foxe. According to Morice, when Henry at last agreed to spare Mary's life, he warned Cranmer that he would live to regret it; and he told Queen Jane, who also interceded for Mary, that she was a fool to do so, because Mary would be an enemy to any children which he and Jane might have.[28]

Henry's anger was directed not only against Mary, but even more against the members of his Council and the courtiers who had spread the rumour that he had forgiven Mary and was intending to make her heiress presumptive to the throne. He would not tolerate a pro-Mary faction at court, or any attempt to force his hand; and as he had frightened the Lutherans by destroying Anne, it was time to frighten the Catholics too. He had Lady Hussey arrested, and sent to the Tower. He expelled the Marquess of Exeter and Sir William Fitzwilliam from the Council. Cromwell told Mary that he had got into serious trouble on her account, and confided to Chapuys that for four or five days he believed that Henry had decided to get rid of him. But Henry ordered him and Audley to examine the other offenders.

They examined Sir Anthony Browne and Sir Francis Bryan. They asked them whether they wished to legitimise the Lady Mary because they believed that the King had formerly been lawfully married to the Princess Dowager. Had they discussed the question of Lady Mary's future with Dr Wolman, Dr Bell, or Dr Knight? Had Sir Nicholas Carey or Sir Thomas Cheyney said anything on the subject? Had they any special reason to feel affection towards the Lady Mary? If, before the Lady Elizabeth had been declared a bastard, it had pleased God to call the King to His mercy (which God defend), leaving the Lady Elizabeth in the degree of a Princess, would they then have adhered to her, or would they have advanced the Lady Mary? All the suspects gave the right answers to the questions, and none of them was sent to join Lady Hussey in the Tower. When Bryan went hunting with Henry near Chertsey in August, Henry told him not to worry, as 'naughty bruits [rumours] were soon blown'.[29]

Chapuys was seriously alarmed when Cromwell told him about Henry's threat to Mary. He managed to smuggle a letter to Mary, advising her that as she had been threatened with violence, she should now submit and take the oath of supremacy, as she would be entitled to claim that she had done so under duress. He advised her to make a secret protestation, before she took the oath, that she did not intend to be bound by it, and he promised to ask the Pope to grant her a dispensation to take the oath and break it. Mary reluctantly agreed to do this; but in fact, thanks undoubtedly to Cromwell's efforts, Henry did not require her to take the oath, and was satisfied with a statement in writing signed by Mary to the same effect.

On 13 June, Mary wrote to Cromwell that she had hardly been able to sleep for the last two or three nights because of her toothache. She stated that though he had urged her to write a more submissive letter to Henry, 'I cannot devise what I should write more'. So she would leave it to Cromwell to draft a suitable letter, and she would sign anything which he required.

Cromwell drafted both a submission and an accompanying letter for Mary to sign. In the letter, she wrote that, 'most humbly prostrate before the feet of Your Most Excellent Majesty', she realised that she had 'so extremely offended Your Most Gracious Highness, that my heavy and fearful heart dare not presume to call you father', and that Henry had no reason to forgive her offences 'saving the benignity of your most blessed nature doth surmount all evils, offences and trespasses, and is ever merciful and ready to accept the penitent calling for grace'. She promised that 'I have and shall, knowing your excellent learning, virtue, wisdom and knowledge, put my soul into your direction . . . beseeching your mercy, most gracious sovereign lord and benign father, to have pity and compassion of your miserable and sorrowful child'. She signed it at 11 p.m. on 15 June. She was utterly exhausted.

She also signed the submission which Cromwell had drafted for her. It stated that, having 'obstinately and inobediently offended' the King her father, she recognised him to be 'Supreme Head in earth under Christ of the Church of England, and do utterly refuse the Bishop of Rome's pretended authority, power and jurisdiction within this realm, heretofore usurped'. She also recognised 'that the marriage heretofore had between His Majesty and my mother the late Princess Dowager was by God's law, and man's law, incestuous and unlawful'.[30]

Henry had insisted on her complete submission, and having obtained it, he was satisfied. He sent Cromwell and Norfolk and other counsellors to Mary to give her his blessing and a loving message. They treated her with the greatest respect, and asked her forgiveness on their knees for the way in which they had been obliged to behave on the last occasion they had visited her. She wrote two more letters to Henry, thanking him, in the most abject language, for having shown mercy to her. At the end of June, Henry gave her a household of forty-two servants, having reduced Elizabeth's household to thirty-two.[31]

On 6 July, Henry and Jane visited Mary at Hunsdon. It was the first time that Henry had spoken to Mary for nearly five years, and both he and Jane showed her great affection. Mary afterwards told Chapuys that Henry said that he suspected that her former disobedience had been due to the encouragement that she had received from the Emperor, and pointed out that Charles was powerless to help her as long as he was alive. He asked her whether she had ever received letters from Charles or Chapuys; she coolly lied, and said that she had not. He asked her whether her submission had been sincere or simulated, for he hated nothing more than dissemblers. He said that sometimes his counsellors advised him to dissemble with foreign ambassadors, but he always refused to do so, and he begged Mary to show that she was his daughter by refusing to dissemble. Chapuys wrote to Granvelle that Mary had given the proper reply to his question, and would continue to dissemble very ably.[32] Henry probably guessed that she was lying, and had asked her the question because his question and her answer were necessary in order to establish the proper picture of the benign Prince and father and the obedient daughter and subject.

A few weeks later, Cromwell asked Henry's permission to present a ring to Mary as a gift. It was inscribed with a suitable poem, pointing out that Christ had set an example to all children by His humility and obedience to God the Father. Henry was so pleased with the inscription that he told Cromwell that he would take the ring and send it to Mary as a gift from himself.[33]

In July, Henry went on his postponed visit to Dover. He took Jane with him on the journey which he had originally intended to make with Anne.[34]

Lady Hussey was in due course released from the Tower. Contrary to what was reported abroad, Wiltshire was not required to play an active part at the trial of his son and daughter. He and his wife were allowed to leave court and retire to Hever, after he had resigned all his offices and granted annuities in favour of people chosen by Henry. His daughter-in-law, Lady Rochford, was allowed to retain part of her husband's property, and to remain at court. Thomas Wyatt was released from the Tower, after his father had promised to ensure that he was obedient in all things to the King's pleasure and that he abandoned the shameless fashions which had caused him to incur the displeasure of God and his master the King.[35] Cromwell emerged with greater wealth and influence. Within a few weeks he had been created Lord Cromwell of Oakham and was granted Wiltshire's office of Lord Privy Seal, as well as gifts of some of the traitors' forfeited lands. But Henry made a mental note of the fact that Cromwell had befriended Mary, and remembered it four years later.

20

POLE

By the summer of 1536, Henry was more powerful than he had ever been. In July, his Parliament passed a statute which enabled him to issue proclamations which would have the same force of law as an Act of Parliament – a power which has never been granted to any other King or Prime Minister in England before or since. Another Act allowed him to nominate his successor to the crown until such time as he and Jane Seymour had issue of their marriage. It was widely believed that Henry had induced Parliament to pass this Act because he intended to appoint his illegitimate son, the Duke of Richmond, to succeed him as King; but Richmond died on 22 July 1536, soon after his seventeenth birthday. It was rumoured that he had been poisoned with a slow-working poison which Anne Boleyn had given him before her death.[1]

There is certainly some mystery about his funeral. He had recently married the Duke of Norfolk's daughter, and Henry ordered Norfolk to take his body to Thetford in a cart, covered with straw, and escorted by only two attendants, and to bury it there secretly. At least, this is what Norfolk understood Henry to say; but after the funeral, Henry reprimanded Norfolk for failing to show proper respect to Richmond's corpse.[2]

Henry knew that he had nothing to fear from either Charles or François. Far from being prepared to enforce a Papal bull depriving him of his throne, they were both courting him, urging him to enter the war on their side. They both made tentative proposals to him for a marriage of his daughter Mary; Charles wished her to marry Dom Luiz, the King of Portugal's brother, and François proposed his third son, the Duke of Angoulême. Henry neither accepted nor rejected these offers, but encouraged the hopes of both suitors without promising anything. One difficulty was that neither Dom Luiz of Portugal nor the Duke of Angoulême could be expected to demean themselves by marrying the King of England's illegitimate daughter, and Charles and François made it plain that their proposal for Mary's hand was conditional on Henry legitimising her by Act of Parliament. Henry refused to legitimise her.[3] He would wait; as Charles and François were so eager to gain his friendship, they might yet be prepared to marry Dom Luiz or the Duke of Angoulême to his bastard daughter. This would indeed be a boost to his prestige.

Henry invited Chapuys and the Bailly of Troyes to come together before his Council and argue the justice of Charles's and François' cause in the war, and to give reasons why Henry should join one side or the other. There they were, the two of them together, contending for his favour. A few days later, he himself gave audience to each of them separately, while the other ambassador waited his turn in the antechamber. After hearing their lengthy arguments, in which both of them tried to prove that the other sovereign was the aggressor and had no right to Milan, Henry announced that after careful consideration he had decided to remain neutral.[4]

His neutrality was a little more friendly to François than to Charles. He excused François from paying his annual pensions to him for the duration of the war; and in September he summoned Chapuys to Ampthill and told him that he thought that François had more right on his side than Charles had in the war, and that he was thinking of entering the war on François' side. He also protested to Chapuys against the persecution by the Inquisition of English merchants in Spain who asserted that he was the Supreme Head of the Church of England. But he refused François' requests for aid. Having first insisted that he was not bound, under his treaty with François, to help him unless Charles invaded France, he continued to refuse him aid when Mary of Hungary's armies entered Picardy and captured Montreuil and besieged Therouanne.[5]

It was not easy for Henry to defend his neutrality with the fighting going on all around Calais and between the opposing navies at sea. Both sides occasionally sent raiding parties through the Marches of Calais to attack the enemy from an unexpected quarter. Henry strengthened the garrison and the defences of Calais, and as usual gave his close personal attention to the problems and decisions involved, whether he was at Whitehall and Greenwich, or hunting in Surrey or Bedfordshire. The authorities at Falmouth were unable to prevent Charles's warships from entering the harbour and attacking French ships in English territorial waters; but Henry sent a fleet to patrol the Channel to protect English merchant ships. His sea captains captured one of Charles's naval commanders, the Admiral of Sluys, who had seized English ships on the grounds that they had been trading with France. The Admiral of Sluys was brought back to England and prosecuted in Henry's courts on a charge of piracy, though Henry afterwards released him at Chapuys's request.[6]

Henry drew nearer to the Lutherans. Just when everyone at home and abroad was expecting him to turn sharply away from Lutheranism, he allowed his bishops to issue Articles of Religion which by implication accepted the doctrine of the Lutheran Confession of Augsburg that there were only three sacraments. In the Ten Articles of July 1536, the Eucharist, Baptism and Penance were listed as sacraments, but the other four sacraments of the Church – Matrimony, Confirmation, Orders and Extreme Unction – were ignored. But the Ten Articles were a compromise; auricular confession, images, prayers to the saints, and even Purgatory, were expressly upheld, and good works as well as faith were declared to be necessary for justification.[7]

In the discussions which took place between March and July 1536 on the committee which drafted the Articles, the bishops clearly formed themselves into two factions. Cranmer was supported in his reforming views by Latimer and Shaxton, two well-known reformers who had been appointed Bishops of Worcester and Salisbury in the place of the two Italians, Ghinucci and Campeggio, and by Edward Fox, Bishop of Hereford, and Hilsey, Bishop of Rochester. Stokesley, Longland, Tunstal, and Archbishop Lee of York were the most active leaders of the orthodox Catholic faction, for Gardiner, the Bishop of Winchester, who was the ablest of them, was absent as ambassador in France. The Catholic bishops were in the majority, but this was outweighed by the authority of Cromwell, the King's Vicegerent, who took part in their discussions and used his influence on the side of the reformers.[8]

The Ten Articles were published as an authoritative statement of faith which all Henry's subjects were required to believe. In order to stifle opposition, Henry issued an order in July placing a complete ban on all preaching until Michaelmas except by bishops in their cathedrals. After the two months' interval, preaching was to be resumed, but no preacher was to discuss the meaning of the Articles, which he was required to read aloud without comment. Anyone who broke this order was to be immediately arrested.[9]

Henry also issued a proclamation suppressing a number of holy days, including all holy days in harvest time, which was defined as being between 1 July and Michaelmas. This suppressed the greater feast of St Thomas of Canterbury on 7 July. The suppression of holy days pleased the gentlemen, merchants and farmers who wanted their servants to work on these days instead of spending them in church and in festivities; but it aroused opposition in the country. Cranmer complained that it was also ignored at Henry's court, and warned Henry that his courtiers were setting a bad example to his subjects by keeping the suppressed holy days.[10]

In 1536, Henry at last felt able to take steps to reorganise the government of Wales, which hitherto had been ruled from Ludlow by the Council of the Marches of Wales under the energetic presidency of Roland Lee, the Bishop of Coventry and Lichfield. Lee and his colleagues had recently had more success than usual in enforcing law and order in Wales. They had captured and hanged a notorious outlaw for whom they had been vainly searching for sixteen years; but Lee wished that it were possible for him to hang some Welsh gentlemen. He was sure that many gentlemen in Wales were in league with the robbers, and thought that if even one gentleman could be hanged, this would have a more salutory effect on the people than the execution of low-born felons. Lee had always been sceptical about the proposal, which had been mooted for some time in London, that justice should be administered in Wales, as it was in England, by the local gentry sitting as justices of the peace, instead of by the Council of the Marches.[11]

But in 1536, Henry and the Council in London decided to go ahead with the scheme. The Council of the Marches of Wales was to be retained, but most of its powers would be exercised by the local JPs. Wales was to be divided into a number of counties, which continued to exist, almost unchanged, as territorial units for local government purposes, until 1974. The county of Monmouth was incorporated into England. Measures were taken to suppress the old Welsh customs which Edward I had allowed to continue after the conquest in the thirteenth century. Gavelkind, the system by which a man's sons all inherited his land in equal shares, was abolished, and replaced by the English system of inheritance by the eldest son. The use of the Welsh language on official business was prohibited, and all proceedings and evidence in the law courts had to be given in English, although many Welshmen could not speak English. Welsh historians have often commented on the irony of the fact that it was a Tudor King, the great-grandson of the Welshman Owain ap Meredith ap Tewdwr, who struck this blow at the land of his origin; but one could hardly expect a King who had just beheaded his wife, imprisoned his niece, and contemplated executing his daughter, to show sympathy for the national feelings of his great-grandfather's fellow-countrymen.

Henry pleased the gentlemen of England, that class on whom he chiefly relied for his political support, by his action against vagabonds. These men refused to conform to the regimented society in which they lived; many of them were the discharged servants and retainers of the household of some great nobleman who had died without heirs or who had been executed as a traitor and lost his lands. They did not relish working in the fields for ten hours a day at a daily wage of fourpence, after the comparatively easy life which they had led in their lord's establishment; but the country gentlemen, who needed their labour, wished to compel them to do so.

In 1530, Parliament passed an Act against vagabonds. Persons who were too old or ill to work could apply to a local JP for a licence to beg; but any vagabond who begged without a licence was to be severely punished. If any able-bodied man or woman, who did not own land or carry on a recognised profession or was a trader in merchandise, was found outside his native parish and could not account for his presence there, the local JP was to send him to the nearest market town, where he was to be tied naked to the end of a cart and 'beaten with whips throughout some market town or other place till his body be bloody by reason of such whipping'. He was then to be sent back to his native parish, and if he did not go, he was to be whipped again. Anyone who sheltered or helped him was to be fined.[12]

This Act did not eliminate vagabonds, and the dissolution of the smaller monasteries greatly increased the number. By the beginning of July 1536, Chapuys was reporting that legions of monks, nuns, and the servants employed in the suppressed religious houses, were roaming the countryside, homeless and penniless, begging for relief. He had been told that there were as many as 20,000 of them. This figure is almost certainly greatly exaggerated. The monks and nuns were in nearly every case granted small annual pensions; but a pension of 40 shillings a year compared unfavourably even with the fourpence a day of the unskilled labourer, and the servants and dependents of the monasteries were normally not granted pensions. An Act was passed in 1536 to increase the penalties for vagabonds. For the second offence a vagabond was not only to be whipped again, but was also to have part of his ear cut off. For the third offence, he was to be hanged. There was obviously some sympathy for the vagabonds among the lower classes, for the Act provided that anyone who refused to whip a vagabond child when ordered to do so, was to be put in the stocks for two days.[13]

Hanging had for long been the punishment for all felonies – that is to say, murder, rape, sodomy, arson, forgery and coining, and the most common of all crimes, robbery and theft – and was to remain so for the next three hundred years. Henry vigorously enforced the law against thieves, which pleased the gentry, the merchant class, and most of the law-abiding population. According to Holinshed, who wrote twenty-five years after Henry's death, 72,000 thieves and vagabonds were hanged during his reign.[14] Historians, who are aware of the tendency of sixteenth-century chroniclers to exaggerate numbers, have usually assumed that 72,000 is an absurd over-estimate which bears no relation to the truth. It is probably an exaggeration, but perhaps not by so very much. Many letters have survived from judges and government officials which give the number of malefactors executed after a recent assize or quarter sessions – some of them for high treason or murder, but the great majority for theft. The figures usually vary from six or eight to twelve or fourteen. If an average of ten persons were hanged at every sessions, this means that forty a year would be hanged in every county, which means 1,600 a year in the forty counties of England, even if we disregard Wales, where different circumstances prevailed. This would amount to about 60,000 during the thirty-eight years of Henry's reign. It is over 2 per cent of the 2,800,000 inhabitants of England, which equals the proportion of the 6,000,000 Jews exterminated by Hitler, who constituted 2 per cent of the population of occupied Europe, though it falls short of the 10,000,000 Russians who are said to have been put to death under Stalin's régime – more than 5 per cent of the population of the U.S.S.R.

But there was one man whom Henry could not hang, burn, imprison, or even murder. This was his cousin, Reginald Pole, the son of Margaret Plantagenet, the daughter of Edward IV's brother the Duke of Clarence, and the widow of Sir Edward Pole. Reginald Pole was born in 1500, a few months after Henry VII executed his mother's brother, the Earl of Warwick, because he was too close to the throne; but Henry VIII had shown favour to the family, creating Margaret Countess of Salisbury in her own right, and granting her eldest son, Henry Pole, the title of Lord Montagu. Henry paid for the education of her third son, Reginald. He was studying at Paris University when the Sorbonne discussed the legality of Henry's marriage to Catherine, and he used his great intellectual abilities and his theological knowledge to argue the case for Henry at the Sorbonne. Next year he went to Padua, and again argued for Henry when Padua University gave its opinion on the divorce issue in 1531. But by then he had come to the conclusion that Henry was wrong, and that the marriage to Catherine was valid. He wrote a treatise on the subject which he sent to Henry, though he did not publish it.[15] Henry thanked him, and expressed the hope that he would change his mind. Pole remained in Italy pursuing his studies, and when Henry urged him to return to England and enter his service, he found excuses for not doing so.

In 1535, Henry put greater pressure on Pole. The well-known humanist intellectual, Starkey, who was a friend of Pole and was one of Henry's chaplains, wrote to Pole in Venice that Henry wished him to write his opinion about the validity of his marriage to Catherine. Starkey emphasized that Henry was eager to obtain Pole's honest and frank opinion; he told Pole that Henry had recently said to him that 'he would rather you were buried there than you should for any worldly promotion or profit to yourself dissemble with him in these great and weighty causes'. In a series of letters, Starkey told Pole that he could not permanently spend his time in study, while completely ignoring his duty to his Prince and benefactor; and while he continued to emphasize that Henry wanted Pole to give his honest opinion, he also threw out hints of the benefits which Pole would obtain if he exercised his great gifts in Henry's service.

It was the executions of the Carthusians and Fisher and More which decided Pole to come out into the open and to become Henry's greatest enemy. He was conscious of the debt of gratitude which he owed to Henry for his education; he was, indeed, being constantly reminded of it by Henry's counsellors and spokesmen. But he became more and more convinced that his duty to God required him to denounce his benefactor as a bloody tyrant who had martyred the champions of the Faith in England. Cromwell, as well as Starkey, now wrote to Pole, asking him to send his honest opinion – it need not be a lengthy work – about the royal supremacy over the Church of England.[16]

Pole wrote at last on 27 May 1536. It *was* long – a whole book – and it did contain his honest opinion. He wrote with passion about the shameful executions of Fisher and More, of More's daughter Margaret Roper breaking through the cordon of guards to greet her father on his way to execution, and of the constancy of Reynolds and the other Carthusian martyrs. He told Henry that he was like Nero and Domitian; he had plundered his subjects for twenty-seven years, and at the very time of the Emperor's glorious expedition to Africa, he , who was so falsely called the Defender of the Faith, had torn to pieces, like a wild beast, all the true defenders of the Faith. He informed Henry that he had appealed to the Emperor to intervene to protect thousands of Christians from Henry, who was a far greater danger than the Turk, and warned him that he would be confronted with a revolution by his own subjects, and would meet with the fate of Richard III.[17]

Pole wrote to his friend Prioli that he had written frankly to Henry for the King's benefit, but that he feared that Henry would not read the book; after glancing at a few sentences, he would throw it away and rage against him and his friends. But Henry did not react as Pole had expected. He replied almost by return of post with a personal letter. He wrote that he had read the book with interest, and was not in the least offended with Pole for writing it; but they obviously disagreed on certain points, and there were things in the book which he would like to discuss personally with Pole. He therefore invited him to come to England.[18] Henry wrote this letter to Pole only two or three days after he had told his counsellors that he had decided to send Mary to the Tower and execute her for refusing to take the oath of supremacy. There was always cold calculation behind every threat that he made and every olive branch that he offered.

Pole replied that he must be excused from accepting Henry's invitation to come to England, because if he did, he would be asked if he believed that Henry was Supreme Head of the Church of England, and would be executed as a traitor if he gave a truthful answer. He told Henry that he had been led astray, like Solomon, by his passion for a woman; but God had now rid Henry of this woman, 'and with her head, I trust, cut away all occasion of such offences as did separate you from the light of God'. Now, 'that in place of her, of whom descended all disorders, the goodness of God hath given you one full of all goodness to whom, I understand, Your Grace is now married', he hoped that Henry would return to his obedience to the Pope.[19]

Pole now received a stream of lettters from his friend Starkey, from Tunstal – the bishop whom he most admired for his support of Catherine and opposition to Henry – and from his mother and his brother Lord Montagu, all expressing the indignation which they had felt when Henry had shown them his book, and their amazement that he could write in such a way about Henry. Starkey wrote that he loved Henry more than his own life.

Lady Salisbury wrote that his book had grieved her far more than the loss of her husband and children. Pole wrote and reminded her that she had taught him from his childhood to serve God. She replied that he could not serve God if he was disloyal to his Prince. Montagu wrote that Reginald's book had hurt him more than if he had lost his mother, wife and children, 'for that had been but natural'. But Reginald had shown himself 'so unnatural to so noble a Prince. . . . For our family, which was clear trodden under foot, he set up nobly, which showeth his charity, his clemency, and his mercy'.[20] Montagu was soon to have personal experience of how much charity, clemency and mercy was in Henry.

In the autumn, the Pope decided to make Pole a cardinal to fill the vacancy caused by Fisher's death. When Henry and Cromwell were informed of this by their agents in Italy, Starkey, Tunstal and Pole's family wrote to warn Pole that if he went to Rome and accepted the cardinal's hat, he would be adhering to the King's enemy and proving himself to be a traitor to his Prince, his country and his family. But Pole went to Rome, taking precautions against being assassinated by Henry's agents on the journey from Venice, and on 22 December 1536 was created a cardinal.[21]

21

THE PILGRIMAGE OF GRACE

On 28 September 1536, the King's commissioners for the suppression of monasteries in Northumberland rode from Corbridge to Hexham to take possession of Hexham Abbey and eject the monks. They found the streets of the town full of armed men, and the abbey gates locked and barricaded. A monk appeared on the roof of the abbey, dressed in armour; he said that there were twenty brothers in the abbey armed with guns and cannon, who would all die before the commissioners should take it, for the abbey had been granted a charter by 'King Henry VIII, God save His Grace'. The commissioners retired to Corbridge, and informed Cromwell of what had happened. Henry ordered them to occupy the abbey by armed force; if the monks resisted, they were to be treated as traitors.[1]

On 1 October, two of Cromwell's officials arrived at Louth in Lincolnshire to collect the taxes. The people rose in revolt, and seized the officials. They hanged one of them, and killed the other by sewing him up in a cowskin and giving him to dogs to eat. Within a few days, the rising had spread to Horncastle, Ancaster, and the whole of Lindsey; 30,000 rebels were marching on Lincoln; and Cromwell was informed that the journeymen would not abide with their masters, and that no one was left in the towns who could wear harness.[2]

It was a popular counter-revolution, a spontaneous resistance of the normally silent majority against all the innovations introduced by the religious *avantgarde* and against the new régime that was being imposed on them: for Professor Elton's theory that the rising was organised by Cromwell's opponents at court seems far-fetched.[3] The rebels objected first and foremost to the suppression of the monasteries. They objected to Henry's low-born counsellors – the 'villein blood' – who had replaced the nobles through whom the King ought to govern his realm; and they objected above all to Cromwell. They objected to Cranmer and Latimer and the heretic bishops, and demanded that they should be handed over to them, or banished from the realm, and that the books of Wycliffe, Tyndale and other heretics should be burned. They objected to the Statute of Uses, which, in order to prevent the evasion of death duties, had restricted the right of testators to leave their property by will. They were alarmed at the rumours that the Council were planning to seize the gold, jewels, and ornaments in the parish churches and to suppress many churches throughout the country, so that there would be only one church every five miles. They were also alarmed at the reports that a tax was to be imposed on every baptism of a child, on every head of cattle, and every time anyone ate a goose.[4]

They were loyal subjects of the King, and looked to the nobles and the gentlemen to lead them. In every town and village where the people rose, they went first to the local squire and asked him to be their leader and to take an oath 'to be true to Almighty God, to Christ's Catholic Church, to our sovereign lord the King, and unto the commons of this realm'.[5] The gentlemen all reacted in the same way. When they heard that a revolt had broken out in the neighbouring villages, they wrote at once to the King's Council, warning them of the danger, and offering to serve the King against the rebels. When the rebels arrived at their house, they agreed to join them and lead them, and smuggled a letter to the Council stating that they had joined the rebels under duress, because otherwise their families would have been killed and their houses burned. Having gained the local gentlemen, the rebels then marched to the house of the nearest nobleman, who reacted in the same way as the gentlemen, and became the leader of all the rebels in the district, while secretly professing his loyalty to the King.

Henry, who was at Windsor, informed the noblemen and gentlemen of his realm that there was a traitorous assembly in Lincolnshire, which aimed at the destruction of his person and at the murder and robbery of all true subjects and the rape and deflowering of their wives and daughters. He ordered the gentlemen of the West Midlands to raise an army from among their tenants and servants, who were to come with horses, pikes, bows and arrows, and other arms, to meet the Earl of Shrewsbury and the Duke of Suffolk at Mansfield and Nottingham and to serve under their command against the rebels of Lincolnshire. He ordered the noblemen and gentlemen of the other counties in the south of England to form a reserve army which would assemble at Ampthill, where he would take command of them, and if the rebellion had not yet been suppressed by the advance-guard, he would lead them against the rebels. Great emphasis was placed on the fact that the men who came to Ampthill would serve under their King's personal command; but Henry probably never intended to lead the army himself, and as usual he left the dirty work to his officers.[6]

Lord Hussey, whose wife had only recently been released from the Tower, joined the rebels when they came to his house – against his will, he said. He and the gentlemen of Lincolnshire wrote to Henry, asking him to send a pardon to the rebels, after which it would be possible to persuade them to go home. Henry sent Lancaster Herald to tell the rebels that the rumours that he intended to suppress churches, and seize the ornaments in them, were untrue, and that it was unreasonable of the rebels to object to paying taxes. Only 10 per cent of them were wealthy enough to be liable for taxes, which were levied on those who owned property worth more than £20. As the tax was sixpence in the pound, a man who owned land worth £40 paid only 10 shillings in tax; and how could anyone justify rebellion for 10 shillings?[7] As for their demands about the base-born counsellors and heretic bishops, 'I never have read, heard, nor known that Princes' counsellors and prelates should be appointed by rude and ignorant common people; nor that they were persons meet or of ability to discern and choose meet and sufficient counsellors for a Prince. How presumptuous then are ye, the rude commons of one shire, and that one of the most brute and beastly of the whole realm, and of least experience, to find fault with your Prince, for th'electing of his counsellors and prelates, and to take upon you, contrary to God's law and man's law, to rule your Prince'.[8]

He ordered them to submit, and to send a hundred of their leaders with halters around their necks to ask his pardon; otherwise he would send a great army against them, which would burn, spoil and destroy their goods, wives and children with all extremity, to the fearful example of all lewd subjects.[9]

On 6 October, Lord Darcy wrote to Henry from his house at Templehurst near Leeds that the West and North Ridings were peaceful, but that revolts had broken out at Dent, Sedbergh, and in Wensleydale. But four days later, the men of Beverley were up. Robert Aske, a barrister from the East Riding of Yorkshire, was travelling through Lincolnshire when the rising began there, and when he arrived home, he persuaded the people to rise in support of the Lincolnshire rebels. Within a day or two, 40,000 men had risen in Howdenshire, Mashamshire, and the whole of the East Riding and were marching on York. Aske called on his men to take an oath to join 'our Pilgrimage of Grace' for 'the common wealth . . . the maintenance of God's Faith and Church militant, preservation of the King's person and issue, and purifying of the nobility of all villeins' blood and evil counsellors, to the restitution of Christ's Church and suppression of heretics' opinions'. As they marched with the cross borne before them, they sang their song:

Christ crucified
For thy wounds wide
Us commons guide
Which pilgrims be,
Through God's grace
For to purchase
Old wealth and peace

For the spiritualty . . .
Crim, Crame and Rich,
With three Ls and the Lich,*
As some now teach
God them amend.
And that Aske may
Without delay
Here make a stay,
And well to end.[10]

Lord Darcy told Henry that he had not enough force to resist the rebels, and that he would have to retire to Pontefract Castle and try to hold it. Henry wrote to Darcy that he was surprised that he could do nothing more effective against the rebels, but assured him that he had no doubts as to his loyalty. Privately, Henry told his counsellors that he suspected that Darcy was a traitor.[11]

Shrewsbury and Suffolk found that the Lincolnshire rebels were ready to submit; according to Shrewsbury, this was thanks to the valiant efforts of Lancaster Herald. Suffolk advised Henry to grant them a general pardon, for then they would surrender their arms and go home, and Suffolk could lead his army against the rebels in Yorkshire. Henry refused to grant a general pardon; he intended to pardon all except a few ringleaders, but thought that it was essential for his 'honour' that there should be a few executions, for otherwise it would be said, at home and abroad, that he had been forced to capitulate to his rebels. Suffolk wished to hang one prominent rebel; but Henry told him that this was not enough, and sent him a list of nine rebels who were to be detained for execution. Suffolk thought that it would be unwise to hang them until after all the rebels had handed in their arms, and though he held the nine men in prison, he did not put them to death for the moment.[12]

Henry agreed to this, and ordered Suffolk to proceed cautiously until the rebels had surrendered all their arms. Then, if there was any new disturbance, he was to 'destroy, burn and kill man, woman and child, to the terrible example of all others, and specially the town of Louth, because that this rebellion took his beginning in the same'.[13]

While Suffolk disarmed the Lincolnshire men, the Earls of Shrewsbury, Rutland and Huntingdon took command of the army which was to deal with the Yorkshire rebels. But though Henry wrote to Gardiner at Valence that he had raised an army of 40,000 men in six days, he had in fact been able to send only 7,000 men to Shrewsbury and his colleagues at Newark. He was also in

*This probably refers to Cromwell, Cranmer and Rich; to Layton, Dr Legh and Dr London, the visitors to the monasteries; and to Roland Lee, the Bishop of Coventry and Lichfield.

Jane Seymour, by Hans Holbein

Thomas Howard, Duke of Norfolk, after Holbein

difficulties about money, for the horsemen in his army were grumbling at receiving only eightpence a day. He ordered Cromwell to raise money as soon as possible in London and other places, and particularly to make the 'fat priests' pay. In his conversation and letters, Henry was now showing a new hatred of priests and monks.[14]

Shrewsbury could not take the offensive with his 7,000 men against Aske's 40,000 rebels. All he could do for the moment was to stop the rebels from crossing the Trent. He stationed men at all the fords in the river; but it had been a very dry autumn, and the water levels were falling fast. If there was no change in the weather, it would soon be possible for the rebels to ford the Trent at almost any point, and Shrewsbury would then be unable to hold this line.[15]

On 16 October, Aske's men entered York. Next day they came to Doncaster, where the Mayor joined them; Shrewsbury heard that 'never sheep ran faster in a morning out of their fold' than did the people of Doncaster to join the rebels. They marched to Pontefract, where Lord Darcy and Archbishop Lee joined them. They were also joined by Lord Latimer, Lord Scrope, Sir Robert Bowes, Sir Ralph Ellerker, Sir Robert Constable, and nearly all the gentlemen of Yorkshire.[16]

By the third week of October, the rising had spread to Lancashire, Furness, Westmorland and Cumberland. At Sawley near Clitheroe the people went to the abbey, ejected the gentleman who had recently leased it from Henry, and put back the Abbot and the monks. Henry told the Earl of Derby to raise an army by summoning the gentlemen of Lancashire and Cheshire to come to him with their tenants and servants. He ordered Derby to go with this army to Sawley, to seize possession of the abbey, and hang the Abbot and all the monks without trial. They were to be hanged in their monks' habits, the Abbot and some of the chief monks on long pieces of timber protruding from the steeple, and the rest at suitable places in the surrounding villages. Derby explained to Henry that he did not have enough troops to carry out these orders in the face of the opposition of the whole countryside.[17]

Chapuys had heard the gossip in London and at court that Norfolk was a secret sympathiser with the rebels and that at the appropriate moment he would reveal himself as their leader.[18] Norfolk was still very active at the age of sixty, after many years of loyal service to Henry – against Andrew Barton, at Flodden, in Ireland, in the Boulonnais, and as a counsellor, administrator and diplomat; but he was known to resent the ascendancy of low-born counsellors like Wolsey and Cromwell, and he was opposed to Lutheran doctrines. He was therefore in sympathy with the rebels' chief demands; and his brother Thomas was a prisoner in the Tower for having become engaged to Lady Margaret Douglas.

Henry sent for Norfolk and had a private talk with him at Windsor. We do not know what they said, except that they discussed religion;[19] no doubt Henry told Norfolk that he trusted in his loyalty, and assured him that he would never allow the Catholic doctrine of the Church of England to be subverted by the heretics. He appointed Norfolk to command his armies at Newark. He could not have chosen a better man either to negotiate with the Yorkshire rebels or to fight them. None of them would accuse Norfolk of being a low-born heretic; and as Norfolk knew that he was under suspicion in some quarters, he was determined to prove his loyalty to Henry.

Norfolk and Shrewsbury reluctantly advised Henry that he would have to grant a pardon to the Yorkshire rebels and promise to consider their demands. Henry insisted that his honour required that there should be a few executions, and that six men, whom he named, including Aske, along with four others to be selected later, should be excepted from the pardon. He tried to persuade Darcy and the other Yorkshire nobles and gentlemen to regain his favour by handing over 'that villain Aske', for he wondered how noblemen could follow the leadership of a common pedlar in the law. But they would not desert Aske; and after Norfolk had met the rebel leaders at Doncaster, he persuaded Henry that there was no alternative to pardoning all the northern rebels without any exception. Henry eventually granted a pardon to everyone living north of Doncaster for any act of rebellion committed before the Eve of the Nativity of the Virgin, 7 December 1536.[20]

Henry wrote to Aske that he understood that he had repented of his offences, and invited him to come to London to discuss the grievances of the Yorkshiremen. Aske accepted the invitation, after Henry had granted him a safe-conduct which was valid until 5 January.[21]

It was a very cold winter. When Henry and Jane went from Whitehall to Greenwich three days before Christmas, they could not go by barge, because the Thames was frozen. So they went overland, riding through the city of London, and received a welcome which proved that London at least was loyal.[22] The risings of 1536 showed that England was politically divided between the north and the south, as was often to be the case in future centuries; but in the sixteenth century, it was the south which was economically advanced and politically radical, and the north which was traditional and conservative. For all Chapuys's accounts, a few years earlier, of the many Papist supporters who came to his embassy to ask the Emperor to save them from heresy, and despite the many reports which Cromwell had received of seditious utterances by Papists in Northamptonshire, Worcestershire and elsewhere, only one town in the south of England stirred in support of the rebels of Lincolnshire and Yorkshire. This was Walsingham in Norfolk, whose shrine of the Virgin was, with Becket's tomb at Canterbury, the most famous place of pilgrimage in the kingdom. Apart from this, there are only two or three recorded cases of sympathy for the rebels being expressed in the south.[23] In the north, only Newcastle, Hull and a few isolated areas remained loyal to Henry, as the Pilgrimage of Grace spread from the Trent and the Mersey to the Tyne and the Solway.

Aske spent Christmas at Greenwich as Henry's guest. Henry was very friendly, and Aske was flattered, charmed and completely fooled. Henry told him that in the summer he would go to Yorkshire, a part of his realm which he had never visited. Queen Jane would come with him, and as she had not yet been crowned, he would have her crowned in the Minster at York. He would also hold a Parliament in York, which would doubtless enact legislation which would satisfy the demands of Aske and his supporters. In the meantime, he would send the Duke of Norfolk to York to reassure the people as to his intentions. Aske returned to Pontefract to tell the good news.[24]

Within a few days, a revolt broke out in the East Riding. It was led by Sir Francis Bigod, which was a little surprising, for Bigod had been an active anti-Papist, and had hitherto played no part in the Pilgrimage of Grace. He tried to capture Hull, but was repulsed by the citizens. The rising was immediately condemned by Aske, Darcy and Constable, who did all they could to prevent it from spreading, for they feared that it would result in the withdrawal of the concessions which they had obtained from Henry. They sent messengers to the villages to tell the inhabitants of the promise made personally by Henry to Aske, that the King would come to Yorkshire in the summer and hold a Parliament at York. They also played an active part in suppressing the rising. But many of the commons supported Bigod, and said that Aske and the gentlemen had betrayed them. In the neighbourhood of York, placards were fixed on the church door in nearly every village denouncing the gentlemen, who began to fear that they were threatened by a class war, a peasant revolt.[25] Bigod and his supporters, though they declared that they would 'put down the Lord Cromwell, that heretic, and all his sect', also announced that 'we serve our sovereign lord King Henry VIII, God save his noble Grace'.[26] Bigod and the rebels agreed with Aske, Constable and Darcy in one point only – their loyalty to the King who was preparing to have them all executed.

There was a rising near Cockermouth in Cumberland, and soon 6,000 men were marching on Carlisle. The Earls of Cumberland and Westmorland had insufficient forces to suppress it; but in Westmorland's absence, Lady Westmorland appeased the district around his house at Brancepeth. Sir Thomas Tempest told Norfolk that 'she rather playeth the part of a knight than of a lady'.[27]

Aske and Darcy wrote to Henry, telling him that they had suppressed Bigod's revolt, but urging him to send Norfolk to York as soon as possible to reassure the people. Norfolk came soon, but not in the spirit that Aske and Darcy expected. The general pardon covered all acts of rebellion committed before 7 December; anyone who rebelled after that date could legally be punished as a traitor. Henry ordered Norfolk to advance with his army against the rebels with the King's banner raised, which meant that he could hang rebels without trial under martial law. Loyal subjects in the north were invited to wear the King's uniform, the red cross of St George on a white coat, to show their loyalty.[28]

Norfolk asked Henry whether he wished him to hang twenty, forty, sixty or a hundred rebels, and warned Cromwell that people would talk if more than twenty were hanged at Durham and York. Henry refused to be specific. At York, Norfolk ordered that only eight should be hanged, but the people were suitably terrorized. The word spread that Norfolk had come to hang and draw from Doncaster to Berwick. The people hastened to wear the red cross of St George; even children stuck makeshift red crosses on their white smocks.[29]

Tynedale and Redesdale had been unaffected by the Pilgrimage of Grace. The inhabitants had continued to live their usual lawless lives, robbing the neighbouring districts of Northumberland and carrying on their traditional family bloodfeuds. Henry now announced that he had decided to take back into his own hands the office of Warden of the Marches, and to appoint as his Deputy Wardens Sir William Evers and Sir John Widdington, who were two of the most notorious robbers in the Marches. He then ordered them to assemble their friends and servants and join the army operating against the rebels in Cumberland and Westmorland. Norfolk warned Henry that there might be disastrous consequences if the Border robbers were let loose in the normally law-abiding districts of Cumberland and Westmorland. Henry replied that he was surprised that Norfolk thought that robbers were worse than traitors.[30]

The Earl of Cumberland's illegitimate son, Sir Thomas Clifford, raised a force of Border robbers and went to Kirkby Stephen in Westmorland to arrest two of the rebels. The Borderers proceeded to loot the village. The people of Kirkby Stephen and the neighbouring villages rose and attacked them. Norfolk wrote that Clifford's men were wholly to blame for what had occurred, and that there would have been no trouble in Kirkby Stephen but for them; but this did not prevent him from doing his duty and proving his loyalty to Henry once the revolt had broken out there. He ordered his troops to burn the people's houses and not to spare the shedding of blood; for he believed that 'this pageant well played, this realm shall be the quieter'.[31]

The 6,000 rebels in Cumberland submitted without resistance after Norfolk had told them that this was their only chance of persuading Henry to be merciful. Norfolk picked out 74 of them, and hanged them in chains in the villages where they lived, leaving their bodies to hang on the gibbets till they rotted.[32] Henry wanted more than 74 hanged; he ordered 'dreadful execution to be done upon a good number of th'inhabitants of every town, village and hamlet that have offended in this rebellion, as well by the hanging of them up in trees as by the quartering of them'. He insisted that all the monks of Sawley, Hexham, Newminster, Lanercost, and St Agatha's Abbey at Richmond in Yorkshire 'that be in any wise faulty' should be hanged 'without further delay or ceremony'.[33]

Norfolk assured him that if he had spared all those who claimed that they had been forced to join the rebels by threats to their lives, he would have hanged far fewer; and he thought that if they had been tried by jury, and not under martial law, not one in five of them would have been convicted. He could not hang them all in chains, for there was not enough iron in the district to make all the chains required; so he hanged some in chains and the others in ropes. This meant that their corpses could not be left hanging for very long before the ropes rotted away. When he reached Durham, he was doubtful if he could legally proceed there by martial law, as there had been no rising in the district; but he induced a jury to find twenty-one people guilty of high treason, and hanged them. He felt an occasional twinge of pity for the inhabitants of the region which he was terrorizing. He sometimes showed this in his letters to Cromwell, but never in his letters to the King.[34]

In Lancashire, the Earls of Sussex and Derby were also hanging rebels, but on a smaller scale. They hanged the Abbots of Sawley and Whalley and several monks there and in Furness; but they did not hang all the monks. At one of their drumhead courts-martial, they were moved when an old man, who had been sentenced to death for joining the rebels, broke down, and asked for mercy as he had three times served in the King's army in the wars against the Scots. They agreed to respite his execution until they had consulted the King. Henry wrote back that their inclination to mercy did them credit, but that if the old man had served in his army and had taken his wages, this made his treason particularly heinous, and the old man was therefore to be executed.[35]

In March, Norfolk returned to York for more trials and executions. Here he proceeded by the ordinary process of law and trial by jury. He knew that there had been strong local sympathy for the rebels, but was all the more eager to give the inhabitants the opportunity to prove their loyalty by playing their part in the punishment of their former comrades. He often selected friends and relatives of the defendants to sit on the juries, and was pleased to note how ready they were to convict, and to show that they loved their King more than their kinsmen.[36]

On one occasion, something went wrong. William Levening, a labourer from the village of Acomb near York, had taken part in Bigod's rising. He put forward the usual plea that he had acted under duress. When he was tried before Norfolk at York, the jury were out from 8 a.m. on Saturday morning till midday on Sunday. Norfolk then asked them if they had agreed on their verdict, and when they told him that they were not yet unanimous, he ordered that they should be deprived of food, drink, fire and warm covering until they had reached their decision, which was the accepted legal procedure in such cases. In the evening, they reached their unanimous verdict of Not Guilty.

Levening was set free, but Norfolk had him rearrested next day, and examined him again about his part in Bigod's rising. He questioned one of the jurors as to why they had acquitted him. The juror said that he and four of his colleagues had been in favour of convicting Levening, but that the other seven jurors thought that he should be acquitted because he was no more guilty than many others who had not been charged, and after their thirty-six hours discussion, and their lack of food, drink and warmth, he and the other four had concurred in the verdict of Not Guilty. Cromwell ordered Norfolk to send him the names of the jurors who had acquitted Levening. Norfolk promised to do so, but thought that if the jurors were arrested and sent to London, people would say that it was an attempt to make juries give verdicts which were against their consciences.[37]

The corpses hanging in chains on the gibbets became a familiar sight throughout the North of England. But in Cumberland and Westmorland, after they had hung there for about two months, many of the bodies were taken down and removed one night. When the Earl of Cumberland was informed, he ordered that inquiries should be made. He found that only 74 bodies had been removed, and that it was the work of nine women, who were the wives of some of the executed men. They had taken the bodies to the local churchyards, and asked the vicars to bury them. If the vicars refused, the women took the corpses away, and came back at night and buried them themselves. Henry was sure that the idea of taking down the bodies could not have come only of women's heads, and thought that Lord Cumberland would have found out who was behind it if he had been more zealous in detecting treason. Henry ordered that those responsible should be found and punished.[38]

Henry wrote to Darcy and Aske, thanking them for their part in suppressing Bigod's rising; but he was determined to put them to death, as they had shown that they were dangerous rebels. He could not punish them for what they had done in October 1536, because he had granted them their pardon; so it was necessary to prove that they had committed some new act of high treason since 7 December. He invited Aske, Darcy and Constable to come to London to discuss the situation with him. Soon after they arrived, they were sent to the Tower on a charge of high treason. When Aske claimed that Henry had sent him a safe-conduct when he came at Christmas, he was told that this safe-conduct had expired on 5 January, and that no new safe-conduct had been issued for this visit.[39]

Cromwell conducted their examination, and searched for evidence of acts of treason committed since the pardon. He managed to find it in the documents which he seized and in the statements of the many prisoners who were interrogated. When Bigod's revolt broke out, Aske, Darcy and Constable had called on the people not to join him, but to remain in their homes; but by urging them to stay in their homes, they were by implication telling them not to join the King's forces and not to assist in the suppression of the rising. This was treason. They had urged the people not to rise, because the King had promised Aske that he would come to York and hold a Parliament there to remedy their grievances; this implied that if the King had not made this promise, the people would have been justified in revolting; and this, too, was treason.[40]

Nearly all the noblemen and gentlemen of Yorkshire had joined the Pilgrimage of Grace in the autumn. Henry could not execute them all. He divided them, somewhat arbitrarily, into two groups – those who were to be forgiven and restored to office and favour, and those who were to be executed on framed-up charges of having committed fresh acts of rebellion after the general pardon. Archbishop Lee, Lord Scrope, Lord Latimer, Sir Robert Bowes, Sir Ralph Ellerker and Sir Marmaduke Constable continued to serve as Henry's loyal servants; Darcy, Aske, Sir Robert Constable, and Bigod were to die. So were Sir John Bulmer and his mistress, Margaret Cheyney, who was known as Lady Bulmer but was not lawfully married to him. Henry had given special orders to arrest the Earl of Northumberland's brother, Sir Thomas Percy, though Northumberland, who was dying of sickness, was allowed to spend his last days in freedom in his house in London.[41]

The Lincolnshire rebels had not been granted a pardon, for they had gone home on a vague promise of mercy. It was now safe to proceed with executions in Lincolnshire. Forty-six of the rebels were executed, and eleven of the Walsingham rebels were hanged, drawn and quartered in Norfolk. Lord Hussey was sent to London to be tried with Lord Darcy before the Court of the Lord High Steward. The Marquess of Exeter was selected to preside at the trial; he himself was not to be beheaded for another eighteen months. The peers unanimously found Hussey and Darcy guilty.

Aske, Constable, Bigod, Sir Thomas Percy, Sir John and Lady Bulmer and their son Ralph, the Abbots of Jervaulx and Fountains and the Prior of Bridlington – three of the most important monasteries in Yorkshire – and five other rebels were tried at Westminster by special commissioners and a jury. Audley presided at the trial, with Cromwell and other members of the King's Council sitting on the court. This time, no chances were taken with the jury; the twelve jurors included Henry's secretary, Hennege, the Deputy Constable of the Tower, Knivet, and Sir Edmund Bedingfield, who had been Catherine of Aragon's jailer at Kimbolton. Sir John and Lady Bulmer pleaded guilty, perhaps as part of a bargain by which the case against their son was dropped, though he was kept in prison in the Tower. There was one other plea of guilty, and the others were found guilty by the jury.[42]

They had all been executed by the middle of July. Darcy and Hussey were beheaded on Tower Hill. Sir Thomas Percy was hanged and beheaded at Tyburn; Bigod, Bulmer, the Abbots and the Prior were hanged, drawn and quartered there. Aske was hanged in chains at York, and Constable at Hull, where his body was so well encased in the chains that Norfolk thought it would hang there for a hundred years. Lady Bulmer was burned at Smithfield. The herald, Charles Wriothesley, who saw her dragged on a hurdle through London to the place of execution, wrote that 'she was a very fair creature, and a beautiful'.[43]

Robert Johns, a monk of Thame Priory, pitied her. 'It is pity she should suffer', he said at breakfast in the chantry on Whit Sunday, five days before her execution. 'It is no pity if she be a traitor to her Prince', said Strebilhill, another monk. 'Let us speak no more of this matter', said Johns, 'for men may be blamed for speaking of the truth'. Strebilhill duly reported the conversation to the authorities.[44]

The King was very merry in the summer of 1537, for his Queen was pregnant with a child which Henry had fathered at Greenwich, while Aske was spending Christmas with him. Lord Lisle, the Governor of Calais, sent Jane two dozen quails, which she liked, and which Henry also enjoyed. They ate a dozen for dinner and the other dozen for supper. Henry thanked Lisle for the quails, but said that he would like twenty or thirty dozen, that they should have been fatter, and would have been better if they had been fresher. So on 24 May, the day before Lady Bulmer was burned, instructions were duly sent to Calais. The quails must be brought alive as far as Dover, and killed there, for then they would be just right for the King's table at Hampton Court.[45]

While the executions were taking place, Henry wrote to Norfolk on 12 June to tell him that he had changed his mind and would not be coming to York this summer. As the Queen was pregnant, she might be distressed if he went so far away from her; the Emperor was sending an important personage to Henry to discuss the possibility of peace negotiations with François; and as long as the war in Europe continued, Henry must be on the spot to take the necessary steps to protect his neutrality. It would be much better to postpone his visit to Yorkshire to another year, for he had never been to the North of England, and if there were more time to make preparations, he would be able to go not only to York but also to Hull, Carlisle, Newcastle, Durham and Berwick.[46] He did not refer to his promise to hold a Parliament at York at which the demands of the Pilgrimage of Grace should be satisfied. No Parliament was ever held at York, and the only step which was taken to satisfy the rebels' complaints was the Statute of Wills, which Parliament passed in 1540 to allow testators to dispose of part of their property by will.

The chief result of the Pilgrimage of Grace was to create the myth of Thomas Cromwell as the arch-villain and mastermind behind the Henrician Reformation. More than two years before Pole wrote his *Apology* to Charles V, the rebels of Lincolnshire and Yorkshire had chosen Cromwell for this role. Cromwell had become the most influential of Henry's counsellors by the end of 1532, if not earlier. Chapuys had soon recognised his abilities as an administrator and diplomat; and in November 1533 he wrote that Cromwell 'rules everything'.[47] But he probably only meant that Cromwell managed everything and dominated his colleagues on the Council; he did not really think that he was the power behind the throne. Neither Chapuys nor anyone else spoke of Cromwell in the same breath with Henry, as they had spoken about 'the King and the Cardinal' in Wolsey's time.

When Cromwell was appointed to be the King's Vicegerent, and this low-born layman was given precedence over the Archbishops and power over the Church, the people became aware of his importance and grumbled about him; but he was not yet seen as the chief cause of the mischief. It was not Cromwell, but Anne Boleyn – 'the Lady', 'the Concubine', 'that woman', '*la Ana*' – who was held responsible for all the evils which the people were too frightened or too loyal to blame on the King himself.

After Anne was beheaded, and Henry did not return to his obedience to the Pope as most people expected, another scapegoat had to be found. It was natural that the rebels in Lincolnshire and the North, whose chief complaint was the suppression of the monasteries and who thought that the nobility should rule the realm under the King, picked on the man with 'villein blood' who had sent the visitors to the monasteries and by whose orders the houses were suppressed. Pole, who was more ready than most of his contemporaries to blame Henry personally, followed the rebels' lead, especially when he was writing to the Emperor and wished to excuse himself for opposing his King and benefactor. He remembered, and probably exaggerated, what Cromwell had said to him on the only two occasions when they had met, more than ten years earlier and before Cromwell had even entered Henry's service.[48]

Twenty years after Cromwell's death, John Foxe took up the same theme from the opposite point of view. He saw Cromwell as the great instrument of God who had persuaded Henry to make England Protestant.[49] He knew that Cromwell had been in power when the monasteries and the shrines were suppressed and when the English Bible was first permitted; he had heard from Cranmer's secretary, Ralph Morice, and other sources, how Cromwell had tried to protect the Protestants during the difficult times which followed the enactment of the Six Articles; and he knew that when Cromwell was overthrown, he was officially denounced as a heretic, and that his death was followed by the years of Catholic reaction. Foxe ignored the active part which Cromwell had played on several occasions in burning sacramentaries – that is to say, those Protestants who in the 1530s held the same view about the Eucharist which Foxe, Elizabeth I and the Church of England held when Foxe wrote his eulogy of Cromwell in his *Book of Martyrs*. He did not realise that though Cromwell sympathised with the Protestants, he promoted them, and suppressed them, whenever Henry told him to do so, and remained at all times an obedient, loyal and efficient royal servant, and nothing more.

22

THE DUCHESS OF MILAN AND MARY OF GUISE

THE Papists in Europe had welcomed the news of the risings in Lincolnshire and Yorkshire; but it was not until May 1537, when the corpses of the defeated rebels were already hanging in chains on the gibbets in the North of England, that Paul III sent Cardinal Pole as Papal Legate to François I and Mary of Hungary to urge them to help in restoring England to its obedience to the Apostolic See. On 10 April, Pole entered Paris in great state with his Legate's cross borne before him, and asked for an audience with François, who was at Amiens; but Henry ordered Gardiner to demand that Pole be arrested and extradited to England as a traitor under the terms of the extradition treaties. François protested that it was out of the question for him to arrest and extradite a Papal Legate who had come on a diplomatic mission from the Pope. Henry replied that there was no clause in the extradition treaty which stated that it should not apply to Papal Legates.

François was anxious to please Henry, for he did not wish him to enter the war on Charles's side. He agreed not to receive Pole and to order him to leave France at once. Pole was given a pass through the battle lines, and went to Cambrai in the Netherlands. He was shocked at the extent of Henry's power, and that the Most Christian King of France was prepared to expel a Papal Legate from his realm in order to please Henry; but Henry was far from satisfied. He insisted that his treaties with François stipulated that traitors should be extradited, not expelled, and blamed Gardiner for his failure to obtain Pole's extradition.[1]

Pole had intended to visit Mary of Hungary in Brussels; but Hutten, Henry's ambassador at her court, had already asked her to extradite him. She was as eager as François not to offend Henry, as she did not wish to provoke him into entering the war on François' side; and when Pole reached Cambrai, he was informed, with the greatest courtesy, that he could not proceed to Brussels, but must go to Liège and stay there as a guest of the Bishop. Liège was governed by the Bishop as a semi-autonomous territory, and though it was really part of the Netherlands, the Bishop's nominal authority there would give Mary of Hungary an excuse for not extraditing Pole.[2]

Hutten was approached by an English criminal, Vaughan, who had been convicted of manslaughter in England. Vaughan offered, in return for a pardon and money, to infiltrate himself into Pole's household, and to persuade Pole to come with him on a secret visit to Papist supporters in England. They would land at a remote cove in Cornwall, and Vaughan would tip off the authorities in advance so that they could arrest Pole when he landed. Vaughan went to Liège and spoke to Pole, who greeted him as a fellow-exile from England; but his correspondence with Hutten was intercepted, and he fled from Liège only just in time to avoid arrest by the Bishop's officers. Hutten, who had paid Vaughan 40 shillings in advance, did nothing more; for Cromwell had told the English agents abroad that Henry did not think it worth while to spend a great deal of money in order to catch Pole, though he would reimburse the agent for any expenses which he had incurred if the attempt to seize Pole was successful.[3]

Pole stayed at Liège for two months, but was unable to make any contact with England or to achieve anything. In July the Pope recalled him to Italy to take part in the General Council of the Church which was to be held at Mantua in the autumn; and Pole obeyed, with great reluctance. As François refused to allow him to travel through France, he had to return through Germany, where travellers ran great risks from highway robbers, apart from the danger that he might fall into the hands of the German Lutherans, or be murdered by Henry's agents; but the Pope asked King Ferdinand of Bohemia to ensure his safety on the journey.[4]

Only James V was prepared to defy Henry. He made a treaty with François by which he was to marry François' daughter Madeleine. Henry was angry that James had not consulted him about his marriage, and had renewed the old alliance with France; but James sailed to France and married Madeleine at a splendid ceremony in Notre Dame in Paris on New Year's Day 1537. As Madeleine's health was poor, and the winter seas were stormy, James asked for a safe-conduct for them to travel overland through England on the journey to Scotland. After consulting Norfolk, Henry refused. He did not relish the idea of James travelling through the North of England so soon after the suppression of the Pilgrimage of Grace, as some of the rebels had hoped for help from Scotland.

In view of Henry's attitude, James was worried about making the journey by sea, and waited for some weeks at Rouen before embarking. One of Henry's agents gleefully reported that James was too frightened of Henry to dare to sail to Scotland; and James complained that Henry's refusal of the safe-conduct had delayed his return to Scotland for forty days. Eventually he sailed with his bride from Rouen in May, escorted by four Scottish and ten

French warships. As they passed Whitby and Berwick, in full view of the people on land, the rumour spread through the North that James had put into a little village near Scarborough to take in fresh water, and that some of the villagers had implored him, on their knees, to save them from Henry. Norfolk investigated the story, and found that it was untrue, though one man had rowed out to James's ships to speak to him. A few weeks earlier, four Scottish Protestants had arrived at Appleby in Westmorland and had asked for asylum from persecution in Scotland.[5]

Henry's officials on the Borders expected that James would avenge Henry's refusal of the safe-conduct by declaring war and invading England.[6] But James struck only at Henry's Scottish supporters. He ordered that Angus's sister, Janet, Lady Glamis, should be prosecuted for the murder of her first husband. She was found guilty, and burned on Castle Hill in Edinburgh. Other relatives of Angus were executed on other charges during the summer of 1537.

Henry was merry. His rebels were defeated, his brother-kings dared not affront him, and his Queen was pregnant. At the end of May, prayers were held in the churches, and bonfires lit in the streets, in London, York, Oxford and throughout the realm, to give thanks 'that our most excellent lady and mistress, Queen Jane, our noble and godly Prince's King Henry VIII's wife, hath conceived and is great with child, and upon Trinity Sunday, like one given by God, the child quickened in the mother's womb'. The people were ordered to pray that it might be a Prince. By the middle of July, the Queen was unlaced.[7]

There was an outbreak of plague in London that summer, and Henry took great care to preserve Jane from infection. He took her to Guildford in July. Cromwell asked if he could come to court, as one of his servants had been ill. Henry said that this was no reason for him not to come; but then, seeing that Jane looked alarmed, he changed his mind, and told Cromwell to stay away. In September, as Jane's time approached, he established her at Hampton Court with a small number of servants, while he himself went to Esher, to lessen the chances of him and his servants infecting her.[8]

He had trouble with his own health. Ever since 1528 he had occasionally been affected by a painful ulcer in his leg. His fall from his horse in January 1536 seems to have made the leg worse; and by the spring of 1537 it had developed into a chronic ulcer. For some days in April he could not go out. He soon recovered, but had a more severe attack in May 1538, when for some days his life seemed to be in danger; and he was ill with a fever, which probably had nothing to do with his leg, when he was at Ampthill in September 1539. His disease has often been diagnosed as syphillis, which was very prevalent in Western Europe in the early sixteenth century, and as it was particularly rife at the French court, Henry might well have caught it from Mary Boleyn; but this, of course, does not mean that he did, and though his trouble with his leg has some of the symptoms of syphillis, the weight of evidence is against this theory. Sir Arthur MacNalty in 1952 believed that it was not syphillis, but was probably a thrombosed vein with detachment of the clot causing pulmonary embolism.*[9]

Several years were to elapse before Henry could no longer walk or ride; but though he still went hunting, he hunted less energetically. He could no longer chase stags for thirty miles. He would wait for the huntsmen to round up the deer and drive them past him; and he more often went hawking than hunting. Since his fall, he did not joust in tournaments. Although he took much less exercise than when he was young, he ate and drank as much as ever, and as he approached the age of fifty, he began rapidly to put on weight.

The defeat of the Northern rebels had left the low-born Cromwell and the heretic bishops more safely ensconced in power than ever. In July 1537 the bishops agreed on a new formulary of faith to replace the Ten Articles of 1536. It was published in a book which was officially named *The Institution of a Christian Man*, but was popularly known as 'the Bishops' Book'. The book was compiled, like the Ten Articles, after the bishops had held almost daily discussions for several months, often under the chairmanship of Cromwell. Henry did not attend the discussions, but he took an active part in producing the book. He studied the proposed drafts, suggested amendments, argued about the precise theological significance of one word as compared to another, and carried on a controversy in writing with Latimer about Purgatory; but as the doctrine put forward in the book showed a movement towards Lutheranism, it was to be the 'Bishops' Book', for Henry wanted the bishops, and not himself, to bear the responsibility for it. The book declared that Marriage, Orders, Confirmation and Extreme Unction were sacraments, but lesser in degree than the three sacraments of Baptism, the Lord's Supper and Penance. This would have been regarded as a Lutheran heresy in the days when Henry wrote his *Assertion of the Seven Sacraments*.

The book repeatedly proclaimed the royal supremacy over the Church and the duty of all good subjects to obey the King. The commentary on the Ten Commandments explained that 'Thou shalt not bear false witness against thy neighbour' meant that no one should spread heretical doctrines. In obeying the commandment 'Honour thy father and thy mother' all loyal subjects must remember that their true father was the King, whom they must love more than their natural father; and above all the commandment meant that they must be prepared to denounce to the authorities anyone whom they suspected of being a traitor.

In the preface to the book, the bishops declared that they 'rejoice and give thanks unto Almighty God with all our hearts that it hath pleased Him to send such a King to reign over us', and asked Henry's permission to publish

*Sir Arthur MacNalty follows Froude in rejecting the story of Henry's affair with Mary Boleyn; but the evidence for it seems to me to be overwhelming.

the book, 'without the which power and licence of Your Majesty, we knowledge and confess that we have none authority either to assemble ourselves together for any pretence or purpose, or to publish anything that might be by us agreed on and compiled'. They assured him that 'if Your Grace shall find any word or sentence in it meet to be changed, qualified, or further expounded, for the plain setting forth of Your Highness's most virtuous desire and purpose . . . we shall in that case conform ourselves, as to our most bounden duties to God and to Your Highness appertaineth'.[10]

Almost as soon as the Bishops' Book was published, a new edition was being prepared. Henry drafted some amendments to the Bishops' Book, and asked Cranmer to comment on them. Henry always expected his bishops and counsellors to show absolute obedience in public, but to give him honest and frank advice in private. Cranmer criticised Henry's draft very freely, objecting to 82 of Henry's 250 suggested amendments to the Bishops' Book; Cranmer sometimes objected to Henry's doctrine, sometimes to his way of expressing it, and occasionally to his grammar. Where the Bishops' Book stated that the tenth commandment meant that no one should take another man's wife, house or lands, Henry suggested that the words 'without due recompense' should be added; but Cranmer thought that 'this addition agreeth not well with the coveting of another man's wife'. The Bishops' Book stated that 'Thou shalt not kill' meant that no one should kill except Princes and those acting under their orders, and that Princes should only kill in accordance with their laws. Henry wished to change this and to state that only 'inferior rulers', not Princes, were required to obey their laws; but Cranmer thought that this change would be undesirable.[11] This was one of several occasions on which Henry put forward the doctrine – which was never officially accepted in words by the judges in his courts – that the King was above the law of the realm, and subject only to the law of God.[12]

In the autumn of 1536, Cromwell and Cranmer persuaded Henry to authorise the publication of an English translation of the Bible, and to order that a copy should be available in every church by Michaelmas 1537.[13] Officially, this did not involve any change from the position which had been adopted in 1530, when Thomas More and the Catholic bishops had formulated the doctrine that whether or not the Bible should be translated into English, and read by Henry's subjects, was entirely a matter for him, and that, though anyone who read Tyndale's New Testament was to be punished, Henry might decide at some time in the future to authorise a translation made by bishops and learned men. But to allow the publication and reading of an English Bible was a great step towards Protestantism, and a repudiation of orthodox Catholicism; and it was a step which Henry never really liked, and agreed to take rather reluctantly and against his better judgment.

After various tentative attempts had been made to produce a satisfactory translation, the English Bible was published and placed in the churches throughout Henry's realm in August 1537. It was known as 'Matthew's Bible', but was in fact nothing less than Tyndale's New Testament without the marginal notes, and the Old Testament which Tyndale had translated, though not published, as far as the Books of Chronicles. The text of the Old Testament, from Chronicles onwards, was the work of Tyndale's colleague, the Protestant John Rogers. Another notorious Protestant heretic, Miles Coverdale, who had himself made another translation of the Bible, worked closely with Cromwell in the publication of 'Matthew's Bible'.

Did Henry know that his Vicegerent, acting in his name, had placed in the churches the same book which he had so strongly denounced and which he had punished people for reading a few years earlier? It has often been assumed that Cromwell and Cranmer deceived Henry about this; but it is unlikely that they would have ventured to do so, and still more unlikely that Henry, with his interest in theological questions, would not have been familiar with the text of Tyndale's New Testament, and would not have recognised it when he studied Matthew's Bible, even if no one told him. He would never have agreed to compromise himself with his Catholic subjects by publishing the translation with Tyndale's name on the title page; but he would not have objected to Tyndale's book being published as Matthew's Bible, as long as he was not officially informed about the connection with Tyndale and could deny that he knew about it.

On 12 October, Queen Jane gave birth to a son. She was delivered by caesarean operation, but the child was healthy, and survived. At last Henry had a son and heir, and proof that God looked on him with favour, and approved of all his policies. Twelve days after the birth, Queen Jane died, apparently of septicaemia. Her body lay in state for more than a fortnight in her chamber at Hampton Court, while the bishops, in relays, said Mass; and Richard Gresham, the Lord Mayor of London, ordered that twelve hundred masses should be sung in the city for her soul. On 12 November, the corpse was borne in procession from Hampton Court to Windsor, with the King's daughter, the Lady Mary, riding behind the body as chief mourner, and all the counsellors, bishops, nobles and courtiers in attendance.[14] Henry himself did not attend the funeral, in accordance with the usual practice.

It was generally believed in the country that Henry was deeply distressed at Jane's death; but there is no evidence for this. The idea that he loved Jane Seymour more than any of his other wives, and was inconsolable when she died, seems to be based merely on the fact that he neither divorced nor beheaded her. Immediately after her death, and a fortnight before her funeral, Henry's counsellors were urging him to remarry. When Cromwell informed the English ambassadors abroad that the Queen had died, he wrote that the King, though he was taking this misfortune reasonably, was little disposed to marry again, but that some of his counsellors had advised him that he ought to do so for the sake of his realm, and that he had 'framed his mind both to be indifferent to the thing and to the election of any person from any part that with deliberation shall be thought meet for him'. On 3 November, Norfolk spoke to Henry. He urged him to accept God's pleasure in taking the Queen, to comfort himself with the treasure that she had left for him and the realm – the infant Prince – and to marry again. On the same day, Sir John Wallop wrote that Henry was 'merry as a widower may be'.[15]

Henry himself, as well as his daughter Mary, was now in the marriage market, and he was immediately sought by both Charles and François. Charles offered him his niece Christina, who was the daughter of his sister and the imprisoned King Christian II of Denmark, and was the widow of Francesco Sforza, Duke of Milan. She had been married and widowed early, for she was still only sixteen, and was living at the court of her aunt, Mary of Hungary, in the Netherlands. Hutten wrote to Cromwell that she was reasonably beautiful, very tall, soft of speech and gentle of countenance, and was said to be a maid as well as a widow. She normally spoke French, with a charming lisp, but she could also speak Italian and German; and she enjoyed hunting, played cards, and could talk on serious topics with great wisdom. She was certainly a possible bride for Henry, though there would of course have to be a great deal of bargaining about the dowry and other terms in the marriage treaty. Henry wished to negotiate it as part of a treaty by which he would marry the Duchess of Milan, his daughter Mary would marry Dom Luiz of Portugal, and his daughter Elizabeth would marry a son of the Duke of Savoy or of King Ferdinand of Bohemia. Charles did not want the three marriages to be negotiated as part of one package deal; and Mary of Hungary was anxious to ensure that if Henry married Christina, he could not claim the throne of Denmark through his wife.[16]

There was the alternative of a French marriage, and this raised a possibility which was very tempting to Henry. James V's bride, Madeleine, had died soon after she reached Scotland, which in view of her health was no great surprise; and François thereupon offered him another high-born French lady, Mary of Lorraine, the Duke of Guise's daughter, who became known to history as Mary of Guise and the mother of Mary, Queen of Scots. She was another young widow, though older than the Duchess of Milan. At the age of nineteen she had married the Duke of Longueville, and bore him two sons before he died, three years after the marriage. She had hardly become a widow before François arranged for her to marry the King of Scots.

Henry conceived the idea of inducing François to break the engagement between James and Mary and to offer Mary to him. He had heard the usual tributes to her beauty and other virtues, but his only object in picking her must have been to humiliate James, to show the world that he could make François do anything he wanted, and to damage relations between François and James.

In November 1537, François sent a new ambassador to England, Louis de Perreau, Sieur de Castillon. He was a few years older than Henry, and an exceptionally able diplomat. He soon learned how to handle Henry by adopting Henry's own tactics of disarming frankness, jovial good humour, and calculated deception. He established a friendly personal relationship with Henry, while advising François that Henry could not be trusted and should be treated as a dangerous enemy. Castillon arrived in England at a time when François' hand was strengthened in the diplomatic negotiations with Henry, for on 16 November Charles and François agreed on a three months' truce and opened secret peace negotiations. This was bad news for Henry, and he and his ministers did not hide their annoyance from Castillon.[17]

During his first talk with Castillon, Henry raised the question of a marriage with Madame de Longueville. Castillon said that she was going to marry the King of Scots; but Henry would not accept this, and insisted on returning to the subject. Castillon wrote to François that Henry 'is so much in love with Madame de Longueville that he cannot prevent himself from returning to it'. Henry told Castillon that he was a much more valuable ally for François than 'this beggarly and idiotic King of Scotland'. He said that he had been informed that François had arranged for Madame de Longueville to marry James V without consulting her, and that she herself and her family would much prefer it if she married *him*. Castillon denied this; but Henry sent Sir Peter Mewtas, a gentleman of his chamber, to visit Madame de Longueville at Châteaudun and to persuade her that a marriage to the King of England would be an even better match than a marriage to the King of Scots.[18]

But François was firm. He refused to break his promise to James, and at the end of January 1538 he persuaded Guise and Mary to sign a formal precontract with James. The marriage took place in May. Henry was annoyed, but said to Castillon: 'Well, if that is so, I am receiving offers from many quarters'. This was certainly true, for Charles had sent one of his leading nobles, Don Diego Hurtado de Mendoza, to Henry to reinforce Chapuys's arguments in favour of a marriage with the Duchess of Milan. Henry entertained Don Diego and Chapuys at a magnificent banquet at Hampton Court, which Castillon duly noted. Chapuys believed that Henry had only done it in order to make the French jealous.[19]

François offered Henry any French lady that he wanted except Madame de Longueville. Castillon assured him that there were other beautiful ladies in France, and that the Duke of Guise had another daughter, Madame de Longueville's younger sister Louise, who was even more beautiful than she. Louise had the additional advantage over Madame de Longueville that she was a virgin. 'Take her', said Castillon to Henry, 'she is a virgin, so you will have this advantage of being able to make the hole to fit your measure'.

Henry laughed, slapped Castillon on the shoulder, and went to Mass.[20]

Henry sent his court painter, Hans Holbein the younger, to paint the portraits of Mademoiselle de Guise and of the Duchess of Milan; but he told Castillon that he wished to see his bride before he agreed to marry her. He thought that this was only reasonable, as marriage should be a permanent union based on love and affection between the spouses. He proposed that he and François should meet again, in a pavilion erected on the frontier between France and the Marches of Calais. François could bring a number of beautiful ladies to the meeting, and Henry would be able to choose the one whom he wished to marry. Both Castillon and François were shocked at this suggestion. They thought that Henry should rely on François to choose a bride for him who would be beautiful and virtuous. It would be an insult to the ladies to parade them before Henry so that he could see which of them he fancied most; and it would be an intolerable humiliation for the ladies whom he did not choose.[21]

Henry said that this would not apply if they came to Calais under the guise of attending his meeting with François; but Castillon would not agree, and asked Henry: 'Wouldn't you like to go further, Sire, and ride them all, one after the other, and afterwards keep the one who was the nicest?' Castillon reported that Henry blushed and laughed at this.[22]

The searches continued for prayer books in the churches in which the word 'Pope' had not been erased, and reports still came in to Cromwell and to the local JPs of things said in inns which might be construed as seditious. One source of danger was unfounded rumours, which greatly alarmed the authorities, for they thought that it was the spread of rumours about the King's intentions to suppress churches and levy new taxes which had caused the risings in Lincolnshire and Yorkshire. The authorities dealt with a false rumour by asking everyone who repeated it to say where he had heard it, until they found someone who could not or would not reveal the source of this information; they then treated this person as the malicious inventor of the rumour, and punished him.

In December 1537, the rumour that the King had died was circulating in Kent and Sussex, and in Northamptonshire, Berkshire and Oxfordshire. Cranmer traced the rumour in his diocese to a housewife in Canterbury, who had heard it from a fishmonger who called at her house to sell fish. The fishmonger was questioned, and said that he had been told it by a man dressed like a merchant whom he had met on Barham Down as he came to Canterbury from Dover. The rumour had been spread by some friars in Lewes, by a husbandman at Kingsthorpe near Northampton, a wheelwright at Lutterworth, a goldsmith at Oxford, a traveller at Dorchester in Oxfordshire, a woman at Higham near Tonbridge, and by the vicar of Bradfield, an almsman of Donnington near Newbury, and several other persons in Berkshire.[23]

The authorities decided that a fuller of Wallingford should be punished as one of the worst rumourmongers, because he had been unable to say where he had heard the story. He was made to stand in the pillory at Wallingford for an hour on a Friday, which was market day, with his ear nailed to the pillory. Then his ear was cut off, and he was stripped to the waist, tied to a cart, and whipped through the town. Next day he was taken to Reading, where Saturday was market day, and placed for an hour in the pillory, nailed to it by his other ear, which was then cut off, and he was whipped again at the cartarse through Reading. Several other men and women were put in the pillory without losing their ears, and one woman was pardoned because she was pregnant.[24]

Henry was personally informed about the inquiries, and was consulted about the punishments. He gave orders that the cook Wilkinson at Newbury and the almsman at Donnington were to be severely punished. But when his secretary, Wriothesley, wrote to the officers in Berkshire, he stated that Hynd and the almsman were to suffer the worst punishment with loss of ears. Cromwell's agent, Vachell, thought that there had been some mistake, and that Sergeant Chalcott at Colley had been ordered to punish the wrong man.[25]

Within a few weeks, another rumour was circulating. A smith from a village near Lewes, who was employed part-time as a tax collector, called with his colleague on Master Apsley, a gentleman at Pulborough, to collect the fifteenth. They found Apsley ferreting in his woods, but as they walked back to the house with him to fetch the money, Apsley said that this was the last tax which he would have to pay this year. No, said the tax collector, he would soon have to pay 'horn tax' – a tax which the King had imposed on every head of cattle. Apsley wrote to the Earl of Southampton at Guildford for confirmation of the story. Southampton knew that it was untrue, and just the kind of rumour which had started the rising in Lincolnshire. He questioned the tax collector, and made further inquiries in the Lewes area. He found a man who had repeated the story, but could not remember where he had first heard it, so Southampton told him that he would be tortured to compel him to reveal the truth. Southampton eventually decided that this man was innocent, and that it was the tax collector who was responsible. He informed Cromwell that he would be suitably punished.[26]

People sometimes spoke disrespectfully now, not only about Cromwell and the heretic bishops, but about the King himself. A man at Walden in Essex said he wished that the King would fall from his horse and break his neck. Another man, in the Forest of Dean, said that no previous King had taken half as much from his subjects in taxes, for Henry just wanted 'money, money'. A balladsinger invented an imaginary story about 'a King' who one day met a woman when he was out riding, and promptly seduced her. When he protested that he had not intended to refer to Henry, he was told that he had no business to make up stories like this about Kings.[27]

Every year in August or September, Henry hunted at Ampthill, and in February 1536 the gamekeepers thought it necessary to replenish the stock of deer there from the 2,067 red deer and the 6,352 fallow deer in the other royal forests.[28] Arrangements were made to bring the deer from Beskwood Park in Nottinghamshire to Ampthill. The villagers of Lowdham near Nottingham were required to help with the transport of the deer, and all of them, except one husbandman named Sanderson, turned out at the summons of the two village constables. The constables knew that Sanderson had a good pair of wheels on his cart which would be useful for fixing to a cart to carry the deer, and they went to his house to fetch the wheels. Sanderson became very angry with the constables, but they told him that they were only carrying out the orders of the King's Council. 'A vengeance on the King and on such false Council', said Sanderson, 'and also on such polling [thieving] harlots as you are that taketh my goods so!' But they took his wheels.

The constables forgot all about the case, until two years later, one day in March 1538, when they were drinking in the inn at Lowdham, they were told that someone was suing them at Leicester Assizes for taking the wheels of his cart. They supposed that it must be Sanderson, that man who had said, two years ago, 'A vengeance on the King'. Master Gabriel Barwick and other gentlemen were drinking in the inn and overheard what the constables said. Now Sanderson and the constables were all in trouble, Sanderson for having spoken the treasonable words, and the constables for not having reported him to the authorities. Sir Nicholas Strelley, the Sheriff of Nottinghamshire and Derbyshire, apparently accepted the constables' explanation that they had not realised how heinous Sanderson's words were; but Sanderson was prosecuted for high treason at Nottingham Assizes.[29]

This was not the only case in which a man was denounced for something that he had said a long time before, perhaps because, when neighbours had a quarrel, they remembered rash sayings in the past. It was not until January 1538 that the authorities discovered that a man in the village of Over in Cambridgeshire had said in July 1536: 'Was not my Lord Cardinal a great man, and ruled all the realm, as he would? What became of him? Is he not gone? Also Sir Thomas More, High Chancellor of England, did not he in like wise rule all the whole realm? What became of him? Is he not gone? And now my Lord Privy Seal [Cromwell] in like manner ruleth all and we shall see once the day that he shall have as great a fall as any of them had'. The village constable warned him that he could be hanged for saying this. A gunner in the navy got into trouble at Portsmouth in September 1539 for an unwise remark which he had made when he was in port at Corunna in Spain three years earlier. He had said that if the King's blood and his blood were side by side in a saucer, no one would be able to tell which was which.[30]

Not everyone who grumbled, and spoke against the King and his counsellors, was reported to the authorities; not everyone who was reported was arrested; and not everyone who was arrested was executed or held in prison for very long.[31] But anyone who spoke unwisely was taking a risk, and this was generally known; and the parson of Colmere in Hampshire, who said: 'I trust to see the day that all this shall be turned ups and down. A man may say what he will in his own house', was soon taught that this second statement was far from the truth. Men who were denounced were sometimes imprisoned for months, and occasionally for years, without trial, in prisons where they complained of 'corrupt and stinking smells', of cold and hunger. One of Henry's officials reported to Cromwell in June 1537 that the monks of the Charterhouse of London, after two years in prison at Newgate, had been 'almost dispatched by the hand of God'; and he added that, in view of their opposition to the King, he was not sorry.[32]

Sometimes people were accused merely out of personal spite. In July 1538 Lancaster Herald, who, according to the Earl of Shrewsbury, had been chiefly responsible for appeasing the rising in Lincolnshire, was arrested and charged with high treason. It was said that when he was sent to Aske and the rebel leaders at Pontefract on 20 October 1536, he knelt before Aske in order to encourage him in his treason, and promised Aske that the King would grant his demands to hand over Cromwell to the rebels. He was also said to have exaggerated the rebels's strength in his reports to Norfolk and the Council, in the hope of inducing the King and his counsellors to grant Aske's demands. He denied the charges, and said that they had been brought against him by his colleague, Clarencieux Herald, because he and Clarencieux had had a quarrel at Hampton Court after Queen Jane's funeral, during which Clarencieux fell downstairs. But he was convicted of high treason, and hanged, drawn and quartered at York. All the other heralds went to York to be present at his execution. His head was stuck up on the gibbet high above York Castle where Aske's bones had been hanging for the last twelve months.[33]

In July 1538, Henry faced a new and unexpected source of trouble. Twenty-two men who were employed by the shoemakers at Wisbech in Cambridgeshire formed a trade union. They were dissatisfied with their wages of fifteen pence for every dozen pairs of shoes that they made, and took an oath not to work for less than eighteen pence per dozen pairs of shoes. After consulting Cromwell, Norfolk arrested and punished them.[34]

23

THE SHRINES

THE Pilgrimage of Grace had shown the extent of the opposition to the suppression of the religious houses, and had made Henry proceed a little cautiously towards achieving his target of seizing the rents, the gold and silver, and the lead from the roofs, of the wealthier monasteries. He repeatedly stated that he had no intention of suppressing all monasteries, but wished only to ensure that they were properly run, by closing down those in which vice prevailed. To prove his sincerity, he actually founded a new monastery and two new nunneries. On 9 July 1537 he delivered the foundation charter of a nunnery at Stixwold in Lincolnshire, and granted it lands which brought in an income of £152 a year; it was to be a model of a properly run and virtuous house. Rumourmongers who said that he was planning to seize the larger monasteries were arrested; but he let it be known that if the Prior and brothers of any monastery felt that they were unable to carry on running a well-ordered house, and wished voluntarily to surrender the monastery to the King, he would be prepared to accept the surrender.[1]

In a little over three and a half years, between the summer of 1537 and the end of 1540, every one of the remaining three hundred monasteries and nunneries in England, Wales and Ireland were suppressed, and nearly all of them were induced to surrender voluntarily. This was achieved by bribing the abbot or prior, with the promise of a large annual pension, to persuade and bully his monks into agreeing to close down the house and give its assets to Henry. The monks, too, were granted pensions, but of much lower value than their head's. The pensions to be granted were negotiated separately in the case of every monastery, but the general pattern, which was usually followed, was a pension of £100 a year for the Prior, £12 a year for the Sub-Prior, £8 for the cellarer and two or three of the leading monks, £6.13s.4d. (10 marks) or £5 for the other monks, and 40s. for the gardener and for some, if not all, of the servants of the monasteries. A few of the leading abbots and priors were created bishops as an additional reward; for Henry created six new bishoprics – Westminster, Peterborough, Oxford, Gloucester, Bristol and Chester. The abbots and priors, if not their monks, thought that they had made a wise bargain, in view of the rumours that Henry was intending to seize all monasteries, in which case no compensation might be offered; and several abbots had recently been hanged, drawn and quartered.

The abbots, priors and monks received their pensions for the rest of their lives. One young monk, who was barely twenty when his monastery was dissolved, continued to receive his pension for seventy years. He was paid for the last time by the Treasury of King James I in 1608.[2]

Henry's chief agent in procuring the voluntary surrender of the houses was Richard Thornden, Cranmer's suffragan Bishop of Dover, who was disrespectfully called 'Dick of Dover' by those who watched his activities with disapproval or cynicism. He travelled all over England and Wales, visiting one house after another, and pointing out to the Prior the advantages which they would gain by surrendering their monastery to the King. In the autumn of 1538, monasteries were surrendering at the rate of more than one a day. Only a handful of them were obstinate. The Abbot of Reading refused point blank to surrender the abbey. This did not weigh in his favour when he was charged with high treason.

The model nunnery of Stixwold, which Henry had founded in July 1537, lasted just over two years before it surrendered at Michaelmas 1539. The Prioress, having served for so short a time, did much less well than most abbesses and prioresses, and received a pension of only £15 a year.[3]

While the larger monasteries were surrendering, the authorities launched a vigorous campaign against the shrines, with their images and sacred relics. Here again, Henry disclaimed any intention of adopting the Protestant position that all images were idolatrous; he wished to suppress only those images which had been abused by being made the object of superstitious worship. By closing down the shrines and seizing the valuable ornaments which had been given to them by pious worshippers, the 'heretic bishops' and their Protestant supporters could strike a blow against pilgrimages, prayers to the saints, and superstitious reverence to relics, and Henry could acquire the confiscated gold, silver and jewels for himself.

The campaign against the shrines was helped by the discovery that some of the most famous relics were frauds. For many years, both local residents and visitors from afar had gazed reverently at the Rood of Grace, the great cross in Boxley Abbey near Maidstone; for after penitents had given money to the monks, in order to gain absolution by 'good works', the figure of Christ on the cross would roll its eyes, move its lips, and nod its head to show that the penitent was forgiven. When Cromwell's agents visited Boxley, they found that the nodding Christ on the crucifix was operated by hidden levers which were secretly manipulated by the monks. The holy blood at Hailes Abbey in Gloucestershire, which liquified when paying penitents worshipped it and gave money to the abbey, was the blood of a duck, replenished regularly by the monks.

The hidden pulleys on the Rood of Grace, and the way in which they worked, were shown by Henry's officers to an angry crowd of local residents at Boxley. The rood was then taken to Maidstone, and similarly exhibited to the people on market day. It was then shown to Henry and his courtiers at Whitehall, and finally to a large crowd of Londoners at Paul's Cross before being publicly burned there.[4] Some of the most sacred relics in the kingdom were seized, brought to London, and burned, including the dagger which had stabbed Henry VI from Caversham in Berkshire, St Cecilia's toe from Coventry Cathedral, and the ear of the centurion which St Peter had struck off when defending Christ in the garden at Gethsemane, which had for long been exhibited at Marlow. Henry ordered that the bones of St Richard should be removed from Chichester Cathedral and burned, because they had been superstitiously worshipped. The shrine of Our Lady of Walsingham was closed, and the image of the Virgin was taken to London and burned.[5]

The suppression of the relics aroused opposition in many places. The vicar of Ticehurst in Sussex was rash enough to say, in a sermon in his church, that anyone who spat at the King's picture on a coin would be punished for his disrespect to the King, yet now people in authority were offering insults to the images of the saints, which was like spitting at God. Other people were overheard making the same comparison at Chesterfield and elsewhere. The vicar of Highley in Shropshire illegally regilded the statue of the Virgin in his church, because the people believed that a blind woman had once recovered her sight by touching it. As late as January 1540, nearly two years after the image of the Virgin had been removed from Walsingham and burned in London, an old woman in the nearby village of Wells-next-the-Sea said that the image was still working miracles in London, as it had formerly done at Walsingham. She was put in the stocks at Walsingham on market day, with a paper on her head on which was written 'A reporter of false tales', and was taken round the town in a cart, while the youths were encouraged by the authorities to throw snowballs at her.[6]

In North Wales, the removal from St Asaph of the image of a local saint, Davelgarthen, caused consternation. The people believed that the wooden image could ride into Hell and release the souls of the damned; on 5 April 1538, one of Cromwell's officials saw six hundred people come in one day to the image, bringing sheep, oxen, horses, and money to the shrine, and he was told that the same thing happened every day. The parson and the parishioners offered him £40 if he would allow Davelgarthen to remain; but he carted it off to London to be destroyed.[7]

There was an ancient saying in Wales, that one day Davelgarthen would burn a forest. Catherine of Aragon's confessor, Friar Forest, had publicly opposed Henry's divorce from Catherine in 1532, and had been imprisoned in very harsh conditions after the break with Rome. The old man reluctantly agreed to take the oath of supremacy; but in April 1538 it was decided to proceed against him as a heretic. The idea seems to have originated with Cromwell, who consulted Cranmer and Latimer, and afterwards discussed the case in detail with the King.

Forest was the only orthodox Catholic and Papist supporter who was accused of heresy by the Protestants in England during the sixteenth century; all the others, under Henry VIII and Elizabeth I, were treated as traitors. He was tried before Cranmer and other commissioners for heresy for having stated that the Holy Catholic Church referred to in the Creed was the Church of Rome; that Fisher and 'other holy fathers' had recently died, like St Thomas of Canterbury, for the rights of the Church and that their souls were now in Heaven; and that he believed that he owed a double obedience, both to the King and to the Pope.

As he refused to recant, he was burned at Smithfield on 22 May. Latimer preached the customary sermon before the burning; Forest told him that he would not have dared to preach such a sermon seven years ago. Instead of fastening Forest to the stake in the usual way, he was hung in chains under his armpits on a gibbet above the fire, apparently so that he should be hanged as a traitor as well as being burned as a heretic. When the faggots were lit, he tried to climb up the gibbet in order to escape the flames, thus proving to the hostile onlookers that he was not inspired by God to suffer martyrdom for a just cause. It occurred to someone with a grim sense of humour to use the wooden image of Davelgarthen as part of the fuel at Forest's burning, in mockery of the saying that Davelgarthen would one day burn a forest. Somebody had even written a suitable poem for the occasion, which was fixed to the scaffold:

> David Davelgarthen,
> As sayeth the Welshmen,
> Fetched outlaws out of Hell.
> Now he is come, with spear and shield,
> In harness to burn in Smithfield,
> For in Wales he may not dwell.
> And Forest the friar,
> That obstinate liar,
> That wilfully shall be dead,
> In his contumacy
> The Gospel doth deny,
> And the King to be Supreme Head.[8]

The shrine of St Thomas of Canterbury in Canterbury Cathedral was left almost to the last, but was the greatest prize of all. In September 1538 the shrine was closed, Becket's bones were removed, and all the jewels and ornaments which had been given to the shrine by pilgrims from all over England and Europe in the past three hundred years were taken to London and appropriated by Henry. The Papist writers stated that it needed twenty-six carts, piled high with the treasures, to take them all to London. This was an exaggeration, for in fact twenty carts were used.[9]

The closure of Becket's shrine outraged the Papists abroad as much as anything that Henry had done. They invented a story, which is almost certainly untrue, that Becket was solemnly prosecuted in the Court of King's Bench for high treason against his King, Henry II, and that as he did not appear when summoned, he was tried in his absence, found guilty, and sentenced. They also alleged that the saint's bones had been burned, which they regarded as a dreadful act of sacrilege. Henry's propagandists denied that the bones had been burned; they said that they had been removed from the cathedral, and buried.[10]

Henry's prominent courtiers were often able to enrich themselves by obtaining grants of monastic lands and the confiscated valuables of the Church. The Duke of Suffolk obtained the lands of thirteen monasteries.[11] In the seventeenth century, many stories were told of how the ancestors of prosperous gentlemen had acquired the monastic lands. Fuller in 1655 wrote of how Master John Chapernoun of Devon obtained the lands of the priory of St German's in Cornwall by kneeling down with other courtiers when the King passed by, and receiving, to his surprise, a grant for which he had not asked, because of a misunderstanding by some officials. Fuller also described how Sir Miles Partridge won the Jesus bells in one of the steeples of St Paul's Cathedral at dice one night from Henry.[12] Most of these stories are probably untrue, but they were the stories which the men and women of the 1530s handed down to their children and grandchildren.

But one of the disadvantages of being a courtier was that Henry might take a fancy to his property and suggest an 'exchange' by which the courtier would grant the property to the King in exchange for other lands granted by Henry. The bishops were particularly liable to be asked to make exchanges; for Henry could not only enrich himself, but could also weaken the power and prestige of his bishops by compelling them to agree to unequal exchanges to the disadvantage of the see. The exchanges were supposed to be voluntary transactions. Henry would propose an exchange to a bishop, which the bishop was free to accept or refuse; but if he refused, or even hesitated before accepting, he was at once made aware that he had incurred the King's displeasure. When Roland Lee was invited to agree to an exchange by which he would surrender the house of the Bishop of Coventry and Lichfield in the Strand in London, he pointed out that if he had no residence in London or Westminster he would be at a grave disadvantage when he had to attend Parliament or come to court; but after receiving a message from Cromwell, he expressed his willingness to serve the King in all things, and to agree to the exchange.[13]

Cranmer was pressurized into agreeing to exchanges with Henry which were very disadvantageous to the see of Canterbury. In the course of a number of exchanges with Henry between 1536 and 1542, he granted many of his lands to the King, including seven of the Archbishop's eleven palaces.[14] When Cranmer's secretary, Ralph Morice, wrote to the Archbishop of Canterbury, Matthew Parker, in about 1565, he was anxious to defend Cranmer from the charge of having given away the property of the see to the disadvantage of future archbishops. Morice wrote that he prayed that Parker and the bishops 'may maintain, in this mild and quiet time, that which he in a most dangerous world did uphold and left to his successors. . . . For as touching his exchanges, men ought to consider with whom he had to do, specially with such a Prince as would not be bridled, nor be against-said in any of his requests'.[15]

Morice told Parker about a conversation between Henry and Cranmer at which he himself was present. Henry asked Cranmer to agree to an exchange by which he granted to him the Archbishop's palace at Knole in Sevenoaks. Cranmer, who was particularly fond of Knole, suggested to Henry that Knole was too small to house all the royal retinue, and that Henry might prefer to take his larger palace at Otford a few miles away, on which Cranmer's predecessor, Archbishop Warham, had spent £30,000 in improvements. Henry said that he preferred Knole, because Knole was on higher ground than Otford, and was therefore healthier – the idea that houses on high ground were healthier was generally accepted in the sixteenth century – and that his health had suffered whenever he had stayed at Otford; but in view of what Cranmer had said, he would take both Knole and Otford, so that his servants could stay in the large unhealthy house at Otford, while he himself stayed at Knole. Cranmer was therefore compelled to surrender both Otford and Knole to Henry in November 1537.[16]

Mary of Guise married James V and sailed to Scotland. She was escorted on her journey by a number of noble French ladies, headed by Madame de Montreuil. James asked Henry if he would grant a safe-conduct to the French ladies to travel through England on their return journey to France. In view of Henry's resentment at James's marriage to Mary, they were not optimistic that the safe-conduct would be granted; but Henry not only agreed to grant it, but said that he would like to meet the ladies. He was on a progress in Sussex, and was at Petworth when they reached London; but as he was intending to go to Dover, he gave orders that they were to be entertained in London before meeting him in Dover. Henry's courtiers and the Lord Mayor invited them to banquets, and showed them Whitehall and Hampton Court; and Henry, going by Lewes, Eridge, Bedgebury and Birling, reached Dover two days earlier than he had planned, so as not to miss the French ladies. He entertained them at a great banquet in Dover Castle, and gave diamonds to Madame de Montreuil and her daughter, and paternosters to the other ladies.[17]

Don Diego Hurtado de Mendoza had been in England for six months, but no definite agreement had been reached about Henry's marriage to the Duchess of Milan. Cromwell favoured a marriage with her and an alliance with the Emperor; but Norfolk preferred a French marriage and alliance. Castillon found Cromwell so hostile that he mentioned it to Henry, and said that in view of Cromwell's attitude he wondered whether there was any point in continuing negotiations. Henry told him not to pay too much attention to what Cromwell said, for although Cromwell was an excellent administrator, he was not competent to handle the business of Kings. Henry added that he could say exactly the same about three or four other members of his Council. Castillon had established a very good relationship with Henry, who on another occasion confided in him that Bryan was usually drunk.[18]

Don Diego had his last talk with Henry at Arundel on 17 August; but he delayed his departure from England, and was at Dover, ready to embark, in the first week of September, when Henry was there with the French ladies. Diego asked Henry for a final audience to say goodbye, but Henry sent him a message that he was too busy to see him. Diego noticed that he was not too busy to spend the day with the French ladies; but Diego had the consolation that Henry had given him a parting gift of £400 at Arundel.[19]

The international situation had taken an unsatisfactory turn for Henry. When Charles and François first made a truce in November 1537, Henry was confident that it would not last long; but when it became clear that they both wished to make peace, Henry offered to mediate. To Henry's great annoyance, Charles and François refused his offer and asked the Pope to mediate. In June 1538 they met the Pope at Nice, where they made a truce for ten years which left most of their differences unresolved. This was followed by a meeting between François and Charles at Aiguesmortes in July, at which the two sovereigns made an ostentatious display of friendship.[20] Henry believed, or pretended to believe, that they would soon be again at loggerheads about Milan. When Castillon told him that François and Charles were now close friends, he made the cryptic comment: 'This will not last long. I once spent three weeks with the Emperor'.[21]

Neither François nor Charles were as keen to make a marriage alliance with Henry as they had been a year before. Charles and Mary of Hungary would not commit themselves on the marriage with the Duchess of Milan. In December 1538, Henry pressed Mary of Hungary for a definite answer, pointing out that at his age he could not afford to wait too long before marrying again; but she would not commit herself. Charles stated that as the Duchess of Milan was related to Catherine of Aragon, she would have to obtain a dispensation from the Pope before she could marry Henry. This was something which it would be very difficult for Henry to accept. By the winter, Charles had opened negotiations for the marriage of the Duchess of Milan to the young Duke of Cleves, and Henry was negotiating for his marriage to one of the Duke of Cleves's sisters.[22]

The Duke of Cleves himself was not a Lutheran, but his quarrels with Charles V about his right to the duchy of Gelders on the borders of the Netherlands had made him a close ally of the German Lutheran Princes. If Henry married one of his sisters, this would mean an alliance not only with Cleves but with the German Lutherans, which would counter to some extent the possible danger of Charles and François uniting against him. But though Henry was ready to make an alliance with the German Lutherans, he had no intention of moving any further towards Lutheranism in England. On the contrary, the greater the danger from foreign Papists, the more he was determined to win the support of the orthodox Catholics who were still the great majority of his subjects, by convincing them that, apart from repudiating the supremacy of the foreign Pope, he was as good a Catholic as ever, and as ardent a persecutor of heretics, especially sacramentaries, as any other sovereign.

In the summer of 1538, Cranmer renewed his efforts to reach a closer understanding with the German Lutherans. In May, a delegation of German Lutheran theologians arrived in London, and discussed with Cranmer and the English bishops the possibility of issuing a joint formulary of faith. Despite the opposition of some of the more orthodox English bishops, they were able to agree on draft articles, which ignored their differences about transubstantiation by merely stating that they believed in the Real Presence, and adopted a compromise position about justification by faith. There remained the disagreements about the 'three abuses' – private masses, the administration of the bread but not the wine to the congregation at communion, and the prohibition of the marriage of priests. Henry, who followed the theological discussions between his bishops and the Germans with close attention, informed them that he himself would deal with these three points, and that the German delegates, instead of raising them in their discussions with the bishops, should write to him about them. He chose Tunstal to help him in the arguments, which was not a good sign for the Lutherans and their English sympathisers.

On 5 August, the Germans sent Henry a full statement of their objections to the three abuses. Henry, who was on his progress in Sussex, found time to work on his reply to the Germans as well as to hunt, and before the end of August had sent them a twenty-two page document in Latin, giving his reasons for maintaining the three abuses, with the relevant Biblical and patristic texts. He was obviously not prepared to compromise about this, and as the Germans refused to agree to any articles of faith which ignored their differences about the abuses, they left for home at the end of August without any agreement having been reached.[23]

The struggle between the Protestant reformers and the orthodox Catholics came to a head in Calais. The Deputy of Calais was the sixty-year-old Arthur Plantagenet, the illegitimate son of Edward IV, whom Henry VIII had created Viscount Lisle. He and his formidable wife Honor were orthodox Catholics, and they and their chaplains and supporters in Calais were zealous in punishing heretics. But the Marches of Calais were in Cranmer's diocese of Canterbury. Cranmer appointed John Butler as his commissary in Calais. Butler was sympathetic to the reformers. He was reluctant to persecute heretics, but eager to denounce Papist sympathisers in Calais who questioned the royal supremacy. Lisle protested to Cranmer against Butler's toleration of sacramentaries; Cromwell urged Lisle to be more zealous against Papist supporters.

Cromwell and Lisle wrote courteous letters to each other, but Lisle suspected that Cromwell was intriguing against him at court. He was therefore very eager to come to England to see the King and gain his favour: Cromwell wrote that Henry wished him to remain at his post in Calais; but when Henry went to Dover in the summer of 1536, Lisle was granted permission to come over from Calais to meet him there.[24]

Lady Lisle had three daughters by her previous marriage to Sir John Basset, a gentleman of Devon. By the autumn of 1537, two of them, Anne and Katherine Basset, were old enough to go to court where they were entrusted to the care of Sir Peter and Lady Mewtas. Henry noticed Anne Basset; when Mewtas assured him that her youngest sister, Mary, was even more beautiful than she, Henry said that he was sure that Anne was the fairest.[25]

Lisle had an agent in London, John Husee, whom he employed to lobby at court and obtain his slice of monastic lands and the property of attainted traitors. Lisle was offering bribes to Cromwell in the hopes of obtaining an annuity of £400; but Cromwell told him that the King would only grant him a pension of £200 a year. When Henry was in Dover in September 1538, inspecting the defences and entertaining Madame de Montreuil and the French ladies, Lisle and Lady Lisle were again given leave to come over from Calais. Henry was charming, and they returned to Calais much comforted.[26]

In November 1538, Lady Lisle went to London to see if she could do better than Husee and obtain the full annuity of £400. Henry was very friendly. One evening she received an unexpected invitation to come to a party at Hampton Court. Henry sent his barge for her, and treated her as the guest of honour. She wrote to her husband in Calais that it was the best banquet she had ever attended. After the banquet, she stayed the night in a splendid room in the palace which Henry put at her disposal. But when she came to talking business with Cromwell, he insisted that Henry would not grant Lisle more than £200 a year.[27]

When Lisle and Lady Lisle wished to obtain some favour at court, and Lisle's letters and Husee's efforts were unsuccessful, they asked Anne Basset to approach Henry. He was very kind to her. He gave her a horse as a gift, and when she fell ill, he ordered Lady Mewtas to take her to Mewtas's country house at Guildford, because it had a larger garden than Mewtas's London house.[28]

The looting of Becket's shrine in September 1538 was the high-water mark of the Henrician Reformation. Immediately afterwards, Henry changed course, and what appeared at the time to be merely another demonstration against the extremists soon became a clear swing towards orthodoxy which was not reversed until the last months of his reign. By espousing the cause of the Reformation, Henry had obtained a divorce from Catherine of Aragon, complete power over the Church, more absolute authority over his subjects than any of his predecessors or contemporary monarchs, the property of the monasteries and the spoils of the shrines. He had nothing more to gain from being a Protestant, but he could win the goodwill of many of his subjects by being an orthodox Catholic.

On 1 October, Cromwell as Viceregent ordered Cranmer and the bishops to search for Anabaptists, to deliver those who refused to recant to the secular arm for punishment, and to burn all books which expounded the doctrines of that detestable sect. We do not know which of the various Anabaptist sects Henry and Cromwell had in mind, but it was probably the followers of Peter Tasch, the Hessian disciple of Melchior Hofmann; because in the summer of 1538, Tasch wrote that his sect was quietly making converts in England despite the persecution which they faced. Cranmer and his fellow-commissioners did not trouble about the Anabaptists' wilder doctrines; they were condemned as heretics for denying the Real Presence in the Eucharist, for this was the heresy which Henry was most eager to be seen to be suppressing. On 29 November a Dutchman and a Dutch woman, both of them 'Anabaptists', were burned at Smithfield for being sacramentaries; and next day this woman's husband, a Dutchman whom Charles Wriothesley described as 'a goodly young man and about twenty-two years of age', was burned for the same heresy at Colchester.[29]

John Nicolson, who had adopted the name of Lambert, was an English sacramentary. He had been in trouble on several occasions in the last ten years as a suspected heretic. In the autumn of 1538 he told the Protestant reformer, John Taylor, that he did not believe in the Real Presence. Taylor persuaded Lambert to put his views about the Real Presence into writing, and sent the document to Barnes, who, with his usual Lutheran zeal against sacramentaries, sent it to Cranmer. Lambert was summoned to appear before Cranmer on a charge of heresy. Apparently Lambert said that he wished to appeal to Henry; and this gave Henry the idea of staging a show-trial in which the King, as Supreme Head of the Church of England, would in person sit in judgement on a notorious sacramentary and condemn him as a heretic.[30]

The trial took place at Whitehall on 16 November. Henry, dressed all in white, entered the hall escorted by his men-at-arms, and took his seat on a throne. Cranmer and the bishops and lawyers were on his right, and Cromwell and the temporal peers on his left. Lambert was at a great disadvantage. He was forced to stand throughout the whole proceedings, which lasted without a break from noon to 5 p.m., whereas everyone else was seated. He had been ordered to submit a written statement to Henry, giving his reasons for rejecting the doctrine of the Real Presence, and he had set out ten reasons. A different spokesman – a bishop or learned divine – was chosen to argue against each of his ten reasons, whereas he had to argue, alone, against them all without a pause during the five hours. According to John Foxe, who described the trial in some detail in his *Book of Martyrs* twenty-five years later, Lambert was also overawed by Henry's 'look, his cruel countenance, and his brows bent unto severity'. The proceedings were conducted in Latin.

If Foxe's account is at all accurate – and he probably consulted a contemporary report of the proceedings – Henry treated Lambert in a bullying manner, rising to his feet and leaning on a cushion of white cloth as he addressed the prisoner. He made caustic comments on the fact that Lambert had assumed this pseudonym when his real name was Nicolson – 'I would not thrust you, having two names, although you were my brother' – and disregarded Lambert's explanation that he had been forced to take a false name because he was persecuted by the bishops. When Lambert thanked the King for condescending to hear the case himself, and praised his learning and piety, Henry interrupted him, saying that he had not come there to hear himself praised, and asked Lambert to say whether he did, or did not, believe that the consecrated bread and wine was the body of Christ – and Henry removed his cap as he spoke these words. 'I answer, with St Augustine', replied Lambert, 'that it is the body of Christ after a certain manner'. 'Answer me neither out of St Augustine', said Henry, 'nor by the authority of any other, but tell me plainly whether thou sayest it is the body of Christ, or no'. Lambert then said that it was not. 'Mark well', said Henry, 'for now thou shalt be condemned even by Christ's own words, This is my body'. Henry could argue theological issues much better than this; but his object now was to impress the people, not with the subtlety of his arguments, but with his hatred of heretics.

He then ordered Cranmer to argue against Lambert's second point. Gardiner, who had returned from France, argued against the third point, and Tunstal, Stokesley and the other bishops took their turn. By the time that the winter daylight was fading, and the servants brought torches to light the hall, Lambert was exhausted, and browbeaten into silence. He gave the

Christina of Denmark, Duchess of Milan,
by Hans Holbein the younger, 1538

Henry reading in his bedroom. Miniature painting by Jean Maillard, in the King's Psalter, c.1540

pitiable exhibition which the authorities had hoped for. At the end of the hearing, Henry said that he would not be a patron of heretics, so Lambert must die; and he called on Cromwell to pronounce the sentence excommunicating Lambert as a heretic and delivering him for punishment to the secular arm. Foxe in 1563 commented sadly on the fact that the four men who played the leading part in bringing Lambert to his trial and condemnation – John Taylor, Barnes, Cranmer and Cromwell – all suffered death in their turn as heretics in later years.[31]

Lambert was burned at Smithfield on 22 November. For some reason, he was made to suffer unusual refinements of cruelty. He was hoisted on a pike out of the reach of the flames, and then put back into the fire, and hauled out again, in order to prolong his sufferings.[32]

John Foxe did not approve of criticising Kings, and did not wish to cast any reflection on Queen Elizabeth's father; but he could not refrain from doing so in connection with Lambert's trial and death, even though he tried to place the blame on Gardiner. 'How much more commendable for thee, O King Henry (if that I may a little talk with thee, wheresoever thou art) if thou hadst aided and holpen that poor little sheep, being in so great perils and dangers, requiring thy aid and help against so many vultures and leopards. . . . For what hath that poor man Lambert offended against you, who never so much as once willed you evil, neither could resist against you. . . . But, O King Henry, I know you did not follow your own nature therein, but the pernicious counsels of the Bishop of Winchester'. But Foxe had gone too far, and the passage was deleted from his second edition in 1570.[33]

Most of Henry's subjects in 1538 thought differently. Cromwell wrote to Wyatt at the Emperor's court in Toledo that Henry had sat in judgement on 'a miserable heretic sacramentary', and that 'it was a wonder to see how princely, with how excellent gravity and inestimable majesty, His Highness exercised there the very office of a Supreme Head of his Church of England, how benignly His Grace assayed to convert the miserable man, how strong and manifest reasons His Highness alleged against him'. If foreign sovereigns had been present, they would have agreed that Henry was 'the mirror and light of all other Kings and Princes in Christendom'.[34]

Husee wrote to Lord Lisle on the evening of the trial that Henry had confounded Lambert and 'that His Grace alone had been sufficient to confound them and they had been a thousand of like opinion. It was not a little rejoicing unto all His Grace's commons and also to all others that saw and heard how His Grace handled and used this matter, for it shall be a precedent while the world standeth, for I think there will be none so bold hereafter to attempt any such like cause'.[35]

Sir Thomas Elyot, who had once been Henry's ambassador to Charles V, had been spending the last two years compiling a Latin-English dictionary, as well as trying to explain away his former friendship for Sir Thomas More. He published the dictionary and dedicated it to Henry a few weeks after Lambert's trial, and wrote in the preface about 'a divine influence or spark of divinity which late appeared to all them that beheld Your Grace sitting in the throne of your royal estate as Supreme Head of the Church of England next under Christ, about the decision and condemnation of the pernicious errors of the most detestable heretic John Nicolson called Lambert'. Elyot praised Henry's 'wonderful patience in the long suffering of the foolish and tedious objections of the said Lambert; as also of your most Christian charity in moving and exhorting so stubborn an heretic, with the most gentle and persuasible language, to recant'. The people present had wept for joy at seeing it.[36]

On the day of Lambert's trial, Henry issued a proclamation, which shocked the Lutherans and drew a protest from Melanchthon. Henry had worked on the text himself, making corrections to the original draft in his own hand. No one was to import or sell any book in English, or to print any copy of the Bible, without a licence from the Privy Council or from someone appointed by the King. Every subject was ordered to denounce to the authorities any Anabaptist or sacramentary whom he encounterd. No one except doctors and scholars of divinity was to argue about the Eucharist. A number of practices which the Lutherans and Protestants condemned, including holy water, creeping to the cross on Good Friday, and candles at Candlemas, were to continue in use until the King ordered otherwise. Married priests were to be deprived of their benefices, and any who married in future were to be imprisoned during the King's pleasure. The proclamation also contained a strong denunciation of Becket, as a rebel against his Prince who had fled abroad to France and to the Bishop of Rome, and was killed in an attempt by his supporters to rescue him from those who were advising him to leave his stubbornness. His picture was to be pulled down throughout the realm; his two saints' days were abolished; and references to him were to be erased from all books.[37]

The Papists did not escape. In August 1538 the authorities arrested a Breton priest who had once been Cardinal Pole's chaplain. They then arrested Pole's brother, Sir Geoffrey Pole, who was persuaded to talk, and to reveal things that he had heard in private conversations with his brother Lord Montagu. By October, the secret Papist sympathisers at court, who had been giving inside information to Chapuys for more than five years, had all been arrested – Lord Montagu, his mother the Countess of Salisbury, the Marquess and Lady Marquess of Exeter, Sir Edward Nevill, Lord Delawarr, and several of their priests and servants. Exeter was very close to Henry. He was the only courtier who was allowed to enter Henry's chamber without being summoned, for he was 'the King's near kinsman and had been brought up of a child with His Grace in his chamber.'[38] Lord Delawarr, Lady

Salisbury and Lady Exeter were imprisoned in the Tower without trial. The others were tried for high treason, ten days after Lambert was burned, charged with having been in contact with 'one Reginald Pole of London, Esquire', who had adhered to the King's enemy, the Bishop of Rome.

Their treason was proved by the confession and evidence of Sir Geoffrey Pole. Sir Geoffrey had said to Lord Montagu: 'Brother, I like well the proceedings of my brother Reginald Pole, Cardinal at Rome'. The Marquess of Exeter had said in London on 26 July 1536: 'I like well the proceedings of the Cardinal Pole', and on 20 September 1537 he had said: 'Knaves rule about the King'. Lord Montagu had said in London on 24 March 1537: 'I like well the doings of my brother the Cardinal, and I would we were both over the sea'; and he had said that he had dreamed that the King was dead. Four days later, he had said about the King: 'He will die one day suddenly. His leg will kill him, and then we shall have jolly stirring'. On 1 April 1537, Montagu had said that he had disliked the King when they were children, and that 'Cardinal Wolsey had been an honest man if he had had an honest master'. Sir Edward Neville had said at Cowdrey in Sussex on 4 August 1538: 'The King is a beast, and worse than a beast', and 'I trust knaves shall be put down and lords reign one day, and that the world will amend one day'. On this evidence, they were found guilty, and sentenced to be hanged, drawn and quartered.[39]

Sir Geoffrey Pole, who tried to commit suicide in the Tower out of remorse at having betrayed his brother and friends, was pardoned and released. Lord Delawarr was pardoned and released after he had granted his house at Halnaker near Chichester to the King. Lady Exeter was freed after a year in prison. Lady Salisbury remained in the Tower. Exeter, Montagu and Sir Edward Neville were beheaded on Tower Hill. The other three suffered the full sentence at Tyburn.[40]

Sir Nicholas Carey, the Master of the Horse, was one of the commissioners who interrogated Exeter and Montagu in the Tower. On 29 November, three days before their trial, Carey said to a friend in his house at Beddington in Surrey that he thought that the Marquess was not guilty. His words were reported, and two months later he was sent to the Tower on a charge of high treason, having been an accomplice of Exeter and Montagu in their treasonable designs. Carey was closely questioned about his correspondence, five years before, with the late Princess Dowager and the King's daughter, the Lady Mary; but he did not implicate Mary. He was found guilty, and beheaded on Tower Hill.[41]

Mary was being very cautious and obedient. Chapuys had hoped that if she submitted to Henry and returned to court, she would be able to use her influence in favour of an alliance with the Emperor; but she made no attempt to do so, and broke off her secret connections with Chapuys.[42] In 1539, Henry thought of marrying her to Duke Philip of Bavaria; but though she was very distressed at the prospect of marrying a Protestant, she was prepared to do so. Wriothesley wrote to Cromwell that Mary had told him that although, 'the King's Majesty not offended, she would wish a desire never to enter that kind of religion, but to continue still a maid during her life, yet remembering how, by the laws of God and nature, she was bound to be in this and all other things obedient to the King's Highness . . . wholly and entirely, without qualification, she committed herself to the King's Majesty as to her most benign and merciful father and most gracious sovereign lord'.[43]

24

THE DESTRUCTION OF CROMWELL

On 17 December 1538, the Pope issued a bull. It declared that although he had excommunicated and deposed Henry by a bull of 30 August 1535, he had suspended its operation in the hope that Henry would repent; but now he was publishing it, because Henry, far from repenting, had committed a new atrocity. He had dug up and burned the bones of St Thomas of Canterbury and scattered the ashes to the winds, after putting the saint on trial in his absence and proclaiming him to be a traitor. He had looted St Thomas's shrine and put deer into St Augustine's Abbey in Canterbury. The Pope was therefore calling on all the Kings of Christendom to enforce the sentence of deposition against Henry. In view of the difficulties of publishing this bull in England, it was to be published as near to England as possible – at Dieppe and Boulogne in France, at St Andrews and Coldstream in Scotland, and at Tuam and Ardfert in Ireland.[1]

The Pope sent Pole on a mission to the Emperor in Spain. His instructions were to urge Charles to make a truce with the Turk and send his armies against Henry, who was worse than the Turk; at least Charles should place an embargo on all trade with England. Pole, who had heard of the execution of his brother and the arrest of his mother, was appalled that the 'Pharaoh of England',[2] after oppressing first the priests, then the people, and then the nobility, had now affronted saints who had reigned with the Heavenly Majesty in Heaven for three hundred years. He left Rome on 2 January, crossed the Apennines in the snow, travelled incognito through the South of France in case Henry's agents tried to assassinate him, and reached Toledo in the middle of February.[3]

Henry ordered Wyatt, his ambassador at Toledo, to ask Charles to extradite Pole as a traitor and rebel. Charles replied that he would not lay hands on a Papal Legate even if he were his own rebel, and that as Pole came to him on a diplomatic mission from the Pope, he would grant an audience. But this was the only comfort that Pole received from the Emperor. Charles told him that he much regretted that the Pope had published the bull against

Henry without consulting him, and to Pole's dismay refused to take action against Henry, even now when he was at peace with François. He said that he could not betray the Venetians by making peace with the Turk, and that if he went to war with Henry, the German Lutherans would rise in Henry's support, and there would be civil war in Germany. He refused to ban trade between the Netherlands and England, and said that he would try to suppress the Lutherans in Germany before tackling Henry. He advised Pole to go to François and urge him to act against Henry.[4]

Pole travelled to Carpentras, avoiding what was probably an attempt by Wyatt to have him assassinated at Gerona on his journey; but he was so discouraged by Charles's attitude that he did not go on to François' court at Nogent-sur-Seine, but sent his deputy, the Abbot of Turin, instead. This saved François from the embarrassment of having to refuse Henry's request for Pole's extradition. François told the Abbot of Turin that he would help in any action against England if Charles also took part in it.[5]

Henry, hearing that the Pope was intending to invade the territory of the Duke of Urbino, sent an envoy to encourage the Duke to resist the Bishop of Rome and his 'false prophets and sheepclothed wolves', the 'enemies of God and ours' and 'the adversary general of Princes';[6] but he could not expect any help from the Duke of Urbino if Charles and François tried to enforce the Pope's bull of deposition. This now seemed to be a real possibility; and to defeat it, Henry could rely only on the loyalty and patriotism of his people. He took energetic steps to defend his kingdom. He ordered that his ships in the Thames should be put in a state of readiness; but there was a shortage of sail-cloth. He asked François for a licence to import sail-cloth from France. Castillon, who found Henry more tractable since the publication of the Pope's bull than he had ever known him, believed that now was the opportunity for François to get rid of a dangerous enemy by joining with Charles to enforce the interdict against England. While continuing his jolly conversations with Henry, he strongly urged François to refuse a licence for the export of the sail-cloth. Meanwhile Henry, hearing that a friar in Paris had denounced him in a sermon for having desecrated the tomb of St Thomas of Canterbury, asked François to punish the friar. François believed in the solidarity of Kings; he severely censured the friar, and forced him to retract his sermon. But he refused the licence for the sail-cloth.[7]

Henry bought a consignment of gunpowder in Germany, and arranged to have it shipped from Antwerp. Charles prohibited all ships from leaving Antwerp, saying that he needed the sailors for an expedition against the Turk. Henry retaliated by arresting ships at Lowestoft which had been loaded at Newcastle with corn for the Netherlands. Both Charles and François withdrew their ambassadors from Henry's court. François sent a young diplomat, Charles de Marillac, who had just returned from a mission to Constantinople, to replace Castillon as ambassador in England; but

Charles did not send a new ambassador to replace Chapuys.[8]

In Spain, France and the Netherlands people were expecting the Pope, the Emperor and the King of France to unite against Henry and invade his heretic realm. English merchants in Spain were alarmed to hear the Spaniards in Galicia and at Seville say that the English were heretics and Lutherans whom they hated worse than the Turks, and that when they conquered England they would treat the English like Jews and infidels. Lisle complained that across the frontier in France, the English were thought to be heretics, and he considered that the sacramentaries of Calais were responsible for this. At a church in Picardy, the priest had refused to begin the service because there was an Englishman among the congregation; so the people had thrown the English heretic out by the ears. The ecclesiastical authorities at Marquise had refused to bury an English child, but had sent the corpse to Calais without ceremony as if it had been a dead calf. Wyatt wished that at Toledo the people would sometimes talk about Henry's firm measures against the sacramentaries and the Anabaptists, and not only about Becket's bones.[9]

Henry ordered musters to be held in every part of the kingdom. All men over seventeen were to be called up for service in the army, except sea-faring men, who were reserved for the navy, and the citizens of London, who were enrolled in a guard for the defence of the capital. Henry divided the realm into eleven defence zones*, and appointed the leading noblemen to take command in each area. The defences at Calais, Guisnes, Berwick, Carlisle and Tilbury were strenghtened, and new fortresses were built at Sandown, Deal and Walmer 'in the Downs', at Sandgate near Folkestone, at Camber in Sussex, at Hurst and Calshot near Southampton, at Portland, and in the Isle of Wight. Bulwarks were erected in the Thames.[10]

Propaganda works were published to arouse the people's loyalty. Richard Morison wrote *An Invective against the great and detestable vice of treason, wherein the secret practices and traitorous workings of them that suffered of late are disclosed*. Another publication, *A Summary declaration of the Faith, uses and observations in England*, emphasized that Henry was a pious and orthodox Catholic; he had merely abolished those practices which allowed Jews, Turks and Saracens to accuse the English of idolatry. Thomas Becket was a traitor; and should Henry have suffered these traitors to live, 'Thomas More the jester, Fisher of Rochester the glorious hypocrite . . . the Carthusians and friars obstinate, and other wool-clothed wolves,' the Holy Nun of Kent, whose feet were kissed by the Papal Nuncios, the heads of the insurrection in Yorkshire who had relapsed after being pardoned, the

*1. The Thames and the Essex coast; 2. Suffolk; 3. Norfolk; 4. Kent; 5. Sussex; 6. Hampshire; 7. Somerset, Dorset, Devon and Cornwall; 8. Lincolnshire; 9. Yorkshire, Westmorland, Northumberland, Cumberland, Durham, Derbyshire, Lancashire and Cheshire; 10. South Wales; 11. North Wales.

Marquess of Exeter, Lord Montague and their accomplices, who plotted to destroy the King and his issue and seize the crown – 'were they not worthy to die?'[11]

At the beginning of April 1539, Henry's spies reported that 8,000 German mercenaries were stationed in Friesland, that ten warships with 5,000 soldiers on board were waiting in the Texel, and that the Scots would attack Berwick on 15 May. What was the intended destination of the mercenaries and the warships? Henry wrote to the noblemen and gentlemen of his realm, informing them that 'the pestilent idol, enemy of all truth and usurpator of Princes, the Bishop of Rome' was planning to rob and spoil the realm and corrupt its good religion. So they were each to furnish forty men, as many as possible to be archers and gunners, to serve at sea and to be ready at one hour's notice. The land forces were to be ready to come out when the beacons were lit, which would be the signal that the invading armies had landed.[12] Meanwhile Henry, spending Easter at Whitehall, let it be known that on Good Friday he had crept to the cross on his knees from the door of the chapel royal, and had himself served the priest at Mass, with 'his own person kneeling on His Grace's knees'.[13]

On Easter Monday, 7 April, 54 warships sailed from Flushing; by Wednesday the 9th, they were anchored off Margate, where they were joined by 14 other ships. At Hayling Island and Ashford in Kent, the word went round that the Emperor's armies had landed, and the defence forces were called out. On 22 April, the 68 ships off Margate sailed through the Narrow Seas. There were another 56 ships in port at Flushing. But soon it was known that the 68 ships in the Channel were bound for Andalusia, on their way to join the Emperor's navy which was operating against the Turks in the Mediterranean; and the 56 ships at Flushing took the 8,000 mercenaries in Friesland to the Baltic.[14]

By 8 May, when the great muster was held in London, the danger had passed. On that day, 16,500 men marched in harness from Mile End and Stepney to St James's Park, then across the fields to Holborn, and into the city at Newgate. They were marching from 9 a.m. to 5 p.m. Henry stood at the gatehouse of Whitehall from noon till 5 p.m. to see them pass before him.[15] The marching men responded enthusiastically to the call to arms, for they knew 'that the cankered and venomous serpent, Paul, Bishop of Rome, by that arch-traitor Reginald Pole, enemy to God's Word and his own natural country, had moved, excited and stirred divers great Princes and potentates of Christendom not alonely to invade this realm of England with mortal war, but also by fire and sword to extermine and utterly to destroy the whole nation and generation of the same'.[16] At Harwich, men, women and children worked on the defences, though one man there said that there would soon be a Pope again and no King. A few men refused to serve in the army. They were arrested.[17]

Parliament had met on 28 April. An Act was passed condemning the Countess of Salisbury as a traitor.[18] The old lady had been imprisoned in the Tower since the arrest and execution of her son Lord Montagu and his associates. Southampton and Henry's other officers had searched unsuccessfully for any real evidence of her guilt; but in the summer of 1539, it was enough that she was the mother of Cardinal Pole. It had become the usual practice, after a prominent public figure had been convicted of high treason, for Parliament to pass an Act of Attainder confirming the verdict of the court. Now, in the Countess of Salisbury's case, the Act of Attainder was passed without holding any kind of trial. This was not unprecedented; it had been done on several occasions in the fourteenth and fifteenth centuries, and more recently in the case of traitors who had fled abroad. But to use the Act of Attainder as a substitute for a trial of a defendant who could have been proceeded against in the usual way, was an innovation for the generation who were living in 1539.

But Henry required his Parliament to strike first and foremost at the Protestants. On 16 May, the Duke of Norfolk announced in the House of Lords that the King expected Parliament to pass an Act establishing six articles of religion. The first stated that the body of Christ was really present in the consecrated bread and wine, and by transubstantiation. The other five articles upheld private masses, the administration of communion in only one kind to the congregation, the value of confession, the validity of vows of celibacy by monks and nuns, and the prohibition of the marriage of priests. Anyone who denied the first article was to be burned for the first offence, even if he recanted at his trial, which was an unprecedented provision. Those who denied the last five articles were to be hanged. Married priests were to separate from their wives before the bill became law; those who failed to do so, or who married after the Act came into force, were to be hanged. Anyone who tried to leave the kingdom in order to escape prosecution for breaking the law was to be hanged, drawn and quartered as a traitor.[19]

Norfolk's statement caused consternation among the Lutherans in England and abroad. Cranmer took the unprecedented step of asking Henry's permission to oppose the proposed Six Articles in the House of Lords. Henry granted his request, and a disputation on the Six Articles took place in the House on three successive days on 19th, 20th and 21 May. The orthodox bishops, led by Gardiner, disputed in favour of the Articles, and Cranmer and his supporters opposed them. But Henry himself came to the House of Lords and took part in the disputation on each of the three days. He argued strongly in favour of the Six Articles. Cranmer believed that his intervention was decisive. He wrote ten years later that the Six Articles would never have passed if the King had not come in person to the House of Lords.[20]

The temporal peers were delighted. One of them wrote that 'never Prince showed himself so wise, learned, Catholic as the King has done in this Parliament'. The Six Articles had been approved, for 'notwithstanding my lord of Canterbury, my lord of Ely, my lord of Salisbury, my lord of Worcester, Rochester and St David's* defended the contrary long time, yet finally His Highness confounded them all with God's learning'. The writer added that Archbishop Lee, Tunstal, Gardiner, Stokesley and other bishops 'have showed themselves honest and well-learned men. We of the temporalty have be all of one opinion'.[21]

On the evening of the last day of the disputation, Henry gave a great banquet at Whitehall. Husee wrote to Lady Lisle that most of the great ladies were there, and that her daughters, Mistress Anne and Mistress Katherine had attended, and had stayed the night at the palace.[22]

Henry had allowed the Protestant bishops to oppose the Six Articles in the disputation, but now he expected compliance. Cranmer, who was personally affected by the provisions against married priests – for seven years he had been living secretly with the German wife whom he married at Nuremberg in 1532 – duly submitted, and voted for the bill at its three readings in the House of Lords. So did all the bishops except Latimer and Shaxton. They made the only form of protest open to them, and stayed away from the House when the bill was read for the first time on 7 June; but they were obviously put under pressure to comply, for on 9 June Latimer attended and voted in favour of the second reading. Shaxton still held out, but he as well as Latimer attended and voted for the third reading next day.[23]

In the House of Commons, Thomas Broke, one of the two MPs for Calais, spoke against the bill. Lisle was indignant at this fresh manifestation of heresy in Calais. He suggested to Gardiner, who with Norfolk was playing the most active part in piloting the bill through Parliament, that Broke should be arrested. Gardiner had some qualms about arresting a MP for words spoken in the House of Commons; but Henry had none, and Broke was sent to the Tower.[24]

The Act came into force on 12 July. It created a great impression. The French ambassador, Marillac, the Lutherans in Germany, and Henry's subjects in London and throughout the realm, all saw it as a great defeat for the reformers in England. Once again rumours circulated, as they had done after the execution of Anne Boleyn, about the arrest or flight of Cranmer and the heretic bishops. At the beginning of July, it was reported that Latimer had been caught at Gravesend trying to leave the kingdom in disguise without a passport, and that he had been sent to the Tower. In fact, he and Shaxton, who had an audience with Henry, asked permission to resign their bishoprics of Worcester and Salisbury. They were allowed to do so, but Latimer was placed under house arrest in the London house of Sampson, the

*Cranmer, Goodrich, Shaxton, Latimer, Hilsey and Barlow.

Bishop of Chichester, and Shaxton was imprisoned in the custody of the Bishop of Bath and Wells.[25]

Francis Hall, a soldier in the Calais garrison, was surprised that Latimer and Shaxton had resigned their bishoprics. 'They be not of the wisest sort, methinks', he wrote to Lady Lisle, 'for few nowadays will leave and give over such promotions for keeping of opinion'.[26]

The Act of the Six Articles – the 'whip with six strings', as the Protestants called it – had an immediate effect on married priests and on those who had concubines. Many of them separated from the women with whom they had been living more or less openly for many years. Cranmer himself sent his wife back to Germany.[27] At the end of July, he presided at the trial of a priest of Croydon who was accused of fornication with the woman with whom he had lived for three years. They had separated before the Act came into force, but the woman confessed that they had had sexual intercourse since 12 July, the relevant date. Fortunately for both of them, they had not been through any form of marriage ceremony, so they were not liable to the death penalty under the Act of the Six Articles, but only to imprisonment for fornication.[28] The Protestants were outraged that the law made it a more serious offence for priests to marry than to have illicit sexual intercourse; but the Catholics had always considered it a more serious crime flagrantly to defy the law of the Church by marriage than merely to sin by fornication, or even adultery.

Henry had his own special reasons for opposing the marriage of priests. In April 1541, he told Marillac that he was even more opposed to the marriage of priests than to Papal supremacy, for if priests were allowed to marry, benefices would become hereditary, and the priests would form a powerful hereditary class which would threaten the royal power.[29]

The monks and nuns who had left their monasteries and nunneries now found that they had lost both ways. Many of them had been induced to leave their houses, and to concur in the surrender of them to Henry, because they thought that they would then be able to marry. But under the Act of the Six Articles, no monk or nun who had taken a vow of celibacy was allowed to marry or to break their vow, even though they had left their houses and put off their monk's or nun's habits.[30]

This was a suitable moment, when the nation was united against the threat of foreign invasion and impressed by Henry's orthodoxy in promulgating the Six Articles, for Henry, in breach of his earlier promises, to introduce a bill in Parliament to suppress the few remaining monasteries which had refused to surrender voluntarily. The bill passed without opposition, and almost unnoticed, in the summer of 1539.[31]

The Lisles were very happy about the Six Articles, and drove home their advantage in Calais. Cranmer's commissary, Butler, the MP Broke, and several parish priests and soldiers of the garrison, were arrested, sent to London, and imprisoned in the Tower and other prisons. Cranmer could do nothing more for them, and presided at their trial for heresy in London. They were accused of denying the Real Presence, but as they had committed the offences before the Act of the Six Articles came into force, they were able to save their lives by recanting and carrying their faggots.[32] The victory had gone to Lisle; but Henry was angry that there should be so much contention in an important garrison town on the frontier of his realm, and that Lisle was always writing about it to the Council instead of dealing with the trouble himself. When Lisle's officer, Ferding, visited Henry at the beginning of July, while the trial of the Calais heretics was taking place in London, he found Henry very hostile. 'I have more ado with you Calais men', said Henry 'than with all my realm after. Therefore get you home'.[33]

The foreign Protestants were in despair. Bucer wrote from Strasbourg to Philip of Hesse that in England 'Cruelty, the Bishop of Winchester, rules', and that Gardiner had persuaded Henry to wait until Parliament reassembled in November and then put to death all the Protestants who were in prison in England. None could escape from the kingdom, because a close watch was being kept on the ports to stop anyone leaving without a passport.[34] This much at least was true. Tunstal's chaplain, Dr Hillyard, wished to leave the realm illegally, not in order to escape from the Six Articles but to join Pole in Italy. He decided that it was easier to go the other way. He was given permission to preach in the diocese of Durham, and travelled from London by Ware, Huntingdon, Lincolnshire and Bridlington to Tunstal's palace at Bishop Auckland, and then preached throughout Durham and Northumberland. When he reached Cornhill-on-Tweed he walked to the river bank, seized a rowing boat when the boatmen's attention was distracted, and rowed across the Tweed to the nunnery of Coldstream, and asked for asylum in Scotland.

This put the Prioress of Coldstream in an embarrassing position. She had for some time been an English spy, and had often sent information to Henry's officers in Northumberland about the Scottish defences and troop movements. She could not hand back Hillyard to the English across the Tweed without revealing to the Scottish authorities that she was an English agent. So she gave him money, and sent him on to Cardinal Beaton in Edinburgh, and secretly informed Sir William Evers at Berwick.

The authorities in England searched for Hillyard's accomplices. They traced his steps back from the Tweed to London, and questioned the people whom he had met on his journey; but no one incriminated himself. Henry asked James to extradite Hillyard as a traitor, under the treaty which provided for the extradition of Border robbers and rebels. James replied that the treaty did not apply to priests.[35]

Henry was merry in the summer of 1539. He held many parties on his barge in the Thames, with his musicians playing. On 17 June he watched a pageant on the Thames, in which two barges, one representing the King's barge and the other the Bishop of Rome's, engaged in a mock combat, which naturally ended in the victory of the King's barge. According to Marillac, pageants against the Pope were performed in nearly every village in England.[36]

Henry had reason to be merry. In May, Charles raised the embargo on ships sailing from the Netherlands, and Henry was able to bring to England the gunpowder which he had bought in Germany. When François heard that Charles was once again allowing trade between the Netherlands and England, he reversed his earlier decision and granted a licence for the export of the sail-cloth to England.[37]

Although there was now no longer any danger of invasion, Henry thought it worth while to try to sow discord between François and Charles. He went about it more subtly than usual. On 23 July, he spoke to Marillac at Guildford, and confided in him that he faced a moral dilemma. He had obtained, from his spies, information which would be of great value to François, and he felt that it was his duty, as a good brother, to pass it on to him; but if he did, it would create ill-feeling between François and the Emperor, and he did not wish to be accused of trying to start a quarrel between two friendly sovereigns. What did Marillac think he ought to do? Marillac wrote to François, who ordered him to try, if possible, to get Henry to put the information into writing, but that if Henry refused to do this, Marillac was to ask Henry to tell it to him verbally. Henry refused to put it into writing, but told Marillac that his information was that one of Charles's leading officers in Milan was prepared to surrender the city to François, who would thus be able to acquire Milan by sudden secret *coup* without war. François thanked Henry for passing on the information, but explained that his excellent relations with the Emperor made it impossible for him to take advantage of the traitor's offer.[38]

Marillac was a little alarmed at the mood in England. The fleet which had anchored off Margate in April, and had caused the invasion scare, had sailed from the Emperor's harbours; but the Englishmen who rallied to the musters were animated by the usual national hatred of the French. Henry assured Marillac that he would not allow anti-French sentiment to get out of hand. When Marillac visited him at Grafton in August, he told Marillac that he was satisfied with what he had, and wished to remain within his island, ready to defend himself, and not to invade his neighbours; for he did not envy their grandeur, provided that they left him the little that he had, which was nevertheless enough to guarantee him against those who wished to annoy him.[39]

In September, the Duke of Cleves's envoys came to London, and signed a treaty for a marriage alliance between Henry and the Duke's sister, Anne. There was a difficulty about Anne's alleged precontract with the Duke of Lorraine's son, the Marquis of Pont-à-Mousson; but the Duke of Cleves assured Henry that there was no precontract. The English representatives stated that Henry had decided to marry Anne of Cleves because he considered it his duty to provide additional male heirs; but there were other reasons why Henry wished to marry her. Cromwell had told him that he had received reports that the Lady Anne of Cleves was very beautiful, 'as well for the face as for the whole body, above all other ladies excellent', and that she excelled the Duchess of Milan 'as the golden sun excelleth the silver moon'. Hans Holbein the younger was sent to Cleves to paint a portrait of her for Henry.[40]

The marriage contract with Cleves revived the hopes of the German Lutherans that the situation in England was not hopeless. They also discovered that, despite all the initial excitement over the Six Articles, the Act was not being enforced, and that Cromwell was surreptitiously using his position to protect Lutherans and make the Act inoperative. In October, the Abbots of Glastonbury, Reading and Colchester were sent to the Tower and charged with high treason. They were accused of having hidden or sold their gold and silver ornaments and plate to prevent Henry from acquiring them when their abbeys were dissolved, and with having said to their monks, in private, that the Pope was the head of the Church, and that they regarded Fisher, More and the Carthusians as martyrs.[41]

Cromwell had no doubt as to what the result of their trials would be, because even before the trials had begun, he noted that the Abbot of Reading was 'to be sent down to be tried and executed at Reading with his complices' and 'the Abbot of Glaston to be tried at Glaston and also executed there'. Cromwell then made another note of possible witnesses who could give evidence for the prosecution.[42]

All went as Henry and Cromwell had planned. The three abbots were found guilty by the juries that tried them. The Abbot of Glastonbury was brought from his prison at Wells to Glastonbury, dragged through the town on a hurdle, and taken to the top of Tor Hill and hanged, drawn and quartered there. The Abbots of Reading and Colchester were also hanged, drawn and quartered. Henry's propagandists wrote their usual diatribes against the traitors. The fact that the Abbot of Reading's name was Cook gave them the opportunity to make jokes. This Cook had thought that he could dress the Bishop of Rome's dinner, but the King had given him a breakfast for his labour.[43]

Anne of Cleves travelled from Düsseldorf to Calais with a retinue of 263 persons and 228 horses,[44] and arrived there in the middle of December 1539. She was detained in Calais for a fortnight by contrary winds which blew west-north-west across the Channel, but she landed at Dover on 27 December. Elaborate preparations had been made for her reception at every stage of the journey, culminating in her meeting with the King on Shooters Hill at Blackheath on 3 January. But Henry, having heard about her beauty, was so eager to meet her that he came in disguise, with a small escort, to Rochester on New Year's Day. He went to her, and disclosed who he was, and dined with her and her ladies; but he was very disappointed, for Anne was far from beautiful, lacked all the social graces, and was not suitably dressed for a great King's court. The ladies-in-waiting that she had brought with her from Düsseldorf were even less attractive, and even worse dressed, than Anne herself.

When Henry returned to Greenwich next day, he told Cromwell that he did not like Anne at all. On 3 January, he went with his courtiers, the nobles and gentlemen, the city dignitaries, and an escort of five or six thousand horsemen, to greet Anne at Shooters Hill. He showed her every sign of respect in public; but he spent next day discussing with his counsellors how he could avoid having to marry her. He told them that he believed that Anne had been precontracted to the Marquis of Pont-à-Mousson, although this matter had been investigated at length during the marriage negotiations, and said that he had agreed to marry her only because of the untrue reports which he had received about her beauty. After Cranmer and Tunstal had inquired again into the precontract, and had ruled that there was no legal bar to Henry marrying Anne, Henry asked Cromwell if there was any way in which he could avoid having to marry her; and when Cromwell said that he feared that there was none, Henry said: 'Is there none other remedy but that I must need against my will put my neck in the yoke?'

As usual, he decided to think about his problem overnight, and next morning, on 5 January, he announced that he would marry her next day. The marriage ceremony was performed in Henry's chapel at Greenwich on Twelfth Day, in the presence of a number of counsellors and noblemen and the envoys of Cleves. According to Henry, the marriage was never consummated. He slept with Anne every night, or every other night, but afterwards said that he had left her as much a maid as he had found her. He also said that he had felt her belly and her breasts, and was sure that she was not a virgin.[45]

Although Henry decided that he must go through with the marriage, it shows the extent of his self-confidence and his utter disregard of all proprieties and international usage, to say nothing of Anne's personal feelings, that he was prepared even to consider the possibility of refusing to marry her after the many weeks of diplomatic negotiations, the political alliances which depended on the marriage, and the public ceremony with which Anne had been received at Calais, Dover and Blackheath. Every other King in Christendom accepted the necessity of having sometimes to marry an unattractive Princess in order to make a useful diplomatic alliance; for Kings did not marry for pleasure, and could always console themselves with mistresses. But Henry had almost certainly not had a mistress since he married Anne Boleyn; and we know from what he said to Castillon during his marriage negotiations in 1538, that he hoped to find a suitable bride whom he could marry for love as well as for political advantage. Did his assumption of the office of Supreme Head of the Church of England, and his repeated declarations of his determination to eliminate vice in the religious houses and to punish fornicating priests and adulterous Queens, lead him to feel that he ought to set an example by practising a new and unfashionable purity in his own sexual life? Or was it just another example of the characteristic which was commented on by so many of the people who knew him – his absolute determination to get his own way on every point, great or small, and only to marry a wife if he wanted her?

And why not? Both Chapuys and Castillon had independently come to the same conclusion, that the more Henry was threatened, the more conciliatory he became, and the more he was placated, the more truculent he was. Nobody was daring to oppose him in 1540, and he saw no reason why he should do anything that he did not wish to do. If, by jilting Anne at the last moment, he deeply offended the Duke of Cleves, this did not matter; the Duke of Cleves was not a very powerful sovereign. If it disrupted the whole plan for an alliance with the German Lutherans which Cromwell now favoured, this did not matter either; for it was obvious, after what had happened in 1533, in 1535, and in 1539, that the Emperor would never dare to invade his realm, or even to place an embargo on trade between England and the Netherlands; and as for François, he had always been able to manipulate him. If he needed the support of the Lutherans, he could always obtain it by beheading some Papist noblemen and having a few abbots hanged, drawn and quartered, just as he could always win the approval of the majority of his subjects by burning heretics. He would not offend his people by discarding Anne of Cleves as much as he had done by divorcing Catherine of Aragon, by suppressing the monasteries, and by looting the shrines; but he had crushed all opposition to those measures, and the great majority of his subjects still served him loyally, especially when confronted with a threat of invasion, and acclaimed him as 'our Prince, our Governor, our Protector, our Head under Christ'.[46]

The handful of refugees abroad were an irritant. When Wriothesley was ambassador to Mary of Hungary in February 1539, he tried to catch the English Papist, Henry Phillips, who was studying at Louvain University. He succeeded in luring Phillips into the English embassy in Brussels; but Phillips escaped one night before Wriothesley could send him to England. Wriothesley asked the authorities in the Netherlands to help him catch Phillips, and invented the story that Phillips was a thief who had stolen money from his own father; but the Papist students of Louvain did not believe him, and hid Phillips. Wriothesley thought it would be wiser if no English scholar was ever permitted to study abroad.[47]

An English gentleman, Robert Branceter, had entered the Emperor's service in 1527; he had served under Charles in North Africa, and had been sent on a diplomatic mission to Persia. The English authorities were informed that Branceter had talked to English merchants in Spain, and had urged them to continue in their obedience to the Pope and not to recognise Henry as Supreme Head of the Church of England; so Parliament in 1539 passed an Act attainting Branceter as a traitor. Wyatt made no attempt to persuade Charles to extradite Branceter; but in December 1539 Charles travelled from Spain to the Netherlands through France, where he had another meeting with François to reassert their friendship. Wyatt accompanied Charles's court, and Branceter came as a gentleman in Charles's retinue. Wyatt told the French authorities that an English traitor named Branceter was in France, without mentioning that he was in the Emperor's train. He obtained an extradition warrant, broke into Branceter's rooms in Paris, overpowered him, and took him prisoner; but the French authorities then discovered that he was in the Emperor's service, and released him. Charles protested strongly to Wyatt, and François had an equally stormy interview with Bonner, Henry's ambassador in France.

Bonner behaved with his usual rudeness, and François demanded that Henry should recall him. Henry apologised for Bonner's behaviour, recalled him, and sent Norfolk, whom the French regarded as one of their supporters in Henry's Council, to appease François' indignation. But Henry promoted Bonner to be Bishop of London, to fill the vacancy caused by Stokesley's death.[48]

Norfolk dropped a hint to François' ministers, while he was in France, that Cromwell might soon fall from power. By April, Marillac was reporting that a fierce power struggle was taking place behind the scenes at Henry's court.[49] Although we have very little reliable evidence about this struggle, there can be no doubt that Marillac and other contemporary commentators were right in believing that Norfolk, with his hatred of base-born counsellors and the new learning, and Gardiner were the leaders of the plot to overthrow Cromwell. Gardiner was the ablest of the orthodox Catholic bishops, and when he was recalled to England in September 1538, after his three years' service as ambassador in France, he used his influence against the Reformation and against Cromwell. It was as wrong of the Protestants to blame Gardiner for the persecution which they suffered under Henry as it was of the Papists to blame Cromwell for the Henrician Reformation; but Gardiner's influence was an important factor in the religious struggle at court.

After Henry's death, Gardiner wrote with affection as well as respect about that 'noble Prince', and implied that he and Henry were on excellent terms.[50] This is very likely true, because Gardiner had all the qualities which Henry required in a counsellor. He was a learned theologian, an able lawyer, a forceful and effective debater in theological disputations, and a very successful diplomat. His lawyer's mind and his independence of character sometimes led him into dangerous differences of opinion with Henry; but he fully accepted the rule, on which Henry always insisted, that his counsellors must give him honest advice, and even frank criticism, in private, and absolute obedience in public. Gardiner was a firm believer in authority and discipline, in State and Church, in the armed forces and in the universities. He considered that even the new method of pronouncing Greek, which Erasmus had favoured, was subversive, because it caused undergraduates to question the correctness of the pronunciation which was adopted by some of their teachers; and as Chancellor of Cambridge University in 1542, he gave orders that any student who pronounced Greek in the modern way was to be punished.[51]

There is evidence that Henry liked Gardiner, as he liked Wolsey, More and Cranmer; but there is no reason to believe that he ever liked Cromwell very much, though he realised that he was a loyal and useful servant, and an efficient administrator. Cromwell was particularly useful in dealing with matters which did not interest Henry, like the reorganisation of government administration and the regulation of the business of the King's Council and Privy Council. The stories which were circulating at court in 1537, that Henry stormed at Cromwell three times a week, and sometimes punched his head and shook him by the scruff of his neck like a dog, are probably not merely exaggerations but complete fabrications and wishful thinking; but Henry made disparaging remarks to Castillon about Cromwell in 1538, and there is no recorded instance of his making such remarks about Wolsey, More, Cranmer or Gardiner.[52]

In the spring of 1540, Henry was falling in love with Katherine Howard, the twenty-year-old daughter of Norfolk's brother, Lord Edmund Howard. She was one of Anne of Cleves's ladies-in-waiting. She had spent some years in the household of her grandmother, the old Duchess of Norfolk. Henry did not know that she had led an immoral life under the old Duchess's roof, undeterred by the beatings which she sometimes received as a result; that she had entered into a secret precontract of marriage with a young gentleman of the household, Francis Derham, and had fornicated with him; and that she had also been the mistress of her cousin, Thomas Culpepper, who was a gentleman of Henry's privy chamber, and of a young musician in the Duchess's household, Henry Mannox.[53]

During the long hot summer of 1540, when the water in the ponds was drying up and cattle were dying of thirst,[54] Henry often crossed the river from Whitehall in his barge to visit Katherine Howard in Southwark. On several occasions he met her there at parties in Gardiner's house.[55] There is a well-established tradition that Norfolk and Gardiner introduced her to Henry in the hope that she would become his mistress and persuade him to adopt Gardiner's pro-Catholic policy and destroy Cromwell; but there is not a shred of evidence that Katherine Howard played any part whatever in Cromwell's downfall or in the shift in Henry's policy in 1540. It seems unlikely that this weak and silly girl would have been capable of carrying on a subtle political intrigue; and if Norfolk or Gardiner had made any obvious attempt to use her to influence Henry's policy, Henry would have reacted very adversely, and would probably have done in the opposite direction from what they intended.

He found the petite and wanton Katherine Howard much more attractive than his new Queen. By the end of April, he was granting her the lands of convicted felons which had been forfeited to him.[56] Once again, as in 1536, his love for a young woman, and his desire to marry her, coincided with his political advantage. If he wished to convince his subjects and foreign rulers that he was an orthodox Catholic, there was no better way of doing it than by executing Cromwell, who had deceived him into believing that Anne of Cleves was very beautiful. Cromwell had not only lied to him, but had made him feel a fool. The idea of getting rid of both Cromwell and Anne of Cleves, of marrying Katherine Howard and turning to Norfolk and Gardiner, was forming in Henry's mind; but Henry never acted in a hurry.

There was more trouble in Calais, with Lisle and his supporters ferreting out heretics. They discovered that Broke, the MP who had recanted the speech against the Six Articles which he had made in the House of Commons, had eaten meat in Lent. Lisle reported to Henry that he wished to banish Broke and three others from the Marches. Henry replied that he thought it would be better to hang two rather than to banish four. If Broke had eaten meat in Lent without a licence, was this not evidence of a relapse into the former heresy which he committed when he criticised the Six Articles? Henry urged the authorities in Calais to try to find some reason for putting Broke to death either as a traitor or as a heretic.[57]

The sermons preached at Paul's Cross on the Sundays in Lent were often an occasion for important pronouncements by leading government propagandists. On the first Sunday in Lent in 1540, Gardiner preached there, and attacked the growth of novelties and heresies. A fortnight later, Barnes preached at Paul's Cross, and criticised Gardiner's sermon. Gardiner complained to Henry, who ordered Barnes and Gardiner to dispute before him. Having heard them, he ordered Barnes to recant and ask Gardiner's forgiveness in another sermon in London. Two other Protestants, Thomas Garrett, the parson of Honey Lane in London, and William Jerome, the vicar of Stepney, both of whom had been in trouble as heretics in the time of Wolsey and More, also preached sermons in London of which Gardiner disapproved; and they, too, were ordered to make a public recantation.[58] On 31 March, Wallop wrote the good news to Lisle in Calais. He told him that Barnes, Garrett and Jerome had all recanted 'from their lewd opinions, and, to be plain, His Highness is of such sort that I think all Christendom shall shortly say, the King of England is the only perfect of good faith, God save him'.[59]

A few days later, Henry ordered that Barnes, Garrett and Jerome should be arrested and sent to the Tower, as their recantations had been inadequate. This was more than another drive against sacramentaries; for the last nine years, Barnes had been in great favour with Henry, and had persecuted sacramentaries from a Lutheran position. The arrest of Barnes was an attack on Lutheranism, and was generally interpreted as a blow at Cromwell. On 10 April, Marillac wrote that 'Cromwell is tottering', and that he and Cranmer did not know what was happening to them.[60]

But the power struggle swayed first one way and then the other. The authorities discovered that Gregory Botolph, who had once been Lord Lisle's chaplain but had joined Cardinal Pole in Rome, had now come to Gravelines and was secretly corresponding with Philpot, a priest in Calais. Philpot was sent to the Tower.[61] Henry ordered Philpot to write to Botolph, inviting him to return to Calais, as the authorities were prepared to forgive him for having gone to Rome and to appoint him as vicar of Arderne in the Marches of Calais. 'Bread and drink ye shall find', wrote Philpot, 'cheese and eggs, but none other cares'.[62] Botolph did not fall into Henry's trap, so Pate, the English ambassador in Ghent, asked the authorities in the Netherlands to extradite him. He invented a story that Botolph had stolen ornaments from a church, because he thought that they would find this very shocking; but they refused to extradite Botolph.[63]

On 17 April, Henry wrote to his 'right trusty and right well beloved cousin and counsellor', Lord Lisle, ordering him to hand over his authority in Calais to the Earl of Sussex and to come to court. Next day, Henry created Cromwell Earl of Essex – the former Earl had recently died from a fall from his horse – and appointed him Lord Great Chamberlain of England.[64]

Lord Lisle arrived in London in the middle of May. A few days later, he was arrested at ten o'clock one night and taken to the Tower, charged with high treason for having plotted with his former chaplain, Botolph, to deliver Calais to the Bishop of Rome and the traitor Reginald Pole. Several of Lisle's servants were arrested with him. The authorities had discovered that he had once granted Botolph a passport to go abroad from Calais, and had written a letter of recommendation in his favour; and no doubt more evidence would soon be forthcoming.[65]

Lisle's friend Sampson, the Bishop of Chichester and Dean of the Chapel Royal, was sent to the Tower on 31 May. Next day, Marillac wrote to Montmorency, the Constable of France, that he had heard that Cromwell had said that there were five other bishops who deserved to be treated in the same way as Sampson, but that he would not yet name them. 'Things have reached a stage', wrote Marillac, 'at which either the party of the said Cromwell, or that of the Bishop of Winchester and his supporters, must fall; and though both are in great authority and favour with the King their master, things seem to be going in Cromwell's favour, because the said Bishop of

Winchester's chief friend, the said Dean of the Chapel, has been struck down'.[66]

Sampson's arrest raised the problem of what to do with Latimer, who for the past eleven months had been held as a prisoner in Sampson's house in London. The matter was referred to the King. Henry did not see that there was any difficulty; he said that as Sampson's household would presumably not be immediately broken up, Latimer could continue to be held as a prisoner in Sampson's house while Sampson was a prisoner in the Tower.[67]

There were also difficulties in Ireland. The Deputy, Lord Leonard Grey, sent encouraging reports to Henry of his successful campaigns against the Geraldines and the leading rebel, O'Conor; but his raids into O'Conor's territory were always followed by his return to Dublin, leaving O'Conor still at large and undefeated. There were intrigues against the Lord Deputy among the members of his Council; the Archbishop of Dublin and other counsellors spread rumours about his incompetence, and even hinted that he might have been in secret contact with Pole. They stated that he had sent artillery and ammunition to places in Galway and Limerick, so that they would be available for use by an invading force if Pole and the Spaniards landed on the west coast.[68]

Henry summoned Grey to come to court for consultations about the military problems, so that he could return to Ireland with reinforcements for a new drive against O'Conor. When he arrived in London at the beginning of June, he was arrested and sent to the Tower on a charge of high treason.[69]

On 7 June, Sampson sent to Cromwell from the Tower a statement about his conversations with Tunstal, Stokesley and Gardiner, which suggests that Cromwell had hoped to induce him to incriminate Tunstal; but on 10 June, Norfolk arrested Cromwell at a meeting of the Council on a charge of high treason, and he was sent to the Tower.[70] The practice which had recently been adopted in Lady Salisbury's case was followed, and Cromwell, too, was condemned without trial by an Act of Attainder passed by Parliament. It declared that although the King's other counsellors had always pursued Henry's 'most godly and princely purpose', Thomas Cromwell, Earl of Essex, 'being a person of as poor and low degree as few be within this your realm', had been so ungrateful for the promotion and gifts which Henry had bestowed on him that he had now been found 'to be the most false and corrupt traitor, deceiver and circumventor against your most royal person and the imperial crown of this your realm, that hath been known, seen or heard of in all the time of your most noble reign'. He was also a 'detestable heretic', who had protected and encouraged heretics and their heresies, including sacramentaries. He had taken bribes; he had planned to marry the King's daughter, the Lady Mary; he had said on a number of occasions since 31 March 1539 that he was 'sure' of the King, and that he would soon be so strong that he would be able to force the King to pursue any policy that he wished. The Act therefore condemned him to be either hanged, drawn and quartered, or burned, according to Henry's pleasure.[71]

Cromwell was kept alive in the Tower until he had provided the necessary evidence for Henry to obtain a divorce from Anne of Cleves. Convocation then asked, and obtained, Henry's permission to examine the validity of his marriage to the Queen. Henry submitted a statement in writing, in his own hand, stating that he had first agreed to marry Anne of Cleves, 'trusting to have some assured friend by it, I much doubting that time both the Emperor and France and the Bishop of Rome; and also because I heard so much, both of her excellent beauty and virtuous conditions'. But the first time that he saw her at Rochester, 'I assure you I liked her so ill, and so far contrary to that she was praised, that I was woe that ever she came into England'. He therefore claimed that he had not married her of his own free will, and that the marriage was void for lack of consent between the parties.

To prove this, he called not only the evidence of Lord Southampton and Sir Anthony Browne, but also the statement of Lord Essex, 'not doubting that but since he is a person which knoweth himself condemned to die by Act of Parliament, will not damn his soul but truly declare the truth'.[72] He also claimed that he had been unable to consummate his marriage to Anne. This was confirmed by the evidence of his physician, Dr Butts, who said that Henry had had nocturnal emissions during the months when he was married to Anne, which proved that he could not have had sexual intercourse with a woman during this time. On the strength of this evidence, Convocation gave judgement that the marriage was annulled, and that Henry and Anne were both free to marry again.[73]

The divorce involved fewer difficulties with Cleves than Henry and his counsellors had expected. Anne agreed to be divorced, to stay in England, to accept the settlement which Henry gave her, and to write to her brother, the Duke of Cleves, assuring him that she was satisfied.[74] Henry gave her two residences, one at Richmond and one at Bletchingley in Surrey, and sometimes visited her at Richmond. He also gave her lands, many of which he had previously granted to Cromwell, and which had reverted to him when Cromwell's property was forfeited on his attainder.

Henry commuted Cromwell's sentence to beheading, and he was executed on Tower Hill on 28 July. Lord Hungerford was beheaded with him; he had been condemned by Act of Attainder for sodomy and raping his daughter, for having a chaplain who had sympathised with the Pilgrimage of Grace, and for asking magicians to foretell when the King would die.[75] Two days later, Henry staged a striking exhibition of his determination to suppress both Papists and heretics. He ordered that the three heretics, Barnes, Garrett and Jerome, should be burned at Smithfield at the same time that three Papists – Abel, Powell and Featherstone – were hanged, drawn and quartered there as traitors for denying the royal supremacy. Abel, who had been Catherine of Aragon's confessor, had been arrested in 1533, when Catherine's household was dispersed after Cranmer's judgement at Dunstable. He had been in prison for more than six years; and Powell and Featherstone had spent nearly as long in jail for refusing to take the oath of the succession to the issue of Henry and Anne Boleyn. Like Barnes, Garrett and Jerome, they were now sentenced to death by Act of Parliament without any form of trial.

The three heretics and the three Papists were dragged through the streets of London on three hurdles, with one heretic and one Papist tied to each hurdle. Barnes and Powell were fastened to the same hurdle. All the way, as they were dragged through the jeering crowds, they argued violently with each other, each claiming that he was a martyr for the Faith and that the other was being most justly punished.[76]

Barnes made a speech at the stake. He said that he had no idea why he was about to be executed, as he had never been charged with any offence, or told why he was to die; but as he understood that he was going to be burned, he supposed that it must be for heresy. He asked the Sheriff, who was in charge of the execution, if he knew why he was to die; but the Sheriff did not know. Barnes pointed out that he had always persecuted Anabaptists, and asked the people to pray for the King, as he himself had done in his prison, praying that Henry might long reign over them. 'I have been reported a preacher of sedition and disobedience to the King's Majesty; but here I say to you that you are all bound by the commandment of God to obey your Prince with all humility, and with all your heart, yea, not so much as in a look to show yourselves disobedient unto him'.[77]

John Foxe in his *Book of Martyrs* wrote that Henry's Council was divided in the summer of 1540 into a Protestant and a 'Papist' faction. The Protestants were Cranmer, Suffolk, Edward Seymour (afterwards Duke of Somerset), Dudley (afterwards Duke of Northumberland), Russell, Paget, Sadler and Audley. The 'Papists' were Gardiner, Tunstal, Norfolk, Southampton, Anthony Browne, Paulet, Baker, Rich and Wingfield. He wrote that the Protestants wished to execute Abel, Powell and Featherstone, while the Papists wished to burn Barnes, Garrett and Jerome; so it was decided, as a compromise, to execute all six together. Dr Scarisbrick, who for some reason assumes that Barnes was accused of being an Anabaptist, writes that 'Henry was not the author of his death and probably never knew exactly how it came about'.[78]

So neither Barnes himself at the stake in 1540, Foxe in 1563, nor Scarisbrick in 1968, blamed the one man who undoubtedly was, and alone could be, responsible for the decision to have the three heretics burned and the three Papists hanged, drawn and quartered. It was only a more perfect expression of the policy which in 1533 had burned Frith the sacramentary at the time of the final break with Rome, in 1535 had burned fourteen

Anabaptists within a month of the executions of Fisher, More and the Carthusians, and in 1538 had burned Lambert ten days before Exeter, Montagu and the leading Papist supporters were condemned. Norfolk, Gardiner and the other orthodox Catholics on the Council would never have dared to have anyone executed without Henry's authority – they rarely ventured to take even unimportant decisions without referring the matter to him – and certainly not a prominent theologian like Barnes, who had been active as a preacher and a diplomat at court and abroad for the past nine years.

For Henry, Barnes had now become the ideal sacrificial victim. After Cromwell, he was the most hated of the heretics around the King who were thought to be responsible for the heretical innovations which had been introduced into the Church of England. Henry's orthodox subjects, unlike their King, were not interested in theological subtleties; they only knew that Barnes was a 'detestable heretic', [79] as the Act of Attainder stated, who had already once been condemned as a heretic many years ago.

While Cromwell was in the Tower awaiting execution, the bishops and learned divines were sitting, by virtue of the commission which he had issued as Vicegerent two months before, to examine the nature of the sacraments and questions concerning the ordination of bishops and priests. They were instructed to reach their conclusions in the light of Scriptural authority and patristic texts. When Cranmer delivered his opinion on these subtle theological questions, he stated that he would be willing to change his mind and reach different conclusions if Henry ordered him to do so. 'This is mine opinion and sentence at this present, which I do not temerariously define, but do remit the judgment thereof wholly unto Your Majesty'.[80] The bishops and courtiers would change their religious opinions, approve a marriage and then invalidate it, curry favour with Henry's ministers and then vilify them as traitors, and sentence their closest colleagues and relations to death, until it was their turn to go to the Tower and to the place of execution. Then they would praise Henry in their last words as they waited for death at the scaffold or the stake.

Henry found time, during this hot and grim summer, to pay attention to the affairs of the Order of the Garter, which always delighted him. The names of the knights of the most noble order were impressively inscribed in the books; but a growing number of them had been executed for high treason. The officials were uncertain whether their names should be erased from the list, as they so richly deserved; for the appearance of the books would be disfigured by a large number of erasures. The matter was referred to the King. He orderd that the names should remain on the list, but that opposite each name there should be added the words: '*Vah, proditor*' (Oh! a traitor!)[81]

25

KATHERINE HOWARD

On 28 July, the day on which Cromwell was executed, Henry married Katherine Howard at the usual private ceremony at Oatlands; and on 8 August she was publicly recognised as Queen when she dined under a cloth-of-state at Hampton Court. Marillac, like other people who saw her, commented on how small she was; he thought that she was graceful rather than beautiful. Henry was passionately in love with her, and treated her with the greatest respect and solicitude; but many people did not like her. Marillac wrote that her motto was 'No other will but her own', and though she behaved graciously to Anne of Cleves, she soon quarrelled with the Lady Mary. She complained that Mary did not treat her with as much respect as she had treated Jane Seymour and Anne of Cleves when they were Queen, and she revenged herself by forcing Mary to dismiss two of her favourite ladies-in-waiting.[1]

She was indiscreet. She appointed two of her former lovers, Derham and Mannox, to be members of her household; and she saw a great deal of her other lover, Culpepper, as he was a gentleman of Henry's privy chamber.

There was a general feeling in the air that great changes were about to take place now that Cromwell had fallen. Even in Protestant London, according to Hall, 'many lamented but more rejoiced' when he was sent to the Tower. The former monks were especially happy. 'They banquetted and triumphed together that night, many wishing that that day had been seven years before'.[2] Norfolk's twenty-three-year-old son, the Earl of Surrey, was of course delighted when Cromwell was executed. 'Now is that foul churl dead, so ambitious of others' blood', he said to his cousin Sir Edmund Knyvett, 'now is he stricken with his own staff'. He added that 'these new erected men would by their wills leave no nobleman on life'.[3]

The Protestants were in despair. The Zwinglian merchant, Richard Hilles, who was able to write informative letters about England once he was safely out of the country on his visits to the Frankfort fair, wrote to Bullinger in Zürich that 'a man may now travel from the east of England to the west, and from north to south, without being able to discover a single preacher who out of a pure heart and faith unfeigned is seeking the glory of our God'. Henry had got rid of them all.[4]

The burning of Barnes shocked the German Lutherans, who published Barnes's speech at the stake. Luther wrote, in the preface, that Barnes had been utterly loyal to Henry, and always referred to him as 'my King'; but 'Junker Harry will be God and do as he craves'. Luther thought that the failure to give any reason for Barnes's execution showed that Henry was ashamed of it, and that Barnes had died as a gift to Henry's new bride, like John the Baptist's head had been Herod's gift to the daughter of Herodias. He revelaed that Barnes had said to him, in private conversation, that Henry had similarly sacrificed Fisher and More to please Anne Boleyn.[5] This was an admission that neither Barnes nor any other English Lutheran would have made in public.

But Hilles believed that most people in England did not really care why Barnes and his colleagues had been put to death, 'because it is now no novelty among us to see men slain, hung, quartered, beheaded; some for trifling expressions, which were explained or interpreted as having been spoken against the King; others for the Pope's supremacy; some for one thing, some for another'. Zwinglian though he was, he was quite prepared to believe the assertions of the Papists that their champion Abel, who died with Barnes, had 'long been kept in a most filthy prison . . . almost eaten up by vermin.'[6]

Henry was merry, very much in love with his new wife, afraid of nobody, and prepared to quarrel simultaneously with both Charles and François. He had pleased his subjects by asking Parliament to pass an Act, in the summer of 1540, which revived a statute of Richard III which had not been enforced for many years. It placed various burdens on aliens: they were not permitted to own land in England, or to employ more than two servants; and a new Subsidy Act taxed them at one shilling in the pound, whereas Englishmen were to pay sixpence in the pound. Both Charles and François protested that this legislation violated their treaties with Henry which provided that there should be no discrimination against each other's subjects. Henry rejected this claim, arguing that as the Act of Richard III was in force when the treaties were made, the treaties must be interpreted as being modified by the Act. He also refused to pay compensation to those aliens whose lands were forfeited under the Act, as he claimed that they should have known about the Act when they bought the land.

Charles, after withdrawing his ambassador from England for just over a year, sent Chapuys back in August 1540, though Chapuys was ill, and had to be carried in a litter. He raised the question of the anti-alien legislation in many conversations with the Council and with Henry personally, and Marillac protested equally strongly. As Henry did not give way, Mary of

Hungary retaliated by imposing restrictions on English merchants at Antwerp, and banning the export from the Netherlands of a consignment of armour that Henry had ordered. Henry thereupon refused to grant the annual licence for the export of timber which the municipal authorities of Dunkirk obtained every year from Rye. Henry and his lawyers found subtle reasons to prove that Mary of Hungary's ban on the export of the armour was a breach of the treaty, but that his own ban on the export of the timber was not; but he hinted that if Mary of Hungary rescinded the ban on the export of armour, he might look favourably on a polite request from Chapuys that he should remove the ban on the export of the timber to Dunkirk. This was not good enough for Mary of Hungary, and the dispute continued.[7]

Henry became involved in a more serious confrontation with François. On the frontier between France and the Marches of Calais, along the river between Ardres and Balinghem, there was a meadow which the French called 'Le Cauchoire' and the English 'the Cowslade'. It had been included in the territory which King John of France had ceded to Edward III under the Treaty of Brétigny; but the line of tall trees which marked the frontier in 1360 had long since been felled; only a few of the oldest local inhabitants could remember them. There had been friction about the Cowslade in Henry VII's reign, when the French had built houses on the meadow, and the English had driven them off and pulled down the houses and seized the building materials.

In July 1540, the French garrison at Ardres sent labourers to build a bridge across the river from the French to the English side. Lord Maltravers, who had replaced Lisle as Deputy of Calais, was alarmed, for he thought that the only reason for building the bridge was to enable the French to march across it if they wished to invade the English Pale in wartime. Henry ordered Maltravers to destroy the bridge, and on 7 September workmen were sent to pull it down. On 29 September, the French rebuilt it. Maltravers sent 200 workmen, with an escort of 300 soldiers, and archers on horseback, who broke it down again. The French rebuilt it again. When Maltravers rode out to see the bridge, a hundred hagbutters,* emerged from a house on the French side of the river. One of them fired a shot in his direction, and he retreated. He was preparing to destroy the bridge for the third time when, to his disappointment, he received an order from Henry to take no further action, as Henry had agreed with Marillac to open diplomatic negotiations with François on the subjet. The dispute dragged on for more than a year while the English and French lawyers examined the evidence of the frontier demarcation.[8]

Henry ordered that extensive work should be carried out to strengthen the fortifications at Calais and Guisnes. He also reinforced the garrison, sending

*'Hagbutters' (infantrymen armed with the new arquebus firearm) were an important element in sixteenth-century warfare.

an additional 2,000 soldiers there. The French thought that he had sent not 2,000, but 20,000, men to Calais.[9]

Henry became involved in another dispute with François when he was informed that there was a weak-minded tailor in Orleans who claimed that he was descended from Edward IV and was the Yorkist heir to the throne. The tailor called himself 'Blanche Rose', but Henry's agents discovered that he was an Englishman named Richard Hosier who had left England in 1531. Henry demanded that he should be extradited as a traitor. The French authorities alleged that he was the son of an English father and a French mother who had been born in Orleans, and was not an English subject; he was therefore not liable to extradition under the treaty. Henry insisted that he should be extradited, and claimed that it was an unfriendly act of François to believe the word of this low-born tailor that he was a Frenchman rather than the assertion of Henry, a King, that he was an Englishman. It was only when the French had made it clear that Blanche Rose would not be extradited that Henry announced that it was beneath his dignity to concern himself with the activities of a tailor, and that he was taking no further action in the matter.[10]

Henry was not afraid of François or Charles, but he was afraid of the plague which raged fiercely in London in the autumn of 1540, with three hundred people dying every week. At the end of his annual progress he did not return to Greenwich or Hampton Court, but spent the winter at Windsor. He issued an order forbidding anyone to come from London to the court. When there were cases of plague in the town of Windsor, he ordered that everyone who had caught it was expelled from the town. The sick and the dying were dragged from their beds, carried into the fields outside the town, and left to die there, unless they were able to find somewhere else to go.[11] This was not a novel idea on Henry's part, but the accepted practice during an epidemic of plague.

Henry did not catch the plague, but he was troubled by his leg, and his health was deteriorating. He had become very fat; we know from his suit of armour in the Tower that he was fifty-four inches round the waist. But he continued to eat and drink enormous quantities. When Marillac visited him at Woking in December 1540 he found him in good spirits, and spending most of his time hawking, now that the hunting season was over. He told Marillac that he had changed his daily routine; he now rose between 5 and 6 a.m., went to Mass at 7 a.m., and then rode for three hours till dinner time at 10 a.m. He said that he felt much better at Woking than he had done in past years when he spent the winter at his houses just outside London. But this boost to his spirits was followed by a set-back when the hole in his leg closed up and caused a violent fever, as it had done three years before. In February 1541 it was thought, for a few days, that he was dying; but he recovered.[12]

With his leg and his enormous girth, he could no longer take any exercise, but he still spent the greater part of every day out of doors, as he had done all his life. During the cold winter of 1540–1, when the roads further north were blocked for many days by snow, he went out hawking; he would sit on his horse, well wrapped up against the cold, and watch his hawk chase its prey. Lord William Howard told François I, in February 1541, that Henry insisted on going out in the coldest weather, when most of his servants would have preferred to stay indoors.[13]

His height and his natural dignity obscured to some extent the grossness of his fat body. His manners, especially to women, were usually impeccable, and he could make a very favourable impression on those who saw him and spoke to him. When the widowed Countess of Northumberland presented a petition to him, complaining that she did not receive a sufficient allowance from her deceased husband's estate, Swyfoe wrote to Lady Northumberland's brother, the Earl of Shrewsbury, that Henry heard her very gently, and 'bowed down upon his staff unto her, and said: "Madam, how can your ladyship desire any living of your husband's lands, seeing your father gave no money to your husband in marriage with your ladyship? Or what think you that I should do herein?"' She answered: 'What shall please Your Grace'. 'Madam', said the King, 'I marvel greatly that my lord your father, being so great a wise man as he was, would see no direction taken in this matter in his time. Howbeit, Madam, we will be contented to refer the matter unto our Council'. He then conferred with Tunstal and Sir Anthony Browne, and gave the petition to Tunstal. She asked him to be good and gracious to her, and he replied: 'We will'.[14]

But Marillac wrote that he had heard from reliable sources that Henry's leg and his intemperate eating and drinking made him irrascible and unpredictable, so that he often had a completely different opinion after dinner from what he had had in the morning. According to Marillac, he cursed his subjects, and threatened to impose taxes which would make them so poor that they would not dare to rebel against him; and he accused his counsellors of disloyalty, saying that they had made him get rid of Cromwell, who was the best servant that he had ever had. But Marillac's 'reliable' informants were often very unreliable. He was a much less intelligent and experienced diplomat than his predecessor, Castillon. Ever since he first arrived in England at the height of the invasion danger in 1539, when he repeatedly informed François that Henry had a fleet of 90 warships ready for action in Portsmouth harbour – the correct figure was 56 – he had been sending inaccurate information to his government. The story that Henry said that he wished to impoverish his people in order to make them too weak to resist him, had been in circulation for many years; and the report that he blamed his counsellors for having persuaded him to get rid of Cromwell is suspiciously similar to the story that was being told in 1530 that he blamed his counsellors at that time for having allowed him to overthrow Wolsey.[15]

After the executions of Cromwell and Barnes and his fellow-sufferers, no more death sentences were carried out for the time being; but Lisle and Lord Leonard Grey, whom Cromwell had sent to the Tower before his downfall, remained there after Cromwell joined them in the Tower and after he was executed. The old Countess of Salisbury was also there. All of them had been condemned to death by Act of Attainder, and neither executed nor reprieved. Edward Courtenay, the son of the executed Marquess of Exeter, had been sent to the Tower at the time of his father's arrest, when he was twelve, and had been kept there without charge ever since. After Lisle and Grey, the Deputies of Calais and Ireland, had been recalled for consultations and promptly arrested, Henry's ambassadors abroad were not as eager as usual to be summoned home. They might be safer abroad, even though this meant that they would be unable to join in the scramble at court for monastic lands and the forfeited property of traitors.

The Archdeacon of Lincoln, Richard Pate – his uncle was Henry's confessor, Longland, the Bishop of Lincoln – was Henry's ambassador in the Netherlands. He had done all that could be expected of him in diplomatic negotiations and in demanding the extradition of English dissidents in the Emperor's territories; and he had written the right letters to Henry and his counsellors, assuring Cromwell on 27 April 1540 'that neither you have a faithfuller servant than I am to you . . . nor a truer bedesman living in this world', and writing to Henry on 27 June that Cromwell, after Henry had 'advanced him from the dunghill to great honour', had shown the ingratitude of a 'traitor far passing Lucifer's'. But Henry's agents discovered that Dr Hillyard, the Papist who had escaped across the Tweed into Scotland, had written a letter to Pate's chaplain. The Council wrote to Pate and assured him that, despite Hillyard's letter, the King had complete confidence in his loyalty; but in December 1540 he was ordered to return home.[16]

Pate, who was at the Emperor's court at Namur, told his servants that he would be leaving for England early next morning. He ordered his groom to make sure that his horse was well shod for the journey, and told his page to bring the key of his strongbox to him in bed, as he wished to refer to a letter that was in the box. When the page came again, to wake him and light his fire as usual at 5 a.m., the room was empty. Pate had defected, together with his secretary and a servant. He had unlocked his strongbox, removed money and papers, and left during the night on his well-shod horse, crossing the Meuse at the back of the house on a boat which he had long since arranged should be kept available for him at all hours of day and night, and had ridden to the territory of the Bishop of Liège, who always refused demands for extradition. He travelled safely through Germany to Rome, and a few months later was created Bishop of Worcester by the Pope, though he was not able to enjoy the revenues of his see till he returned to England under Queen Mary.[17]

Wyatt, who had been recalled from his post as ambassador to the Emperor some months before, was sent to the Tower in January 1541 on a charge of high treason. He was accused of having been in secret contact with English traitors abroad while he was ambassador at Charles's court. Henry wrote to Sir John Wallop, his ambassador in Paris, that he was recalling him because he had decided to promote him to higher office, but made arrangements for him to be arrested at Sittingbourne on his journey home and brought secretly to a house in Southwark for interrogation. But Wallop discovered that he was to be arrested at Sittingbourne before he left Paris. Henry cancelled the plan to arrest him at Sittingbourne, and assured him that he had complete trust in him. Wallop returned to England, and Henry allowed him to come to London and had him examined by the Council without arresting him. He then decided not to arrest him, and appointed him Governor of Guisnes; and Wyatt, too, was pardoned without being brought to trial.[18]

But more executions were to come. Sir John Neville and other gentlemen and priests in Yorkshire were accused of plotting a new insurrection and of being in contact with the Scots; and Neville and two of his accomplices were hanged, drawn and quartered in June 1541. At the same time, Henry suddenly ordered that the Countess of Salisbury was to be executed. The old lady, who had heard nothing since the Act of Attainder had been passed more than two years before, seemed bewildered when they told her that she was to die, for she had never been accused of any specific offence. The only evidence against her was that she had forbidden her servants to read the English Bible, and had once been seen burning a letter.[19]

She was brought out to Tower Green, and beheaded on 27 May by a young and inexperienced headsman who failed to cut off her head at the first attempt, panicked, and hacked repeatedly at her head, neck and body. When Cardinal Pole heard of her death, he wrote that he would have grieved if she had died a natural death, but that he was proud to be the son of a martyr. The guilt of Herod, Nero and Caiaphas had been exceeded by that of this man who had slain a most innocent woman, related to him in blood, aged and feeble, and famous for her virtue – a woman whom he had once venerated as a mother.[20]

Lord Leonard Grey was tried in the Court of King's Bench on 25 June. He pleaded not guilty, and said that he had sent the ordnance and ammunition to Galway and Limerick, and had done all the other acts of which he was accused, with the authority of his Council in Ireland; and he said that he had documents which could prove this, but they had been taken from him when he was arrested, and he was unable to produce them at the trial. He later changed his plea to guilty, and was sentenced to be hanged, drawn and quartered. The clerk to the Privy Council, William Paget, wrote to Wriothesley, the Secretary of State, that the lords of the Council went to Henry next day, and urged him to pardon Lord Leonard; but the King 'would not hear of it, but slipped them on, saying that he appointed Cox to resort to the Lord Leonard for his ghostly father'. Henry respited the execution long enough for Cox to hear Grey's last confession, and commuted the sentence to death by the axe. Lord Leonard was beheaded on Tower Hill on 28 June.[21]

On the previous day, Lord Dacre of Hurstmonceux in Sussex, who was often called 'Lord Dacre of the South' to distinguish him from Lord Dacre of Gilsland in Cumberland, was sentenced to death, not for high treason, but for murder. Lord Dacre was a young daredevil of twenty-four. On the night of 30 April 1541, he and thirteen other young men from London, Kent and Sussex, some of them gentlemen and some yeomen, set out from Hurstmonceux on a poaching expedition in the park of a neighbouring gentleman at Hellingly. They divided into two parties, and went to the park by different ways. Lord Dacre and the seven other men in his party encountered three gamekeepers on the way; a fight ensued, and one of the gamekeepers was seriously wounded, and died two days later. Lord Dacre and his seven colleagues were charged with murder.*

The seven were tried in the Court of King's Bench in Westminster, and found guilty by the jury. They were all sentenced to be hanged. Lord Dacre was tried in the Court of the Lord High Steward by Audley and other peers. He pleaded not guilty, and denied that he had any intention of killing the gamekeeper; but the judges then held a meeting in the Star Chamber with several members of the King's Council, after which Dacre changed his plea to guilty, and was sentenced to be hanged. This was the only sentence which the court could impose; but Paget understood that Dacre had been led to believe that the death sentence would be commuted if he pleaded guilty. Dacre's youth, and his calm, dignified and repentant conduct at his trial, aroused much sympathy among the spectators and the public; and there were few countries in Christendom where a nobleman would be hanged for killing a gamekeeper.

Immediately the trial was over, the lords of the Council, who on the day before had failed to persuade Henry to pardon Lord Leonard Grey, went to him again to ask mercy for Lord Dacre; but Paget wrote to Wriothesley that their plea 'took no effect'. Henry ordered that Dacre and three of his companions should die, and pardoned the other four. The sentence was carried out at Tyburn on 28 June. When Dacre was on the gallows at 11 a.m., the execution was postponed for some reason – perhaps yet another plea for his life was made to Henry. The spectators thought that he had been pardoned, and rejoiced; but three hours later, he was hanged.[22]

As Dacre had been convicted of felony, his property was forfeited to the crown; but his grandfather had drafted his will with care. It provided that the

*The story, which has been widely accepted for four hundred years, that Lord Dacre was in the other party which did not encounter the gamekeepers, is incorrect. The report of the trial shows that the six members of the other party were not charged with murder.

land should be entailed in such a manner that, according to Henry's law officers, it was exempt from forfeiture. Henry did not agree. Wriothesley wrote that 'His Majesty thinketh the will of the grandfather should not be so perfect' as to prevent the King from taking it.[23] Rich was ordered to look more closely into the matter.

There were other executions in June 1541. Two archers of Henry's guard were hanged for robbing a merchant near the court. One of the workmen at Guisnes, the Welshman Morris ap Powell, tried to organise a strike among the labourers working on the fortifications. Henry ordered Wallop to punish him 'to the fearful example of all others'. Wallop hanged him, and wrote to Henry that, since then, the labourers had done their duty 'more quietly'.[24]

Sir Edmund Knyvett was luckier. He had been involved in a quarrel with his opponent at tennis in the tennis court at Hampton Court; they had drawn their swords, and he had wounded the other player. Duels between courtiers were commonplace occurences at François I's court; but Henry was determined to prevent them in England, and an Act of Parliament had been passed which enacted that anyone who drew his sword within the precincts of the court should lose his right hand. Knyvett was tried in the Court of King's Bench and sentenced to undergo this penalty; but when the sentence was about to be carried out, when the King's master cook was ready with the knife, 'the Sergeant of the Scullery with his mallet, the irons laid in the fire to have seared him, and the King's master surgeon with searing cloth ready', Henry sent Sir Richard Long to postpone the execution till after dinner, and then pardoned Sir Edmund Knyvett; but he issued a proclamation that if a similar case occurred in future, the sentence would be carried out.[25]

The situation was improving a little in the lawless parts of the realm. Wales was more orderly since the Act of 1536, and an effort had been made, not wholly successfully, to enforce law and order in Tynedale and Redesdale. Affairs in Ireland were still unsatisfactory. Most of the country was unsubdued; O'Neill, in Ulster, was especially troublesome. There were constant reports that James V was planning to invade Ireland, or at least send aid to the Ulster rebels. Papal Nuncios and less eminent agents travelled from Rome to Ireland through Scotland with James's assistance, and Irish priests and monks made the journey the other way to Rome. Two of them were unlucky enough to be in a ship which, on the voyage from Scotland to France, was forced by storms to enter the port of Newcastle. They were identified, arrested, and ultimately executed by Henry's officers.[26]

Henry was worried about Gerald Fitzgerald, whom he and his agents called 'young Gerald', though the Pope recognised him as the eleventh Earl of Kildare. He was aged twelve when Henry executed his father in 1537. He escaped to France, but as Henry asked François to extradite him, he took refuge in the Bishop of Liège's territories. In 1541, when Wallop was ambassador in France, he tried to bribe a Breton in young Gerald's household to kidnap him and bring him to Ireland; but the Breton told Wallop's agent that 'next God he loved the child above all men', and would not betray him for £20,000.[27]

Henry decided to take the new title of 'King of Ireland.' For 370 years, the Kings of England had held the title of 'Lord of Ireland'; but antiquarians now produced documents which proved that the Kings of Britain since before the coming of the Romans had been entitled to be called Kings of Ireland. On 19 June 1541, the Irish Parliament unanimously proclaimed Henry King of Ireland, and the heralds at Greenwich proclaimed him by this title on 7 July. But Henry was not satisfied. He thought that it was derogatory to his honour and to his hereditary claim to Ireland that he should accept a title which had been offered to him by the Irish Parliament; and he insisted that there should be verbal changes in the title to make it clear that it was not a Parliamentary one. It was finally promulgated under the Great Seal in the form in which Henry himself had drafted it: 'Henry VIII, by the grace of God King of England, France and Ireland, Defender of the Faith, and in earth, immediately under Christ, Supreme Head of the Churches of England and Ireland'.[28]

The removal of Lord Leonard Grey had not ended the bickerings in the Lord Deputy's Council. Grey's successor, Sir Anthony St Leger, was denounced in his turn. Henry was informed that St Leger had said, one day at dinner, that the King's father had no just title to the crown till he married King Edward's daughter. St Leger said that he had been misquoted, for he had said that Henry VII's title was not perfect till he married Elizabeth of York, because some of his advisers had urged him to claim the throne by right of conquest; 'but now, thanked be the Lord, all titles be in the King our master'. Henry was satisfied with this explanation.[29]

Henry had reason to be satisfied with St Leger, for he proved to be the most successful Deputy that Henry had sent to Dublin. In October 1541, he invaded O'Neill's lands, and ravaged them for twenty-two days. He raided them again next month, and by Christmas O'Neill had submitted, and delivered his son as a hostage for his good behaviour. Henry was reluctantly persuaded that, in view of the expense involved in maintaining a large army in Ireland and holding down the Irish by force, it would be wiser not to punish O'Neill and other rebels as they deserved, but to win them over by confirming them in the possession of their hereditary lands and by granting them English peerages,* on condition that they abandoned their traditional Irish 'vile and savage life'. He offered to create them Earls if they were prepared to come to his court, for Earls were always created by the King in person; if they did not wish to leave Ireland, he would create them Viscounts or Barons, and send them the letters patent. O'Neill came to England, and

*'English' peerages, as opposed to their Gaelic Irish titles, though they were later called 'Irish peerages' by the English.

Henry created him Earl of Tyrone, after he had agreed to abandon his Irish name and assume whatever name Henry gave him, to wear English dress and speak English, and to put his lands under tillage.[30]

The Irish chiefs were happy with the arrangement. When O'Neill and three others came to Hampton Court, they knelt to Henry and remained on their knees all the time that Henry and his interpreter were speaking to them.[31]

Heretics were burned in London and Salisbury. In January 1541, Henry issued a commission to Bonner, the Bishop of London, and to Sir Richard Gresham, the Lord Mayor, to launch a new drive against sacramentaries under the Act of the Six Articles. Bonner now began to establish the reputation of a cruel persecutor of Protestants which has remained with him for four centuries. He sat in the Guildhall with the Lord Mayor and other officers of the city, dealing not only with those guilty of the capital offence of denying the Six Articles, but with many cases in several London parishes of people who had refused to light a candle at Candlemas, or had shown disrespect for one of the other ceremonies of the Church. One of those brought before Bonner was Richard Mekins, a boy of fifteen; he had denied the Real Presence, and had also praised Barnes, not realising that Barnes had burned sacramentaries like himself. He suffered from neglect and hunger in prison, for his parents were afraid to send him any relief or to visit him there. According to John Foxe, when he was tried at the Guildhall, Bonner had to send the jury back three times before they could be induced to bring in a verdict of guilty; but at the stake, Mekins said that Bonner had been kind to him, and he recanted his heresy. Under the Act of the Six Articles, this could not save him, and he was burned.[32]

Another youth, John Collins, lived across the river in Southwark, and was therefore in Gardiner's diocese of Winchester, which included the whole of Surrey and the south bank of the river and extended half-way across London Bridge. Collins objected to the idolatrous worship of the figure of Christ on a crucifix which hung in a chapel in the port of London; the chapel was frequented by Spanish sailors who went there to give thanks for their safe arrival in London. Collins shot an arrow into the foot of the figure on the crucifix, and called on the crucifix to punish him if it had any power to do so. Many people said that Collins was mad; but a recent Act of Parliament had enacted that insanity should no longer be a defence to a charge of heresy or high treason, and Collins was burned.[33]

The English Bible which Cromwell had promulgated was still legal, and the order that it should be placed in the churches was still in force; but after Cromwell's downfall and Bonner's enforcement of the Six Articles in London, people hesitated to read the Bible, and many parsons removed it from their churches. Then, just when all observed at home and abroad believed that Henry had definitely embarked on an anti-Protestant course, he issued in May 1541 a proclamation in which he reprimanded those parish priests who, in defiance of the law, had no Bibles in their churches. He stated that he had authorised the publication of the English Bible so that the people would 'learn thereby to observe God's commandments, and to obey their sovereign lord and high powers, and to exercise godly charity, and to use themselves according to their vocations in a pure and sincere Christian life, without murmur or grudging'; but they must read it 'humbly, meekly, reverently and obediently', not 'with loud and high voices', nor should they 'presume to take upon them any common disputation, argument, or exposition of the mysteries therein contained'.[34]

Six weeks later, the Council sent a circular letter to JPs. Apart from urging them to administer justice fairly and to enforce the laws against vagabonds, which had not been applied with sufficient vigour, the circular stressed the need for them to root out secret Papists, who were 'the most cankered and venemous worms' in the commonwealth, enemies to God, and traitors. The JPs were warned that Henry hoped that this 'gentle admonition' would cause them to do their duty; but if not, 'the next advice shall be of so sharp a sort as shall bring with it a just punishment of those that shall be found offenders in this behalf'.[35]

On 30 June 1541, Henry set out on the journey to Yorkshire which he had promised to make four years before. Unlike his predecessors and other Kings of his time, he travelled very little. The mediaeval Kings of England travelled continually throughout their realm; Henry VII had been to York and to Exeter. François I moved between Amiens, Paris, Lyons and the castles on the Loire. Charles V went from Burgos and Valladolid to Madrid, Toledo and Granada, from Brussels to Ghent and Bruges, from Regensburg to Vienna, Mantua and Palermo. But after reigning for thirty-three years, Henry VIII had set foot in only eighteen of the forty counties of England. He had three times crossed to Calais, but had never visited Wales or Ireland. Since his visit to Nottingham in 1511, he had never been north of Grafton or west of Bristol.

Travelling was not easy in sixteenth-century England. The roads were less adequate than those in France, Spain and the Netherlands; they had been deteriorating ever since the Romans built them, and were worse than they had been for a thousand years, or than they would ever be again after the improvements introduced in the seventeenth century. But the hardships of travel would not have deterred Henry when he was young and fit enough to chase stags for thirty miles. This was not the reason why he never went more than a hundred and twenty miles from London. It was because he was determined to remain in close contact with political events at home and abroad; and even with couriers riding to him in post, he felt out of touch if he was far off. He had always played a more active part in policy decisions than François I; and he was much more reluctant than Charles V to appoint a Regent to act for him in his absence.

With no war in Europe, and all the traitors put to death – Lord Lisle alone remained in the Tower, uncertain of his fate – Henry felt safe enough, at last, to go to Yorkshire in the summer of 1541. He took steps to see that he was well protected during his visit to the rebel areas of 1536: he was accompanied by five thousand gentlemen, servants and soldiers.[36] Queen Katherine, his daughter Mary, and most of his counsellors and secretaries went with him, though some remained in London with Audley and Cranmer. He proposed to go from one of his manors to another, and to stay with prominent courtiers and local gentlemen, in most cases not travelling more than ten or fifteen miles a day, and remaining two or three days in each place where he stopped, to hunt, and to meet the local gentlemen.

Even at this slow rate of progress, he expected to be in Lincoln within three weeks; but he was held up by the heavy rains. After going from Greenwich, by Enfield, St Albans and Dunstable, to Ampthill, he remained there for a fortnight because of the reports of the floods further north. He then went from Ampthill to Grafton, Northampton, and the suppressed abbey at Pipewell. While he was at Northampton, an envoy arrived from James V, suggesting that as Henry was going to York, James might meet him there. Henry sent a favourable reply to the proposal from Pipewell before moving on to the Bishop of Lincoln's charming little manor house at Liddington in Rutlandshire.[37]

At Liddington, the Queen committed the first of several indiscretions of which she was guilty during the journey to the north. Looking out of the window of her room, she saw her former lover, Thomas Culpepper, walking in the garden, and wrote him a note: 'Master Culpepper, I heartily recommend me unto you . . . I never longed so much for thing as I do to see you and to speak with you. . . . It makes my heart to die to think what fortune I have that I cannot be always in your company. . . . Come when my Lady Rochford is here, for that I shall be best at leisure to be at your commandment. . . . Yours as long as life endures, Katherine'.[38] She was foolish to write this letter, and Culpepper was foolish not to burn it.

Henry moved on to Collyweston and to the Duke of Suffolk's house at Gainsthorpe near Bourne. From Gainsthorpe, he went to Sleaford, and on 9 August entered Lincoln. He was met on the heights of Temple Brewer by the Mayor and the city dignitaries, the clergy, and the gentlemen of Lincolnshire; and after Henry and Katherine had dined, they entered a tent, where they changed out of their riding clothes of green and crimson velvet into robes of cloth-of-gold and silver, before entering the city in state, with the gentlemen of Henry's guard leading the way, then Lord Hastings bearing the sword of state, walking immediately in front of Henry, who rode on a great horse which had been imported from Flanders. Sir Anthony Browne, the Master of the Horse, walked beside him holding the horse by the bridle. The Earl of Rutland rode behind the King, followed by the Queen and her ladies on their smaller English horses, and the Lady Mary, and the rest of the lords and ladies. They went to Mass in the cathedral, where Longland officiated, before going to their lodgings. Here Katherine was even more indiscreet. She met Culpepper in Lady Rochford's room in the middle of the night, while Henry was sleeping off the effects of his usual large supper.[39]

Henry stayed for three days in Lincoln, and then went north to Gainsborough, where he stayed with Sir William Parr. According to local tradition, he met Parr's sister, Katherine Parr, at Gainsborough; but there is no contemporary record of her having come to Gainsborough from her home at Snape Hall in Yorkshire, where she lived with her husband, Lord Latimer. Henry went from Gainsborough to Scrooby in Nottinghamshire, and on 18 August entered Yorkshire on the road to Hatfield. He was met on the county boundary by the Archbishop of York with the nobles, clergy and gentlemen of Yorkshire with their tenants and servants – about five thousand people – who knelt to him and presented him with a petition asking for his clemency. 'We, your humble subjects, the inhabitants of this Your Grace's county of York . . . confess that we wretches, for lack of grace and of sincere and pure knowledge of the verity of God's word . . . have most grievously, heinously and wantonly offended Your Majesty . . . in the unnatural, most odious and detestable offences of outrageous disobedience and traitorous rebellion'. They thanked him for pardoning their rebellion, and assured him that they would always pray for him, for Queen Katherine, and for Prince Edward.[40]

Henry graciously accepted their homage, and invited all the local gentlemen to join him in a great hunt in Hatfield Close. Marillac, who had followed Henry on his progress, thought it was a strange kind of hunt. Two hundred stags were rounded up by the huntsmen into an enclosure, and were then killed with arrows shot at them by gentlemen and servants from boats on a lake, while at the same time other hunters were killing the swans, pike and carp in the lake. Next day, hundreds of stags were killed in a similar way a few miles away in the park. Henry distributed the dead animals and fish among the local gentry, who dined on them and praised the King.[41]

At Pontefract, Henry received a letter from James accepting his invitation to meet him in York. He waited for a month before going to York, while preparations were made for his ceremonial entry into the city and for the visit of the King of Scots. In the meantime, he stayed at the Archbishop of York's palace at Cawood, where Wolsey had been arrested, and at the Earl of Northumberland's house at Wressel near Howden, and then went to Leconfield in the East Riding, a few miles from Beverley and in the district where the Pilgrimage of Grace had first begun. At Hull, he thanked the Mayor and citizens for their loyalty during the rebellion. He entered York on 18 September with the same ceremony that had been used at his entry into Lincoln. At both Pontefract and York, Katherine met Culpepper in Lady Rochford's room after Henry had retired to bed.[42]

Some twelve or fifteen hundred labourers were working day and night to prepare the house where James V would stay; but James did not come. When François heard from Marillac that James was expected at York, he raised the matter with Cardinal Beaton, who was visiting him at Macon. Beaton assured him that James would not meet Henry without first consulting François, and the bishops on James's Council persuaded him not to go to York. Henry heard nothing from James, but received news from Lord Wharton at Carlisle that the Scots had made an inroad across the Border, advancing sixteen miles into England, burning John à Musgrave's house, and killing seven of the Fenwicks. He wrote an angry letter of protest to James.[43]

Henry stayed at York for nine days, and then began the journey home. He went again to Hull, where he drafted a plan for new bulwarks to be built for the defence of the harbour, and sent an order to Cranmer to suppress any shrine or image in cathedrals or elsewhere to which idolatrous worship was still being paid, and to enforce the injunctions which forbade candles to be placed anywhere in churches except before the Sacrament. This order, which was another unexpected move in favour of the Protestants, is generally thought to have been drafted by Cranmer. This may well be so; but Henry had not seen Cranmer for more than three months when he issued the order. It obviously did not need any pressure from Cranmer to persuade Henry in Yorkshire to make a move to counterbalance the recent pro-Catholic trend in religious policy.[44]

On 5 October, Henry crossed the Humber to the Lincolnshire shore and stayed at the suppressed abbey at Thornton, before travelling south. He was eager to get home before the winter weather set in, and it took him only seventeen days to go by Kettleby, Bishop's Norton, Ingoldby, Sleaford, Collyweston, Fotheringhay, Higham Ferrers, Wollington and Ampthill to Windsor. He arrived at Hampton Court on 29 October.[45] He had, as usual, remained in close touch, throughout his visit to the north, with every detail of government. At Kettleby on 10 October he heard that some men had been caught trying to steal valuables from Windsor Castle, and had been committed to the Marshalsea, the King's Bench and Newgate prisons. He was displeased, and ordered his counsellors in London to remove the thieves from these prisons and transfer them to the Tower; for if they were imprisoned in the usual prisons for thieves, it would suggest that robbing the King was no more serious an offence than robbing one of his meanest subjects.[46]

Shortly before his return, Cranmer had been informed by John Lassels, who had been in trouble as a Protestant heretic some months before, that Lassels's sister Mary had told him that when she was in the old Duchess of Norfolk's household at Horsham, Katherine Howard had fornicated with

Derham, Culpepper and Mannox. Cranmer and the other counsellors hardly dared to tell Henry; but four days after Henry's return, Cranmer slipped a piece of paper into his hand after Mass on All Souls' Day, informing him of the Queen's misconduct before her marriage.

There is no doubt that Henry was shaken and hurt, though the stories of his uncontrollable rages and hysterical behaviour come only from the unreliable Marillac. In fact, his conduct was perfectly rational, though typically unforgiving and savage. He immediately ordered that further inquiries should be made, and Mannox, as well as Mary Lassels and other gentlewomen and servants in the Duchess of Norfolk's household were examined during the next three days. Henry completely dissembled his feelings while these inquiries were going on; Marillac, who saw him with the ladies at Hampton Court, had never seen him so gay and happy. By 5 November, if not before, Henry was convinced of Katherine's guilt. He spent that morning in consultation with his Council, and after dinner left Hampton Court by barge and went to Whitehall, having as usual decided to be absent while the unpleasant work was done.

As soon as he had left, Cranmer confronted the Queen, and by a show of sympathy, which may not have been entirely feigned, extorted a confession from her. By 10 November, Chapuys had found out what was happening, though Marillac on the 11th was still in the dark and putting forward various inaccurate explanations for the excitement at court. On 12 November, the Council informed the ambassadors abroad that the Queen had been guilty of incontinence before her marriage, and in view of the fact that she had employed Derham in her service after she became Queen, there were strong grounds for suspicion that she had been guilty of adultery since the marriage.[47]

When Marillac at last found out the truth, he sent sensational reports to François and Montmorency of Henry raging through the palace with a drawn sword searching for Katherine in order to kill her, and expatiating on the dreadful tortures which he would inflict on her. In view of Marillac's unreliability and the inaccuracy of the information which he was sending a few days earlier, we can disregard these stories. But there is no reason to doubt the truth of the account which the Council wrote to the ambassadors abroad on 12 November, that Henry refused to believe that Katherine was guilty until it was clearly proved, but that then 'his heart was so pierced with pensiveness, that long it was before His Majesty could speak and utter the sorrow of his heart unto us, and finally with plenty of tears, which was strange in his courage, opened the same'. He had not recovered his composure a fortnight later; on 26 November, Dudley wrote to the Earl of Rutland that the King was 'not a little troubled with this great affair'.[48]

Katherine was sent as a prisoner to Syon House. Derham and Culpepper were tried at the Guildhall in London on 1 December on a charge of high treason for having committed adultery with the Queen. The indictment stated 'that Katherine, Queen of England, formerly called Katherine Howard, late of Lambeth, Surrey, led an abominable, base, carnal, voluptuous and vicious life like a common harlot with divers persons', including Derham, but that on 20 and 24 May 1540 and at other times she 'led the King by word and gesture to love her and (he believing her to be pure and chaste and free from other matrimonial yoke) arrogantly coupled herself with him in marriage'. She had held illicit meetings with Culpepper at Pontefract on 29 August 1541 and elsewhere 'to invite the said Culpepper to have carnal intercourse with her, and insinuated to him that she loved him above the King and all others; and similarly the said Culpepper incited the Queen'.[49]

Derham and Culpepper both pleaded Not Guilty. Derham argued that he was Katherine's lawful husband on account of the precontract. They later changed their pleas to Guilty, and were sentenced to be hanged, drawn and quartered. Henry commuted the sentence on Culpepper to beheading, but insisted that Derham suffer the full penalty, though by any standard his guilt was less than Culpepper's; for not only had he been precontracted to Katherine, but the evidence that he had committed adultery with her after her marriage to Henry was far less strong in his case than in Culpepper's. On 6 December, Cranmer, Wriothesley and other counsellors wrote to Sir Anthony Browne and Sadler, who were with the King, that 'Derham maketh humble suit for the remission of some part of the extremity of his judgement, wherein we require you to know His Grace's pleasure'. Sadler replied that Henry wanted Derham's execution to be postponed so that he could be examined again and persuaded to incriminate Katherine's other lovers; but 'touching the remission of the extremity of Derham's judgement, the King's Majesty thinketh he hath deserved no such mercy at his hand, and therefore hath determined that he shall suffer the whole execution'.[50]

On 22 December, seven women and four men were tried at Westminster on a charge of misprision of treason; they included Norfolk's brother Lord William Howard and his wife, and Norfolk's sister Lady Bridgewater. The others were ladies and gentlemen in the Duchess of Norfolk's household. Their offence was that, knowing that Katherine, Queen of England, had led an evil and carnal life with Derham and others, and that the King intended to marry her, and that, after her marriage, the Queen had retained Derham in her service, they had traitorously concealed this information. Ten of the eleven pleaded Guilty, and the eleventh was found guilty by the jury. They were all sentenced to imprisonment for life with the forfeiture of their goods.[51]

The case of the Duchess of Norfolk was more difficult. When she heard that Derham had been arrested, she opened his coffers and destroyed some documents; but Norfolk arrived before she had finished, and he seized the remaining papers, arrested her and denounced her to Henry. As there was nothing incriminating against Derham in the letters that Norfolk seized, the judges did not think that there was sufficient evidence to convict the Duchess of misprision of treason. Henry thought differently. Browne and Sadler wrote to the Council that the King believed that if the judges considered the matter fairly, they would find that the fact that the Duchess had destroyed a document proved that the document contained treason; for he did not think that the judges 'have a better ground to make Derham's case treason, and to presume that his coming again to the Queen's service was to an ill intent of the renovation of his former naughty life, than they have, in this case, to presume that the breaking of the coffers was to th'intent to conceal letters of treason'.[52]

In view of the judges' doubts, the Duchess was not brought to trial. When Parliament met in January 1542, she was sentenced to life imprisonment for misprision of treason by the same Act of Attainder which pronounced that the Queen and Lady Rochford were guilty of high treason and should suffer death by burning or otherwise according to the King's pleasure. The royal consent to the bill was given by Audley on Henry's behalf, in order to spare him from the painful duty of giving it in person. Katherine and Lady Rochford were beheaded on 13 February on Tower Green. Before they died, they both made short speeches, saying that they had been justly punished, and urging the people to obey the King in all things.[53]

Henry decided to pardon the Duchess of Norfolk and the others who had been convicted of misprision of treason, but not to tell them this too soon.[54] They were all released within nine months.

It was the Protestant, John Lassels, and Cranmer who had exposed Katherine Howard, and Norfolk's brother, sister and stepmother had been sentenced to imprisonment for life; but Henry did not destroy Norfolk, and if the downfall of Katherine Howard had any effect on Henry's religious policy, it was the opposite of what the Protestants had hoped. Norfolk wrote to Henry condemning 'mine ungracious mother-in-law [stepmother], mine unhappy brother and his wife, with my lewd sister of Bridgewater', and pointed out that it was he who had caught and denounced the Duchess. He spent a few weeks on his estates in Norfolk, and then returned to court. Marillac thought that this was a sign that Henry was about to go to war, for Norfolk was his best general.[55]

Just as the execution of Anne Boleyn led, not to the Catholic reaction that everyone expected, but to a move towards Lutheranism, so now, within a month of the execution of Katherine Howard, Henry issued a proclamation against Protestant books. All English translations of the Bible, except the Great Bible of 1539, including 'Matthew's Bible', were banned, along with all the works of Tyndale, Coverdale, Frith, Wycliffe, Luther and Calvin, and other Protestant tracts. Anyone possessing a copy was to hand it in within forty days to his master or to the Sheriff or Bishop's officer to be publicly burned. This was followed in May 1542 by injunctions from Bonner which placed more restrictions on preaching, and prohibited anyone from expounding a heresy under pretence of refuting it, unless he was authorised to do so by the King or his bishop.[56]

After a few weeks, Henry threw off his grief, and consoled himself as usual with banquets, parties, and the company of ladies. The ladies were invited to stay the night, and Henry himself went round from room to room to make sure that everything was prepared for them. On 29 January, a few days before the Bill of Attainder against Katherine was introduced in Parliament, Henry gave a supper party at Whitehall. He sat among the guests at a table with twenty-six ladies and a few gentlemen, while thirty-five ladies and gentlemen sat at another table. The courtiers, seeing him so gay and attentive to the ladies, wondered whether he was planning to marry one of them. Would it be Lord Cobham's sister? Chapuys thought that she was a pretty young creature, who was bright enough to come to grief like the others if she were to try. Would it be Sir Anthony Browne's niece? Or would it be Anne Basset? For was it not because of her that Henry had just released and pardoned her stepfather, Lord Lisle, after he had spent twenty months in the Tower? Lisle was old, ill, and a broken man, and died a few days after his release. Lady Lisle had gone mad during his imprisonment.[57]

A woman in London spoke too loudly. 'What a man is the King', she said, 'how many wives will he have?' She was arrested, and examined; but Henry ordered that she was to be discharged with a warning.[58]

26

SOLWAY MOSS

IN the summer of 1541, François' ambassador in Constantinople, Rincón, who by birth was a Spaniard and Charles's subject, travelled back to Constantinople after a visit to François' court. He was stopped near Cremona by Charles's soldiers, his papers were seized, and he was never heard of again. François asserted that he had been murdered on Charles's orders. Charles denied this, and claimed that the documents which had been taken from Rincón proved that François was plotting against Charles with the enemy of Christendom, the Turk.

François made it clear that he intended to make the assassination of Rincón a *casus belli*. He postponed the beginning of hostilities and the declaration of war for nearly a year, but both he and Charles wasted no time in wooing Henry. François proposed that his son, the Duke of Orleans, should marry Mary, and offered to take her without her being legitimised by Act of Parliament, after Norfolk had told Marillac, in the strictest confidence, that Henry was intending to nominate her to succeed to the crown in default of Prince Edward and his issue. François also proposed that, instead of giving the usual dowry with Mary, Henry should release the Kings of France from the liability to pay the pensions which they owed the Kings of England under the old treaties; but Henry vehemently rejected this proposal. François then reduced his terms, and offered to take Mary without a dowry if he were released from all the arrears which were due on the pensions. Henry turned down this suggestion too, because the arrears now amounted to two million crowns, and no woman in Christendom had ever been thought to be worth even one million crowns by way of dowry.[1]

Henry thought that Charles might make a better offer. On 18 November 1541 – a fortnight after the exposure of Katherine Howard, when Marillac imagined that Henry was raging through the palace in an insane fury with a drawn sword – he was in fact sending the Earl of Southampton to tell Chapuys that François had made an unsatisfactory offer of a marriage alliance with Mary, and hinting that Charles might wish to make a more acceptable proposal. Chapuys held talks with some of Henry's counsellors, and found that Henry was as usual unwilling to commit himself in a hurry; but by May 1542, Charles had proposed, not a marriage, but a defensive and offensive military alliance against France.[2]

Throughout the summer, Chapuys and Marillac watched each other. Chapuys was too ill to travel regularly between his house in London and the court, or to meet Henry's ministers secretly, as he had once met Cromwell, in a half-built house in the city. He was taken to Hampton Court by barge, and remained there for several weeks, in a suite of rooms which was allotted to him, while he negotiated with Gardiner, Tunstal and other counsellors. Marillac noticed this, and drew the obvious conclusion that important negotiations were in progress. He did not know that one of his secretaries was a spy of Chapuys, and that Chapuys had succeeded in breaking the code in which he communicated with François and Montmorency.[3]

Henry had the satisfaction not only of being wooed again by Charles, but of hearing Chapuys adopt a very different tone than he had done in the days when he was championing Catherine of Aragon. Chapuys told Gardiner that he knew that Henry did not need to rely on the friendship of either Charles or François, but that a Prince who was so endowed by God with riches and wisdom as Henry was, should use these gifts for the pacification of Christendom, and thus win renown in this world and God's reward in the next; if Henry joined with the Emperor, who regarded him as a father, he would be called the father of Christendom. Chapuys suggested that if Charles and Henry went to war with François, Henry could acquire Boulogne, Ardres, Montreuil and Thérouanne, while Charles would see that the Duke of Savoy regained his territories.[4]

The offer tempted Henry, but there were difficulties about making a military alliance with Charles. There was the question of financial aid to be discussed; and the religious differences created obstacles. If the treaty contained the usual clauses that it was to take effect subject to both parties' engagements in their treaties with other Princes and potentates, did the insertion of the word 'potentate' include the Bishop of Rome, and did Charles's engagements to the Pope involve obligations which would prejudice Henry? And should Henry be described, in the treaty, as Supreme Head of the Church of England along with his other titles, when Charles did not recognise him as Supreme Head, and would be compromised with the Pope if he did so?

In June, François made a military alliance against Charles with Gustavus Vasa of Sweden and Henry's one-time brother-in-law, the Duke of Cleves. He invited Henry to join the alliance, but Henry refused, and spoke disparagingly to Marillac about 'that poor little King of Sweden', who, like James V, was too poor to be able to give any effective help to François in a war.[5] But Henry was making every difficulty which he could in the negotiations with Charles. He blamed Charles for not having allowed him to conquer France when François was a prisoner after Pavia. Chapuys admitted that Charles had made an error of judgment here, and he agreed with everything that Henry said; for he believed, as he wrote to Granvelle, that it was absolutely essential for the Emperor to have Henry on his side in the forthcoming war. On 29 June, he complained that no progress whatever had been made during the months of negotiations; but the same day he persuaded Henry to make a secret treaty by which Henry and Charles agreed that they would not make a treaty with any other power before October, and that in the meantime Henry would send Thirlby, the Bishop of Westminster, to Spain to negotiate with Charles in person about the terms of the alliance. But Chapuys was still anxious. He wrote to Mary of Hungary and urged her to lift the restrictions which she had imposed on the export of goods from the Netherlands by English merchants, as a unilateral act, without waiting until Henry agreed to grant the relief which she was demanding for the Flemish merchants in London; and she told him that she had already done so.[6]

It was a term of the agreement that it should be kept absolutely secret. When Marillac asked Henry if he was negotiating an alliance with Charles, Henry denied it. Marillac asked why, in that case, was Chapuys spending so much time at Hampton Court? Henry said that they were negotiating only about the commercial restrictions which had been imposed on English and Flemish merchants in the Netherlands and in England.[7]

On 12 July 1542, François declared war on Charles, and sent his armies to invade the Netherlands and attack Perpignan. Almost at the same time, the Scots resumed their raids across the Border. Henry saw the outbreak of war in Europe, and the prospect of a military alliance with the Emperor, primarily as an opportunity to dominate Scotland, to destroy French influence there, and to force James V to abandon his hostile policy. He ordered musters throughout all the northern counties of England, and gave the maximum publicity to his military preparations. James expressed a wish for a peaceful solution, and sent envoys to London to negotiate. Henry ordered the Wardens of the Marches to make a retaliatory raid into Scotland, but, having done so, to take no further action while he was negotiating with the Scottish envoys at Windsor. Next day, he changed his mind, and sent new orders to the Earl of Rutland in the north; he was willing to forbear taking this 'last revenge' on the Scots if the scores between them were more or less equal.[8]

Meanwhile François' armies and the Duke of Cleves had invaded Luxemburg and the Netherlands. Mary of Hungary asked Henry to send her help at once; but Henry had no intention of doing this until Charles had agreed to the treaty of alliance, though Chapuys reminded him that 'while the Romans deliberate, Saguntum falls'. Chapuys said that when Henry had refused aid against the Turks, his excuse had been that Hungary was too far away; but what excuse could he give now for not helping the Netherlands? Henry first said that he had heard that the French had retreated from the Netherlands. Then he blamed Charles for neglecting the defences of his territories and allowing the French to invade them.[9]

Henry was moving towards his third war with France. In the summer of 1542, French warships and privateers were robbing and capturing English fishermen in the Channel. In England, there was an outburst of anti-French hatred. The people called the French King 'the Turk'. When they found a Frenchman alone, they attacked him; at Dover, fifteen French sailors from Dieppe were imprisoned and beaten up. In France, the people defied Henry to do his worst, and sang:

Weh! que sait-il faire,
Le Roi d'Angleterre?[10]

But Henry was still keeping his options open. As Charles was haggling with Thirlby in Spain about the terms of the alliance, Henry, after waiting till October to comply with the terms of his agreement with Chapuys, offered François an alliance against Charles. He told Marillac that if François would cede him Ardres, Tournehem and Montreuil as a pledge for the payment of the pensions and the arrears due to him, he would make an alliance with him against Charles; and if the two Kings were thus knit together, and united with some of the German Princes, they could do great things for Christendom.[11]

In the middle of August, James V recalled his envoys from Windsor, and Henry ordered the gentlemen in the North and their tenants and servants to be ready to march against the Scots at one hour's notice. Sir Robert Bowes and Angus decided to retaliate for the Scottish raids by a raid into Teviotdale, and on 24 August crossed the Border between Kelso and Jedburgh and burned several farms and hamlets. On their homeward journey, they were attacked by 2,000 Scots, and Bowes and several gentlemen were taken prisoner, though Angus and Sir George Douglas escaped into England. It was a blow to Henry's pride, as well as weakening his bargaining position; but he was determined to retrieve the situation. He ordered his army to assemble at Newcastle under Norfolk's command, and invade Scotland; they were to march forward from Newcastle on 29 September. But the Scots then offered to reopen negotiations, and Henry agreed that Norfolk, Southampton and Tunstal should meet the Scottish envoys at York on 18 September. The date for the army's advance from Newcastle was postponed by a week to 6 October; and Henry ordered that the negotiations at York were to be broken off if the Scots had not accepted his terms by 29 September.[12]

Henry's terms to the Scots were that they should release Bowes and his fellow-prisoners without ransom, though he agreed that if the Scots insisted, a reasonale ransom might be paid; that the Scots should agree to a new treaty for the extradition of traitors, which should include churchmen; that James should come on a state visit to Henry's court; and that the Scots should deliver hostages of noble rank till the terms of the treaty had been carried out. The Scots agreed to all these demands, except that James would not agree to go further south than York to meet Henry. The English replied that as James had failed to come to York in 1541, Henry would not go there again. James then agreed to go as far as Huntingdon for the meeting, but that, as his Queen was pregnant, he could not meet Henry before 15 January. Henry insisted that James should agree to meet him at any place that he named, and that the meeting could not be postponed till January. On this point, the talks broke down, and both sides prepared for war.[13]

But Norfolk was not ready to advance, for the ships bringing victuals and beer from London had not arrived at Newcastle. Ever since the mutiny at Fuentarrabia in 1512, all English generals had been conscious that it was essential that there should be an adequate supply of beer for the soldiers; so Norfolk put back the date for the assembly of the army at Newcastle from 1 October to the 7th, and then to 11 October. He promised Henry that he would launch the biggest invasion of Scotland that had been seen for a hundred years; but he was worried, because when the ships from London at last reached Newcastle on 7 October, he realised that there would only be enough beer for six days, even if he rationed the men to two drinks a day, which he feared might cause trouble.[14]

He led his army across the Border at Berwick on 22 October, and burned Eccles, Kelso and twenty villages; but he had miscalculated about the beer, which had almost run out after four days, so he retreated into England. He wrote an apologetic report to Henry, who accepted his explanation, though he regretted that so powerful an army had accomplished so little. The Scots claimed a victory. Beaton wrote to the Pope that 40,000 Englishmen had advanced only two miles into Scotland when they heard that James was leading his army against them, whereupon they fled back into England. James took personal command of his army, and prepared to invade the Western Marches.[15]

On 24 November, 18,000 Scots crossed the Border near Gretna, and burned some houses along the River Esk. When they reached the marshy ground of Solway Moss, less than a mile into England, they were attacked by 3,000 English soldiers and fled in confusion. Only 7 Englishmen and 20 Scots were killed in the battle, but more Scots were drowned in their flight. The English captured 1,200 prisoners, including two Earls, five Lords, and 500 lairds and gentlemen, as well as 3,000 horses, 30 standards, 20 cannons, 120 handguns, and 4 cartloads of spears. John Knox and the later Scottish Protestant writers attributed the defeat to the incompetence of James's favourite, Oliver Sinclair, to whom he had entrusted the command of the army; the Catholics suspected that Lord Maxwell, another of the Scottish commanders, was a Protestant sympathiser and a traitor who deliberately engineered the defeat. It was a disaster for the Scots, and completely retrieved the situation for Henry, just when things seemed to be going wrong.[16]

James, who had watched the rout of his army from a hilltop in Scotland six miles away, had another bitter disappointment a fortnight later, when his Queen gave birth to a daughter, not a son; and on 14 December he died, leaving the baby Princess to succeed to the crown as Mary, Queen of Scots, when she was six days old.

Henry made the most of his luck, and handled the situation, at least in the early stages, with skill. He ordered that his twenty eminent Scottish prisoners-of-war should be brought to London, and that they should not be allowed to speak to each other on the way. When they rode into London on the afternoon of 19 December, they were sent to the Tower; but after being imprisoned there for barely thirty-six hours, they were brought before the King's Council at 8 a.m. on 21 December, and released on parole, being placed in the custody of various noblemen and gentlemen of suitable rank at their London houses. On St John's Day they were taken to Hampton Court, and spent three days at Henry's court during the Christmas festivities. Henry treated them with the greatest courtesy, and invited them to walk immediately in front of him when he went to Mass. After being entertained at a banquet in the city by the Lord Mayor on 31 December, they left London on their return journey to Scotland on New Year's Day.[17]

Henry and his counsellors told them at Hampton Court that although Henry was the lawful overlord of Scotland, because the Kings of Scots had sworn fealty to the Kings of England in 1097, 1189 and 1291, he had not asserted his claim against his dearest nephew James V, and would not do so against James's child. He wished only to ensure future amity between England and Scotland, which was to the interests of every Scot. The hostility between the realms was solely due to Beaton, the Cardinal of St Andrews, who, forgetting his duty to his King and the interests of his native country, had acted on the orders of his true master, the Bishop of Rome, and had sided with the French King because he hated the godly reformation of religion which Henry had carried out in England. Peace and friendship between the two realms would be ensured if 'the daughter of Scotland' married Henry's son, Prince Edward, when they reached marriageable age.[18]

Before the Scottish lords and lairds returned to Scotland, all twenty of them signed a declaration that Henry should have the custody of Mary, Queen of Scots, and that she should marry Prince Edward; but ten of the twenty, including the two Earls, Glencairn and Cassillis, also signed another agreement which they did not disclose to their ten fellow-prisoners. By this secret agreement, they promised that if Mary died, they would regard Henry as King of Scots and serve him as his subjects.[19]

James V had set up a Regency Council in his will; but James Hamilton, Earl of Arran, who was the next heir to the crown after 'the child', claimed that Beaton had forged the will. The other lords agreed to appoint Arran Governor of Scotland as Regent for the Queen. He arrested Beaton, and imprisoned him in Blackness Castle on the Forth. He extradited two English Papist refugees, who had fled to Scotland after the Pilgrimage of Grace, and a few days after Solway Moss had murdered Henry's herald who was returning from Edinburgh to Berwick; he unconditionally released Sir Robert Bowes and the other English prisoners-of-war; and he pardoned Angus and Sir George Douglas for their treason. Angus and his brother returned to Scotland with some trepidation, after Henry had assured them that he was strong enough to defend and advance them 'as long as they shall go on a straight foot with him'.[20]

The Scots had good reason for wishing to be friendly with Henry. He had shown that he could usually defeat them in war, even if they occasionally won a battle, that he could do them much more harm than the King of France could do them good, and that he was rich enough to be able to pay suitable bribes and annuities to the lords and influential lairds. There was also the religious question. The great majority of the Scots were Catholics, but there were Protestant sects in the Kyle in Ayrshire and in the port of Dundee, which carried on a busy trade with the Lutheran Hansa towns. The Scottish Protestants, whose martyrs had suffered at the stake under James V and Cardinal Beaton, had been told that the King of England was an excommunicated heretic, and many of them therefore regarded him as a saviour whose armies would liberate them from oppression. Those of them who had fled to England to escape persecution had discovered the truth about Henry. One of the most eminent Scottish Protestant preachers, George Wishart, had got into trouble when he preached at Bristol in May 1538: 'the said stiffnecked Scot' had been denounced as a heretic, tried before Cranmer and other commissioners, and forced to carry his faggot.[21] But ever since the days of Henry's alliance with Wullenweber and Meyer, he had found that heretics could be as useful abroad as they were troublesome in his own realm.

Henry's commander at Berwick was Sir John Dudley, the son of Edmund Dudley whom he had executed when he first came to the throne. After Lord Lisle died in March 1542, Henry created Dudley Viscount Lisle. The fact that Henry had put Dudley's father to death did not prevent Dudley from becoming one of the King's best counsellors and generals, and his companion at the gaming tables; for Henry had restored to him his father's forfeited lands, and he had his own career to think of, as well as his duty to his King to perform. It was only after Henry's death that he once ventured to make a passing reference in a letter to the fate of 'my poor father', who 'suffered death for doing his master's commandments'. During Henry's lifetime, he proved the truth of Machiavelli's statement that 'men more quickly forget the death of their father than the loss of their patrimony'; for he told Arran that Henry was 'the most noble Prince and father of wisdom of all the world'.[22]

Dudley was regarded by John Foxe as being one of the Protestants on Henry's Council, and he believed that on religious as well as on national grounds, Henry should perform a civilising mission among the Scottish barbarians. He urged Henry to annex the south of Scotland up to the Forth and the Clyde; it would be 'an acceptable deed before God, considering how brutely and beastly the people now be governed. . . . O what godly act should it be to your excellent Highness to bring such a sort of people to the knowledge of God's laws!'[23]

The persecuted English sacramentaries saw things differently. Butler wrote to Bullinger that Henry was threatening the Scots with 'a terrible war . . . with the soldiers in arms thirsting for blood', unless they agreed to abolish Papist practices 'which this Proteus obstinately retains in his own kingdom with more than tyrannical cruelty'. Hilles thought that Henry had invaded Scotland 'trusting, I fear, in chariots and horses and in the multitude of men, rather than in the name of God'.[24]

Henry sent the very able Sir Ralph Sadler, who was one of his two Secretaries of State, as his ambassador to Edinburgh with instructions to see that Arran pursued a pro-English policy, and that Angus and Sir George Douglas carried out Henry's wishes. Henry told Sadler and Angus to persuade Arran to send both Mary, Queen of Scots, and his prisoner Beaton to England, and to surrender to Henry's officers the castle of Dunbar and Angus's castle of Tantallon at North Berwick on the east coast, and Dumbarton Castle at the mouth of the Clyde, where the castle guns could virtually prevent any foreign fleet from entering the estuary and disembarking an invading army. But Arran was very reluctant to do any of these things. Sir George Douglas told Lisle that he would be suspected of being an English agent if he handed over Beaton to Henry; but he would see to it that Arran kept the Cardinal in safe custody at Blackness Castle. Since his return to Scotland, he had become aware that all the arguments in favour of friendship with England – the national interest, the greed for Henry's gold, and Protestant zeal – were more than countered by the gut reaction of Scottish nationalism and hatred of the English. He told Sadler that he and Angus were hated for Henry's sake, and were called 'the English Lords', and that any attempt 'to bring the obedience of this realm to England . . . is impossible to be done at this time', for 'there is not so little a boy that he will hurl stones against it, the wives will come out with their distaffs, and the commons unequivocally will rather die in it, yea, and many noblemen and all the clergy fully against it'.[25]

The people were turning against Arran too. They said that he was 'an heretic and a good Englishman', and had sold Scotland to Henry; for the Scottish Parliament had passed an Act which for the first time made it lawful to read an English translation of the Bible, and Arran asked Henry to send copies of the Great Bible to Scotland. Henry sent the bibles, but warned Arran not to allow the Scots to read the unauthorised translations by Tyndale and Coverdale or any of the other Protestant books which he had banned in England; and he urged him not to allow the people to argue about the meaning of the passages in Scripture.[26]

On 11 February 1543 the treaty of alliance between Charles and Henry was finally signed at Whitehall by Gardiner, Wriothesley and Chapuys. The last remaining difficulty, as to whether Henry should be described in the treaty as Supreme Head of the Church of England, was settled by a compromise: the title would be included in Henry's copy of the treaty, and erased in Charles's copy.[27] The treaty provided that Charles and Henry would demand that François should break off relations with the Turk, 'the inveterate enemy of the Christian name and faith', and should compensate Charles for all the damage done to his territories by the Turks, and pay all the arrears of Henry's pensions; if François did not accept these demands within ten days, they would both declare war on him, with Henry 'challenging' for the realm of France, Normandy, Aquitaine and Guienne, and Charles 'challenging' for Burgundy, Abbeville, Amiens, Corbie, Bray, Peronne and St Quentin. Henry and Charles agreed to invade France within two years, and not to make a separate peace unless François agreed to cede Ponthieu, Boulogne, Montreuil, Thérouanne and Ardres to Henry, and Burgundy to Charles. Henry and Charles would extradite each other's rebels and fugitives; and in view of the fact that heretical books were printed in each other's territories and smuggled into their realms, Charles would allow no book to be printed in English in his territories, and Henry would allow no book to be printed in German in England.[28]

The spring and summer of 1543 were wet and cold, and it was a dismal time for the Protestants in England. The Convocation of Canterbury, as well as voting an unprecedented subsidy of six shillings in the pound to Henry for the war, discussed the new edition of the Bishops' Book which had been drafted by the bishops and learned divines. It was more orthodox and Catholic than the formularies of faith of 1536 and 1537; and when it was published in May 1543, under the title *A Necessary doctrine and erudition for any Christian man, set forth by the King's Majesty of England*, it became known as 'the King's Book'. Henry, who had not been officially identified with the Bishop's Book, was happy to see this more Catholic formulary named after him. It laid down that there were seven sacraments of equal importance, except that the Sacrament of the Altar was elevated above the others because of the Real Presence of Christ in the Eucharist, which was expressly stated to be present there by transubtantiation; and the doctrine that it was necessary for the wine as well as the bread to be administered to the congregation was condemned as 'pestiferous' and 'devilish'. Henry sent a copy of the book to Charles V, to show him how Catholic was the doctrine which he was teaching to his people.[29]

From the Protestant point of view, the most retrograde step was the attack on the reading of the Bible. In the preface to the King's Book, Henry stated that by allowing his subjects to read the Bible in English he had succeeded in eliminating 'hypocrisy and superstition', but now 'we find entered into some of our people's hearts an inclination to sinister understanding of Scripture, presumption, arrogancy, carnal liberty and contention'. God 'hath ordered some sort of men to teach other, and some to be taught'; and though it was necessary for the teachers to read the Bible, those 'ordained to be taught' should only read it 'as the Prince and the policy of the realm shall think convenient so to be tolerated as taken from it'. They should therefore read, not the Bible but the King's Book, which 'containeth a perfect and sufficient doctrine'; and, 'praying to God for the spirit of humility', they should 'conform themselves . . . willingly to observe such order as is by us and our laws prescribed'. Thus 'presumption and arrogancy shall be withstanded, malice and contention expelled, and carnal liberty refrained and tempered'. In April, Parliament passed an Act forbidding yeomen and labourers, and women of any rank, to read the Bible, even privately to themselves.[30]

In March, the Council investigated the case of some Portuguese immigrants suspected of Judaism, and imprisoned eight printers who had printed banned books. They ordered a drive in London against those persons who ate meat, cheese and eggs in Lent. The sheriffs and their officers broke into people's houses, unannounced, at dinner time to see what they were eating.[31]

The Catholics also tried to get rid of Cranmer. There had been a great contention at Canterbury among the seven Catholic and the five Protestant canons in the cathedral, and some of the Catholic canons denounced Cranmer for encouraging heretical sermons and practices in his diocese. They acted at the instigation of Dr London, the former visitor to the monasteries, and were probably encouraged by Gardiner. They drew up a long list of cases in which Cranmer had winked at heresy, and presented the document to Henry, who read it when he was passing Lambeth Palace in his barge. Cranmer, knowing that the King was passing by, had come out on to the bridge to salute him, and Henry summoned him to come to his barge. He showed him the document, and, according to Morice, said to Cranmer: 'Ah, my chaplain, I have news for you. I know now who is the greatest heretic in Kent'. Cranmer asked him to appoint an impartial commission to inquire into the truth of the accusations; but Henry appointed Cranmer himself to investigate the conduct of the Catholic canons in making the accusations.

According to Archbishop Parker, Henry asked Cranmer, during this conversation on the barge, whether his bedchamber could pass the test of the Six Articles, and made it plain that he knew that Cranmer had a wife. Cranmer assured Henry that he had sent her back to Germany after the Six Articles were enacted, and begged on his knees for pardon, which Henry granted him. If Parker's story is correct – and he probably obtained his information from Morice – it is another example of the utter cynicism of Henry's attitude towards the marriage of priests.*

Cranmer spent several months examining the evidence that the Catholic canons had presented to Henry, and exonerated the Protestants who had been accused of heresy. This was a clear warning to the Catholic canons, and to Gardiner, that Henry would not, at the moment, allow them to overthrow Cranmer as they had overthrown Cromwell.[32]

Franklin, who had succeeded Sampson as Dean of the Chapel Royal, knew that one of the canons at Windsor, Simon Heynes, was a Protestant. Franklin tried to find evidence on which he could accuse Heynes of heresy. He made inquiries, and discovered that John Marbeck, the organist in the chapel royal, and three men in the town of Windsor – Testwood, Filmer and Pearson – were sacramentaries. When the officers searched Marbeck's lodgings, they found that he was making a concordance of the English and Latin Bibles, and had copied out various heretical passages from the books of Calvin and other Protestant writers. He was frequently interrogated by Gardiner, who told him that he admired him as a musician, and would like to save him; but when Gardiner asked him to give the names of other heretics, he refused; and the authorities found it impossible to bring any charge against Heynes.[33]

In July, to nearly everyone's surprise, Henry married Katherine Parr. After the execution of Katherine Howard, his counsellors believed that he would never remarry, though rumours circulated among the people from time to time that he was about to take back Anne of Cleves. In the summer of 1543, Henry was fifty-two and Katherine Parr was thirty-one. She was the sister of William Parr, whom Henry had recently created a peer. She had been married at a very early age to the aged Lord Brough, and after his death she had married Lord Latimer, who was one of the Yorkshire noblemen who supported the Pilgrimage of Grace, but had been pardoned. He died only a few months before Katherine married Henry.

Nothing is known about Henry's courtship of Katherine. We know at least something about how he met and wooed all his other wives; but there is no

*Neither Morice nor Foxe mention the reference to Cranmer's marriage in their account of the conversation on the barge. Foxe, in another passage, states that Henry allowed Cranmer to keep his wife with him 'all the Six Articles' time, contrary to the law'; but she probably went to Germany in 1539, and returned in 1543. As to this, see my *Thomas Cranmer*, p. 148.

record of when he met Katherine Parr, and when he decided to marry her. We know only that in February 1543 he paid a tailor to make Italian dresses for her, and that on 10 July Cranmer issued a licence which stated that as the King 'deigned' to marry Lady Latimer, the marriage could take place in any church or chapel without publication of banns. Chapuys was surprised that Henry had married her, for she was not beautiful – less beautiful even than Anne of Cleves – and she had been unable to have children by either of her first two husbands.[34]

Katherine had fallen in love with Jane Seymour's brother, Thomas Seymour, whom she eventually married as her fourth husband after Henry's death. She then explained to him that she had wished to marry him in 1543, but that her will was 'overruled by a higher power'. She is traditionally supposed to have said, when Henry proposed to her, that 'it was better to be his mistress than his wife'; but we can be sure that this very wise and responsible woman would never have said this to Henry, and probably did not even whisper it to anyone during his lifetime. Eight days after the wedding, she wrote to her brother, Lord Parr, that it had pleased God to incline the King to take her to be his wife, which was the greatest joy and comfort that could happen to her. Henry and Katherine were married by Gardiner in an upper oratory called the Queen's Privy Chamber at Hampton Court on Thursday, 12 July 1543, with Katherine promising to take Henry 'for better or worse, for richer for poorer, in sickness and in health', and 'to be bonny and buxom in bed and at board till death us depart'.[35]

A week after the wedding, Marbeck, Pearson, Testwood and Filmer were brought from their prison in the Marshalsea in Southwark to Windsor, and put on trial for heresy. Testwood was so ill that they had to bring him on crutches from the Marshalsea; but a fifth man, Bennet, was left in the Marshalsea and not put on trial because he had caught the plague, which saved his life. The others were tried on 26 July before Capon, the Bishop of Salisbury, and the Dean of the Chapel Royal and other judges, and by a jury consisting of tenants of the chapel royal. The defendants objected that the tenants could not be impartial, and asked to be tried by a jury composed of men from the town of Windsor; but this objection was overruled.

The chief witness against Testwood was a priest who said that whenever he celebrated Mass, Testwood lowered his eyes to avoid looking at the Host instead of gazing adoringly at it. Testwood asked why the priest was looking around the church and noticing him at such a solemn moment; but the Attorney-General, who was appearing for the prosecution at the trial, said that the priest 'could not be better occupied than to mark such heretics that so despised the blessed Sacrament'. Marbeck's concordance of the Bible was not a capital offence; but he was charged with denying the Real Presence, under the Act of the Six Articles, because he had written a document about this which was found in his rooms, though he claimed that this was an extract from one of Calvin's books which he had copied out before the Six Articles came into force. The jury at first disagreed, but eventually returned a verdict of Guilty, and they also convicted the other three defendants. All four of them were sentenced to be burned; but Marbeck was reprieved. Gardiner told him that he had interceded for him with Henry because he admired his music, and that Henry had agreed to pardon him.[36]

Testwood, Filmer and Pearson were burned on 28 July in the park below the castle. They all drank a cup of ale before the faggots were lit, toasting the day when they would meet again in Heaven. Hilles, remembering how Cromwell, and Barnes and his fellow-martyrs, had been executed at the time of Henry's marriage to Katherine Howard, wrote that Henry had burned the three 'godly men' at Windsor because he had married Katherine Parr, as 'he is always wont to celebrate his nuptials by some wickedness of this kind'.[37]

But Henry soon righted the balance. Bennet had been saved only by the plague from sharing the fate of his three colleagues; but when he recovered from the plague, his case was further investigated, and it was decided that he had been falsely accused by Dr London and other Catholics. Bennet's friends in Henry's household were exonerated; and London, who had denounced them and had also been associated with the plot of the Catholic canons of Canterbury against Cranmer, was convicted of perjury. He and two of his associates were sentenced to ride through the streets of Windsor, facing their horse's tail, with a paper fixed to their heads proclaiming that they were perjurers, and afterwards to stand in the pillory. They were then imprisoned in the Fleet, where London died a few months later.[38]

The Catholics in Canterbury denounced Richard Turner, the vicar of Chartham, for preaching against ceremonies; but Cranmer, who tried the case, found that there was no evidence that he was guilty of heresy. His parishioners at Chartham were very pleased that he had been acquitted, and planned to give him a great welcoming reception when he arrived home. Turner realised that this might be interpreted by the authorities as a seditious gathering, and returned home by another route, walking through the woods and making a detour of eighteen miles to avoid the demonstration; but the Catholics reported that the demonstration had taken place, without mentioning that Turner had not taken part in it. When Henry heard about the incident, he regarded it as a dangerous defiance of authority, and ordered that Turner should be whipped out of the county as a seditious person.

Morice, who had presented Turner to his benefice at Chartham, asked Cranmer to intercede with Henry for Turner; but Cranmer, who had already become involved in the case by acquitting Turner, was afraid to compromise himself further, and refused to help. He would not even allow Morice to contact the witnesses at Chartham who could have proved that Turner had avoided taking part in the demonstration. So Morice acted without Cranmer. He wrote to Anthony Denny, who was a gentleman of Henry's privy chamber, and to Dr Butts. Butts was in the habit of being in attendance when Henry had his hair and beard trimmed by his barber; and he took the opportunity, when Henry was at the barber's, of mentioning Turner's case and telling Henry the true facts. Henry thereupon rescinded his order to have Turner whipped, and commended him as a loyal subject.[39]

27

THE WAR FOR BOULOGNE

THE war in Europe was going well for Charles and Henry. Charles marched against the Duke of Cleves, and in August 1543 captured Düren and massacred the inhabitants. The Duke of Cleves thereupon capitulated, and accepted the very favourable terms which Charles offered him. Charles was then free to turn against François. Henry sent 5,600 English troops under Wallop to help Charles besiege Landrecies, as well as sending 20,000 crowns to Antwerp to help pay for Charles's mercenaries. Wallop wrote to Henry from Landrecies about Charles's new weapon, the incendiary bombs which were fired by his twenty-one cannons into the town. The bombs ignited as they travelled through the air, and when they fell inside the city they bounced several times, setting fire to the buildings which they passed. Wallop and his men won great praise from Charles for their valour; but Charles was unable to capture Landrecies, and abandoned the siege when François sent an army to relieve the town.[1]

The situation in Scotland had not turned out well for Henry. The Scots were not prepared to hand over Mary, Queen of Scots, to him while she was a child. Arran, who was increasingly conscious of the anti-English feeling in Scotland, was very reluctant to give way over this; and Angus and his brother were not accomplishing anything. Lisle assured Henry that whenever Angus mentioned Henry's name, whether in the Scottish Council or elsewhere, 'he pulleth off his cap and saith "The King's Majesty my master, God says His Grace"'; but Henry ordered Sadler to make it clear to Angus and Sir George Douglas, and also to Glencairn and Maxwell, that there was a difference between words and deeds.[2]

Henry expected Angus and Sir George Douglas to obey him as if they were his subjects. He told Sadler to remind Sir George of their last conversation in the lodge in Windsor Park, when Henry was about to go shooting at the butts; and of another occasion when he had been riding towards Foliejon Park near Windsor with Angus and Sir George, and they had pointed out to him a man in the crowd by the wayside who was one of the greatest thieves in Scotland, and Henry had had him arrested at their request. Did not all this suggest that they were Henry's subjects? And did they imagine that he would have refused James V's demand for their extradition unless they had been his subjects?[3]

Instead of sending Beaton to Berwick, as Henry demanded, Arran transferred him from Blackness Castle to Beaton's own castle at St Andrews. This alarmed Henry,[4] and soon afterwards Beaton was at liberty and had joined the Earl of Argyll and other lords. It was a consolation for Henry when Matthew Stewart, Earl of Lennox, who was sent from France by François I to oppose Arran's pro-English policy, informed Henry that he would change sides and serve Henry if he was allowed to marry Henry's niece, Lady Margaret Douglas. Henry agreed, and Lennox married Margaret and took an oath to be Henry's subject and to serve him in Scotland.

Henry continued to demand that Arran sign the marriage alliance with England, and at last Arran gave way. He sent Glencairn, Sir George Douglas and other envoys to England, and on 1 July 1543 they signed a treaty with Henry's counsellors at Greenwich. Mary, Queen of Scots, was to be delivered to Henry when she was ten. After her marriage to Prince Edward, Scotland would continue to be called 'the Kingdom of Scotland' and to be governed by its own laws. English and Scottish refugees would be extradited, unless they had been accepted as subjects in their country of refuge.[5]

Arran promised Henry that the treaty would be ratified when the Scottish Parliament met in September; but the Scottish people revolted against the treaty. At this moment, news arrived that Henry's warships had captured some Scottish merchant ships which were carrying exports to France. This caused an outburst of violent anti-English feeling in Edinburgh, and Sadler was warned that he would not leave Edinburgh alive unless the Scottish ships were restored.[6] Henry, who remembered how his herald had been murdered at Dunbar nine months before, sent a stern warning to the city of Edinburgh: if they harmed Sadler, they must expect 'the revenge of our sword to extend to that town and commonalty and all such . . . as shall by any means hereafter come into our hands to . . . the extermination of you to the third and fourth generation'. He explained that he had stopped the Scottish ships because they were trading with his enemy, France, and promised to restore them as a gesture of goodwill; but if any Scots broke the Treaty of Greenwich, he would treat them as enemies to both England and Scotland.[7]

Sadler's servant, hearing a Scot in the streets of Edinburgh speak such despiteful words about Henry 'as no true Englishman could bear, but having any heart and stomach must needs be provoked to revenge it', drew his dagger on the man, but came off worst in the brawl that followed, and escaped to Sadler's house with a wound in the hand. Sadler wrote that 'never man had to do with so rude, so inconstant and beastly a nation as this is'. But

Henry's counsellors promised him that 'in case your finger should ache by their means, all Edinburgh shall rue it for ever after'. Henry ordered him to go to the safety of Angus's castle of Tantallon.[8]

On 14 September, Henry ordered Suffolk, who was at the English army headquarters at Darlington, to lead an army of 8,000 men to Edinburgh to seize Beaton and Arran and burn the city. Suffolk explained to Henry that this was impossible. Arran and Beaton were at St Andrews, not at Edinburgh, and by the time that the expedition was ready to start, the winter weather would have set in. The roads would then be too damp for waggons to pass; and the ordnance and 3,000 castrells of beer could not be carried on horseback. Henry then sent an ultimatum to Arran, telling him that if the townsmen of Edinburgh wrote him 'an honest and humble letter', he would return the Scottish ships, and 'proceed princely with the Scots'; otherwise, he warned them of 'their destruction with fire and sword'. Arran sent a defiant answer to Henry's 'unseemly' letter, and ordered Angus to cease harbouring Sadler, an enemy alien in wartime, at Tantallon. Sadler was safely escorted to Berwick, and both sides prepared for a merciless war.[9]

On 13 January 1544, Angus, Glencairn and Cassillis met Arran's representatives at Greenside Chapel near Edinburgh, and agreed on behalf of Angus and Sir George Douglas that they would join with Arran and Beaton against Henry. When the news reached Hampton Court, Henry, who had just sent some more money to Angus and his brother, announced that, with God's help, he would make their punishment known to all the world. But he quite accepted Suffolk's arguments against the feasibility of attacking Edinburgh before the spring. He ordered Suffolk to prepare to invade Scotland with a large army in March, and in the meantime to carry out smaller raids in the Border regions during the winter. He told him to do the greatest possible damage to the lands of the Douglases and Angus's supporters. But Angus wrote secretly to Henry, telling him that he had only pretended to make friends with Arran, and was intending to betray him at the proper moment. Henry did not believe this, but pretended that he did. He told Angus that he was devastating the Douglas lands in order to make Arran believe that Angus and Sir George were on Arran's side.[10]

Suffolk told Henry that it would not be possible to prepare an invasion in March, and that it would have to be postponed till May. Henry reluctantly agreed; but Teviotdale and Liddisdale were heavily raided during the winter. Whenever the moon was up, the English raided and 'kept the Scots waking'. In October 1543 they raided on 12 nights; on 10 in November, on 3 in December, 4 in January, 9 in February, and 15 in March. They burned 124 villages and hamlets, and carried away with them into England 3,285 oxen, 332 horses, and 4,710 sheep and goats. They killed 35 Scots and took 408 prisoners. Henry ordered that whenever a Scottish town or village was burned, a notice should be left, fixed to the church door or in some other prominent place, containing the words: 'You may thank your Cardinal of this'. Much of the damage was done by the Scottish Border robbers, the Armstrongs and the Grahams, who had fled from justice into England and had enlisted in Henry's forces. But the Scots' houses were primitive dwellings of thatch and earth, which could be rebuilt almost as quickly as they could be burned. In July 1544 the English burned a village and 200 scattered houses which had been rebuilt since they had burned them in the previous winter.[11]

The chief exploit planned against the Scots was an attack on Edinburgh. Henry's former brother-in-law, Edward Seymour, Earl of Hertford, was to take an army of 16,000 men to Leith by sea, thus avoiding the supply difficulties. With four days' provisions, including the all-important beer, they would be able to disembark at Leith and burn Edinburgh; while a smaller force, consisting only of cavalry, would cross the Border and ride by land to a point as near as possible to Edinburgh, for even if they were unable to link up with the seaborne army, they would be able to do a great deal of damage on the way. Henry's Council told Hertford that 'His Majesty's pleasure is that ye shall . . . put all to fire and sword' along both the north and south banks of the Forth, 'putting man, woman and child to fire and sword without exception where any resistance shall be made against you'. He was to burn Edinburgh, including the palace of Holyroodhouse, 'without taking either the castle or town to mercy, though they would yield, for ye know the falsehood of them all'. He was not to forget 'to spoil and turn upside down the Cardinal's town of St Andrews, as th'upper stone may be the nether, and not one stick stand by another, sparing no creature alive within the same, specially such as either in friendship or blood be allied to the Cardinal'. But Henry agreed to abandon this project when Hertford explained that St Andrews was twenty miles from Leith.[12]

By 26 April, the invasion army was embarked on 114 ships at Tynemouth, and 4 May they landed two miles from Leith. After some fighting, they entered Edinburgh on 7 May, and spent two days burning the city. Hertford told the Provost that he had been sent not to treat, but to take vengeance, and after ordering every man, woman and child to go into the fields outside the town, for otherwise he would put them to the sword, he set their town on fire. Nearly every house in the city was burned, including Holyroodhouse, though the castle was not captured, and continued firing at the English throughout the operation. Hertford also burned Leith, and the raiding parties which came overland burned Craigmillar, Preston, Grange, Tranent, Haddington and Dunbar, and part of Musselburgh, as well as Seton Castle, and Newbottle Abbey.[13] Hertford, Lisle and Sadler had the satisfaction, while Edinburgh was burning, of hearing 'the women and poor miserable creatures of the town' blaming Beaton for the disaster, crying out: 'Woe worth the Cardinal!' Hertford and his colleagues wrote to Henry that they would 'devastate this realm and annoy your enemies' so that their falsehood 'shall be revenged and punished to the universal example of the whole world'.[14]

Henry and Charles had agreed that they would invade France by 6 June 1544. In January Henry announced, to the dismay of his counsellors, that he would command his army in person. The counsellors no doubt thought that his presence would hamper military operations: they would have to spend time providing him with suitably lavish accommodation beyond the range of the enemy guns, as well as making arrangements to ensure that his wine was available at every place where he stayed on his journey. Charles, who was commanding his own army, urged Henry not to risk his valuable life by going in person; but Henry replied that if Charles was going, he was going too. Chapuys was confident that Henry would be unable to go, especially after he fell ill again in March with the usual trouble in his leg. On 18 May, Chapuys wrote to Charles that, apart from Henry's age and weight, 'he has the worst legs in the world', and that it was surprising that he did not spend all his time in bed, as he could hardly stand, and could not make the slightest exertion without danger to his life.[15]

There was also a difference of opinion between Charles and Henry about strategy. Charles's plan was that he should invade France through Champagne while Henry invaded from Calais, and that both their armies should converge on Paris; but Henry's motive for entering the war was to capture Boulogne, Montreuil, and other towns and fortresses in the neighbourhood of Calais, and he had quite made up his mind that his armies, instead of advancing on Paris, should besiege and capture Boulogne and Montreuil.[16]

For the first time in any of his wars, Henry decided to augment his English levies by enrolling foreign mercenaries. Charles recommended Captain Landenberg, a German mercenary leader whom he himself had employed in the past. Henry sent two agents, Fane and Chamberlain, to negotiate with Landenberg, and they agreed with him that he would provide and lead 1,000 horsemen and 4,000 foot soldiers, who would be at Aachen by 24 May; and Henry agreed to pay him £8,333.6s.8d. a month. There seems to have been a genuine misunderstanding, caused perhaps because of Henry's inexperience in dealing with mercenaries. Henry did not expect to have to pay Landenberg until he and his men joined Henry's army; and when Landenberg said that by the accepted practice he was entitled to be paid from the day that this men mustered at Aachen, and to receive one month's wages in advance, Henry objected. While Landenberg's men were waiting, without their wages, at Aachen, they invaded the Bishop of Liège's territory and robbed the inhabitants. The Bishop complained to Mary of Hungary and Charles, who told Henry that Landenberg was quite justified in demanding a month's wages in advance from 24 May. Charles insisted that Henry should pay Landenberg, and also compensate the Bishop of Liège for the damage that Landenberg's men had done; but Henry refused. Charles warned Henry that if he did not pay, Landenberg might offer his services to François; and as Henry still refused to pay, Charles finally decided to take Landenberg's men into his own service to stop them from going to François. This placed a further strain on Charles's relations with Henry.[17]

Henry's troops, under Norfolk, Suffolk and Russell, effectively besieged Boulogne; but they were less successful at Montreuil, for they did not have enough men to surround the town, and merely attacked it from one side. Operations were hampered by the weather, and Norfolk, writing from Montreuil on 'this fifth foul night of July', reported that his men were drinking water, and had had no beer for ten days, 'which is strange for Englishmen to do with so little grudging'. This potentially dangerous situation was quickly remedied, for Suffolk sent Norfolk four or five hundred tuns of beer from his camp near Wimereux.[18]

François meanwhile made tentative peace overtures to Henry, assuring Henry that his love for him was undiminished; but Henry, as he had agreed in his treaty with Charles, told François that he would not negotiate with him without Charles being also involved, and he told Charles about François' approach to him.[19] He then prepared to take command of his army. He appointed Queen Katherine to be Regent in his absence, leaving Cranmer, Audley and Wriothesley at Hampton Court as members of her Council.[20] He spent his last night in England at Cranmer's house at Ford near Herne, and crossed to Calais on the evening of 14 July.

Suffolk and Henry's other commanders still hoped that Henry would remain in Calais, and not take personal charge of operations at Boulogne or Montreuil; but any chance of persuading him to do this was eliminated by the outbreak of plague in Calais. Henry decided to go to Boulogne. Twelve years before, he had easily travelled the twenty miles from Calais to Boulogne in a day; but now arrangements were made for him to stay the night at Marquise, which the English had captured, and go on next day to Boulogne. He left Calais on 25 July, dressed in full armour on a great charger. Hertford, who had come to Calais after his triumph in Scotland, carried Henry's helmet and spear. They reached Marquise in a violent thunderstorm, for the weather was as wet and windy around Calais that summer as it had been during Henry's first campaign there in 1513.[21]

Suffolk captured Basse Boulogne five days before Henry arrived, and set out to capture the town of Boulogne on the hill behind the city walls. He had erected a building for Henry to lodge in, on the north side of the town near the sea, in a healthy spot well supplied with water and out of the range of the French cannon. Henry stayed here for seven weeks, directing operations and remaining in close touch with affairs at home. Queen Katherine proved to be more than competent as a Regent, and she and her counsellors carried on the administration of the government with energy; but the correspondence between Hampton Court and Boulogne shows very clearly how Henry governed England. Every decision of importance was referred to him. Were the gipsies arrested in Huntingdonshire to be whipped as vagabonds or banished from the realm as undesirable aliens? Were some old Frenchmen in Cornwall, who had lived there for many years, to be banished under the proclamation which expelled all enemy aliens from England? Was a goldsmith's apprentice, who had stolen from his master, to be hanged, or could he be pardoned on account of his youth, as he had been in such fear of death that it would be as great a deterrent as if the sentence had been carried out? In every case, only Henry in Boulogne could decide.[22]

François continued to make peace overtures to Henry. After making initial difficulties, Henry agreed to Fançois' envoy at his camp at Basse Boulogne; but he told the envoy that even if François offered him half his realm, he would not break faith with Charles and negotiate a separate peace.[23] François' envoy then asked him if he would take part in peace talks if Charles was included, and Henry agreed to do so for the sake of peace in Christendom. But Henry and Charles continued to be in disagreement about their plan of campaign. Charles advanced deep into Champagne, and urged Henry to march on Paris. Henry agreed to do so as soon as he had safeguarded his flank by capturing Montreuil. But Norfolk was no nearer to taking Montreuil, though his men were so close to the walls that they could bandy insults with the Frenchmen in the town. When Chapuys, who had come to Calais with Henry, complained that Henry was taking a long time to capture Montreuil, Henry said that this was the fault of Mary of Hungary in delaying in sending supplies to his army there.[24]

Henry was in excellent spirits, boisterous and confident. When he was told that the Dauphin was advancing with a large army to relieve Boulogne, he said that he would teach the Dauphin his duty to his godfather. On 2 September, Hertford wrote to Queen Katherine that Henry was in better health than he had seen him for seven years. Henry himself dictated a letter to Katherine on 8 September, telling her that he regretted that he did not write with his own hand because he was too busy directing military operations. He acknowledged the valour which the French soldiers had shown in their defence of Boulogne, and said that they had 'fought hand to hand for it, much manfuller than either Burgundians or Flemings would have done', for the Flemish and Burgundian contingents in his army 'will do no good where any danger is'.[25]

Henry's men captured Hardelot Castle, between Boulogne and Montreuil, and Henry chose the castle as the venue for the peace talks. Cardinal Du Bellay met Norfolk and Russell there, and Granvelle's son, Antoine de Perrenot de Granvelle, Bishop of Arras, came to represent Charles. Henry offered to release François from his obligation to pay the pensions including the arrears, if François ceded Boulogne, Montreuil and Ponthieu to him; he thought that this was a very reasonable offer, as he would soon conquer them in any case. François was only prepared to cede Ardres. Charles demanded that François should break his alliance with the Turk, compensate Charles for all the damage that the Turk had done in Hungary and other Habsburg territories, and agree to cede all the territories which he had gained in his recent wars, including Savoy and Milan. Henry told Charles that he thought that they should be prepared to grant the French more favourable terms.[26] But Charles for once was about to get his own back on Henry for all the slights that he had suffered during the last twenty years.

Charles had advanced as far as Château-Thierry, only fifty miles from Paris; but then, running short of supplies, he retreated northwards. On his journey, he was holding secret peace talks with François' envoys, and on 18 September he announced that he had made peace at Crépy-en-Laonnois, though the treaty had in fact almost certainly been agreed a few days earlier. François surrendered Savoy and Milan, and repudiated his alliance with the Turk, while Charles abandoned his claim to Burgundy. François' son, the Duke of Orleans, was to marry Charles's daughter. Nothing was said about Henry, who was left to fend for himself.[27]

Charles sent the Bishop of Arras to tell Henry at Basse Boulogne that he had made a separate peace. Afterwards, Henry and the Bishop of Arras gave contradictory accounts of their talk. The Bishop claimed that Henry had consented to Charles making a separate peace. Henry denied this; but it seems that he accepted the news of the Treaty of Crépy philosophically, and did not then make any strong protest. Afterwards, he claimed that Charles had violated their treaty by making a separate peace, to which Charles replied that Henry had broken the treaty by lingering at Boulogne and Montreuil and not advancing on Paris.[28]

Perhaps the reason why Henry reacted to the Bishop of Arras's declaration with more self control than his counsellors[29] was because he had just taken Boulogne. His archers had won him his first victories in 1513; Boulogne in 1544 was captured by his artillery, which fired 100,000 rounds of ammunition into the town, and after six weeks' bombardment forced the demoralised garrison to capitulate. The surrender agreement was signed by Suffolk and the French envoys in Henry's camp on 13 September, and Henry entered Boulogne next day. By the surrender terms, the French garrison was allowed to march away, and Henry rode for a mile along the Montreuil road to see them leave. He stayed in Boulogne for a fortnight, and after reviewing his army outside the Montreuil gate, and knighting at his lodgings a number of officers who had distinguished themselves during the siege, he sailed for England on 30 September.[30]

He had captured Boulogne just in time. The peace with Charles had transformed the situation to François' advantage. The Dauphin led 36,000 men, who had been fighting against Charles, towards Montreuil. Charles offered to mediate and obtain the best possible terms for Henry; but this was a pretence, for the Emperor adopted a very unfriendly policy. He prevented Henry from continuing to obtain his food supplies from Charles's town of St Omer. He refused to allow German mercenaries to cross his territories to join Henry's forces at Calais, or gunpowder to be exported to England from Antwerp, though his officers allowed French warships to take refuge and to revictual at Dunkirk. Henry even received reports, which Charles denied, that some of the mercenaries who had been serving in Charles's army had joined the Dauphin's forces marching on Calais.[31]

At Otford, on his journey home, Henry received very bad news from Calais. As the Dauphin advanced, Norfolk abandoned the siege of Montreuil, and withdrew the main army from Boulogne, leaving only a token garrison there, although Henry had not authorised this decision. The plague spread both at Calais and among the garrison at Boulogne, and an increasing number of deserters crossed from Calais to Dover. Henry ordered Norfolk to return to Boulogne, and told the authorities at Dover to send the deserters back to Calais; a few of them were hanged. As winter set in, the Dauphin retreated without reaching Boulogne.[32]

During the winter, Henry prepared for a defensive campaign next summer, but he was hampered by Charles's hostility. Some Flemish ships called at the port of London, and loaded a cargo of herrings, intending to sail with them to France. Henry stopped the ships from sailing. Charles immediately retaliated by arresting all the English ships at Antwerp and restricting the movements of the English merchants there. Before the dispute had been solved, Charles was informed by his son, Prince Philip, who was his Regent in Spain, that an English privateer had robbed a Spanish ship returning from the Indies, and that other Spanish ships had been detained in Falmouth. Charles thereupon ordered Philip to arrest all English ships in Spanish ports. Henry protested that the Spanish ships had put in to Falmouth in stormy weather, and that, far from detaining them, he had given the sailors relief, and facilities for repairing their damaged ships.

The tables were turned. It was Henry who was at war with François, and Charles was the neutral who could blackmail the hardpressed belligerent. He refused to negotiate until Henry released the Flemish ships in the Thames with their cargo for France. When Henry did so, Charles still did not release the English ships at Antwerp or in Spanish ports; he demanded compensation for the cargo of herrings which had perished during the detention of the ships, and for the Spanish merchant who had been robbed of his cargo from the Indies. Henry gave way, and agreed to all his demands.[33]

On 3 January 1545, François announced that he was planning to invade England next summer as the best way of forcing Henry to surrender Boulogne, and perhaps, with God's grace, to free the people of England from

Henry's tyranny.[34] Henry also expected the Scots to cross the Border to revenge the burning of Edinburgh and the other towns in Scotland. He decided to forestall them by another destructive raid into Scotland. He was also eager to punish the treachery of Angus and Sir George Douglas, and offered a reward of 2,000 crowns to anyone who captured Angus, and 1,000 crowns to the captor of Sir George; but Sir George wrote to Henry that he had been forced to act as he did because of the 'extreme war that is used of killing women and young children'.[35]

On 25 February, the Warden of the Eastern Marches, Sir William Evers, led a raid into Teviotdale. He marched towards Jedburgh, and burned Melrose; but two days later, on the return journey to England, he was attacked by a Scottish force under Arran and Angus on Ancrum Moor. Evers was killed, and the English were severely defeated, losing many men killed and taken prisoner, and all the good horses in Northumberland. It was the greatest defeat that Henry had suffered since he came to the throne, and it was suitably exaggerated by the propagandists in Edinburgh, Paris and Rome.[36]

But Henry, defeated in Scotland, hard-pressed at Boulogne, threatened with a French invasion in the summer, and thwarted at every turn by the Emperor, could still rely on the loyalty and patriotism of the great majority of his people. He appealed to them to pay the unprecedented taxes which he imposed on them, and to rally to defend the country. Most of his subjects eagerly contributed to the voluntary loan. The inhabitants of the parishes of Tandridge and Reigate in Surrey, where the country was barren and poor, gave eagerly; but one of the London aldermen, Richard Rede, refused to pay. He was conscripted into the army and sent to serve against the Scots. The Council ordered that he was to go into action like any ordinary soldier, so that 'he may feel what pains other poor soldiers abide abroad in the King's service, and know the smart of his folly and sturdy disobediance'. He was to be treated 'after the sharp military discipline of the northern wars'.[37]

Henry declared that though the French King meant to do his uttermost to recover Boulogne, he would, God willing, discover that he had 'to do with a Prince and a nation which have lost no piece of the virtue of their progenitors and forefathers'. Orders were given for three beacons to be placed on the hilltops throughout the country. When an appreciable number of warships were seen approaching the coast, one of the beacons was to be lit. A second beacon would be fired when the invading force approached within four miles of the coast, and the third when the enemy landed. In April, as the time of the expected invasion drew near, Henry called on all the noblemen and gentlemen to be ready with their allotted number of men by the second week in May, as the King's ancient enemies, both Scots and Frenchmen, of their insatiable and deadly malice, intend to annoy this realm both by land and sea.[38]

The French men-of-war were cruising in the Channel; they gained control of the Narrow Seas, and for three weeks prevented any communication between Dover and Calais. Two thousand French soldiers under the Sieur de Lorges arrived in Scotland; and there were rumours that 'young Gerald' was coming to Ireland with a French army. At the beginning of July, it was reported that 40,000 French soldiers were ready to invade England. While Norfolk, Suffolk and Russell were ready, with an army of 90,000 men, to repel an invasion at any point between Lincolnshire and Cornwall, Hertford at Darlington was expecting a French force to land somewhere near Newcastle to coincide with a Scottish invasion by land across the Border.[39]

The latent hostility to priests was as strong as ever among many sections of the English people. A rumour circulated in Dorset and Somerset that Henry had ordered that the houses of priests should be searched to find those of them who were enemy spies, and the imaginary order was carried out in nearly every town and village until Russell put a stop to it.[40]

As the nation rallied to the 'repulse of th'enemies bruiting to invade',* Henry again decided to employ foreign mercenaries, despite all the difficulties which this involved. Charles refused to allow some German hagbutters, who would have been very useful to Henry, and some Italian mercenaries to cross the Netherlands. Henry sent him a message that he cared 'not a groat, neither for the French King nor for him'. Thirteen hundred Spanish mercenaries managed to reach England, and Henry sent them to join his army at Newcastle. They were billetted in private houses in Newcastle, and objected to the English food which their landladies gave them. They bought their own food in the market, and insisted on taking over their landladies' kitchens and dressing and cooking the food there in the Spanish style. The landladies protested to the authorities, and claimed compensation for the damage which the Spaniards did.[41]

Henry appealed to the German Lutherans, asking them, out of their zeal for God's word and the abolishing of the Bishop of Rome's authority, to help him find mercenaries in Germany.[42] Philip of Hesse recommended Captain von Reiffenberck, who agreed to enlist 1,000 horsemen and 8,000 foot at Coblenz for service in Henry's forces at Boulogne, at the rate of 25,897 florins every half-month. The chief difficulty would be obtaining Charles's permission for them to cross his territory; but Henry persuaded Charles to agree to this, on condition that they came through Luxemburg and stayed close to the southern boundary of the Netherlands until they entered English-occupied territory near Boulogne. They were not to vary from this route, and under no circumstances were they to enter Brabant.

Henry's agents, Fane and Chamberlain, impressed this on Reiffenberck; but he nevertheless assembled his men, not at Coblenz but at Aachen, from

*Spreading rumours that they were about to invade.

where they could only reach Boulogne by going through Brabant. Charles refused to allow them to do this, and they were at stopped at Visé and forbidden to cross the Meuse. When Fane and Chamberlain, who accompanied the mercenaries, told Reiffenberck that he should have gone by the agreed southern route and should never have come to Aachen, he replied that no Prince could decide which route a captain of mercenaries should follow, as this must depend on the captain's assessment of the transport problems. Disputes arose between Reiffenberck and Chamberlain and Fane about the terms of the contract of hire. Chamberlain and Fane said that Henry had only hired the mercenaries for three months; Reiffenberck said that it had been agreed that they should be paid for four months – for three months's service in the field plus on month's travelling time. He also claimed that it was an accepted custom that one page could be enrolled as a batman for every twelve horsemen, and that Henry must pay the wages of the pages, although this had not been expressly stated in the contract.

As Chamberlain and Fane would not pay, Reiffenberck seized them as hostages, and refused to release them until he received his money. They indignantly declared that Henry was not a Prince who could be forced to pay money by threats to his commissioners; but in the end they paid under protest, and were freed. Henry's secretary, Paget, wrote to Reiffenberck, demanding that he return the money, for otherwise Reiffenberck could be sure that wherever he might be in Christendom, it would cost him his life, even if Henry had to pay 50,000 crowns for it. But Henry did not get his money back. Henry appealed to Charles to punish Reiffenberck; but Charles refused, and Henry had to be satisfied with a half-hearted apology from Philip of Hesse, who wrote that he was sorry that the captain whom he had recommended had annoyed Henry, but that it had nothing to do with him.[43]

Charles was attempting to mediate between François and Henry, but found that all negotiations broke down on the stumbling block of Boulogne. Henry was determined to retain Boulogne, and François was determined to recover it. Charles suggested to Henry that Boulogne was not worth a war; and he urged François to give way about Boulogne, because Henry would soon die, and it would be easier for François to recover it from an English Regent during the infancy of Prince Edward. But the Emperor's arguments could shake neither Henry nor François.[44]

In July 1545, Henry travelled to Portsmouth, where the Lord Admiral, Lisle, waited with eighty men-of-war to repel the invasion. Henry stayed at Portsmouth while Lisle's ships fought the French in the Channel; they were repulsed at Brest, but defeated the French off Alderney. Charles's new ambassador, van der Delft, who had replaced the ailing Chapuys, came to Portsmouth to persuade Henry to make peace. On Saturday 18 July, Henry invited van der Delft to dinner on board his largest ship, the *Great Harry*; but in an angry interview he rejected the ambassador's suggestion that he should give up Boulogne.

Next day, on Sunday 19 July, Henry dined again on board ship, this time on his second ship, the *Mary Rose*. While they were at dinner, news came that the French fleet was sailing to attack Portsmouth, and had entered the Solent. Henry immediately left the *Mary Rose*, and the whole fleet, led by the *Great Harry*, sailed out to meet the enemy. After a sharp exchange of gunfire, the French sailed away to the east, along the Sussex coast. In the afternoon, after the enemy had disappeared, the *Mary Rose* suddenly capsized, and rapidly sank. Nearly all the crew of 500 were drowned, with the Vice-Admiral of the fleet, Sir George Carey, for there were less than 30 survivors from the *Mary Rose*.[45]

Henry was eager to raise the ship, in order to use her powerful guns. He employed some Italian contractors to do the work, and supplied them with the hulks, hoys and cables that they needed 'for the recovery with the help of God of the *Mary Rose*'. But their first attempt, on 3 August, failed; they failed again on 6 August; and on 9 August they reported that all their efforts had been unsuccessful and that they had broken the ship's mast. They suggested that in six days' time, they should try to drag the *Mary Rose* into shallow ground; but there is no record that this was attempted, and the *Mary Rose* was not raised until 1982.[46]

The French, sailing away from Portsmouth, landed in the Isle of Wight on the evening of 21 July, and four days later they came ashore at Seaford and burned the town and Sir John Gage's house at Firle. The three beacons were all lit on each of the designated hills in the South of England, and the levies of Kent and Sussex assembled at Uckfield; but by the time that they arrived there, they had heard that the local forces at Seaford had counterattacked, and that the French had reembarked. They also withdrew from the Isle of Wight. All the men-of-war had returned to France by 28 July.[47]

On 1 August, Henry left Portsmouth for Petworth, because plague had broken out in the fleet. As he rode in the great heat over Portsdown Hill, he looked out to sea and objected to the position of his warships in the harbour. He gave orders that they were to be moved to better stations. From Petworth he went to Guildford, where he hunted with van der Delft and received Scepperus, another envoy whom the Emperor had sent to persuade him to relinquish Boulogne. He told Scepperus that he was so little afraid of the French King that, trusting in God and the valour of his subjects, he was pursuing his usual pastimes without a care; for the French King had been unable to invade him all the summer, although the weather had been so favourable for an invasion that people called it 'the French God'. Henry had reason to be happy, for the French had suffered setbacks in the Boulonnais and at sea, and Lisle had burned Tréport and the surrounding villages.[48]

Henry was not only hunting at Guildford and hawking at Windsor in the summer and autumn of 1545, but was making plans to ensure a good supply of game in the future. He decided to create a new park near Whitehall, where he could preserve hares, partridges, pheasants and herons 'for his own disport and pastime'. No one was therefore to hunt or hawk in an area between Whitehall and St Giles-in-the-Fields, in the south, and Islington, Our Lady of the Oak, Highgate and Hornsey Park in the north.[49] In wartime, as in peacetime, the King's game, like the King's wines, was an important consideration for government officials.

28

ANNE ASKEW

PLAGUE had spread throughout the navy; of the men in the ships which had raided Tréport, 8,488 were fit and 3,512 were ill. Nearly all the garrison in the Isle of Wight were affected, and the plague was raging in Calais, though it had passed its peak in Boulogne. The two bad harvests of 1543 and 1544 had caused a food shortage throughout England, and indeed in most of Europe. There was a shortage of bread in London, where by May 1545 the price of wheat had risen to 27s. or 28s. per quarter. Henry gave 20,000 quarters, which he had purchased for the army, to the Lord Mayor for the suffering citizens. He sent agents to buy corn in Antwerp, and wheat, rye and bacon in Bremen; but the authorities in both Antwerp and Bremen banned the export of foodstuffs because of the shortage there. He was able to obtain the wheat, rye and bacon, as well as butter and cheese, in Amsterdam; but he had to go as far afield as Danzig to get the ropes that he needed for the navy.[1]

The war was costing Henry more money than ever before, with the additional expense of hiring the mercenaries. After receiving nearly £71,000 from the Benevolent Grant which his subjects were required to pay him, he was forced to find new ways of raising money. He adopted one method which pleased the Protestants: he suppressed the chantries, where prayers were said for the souls in Purgatory of the many testators who bequeathed money for this purpose, and seized the funds to pay for the war. He suppressed a large number of colleges, hospitals and mental asylums, and left the inmates to roam the streets without any relief, unless they were caught by the order which rounded up all vagabonds, as well as actors, and conscripted them into the army. His closure of the hospitals reduced the medical care for the poor to a level from which it did not recover for more than two hundred and fifty years.[2] Most of the proceeds of the seizure of the colleges and hospitals were spent on military expenditure, but several courtiers and government officials succeeded in staking a claim to a share in the spoils.

Henry, who had once lent money to the Emperor and to many petty rulers in Europe, now had to borrow money from the Fuggers and the bankers in Antwerp at 13½ per cent interest. He bought jewels and valuables at Antwerp, not to wear them himself, but to sell them at a profit to pay for the war. But Mary of Hungary prohibited his agents from exporting them from Antwerp, because this would have sent up the price of the gold and jewels which remained in the Netherlands.[3]

In May 1544 Henry devalued the currency, creating new coins of lower gold and silver content than the old coins; the new coins included the sovereign, to be worth 20s., and the half-sovereign, worth 10s. By the autumn of 1545, prices had nearly doubled, and inflation continued to be a factor in a kingdom where prices had been stable for centuries.[4]

The hardships caused dissatisfaction throughout England, and the mood of patriotic resistance to the French and Scots was not unanimous. There were desertions from the army in Boulogne and Calais, and many labourers who had been employed on fortifications in the Isle of Wight deserted and fled from the island. In June 1545 Chapuys reported that every man of any intelligence in England was against the war.[5] This was certainly true of the members of Henry's Council, for many of them felt that Henry was unreasonable in continuing the war for the sake of Boulogne, though his commander there, the dashing young Earl of Surrey, was as determined as Henry not to yield up the town.

Norfolk, who was in favour of peace, was annoyed at his son's attitude. His gentleman-servant, Hussey, wrote to Surrey on 6 November 1545 that as regards Boulogne, 'every counsellor saith Away with it; and the King and your lordship saith, We will keep it'. Hussey wrote that Norfolk was distressed that when all the counsellors, after six days' argument, seemed at last to have persuaded Henry to give way about Boulogne, Surrey had written to the King, urging him to keep it, and had undone in six hours what they had achieved in six days. After stating that Norfolk 'had rather bury you and the rest of his children before he should give his consent to the ruin of this realm', Hussey wrote that he was sure that Surrey would burn this letter, which for safety Norfolk was sending by his own servant. 'Letters have been brought to the King's intelligence written from one friend to another, and if ye shall write any secrecy, send it by a sure person'. Surrey did not burn the letter; perhaps he never received it. Today it is in the Public Record Office, and is endorsed, in another hand: 'Letters to be delivered to the King's Majesty'.[6]

The army in the North had remained inactive throughout the summer, waiting for the French landing near Newcastle and the Scottish invasion across the Border that never came. In September 1545 Hertford took the offensive, and launched an invasion of Scotland with a force which was partly composed of Spanish mercenaries. The operation was designed not only to do the usual damage to the people's homes and crops, but to capture and hold Kelso. Despite very cold weather for late September, and heavy floods, Hertford succeeded in his objective; and he also burned 287 places in 16 days, including 7 monasteries and 5 market towns.[7]

Henry tried a diversion in Scotland. He made contact with Donald, Lord of the Isles and Earl of Ross. Donald and his 'wild Scots' of Argyllshire had no love for the government of Scotland and the people of the Lowlands; he himself had been born in one of James IV's prisons, and had spent the greater part of his life there; one of his relations had been murdered in his bed in Edinburgh; and many of his people had at various times been massacred by the Lowlanders. In the autumn of 1544 he raided Inverness-shire on Henry's behalf, promising that he would keep Christmas at Inverness; but though he caused considerable suffering to the local inhabitants, he did no harm to Arran and the government, and no good to Henry.[8]

Next year, Henry tried to make better use of him. Donald's brother, the Bishop of the Isles, visited Henry at Oatlands in September 1545, and agreed that Donald would suply 8,000 men to serve under Lennox in a campaign in the west of Scotland; but this plan also came to nothing. Henry succeeded, with some difficulty, in raising an army of 2,400 native Irishmen – the 'savages', as Scepperus called them – and they eventually sailed from Dublin under Lennox's command in November 1545, intending to take Dumbarton, where they would be joined by Donald's wild Scots. But Lennox failed to take Dumbarton, and sailed back to England. Henry abandoned his attempt to make use of the Lord of the Isles.[9]

A more promising line of attack in Scotland had been suggested to Henry in May 1545. The Earl of Cassillis wrote to Sadler and offered to arrange for the assassination of Beaton, Arran and other prominent members of the Scottish government. The matter was referred to Henry. On 30 May, Henry's counsellors wrote from Greenwich to Hertford at Darlington that Henry had seen Cassillis's letter to Sadler, with the offer to kill the Cardinal and the others, but that Henry, 'reputing the fact not meet to be set forward expressly by His Majesty, will not seem to have to do in it; and yet not misliking the offer', thought that Sadler should write to Cassillis 'that if he were in th'Earl of Cassillis's place . . . he would surely do what he could for th'execution of it, believing verily to do thereby not only acceptable service to the King's Majesty, but also a special benefit to the realm of Scotland'.[10]

Sadler duly wrote to Cassillis, but received no reply from him. Instead, it was Alexander Crichton, the laird of Brunstane, who took the matter further. He had for some time been an English agent, and Sadler told Henry that, 'except there be no truth in Scottishmen', Brunstane was reliable. In July, Brunstane wrote two letters, one to Henry and one to Sadler, which he sent to Sadler, who was with Hertford at Darlington. On 12 July, Hertford, Tunstal and Sadler wrote to Paget that as Brunstane's letters referred to the killing of the Cardinal, and as 'His Majesty will not seem to have to do in that matter', they had referred it to Sadler; and Sadler wrote to Brunstane that though Henry would not meddle with the offer to kill Beaton, it would be 'an acceptable service to God to take him out of the way'.[11]

When Hertford captured Kelso in September, he took some French soldiers who were serving in the force which François had sent to Scotland under the command of the Sieur de Lorges. Some of them offered to serve in Henry's army. On 9 September, the Council wrote to Hertford that the Frenchmen should be told that the King thought that if they wished to enter his service, they should first 'do some notable damage or displeasure to th'enemies . . . as trapping or killing the Cardinal, Lorges, the Governor [Arran] or some other man of estimation'. They would then not only be accepted into Henry's service, but well rewarded.[12]

The Emperor offered to mediate between François and Henry, and invited them to send delegates to peace talks in the Netherlands. But the German Lutherans were also eager to mediate. They knew that Charles was preparing to wage war against them next summer, and hoped that if Henry and François made peace, they would follow this up by making an alliance with each other and with the German Lutherans against Charles. For this reason, Charles was anxious that it should be he, and not the Lutherans, who induced Henry and François to make peace. This was just the sort of situation which Henry relished. If there was a competition between Charles and the German Lutherans to be the successful mediator, and if he made it clear that he would not compromise on his demands, Charles and the Lutherans would both have a strong motive to put pressure on François to give way and accept Henry's terms. So while Henry sent a top-level delegation headed by Gardiner to negotiate with the representatives of François and Charles in a church in Utrecht, he sent his secretary, Paget, to meet the French and Lutheran envoys in a tent on the frontier between Guisnes and Ardres. Paget was inferior in rank to Gardiner; but when van der Delft visited Henry at Guildford in August 1545, he noted that Paget was the most influential person at court.

Henry repeatedly made it clear that he would not give way on two points: he would not give up Boulogne, and he would not agree to Scotland being included in any peace treaty with France. François was equally determined to recover Boulogne, and he would not abandon the Scots to Henry's mercy. The apparent deadlock made Charles and the German Lutherans redouble their efforts to find an acceptable compromise before the other mediator did. The German Lutherans were alarmed when they heard that Henry had sent Gardiner to carry on parallel peace negotiations at the Emperor's court; and Gardiner thought that it would be highly undesirable to have the German Lutherans acting as mediators between Princes.[13]

Gardiner was surprised that Paget did not send him any information about how the talks at Guisnes were progressing. He did not know that

Henry had expressly ordered Paget to keep Gardiner in the dark. On 29 November, Henry wrote to Paget that he was not to tell Gardiner the terms of the German Lutherans' latest proposals until he received orders from him to do so.[14]

Just as he played off the two mediators against each other, he continued to encourage and suppress the Catholics and the Protestants. Not long after the burning of the Protestants in the summer of 1543, he had Gardiner's cousin and secretary, Germain Gardiner, executed as a Papist in January 1544. According to John Foxe, he contemplated sending Gardiner himself to the Tower, but changed his mind and maintained him in office. Four months later, after the burning of Edinburgh and shortly before he left to take command of his armies at Boulogne, he authorised Cranmer to order that the prayers said by the priest in the processions which were often held in the streets in towns and villages, should be spoken in English, and not, as hitherto, in Latin. Cranmer's English Litany included a new verse: 'From all sedition and privy conspiracy; from the tyranny of the Bishop of Rome and all his detestable enormities; from all false doctrine and heresy; from hardness of heart, and contempt of thy word and commandment, Good Lord deliver us'. It also contained a special prayer for 'our most dear and sovereign lord the King's Majesty', who 'spareth not to spend his substance and treasure, yea, ready at all times to endanger himself, for the tender love and fatherly zeal that he beareth toward this his realm and the subjects of the same'. In the summer of 1545, Cranmer was allowed to publish an English Primer.[15] These measures were rightly seen as a further movement towards a religious reformation and a setback for Gardiner and the orthodox faction.

The most remarkable step in the religious contest at court was the well-known incident when the Catholic faction suggested to Henry that Cranmer should be sent to the Tower, and he was saved by Henry. The story was told by Morice in a document which he wrote for Archbishop Parker in about 1565. Parker almost certainly sent the document to Foxe, who also spoke to Morice, and Foxe included the story in his *Book of Martyrs*. Shakespeare, who had doubtless read Foxe, included the incident in his play, *Henry VIII*. Morice's original manuscript has survived, and is very reliable evidence, for Morice witnessed part of the events himself, and heard the rest of the story from Cranmer.*

* It is impossible to fix the date on which the incident took place, as a very plausible case can be made out both for the spring of 1543 and the autumn of 1545. Gairdner, after stating in his *English Church in the Sixteenth Century* that it was 1543, changed his mind, and suggested in his *Lollardy and the Reformation* that it was 22 November 1545. This date has generally been accepted. In my *Thomas Cranmer*, I suggested that 26 April 1543 was more likely, but I now incline to the later date. Whichever date is chosen involves rejecting as an error at least one of the minor details mentioned by Morice. If it took place in November 1545, Gardiner, who was in the Netherlands, cannot have been directly involved in it; but Morice, unlike Foxe and Shakespeare, does not say that he was.

Morice wrote that some of Henry's counsellors went to him and accused Cranmer of heresy, and urged him to send Cranmer to the Tower. Henry agreed that Cranmer should be arrested at the Council table next day; but that evening, he sent a message to Cranmer to come to him at Whitehall. He spoke to Cranmer in the gallery; he told him that he was to be sent to the Tower next day, and asked for his comments. Cranmer said that he was very willing to go to the Tower, as this would give him the opportunity to prove his innocence of the charge of heresy, provided that he had a fair trial before an impartial judge. According to Morice, Henry replied: 'Oh, Lord God! what fond simplicity have you, so to permit yourself to be imprisoned, that every enemy of yours may take vantage against you. Do not you think that if they have you once in prison, three or four false knaves will be soon procured to witness against you and to condemn you, which else now being at your liberty dare not once open their lips or appear before your face. No, not so, my lord, I have better regard unto you than to permit your enemies so to overthrow you'. Henry then gave Cranmer his ring, and told him to produce it when he was arrested next day, as this would mean that the counsellors would have to refer the case to Henry himself.

When Cranmer attended the meeting of the Council next day, he was not allowed to enter the Council chamber, and was kept waiting for three-quarters of an hour in the anteroom with servants and suitors. Morice, who saw him there, went to Dr Butts, who informed Henry of the indignity to which Cranmer was being subjected; but though Henry was angry, he did not interfere at this stage. When Cranmer was at last called before the Council, he was informed that he was being sent to the Tower on a charge of heresy; but he then produced the ring. At this, Russell said that he had always told his fellow-counsellors that the King would never allow Cranmer to be sent to the Tower, unless he believed that Cranmer was guilty of high treason. They all then went to Henry, who strongly criticised them for having attempted to send Cranmer to the Tower, though Norfolk protested that they had only done so in order to give him the opportunity to prove his innocence. Henry then ordered them all to shake hands with Cranmer, and told Cranmer to invite them to dinner.[16]

Although both Morice and Foxe tell the story to show Henry's affection for Cranmer – Foxe wrote that Henry handled the case 'benignly and mercifully' – in fact it is a perfect illustration of the cold-blooded way in which he preserved a balance of power in his Council and at court by deliberately sowing mistrust and fear among the Catholic and Protestant factions. If there is any truth at all in Morice's account of the words that Henry spoke to Cranmer in the Gallery at Whitehall on the previous evening, it shows that Henry perfectly understood that many of the people whom he executed were convicted on perjured evidence. The counsellors would not have ordered Cranmer to be sent to the Tower unless they believed that Henry had authorised it; but Henry had deliberately led them on so that they could be humiliated after they themselves had first humiliated Cranmer. He did not punish the counsellors who had brought a false charge against his Archbishop, but insisted that Cranmer should entertain to dinner the men who had wished to have him burned, and then return to the Council table and work together with them as colleagues, as he had been doing for ten years before they denounced him as a heretic.

On Christmas Eve, Henry went to the House of Lords to prorogue Parliament. He was received with the usual adulatory address by Wriothesley, who had been appointed Lord Chancellor after Audley died in 1544. In his speech in reply, Henry said that for 'such small qualities as God hath endowed me withal, I render to his goodness my most humble thanks'. He thanked the peers and MPs for granting him, without his request, the chantries and hospitals, claimed that by capturing Boulogne he had removed a threat and acquired a valuable asset, and stated that 'no Prince in the world more favoureth his subjects than I do you, nor no subjects or commons more love and obey their sovereign lord than I perceive you do me'.

But he found fault with them in one respect: they did not obey the exhortation in the thirteenth chapter of St Paul's epistle to the Corinthians to show charity; for 'what charity is amongst you, when the one calleth the other heretic and Anabaptist, and he calleth him again Papist, hypocrite and Pharisee. . . . Some be too stiff in their old Mumpsimus, other be too busy and curious in their new Sumpsimus'. He told them to behave better, 'or else I, whom God hath appointed his Vicar and high minister here, will see these divisions extinct and these enormities corrected, according to my duty'. He reminded them that though he had permitted them to read the Bible in English, this was so that they could read it to themselves and instruct their children, 'and not to dispute and make Scripture a railing and a taunting stock against priests and preachers, as many light persons do. I am very sorry to know and hear how unreverently that most precious jewel, the word of God, is disputed, rhymed, sung and jangled in every alehouse and tavern, contrary to the true meaning and doctrine of the same'.[17]

William Petre, who was deputising as Henry's Secretary of State while Paget was at Guisnes, wrote to Paget that Henry had addressed Parliament with a gravity 'so sententiously, so kingly, or rather fatherly, as peradventure to you that hath been used to his daily talks should have been no great wonder . . . but to us, that have not heard him often, was such a joy and marvellous comfort as I reckon this day one of the happiest of my life'. Paget thanked Petre for sending him 'the most godly, wise and kingly oration' which Henry had made, and said that he would have eaten fish, which he hated, every day for a year if he could have had the privilege of hearing the speech.[18]

The peace talks at Guisnes and at Utrecht broke down, and the war continued, with clashes taking place at sea and on land around Boulogne. On

7 January 1546, a force of 4,000 French soldiers from Montreuil and 2,000 English soldiers from Boulogne fought a battle at St Etienne. There was no doubt that it was a French victory, for the English lost 205 men killed, including Edward Poynings, Surrey's second-in-command, and eleven other captains. The French made the greatest propaganda use of the victory, but it did not shake Henry's determination to carry on the war; and Paget wrote to Surrey that 'His Majesty, like a Prince of wisdom, knows that who plays at a game of chance must sometimes lose'.[19]

Henry took his usual interest in every detail of military operations, giving orders about the depth of the new harbour being built at Ambleteuse. He interested himself in the education of his eight-year-old son, Prince Edward, and from time to time visited him at Hertford, where he had been set up with his own household. The boy was intelligent; his tutor, Dr Cox, described him to Cranmer as 'an imp worthy of such a father'. Henry's health continued to trouble him. In March he caught a fever which prevented him from engaging in his usual out-door activities; but he was well enough to pass the time playing cards with Lisle and other courtiers. Before the end of the month, he was talking about going on a progress to the end of his kingdom next summer; this was probably to Wales, because he was contemplating going to Wales in 1542. But when Scepperus and van der Delft visited him at Greenwich on 21 March, they thought, from his appearance, that his illness was more serious than he made out.[20]

In April, d'Annebaut, the Admiral of France, proposed that he and his English counterpart, Lord Lisle, should reopen peace negotiations. Henry agreed, and the two admirals met at Calais, without the help of any mediators, on 24 April. Henry had the satisfaction that the overtures for peace had again come from François, and that the negotiations were being conducted on English soil at Calais; but on the day after the talks began, on Easter Sunday, Sir Ralph Ellerker was killed in a skirmish near Boulogne.[21] The war was no longer going Henry's way, and the expense of the war and the opposition to it in his Council eventually led him to modify his position and to show a readiness to compromise.

The talks between d'Annebaut and Lisle involved long, hard bargaining, but after a month they had reached agreement on all essential points. François would pay all arrears of pensions due to Henry under the treaty of 1525 and the current annual pensions. If two million crowns had been paid by Michaelmas 1554, Henry would surrender Boulogne to François; but if the money was not paid, François would forfeit his right to Boulogne. The Scots were included in the peace under a complicated formula which was designed to obscure the fact that Henry had given way on this point; they were to be comprehended in the peace on condition that their representatives negotiated their own peace treaty with Henry, and in the meantime Henry would not wage war against Scotland unless a new cause of war arose.

Neither the French nor the English were to build any new fortifications at Boulogne, but existing defences could be completed and repaired. Henry and François would extradite each other's subjects who were guilty of treason or *lèse-majesté*.[22]

On 24 May, the rumour spread in London that peace had been signed in Calais; but it was a premature report. Five days later, a draft peace treaty was agreed between Lisle and d'Annebaut; but Henry objected to a relatively minor clause, which provided that those Frenchmen who had left Boulogne after he captured it, might return if they took the oath of allegiance to him. On 3 June, Paget feared that the talks would fail on this point, and that the war would continue; but next day, after an acrimonious argument between Lisle and d'Annebaut, the French gave way, and the clause to which Henry objected was deleted. On Monday 7 June the peace treaty was signed at Camp (today Campagne-les-Guisnes), on the frontier a mile to the south of the Field of Cloth-of-gold. Six days later, on Whit Sunday, peace was proclaimed in London.[23]

But there was to be no peace in Scotland. On 29 May, sixteen Scottish Protestant gentlemen, led by Norman Leslie, the Master of Rothes, broke into Beaton's castle of St Andrews, killed Beaton, and held the castle in defiance of Arran and the government. Leslie and his colleagues had been outraged by Beaton's action in burning the Protestant preacher, George Wishart, for heresy outside the castle walls three months before. Henry's ministers did not conceal their delight at the news.[24] The Cardinal had been assassinated, and it had cost Henry nothing; for Protestant idealists had acted before Brunstane or Cassillis. Here was a situation which Henry could perhaps exploit.

Henry had never hesitated to combine a pro-Protestant policy abroad with an anti-Protestant policy at home, and in the summer of 1546 he launched the sharpest attack on them since 1540. Gardiner and Norfolk undoubtedly sympathised with the new drive against the heretics, but the leading part in it was played by Wriothesley, the Lord Chancellor. A number of prominent heretics were summoned before the Council. Dr Crome, a well-known divine who had always been suspected of Protestant sympathies and had got into serious trouble in 1541, again ventured to preach a sermon which came near to denying the Real Presence. The Council ordered him to recant at Paul's Cross. His recantation sermon was unsatisfactory, and the Council took up the case again; but the counsellors knew that Henry liked Crome, and referred the case to him. Henry contented himself with ordering Crome to recant again in another sermon at Paul's Cross, and this time his submission was complete. Latimer was suspected, but he too escaped with a warning. Lord Thomas Howard was reprimanded by the Council for arguing about Scripture in the Queen's apartments, and a page was imprisoned in the porter's lodge for the same offence. John Taylor was examined before the

Katherine Parr, painting attributed to William Scrots, c.1545

The family of Henry VIII, by an unknown artist. On the left is Princess Mary, on the right Princess Elizabeth. On the King's right is Prince Edward; on his left is Jane Seymour, painted after her death

Edward, Prince of Wales, painting from the studio of William Scrots, c.1546

Council for a sermon which he had preached at Bury St Edmunds; but, like the curate of Tenterden, he was allowed to go free after being warned not to repeat the offence.[25]

The Council took a more serious view of six cases, which they sent for trial in the city of London. The defendants included Shaxton, the former Bishop of Salisbury; John Lassels, who had first exposed the misconduct of Katherine Howard; and Anne Askew. This brave, cool, and very intelligent young gentlewoman of twenty-five, the daughter of Sir William Askew of Lincolnshire, had married Master Kyme, a Lincolnshire gentleman; but he had strongly objected to the Protestant doctrines which she advocated, and turned her out of his house. She came to London, and distributed illegal Protestant books. She had contacts at court with some of the most eminent ladies there – some said with the Queen herself. In March 1545 she was arrested, and examined by Bonner; but he was impressed by her intelligence and good manners, and he and other officials made it easy for her to recant.[26]

But Anne Askew continued her heretical activities, and was summoned before the Council. Her husband was brought up from Lincolnshire to confront her there; but she refused to recognise him as her husband, or to use her married name of Kyme. She was sent to the Tower, and he was told to return to Lincolnshire. She was questioned in the Tower by Wriothesley and Rich, who wanted to know the names of her contacts at court. As she would not tell them, they ordered Sir Anthony Kingston, the Constable of the Tower, to torture her on the rack. Kingston had often administered torture, and he tortured Anne Askew; but after she had been removed from the rack, he was so moved by her calm courage that he refused to comply when Wriothesley ordered him to torture her again, even though Wriothesley told him that by refusing to do so, he was guilty of disobedience to the King. So Wriothesley and Rich had to torture her themselves, while Kingston, realising that they would be reporting him to the King, forestalled them by going at once to Henry, informing him of what he had done, and imploring his pardon. Henry pardoned him for his disobedience. According to Foxe, the King 'seemed not very well to like' the 'so extreme handling' of Anne Askew by Wriothesley and Rich. If he had really disliked it, he could of course have put a stop to it.[27]

Anne afterwards wrote her own account of her interrogation. 'Then they did put me on the rack, because I confessed no ladies or gentlemen, to be of my opinion, and thereon they kept me a long time; and because I lay still and did not cry, my Lord Chancellor and Master Rich took pains to rack me with their own hands, till I was nigh dead. Then the Lieutenant caused me to be loosed from the rack. Incontinently I swooned, and then they recovered me again. After that I sat two long hours reasoning with my Lord Chancellor upon the bare floor; where he, with many flattering words, persuaded me to leave my opinion. But my Lord God (I thank his everlasting goodness) gave me the grace to persevere, and will do, I hope, to the very end. Then was I brought to a house and laid in a bed, with as weary and painful bones as ever had patient Job'.[28]

She could not stand or walk after the racking, and had to be carried in a chair to the Guildhall for her trial before Bonner, Norfolk and other judges on 18 June. Shaxton, Lassels, and three others were tried with her. They all pleaded guilty to denying the Real Presence, and were sentenced to be burned. Henry offered them a pardon if they recanted. Shaxton and one other agreed to recant, and Henry ordered that Shaxton should preach the sermon at the stake before the others were burned. Anne Askew, Lassels, and the two others were burned at Smithfield on 16 July, with Anne, still unable to stand, being strapped to the stake in her chair.[29]

The drive against the Protestants threatened Queen Katherine. According to John Foxe, Henry played the same trick with her as he had done with Cranmer; he led his Catholic counsellors to believe that he would send her to the Tower and proceed against her as a heretic, in order to be able to expose their wicked machinations against her.

Foxe wrote that Katherine Parr was a model wife, who nursed Henry during his increasing trouble with his leg; but she was also a Protestant and an eager reader of the Bible, and often engaged in theological arguments with him. On one occasion, when Henry was in a bad mood because his leg was hurting, he lost his temper, and said: 'A good hearing it is, when women become such clerks; and a thing much to my comfort, to come in mine old days to be taught by my wife'. Gardiner seized his opportunity, and he and Wriothesley urged Henry to send her to the Tower. Henry pretended to agree, and signed an order for her arrest on a charge of heresy. His physician, Dr Wendy, discovered about the order, and showed it to Katherine. She told her ladies to get rid of their banned Protestant books, and went to Henry; but when he suggested that they should have their usual theological discussion, she refused. She told him that she knew 'what great imperfection and weakness by our first creation is allotted unto us women, to be ordained and appointed as inferiors and subject unto men as our head. . . . Since therefore God hath appointed such a natural difference between men and women, and Your Majesty being so excellent in gifts and ornaments of wisdom, and I a silly poor woman, so much inferior in all respects of nature unto you, how then cometh it now to pass that Your Majesty, in such diffuse causes of religion, will seem to require my judgment?' She explained that she had only argued with Henry in the past, in order to have the opportunity of listening to his learned arguments. 'And is it even so, sweetheart?' said Henry, who was very pleased with her attitude.

Next day, when Henry and Katherine and her ladies were in the garden at Hampton Court, Wriothesley arrived with an escort of forty of the King's guard to arrest the Queen and take her to the Tower; but Henry had a whispered conversation with him. Most of what they said could not be overheard by Foxe's informants; but they heard Henry call Wriothesley 'arrant knave, beast and fool'. Wriothesley and the guard departed in haste, and Katherine was saved.[30]

THE LAST PURGE

In August 1546, Henry surpassed himself at his game of being alternately, or even simultaneously, a Catholic and a Protestant. Within the space of three weeks he carried on secret negotiations at Whitehall with a Papal envoy about the possibility of his submitting once again to Papal supremacy, and also announced his intention of becoming a sacramentary – actions which, if they had been committed by any of his subjects, would have made him liable to be both hanged, drawn and quartered, and burned.

When the Pope heard that François and Henry had made peace, he asked François to persuade Henry to receive an unofficial and secret emissary who could discuss the possibility of Henry returning to his obedience to the Apostolic See. He proposed to send Guron Bertano, who had been employed by Henry as one of his Italian agents when he was seeking a divorce from Catherine of Aragon, and had visited Henry's court in 1530. Henry agreed to receive Bertano, who arrived in London on 30 July and stayed in the house of Odet de Selve, the new French ambassador. On 2 August he met Paget, and spoke with Henry next day. Henry told Bertano that he would be willing to submit his case to the authority of the General Council of the Church, which was meeting at Trent, if the Council was transferred from Trent to some place in France.

Bertano sent a report about his talk to Rome, and waited in London for a reply; but to his disappointment, no reply had arrived after nearly two months. On 30 September Wriothesley and St John came to Selve's house and ordered Bertano to leave England immediately, for Henry had realised that the Pope was making a fool of him; and as the secret of Bertano's presence in England was beginning to be known, he must go at once without coming to court again. Wriothesley and St John declared that Henry would never renounce his supremacy over the Church of England, which was in accordance with the word of God and was supported by all his people. We can be sure that Henry never intended to return to his allegiance to Rome, for he could have gained nothing by it, and it would inevitably have been seen as a surrender on his part. But he realised that no harm could come of his meeting Bertano and discovering what the Pope was prepared to offer him, and that the more options which he had, or which people thought he had, the stronger his bargaining position would be. If a reply had come from Rome in time, he would have found some other excuse for breaking off the negotiations.[1]

On 20 August d'Annebaut arrived in the Thames in the *Great Zachary* of Dieppe, escorted by fourteen galleys; it was a return visit after Sir Thomas Cheyney's reception by François at Fontainebleau in July. After spending three days at Greenwich and London, the Admiral went to Hampton Court on 23 August, and was met by Prince Edward, who brought him to Henry's presence. He spent four days with Henry at Hampton Court, 'with banqueting and hunting and rich masques every night with the Queen and ladies, with dancing in two new banqueting houses, which were richly hanged, and had rich cupboards of gold plate all gilt, and set with rich stones and pearls, which shone richly'.[2]

After the banquet on the first evening, Henry, who could no longer walk or stand by himself, was helped up from the table by d'Annebaut and Cranmer. According to what Cranmer told Morice a few years later, as Henry stood there, leaning on the Admiral and the Archbishop, he made proposals 'concerning the establishment of sincere religion then' which went far beyond anything that Cranmer or anyone else would have thought Henry capable of. Cranmer told Morice that Henry and François agreed that within six months they would 'have changed the Mass into a communion (as we now use it)' and that, after François had repudiated Papal surpremacy, he and Henry would send an ultimatum to Charles demanding that he should do likewise, 'or else they would break off from him'. Henry told Cranmer to put these proposals into writing for François to consider; but Henry died before this could be done.[3]

Cranmer's story is at least partly confirmed by the correspondence of Wotton, Henry's ambassador at François' court;[4] but it is very unlikely that Henry was seriously proposing to abolish the Mass and to introduce a communion service like that which was established by the first Book of Common prayer in 1549, and which, at least by implication, denied the Real Presence. He may have been talking less than half seriously, as he did when he suggested that he might go to live among the Anabaptists in Lübeck; and he was perhaps a little drunk, and thinking aloud about a possible policy which he might one day pursue. But he said as much, on 23 August, as Anne Askew and her fellow-martyrs had been burned for saying on 16 July.

While Henry and d'Annebaut at Hampton Court were inaugurating the new era of peace and friendship between England and France, Henry received news from Boulogne which nearly precipitated a new war. Lord

Grey wrote to him that the French were erecting fortifications on the hill of Le Portet across the harbour from Boulogne. The French had carried out some work on the hill before Henry captured Boulogne, but had not occupied it for more than a year. The English therefore claimed that the French action was a breach of the peace treaty, which stipulated that no new fortifications should be erected. Lord Grey asked the French commander, Du Bies, for permission to inspect the work which was being carried out, but Du Bies refused. Henry protested strongly to d'Annebaut, and said that he would not permit this violation of the peace treaty. D'Annebaut said that he knew nothing about it, but that Selve would tell François what Henry had said.

On 4 September, Henry left Hampton Court on his annual progress; but next day a courier arrived at Woking with another letter from Lord Grey asking Henry for instructions, for in the last few days the number of French pioneers working on Le Portet had increased from eighty or a hundred to four or five thousand. Henry dictated a letter to Paget, which was taken to London and written in the Council's name to Grey, and signed by Wriothesley, Gardiner and St John. Henry ordered Grey to ask Du Bies to stop work on the fortifications till he received further orders from François; if Du Bies continued the work, Grey was to send troops to destroy the fortifications, if he had sufficient force to do so. Grey apparently acted on his own initiative without waiting for Henry's orders. He sent 500 pioneers, with an escort of cavalry, across the harbour at low tide to Le Portet, where they found the fortifications, 12 to 13 feet deep, 700 feet long, and 14 feet wide, and no French soldiers guarding them. They destroyed them, and returned to Boulogne before the tide came in.

According to what Grey's son told Holinshed, the Council were alarmed when they heard what Grey had done, as they feared that it would lead to a renewal of the war. One of the counsellors said that Grey ought to lose his head for having acted without authority; but Henry said that he would prefer it if a dozen men like this counsellor lost their heads. He sent Hertford to Boulogne to reinforce the garrison with 7,000 additional soldiers and 500 more pioneers. In London, people made wagers as to whether or not there would be war with France within eight months. But François, though he insisted that he was justified under the treaty in fortifying Le Portet, because work had been carried out there more than a year before, agreed not to proceed with the work. He proposed instead that all fortifications which had been begun, but not finished, by either the French or the English before the treaty was signed, should be demolished; and Henry agreed.[5]

As Henry, despite his legs, travelled on his progress to Guildford, Chobham and Windsor, he was in touch with events in Scotland as well as at Boulogne. Arran had no doubt that Henry had instigated the assassination of Beaton, and that Leslie and his companions were holding St Andrews Castle for Henry; and at the end of August he marched to St Andrews and besieged the castle. There is no evidence that Henry had known about the plan to kill Beaton and seize the castle; but the Protestants in the castle, who became known as the 'Castillians', sent the young William Kirkcaldy of Grange, who was one of Beaton's assassins, to Henry's court to ask Henry to send them aid. This was an opportunity which Henry could not miss. The complicated formula, in his peace treaty with François, about the inclusion of the Scots in the peace, made it possible for him to argue that he was adhering to the treaty as long as he refrained from open war. The little castle of St Andrews, which, as Arran pointed out to the Pope, was 'scarcely four hours' sail from England', gave Henry a bridgehead, less than 80 yards long and 60 yards wide, but of great strategical importance, as was clearly recognised in Rome, at François' court at Beaune, and in Charles's camp at Donauwerth. Henry agreed to help the Castillians. When the assassins captured the castle, they found that Arran's son was staying there with the Cardinal, and they had held him ever since as a hostage. Henry demanded that he should be sent to England, and Kirkcaldy agreed to hand him over to Henry.[6]

On 18 September, Henry sent orders from Chobham that his sea-captain, William Tyrrel, should sail with a fleet of six ships from Southampton to St Andrews with victuals and munitions for the Castillians. When Tyrrel reached the Forth, he was to land and burn some small village as a feint, so as to draw off Arran's army from St Andrews, and was then to land at St Andrews and take in the supplies to the castle. He was then to return to England with Arran's son.[7]

It took longer than expected to equip the fleet for St Andrews, and on 3 October Henry wrote impatiently from Windsor, ordering the Council in London to hasten Tyrrel's departure, as winter was approaching. A week later, the ships were on their way north, and Selve was at Windsor asking Henry where they were going. Henry said that they were sailing to Scotland to deal with Scottish pirates; but Selve, who had received exaggerated reports of 14, 20, 25 or even 40 ships sailing north from Harwich and Yarmouth, suspected that they were going to revictual St Andrews Castle.[8]

When Tyrrel arrived off St Andrews, he was unable to unload his supplies, for his ships were bombarded from the shore by Arran's cannons. But Norman and John Leslie, and Henry Balnaves, were daring enough to clamber down the rocks from the castle and row out through the winter seas and under enemy gunfire to the English fleet. They sailed away with Tyrrel's ships to London for a conference with Henry. They did not bring Arran's son with them. Henry was making preparations for an invasion of Scotland next summer; he negotiated with mercenary captains to hire 12,000 German *landsknechts*, 2,000 horsemen from Cleves, and 1,500 Albanians for next year's campaign. Arran appealed to François for help.[9]

On 19 December the Scottish Privy Council met at St Andrews, with

Arran and Mary of Guise in attendance. They decided that, as the siege of the castle had been long and costly, and as the King of England was preparing to invade the realm and take over the castle from the holders of it, who could not otherwise save their lives, it would be best to come to terms with them, rather than to allow the Governor's son to fall into the hands of the English. They therefore agreed to a truce, which left the Castillians in possession of the castle. Henry retained his bridgehead for next year's invasion.[10]

Reports began to circulate that Henry was seriously ill. On 19 September, when Henry was at Chobham, Wriothesley assured Selve in London that the stories of his illness were greatly exaggerated, as he had merely had a cold. Two days later, van der Delft, too, heard that the King had been dangerously ill, but that, though his physicians at one time had despaired of his life, he was now convalescing.[11]

At the end of October, rumours were circulating in Italy that Henry was so ill that he could not live many weeks. Henry's agent in Venice, Ludovico dall'Armi, tried to trace the rumour. But Ludovico had got into serious trouble with the Venetian government. The Doge and Senate believed that Henry had instructed Ludovico to arrange for the assassination of Cardinal Pole; and whether this was true or not, Ludovico had certainly killed a personal enemy in Venice, for which he would have been tried and executed if Henry had not intervened with the Doge in his favour. The Venetians, conscious as always of the advantage of maintaining good trading relations with Henry had merely banished Ludovico; but he returned to Venice and murdered another man. The Doge now raised the matter with Henry, and threatened to prosecute Ludovico for murder if he did not leave Venice at once.[12]

On 10 November, Henry returned from Windsor to Whitehall, but only to take a medicinal bath; within twenty-four hours he had left for Oatlands. On 17 November, the Scottish ambassadors, who had come to negotiate their separate peace treaty, asked for an audience with Henry, but were told that they could not see him because he was indisposed. Selve thought that this was an excuse, and that Henry wished to postpone the meeting until he had received news from St Andrews; but Henry agreed to receive the Scots on 21 November. It was a stormy encounter. The Ambassadors protested against the intervention of the English fleet at St Andrews; Henry rejected the protest, accused the Scots of aggressive acts against him, and threatened to refuse to make peace.[13]

Van der Delft spoke with Henry at Oatlands on 5 December. Henry told him that he had recently had a fever for thirty hours, but was now well again. Van der Delft thought that he still looked very ill. On Wednesday 8 December, it was Selve's turn to ask for an audience. He was told that Henry could not see him before Sunday or Monday, because he had such a bad cold that he was unable to speak; but Selve was informed that Henry went hunting every day, though the weather had turned bitterly cold.[14]

Henry, dying at fifty-five, unable to walk or stand, with his painful leg and his recurring colds and fevers, could still be lifted on to a horse and spend hours in the freezing temperatures watching his huntsmen round up the deer and slaughter them with their arrows. He could also direct another great political *coup*. On 26 September Bonner, in compliance with Henry's orders, presided at the public burning of heretical books at Paul's Cross.[15] It was the culmination of a year of persecution of Protestants; but things were about to change.

Gardiner had misjudged the situation. He told Paget that though he was worried about the future, when the younger generation took control, he had no fear that subversive elements would ever gain control as long as Henry lived.[16] He felt sufficiently sure of his position that when the Council wrote to him and asked him to agree to an exchange of lands with Henry, he refused to do so until he had spoken to Henry about the matter. The Council thereupon wrote to him again, and on 2 December he wrote to Henry, asking his pardon, on his knees, for having offended him.

Henry replied to Gardiner two days later. He wrote that he would always be prepared to grant Gardiner an audience, to discuss the exchange of lands or anything else; but 'we must, in the meantime, think that if the remembrance of our benefits towards you had earnestly remained in your heart in deed, as you have now touched the same in words, you would not have been so precise in such a matter'. He added that even if he had asked Gardiner to agree, not to an exchange but to make a voluntary surrender of some of his lands, 'your duty had been to have done otherwise in this matter than you have'.[17]

On 12 December, Norfolk, who had been staying on his estates in Norfolk, came to court. When he arrived at Whitehall, he was informed that his son, the Earl of Surrey, had been sent to the Tower earlier in the day on a charge of high treason, and that he himself was also to be sent to the Tower on the same charge.[18] He was as surprised as everyone else. This had been a well-kept secret; there had been none of the gossip which had preceded the downfall of Wolsey and Cromwell.

The file on the Earl of Surrey went back for some years. This handsome, brave, bragging and much admired young nobleman, soldier and poet wrote charming love poems to the ladies of the court; but he had a less delicate side to his nature, and took rooms in the city of London, where he could indulge his vices more safely than at court or in his father's household. In 1543, he and some young companions ate meat in Lent and went out at night shooting with their stonebows and breaking the windows of respectable London merchants.

His landlady was very proud to have the handsome young nobleman as her lodger. When her butcher sent her a knuckle of veal, she sent her maidservant to complain, and to insist that he supply her with the best cuts, because 'peers of the realm should thereof eat, and beside that a Prince'. A tailor who was in the butcher's shop asked 'What Prince?'. The maidservant said 'The Earl of Surrey'. The tailor said that 'he was no Prince, but a man of honour, and of more honour like to be. To which said she. Yes, and if ought other than good should become of the King, he is like to be King'. The tailor said 'Is it not so', but she said 'It is said so'.

The King's Council looked into the matter. The maidservant and her mistress told them that Surrey had said that if the King died, his father, the Duke of Norfolk, would probably be King; and Surrey had a coat-of-arms in his lodgings on which, in the first quarter, was the cross and martlets which was the shield of Edward the Confessor, from whom he was descended. The Council sent Surrey to prison in the Fleet for eight days for eating meat in Lent and breaking the windows, and took no action about the other business; but the statements of the butcher, the maidservant and the landlady were filed for future reference, though no one mentioned them while Surrey was distinguishing himself by his valour at Landrecies and Boulogne.[19]

In December 1546, Surrey was arrested and detained in Wriothesley's house for several days before being taken through the streets of London to the Tower. He strongly denied his guilt, and wrote to Henry protesting his innocence; but both François and Mary of Hungary were officially informed by the English ambassadors that he and Norfolk had confessed to plotting to make Norfolk Regent for Prince Edward when Henry died, and then to murder Edward and make Norfolk King. When Wotton told François about the 'abominable intent' of Norfolk and Surrey, François said that they should be put to death if their guilt was clearly proved. Wotton said that it was, by Surrey's own confession.[20]

The witnesses duly came forward. Sir Edmund Knyvett said that once, when he had accused Surrey of bearing malice towards him, Surrey replied: 'No, no, cousin Knyvett, I malice not so low; my malice climbs higher'. The statements of the tailor, the landlady and the maidservant in 1543 were brought up against him. A witness testified that Surrey had urged his sister, the Duchess of Richmond, the widow of Henry's illegitimate son, 'to become the King's harlot'; he had advised her, when the King summoned her to his presence, to be reluctant to go, so that the King would send for her again, 'and so, possibly, that His Majesty might cast some love unto her, whereby in process she should bear as great a stroke about him as Madame d'Etampes doth about the French King'. Other witnesses had seen Norfolk going to Marillac's house at night, when Marillac had been François' ambassador in London more than four years before; and the arms of Edward the Confessor were quartered on Norfolk's coat-of-arms engraved in his house in Norfolk.[21]

Norfolk wrote to Henry denying his guilt, begging for mercy, and saying that he thought that he had offended no man, 'unless it were such as are angry with me for being quick against such as have been accused for sacramentaries'. As for religious questions, he would always obey any law that Henry made, knowing that Henry was 'a Prince of such virtue and knowledge'; and this was the only reason why people bore him ill will. He wrote to the Council, reminding them of his long service, how he had been hated by those traitors, Buckingham, the Cardinal, and Cromwell. 'Who tried out the falsehood of the Lord Darcy, Sir Robert Constable, Sir John Bulmer, Aske, and many others, but only I? Who showed His Majesty of the words of my mother-in-law for which she was attainted of misprision, but I?'[22]

Henry had announced that he would spend Christmas at Greenwich; but instead he sent Queen Katherine to hold the Christmas festivities there, while he himself went to Whitehall to direct the proceedings against Norfolk. On some days he was too ill to get up, and stayed in bed; then next day he would be better, and would rise and dress. But whether up, or from his bed, he personally planned the moves in the destruction of Norfolk and Surrey.[23] It is not difficult to guess his motives. He himself could handle, and draw the maximum advantage, from a bitterly divided Council; but his infant son and his Regent could not do so. He had decided that the Protestant faction should hold power after his death, and meant to get rid of their enemies before he died.

On 30 December, Henry made his will. Repenting his life, he bequeathed his soul to God. Although personally he would be happy to be buried in any place accustomed for Christian folks, the reputation of the dignity to which he had been called made it necessary for him to be buried in the choir of his college at Windsor. He directed that the tombs of Henry VI and Edward IV be embellished, and that 1,000 marks be given to common beggars who prayed for his soul. He bequeathed the crown – as the Act of Parliament empowered him to do – to Prince Edward and his heirs; failing them, to any issue which he might have by Queen Katherine; failing this, to his daughter Mary and her heirs, on condition that she did not marry without the written consent of the majority of the surviving members of the Regency Council that he was appointing for his son; failing her, to his daughter Elizabeth and her heirs on the same condition; and failing her, to the daughters of his sister the French Queen and their next-of-kin. He appointed a Regency Council of sixteen members; they included Cranmer, Wriothesley, Hertford, Lisle, St John, Russell, Tunstal, Paget and Denny. Gardiner was not included, and did not receive the pecuniary legacies which Henry gave to his other ministers.[24]

Henry announced that he intended to create his son Edward Prince of Wales, and preparations were made to celebrate the event with a great tournament; but though his counsellors made every attempt to minimize the gravity of his illness, it was clear to both Selve and van der Delft that he was very ill. When Selve asked for an audience with Henry on New Year's Eve to discuss the situation in Scotland, Paget said that this was impossible because Henry was troubled by his leg, and referred him to Hertford instead. Henry was too ill to see van der Delft on 8 January. The ambassadors now wrote to their sovereigns, speculating about Henry's illness and who would be the Regent for the new King, and they guessed, rightly, that power would pass to Hertford, who would pursue a pro-Protestant policy. There was a general feeling among the people, too, that the Protestants were coming to power. Henry recovered again, and was well enough to see Selve, van der Delft and other ambassadors at Whitehall on 17 January; and Selve formed the impression that he was now fairly well.[25]

The counsellors went to the Tower every day to question Norfolk and Surrey, and on 12 January Norfolk signed a confession. He admitted that he was guilty of high treason for having worn the arms of Edward the Confessor in the first quarter of his coat-of-arms ever since his father died in 1524, and of misprision of treason for not revealing that his son Surrey had done the same. He asked the King for mercy, although he admitted that he did not deserve it.[26]

In the end, the arms of Edward the Confessor was the only charge brought against them. Surrey was tried at the Guildhall before Wriothesley, the Lord Mayor, and Hertford and other members of the King's Council. He pleaded Not Guilty, but the jury found him guilty. Henry commuted the sentence to beheading, and he was executed on Tower Hill on 19 January. Norfolk was condemned without trial by an Act of Attainder, which declared that he had confessed that he was a traitor, and sentences him to be hanged, drawn and quartered.[27]

There had been rumours that Norfolk would be pardoned, but Henry had decided that he should die. The Bill of Attainder was introduced on 18 January, and it had passed in both Houses by 24 January. Wriothesley then announced in the House of Lords that the King was not well enough to come to the House to give his royal assent to the bill in person, but that his assent would be given by commissioners – as had been done in the case of Katherine Howard – because Henry wished the bill to become law as soon as possible. Everyone must have guessed why there was a need for urgency, because Parliament would automatically be dissolved, and the bill would fall, if the King died.

On the afternoon of 27 January, Wriothesley, St John, Russell and Hertford came to the House of Lords and gave the royal assent to the bill.[28] That night, Henry's physicians realised that he would die within a few hours. They hesitated to tell him, for fear of the Act of Parliament which had been passed after the execution of Lord Hungerford, making it high treason to foretell the date of the King's death; but Sir Anthony Denny told him. Henry said that though he had sinned during his life, 'yet is the mercy of Christ able to pardon me all my sins, though they were greater than they be'. According to John Foxe, Denny asked Henry if he wished to confer with some learned man; but as Henry, unlike Foxe, believed in confession and extreme unction, it is more likely that Denny asked him to name the priest whom he selected to hear his last confession. Henry said that he would like it to be Cranmer; but when Denny asked him if he wanted them to summon Cranmer from Croydon, Henry, as so often when he had to take an important decision, said that he would sleep first and decide when he woke up. He slept for a few hours, and shortly before midnight asked them to send for Cranmer.

It was a very cold night, for the rivers were frozen all over Western Europe, and Cranmer could not make rapid progress on the icy roads. By the time he arrived, Henry was unconscious. But Cranmer urged him, if he could not speak, to give some sign with his eyes or his hand that he put his trust in the mercy of Christ; and Henry took Cranmer's hand and squeezed it as hard as he could. He died at two o'clock in the morning of 28 January 1547.[29]

His counsellors were stunned and grief-stricken by his death, as were the members of the Politburo when Stalin died. His death was not announced for some days, and the secret was well kept. On 29 January, more than twenty-four hours after he died, Selve asked for an audience, and was told that the King was unable to see him as he was indisposed. The Venetian ambassador was given the same answer when he asked for an audience on 30 January to protest about the activities of Ludovico dall'Armi. It was only on 31 January that the heralds proclaimed King Edward VI.[30]

The severity of the régime was immediately relaxed. Hertford and the Protestants whom Henry had placed in power before he died did not execute their enemy, Norfolk, though they had only to allow the Act of Attainder to take effect. He was kept in the Tower for the whole of Edward's reign, and emerged six years later at Mary's accession, when he was nearly eighty, to suppress a Protestant revolt on her behalf. Hertford, who set aside the Regency Council which Henry had appointed, became Duke of Somerset and Lord Protector and pursued a Protestant policy, with the Protestants, as Foxe wrote in 1563, 'wading also through dangerous tempests of King Henry's time . . . to the mild and halcyon days of King Edward VI'. But Cranmer hardly dared to seize his opportunity. When Morice said that the Reformation could advance much faster now that Henry was dead, Cranmer replied that it would be necessary to go much more slowly, because now, under Edward VI, they would encounter resistance from the Catholics; but 'if the King's father had set forth anything for the reformation of abuses, who was he that durst gainsay it?' Cranmer was so distressed at Henry's death that he allowed his beard to grow, and and commented: 'He was evermore too good for us all'.[31]

Henry had told his daughter Mary in 1536 that as long as he was alive, the Emperor would not be able to help her. As soon as Henry died, Charles proceeded to bully the government of Edward VI on her behalf in a way that he would never have dared to do in Henry's days. He threatened the English with war if they attempted to punish her for celebrating the old Catholic Mass which was suppressed in 1549; and she defied them, and dared them to do their worst, telling them that their laws were too mild to frighten her or her chaplains.[32]

Six months after Henry died, St Andrews Castle surrendered to the French fleet, and in 1550 the English Protestant government ceded Boulogne to the French King. When Mary came to the throne, she burned sacramentaries with a vigour of which Henry would have approved; but she restored the foreign Pope, and married a foreign Prince who involved England in an unsuccessful war. Less than eleven years after Henry died, Guisnes, Calais and the whole of the English Pale were lost for ever to the French; and in 1559 John Aylmer, lamenting the triumph of the French, remembered wistfully 'how did King Henry VIII scourge them? In his youth, won Thérouanne and Tournai, and in his age Boulogne, Blackness [Blanc Nez], Newhaven [Ambleteuse], the Old Man, and all that country', as well as chastising 'the piddling Scots'. In 1575, Ulpian Fulwell praised Henry in verse and prose as being 'to the world an ornament, to England a treasure', and 'to his faithful and loving subjects a tender father'. Fulwell thought that Henry's success in war was 'an evident token that God was on his side'.[33]

The Protestant readers of the Bible, whom Henry so rightly regarded as a subversive threat to absolute monarchy, had already turned against him, in secret if not openly, before he died. It was they, not the Papists, who were the real threat to his régime. By 1558, Anthony Gilby was writing in Geneva that 'thus was there no Reformation, but a deformation, in the time of that tyrant and lecherous monster'; and Gilby and John Knox, who had been with the Castillians in St Andrews, were reminding the readers of their Geneva Bible, in the marginal notes, that 'Jehu slew two Kings at God's appointment'. Fifty years later, that stalwart champion of the Protestant Cause, Sir Walter Raleigh, wrote: 'Now, for King Henry VIII, if all the pictures and patterns of a merciless Prince were lost in the world, they might all again be painted to the life out of the story of this King'.[34]

A hundred and two years and two days after Henry VIII died at Whitehall, Charles I died there, beheaded by Protestant extremists who thought that he was too tyrannical and not Protestant enough; but he was certainly more Protestant than Henry VIII, and far less tyrannical.

In more recent times, assessments of Henry have varied from H.A.L. Fisher's champion of the Anglican *via media* between Roman Catholicism and Presbyterianism, Sir Arthur Bryant's 'natural leader' who, unlike 'arbitrary sovereigns' like Charles I, believed in carrying his people with him, and Thomas Gray's 'majestic lord that broke the bonds of Rome', to Sir

Charles Oman's Henry, with his 'selfishness', and 'ruthless cruelty'; Charles Dickens's 'most intolerable ruffian, a disgrace to human nature, and a blot of blood and grease upon the history of England'; and Geoffrey Baskerville's '*faux bonhomme*'.[35]

Fulwell was almost the last man to write about Henry VIII with unqualified enthusiasm. His later champions have written more as apologists than as admirers, excusing his actions on the grounds that the severity of his dictatorship prevented disorders and civil war which would have led to far greater evils and loss of life. This argument has been repeated throughout the centuries, ever since William Thomas wrote *The Pilgrim* a month after Henry's death. When an Italian said to him in February 1547 that Henry was 'the greatest tyrant that ever was in England', Thomas replied that he had engaged, like a good physician, in blood-letting; for 'it was better to draw blood of a few persons who were the corruption of a whole realm, than to suffer the whole realm to perish'.[36]

Lord Herbert published his book on Henry in the year of Charles I's execution. By then, public opinion had decisively turned against Henry; but Herbert thought that 'with all his crimes, yet he was one of the most glorious Princes of his time'. He regretted that Henry 'was exposed to obloquy, as his accusers will neither admit Reason of State to cover anywhere, or Necessity to excuse his actions'; for it was 'discontented clergymen (for his relinquishing the Pope's authority and overthrowing the monasteries), or affronted women (for divers examples against their sex) that first opposed and cried him down'.[37]

In the nineteenth century, Froude adopted the same line. 'His personal faults were great . . . but far deeper blemishes would be but scars upon the features of a sovereign who in trying times sustained nobly the honour of the English name, and carried the commonwealth securely through the hardest crisis of its history'.[38] Pollard, who believed that 'his dictatorship was the child of the Wars of the Roses', claimed that 'every drop of blood shed under Henry VIII might have been a river under a feebler King'. It is an argument which can be, and has been, used to justify every successful tyrant who was not overthrown by a revolution or by an invading foreign army.

Pollard tried to make his readers in 1902 understand that it was possible in the sixteenth century for a dictator to be worshipped by his people, and that the victims whom he executed were expected to praise him and vilify themselves at their trial and on the scaffold. We do not need to have this explained to us in 1984.

Pollard described Henry VIII as 'Machivaelli's Prince in action'.[39] We do not know if Henry read *The Prince*. Pole wrote that Cromwell admired it, and Lord Morley sent Henry Machiavelli's *History of Florence* and advised him to read *The Prince*, which he highly recommended. But Henry did not need to read *The Prince* to realise the wisdom of using his ministers to do unpopular actions, and if necessary punishing them afterwards for carrying out his orders; and not even Machiavelli thought of brainwashing the people by arranging for every preacher in the country to tell them from the pulpit, again and again, week after week, that the Prince was 'next under Christ'.[40]

Apart from his weapons of terror and propaganda, Henry won the suport of the majority of his people by appealing to their worst instincts – to their hatred of Scots and Frenchmen, of idealists, martyrs, and 'do-gooders', to their willingness to denounce their neighbours to the authorities. He relied on the support of the gentry with their greed for land and money, and on the ambition and optimism of noblemen and courtiers who always believed that they would be the survivors and beneficiaries, not the victims, of the next purge of Papists or heretics.

The eminent historians who, in the course of four centuries, have written about Henry, all suffer from one disadvantage: none of them ever met him. But More, Roper, Wolsey, Cavendish, Cranmer, Morice, Chapuys and Castillon all met Henry, and all agreed in their estimate of his character. The lion who, knowing his strength, cannot be ruled; the Prince of a royal courage who cannot be persuaded from his will and appetite, and who will not be bridled nor be against-said in any of his requests;[41] who reacts to every concession and sign of weakness by pressing home his advantage and demanding more, but when confronted by firmness and resistance, becomes affable, and retreats. During his thirty-eight-year reign, from the age of seventeen to fifty-five, he used the services of others and listened to their advice, but took all the decisions, whether in the hunting field, at the butts in the park at Hampton Court, in camp at Boulogne, or on his sickbed at Whitehall. He was always the tall, jovial *bon vivant*, with his zest for life, his love of music and the company of ladies, and his cruel, piggy eyes.

REFERENCES

ABBREVIATIONS USED IN THE REFERENCES

E.H.R.	*English Historical Review.*
Ep.Reg.Scot.	*Epistolae Jacobi Quarti, Jacobi Quinti, et Mariae, Regum Scotorum.*
Ham.P.	*Hamilton Papers.*
L.P.	*Letters and Papers of the Reign of King Henry VIII.*
Narr.Ref.	*Narratives of the days of the Reformation.*
Pet.Mart.Ep.	*Opus Epistolarum Petri Martyris Anglerii Mediolanensis.*
Poli Ep.	*Epistolarum Reginaldi Poli S.R.E.Cardinalis.*
Sp.Cal.	Spanish Calendar.
St.P.	*State Papers . . . King Henry the Eighth.*
Ven.Cal.	Venetian Calendar.

Unless otherwise stated, references to numbers in *Ham.P.*, *Lisle Letters*, *L.P.*, *Sp.Cal.*, and *Ven.Cal.*, are to the numbers of the documents. In all other cases, unless otherwise stated, references to numbers are to the page numbers.

Unless otherwise stated, references to *L.P.*, vol.i, are to the second edition.

Chapter 1 – Henry Tudor and his England

1. Ellis, iii(i).360.
2. Elton, *Studies in Tudor and Stuart Politics and Government*, i.104.
3. *Sp.Cal.*, i.205
4. Machiavelli, *The Prince*, 7, 11.
5. *Cal. Pat. Rolls 1485–94*, 423; *Letters and Papers of Richard III and Henry VII*, i.388; ii.57*n*., 374; Austis, *Register of the Order of the Garter*, i.236.
6. Pollard, *Reign of Henry VIII*, i.147.
7. Skelton, *Works*, i.135.

8. Allen, *Opus Epistelarum Erasmi*, i.6, 239–41.
9. *Sp.Cal.*, i.205.
10. Muller, *Letters of Stephen Gardiner*, 280.

Chapter 2 – The Prince of Wales

1. *Sp.Cal.*, i.203
2. Pollard, *Henry VIII*, 25; Scarisbrick, *Henry VIII*, 5. The date is sometimes wrongly given as 18 Feb. 1503/4.
3. *Sp.Cal.*, i.360.
4. Ibid, i.339; Ellis, i(i).46.
5. Pollard, *Reign of Henry VII*, i.240–50.
6. *Sp.Cal.*, i.210, 239, 511; *Ven.Cal.*, i.942.
7. *Sp.Cal.*, i.210.
8. Ibid, i.364, 370; Burnet, *History of the Reformation*, iv.15–16.
9. Collier, *Ecclesiastical History*, ix.66.
10. *Letters and Papers of Ric. III and Hen. VII*, ii.188.
11. *Correspondencia de Fuensalida*, 449
12. *Sp.Cal.*, i.204, 216.
13. Camden, *Remaines concerning Britain*, 271.
14. Bacon, *Life of Henry VII*, 190; Harrison, 'The Petition of Edmund Dudley' (*English Historical Review*, lxxxvii.82–99); *L.P.Add.*, i.92.
15. *Correspondencia de Fuensalida*, 449; *L.P.*, xiii(ii).804.
16. *Ven.Cal.*, i.939, 941, 945; Chrimes, *Henry VII*, 313–14.
17. *The Will of Henry VII*, 1–47. *L.P.*, i.1; Chrimes, 314.

Chapter 3 – The Young King

1. *L.P.*, i.11(1) and (10); Hall, 505–6; Chrimes, 309–16.
2. Rogers, *Correspondence of Sir Thomas More*, 14–15; Allen, i.450.
3. Hall, 506–7; Fisher, *English Works*, 268–88.
4. *L.P.*, i.6; *Sp.Cal.*, ii.3–5, 10–11.
5. *Letters of Henry VIII*, 8–10.
6. *Sp.Cal.*, ii.17.
7. For the coronation, see Hall, 507–12.
8. Ibid, 512.
9. *L.P.*, i.559; Harrison, op. cit. (*E.H.R.*, lxxxvii.82–99); Hall, 515.
10. Hall, 513.
11. *L.P.*, iii.942.
12. *L.P.*, iv.1939.
13. *Giustiniani's Dispatches*, ii.312.
14. Muller, 32–33.
15. *L.P.*, ii.3765.
16. Allen, ii.504, iii.192.
17. *L.P.*, i.158(31), (32), (55), 89, 190(15) (36).

18. *Sp.Cal.*, ii.43; Hall, 516–19; *L.P.*, i.698; *Sp.Cal.Supp.*, pp. 36–44.
19. *Sp.Cal.*, ii.43; *Sp.Cal.Supp.*, pp. 36–44.
20. *Sp.Cal.*, i.551, 603–4; ii.13, 50; *Sp.Cal.Supp.*, pp. xiii–xviii, xxii–xxiii, 13–29, 33–34, 36–44, 102–5.

Chapter 4 – Guinegatte and Flodden

1. *Ven.Cal.*, ii.11.
2. Burnet, iv.7.
3. Green, *Letters of Royal Ladies*, i.159.
4. *L.P.*, i.354, 564, 681.
5. *St.P.*, vi.173.
6. *L.P.*, viii.1178; *Aeneas Silvius in Europam* (in Hume Brown, *Early Travellers in Scotland*, 25–26).
7. *Sp.Cal.*, i.210.
8. For Andrew Barton, see Hall, 525; *Ep.Reg.Scot.*, i.111–12, 120–1; *L.P.*, i.855; 'Ballad of Andrew Barton' (Child, *Ballads*, iii.334–50).
9. *Sp.Cal.*, ii.67.
10. *L.P.*, i.1100, 1206, 1287, 1347; Rymer, *Foedera*, xiii.343–4.
11. *Sp.Cal.*, ii.44.
12. Cavendish, 12.
13. Rymer, xiii.342–3; *Sp.Cal.*, ii.58.
14. *Ven.Cal.*, ii.178.
15. *Letters of Henry VIII*, 16.
16. *L.P.*, i.1326.
17. For the mutiny at Fuentarrabia, see *L.P.*, i.730, 1239, 1286, 1292, 1320, 1326–7, 1422; *Sp.Cal.*, ii.65, 68, 70, 72; Polydore Vergil, xxvii.13.
18. Rymer, xiii.342–3; *L.P.*, i.1661, 1834; *Ven.Cal.*, ii.211, 219, 225, 229, 237, 239, 241, 250, 252–3.
19. *L.P.*, i.1735, 1769.
20. *Sp.Cal.*, ii.91, 95–97, 101, 104–7, 110–11, 114–15, 119, 122, 125–7, 130.
21. *Ven.Cal.*, ii.229, 248, 253–4.
22. Brixius, *Antimorus*, passim; *L.P.*, i.1046.
23. Allen, iv.525–6.
24. Du Bellay, *Mémoires*, i.47; *Pet.Mart.Ep.* 286.
25. For Henry's Campaign in France, see *L.P.*, i.2391–2; Hall, 537–45, 548–55, 564–7.
26. *L.P.*, i.2391.
27. *Lettres de Louis XII*, iv.190–1.
28. *L.P.*, i.2122; Hall, 545–8; *Letters of Henry VIII*, 17–19.
29. For the Battle of Guinegatte and operations at Thérouanne, see *L.P.*, i.2186, 2188, 2195, 2391; Le Glay, *Négociations diplomatiques entre la France et l'Autriche*, i.531–47; *Pet.Mart.Ep.*, 288; Hall, 549–51; *Archaeologia*, xxvi.475–8; *Lettres de Louis XII*, iv.189–97.
30. For Henry's visit to Lille and operations at Tournai, see *L.P.*, i.2391.
31. *L.P.*, ii.1664.

32. Pitscottie, 262–4, 266.
33. For Flodden, see *St.P.*, iv.1; *L.P.*, i.2246, Hall, 555–64; R.L. Mackie, *King James IV of Scotland*, 259–76; J.D. Mackie, in *Scottish Historical Review*, xxxviii.135; Mackenzie, *The Secret of Flodden*, 75–93; J.D. Mackie, in *Scottish History Society*, (3rd Series) xliii.38–85.
34. *L.P.*, i.2391.
35. Ellis, i(i).88.
36. *L.P.*, i.2391; *Archaeologia*, xxvii.258–60; *Ven.Cal.*, ii.316.

Chapter 5 – Suffolk and Mary

1. *L.P.*, i.2318, 2331, 2338, 2385, 2391.
2. *Chronicle of Calais*, 71–74.
3. *L.P.*, i.2391.
4. *L.P.*, i.2377, 2446; *Sp.Cal.*, ii.138.
5. *Chron. of Calais*, 73.
6. *L.P.*, i.2391; Theiner, 511–13; Rymer, xiii.385.
7. *Pet.Mart.Ep.*, 294; Allen, i.550; *L.P.*, i.2634; *Ven.Cal.*, ii.382, 386.
8. *L.P.*, i.2592.
9. *Sp.Cal.*, ii,141.
10. *Chron. of Calais*, 71–76; *Lettres de Louis XII*, iv.274–6, 308–11.
11. *L.P.*, ii.3343.
12. *Lettres de Louis XII*, iv.338.
13. *L.P.*, i.2867–8, 3035; *Lettres de Louis XII*, iv.303–8, 318–20, 328, 335–41; *Pet.Mart.Ep.*, 539.
14. *Lettres de Louis XII*, iv. 328.
15. Ibid, iv.328, 335.
16. *Sp.Cal.*, ii.178.
17. Rymer, xiii.407–7, 409–12, 432–5; Halliwell, *Letters of Kings of England*, i.225–8; *L.P.*, i.3136, 3226(17).
18. *L.P.*, i.3171.
19. Ibid, i.3153, 3247.
20. *Pet.Mart.Ep.*, 297–8.
21. *L.P.*, ii.p. xviii–xxxii; Green, *Letters of Royal Ladies*, i.187–8, 2004–6.
22. 'The King's Book of Payments' (*L.P.*, ii., p. 1465).
23. Ibid, p. xxvii.
24. Ibid, i.3376, 3387.
25. Ibid, 3472,3478–9; *Sp.Cal.*, ii.192; *Pet.Mart.Ep.*, 299; Scarisbrick, 55–56.
26. *Ven.Cal.*, ii.600.
27. Ibid.
28. *L.P.*, ii.140, 146, 175.
29. Ibid, 15; Ellis, i(i).121.
30. *L.P.*, ii.106, 133–5; Green, *Letters of Royal and Illustrious Ladies*, i.190–2.
31. *L.P.*, ii.113, 203.
32. Ibid, 138, 180, 197, 199, 226; p. xxiii–xxiv; Green, *Letters*, i.199–200.
33. *L.P.*, ii.222.

34. Ibid, 224; p. xxvii–xxix.
35. Ibid, ii. p. xxiv–xxv, Green, i.199–200.
36. *L.P.*, ii.237, 343, 367; p. xxxi.
37. Ibid, 227, p. xxxii; Green, *Letters*, 204–6.
38. *L.P.*, ii.399.
39. Ibid, 1652.

Chapter 6 – Wolsey

1. Ellis, ii(i).108, 227; Rymer, xiii.414; *Lettres de Louis XII*, iv.342–3; *L.P.*, i.3197, 3204.
2. Fiddes, *Collections*, 251–3; *L.P.*, i.3140, 3300.
3. Allen, ii.69–70; *L.P.*, ii.666, 1300, 2500; *Ven.Cal.*, ii.635, 671, 788, 801, 875, 878.
4. *Giustiniani's Dispatches*, ii.216.
5. Ibid, 268–9.
6. Elton, *The Tudor Revolution in Government*, 320.
7. *L.P.*, ii.4060, 4458; Cavendish, 13; Lord Herbert, 269.
8. *Giustiniani*, i.283; ii.314
9. Ibid, ii.55.
10. Ibid, 312.
11. Ibid, i.83–87; ii.312.
12. Ibid, i.74–81, 83–87, 90–92.
13. Ellis, ii(i).253; *L.P.*, ii.267.
14. *L.P.*, i.3468; ii.66, 788, 795, 826, 832, 850, 871–2, 885; *Ep.Reg.Scot.*, i.233; Ellis, i(i).127, 130; Green, *Lives of the Princesses*, iv.224–5.
15. Green, *Letters*, i.218–19.
16. *Giustiniani*, i.179–82.
17. *L.P.*, ii.1652.
18. Ibid, 1024–7, 1030, 1044, 1171, 1350, 1493, 1598, 1671–2, 1710, 1720, 1734, 1757, 1759, 1779, 1797, 1830; Green, *Princesses*, iv.234–6; *Giustiniani*, i.157, 161–71; 219–20. Lodge, i.8, 13.
19. *Ven.Cal.*, iii.232.
20. *L.P.*, ii.838, 1265, 1377, 2201, 2605, 2626.
21. Ibid, 2909.
22. *Giustiniani*, ii.17, 132.
23. Ibid, i.101; *Ven.Cal.*, ii.594.
24. *Giustiniani*, i.133–6.
25. Ibid, 138–9; *L.P.*, ii, p. xlix–l; *Ven.Cal.*, ii.662.
26. *L.P.*, ii., p. lxx–xxii.
27. For Maximilian's Italian campaign and English policy, see *St.p.*, vi.36, 39, 46–50; *Correspondance de Maximilian et de Marguerite d'Autriche*, ii.304–5; *Negac. Dip.*, ii.101–8; *Giustiniani*, i.153–5, 221–3; *L.P.*, ii.1065, 1095, 1146, 1193, 1328, 1483, 1489, 1542, 1559–60, 1564, 1593, 1609, 1613–14, 1617–18, 1634, 1696, 1718, 1729, 1753–4, 1792, 1799, 1813, 1816, 1865, 1877–9, 1885, p. lxix–lxxx; *Ven.Cal.*, ii.692.

28. *L.P.*, ii.1793.
29. *Giustiniani*, i.214–19, 265–70; ii.37–42.
30. *L.P.*, ii.1721, 1965, 2253, 2255, 2611; p. lxxii.
31. Ibid, 1902, 1923, 1931, 2218; Ellis, i(i).134–8.
32. *Negoc. Dip.* ii.109–11; *L.P.*, ii.1896, 1902, 1923, 1937, 1942–3, 1965, 1967, 2010, 2014–15, 2017, 2023, 2045–6, 2055, 2070, 2076, 2082, 2090, 2095, 2100, 2104, 2113, 2151–4, 2156–7, 2176–8, 2185, 2201, 2218, 2224, 2228, 2286, 2291, 2319, 2328, 2330, 2405, 2501, 2632, 2648, 2678, 2713, 2791; pp. lxxix–lxxx, xcv–xcvii.
33. *Giustiniani*, i.181; *L.P.*, ii.1546.
34. L.P., ii.2632.
35. *Negoc. Dip.*, ii.101–8; *L.P.*, ii.1928, 1943; Scarisbrick, 62–63.
36. *L.P.*, ii.2387; Rymer, xiii.556.
37. *Giustiniani*, ii.29–31.
38. *L.P.*, ii., pp. cxx–cxxv.
39. Ibid, 827.
40. Ellis, iii(i).201–8; *L.P.*, ii.1478, 1516, 1973, 2418, 2767, 2846, 3690; *Ven.Cal.*, ii.921.
41. *L.P.*, ii.1478–9, 1517, 1541, 1665, 1783, 2081, 2136.

Chapter 7 – Evil May Day

1. *L.P.*, i.2929; *Ven.Cal.*, ii.445.
2. Theiner, 511–12; *L.P.*, ii.1282.
3. *L.P.*, ii.3815–16.
4. *Ven.Cal.*, ii.400, 868.
5. *Giustiniani*, ii.12–16, 63–66, 166–77; *L.P.*, ii.1446.
6. *Giustiniani*, ii.113–25; *L.P.*, ii.3352, 3781, 3828, 3973; *Ven.Cal.*, ii.954, 1023, 1026, 1045; Creighton, *History of the Papacy*, v.279–86.
7. Foxe, iv.179.
8. *Ven.Cal.*, iv.430, 434.
9. For Hunne's case, see Foxe, iv.183–205; *Keilwey's Reports*, 180–5; Hall, 573–80; *L.P.*, ii.1313–14.
10. For Evil May Day, see Hall, 586–91; *Giustiniani*, ii.68–72, 77; *L.P.*, ii.3259; *Ven.Cal.*, ii.910.
11. *L.P.Add.*, i.185, 188.
12. *Giustiniani*, ii.96–99, 101–3; *L.P.*, ii.3446; *Ven.Cal.*, ii.918–19.
13. Hall, 592; *Giustiniani*, ii.113–14; *L.P..*, iv.4510; *Ven.Cal.*, ii.944.
14. *Giustiniani*, ii. 126–7, 141–50, 166–73; *L.P.*, ii.3603, 3747, 3807, 3985, 4058, 4060–1, 4276, 4308, 4326.
15. *L.P.*, ii.3951.
16. Ibid, 4045, 4124–5.
17. Ibid, 147, 165, 325, 812, 824–5, 890, 918, 964, 1055, 1255, 1259, 1509–10, 1894, 2236, 3886, 3907, 3979.
18. *Giustiniani*, ii.213; *L.P.*, ii.3723, 3764, 3872, 4303, 4439.
19. *L.P.*, ii.4040, 4073, 4084, 4139, 4179, 4271, 4289; *Ven.Cal.*, ii.1023, 1026, 1045.

20. *Giustiniani*, ii. 202–3, 218–22; *L.P.*, ii.4333, 4362, 4468, 4473, 4479–80; *Ven.Cal.*, ii.1062, 1066; Rymer, xiii.624–53.
21. Rymer, ibid.; *Sp.Cal.*, ii.264; *L.P.*, ii.4470.
22. Margaret, Queen of Navarre, *The Heptameron*, Novel iv; see also Novel xiv.
23. *Giustiniani*, ii.224–32; *L.P.*, ii.4479; pp. 1441–1518; *Ven.Cal.*, ii.1088, 1095.
24. *St.P.*, i.1–2; *Giustiniani*, ii.189–90, 235–7, 240; *L.P.*, ii.4398.

Chapter 8 – The Destruction of Buckingham

1. Hall, 703.
2. *L.P.*, ii.1902, 1923, 1931; iii.App.C. to Pref.
3. Ibid, iii., p. i–xviii, Nos. 87–88, 100, 164, 192, 215, 222, 236, 239–41, 274, 277, 283, 296–7, 299–300, 304, 307–8, 310, 318, 323, 326; *Negoc. Dip.*, 265–8; *Giustiniani*, ii.263–4; Spalatin, Historishe Nachlass, 108–10; Bucholtz, *Ferdinand I*, iii.673.
4. *St.P.*, i.3.
5. Ibid, 8; *L.P.*, iii.339, 351, 353-4, 409, 416, 419; Ellis, i(i).154–8.
6. For the negotiations for the meeting, see *L.P.*, iii.111, 415–16, 609, 622–5, 632, 642–3, 645, 666, 673, 677, 681, 692, 698–700, 702–4, 738, 746, 764, 778, 797, 806–8, 821, 830–3, 835, 841–2; Rymer, xiii.691, 695; *St.P.*, vi.54; Ellis, i(i).168–74; *Giustiniani*, ii.263.
7. *L.P.*, iii.514.
8. Ibid, 803–4.
9. *Ven.Cal.*, iii.50, 53–56, 58; Hall, 603–4.
10. For the Field of Cloth-of-gold, see *L.P.*, iii.700, 702, 869–70, 878; *Ven.Cal.*, iii.50, 67–69, 80–85, 88–94; Hall, 605–20; Fleuranges, *Memoires*, 318–31.
11. *L.P.*, iii.803–4, 908, 914, 1127; *Ven.Cal.*, iii.106; Hall, 620–2; Rymer xiii.721; Teulet,i.17–23.
12. *L.P.*, iii.950, 957, 964, 1008, 1013.
13. Rogers, 212–39; Allen, iii.579–83.
14. *L.P.*, iii.1165, 1313.
15. St.P., ii.40–41, 47–48, 61–62, 72–75.
16. Ibid, 65–72.
17. *L.P.*, iii.1212, 1295.
18. Ibid, 1893; Polydore Vergil, xxvii.50–52.
19. Ibid, 1.
20. Ibid, p.cxix.
21. For Buckingham's case, see ibid, 1284–8, 1290–3; *Ven.Cal.*, iii.213, 219; *Sp.Cal.*, ii.336; Hall, 622–4; Brewer's Pref. to *L.P.*, iii., pp. cviii–cxxxvii; Wriothesley, i.13; *Greyfriars' Chron.*, 30.
22. *L.P.*, iii.1293.
23. Hess, *Erasmu of Rotterdam*, ii.607.
24. *L.P.*, iii.1123, 1210, 1216; *St.P.*, vi.67.
25. Fisher, *Opera*, 1375–92; Roscoe, *Leo X*, ii.420–1; *Ven.Cal.*, ii.210, 213.
26. Ellis, ii(i).286; Roper, 67; Brewer's Pref. to *L.P.*, iii., pp. ccccxix–ccccxxv; Notes to More's *Works*, v.720–1.

27. Henry VIII, *Assertio Septem Sacramentarum*, especially pp. 193, 202, 216, 222, 312, 364, 384, 388, 414, 452, 462.
28. Ibid, 156–79; Rymer, xiii.760; Ellis iii(i).254–68.

Chapter 9 – The Great Enterprise

1. *L.P.*, iii.1150, 1162, 1213–14, 1340, 1362, 1371, 1395, 1418, 1422, 1432.
2. *Papiers d'Etat de Granvelle*, i.128–241; *L.P.*, iii.1395, 1479, 1536.
3. *L.P.*, iii.1508; *Sp.Cal.*, ii.355.
4. *St.P.*, i.25; 79; *L.P.*, iii.1448, 1455, 1479, 1536.
5. St.P., i.50.
6. *Negoc. Dip.*, ii.529–86; Granvelle, i.125–241; *L.P.*, iii.1549, 1560, 1615, 1625, 1694–6, 1705, 1724, 1729, 1732, 1736, 1742, 1748, 1753, 1769–70, 1802–3, 1816–17.
7. *St.P.*, i.68, 71.
8. *Negoc. Dip.*, ii.490.
9. *St.P.*, i.47, 51–52, 54–68; *L.P.*, iii.1544, 1629.
10. *St.P.*, i.74–75.
11. Ibid, 84–92.
12. *L.P.*, iii.1765, 1802.
13. Ellis, iii(i).274–8.
14. *L.P.*, iii.1869, 1879, 1895, 1932, 1945, 1952, 1960; *Sp.Cal.*, ii.366, 375.
15. *Sp.Cal.*, ii.378.
16. *St.P.*, i.23; *L.P.*, iii.1448.
17. *Sp.Cal. Further Supp.*, 42–46.
18. *L.P.*, iii.2292.
19. For Charles V's visit to England, see Rymer, xiii.767–8; *L.P.*, iii.2288–9, 2306, 2309; *Sp.Cal.*, ii.420, 437, 441; *Ven.Cal.*, iii.462–3, 465–7, 470, 484, 486, 493, 495; Hall, 634–42.
20. *L.P.*, iii.2322, 2333, 2360; *Sp.Cal.*, ii.442.
21. For Surrey's campaign, see *L.P.*, iii.2530, 2540–1, 2549, 2551, 2560, 2568, 2579, 2581, 2592, 2614; *St.P.*, i.112; Hall, 646–8.
22. *Ven.Cal.*, iii.467, 470, 474, 480, 486, 495, 502, 513, 515, 528, 537, 550, 555, 595, 608, 637, 650, 683, 700–1.
23. Rymer, xiii.772–3; *L.P.*, iii.2439, 2531, 2536, 2538, 2564–5, 2571–4; *St.P.* i.107–9; vi.106–7.
24. *Negoc. Dip.*, ii.589–92; Rogers, 286–8; Bradford, 80–82; *St.P.*, i.133–4; vi.131–41, 151*n.*, 174–5; *L.P.*, iii.3030, 3225, 3308, 3326.
25. *St.P.*, vi.153–4*n.*
26. *L.P.*, iii.3315, 3317–19, 3371; *St.P.*, i.131–2; *Sp.Cal. Further Supp.*, 274–6.
27. *St.P.*, i.135–40.
28. *L.P.*, iii.3348, 3516; Rogers, 299–301; Hall, 667–72.
29. *St.P.*, i.142; iv.27–44; *L.P.*, iii.3360; Ellis, i(i).232–5.
30. Luther, *Antwortt deutsch Mart. Luthers auff König Henrichs von Engelland buch*, Ai, Aii, Diii, Fiii.
31. *L.P.*, iv.40, 301.

32. Burnet, vi.11–16; *L.P.*, iii.3547, 3592, 3629, 3647; *Sp.Cal.*, ii.611; Brewer's Pref. to *L.P.*, iii., pp. ccclxxxiv.
33. *L.P.*, iv.441, 510.
34. *Captivité de François Ier*, 53–57; *St.P.*, i.151, 153–6; vi. 305–11, 364–5; *L.P.*, iv.752, 1093, 1160, 1729; *Sp.Cal. Further Supp.*, 367–75.
35. *L.P.*, iv.1083, 1190, 1247–8; *Sp.Cal.*, iii(i).20, 28, 31–33; Lanz, i.157–9.
36. *Greyfriars Chron.*, 32; Ellis, iii(i).377; Hall, 692–3.
37. *St.P.*, vi.412–36; Lanz, i.157.
38. *St.P.*, vi.444–5; *L.P.*, iv.1378–9, 1390–1, 1409; *Sp.Cal. Further Supp.*, 443–7.

Chapter 10 – The Holy League

1. *L.P.*, ii., p. lxx.
2. Green, *Lives of Princesses*, iv.349, 387–8, 522–3; *St.P.*, iv.84–110, 115–25, 136–8, 150–65, 167–72, 185–223, 321–32, 347–57, 360–6; *L.P.*, iv.516, 528, 530, 562, 573, 599, 668, 673–4, 704, 713, 728, 745, 768, 1111, 2487, 2575, 2592.
3. Foxe, v.415.
4. *L.P.*, iv.995.
5. Foxe, iv.619–22; v.415–18.
6. Luther, *Briefe*, iii.24–26, 58; *L.P.*, iv.1614.
7. Henry VIII, *Assertio Septem Sacramentarum*, App.; *L.P.*, iv.2446.
8. *L.P.*, iii.1978.
9. Ellis, iii(i).359–81; *L.P.*, iv.1260, 1295, 1311, 1318–19, 1321; App.34, 36, 39.
10. Ellis, iii(ii).3–7; *L.P.*, iv.1324, 1343.
11. *L.P.*, iv.1397, 1459, 1470–1.
12. Ibid, 1431.
13. Ibid, x.450.
14. Ibid, xii(ii).952.
15. Harpsfield, *Life and Death of Sir Thomas More*, 41.
16. *L.P.*, iv.2036, 2039, 2148.
17. Ibid, 2228, 2266; Ellis, ii(i).341–3; *St.P.*, vi.532.
18. *St.P.*, i.181; vi.549–50.
19. Ibid, i.201–2; vi.527–31; *L.P.*, iv.3095.
20. Rymer, xiv.187; *St.P.*, i.165–8, 177; *L.P.*, iv.2228, 2233, 2236, 2266, 2451; *Ven.Cal.*, iii.1393.
21. St.P., i.181–3; *L.P.*, iv.2559.
22. *L.P.*, iv.2573, 2604, 3065–6; App.81, 94–95.
23. Ibid, 3072, 3114, 3200–1, 3253, 3436.
24. Ibid, 3080.

Chapter 11 – The King's Great Matter

1. Cavendish, 29–35.
2. Sanders, *The Anglican Schism*, 25.
3. Crapelet, *Lettres de Henri VIII à Anne Boleyn*, 102–5 (Letter I).

4. Ibid, 104–7 (Letter II).
5. Ibid, 110–13 (Letter IV).
6. Ibid, 124–5 (Letter X).
7. Harpsfield, *Life of More*, 40–43; Harpsfield, *The Pretended Divorce of Catherine of Aragon*, 175, 288–9; Sanders, 13–16; Cavendish, 82–83.
8. Lev.xx.21; Deut.xxv.2. See also Lev.xviii.16.
9. Scarisbrick, 196.
10. Roper, 20–21.
11. *L.P.*, iv.5791.
12. Ibid, 3140.
13. *St.P.*, i.189.
14. *Sp.Cal.*, iii(ii).113.
15. *St.P.*, i.194–5.
16. *Sp.Cal.*, iii(ii).273; *St.P.*, vii.360; Pocock, *Records of the Reformation*, ii.495.
17. Scarisbrick, 183–97; Elton, *Studies in Tudor and Stuart Politics and Government*, i.104.
18. *Sp.Cal.*, iii(ii).69.
19. *St.P.*, i.196–204.
20. Ibid, 209, 212, 216.
21. Ibid, 215–16, 220–1; *L.P.*, iv.3278, 3312.
22. *L.P.*, iv.3304.
23. Ibid, 3444(2).
24. *St.P.*, i.267–77.
25. Burnet, vi.22; *St.P.*, vii.1–2.
26. *St.P.*, vii.3.
27. Burnet, iv.37–39; *St.P.*, vii.35–37; *L.P.*, iv.3913.
28. Pocock, i.75–77, 86–88.
29. Ibid, 133.
30. Ehses, *Römische Dokumente*, 31.
31. *L.P.*, iv.3412, 3430, 4112; Granvelle, i.310–46; Le Grand, *Histoire du Divorce de Henry VIII*, iii.27–48.
32. *L.P.*, iv.4008, 4147, 4153, 4376, 4426; App.147, 153–4, 158, 164, 166, 169, 179.

Chapter 12 – The Trial at Blackfriars

1. *L.P.*, iv.3625, 3664, 3761, 4141, 4145, 4173, 4188, 4236, 4243, 4287, 4296, 4299–4301, 4414.
2. Ibid, iv.4310, 4331.
3. Crapelet, 108–11, 128–31 (Letters III and XII); Le Grand, iii.137–8; *St.P.*, i.299, 302–4, 307, 311–12; *L.P.*, iv.4404, 4408–9, 4428–9, 4510.
4. Crapelet, 130–5 (Letter XIII); *L.P.*, iv,4408; *St.P.*, i.312–16.
5. Fiddes, *Collections*, 174–6.
6. *St.P.*, i.316–17.
7. Lord Herbert, 174.
8. *St.P.*, i.314*n.*, 317–18; *L.P.*, iv.4529.
9. Crapelet, 150.

10. *St.P.*, vii.29–35.
11. Crapelet, 146, 148.
12. *St.P.*, i.327; iv.505–6, 509–12*n.*, 517–40, 535–9*n.*, 547–9*n.*; *L.P.*, iv.4622, 4716–19, 4812, 4874, 4926, 4940, 4951, 4963.
13. *St.P.*, i.325; *L.P.*, iv.4675.
14. Crapelet, 116, 118 (Letter VI).
15. Porcacchi, *Lett. di xiii Huom. Illus.*, 39–40; Theiner, 567; Laemmer, *Mon.Vit.*, 30; *L.P.*, iv.4736, 4881.
16. Hall, 754–5.
17. *L.P.*, iv.5702.
18. Pocock, ii.590–602.
19. *L.P.*, iv.5613.
20. Hall, 757; Cavendish, 80–85; Theiner, 584; *L.P.*, iv.5694–5, 5702; *Ven.Cal.*, iv.482.
21. *L.P.*, iv.5774; Theiner, 585.
22. B.L., Vit.B xi, f.175.
23. *St.P.*, i.194.
24. *St.P.*, vii.182–4; Le Grand, iii.337–8.
25. Burnet, iv.122–4; Ehses, 31.
26. *St.P.*, vii.193.
27. Cavendish, 89–91.
28. *Sp.Cal.*, iv(i).83; Hall, 758–9; *L.P.*, iv.5803.

Chapter 13 – The Destruction of Wolsey

1. *L.P.*, iv.5821, 5831; *St.P.*, i.340–3, 347.
2. *Narratives of the Reformation*, 240–2; Foxe, viii.6–8; Ridley, *Thomas Cranmer*, 25–28.
3. Theiner, 564.
4. *L.P.*, iv.5911; Rymer, xiv.326–44.
5. *St.P.*, i.344.
6. Cavendish, 92–97.
7. Ibid, 97; Hall, 760; *L.P.*, iv.6035.
8. Cavendish, 98–104.
9. Le Grand, iii.369.
10. *L.P.*, iv.6016.
11. Ibid, iv.6035.
12. Hall, 764; Lord Herbert, 266–74.
13. Cavendish, 120–4, 129–35.
14. *L.P.*, iv.6377, 6510, 6523, 6579, 6663, 6666, 6679.
15. *A Supplication of the Begars*, 7; Foxe, iv.661.
16. Foxe, iv.657; Laemmer, *Mon.Vit.*, 31–32; *L.P.*, iv.5416.
17. *L.P.*, xvi.101.
18. Harpsfield, *Life of More*, 23–24.
19. Ibid, 12–20; Harpsfield, *Life of More*, 26–33; *St.P.*, i.124; Ridley, *The Statesman and the Fanatic*, 143–7.

20. Allen, iv.13–22; Roper, 48–49; Harpsfield, *Life of More*, 65–66.
21. Roper, 20–21.
22. Rogers, 493–6.
23. Hall, 765; Elton, *Studies in Tudor and Stuart Politics*, ii.107–36; Strype, *Cranmer*, ii.695; Wilkins, iii.739.
24. Hall, 771; Wilkins, iii.727–37, 740–2.
25. *L.P.*, iv.6627, 6705; v.75, 176, 555; *Sp.Cal.*, iv.68, 772; Duke of Manchester, *Court and Society*, i.165–7; Lord Herbert, 302; Pocock, ii.9.
26. Lamb, *Cambridge Documents*, 19–27; Burnet, iv.130–3; Cooper, *Annals of Cambridge*, i.342–3; Fiddes, *Collections*, 183; Wilkins, iv.726–7; *St.P.*, i.377–9; Wood, *Annals of Oxford*, ii.43–44.
27. *L.P.*, iv.6321, 6454, 6459, 6550; v.3; Rymer, xiv.392–7; Le Grand, iii.458–71, 507–9.
28. Rymer, xiv.393–401; Theiner, 592; Pocock, i.438–40; *L.P.*, iv.6279, 6548, 6613, 6628–9, 6632, 6640–1; v.3.
29. Rymer, xiv.405–7; Lord Herbert, 303–11.
30. Foxe, viii.9; *L.P.*, iv.6111; Theiner, 591–2; *St.P.*, vii.261–6.
31. Cavendish, 144–52; *St.P.*, i.366; *L.P.*, iv.6447; *Sp.Cal.*, iv.366.
32. Bradford, *Correspondence of Charles V*, 319–80; *Sp.Cal.*, iv.354, 366, 373, 411.
33. Cavendish, 152–81; for the passages cited, see 173, 178–9.
34. Ibid, 183–6.

Chapter 14 – Which Way?

1. Bradford, 334–5; *L.P.*, v.112; *Sp.Cal.*, iv.641.
2. Wilkins, iii.725; *L.P.*, v.70, 105; *Sp.Cal.*, v(i).619, 635.
3. Wilkins, iii.762–5; *L.P.*, v.App.9.
4. Pocock, ii.104–8.
5. *L.P.*, v.105; *Sp.Cal.*, iv.635.
6. Merriman, *Life and Letters of Thomas Cromwell*, i.56.
7. *Poli Ep.*, i.113–40; *L.P.*, xiv(i).200.
8. Foxe, iv.619, 689–94, 698; More, *Works*, ix.117–19; *L.P.*, v.App.29–30; Ridley, *The Statesman and the Fanatic*, 254–8.
9. More, *Works*, viii.14–17, 29.
10. *L.P.*, iv.6752; v.App.7; Pocock, ii.184–9.
11. Tyndale, *Works*, i.174–5, 177–9.
12. Strype, *Mem.*, i(i).172; More, *Works*, viii.29–32.
13. Tyndale, *The Practice of Prelates* (*Works*, ii.319–34).
14. Demaus, *Tyndale*, 295–9; *St.P.*, vii.302–4; *L.P.*, v.65, 153.
15. Merriman, i.335–9.
16. Ibid; Foxe, v.5–7, 9.
17. *L.P.*, v.354.
18. Ibid, v.148, 171; *Sp.Cal.*, iv.664; Schulte Herbrüggen, *Sir Thomas More: Neue Briefe*, 97.
19. *L.P.*, v.120; *Sp.Cal.*, iv.646.
20. *Stat. of Realm*, 22 Hen.VIII, c.9.

21. *L.P.*, v.216, 266, 941; *Sp.Cal.*, iv.934.
22. *St.P.*, vii.297–9; *L.P.*, v.287.
23. *L.P.*, v.274; *St.P.*, vii.339–46.
24. More, *Works*, viii.23–26; Foxe, iv.643–56, 704–5.
25. Vives, *Opera*, vii.134–6.
26. Crapelet, 138, 140 (Letter XVI).
27. *St.P.*, vii.305–16.
28. *L.P.*, v.340, 361, 696; *Sp.Cal.*, iv.765, 775, 880.
29. *L.P.*, v.696, 762; *Sp.Cal.* iv.880, 897.
30. Pocock, ii.166–8.
31. Wilkins, iii.754–5.
32. *L.P.*, v.832, 879; *St.P.*, vii.360–3; *Sp.Cal.*, iv.907, 922.
33. *L.P.*, v.1013; *Sp.Cal.*, iv.951.
34. Rymer, xiv.433–4.
35. Scarisbrick, 502–6.

Chapter 15 – The Break with Rome

1. *L.P.*, v.1097; *Sp.Cal.*, iv.960; Pocock, ii.280.
2. *L.P.*, v.1200; *Sp.Cal.*, iv.979, 984.
3. *L.P.*, v.1191, 1202, 1209; vi.733.
4. Ibid, iii.1681 (15 Oct.1521).
5. For Elizabeth Barton, see Wright, *Letters relating to the Suppression of Monasteries*, 14–34; Cranmer, *Works*, ii.272–4; Rogers, 465–6, 480–8; Hall, 806–14; *L.P.*, vi.1149, 1336, 1382, 1445, 1460, 1464–5, 1468; *Sp.Cal.*, iv. 1153–4.
6. *L.P.*, v.1258, 1277; *Sp.Cal.*, iv.987.
7. *St.P.*, i.387–8; iv.159–65, 586–96, 611–16; *L.P.*, v.1429, 1800 (25 Aug.1532).
8. Le Grand, iii.553–7.
9. Ibid, 555–6.
10. *L.P.*, v.1274, 1370.
11. Ibid, 1231.
12. Ibid, 1377; Strype, *Cranmer*, ii.681–2.
13. *Bishop Cranmer's Recantacyons*, 4; *Spanish Chronicle of Henry VIII*, 19.
14. Parker, *De Antiquitate Britannicae Ecclesiae*, 392–3.
15. For the meeting at Boulogne and Calais, see Camusat, i.105–11; *L.P.*, v.1316, 1337, 1354, 1377, 1429, 1484–5; *Sp.Cal.*, iv.995, 998, 1003, 1008; Hall, 789–94; Hamy, *Entrevue de François Ier avec Henry VIII*, 59–107.
16. Camusat, i.109–11, 172–3.
17. Hall, 794; *L.P.*, v.1531, 1579; *Sp.Cal.*, iv.1024, 1030.
18. *St.P.*, vii.386–91; *L.P.*, v.1551, 1609, 1620; vii.1608; Foxe, viii.55; Harpsfield, *The Pretended Divorce of Catherine of Aragon*, 290.
19. *L.P.*, v.1532, 1536, 1567; *Sp.Cal.*, iv.1025; Lanz, ii.22; Pocock, ii.378–84.
20. Cranmer, *Works*, ii.246; Hall, 794.
21. *L.P.*, vi.160; *St.P.*, vii.417–18.
22. *L.P.*, vi.89, 142, 160, 180, 296; *Sp.Cal.*, iv.1043, 1057; *St.P.*, vii.425.

23. *L.P.*, vi.235; *Sp.Cal.*, iv.1056.
24. *L.P.*, xii(ii).953.
25. Cranmer, *Works*, ii.538, 559–62; Foxe, viii.53–56, 65–66; Ridley, *Thomas Cranmer*, 55–58, and works there cited.
26. Wilkins, iii.756–7.
27. Cranmer, *Works*, ii.237–9.
28. *St.P.*, i.392–3.
29. *L.P.*, vi.391; *Sp.Cal.*, iv.1062.
30. *L.P.*, vi.351; *Sp.Cal.*, iv.1061.
31. *L.P.*, vi.324; *Sp.Cal.*, iv.1058.
32. *L.P.*, vi.465; *Sp.Cal.*, iv.1072.
33. *L.P.*, vi.918, 1125, *Sp.Cal.*, iv.1107, 1127.
34. *St.P.*, i.394–7; Cranmer, *Works*, ii.241–3; Pocock, ii.473–5.
35. Burnet, iv.189–91; Rymer, xiv.470–1; *L.P.*, vi.561—3, 585, 601; *Tudor Tracts*, 9–19; Camusat, ii.17–18; Wriothesley, i.18–22; Hall, 798–805; Cranmer, *Works*, ii.245–6.
36. Lanz, ii.66; Granvelle, ii.30, 33; *L.P.*, vi.517, 541, 568–9; *Sp.Cal.*, iv.1064, 1076.

Chapter 16 – The Princess Dowager

1. Pocock, ii.497–501; *St.P.*, i.397–404.
2. *L.P.*, vii.232; *Sp.Cal.*, v(i).19.
3. Foxe, v.1–18; Tyndale, *Works*, i.,p.lx; Cranmer, *Works*, ii.246; Wriothesley, i.22.
4. *L.P.*, vi.948.
5. *L.P.*, vi.1018; *Sp.Cal.*, iv.1117.
6. *L.P.*, vi.1018; *Sp.Cal.*, iv.1117, 1127.
7. *L.P.*, vi.1201, 1510; *Sp.Cal.*, iv.1158.
8. *L.P.*, vii.873.
9. Ibid, vi.1112.
10. *L.P.*, vi.391, 1186; vii.696.
11. *L.P.*, vi.918.
12. Ibid, 1528, 1538.
13. Ibid, vii.83; *Sp.Cal.*, v(i).4.
14. *St.P.*, i.415–22; *L.P.*, vi.1543, 1558, 1571; *Sp.Cal.*, iv.1164–5.
15. *St.P.*, vii.427–37, 462–5; Camusat, ii.11–12, 79–80; Le Grand, iii.571–88; Granvelle, ii.33; *L.P.*, vi.255, 424, 996.
16. *St.P.*, iv.625–30, 644–6, 648–51, 661–2; Camusat, ii.125–7; Rymer, xiv.480–2; *L.P.*, v.1638; vi.19, 409, 744; *Sp.Cal.*, iv.1041.
17. *Stat. of Realm*, 23 Hen. VIII, c.20, 25 Hen. VIII, c.27; Rymer, xiv.476–9; *L.P.*, vi.953, 1046, 1104.
18. Burnet, vi.56–67; Le Grand, iii.571–88; *St.P.*,vii.526.
19. Camusat, ii.20.
20. *L.P.*, vi.1572.

21. *Stat. of Realm*, 25 Hen.VIII, C.12; Cranmer, *Works*, ii.271–4; Wright, 14–19; Hall, 806–14; *L.P.*, vi.697, 1249, 1336, 1436, 1460, 1464–5, 1467–8; vii.70, 72; *Sp.Cal.*, iv.1184; Rogers, 470, 480–8.
22. Rogers, 490.

Chapter 17 – The Oath

1. *St.P.*, i.411–15.
2. *L.P.*, v.820.
3. *Stat. of Realm*, 26 Hen.VIII, c.1.
4. Pocock, ii.532–3; Le Grand, iii.631–5; *L.P.*, vii.367–70; *Sp.Cal.*, v(i).27–30.
5. Strype, *Mem.*, i(ii).175.
6. Cranmer, *Works*, ii.283–4; *L.P.*, vii.750.
7. Cranmer, *Works*, ii.296–7, 308–9; *L.P.*, vi.572; vii.32.
8. Cranmer, *Works*, ii.460–2; *L.P.*, vii.871; *Sp.Cal.*, v(i).68.
9. *Stat. of Realm*, 25 Hen.VIII, c.22; *H.L.Jo.*, 30 Mar. 1534; Pocock, ii.536.
10. Rogers, 501–7; *L.P.*, vii.1025; Rymer, xiv.487–90.
11. Cranmer, *Works*, ii.285–6.
12. Merriman, i.381.
13. *L.P.*, vii.695–6; *St.P.*, i.419–22.
14. Heylin, ii.70.
15. *L.P.*, vii.1013; *Sp.Cal.*, v(i).75.
16. *L.P.*, vii.490, 530, 1031; *Sp.Cal.*, v(i).44–45; Rymer, xiv.529, 539.
17. *L.P.*, vii.676, 679, 727, 897.
18. Ibid, 962; xiii(ii).803.
19. Ibid, vii.1270.
20. Ibid, 957, 1141, 1336, 1368; *Sp.Cal.*, v(i).70, 87, 109; Lanz, ii.99; *St.P.*, ii.201–2.
21. *L.P.*, vii.970 (see *L.P.*, viii., pp.xx–xxi*n*.)
22. Waitz, *Lübeck unter Jürgen Wullenwever*, ii.319–23, 389–90; *L.P.*, viii.913; pp.xix–xxiii; xiii(ii).702(2).
23. *L.P.*, viii.72, 1178; ix.113, 153, 187, 246, 286, 309, 356, 483, 752, 776, 861, 992, 1110; x.343, 686; Waitz, ii.114–17; iii.470–1; Wegener, iii.232–40; iv.10–12, 42–45.
24. *Stat. of Realm*, 26 Hen.VIII, c.1, 13.
25. *L.P.*, viii.661.
26. Ibid; Cranmer, *Works*, ii.303.
27. *L.P.*, viii.666, 683; *Sp.Cal.*, v(i).156; Wriothesley, i.27–28; Chauncy, *Historia Aliquot Martyrum Anglorum*, 102–3.
28. *L.P.*, viii.771, 826, 846; *Sp.Cal.*, v(i).170; Wriothesley, i.28.
29. *L.P.*, viii.742, 747, 786; *Sp.Cal.*, v(i).169.
30. *St.P.*, vii.604–5; *L.P.*, viii.779, 813, 837.
31. *L.P.*, viii.876; *Sp.Cal.*, v(i).174.
32. Chauncy, 107; *L.P.*, viii.846.
33. *Archaeologia*, xxv.94–99; *L.P.*, viii.856, 858–9, 867, 948; *Sp.Cal.*, v.178; Wriothesley, i.28–29.
34. *L.P.*, viii.949; *Sp.Cal.*, v(i).179.

35. *L.P.*, viii.974, 996; *Sp.Cal.*, v(i).180; Roper 86–97; Harpsfield, *Life of More*, 183–97, 258–64; Derrett, 'The Trial of Sir Thomas More' (*E.H.R.*, lxxix.449–77); Elton, *Policy and Police*, 409–16.
36. *Sp.Cal.*, v(i).180; Harpsfield, *Life of More*, 201–4, 266; Roper, 100–3.
37. *L.P.*, viii.726, 904, 909, 1012, 1060, 1075, 1104–5, 1141; *Sp.Cal.* v(i).176, 183, 185–6; *Mori Lucubrationes*, 511.
38. *L.P.*, viii.985.
39. Hall, 817.

Chapter 18 – The Monasteries

1. *L.P.*, viii.1095, 1115–17; *Sp.Cal.*, v(i).187; Bucholtz, *Ferdinand I*, ix.15–16; Camusat, ii.26–27.
2. *L.P.*, ix.74
3. Ibid, viii.196, 737; ix.46, 883, 1059; x.318.
4. Ibid, viii.1018; *Sp.Cal.*, v(i).181.
5. *L.P.*, viii.1, 48; *Sp.Cal.*, v(i).122, 127.
6. *L.P.*, ix.434, 525; *Sp.Cal.*, v(i).205.
7. *St.P.*, ii.309–11, 341–2.
8. *L.P.*, ix.153, 181; x.53, 285, 343, 490; Bucholtz, ix.352–4.
9. *L.P.*, viii.1118; St.P., vii.633–6
10. *L.P.*, ix.758, 868, 904, 947; x.35.
11. Ibid, ix.17.
12. Ibid, 58, 524, 989.
13. Ibid, 249; *Society of Antiquaries Proclamations*, i.78.
14. *Poli Ep.*, i.118–26; *L.P.*, xiv(i).200.
15. P.R.O., S.P.1/98, ff.26–27; *L.P.*, ix.42, 139, 632.
16. Wright, 75–77; Ellis, iii(ii).288–9.
17. Wright, 59–60.
18. *L.P.*, x.165, 511.
19. Ibid, ix.375, 713, 790, 1170.
20. Ibid, x.49, 364; Wright, 97–98.
21. Wright, 129–30, 136–7.
22. Latimer, *Works*, i.123 (2nd sermon before Edward VI, 15 March 1548/9).
23. *L.P.*, x.531, 749; Hughes, *History of the Reformation*, i.App.i.
24. *L.P.*, vi.1571; vii.83, 530, 726; *Sp.Cal.*, iv.1165; v(i).4, 60; Mattingly, *Catherine of Aragon*, 281.
25. *L.P.*, ix.862.
26. Ibid, vii.871; viii.189, 200, 429; *Sp.Cal.*, v(i).68, 134, 142.
27. *St.P.*, i.215; *L.P.*, vi.1126, 1453; viii.876; ix.596; *Sp.Cal.*, v(i).174; Mattingly, 290–3, 310–11.
28. *L.P.*, viii.200, 501–2, 697. See also *L.P.*, x.307.
29. Ibid, ix.326, 356–7; *Sp.Cal.*, v(i).203–4.
30. *L.P.*, ix.596.
31. Ibid, 443.
32. Luther, *Briefe*, iv.655.

33. *Corp.Ref.*, ii.947–8; iii.10–12; Strype, *Mem.*, i(i).357–8.
34. Wilkins, iii.792–7; *L.P.*, ix.207, 718, 904; *Sp.Cal.*, v(i).220.
35. *L.P.*, ix.1036; *Sp.Cal.*, v(i).246.
36. *L.P.*, x.59, 200, 230.
37. *Archaeologia*, xvi.23; *St.P.*, i.452; *L.P.*, x.28, 59–60, 65, 106, 141, 230, 284.
38. *L.P.*, x.410, 429.
39. Ibid, 25, 54, 235.
40. Burnet, vi.150–64; Wegener, iv.14; Luther, *Briefe*, iv.662–3; *Corp.Ref.*, iii.12, 35–36; Strype, *Mem.*, i(ii).234–43; *L.P.*, x.665.
41. *L.P.*, x.287; *St.P.*, v.39, 44, 50.
42. Lanz, ii.212–13; *L.P.*, x.333, 666, 670, 760.
43. *L.P.*, x.678.

Chapter 19 – The Destruction of Anne Boleyn

1. *L.P.*, x.200, 294.
2. Ibid, ix.776; x.199, 282.
3. Ibid, x.351.
4. Ibid, 601.
5. Ibid, 409.
6. Ibid, 699–700; *St.P.*, vii.683.
7. Austis, i.398–401; *L.P.*, x.752.
8. *Lisle Letters*, 686; Wriothesley, i.36.
9. *L.P.*, x.782; Wriothesley, ibid; *Lisle Letters*, 694.
10. Ellis, i(ii).56.
11. *L.P.*, x.909; *Lisle Letters*, 703a.
12. Ellis, i(ii).54–55.
13. Wriothesley, i.App.189–226; *L.P.*, x.908; Wilkins, iii.803.
14. *L.P.*, x.808.
15. Wriothesley, 39–40.
16. *L.P.*, x.902; Hall, 819; Gachard, *Anal.Hist.*, i–iv.18.
17. Wilkins, iii.803; *L.P.*, x.909; xi.41; Wriothesley, i.40–41; Burnet, vi.167. For the grounds of Henry's divorce from Anne, see Friedmann, *Anne Boleyn*, ii.351–5; Ridley, *Thomas Cranmer*, 106–9.
18. Wriothesley, i.41–42; Gachard, op. cit. i–iv.17*n.*; *L.P.*, x.908, 1107; *Lisle Letters*, 698; Excerpta Hist., 261–5; Crapelet, 167–214.
19. *Cal.For.Pap.Eliz.*, i.1303, p.528.
20. Cranmer, *Works*, ii.323–4.
21. *L.P.*, x.908–9.
22. Ibid, 915; *Lisle Letters*, 706, 848a.
23. Wriothesley, i.44–51; *H.L.Jo.*, 12 June, 18 July 1536.
24. *L.P.*, xi.48, 285, 294; *Lisle Letters*, 902; Wriothesley, i.54.
25. *L.P.*, x.888–9, 909, 965; *St.P.*, v.47.
26. *L.P.*, x.838, 922, 970, 1043; *Corp.Ref.*, iii.89–90; Ellis, i(ii).69.
27. Hearne, *Sylloge*, 124—8, 137–49; *St.P.*, i.445–9; *L.P.*, x.1134, 1150, 1187; xi.7, 9–10, 230.

28. *Narr. Ref.*, 259; Foxe, viii.43; *A Supplicacyon to the Quenes Maiestie*, 4; *L.P.*, x.908.
29. *L.P.*, xi.250; P.R.O., S.P., 1/105, f.261.
30. Hearne, *Sylloge*, 126; *St.P.*, i.457–9.
31. *L.P.*, x.1187.
32. Ibid, xi.40, 219.
33. Ibid, 148.
34. *Lisle Letters*, 748a.
35. *L.P.*, x.1131; xi.17.

Chapter 20 – Pole

1. Wriothesley, i.53–54.
2. *L.P.*, xi.233, 236.
3. Ribier, i.38–39.
4. *L.P.*, xi.7.
5. Ibid, 479.
6. Ibid, xii(i).277, 866.
7. For the Ten Articles, see Burnet, vi.272–90.
8. Aless, *Of the acutorite of the word of god agaynst the Bisshop of london*, A.v.
9. Wilkins, iii.807–8.
10. Ibid, 832–4; Cranmer, *Works*, ii.347.
11. *L.P.*, xii(i).472; x.130, 203; *St.P.*, i.454–5.
12. *Stat. of Realm*, 22 Hen.VIII, c.12.
13. *L.P.*, xi.423; *Stat. of Realm*, 27 Hen.VIII, c.25.
14. Holinshed, i.314.
15. Cranmer, *Works*, ii.229–31.
16. Strype, *Mem.*, i(ii). 279–82; *Poli Ep.*, i.434–7; *L.P.*, viii.217–20, 801; ix.988; *Sp.Cal.*, v(i).244.
17. *L.P.*, x.974–5; Burnet, vi.172–6; Pole, *De Unitate Ecclesiastica*, passim.
18. *Poli Ep.*, i.437–40, 455–7.
19. Strype, *Mem.*, i(ii).295–306 (see p.304 for passages cited).
20. Burnet, vi.177; *L.P.*, xi.73–74, 92–93, 401, 451; Strype, *Mem.*, i(ii).282–95, 306; *Poli Ep.*, i.464, 466–7.
21. *L.P.*, xii(i).105, 125.

Chapter 21 – The Pilgrimage of Grace

1. *L.P.*, xi.504.
2. Ibid, 531, 533–4, 552–3, 567, 585, 714, 854, 970.
3. Elton, *Studies in Tudor and Stuart Politics and Government*, iii.183–215.
4. *St.P.*, i.463–6, 482*n*; Strype, *Mem.*, i(ii).266–8; *L.P.*, xi.585, 705, 828, 848, 853, 860, 892, 902, 1246; xii(i).70.
5. *L.P.*, xi.552, 568.
6. Ibid, 537, 557, 562, 579, 587, 860, 874, 885, 906–7.

7. Ibid, 569.
8. *St.P.*, i.463.
9. *L.P.*, xi.569.
10. Ibid, 563–4, 692, 708, 786(3).
11. Ibid, 611, 687, 749.
12. Ibid, 672, 674, 715, 717, 764.
13. Ibid, 780.
14. Ibid, 656, 754, 758, 768–9, 775, 831; *St.P.*, i.472.
15. *St.P.* i.493–5; *L.P.*, xi.1087.
16. *L.P.*, xi.760, 774.
17. Ibid, 856–7, 894, 947, 1251.
18. Ibid, 576, 1143.
19. Ibid, xii(i).416.
20. *St.P.*, i.498–505, 519–21; Dodds, *Pilgrimage of Grace*, 268–9; *L.P.*, xi.955, 1042, 1045, 1063, 1174–5, 1228, 1237, 1271.
21. *St.P.*, i.523–4.
22. Wriothesley, i.59–60; Hall, 823; *Lisle Letters*, 813.
23. *Lisle Letters*, iii., pp. 566–8; *L.P.*, xi.1231; xii(i).298, 424, 456, 1300.
24. *L.P.*, xii(i), 43–44.
25. *St.P.*, i.526–7; *L.P.*, xii(i).67–68, 102–4, 112, 114, 135–8, 141–8, 154–64, 168–71, 177–8, 184.
26. *L.P.*, xii(i).163.
27. Ibid, 185, 310, 345.
28. Ibid, 136, 234; *St.P.*, i.537–40.
29. *L.P.*, xii(i).259, 292, 338, 410, 416, 609.
30. Ibid, 225, 291, 329, 332.
31. Ibid, 419, 439.
32. Ibid, 448, 468–9, 478, 498; *St.P.*, i.537.
33. *St.P.*, i.538–40.
34. *L.P.*, xii(i).498, 609, 615, 918.
35. Ibid, 632, 666; *St.P.*, i.641.
36. *L.P.*, xii(i).1172.
37. Ibid, 730–1, 777.
38. Ibid, 1214, 1246, 1257, 1307.
39. *St.P.*, i.529; *L.P.*, xii(i).208, 846.
40. *L.P.*, xii(i).847.
41. Ibid, 225, 393.
42. Ibid, 1207, 1227; Wriothesley, i.63.
43. *St.P.*, i.557–9; Wriothesley, i.64.
44. *L.P.*, xii(i).357.
45. *Lisle Letters*, 879, 881, 956.
46. *St.P.*, i.551–5.
47. *L.P.*, vi.1445; *Sp.Cal.*, iv.1153.
48. *Poli Ep.*, i.130–40; *L.P.*, xiv(i).200.
49. Foxe, v.362–8, 378–403.

Chapter 22 – The Duchess of Milan and Mary of Guise

1. *St.P.*, v.72–3; *Poli Ep.*, ii.33–41; Burnet, vi.185; *L.P.*, xii(ii).433–5, 779, 817, 865, 931, 939, 996, 1032.
2. *Poli Ep.*, ii.41–57; *St.P.*, vii.680–3, 688–701; *L.P.*, xii(i).1061, 1306; xii(ii).26.
3. *St.P.*, 696–703; *Poli Ep.*, ii.64–68; *L.P.*, xii(i).1235.
4. *Poli Ep.*, ii.68–71, 73–77, 79–80, 82–84, 88–89; *St.P.*, vii.707; *L.P.*, xii(ii).174.
5. *St.P.*, i.549; v.78–81; *L.P.*, xii(i).445, 703, 1256.
6. *L.P.*, xii(i).839, 843, 892.
7. Ibid, 1325; *Lisle Letters*, 887.
8. *L.P.*, xii(ii).242.
9. *Lisle Letters*, 943; Kaulek, *Correspondance de Castillon et de Marillac*, 50; *L.P.*, xiii(i).1006; xiv(ii).149, 153; MacNalty, *Henry VIII, a difficult patient*, 102–3, 159–65, 198–9.
10. Lloyd, *Formularies of Faith*, 24, 26–27, 128–9, 152–4, 168.
11. Cranmer, *Works*, ii.83–114, especially p.105.
12. See, for example, *St.P.*, i.393; ii.53.
13. Burnet, iv.308–13; vi.214.
14. *St.P.*, i.574; *L.P.*, xii(ii).1060.
15. Merriman, ii.97; *Lisle Letters*, 902; *L.P.*, xiii(ii).1030.
16. *St.P.*, viii.5–6, 7n., 14–20, 29–31; Nott, *Howard and Wyatt*, ii.469–70; Lanz, ii.682; *L.P.*, xiii(i).207, 241, 338, 380, 402, 419; *Sp.Cal.*, v(ii).182, 212–14, 217.
17. Ribier, i.62–64; Kaulek, 9; *L.P.*, xii(ii).1148.
18. Kaulek, 9–15; *St.P.*, viii.10.
19. Kaulek, 17–19, 23–24; Teulet, 131–4; *L.P.*, xiii(i).323, 338; *Sp.Cal.*, v(ii).185, 213.
20. Kaulek, 48, 51–53.
21. Nott, ii.485–9; Kaulek, 57, 64, 68, 70, 73, 75–76, 83; *L.P.*, xiii(ii).73, 262; *St.P.*, viii.17–20.
22. Kaulek, 80–81.
23. *L.P.*, xii(ii).1185, 1205, 1208, 1220, 1252, 1256, 1282; xiii(i).7, 57–58, 76; Cranmer, *Works*, ii.361.
24. *L.P.*, xii(ii).1256, 1298.
25. Ibid, xiii(i).7.
26. Ibid, 392, 440, 475.
27. Ibid, xii(ii).672, App.43; xiv(i).56.
28. Ibid, xiv(ii).119(iii).
29. Ibid, xiii(i).595, 788.
30. Ibid, 95; xiv(ii).165.
31. See Elton, *Policy and Police*, 383–400.
32. *L.P.*, xii(i).877; xiii(i).1141; Wright, 162; Ellis, i(ii).76.
33. *St.P.*, i.560; Ellis, iii(iii).62; *L.P.*, xi.674; xiii(i).1311, 1313.
34. *L.P.*, xiii(i).1454; xiii(ii).57, 91.

Chapter 23 – The Shrines

1. Ellis, iii(iii).159–62; *L.P.*, xiii(i).573, 893.
2. Fuller, *Church History*, ii.300.
3. *L.P.*, xiv(ii).235.
4. Ellis, iii(iii).168–9; Burnet, vi.194–5; *L.P.*, xiii(i).347; Latimer, *Works*, 406; *Lisle P.*, 1108.
5. Wright, 212, 222; *L.P.*, xiv(i).69; Wilkins, iii.840.
6. *L.P.*, xiii,(i).1199, 1345; xiii(ii).1243; xv.86.
7. Wright, 190–1; *L.P.*, xiii(i).863.
8. For Forest's case, see Ellis, iii(ii).249–70; Bourchier, *Historia Ecclesiastica de Martyrio*, 28–69; Cranmer, *Works*, ii.365–6; *L.P.*, xiii(i).877, 1043; Hall, 825–6; Foxe, v.179–80; Wriothesley, i.78–80; *Greyfriars Chronicle*, 42.
9. *L.P.*, xiii(ii).1280, p.534f.34b; xiv(i).1073.
10. Wilkins, iii.835; *L.P.*, xiii(ii).133, 684; Burnet, iv.318; Collier, ix., 162–74.
11. *L.P.*, xiii(ii).1269.
12. Fuller, ii.283–4.
13. *L.P.*, xii(i).806–7, 820.
14. *Stat. of Realm*, 27 Hen.VIII, c.34; 37 Hen.VIII, c.16; *L.P.*, xiii(i).1519(68); xv.613(52); xvii.443(15); Cranmer, *Works*, ii.348.
15. *Narratives of the Reformation*, 264, 266.
16. Ibid, 266; Collier, ix.295; *L.P.*, xiii(i).1319.
17. *St.P.*, i.580–3; *L.P.*, xiii(ii).2, 205, 209, 280, 288, 349.
18. Kaulek, 49; *L.P.*, xiii(ii).280.
19. *L.P.*, xiii(ii). 232, 349; *Sp.Cal.*, vi(i).7, 12.
20. Kaulek, 13–15, 17–19, 24–25, 61–63, 65–66, 68–69, 72–74; Leonard, ii.407–11, *L.P.*, xiii(i).1396; *Sp.Cal.Further Supp.*, 457.
21. Kaulek, 79.
22. *L.P.*, xiii(ii).484; xiv(i).7, 299; *St.P.*, viii.111, 120; *Sp.Cal.*, vi(i).40; Merriman, ii.187.
23. Burnet, iv.352–91; Cranmer, *Works*, ii.371, 377–80, 472–84; Seckendorff, iii.180.
24. *Lisle Letters*, 683–4, 739–42a, 744–48a.
25. Ibid, 899.
26. Ibid, 1215, 1220.
27. Ibid, 1268–70, 1272.
28. Ibid, 1513, 1558.
29. Wilkins, iii.836–7; *Corp.Ref.*, iii.583; Wriothesley, i.80.
30. Foxe, v.181–228; *L.P.*, xiii(ii).849, 851.
31. Foxe, v.229–34.
32. Ibid, 236; Wriothesley, i.88–89; *Greyfriars Chronicle*, 42; Hall, 826–7.
33. Foxe, v.235. Cf. 1563 edition, p.533, and 1570 edition, p.1284.
34. Merriman, ii.162.
35. *Lisle Letters*, 1273.
36. Elyot, *Dictionary*, Pref., Aii.
37. Strype, *Cranmer*, App. No.viii.

38. *L.P.*, iv.1939; xiii(ii).267, 695, 702, 743–4, 754, 765–6, 797, 802–4, 818–22, 827, 838, 855, 873, 987; Ellis, i(ii).96–98; ii(ii).110–16; Ribier, i.247–8.
39. *L.P.*, xiii(ii).979, 986.
40. Wriothesley, i.91–92; *L.P.*, xiii(ii).1056, 1089; xiv(i).191(3); xiv(ii).481.
41. *L.P.*, xiv(i).57, 189–90, 290; Lanz, ii.304–5.
42. *L.P.*, xiii(i).1033; *Sp.Cal.*, v(ii).224.
43. Hearne, 149.

Chapter 24 – The Destruction of Cromwell

1. Burnet, iv.318.
2. *Poli Ep.*, iii.Ep., p.2.
3. Ibid, i.94–113; ii.ccclxxiv–cclxxx, 142–3, 233; *L.P.*, xiii(ii).1110, 1148, xiv(i).13–14, 36, 98, 126; *Sp.Cal.*, vi(i).34.
4. Nott, ii.511–14, 523, 598; *Poli Ep.*, ii.ccxcii, 232–6; *L.P.*, xiv(i).441, 547–9, 603; *Sp.Cal.*, vi(i).45–46.
5. Ribier, i.401–2; *L.P.*, xiv(i).441, 560–1, 594, 602–3; *Poli Ep.*, ii.150–2.
6. Nott, ii.504–7; Ribier, i.357–9; *St.P.*, viii.130.
7. Ribier, i.363–4, 386–91; *L.P.*, xiv(i).143, 353–4; *St.P.*, viii.178.
8. *L.P.*, xiv(i).287, 319, 336, 338, 536, 541; *St.P.*, viii.152–69.
9. *St.P.*, viii.168–9; *Lisle Letters*, 1464; Nott, ii.342; *L.P.*, xiii(ii).323, 429; xiv(i).158.
10. *L.P.*, xiv(i).398, 652–4, 692, 695–6, 712, 714, 722, 726, 733, 769; Kaulek, 87–91; Ribier, i.437–9.
11. Collier, ix.162–74.
12. Halliwell, *Letters*, i.359–60; *St.P.*, v.153, 156; *L.P.*, xiv(i).601, 691.
13. *Lisle Letters*, 1415.
14. *L.P.*, xiv(i).633, 728, 734, 767, 823, 855, 902, 948.
15. *Archaeologia*, xxxii.30–37; *Lisle Letters*, 1406; Wriothesley, i.95–97; Hall, 828–30; Kaulek, 98.
16. *Archaeologia*, xxxii.31.
17. *L.P.*, xiv(i).682, 863, 968, 1071.
18. Statute, 31 Hen.VIII, c.15.
19. *H.L.Jo.*, 5, 16 May 1539; *Stat. of Realm*, 31 Hen.VIII, c.14.
20. *H.L.Jo.*, 19, 20, 21 May 1539; Cranmer, *Works*, ii.168; Foxe, v.264–5; *Lisle Letters*, 1421–3.
21. Burnet, vi.233.
22. *Lisle Letters*, 1425.
23. *H.L.Jo.*, 7, 9, 10 June 1539; Burnet, vi.233.
24. *Lisle Letters*, 1451, 1459; Foxe, v.502–5.
25. Kaulek, 101–4, 106–9; Ribier, i.465; *Corp.Ref.*, iii.742; *Lisle Letters*, 1475–6, 1478; Wriothesley, i.101, 103; *L.P.*, xiv(i).1901–2, 1157, 1207–8, 1217.
26. *Lisle Letters*, 1476.
27. Parker, *De Antiquitate Britannicae Ecclesiae*, 390; Ridley, *Thomas Cranmer*, 148.
28. Cranmer, *Works*, ii.394–5; *L.P.*, xiv(i).1333.

29. *L.P.*, xvi.733; *Sp.Cal.*, vi(i).156.
30. *Original Letters*, i.36.
31. *Stat. of Realm*, 31 Hen.VIII, c.13.
32. Foxe, v.506–13; Cranmer, *Works*, ii.390; *Lisle P.*, 1492.
33. *Lisle Letters*, 1481.
34. *Corp.Ref.*, iii.775–81.
35. *L.P.*, xiv(ii).684, 748–9; xv.31–32, 125, 131, 198; *Sadler P.*, i.3; *St.P.*, v.173.
36. Wriothesley, i.99–100; Kaulek, 105, 114; Ribier, i.465.
37. *L.P.*, xiv(i).1012, 1137, 1173, 1208; Kaulek, 105, 108; Ribier, i.465.
38. Kaulek, 117–22.
39. Ibid, 112–16, 125–6.
40. Teschenmacher, *Annales Cliviae*, App.144–9; *St.P.*, i.605; *L.P.*, xiv(ii).500, 574.
41. *L.P.*, xiv(ii).399, 427, 459, 532–3.
42. Ibid, 399; B.L., Cotton M.S., Titus, B.i., f.441.
43. Wright, 259–62; *L.P.*, xiv(ii).613.
44. For Anne of Cleves's journey and reception, see *Chron. of Calais*, 167–71; *St.P.*, viii.208–13; Wriothesley, i.109–11; Hall, 832–7; Merriman, ii.268–76; Kaulek, 149–51; *L.P.*, xiv(ii).634.
45. Merriman, ii.268–76.
46. B.L., Cotton M.S., Tit. B., i., f.109; *L.P.*, xiv(i).869.
47. Ibid, 247–9, 257, 264.
48. Nott, ii.360, 365; *St.P.*, viii.219, 240, 245; Kaulek, 153, 156; *L.P.*, xv.121, 154–5; Ribier, i.495.
49. Ribier, i.513.
50. Muller, 286–7, 365.
51. Strype, *Mem.*, i(ii).479.
52. *St.P.*, ii.551; *L.P.*, xiii(i).471; Kaulek, 49.
53. Nicolas, *Privy Council Proceedings*, vii.352–6; *Hist.MSS.Com.*, *Bath MSS.*, ii.8–9.
54. Wriothesley, i.123.
55. *Orig.Letters*, i.201–2.
56. *L.P.*, xv.613(12).
57. *Lisle Letters*, vi., p.65; No.1666.
58. Foxe, v.420–1, 428–32; Wriothesley, i.114; Muller, 173–4; Kaulek, 168–9; Ellis, iii(ii).258.
59. *Lisle Letters*, 1663.
60. Ribier, i.513.
61. *Lisle Letters*, vi., pp.53–104.
62. Ibid, No.1674–5; vi., p.111.
63. *St.P.*, viii.343.
64. *Lisle Letters*, 1673; *L.P.*, xv.541.
65. Kaulek, 184–5; *Lisle Letters*, vi., pp.117–34.
66. Kaulek, 187–8.
67. *St.P.*, i.627.
68. Ibid, iii.12–15, 25–27*n*, 36–43, 135–6, 208–9, 213–16.
69. Ibid, 194–5, 216–17.

70. Strype, *Mem.*, i(ii).381–3; Kaulek, 190.
71. Burnet, iv.415–23.
72. Ibid, 430.
73. Ibid, 431–9; *L.P.*, xv.822, 850.
74. *St.P.*, i.637–41, 643–6; Burnet, iv.440–2.
75. Foxe, v.402–3, 438; Wriothesley, i.120; Hall, 838–40.
76. Foxe, v.434–8.
77. Ibid, 434–6.
78. Ibid, 439; Scarisbrick, 383.
79. Stat., 32 Hen.VIII, c.58.
80. Burnet, iv.443–96; vi.241–2, 246–8; see especially iv.494.
81. Austis, i.417.

Chapter 25 – Katherine Howard

1. Wriothesley, i.121–2; Kaulek, 218; *L.P.*, xvi.314; *Sp.Cal.*, vi(i).143.
2. Hall, 838.
3. *L.P.*, xxi(ii).555(1).
4. *Orig.Letters*, i.204.
5. Luther, *Bekantnus des Glaubens die Robertus Barns en Lundon inn Engelland gethan hat*, passim; *L.P.*, xvi.106.
6. *Orig.Letters*, i.211.
7. *Stat. of Realm*, 32 Hen.VIII, c.16; *St.P.*, i.647–50; viii.365, 429, 588; Kaulek, 232; *L.P.*, xvi.13, 182, 188, 214, 347, 662, 733, 864, 954, 962, 1068, 1080; *Sp.Cal.*, vi(i).121, 135, 144, 155, 163, 168.
8. *St.P.*, i.658; viii.441, 458, 460, 479, 553; *Chron. of Calais*, 191–7; Kaulek, 222, 228–30, 235–6, 243, 267, 277, 302; Nicolas, vii.64; *L.P.*, xvi.29, 35, 130, 183–4, 200, 276, 465, 562, 761, 876.
9. Kaulek, 250–1, 289; *L.P.*, xvi.785; Ribier, i.552–3.
10. *St.P.*, i.653; viii.434, 436, 447, 457, 511; Kaulek, 222, 233; *Hist.MSS.Com.*, *Rutland MS.*, 11; *L.P.*, xvi.57, 115, 174.
11. Kaulek, 236–7.
12. Ibid, 247, 273–4; Nicolas, vii.138–9*n*.
13. *St.P.*, viii.519.
14. *Archaeologia*, xxxiii.5–6.
15. Kaulek, 101–4, 274; *L.P.*, xiv(i).1091–2, 1097; xvi.590.
16. *St.P.*, viii.338, 364–5.
17. *L.P.*, xvi.448.
18. Nott, ii.277–308; *St.P.*, viii.530–2, 544–6; *L.P.*, xvi.461, 515–16; *Sp.Cal.*, vi(i).150.
19. *L.P.*, xiii(ii).817–18.
20. Kaulek, 309; *L.P.*, xvi.897; *Sp.Cal.*, vi(i).166; *Poli Ep.*, iii. Ep., pp.35–37.
21. *L.P.*, xvi.932; Wriothesley, i.125.
22. *L.P.*, xvi.931–2; Wriothesley, i.125; Kaulek, 317–18.
23. *St.P.*, i.658.
24. P.R.O., S.P., 1/166, ff.35, 58; *L.P.*, xvi.887, 917.

25. Nicolas, vii.181–2; Wriothesley, i.125.
26. *L.P.*, xiv(i).455; xv.752; *St.P.*, v.151–2; ix.106; Elton, *Policy and Police*, 367.
27. *L.P.*, xvi.429; *St.P.*, iii.281–5.
28. *St.P.*, i.659; iii.304–10, 323–5; *L.P.*, xvi, 927, 974.
29. *L.P.*, xvi.1487.
30. *St.P.*, i.666–7; iii.300–3, 336–8, 350–3, 394–7; *L.P.*, xvii.831–3, 890; *Sp.Cal.*, vi(ii).68.
31. *L.P.*, xvii.468; *Sp.Cal.*, vi(ii).20.
32. Foxe, v.440–9; Hall, 841.
33. *Orig.Letters*, i.200–1; Wriothesley, i.119; Foxe, v.251.
34. Burnet, iv.307.
35. *L.P.*, xvi.945.
36. Kaulek, 317.
37. Nicolas, vii.207, 209–22; *Ham.P.*, i.75, 82; Kaulek, 320.
38. P.R.O., S.P., 1/187, f.14; *L.P.*, xvi.1134.
39. Nicolas, vii.226–7, 230; *L.P.*, xvi.1337, 1339; *Archaeologia*, xxiii.336–8.
40. Nicolas, vii.231–4; Kaulek, 334; *L.P.*, xvi.1131.
41. Kaulek, 326–7, 334–6.
42. Nicolas, vii.236–43; Kaulek, 341; *L.P.*, xvi.1338–9.
43. Kaulek, 337–8; *L.P.*, xvi.1178, 1182; *Ham.P.*, i.87–88.
44. Nicolas, vii.244–52; *L.P.*, xvi.1232; Foxe, v.463.
45. Nicolas, vii.252–63.
46. *St.P.*, i.683–4.
47. Ibid, 689–95; Kaulek, 352–4; Nicolas, vii.267–8, 352–6; *L.P.*, xvi.1320–1, 1328; *Sp.Cal.*, vi(i).204.
48. Kaulek, 363–7, 370–2; Nicolas, vii.355; *L.P.*, xvi.1376; *Hist.MSS.Com.*, *Rutland MS.*, i.28.
49. *L.P.*, xvi.1395.
50. *St.P.*, i.698, 701.
51. *L.P.*, xvi.1470.
52. *St.P.*, i.700.
53. *Stat. of Realm*, 33 Hen.VIII, c.21; Kaulek, 388; *L.P.*, xvii.100, 106.
54. *St.P.*, i.727.
55. Ibid, 721; Kaulek, 383, 426; *L.P.*, xvii.415.
56. *L.P.*, xvii.177; Burnet, iv.510–19.
57. Gachard, *Anal.Hist.*, i–iv.242–5; *L.P.*, xvii.92, 124; *Sp.Cal.*, vi(i).232, 350.
58. *L.P.*, xvi.1407; *St.P.*, 1708–9.

Chapter 26 – Solway Moss

1. Kaulek, 341–5, 390–4, 402–3, 411; *St.P.*, i.728–32; viii.680–5.
2. *L.P.*, xvi.1359; xvii.329; *Sp.Cal.*, vi(i).207.
3. Kaulek, 422–9.
4. *L.P.*, xvii.329.
5. Kaulek, 438.
6. *L.P.*, xvii.App.21–23, 28, 33; *St.P.*, ix.65–66.

7. Kaulek, 432–5.
8. *St.P.*, v.211, 211–12n.; *L.P.*, xvii.586; *Sp.Cal.*, vi(ii).41.
9. *L.P.*, xvii.586, 746, 759; *St.P.*, ix.123; *Sp.Cal.*, vi(ii).58.
10. *L.P.*, xvii.418, 560, 759; Kaulek, 456–7.
11. *St.P.*, ix.65, 202–5.
12. Ibid, v.207–8; *Ham.P.*, i.127, 146(l), 154, 158; *L.P.*, xvii.764.
13. *Ham.P.*, i.175, 181, 189, 197; *St.P.*, v.198–9; *L.P.*, xvii.919.
14. Lodge, i.42–43; *Ham.P.*, 171–3, 178(1), 182, 185, 190(1), 193, 198, 201–2, 211, 218, 221; *L.P.*, xvii.199.
15. *Ham.P.*, i.221, 223–4, 226, 228–9, 231; p.lxxvii, lxxx; *St.P.*, v.213–19; Theiner, 613; *L.P.*, xvii.998, 1060.
16. *Ham.P.*, i.240, 247; pp.lxxii, lxxxvii; Knox, *History of the Reformation in Scotland*, i.35–38; *L.P.*, xvii.1137, 1207; *Ven.Cal.*, v.288.
17. *Ham.P.*, i.241; p.lxxxvii; Wriothesley, i.140–1 (who wrongly states that the court was at Greenwich for Christmas); Dasent, *Acts of the Privy Council*, i.66–69; *L.P.*, xvii.1224, 1230, 1241; *Sp.Cal.*, vi(ii).69, 85, 87, 90.
18. Hall, 846–56; *Ham.P.*, i.269; *L.P.*, xvii.898(2).
19. *Ham.P.*, i.270(2), 276, 276(3).
20. Ibid, 275(1).
21. Ricart, *The Maire of Bristowe is Kalendar*, 55; *L.P.*, xiv(i).184, 1095.
22. See Northumberland to Cecil, 7 Dec. 1552, in Tytler, *England under Edward VI and Mary*, ii.148; Machiavelli, *The Prince*, 131; *St.P.*, v.250n.
23. Foxe, v.439; *Ham.P.*, i.255.
24. *Orig.Letters*, i.237; ii.634.
25. *Ham.P.*, i.269, 275(i); *St.P.*, v.242, 250–1n.; *Sadler P.*, i.160–8.
26. *Ham.P.*, i.348, 408.
27. *L.P.*, xviii(i).150; *Sp.Cal.*, vi(ii).100.
28. Rymer, xiv.768–76.
29. Wilkins, iii.868; Lloyd, 262–3, 266; *St.P.*, ix.615–16.
30. Lloyd, 215, 217–19; *Stat. of Realm*, 34 & 35 Hen.VIII, c.1.
31. Dasent, i.94, 105–8, 113–15.
32. *Narr.Ref.*, 252–3; Foxe, viii.28–31; Parker, *De Antiquitate Britannicae Ecclesiae*, 392–3; *L.P.*, xviii(ii).546.
33. Foxe, v.464–86; Dasent, i.97–98, 126–7, 150–1.
34. *L.P.*, vxiii(i).443, 854, 954; *Sp.Cal.*, v(ii).188.
35. *L.P.*, xviii(i).873, 918.
36. Foxe, v.486–92.
37. Ibid, 493–4; *Orig.Letters*, i.242.
38. Foxe, v.494–6.
39. Ibid, viii.31–34.

Chapter 27 – The War for Boulogne

1. *L.P.*, xviii(i).925, 955; xviii(ii).143, 294, 310; *Sp.Cal.*, vi(ii).190, 204, 249; *St.P.*, ix.489–93, 522–9, 554.
2. *Ham.P.*, i.43, 426.

3. *St.P.*, v.273; *Ham.P.*, i.354, 358; *L.P.*, xviii(i).455.
4. *Ham.P.*, i.345.
5. *St.P.*, v.281–2*n*.; Rymer, xiv.786–97.
6. *Sadler P.*, i.259; *Ham.P.*, i.446, 451; ii.14,19.
7. *St.P.*, v.334–5.
8. *Ham.P.*, ii.27, 33, 46; *St.P.*, v.335.
9. *Ham.P.*, ii.31, 34–35, 51, 93, 123(1).
10. Ibid, 138(b), 149, 154, 159, 162; *St.P.*, v.355; Haynes, *State Papers left by Lord Burghley*, 20; *Hist.MSS.Com.*, *Cecil MSS.*, i.135.
11. *Ham.P.*, ii.98, 130, 160, 307; Haynes, 12–13; *L.P.*, xix(ii).33.
12. *Ham.P.*, ii.189, 207, 209, 217.
13. Ibid, 230, 232–3, 237, 240; 'The late Expedition in Scotlande', passim; 'The Late Expedition by the King's Army' passim (in Dalyell, *Fragments of Scottish History*); *L.P.*, xix(i).355, 481, 518(3), 533; *Sp.Cal.*, vii.85, 89.
14. *Ham.P.*, ii.233.
15. *L.P.*, xviii(ii).525; xix(i).65, 118, 206, 318, 529–30, 714, 964; xix(ii).275; *Sp.Cal.*, vii.17, 22, 50, 65, 99–100; *St.P.*, i.761–2; ix.682–93, 710–12; Haynes, 6.
16. *L.P.*, xviii(ii).525; xix(i).271, 714, 794, 955; *St.P.*, ix.710, 715; *Sp.Cal.*, vii.134, 159–60.
17. *L.P.*, xix(i).427, 682, 730, 765, 767, 769, 776, 789, 793, 799, 827, 829, 850, 856, 858, 896–7, 944, 960; *Sp.Cal.*, vii.77, 124, 128, 131, 138–9, 142, 144, 157; *St.P.*, ix.718–25; Lanz, ii.415.
18. *L.P.*, xix(i).795, 849, 868, 907.
19. Ibid, 291; *Sp.Cal.*, vii.60–61; *St.P.*, ix.391–2.
20. *St.P.*, i.763–5.
21. *L.P.*, xix(i).921, 940, 946; Rymer, xv.52–57; *Sp.Cal.*, vii.152.
22. *L.P.*, xix(i).957, 964; xix(ii).167, 207, 324; *Ham.P.*, ii.322.
23. *L.P.*, xix(i).929, 933, 953, 955, 1024, 1026; xix(ii).20–21, 45, 53, 105, 235; *Sp.Cal.*, vii.156, 159–60, 169, 173, 176, 179, 187, 222; *St.P.*, x.1, 19–20, 23–27, 24–25*n*.
24. *L.P.*, xix(i).866, 903, 921, 955, 989; xix(ii).112; *Sp.Cal.*, vii.152, 164, 159–60.
25. *St.P.*, x.11–12; *L.P.*, xix(ii).174; Rymer, xv.50–52.
26. *St.P.*, x.31–33, 64–65n., 71–75; *L.P.*, xix(ii).218, 236; *Sp.Cal.*, vii.198.
27. Leonard, ii.430–48; Gachard, *Voyages des Souverains des Pays Bas*, ii.292–3; *L.P.*, xix(ii)., p.xxvii*n*.
28. *L.P.*, xix(ii).236, 268, 281, 288, 304, 344, 410, 507, 661; *Sp.Cal.*, vii.198, 209–11, 217, 241, 248, 253; Granvelle, iii.26–29; *St.P.*, x.76–82, 94–96, 147–51, 161–5.
29. *L.P.*, xix(ii).292.
30. *St.P.*, x.66–70; *L.P.*, xix(ii).236, 334, 336; xx(ii).494; *Sp.Cal.*, vii.198, 215;
31. *L.P.*, xix(ii).287, 306–7, 323, 342, 372, 379, 671; xx(i).606, 689, 1092, 1248; *Sp.Cal.*, vii.216; viii.51; *St.P.*, x.101, 358.
32. *L.P.*, xix(ii).347, 352, 355, 399, 515; xx(i).1123; *Sp.Cal.*, vii.219; *St.P.*, x.101, 108; Nott, i.App.No.xvii.
33. *L.P.*, xx(i).7, 21–22, 27, 30, 36, 41, 43, 137, 239, 261, 459, 590; *Sp.Cal.*, viii.4–5, 7, 15–16; *St.P.*, x.241–4, 254–61, 309–19, 321–3, 330–3, 370, 408.
34. *L.P.*, xx(i).11.
35. Haynes, 43; *Ham.P.*, ii.395; *St.P.*, v.417–18.

36. *Ham.P.*, ii.414, 417–20, 422; *Sp.Cal.*, viii.23.
37. *L.P.*, xx(i).16, 85; Lodge, i.99–100.
38. *L.P.*, xx(i).17, 52, 538.
39. Ibid, 1017, 1078, 1101; xx(ii).167; *Sp.Cal.*, viii.124; *St.P.*, iii.517; v.432, 475.
40. *St.P.*, i.827.
41. Dasent, i.174; *L.P.*, xx(i).606, 787.
42. *St.P.*, x.278–83.
43. Ibid, 610–11, 613–16, 657–60, 822; *L.P.*, xx(i).721, 947, 1079, 1138; xx(ii).283, 380, 527, 536, 544, 563, 585, 605–6, 636, 671, 679–80, 689, 710, 715–16, 750, 883, 962, 992; *Sp.Cal.*, viii.151.
44. *L.P.*, xix(ii).373, 555; xx(i).462, 1293; *Sp.Cal.*, vii.233; viii.10,106.
45. *L.P.*, xx(i).1263, 1293; p.lx–lxi; *Sp.Cal.*, viii.101, 106; Du Bellay, iv.282–305; Froude, *History of England*, iv.126–44.
46. *St.P.*, i.796, 801, 803; *L.P.*, xx(ii).81.
47. *L.P.*, xx(i).1245, 1276–7, 1279, 1293, 1297, 1299, 1301.
48. *St.P.*, i.798–9, 801, 820–4, 829; v.508; Dasent, i.225–30; *L.P.*, xx(ii).145, 149, 178, 493; *Sp.Cal.*, viii.122, 126, 143.
49. *Society of Antiquaries Proclamations*, ii.154.

Chapter 28 – Anne Askew

1. *St.P.*, i.831–4; x.581–3; *L.P.*, xx(ii).251, 486, 513, 589, 717, 754; xxi(i).126, 195, 201, 218, 241; *Sp.Cal.*, viii.232, 244; Wriothesley, i.163.
2. Strype, *Mem.*, i(ii).489; MacNalty, 153–5; Parker, *Correspondence*, 34; Wilkins, iii.875–6.
3. *L.P.*, xx(ii).223, 254, 393; xxi(i).56, 197, 296, 375, 409; xxi(ii).42, 51.
4. *Soc.Antiqu.Procl.*, ii.118; *L.P.*, xxi(i).447; xxi(ii).42, 70–71, 97; *Sp.Cal.*, viii.220.
5. *L.P.*, xx(i).984, 1329; xx(ii).200; xxi(i).589; *Sp.Cal.*, viii.70; Dasent, i.276.
6. P.R.O., S.P., 1/210, ff.30–33; *L.P.*, xx(ll).738.
7. *St.P.*, v.486–7, 509–37, 539–43; *L.P.*, xx(ii).97, 401, 456, 458, 525.
8. *Ham.P.*, ii.391.
9. *St.P.*, iii.533–5, 537–8, 541–4, 548–50; v.482–5, 501–8; Dasent, i.188, 240; *L.P.*, xx(ii).231, 714.
10. *St.P.*, v.449–50.
11. Ibid, 470; *Ham.P.*, ii.116.
12. *St.P.*, v.510–12.
13. Ibid, x.640–1, 643–5, 654–7, 667–77, 679–87, 723–9, 744–8, 795–801, 815–16; *L.P.*, xx(ii).149, 773–5, 782, 788, 793–4, 798, 821; *Sp.Cal.*, viii.122; Muller, 201–2.
14. Muller, 210; *St.P.*, x.730–3.
15. Foxe, v.690–1; *Private Prayers of Queen Elizabeth*, 567, 572; Dasent, i.225; Strype, *Cranmer*, i.185; Cranmer, *Works*, ii.412.
16. *Narr.Ref.*, 254–8; Foxe, viii.24–26; Parker, *De Antiquitate Britannicae Ecclesiae*, 393–5; Gairdner, *The English Church in the Sixteenth Century*, 233;

Gairdner, *Lollardy and the Reformation*, ii.418–21; Ridley, *Thomas Cranmer*, 238–9 and n.
17. Hall, 864–6; *H.L.Jo.*, 24 Dec.1545.
18. *L.P.*, xx(ii).1030, 1045.
19. Ibid, 81; *St.P.*, xi.3–5, 16–17.
20. *L.P.*, xxi(i).365, 439, 447, 488; *Sp.Cal.*, viii.208, 216, 220; Foxe, vi.351. *St.P.*, i.842–50, 872, 875, 878; *L.P.*, xxi(i).836; xxi(ii).155; Ellis, ii(ii).176–8.
21. *L.P.*, xxi(i).640, 682; *St.P.*, xi.111–14.
22. Rymer, xv.93.
23. *St.P.*, xi.183–6, 192–6, 193*n.*, 202–8; *L.P.*, xxi(i).938, 949–50, 952, 975–6, 989, 995; *Sp.Cal.*, viii.266–7; Rymer, xv.93.
24. Knox, *History of the Reformation in Scotland*, i.76–78; *St.P.*, v.561; xi.221.
25. Strype, *Mem.*, iii.160; Dasent, i.400, 402, 408, 414, 417–19, 423, 466–7, 492–3; *St.P.*, i.842–50, 872, 875, 878; *L.P.*, xxi(i).836; xxi(ii).155; Ellis, ii(ii).176–8.
26. Foxe, v.537–43.
27. Ibid, 543–8; Bale, *Works*, 137–246; Dasent, i.462.
28. Foxe, v.547.
29. Ibid, 550–1; Wriothesley, i.169–70.
30. Foxe, v.553–61.

Chapter 29 – The Last Purge

1 *Correspondence de Selve*, 17–22; *L.P.*, xxi(ii).194, 203.
2. Wriothesley, i.171–3; *L.P.*, xxi(i).1384.
3. Foxe, v.562–4.
4. *St.P.*, xi.322–6, 330.
5. Ibid, i.858, 862–4, 867–8, 870–1; xi., 283–9, 290*n.*, 293–7, 300, 319, 333–4; Selve, 22–26; *L.P.*, xxi(ii).23, 28–29, 31–32, 69, 83–84, 89–91, 101, 114, 125–6, 128, 131, 151, 245, 330; pp.xi–xviii; *Sp.Cal.*, viii.320; Holinshed, iii.859–61
6. Theiner, 618; *St.P.*, i.867; *L.P.*, xxi(ii).92, 114, 123(2); *Sp.Cal.*, viii.323;
7. *St.P.*, v.563–5.
8. Selve, 39–44; *L.P.*, xxi(ii).212.
9. Selve, 61–65, 67–68, 71; *St.P.*, v.572–4; *L.P.*, xxi(ii).451.
10. *L.P.*, xxi(ii).575.
11. Ibid, 139; Selve, 32.
12. *L.P.*, xx(i).687, 745; xx(ii).269, 287; xxi(ii).384, 567; *Ven.Cal.*, v.335, 337, 356, 439.
13. Selve, 53–61.
14. Ibid, 72–73; *L.P.*, xxi(ii).546, 605; *Sp.Cal.*, viii.364, 370.
15. Foxe, v.566, App.No.xviii; Wriothesley, i.175.
16. Muller, 161.
17. Foxe, vi.138–9.
18. *L.P.*, xxi(ii).546; *Sp.Cal.*, viii.364; Wriothesley, i.176.
19. P.R.O., S.P. 1/175, f.85; *L.P.*, xviii(i).73, 315, 327, 351, 390; xx(ii).App.30; *St.P.*, ix.554; Dasent, i.104; *Sp.Cal.*, vi(ii).127.
20. *L.P.*, xxi(ii).541, 546; *St.P.*, xi.378, 387–8.

21. *L.P.*, xxi(ii).555.
22. Lord Herbert, 566; Burnet, vi.274.
23. *Letters of Henry VIII*, 422–3; *L.P.*, xxi(ii).605–6; *Sp.Cal.*, viii.370.
24. Rymer, xv.110.
25. Selve, 78–83, 88; *L.P.*, xxi(ii).679, 756; *Sp.Cal.*, viii.317, 386; *Orig.Letters*, i.41–42, 256.
26. *L.P.*, xxi(ii).620; *Sp.Cal.*, viii.373; Lord Herbert, 567–9.
27. *L.P.*, xxi(ii).697, 753; Wriothesley, i.177; Statute, 38 Hen.VIII, c.32.
28. *H.L.Jo.*, 18, 24, 27 Jan.1546/7.
29. Foxe, v.689.
30. Selve, 95–96; *Ven.Cal.*, v.452; Wriothesley, i.178.
31. Foxe, v.563, 691, 697.
32. *L.P.*, xi.219; Edward VI, *King Edward's Journal*, 18, 19 Mar. 1550/1 (in Burnet, v.32); *Sp.Cal.*, x.251–61; Dasent, iii.350.
33. Aylmer, *An Harborrowe for Faithfull & Trewe Subiectes*, Q2; Fulwell, *The Flower of Fame* (in *Harleian Miscellany*, ix.343.
34. Gilby, *An Admonition to England and Scotland* (in Knox, *Works*, iv.563); Geneva Bible, note to 1 Sam., xxvi.9; Raleigh, *History of the World*, Preface, B.
35. Fisher, *History of Europe*, 520; Bryant, *Spirit of England*, 227; Gray, 'Ode to Magic' (*Works*, i.65); Oman, *History of England*, 282; Dickens, *A Child's History of England*, 306; Barskerville, *English Monks and the Suppression of the Monasteries*, 12.
36. Thomas, *The Pilgrim*. 9, 54–55.
37. Lord Herbert, 574.
38. Froude, iv.243.
39. Pollard, *Henry VIII*, 429, 434, 439–40.
40. *Poli Ep.*, i.135–7; *L.P.*, xiv(i).200, 285; Machiavelli, *The Prince*, 54; Elyot, *Dictionary*, Pref., Aii.
41. Roper, 56–57; Cavendish, 179; *Narr.Ref.*, 266.

BIBLIOGRAPHY

MANUSCRIPT SOURCES

British Library:
Cotton MSS. Caligula D vii, viii
Galba B ix
Titus, B.i.
Vitellius B ix, xi, xx
Additional MSS. 28578
Public Record Office:
State Papers I/2, 17, 23, 27, 42, 98, 105, 166–7, 175, 210.

PRINTED WORKS

ALESS, A. *Of the auctorite of the word of god agaynst the bisshop of london* (Leipzig (?), 1540).

ALLEN, P.S. and H.M. (eds.) – *Opus Epistolarum Des.Erasmi Rotorodami* (Oxford, 1906–58).

Archaeologia, vols. xxvi, xxxii, xxxiii (London, 1836, 1847, 1849).

AUSTIS, F. (ed.) *The Register of the Most Noble Order of the Garter from its cover in black velvet usually called the Black Book* (London, 1724).

AYLMER, J. *An Harborrowe for Faithfull & Trewe Subiectes agaynst the late blowne Blaste concerninge the Gouvernmēt of Women* (Strasbourg, 1559).

BACON, FRANCIS *History of the Reign of King Henry VIII* (ed. J.R. Lumby) (Cambridge, 1881 edn.).

BALE, J. *Select Workz of John Bale* (Parker Society) (Cambridge, 1849).

BASKERVILLE, G. *English Monks and the Suppression of the Monasteries* (London, 1937).

"Bishop Cranmer's Recantacyons" (*Miscellanies of the Philobiblon Society*, vol.xv) (London, 1877–84).

Bishops' Book. See Lloyd.

BOURCHIER, T. *Historia Ecclesiastica de Martyris Fratrum Ordinis Divi Francisci, dictorum de Observantia* (Paris, 1582).

BOWLE, J. *Henry VIII* (London, 1964).

BRADFORD, W. *Correspondence of the Emperor Charles V and his Ambassadors at the Courts of England and France* (London, 1850).

BREWER, J. Prefaces to *Letters and Papers of Henry VIII*. See Letters and Papers.

BRINKELOW, H. *The cōplaint of Roderyck Mors* (London, 1548).

BRIXIUS, G. *Antimorus* (Basle, 1520(?)).

BROWN, P. HUME *Early Travellers in Scotland* (Edinburgh, 1891).

BRYANT, A. *Spirit of England* (London, 1982).

BUCHANAN, G. *History of Scotland* (Edinburgh, 1752 edn.).

BUCHOLTZ, F.B. VON *Geschichte der Regierung Ferdinand des Ersten* (Vienna, 1831–8).

BURNET, G. *The History of the Reformation of the Church of England* (ed. N. Pocock) (Oxford, 1865 edn.).

Calendar of Letters, Documents and State Papers relating to the Negotiations between England and Spain preserved in the Archives at Simancas and elsewhere (ed. G.A. Bergenroth, P. de Goyangos, G. Mattingly, R. Tyler, etc.) (London, 1862–1965)

Calendar of State Papers and Manuscripts relating to English Affairs in the Archives of Venice and other Libraries in Northern Italy (ed. Rawdon Brown, Cavendish Bentinck, etc.) (London, 1864–1947).

Calendar of State Papers (Foreign Series) in the reign of Elizabeth, vol. i (ed. J. Stevenson) (London, 1863).

Calendar of the Patent Rolls – Henry VII, vol. I, A.D. 1485–1494 (London, 1914).

CAMDEN, W. *Remaines concerning Britain* (London, 1657 edn.)

CAMUSAT, N. *Meslanges historiques* (Troyes, 1619).

Captivité de François Ier (ed. A. Champollion-Figeac) (Paris, 1847).

CAVENDISH, G. *Thomas Wolsey late Cardinall, his lyffe and deathe* (ed. R.S. Sylvester) (Early English Text Society edn.) (Oxford, 1959).

CHAUNCY, M. *Historia aliquot martyrum Anglorum* (Mainz, 1550).

CHILD, F.J. (ed.) *The English and Scottish Popular Ballads* (Dover edn.) (New York, 1965).

CHRIMES, S.B. *Henry VII* (London, 1972).

Chronicle of Calais in the reigns of Henry VII and Henry VIII (ed. J.G. Nichols) (Camden Society) (London, 1846).

COLLIER, J, *The Ecclesiastical History of Great Britain* (London, 1840 edn.).

COOPER, C.H. *Annals of Cambridge* (Cambridge, 1843).

Corpus Reformatorum (ed. C.G. Bretschneider and H.E. Bindseil) (Halle and Brunswick, 1834–1900).

Correspondance de l'Empereur Maximilien Ier et de Marguerite d'Autriche, sa fille (ed. M. Le Glay) (Paris, 1839).

CRANMER, T. *The Works of Thomas Cranmer* (ed. J.E. Cox) (Parker Society) (Cambridge, 1844–6).

CRAPELET, G.A. *Lettres de Henry VIII à Anne Boleyn* (Paris, 1835 edn.)

CREIGHTON, M. *A History of the Papacy from the Great Schism to the Sack of Rome* (London, 1897).

CROMWELL, T. See Merriman.

DALYELL, J.G. *Fragments of Scottish History* (Edinburgh, 1798).

DASENT, J.R. (ed.) *Acts of the Privy Council of England* (London, 1890–1907).
DEMAUS, R. *The Life of William Tyndale* (ed. R. Lovett) (Manchester, 1922 edn.).
DERRETT, J.D.M. 'The Trial of Sir Thomas More' (*English Historical Review*, vol. lxxix (London, 1964).
DICKENS, CHARLES *A Child's History of England* (London, 1898 edn.).
Dictionary of National Biography (Oxford, 1885–1900).
DODDS, MADELEINE AND RUTH. *The Pilgrimage of Grace 1536–1537 and the Exeter Conspiracy 1538* (Cambridge, 1915).
DU BELLAY, M. and G. *Mémoires de Martin et Guillaume Du Bellay* (ed. V.L. Bourrilly and F. Vindry) (Paris, 1908–19 edn.).
EDWARD VI "King Edward's Journal". See Burnet.
EHSES, S. *Römische Dokumente zur Geschichte der Ehescheidung Heinrichs VIII von England 1527–1534* (Paderborn, 1893).
ELLIS, H. *Original Letters illustrative of English History* (London, 1824–46).
ELTON, G.R. *England under the Tudors* (London, 1953).
— *Henry VIII an essay in revision* (London, 1962).
— *Policy and Police* (Cambridge, 1972).
— *Studies in Tudor and Stuart Politics and Government* (Cambridge, 1974–83).
— *The Tudor Revolution in Government* (Cambridge, 1953).
ELYOT, T. *The Dictionary of syr Thomas Eliot knyght* (London, 1538).
Epistolae Jacobi Quarti, Jacobi Quinti, et Mariae, Regum Scotorum (Edinburgh, 1722–4).
ERASMUS, D. See Allen.
Excerpta Historica (ed. S. Bentley) (London, 1831).
FIDDES, R. *Collections*, in the second part of his *The Life of Cardinal Wolsey* (London, 1724).
FISH, S. *A Supplication for the Beggars*. See Four Supplications.
FISHER, H.A.L. *A History of Europe* (London, 1936 edn.).
FISHER, J. *The English Works of John Fisher, Bishop of Rochester* (ed. J.E.B. Mayor) (Early English Text Society) (London, 1876).
— *R.D.D. Ioannis Fischerii . . . Opera* (Würzburg, 1597) (reprint, Farnborough, Hants., 1967).
FLEURANGES, R. DE *Memoires du Maréchal de Fleuranges* (Paris, 1753).
Four Supplications 1529–1533 A.D. (Early English Text Society) (London, 1871).
FOXE, J. The Book of Martyrs;
The Acts and Monuments of John Foxe (ed. J. Pratt) (London, 1877; New York, 1965).
First edition: *Actes and Monuments of these latter and perillous dayes touching matters of the Church* (London, 1563).
Second edition: *The Ecclesiasticall History, contayning the Actes and Monuments of thynges passed in every kynges tyme in this realm, especially in the Church of England* (London, 1570).
FRIEDMANN, P. *Anne Boleyn* (London, 1884).
FROUDE, J.A. *The History of England from the fall of Wolsey to the death of Elizabeth* (London, 1870 edn.).
FUENSALIDA, G.G.DE *Correspondencia de Gutierez Gomez de Fuensalida* (ed. A.P. y Mélia) (Madrid, 1907).

FULLER, T. *Church History of Britain from the birth of Jesus Christ until the year MDCXLVIII* (London, 1868 edn)
FULWELL, U. *The Flower of Fame: containing the bright Renowne and moste fortunate Reigne of King Henry the VIII* (London, 1575). See Harleian.
GACHARD, P. *Analectes historiques* (Brussels, 1856–71).
— *Collection des Voyages des Souverains des Pays-Bas* (Brussels, 1876–82).
GAIRDNER, J. *Lollardy and the Reformation in England* (London, 1908–13).
— Prefaces to *Letters and Papers of Henry VIII.* See Letters and Papers.
— *The English Church in the Sixteenth Century* (London, 1902).
GARDINER, S. *A declaration of such true Articles as George Joye hath gone about to confute as false* (London, 1546). See Muller.
— Letters. See Muller.
GILBY, A. *An Admonition to England and Scotland to bring them to repentance* (Geneva, 1558). See Knox, *Works.*
GIUSTINIANI, S. *Four Years at the Court of Henry VIII: Selections of Despatches written by the Venetian Ambassador Sebastian Giustinian* (ed. Rawdon Brown) (London, 1854).
GRANVELLE, A.P . DE *Papiers d'Etat du Cardinal de Granvelle* (ed. C. Weiss) (Paris, 1841–52).
GRAY, T. *The Works of Thomas Gray* (ed. J. Mitford) (London, 1836–43).
GREEN, MARY ANNE EVERETT *Letters of Royal and Illustrious Ladies of Great Britain* (London, 1846).
— *Lives of the Princesses of England* (London, 1850–5).
Greyfriars Chronicle. *Chronicle of the Greyfriars of London* (ed. J.G. Nichols) (Camden Society) (London, 1852).
HALL, E. *Chronicle* (London, 1809 edn.).
HALLIWELL, J.O. *Letters of the Kings of England* (London, 1846).
Hamilton Papers (ed. J. Bain) (Edinburgh, 1890–2).
HAMY, P.A. *Entrevue de François Premier avec Henry VIII à Boulogne-sur-mer en 1532* (Paris, 1898).
Harleian Miscellany, vol. 9 (London, 1812).
HARPSFIELD, N. *A treatise on the Pretended Divorce between Henry VIII and Catherine of Aragon* (Camden Society) (London, 1878).
— *The life and death of Sr Thomas More, knight* (ed. Elsie Vaughan Hitchcock) (Early English Text Society) (London, 1932).
HARRISON, C.J. "The Petition of Edmund Dudley" (*English Historical Review*, vol. lxxxvii (London, 1972).
HAYNES, S. *A Collection of State Papers . . . left by William Cecill Lord Burghley* (London, 1740).
HEARNE, T. *Titi Livii . . . accedit, Sylloge Epistolarum a variis Angliae Principibus scriptarum* (Oxford, 1716).
HENRY VII *The Will of King Henry VII* (ed. T. Astle) (London, 1775).
HENRY VIII *A Glasse of the Truthe* (London, 1532 (?)). See Pocock.
— *Assertio Septem Sacramentarum or Defence of the Seven Sacraments by Henry VIII, King of England* (ed. Rev. L. O'Donovan) (New York, 1908 edn.).
— *The Letters of King Henry VIII* (ed. M.St. Clare Byrne (London, 1936). See Crapelet. (ed. L. Black) (London, 1933).

Heptameron. See Margaret, Queen of Navarre.
HERBERT OF CHERBURY, EDWARD, LORD *The Life and Raigne of King Henry the Eighth* (London, 1649).
HERBRÜGGEN, H. SCHULTE *Sir Thomas More: Neue Briefe* (Münster, 1966).
HESS, S. *Erasmus von Rotterdam, nach seinem Leben und Schriften* (Zürich, 1790).
HEYLYN, P. *Ecclesia Restaurata, or, The History of the Reformation of the Church of England* (ed. J. Barnard and J.C. Robertson) (Cambridge, 1849 edn.).
Historical Manuscripts Commission Reports:
Calendar of the Manuscripts of the Marquis of Bath (Dublin, 1907).
Calendar of the Manuscripts of the Marquis of Salisbury (London, 1883–5) (cited as "Cecil MSS.").
The Manuscripts of the Duke of Rutland (London, 1905).
HOLINSHED, R. *Chronicles of England, Scotland and Ireland* (London, 1807–8 edn.).
HUGHES, P. *The Reformation in England* (London, 1950–4).
JAMES IV *The Letters of James IV 1505–1513* (ed. R.K. Hannay, R.L. Mackie and Anne Spilman) (Edinburgh, 1953). See *Epistolae*.
JAMES V *Letters of James V* (ed. R.K. Hannay, D. Hay) (Edinburgh, 1954). See *Epistolae*.
KAULEK, J. *Correspondance politique de MM. de Castillon et de Marillac* (Paris, 1885).
KEILWEY, R. *Reports d' ascuns Cases qui ont evenus aux temps du Roy Henry VII et du Roy Henry VIII* (London, 1688).
King's Book. See Lloyd.
KNOX, J. *John Knox's History of the Reformation in Scotland* (ed. W. Croft Dickinson) (Edinburgh and London, 1949 edn.).
— *The Works of John Knox* (ed. D. Laing) (Edinburgh, 1846–64).
LAEMMER, H. *Monumenta Vaticana* (Freiburg im Breisgau, 1856).
LAMB, J, *A Collection of Letters . . . illustrative of the History of the University of Cambridge during the period of the Reformation* (London, 1838).
LANZ, K. *Correspondenz des Kaisers Karl V* (Leipzig, 1844–6).
LATIMER, H. *The Works of Hugh Latimer* (Parker Society) (Cambridge, 1844–5).
LE GRAND, J. *Histoire du Divorce de Henry VIII Roy d'Angleterre et de Catherine d'Arragon* (Paris, 1688).
LEONARD, F. *Recueil des Traitez de Paix, de Treve, de Neutralité, de Conféderation, d'Alliance, et de Commerce, faits par les Rois de France avec tous les Princes et Potentats de l'Europe* (Paris, 1693).
Letters and Papers (Foreign and Domestic) of the Reign of King Henry VIII (ed. J. Brewer and J. Gairdner) (London, 1862–1920).
Letters and Papers illustrative of the Reigns of Richard III and Henry VII (ed. J. Gairdner) (London, 1861–3).
Lettres du Roy Louis XII et du Cardinal G. d'Amboise, avec plusieurs autres lettres (Brussels, 1712).
The Lisle Letters (ed. Muriel St Clare Byrne) (Chicago and London, 1981).
LLOYD, C. *Formularies of Faith put forth by authority during the reign of Henry VIII* (Oxford, 1825).
LODGE, E. *Illustrations of British History, Biography and Manners in the reigns of Henry VIII, Edward VI, Mary, Elizabeth and James I* (London, 1838).

London Chronicle in the times of Henry VII and Henry VIII (ed. C. Hopper) (Camden Miscellany No. iv) (Camden Society) (London, 1859).
LOWER, M.A. "The Trial and Execution of Thomas Lord Dacre" (*Sussex Archaeological Collections*, vol. xix) (Lewes, 1867).
LUTHER, M. *Antwortt deutsch Mart. Luthers auff König Henrichs von Engelland buch* (Wittenberg, 1522).
— *Bekantnus des Glaubens, die Robertus Barns der Heiligen Schrifft Doctor (inn Deutschem Lande D.Antonius genent) zu Lunden inn Engelland gethan het, Anno MDXL, am XXX tag des Monats Julii, Da er zum Fewer one urteil und recht, unschuldig, unverhörter sach, gefurt und verbrant worden ist* (Wittenberg, 1540).
— *Dr Martin Luthers Briefe, Sendschriften und Bedenken* (ed. W.M.L. de Wette) (Berlin, 1825–56).
MACHIAVELLI, N. *The Prince* (ed. W.K. Marriott) (Everyman edn.) (London, 1940).
MACKENZIE, W. MACKAY *The Secret of Flodden* (Edinburgh, 1931).
MACKIE, J.D. "Henry VIII and Scotland" (*Transactions of the Royal Historical Society*, 4th Series, vol. xxix) (London, 1947).
— "King James IV" (*Scottish Historical Review*, vol. xxxviii) (Edinburgh, 1959).
— "The English Army at Flodden" (*Miscellany of the Scottish History Society*) (Scottish History Society, 3rd Series, vol. xliii) (Edinburgh, 1951).
MACKIE, R.L. *King James IV of Scotland* (Edinburgh, 1958).
MACNALTY, A.S. *Henry VIII, a difficult patient* (London, 1952).
MANCHESTER, W.D. MONTAGU, DUKE OF (ed.) *Court and Society from Elizabeth to Anne* (London, 1864).
MARGARET OF ANGOULÊME, QUEEN OF NAVARRE *L'Heptaméron* (ed. M. François) (Paris, 1964 edn.).
MATTINGLY, G. *Catherine of Aragon* (London, 1942).
MERRIMAN, M.H. "The assured Scots" (*Scottish Historical Review*, vol. xlvii) (Edinburgh, 1967–8).
MERRIMAN, R.B. *Life and Letters of Thomas Cromwell* (Oxford, 1902).
MORE, Sir T. Correspondence. See Rogers.
— *Mori Lucubrationes* (Basle, 1563).
— *The Complete Works of St Thomas More* (ed. R.S. Sylvester etc.) (New Haven and London, 1963–79).
MORICE, R. "A declaration concernyng . . . that most Reverent Father in God, Thomas Cranmer, late archebisshop of Canterbury". See Narratives of the Reformation.
MULLER, J.A. (ed.) *The Letters of Stephen Gardiner* (Cambridge, 1933).
Narratives of the Days of the Reformation (ed. J.G. Nichols) (Camden Society) (London, 1859).
Négociations diplomatiques entre la France et l'Autriche durant les trente premières années du XVIe siècle (ed. M. Le Glay) (Paris, 1845).
NICOLAS, H. (ed.) *Proceedings and Ordinances of the Privy Council of England* (London, 1834–7).
NOTT, G.F. (ed.) *The Works of Henry Howard Earl of Surrey and of Sir Thomas Wyatt the Elder* (London, 1815).
OMAN, C. *A History of England* (London, 1921 edn.).

Original Letters relative to the English Reformation (ed. H. Robinson) (Parker Society) (Cambridge, 1846–7).

PARKER, M. *Correspondence of Matthew Parker* (Parker Society) (Cambridge, 1853).

— *De Antiquitate Britannicae Ecclesiae & Priuilegiis Ecclesiae Cantuariensis, cum Archiepiscopis eiusdem LXX* (London, 1572).

PARMITER, G. DE C. *The King's Great Matter* (London, 1967).

PETER MARTYR DE ANGLERÍA *Opus Epistolarum Petri Martyris Anglerii Mediolanensis* (Amsterdam, 1670).

PINKERTON, J. *The History of Scotland from the Accession of the House of Stuart to that of Mary* (London, 1797).

PITSCOTTIE, R. LINDSAY OF *The Historie and Cronicle of Scotland* (ed. A.J.G. Mackay) (Edinburgh and London, 1899 edn.).

PIUS II, POPE *Aeneas Silvius. in Europam* (Memmingen, 1490). See Brown.

POCOCK, N. *Records of the Reformation: The Divorce 1527–1533* (Oxford, 1870).

POLE, P. *Epistolarum Reginaldi Poli S.R.E. Cardinalis* (ed. A.M. Quirini) (Brixen, 1754–67).

POLLARD, A.F. *Henry VIII* (London, 1905 edn.).

— *The Reign of Henry VII from contemporary sources* (London, 1913–14).

PORCACCHI, T. *Lettere di XIII Huomini Illustri* (Venice, 1565).

Private Prayers of the Reign of Queen Elizabeth (Parker Society) (Cambridge, 1851).

RALEIGH, W. *The History of the World* (London, 1614).

RIBIER, G. *Lettres et Mémoires d'Estat des Roys, Princes et Ambassadeurs sous les Regnes de François Ier, Henri II et François II 1537–1559* (Paris, 1666).

RICART, R. *The Maire of Bristowe is Kalendar* (Camden Society) (London, 1872).

RIDLEY, J. *The Statesman and the Fanatic* (London, 1982).

— *Thomas Cranmer* (Oxford, 1962).

ROGERS, ELIZABETH FRANCES (ed.) *The Correspondence of Sir Thomas More* (Princeton, N.J., 1947).

ROPER, W. *The Lyfe of Sir Thomas Moore, knighte* (Early English Text Society) (London, 1935).

ROSCOE, W. *The Life and Pontificate of Leo the Tenth* (London, 1846)

RYMER, T.W. *Foedera, Conventiones, Literae, Et Cujuscunque Generis Acta Publica inter Reges Angliae* (London, 1704–17).

Sadler Papers. *The State Papers and Letters of Sir Ralph Sadler* (ed. A. Clifford) (Edinburgh, 1809).

SANDERS, N. *Rise and Growth of the Anglican Schism* (ed. D. Lewis) (London, 1877 edn.).

SCARISBRICK, J.J. *Henry VIII* (London, 1968).

SELVE, O. DE *Correspondance politique de Odet de Salve* (ed. G. Lefèvre-Pontalis) (Paris, 1888).

SKELTON, J. *The Poetical Works of John Skelton* (ed. F. Henderson) (London and Toronto, 1931).

SMITH, PRESERVED *Erasmus* (New York, 1923).

SPALATIN, G. *Georg Spalatin's historischer Nachlass und Briefe* (Jena, 1851).

Spanish Calender. See Calendar of Letters . . . in Simancas.

Spanish Chronicle. *Chronicle of King Henry VIII of England, being a contemporary record . . . written in Spanish by an unknown hand* (ed. M.A.S. Hume) (London, 1889).

State Papers published under the authority of His Majesty's Commission: King Henry the Eighth (London, 1831–52).

Statutes of the Realm (London, 1810–24).

STRYPE, J. *Ecclesiastical Memorials* (Oxford, 1822 edn.).

— *Memorials of the Most Reverend Father in God Thomas Cranmer* (Oxford, 1840 edn.).

A Supplicacyō to the quenes maiestie (Strasbourg (?), 1556).

Supplication for the Beggars See *Four Supplications.*

TESCHENMACHER, W. *Annales Cliviae, Juliae, Montium, Mancae, Westphalicae, Ravensbergae, Geldriae et Zutphaniae* (Frankfort and Leipzig, 1721 edn.).

TEULET, A. *Papiers d'État, Pièces et Documents relatifs à l'Histoire de l'Ecosse au XVIe siècle* (Paris, 1851–60).

THEINER, A. *Vetera monumenta Hibernorum et Scotorum historiam illustrantia 1216–1547* (Rome, 1864).

THOMAS, W. *The Pilgrim: a dialogue on the Life and actions of King Henry the Eighth* (ed. J.A. Froude) (London, 1861).

Tudor Tracts (ed. A.F. Pollard) (Westminster, 1903).

TYNDALE, W. *Doctrinal Treatises and Introductions to different portions of the Holy Scriptures* (Parker Society) (Cambridge, 1848) (cited as "Tyndale, *Works*, vol. i).

— *Expositions and Notes on sundry portions of Holy Scripture, together with the Practice of Prelates* (Parker Society) (Cambridge, 1849) (cited as "Tyndale, *Works*, vol. ii).

— *An Answer to Sir Thomas More's Dialogue*, etc. (Parker Society) (Cambridge, 1850) (cited as "Tyndale, *Works*, vol. iii").

TYTLER, P.F. *England under the Reigns of Edward VI and Mary* (London, 1839).

Venetian Calendar. See *Calendar of State Papers . . . in the Archives of Venice.*

VERGIL, P. *Historiae Anglicae* (Leyden, 1651 edn.).

VIVES, J.L. *Opera omnia* (Valencia, 1782–90).

WAITZ, G. *Lübeck unter Jürgen Wullenwever und die Europäische Politik* (Berlin, 1855–6).

WEGENER, C.F. (ed.) *Aarsberetninger fra det Kongelige Geheimearchiv* (Copenhagen, 1852–70).

WILKINS, D. *Concilia Magnae Britanniae et Hiberniae a Synodo Veralaniensi A.D. CCCCXLVI ad Londinensem A.D. MDCCXVII* (London, 1737).

WILLIAMS, N. *Henry VIII and his Court* (London, 1971).

WOOD, ANTHONY À. Annals. *The History & Antiquities of the Colleges and Halls in the University of Oxford* (Oxford, 1786–90).

WOOD, MARY ANNE EVERETT. See Green.

WRIGHT, T. *Three chapters of Letters relating to the Suppression of Monasteries* (Camden Society) (London, 1843).

WRIGLEY, E.A. and SCHOFIELD, R.S. *The Population History of England 1541–1871* (London, 1981).

WRIOTHESLEY, C. *A Chronicle of England during the reigns of the Tudors* (ed. W.D. Hamilton) (Camden Society) (London, 1875–7).

INDEX